London 14 July 1778

ought of John Murray, Bookseller,

Stationer at N.º 32 — Fleet Street

London 10 may 1779

Dear Archy

I had your last letter apologising for silence which I submitted to. I do not protest against short

must be extreme hurry indeed you from writing half a day

The family are in

brother at Margate,

write well, altho her

his insolence which

me. Yet it is to be

struggled with.

January 1.º 1780

shillings

ined shares

ase a further

£ 25..

£ 1..10..0

the sum of One pound ten shillings as p.º advice and place the same to account of

Yours hum.º Serv.º

Bennet & J.

To M.º J. Murray
bookseller in Fleet-street
London —

the Grace of God, in good Order

in and upon the good Ship called the Virg
whereof is Master, under God, for this present
and now riding at Anchor in the River

Virginia — to

One Case and One

R.M. N.º 1. Case
2 Box

0..3..6 Freight
0..2..0 Primage
0..5..0 Shipping charges

being mark'd and number'd as in the Margin, a
and well Condition'd, at the aforesaid Port of
of the Seas only excepted) unto M.º Ra

or to his Assigns, he or they paying Freig
Three Shillings & Sixpence
with Primage and Average accustom'd. In Witn
Ship hath affirm'd to 3 Bills of Lading, al
3 Bills being accomplish'd, the other 2
Ship to her desir'd Port in Safety. Amen. Da

Insides & Contents Unknown to

M.º William & Shaw London 4.º May 178

Bought of John Murray, Bookseller,
and Stationer at N.º 32 — Fleet Street

1780

July 18 Scotch Preacher 3 Vols new & neat
24 Farquharsons Sermons 2 Vol. new
Oct.º 18 Do Galic Dictionary Del.º to M.º Alex.º Shaw new

1781 Smiths Galic antiquities boards 2 copies
26 Owens Dictionary of Arts & Sciences
4 Vol. new & neat
Galic Dictionary 2U. Del.º to yourself
Ballance Due to you

9..
7..
1..15..
3..10..
10..6
1..16..
1..15..

Dictionary 2U bds
as the

10..2..6
2..2..6
12..5

1780

M.º Assignees

LETTER
TO
W. MASON, A.M.

20 June 1777

The First
John Murray

and the Late Eighteenth-Century London Book Trade

John Murray, *c.* 1777. Oil on canvas, by David Allan. Murray holds a copy of his *Letter to Mason*, 1777

The First
John Murray

and the Late Eighteenth-Century London Book Trade

With a Checklist of his Publications

＊＊＊＊＊＊

by
William Zachs

*A British Academy
Postdoctoral Fellowship Monograph*

Published for THE BRITISH ACADEMY
by OXFORD UNIVERSITY PRESS

Oxford University Press, Great Clarendon Street, Oxford OX2 6DP

Oxford New York
Athens Auckland Bangkok Bogota Bombay
Buenos Aires Calcutta Cape Town Dar es Salaam
Delhi Florence Hong Kong Istanbul Karachi
Kuala Lumpur Madras Madrid Melbourne
Mexico City Nairobi Paris Singapore
Taipei Tokyo Toronto Warsaw

and associated companies in
Berlin Ibadan

Published in the United States by
Oxford University Press Inc., New York

British Library Cataloguing in Publication Data
Data available

ISBN 0–19–726191–4

Typeset by J&L Composition Ltd, Filey, North Yorkshire
Printed in Great Britain
on acid-free paper by
Creative Print and Design Wales
Ebbw Vale

Contents

List of Plates   viii
List of Tables and Figures   x
Acknowledgements   xi
Notes on the Text   xiii
Chronology   xiv
Family Tree   xvi

Introduction   1

1: **Early Years**   5
    Kith and Kin   5
    On the High Seas   8
    In Search of a Job   9
    Man of Letters   11
    Bookseller and Stationer   19

2: **Thirty-two Fleet Street, at the Sign of the Ship**   25
    Business as Usual   25
    Early Publications   28
    Book Production   32
    Buying and Selling Books   35
    Murray's Correspondence   42
    Other Ventures   43

3: **The Eighteenth-Century Book Trade**   52
    Literary Property — A Brief History   52
    Murray and the 1774 Literary Property Decision   56
    Mysterious 'Murray' Imprints   62

4: **Dealing with Authors**   63
    Judging Literary Merit   63
    Modes of Publication   66
    Style Matters   70

5: **The London Trade**   77
    Co-publication   77
    Murray's Book Trade Associates   81

Advertising 86
Catalogues 87
The Antiquarian Book Trade 89

6: **Trade Outside London** 91
Edinburgh 91
Glasgow 103
Other Cities 106

7: **The Irish Trade** 109
Getting a Foot in the Door 109
The 'Dublin Cartel' 116
Publishing Irish Authors 120

8: **Family Matters** 122
Nancy 122
Sisters 127
The Irish Inheritance 133
The Irish Jaunt 137
Archie 139
Hester and Family 142

9: **Diversity and Specialisation** 153
Novels 153
Poetry 155
Sermons 162
Drama 164
Histories and Historians 165
Translations 172
Medical Works 175

10: **A Litigious and Disputatious Nature** 184
Murray versus Mason, 1777 184
Murray versus the *Encyclopaedia Britannica*, 1783 189
Murray versus Cullen, 1784 191
Murray versus Captain Innes Munro, 1788–90 195
Murray versus _____ 198

11: **Periodical Publications** 200
Early Periodical Ventures 200
The *English Review* 208
Other Periodical Ventures 216

12: **The Politics of a Bookseller** 221
The American Revolution 221
National Affairs 226
The French Revolution 228
India 231

13: **Later Years** 238
Decline and Fall 238
'Printed for H. Murray' 242
'J. Murray and S. Highley (Successors to the Late Mr. Murray)' 246
The Second John Murray 249

A CHECKLIST OF MURRAY PUBLICATIONS, 1768–1795 253
Index of Murray Publications 410

A Bibliography of Pamphlets Written by Murray 415
Bibliography 417
Index 425

List of Plates

Originals are in the Murray Archive except those with an asterisk (*), which belong to the author or to the institution noted.

Frontispiece

John Murray, *c.* 1777. Oil on canvas, by David Allan. Murray holds a copy of his *Letter to Mason*, 1777

Between page 78 and page 79

1. John Murray, *c.* 1785. Oil on canvas, by an unidentified artist of the British School

2a. Believed to be Robert McMurray *c.* 1750. Miniature in watercolour on ivory by an unidentified artist

2b. James Gilliland, jeweller, and his wife Elizabeth, eldest sister of John Murray, *c.* 1770. Miniatures in watercolour on ivory by Henry Raeburn, who was apprenticed to Gilliland

2c. John Murray, *c.* 1791. Miniature in watercolour on ivory, possibly by John Donaldson

3. William Sandby's engraved trade card

4. *St Dunstan's in Fleet Street. Engraving by Thomas Malton, 1797 (Courtesy of the Yale Center for British Art, Paul Mellon Collection)

5. No. 32 Fleet Street in the mid-nineteenth century. Watercolour by an unidentified artist

6. Title pages of the two 1768 editions of Lord Lyttelton's *Dialogues of the Dead*

7. Daybook I, opened at pages 2–3

8. Account Ledger entry (p. 248) for editions of Edmund Cartwright's poem *Armine and Elvira*

9. Receipt for books bought by the Rev. William Shaw, 4 May 1780, entered on Murray's engraved stationery

10. *Title page of Edmund Cartwright's *Armine and Elvira*, sixth edition, 1777

11. Account Ledger entry (p. 40) for David Goodsman, bookbinder

12. An advertisement for 'Books Printed for J. Murray, And Sold by him, at his Shop'

13. A receipt for goods shipped to Robert Miller in Virginia, 2 December 1773

14. Account Ledger entry (p. 183) for Edward Galliard, formulator and proprietor of the 'Edinburgh Febrifuge Powders'

15. Account Ledger entry (p. 295) for James Tassie, modeller in glass

16. Account Ledger entry (p. 41) for Murray's edition of the *Poems by Mr. Gray*, 1776

17. Title page of the *Poems by Mr. Gray*, 1776

18. Booksellers' Book entry (p. 11) for Murray's share in *The Works of the English Poets. With Prefaces, Biographical and Critical, by Samuel Johnson*, including entries for editions of Johnson's *Lives of the Poets*

19. *Title page of *The Works of the English Poets*, 1790 edition

20. *Title page of the spurious 'Murray' edition of *The Vicar of Wakefield*, 1774, probably printed in Ireland

21 *Part II of Johann Kasper Lavater's

& 22a. *Essays on Physiognomy* in its original printed wrappers

22b. *Engraved subscriber's receipt for Part III of the *Essays on Physiognomy*

23. A list of payments made to the engravers of the *Essays on Physiognomy*, including William Blake and James Gillray

24. *Title page of John Gast's *History of Greece*, 1782

Between page 206 and page 207

25. Expenses for the 1793 edition of John Gay's *Fables*, known as the 'Stockdale edition' (loose sheet in Account Ledger)

26. Receipts for Murray's 'syndicate' purchases in shares of fourteen titles, Globe Tavern, 5 June 1783 (loose sheet in the Booksellers' Book)

27. Booksellers' Book entry (p. 23) for Murray's share in *The Works of Laurence Sterne*

28. Title page to *The Works of Laurence Sterne*, 1780

29. Expenses for Millot's *Elements of the History of England* (loose sheet in Account Ledger, p. 123)

30. Title page of Millot's *Elements of the History of England*

31. Advertisements for Murray's publications, some dated in his hand, from his newspaper clipping album

32. *Title page of *Murray's Catalogue of Books in Medicine, Surgery, Anatomy, Natural History for the Use of the Faculty, and Practitioners in General*, 1784 (Courtesy of the Logan Clendening History of Medicine Library, University of Kansas)

33. *Title page of the *Medical and Philosophical Commentaries*, 1774

34. An entry from Murray's Irish diary for 24 June 1775, describing an evening of debauchery

35a. Bill listing clothing and boarding charges for Murray's illegitimate son Archie, 8 June 1779 (loose sheet in Account Ledger, p. 200)

35b. A letter written by Murray to Archie, 10 May 1791

36. John Murray II (born 27 November 1778) about the age of five. Crayon drawing on paper by an unidentified artist

37. Booksellers' Book entry (p. 33) for Murray's share in *Robinson Crusoe*, 1784 and 1791 editions

38. *Title page of Abraham Portal's *Nuptial Elegies*, 1774

39. *Title page of Edmund Cartwright's *The Prince of Peace*, 1779

40. *Title page of Gerald Fitzgerald's *The Injured Islanders*, 1779

41. Booksellers' Book entry (p. 12) for Murray's share in *The Plays of William Shakspeare*

42. *Title page of *The Plays of William Shakspeare*, 1793 edition

43. Title page of the *Foreign Medical Review*, 1779

44. Title page of *A Letter to W. Mason, concerning his Edition of Mr. Gray's Poems and the Practices of Booksellers*, 1777

45. Title page of *An Author's Conduct to the Public*, 1784, Murray's attack on Dr William Cullen

46. *Title page of *The Defence of Innes Munro*, 1790

47. 'Catalogue of the Stock in Trade (with the Valuation) of Mr. J. Murray at the time of his Decease'. The letters of the alphabet refer to the listing of books in the catalogue by the authors' surnames

48. *London Booksellers' trade card about 1800, listing John Murray II as a medical publisher (By permission of the Bodleian Library, John Johnson Collection)

List of Tables and Figures

Table 1.   Murray's Publishing Arrangements   30–1
Table 2.   Murray's Publishing Subjects   158–60

Figure 1.   Murray's Publishing Arrangements, 1768–93   32
Figure 2.   Murray's Publishing by Year, 1768–93   33
Figure 3.   Murray's Publishing Subjects, 1768–93   161
Figure 4.   Murray's Medical and Other Publications by Year   177

Acknowledgements

The first John Murray died over two hundred years ago. However, his name and the publishing house he founded live on to this day in London at 50 Albemarle Street, where the second Murray moved in 1812. It will come as no surprise, therefore, that my greatest debt is to the present John Murray (seventh in the line), for access to his archive and for permission to quote from the material it contains.

The archive is administered by Virginia Murray, whose help and encouragement cannot be adequately acknowledged. Many of my happiest days have been spent with her working in the splendid drawing room — virtually unchanged since the mid-nineteenth century — which has been the scene of so much literary activity and history. There in 1814 the second Murray introduced Lord Byron to Walter Scott, and there the works of such well-known writers as Jane Austen and Charles Darwin first saw the light of day. Many other literary greats have left their marks at the house of Murray since then.

It is not possible to think about 50 Albemarle Street without remembering the late John G. ('Jock') Murray (sixth in the line), who died in the summer of 1993. For me, he was a link to that John Murray whose story I have written. Though occupied with the pressing matters of the firm, he often asked about my research and read parts of this book in manuscript. I am sorry that he did not live to see it published.

At various stages during this project several people offered their help and advice: Anne Kelly, of the Edinburgh University computing centre, created the database for collecting and organising Murray's correspondence; Christopher Fletcher unearthed information about Murray in London libraries and archives; Michael Harris, Donald D. Eddy, David Vander Meulen and Antonia Forster helped with bibliographical queries. Several antiquarian booksellers, both in Britain and America, alerted me to copies of Murray's publications, particularly those containing useful information such as advertisements. A. A. Barnes and Warren McDougall photographed the items which illustrate this work.

Several people were kind enough to read my work in full or in part: O. M. Brack, Donald D. Eddy, Warren McDougall, Patrick Maguire, Diana Patterson, James Raven, Richard B. Sher, Selig Silverman, William St Clair and James. L. W. West III. Diana Patterson deserves special note for her generosity in sharing information. Her interest in John Murray dates back to the 1970s when she produced a University of Toronto M. A. thesis, 'John Murray, 32 Fleet Street: an Investigation of Publishing and Taste with a Catalogue of his Publications'. It has been my good fortune not only to have profited from her research but also to have found someone with a kindred passion for the first John Murray. Patrick Maguire worked closely with me as I wrote each chapter, indeed each paragraph; and I am grateful to him for his thoughtful guidance.

Many institutions allowed me access to their collections or took time to answer queries, bibliographical or otherwise. The list is long but important to record: Aberdeen University Library, Amherst College Library, the Bodleian Library, Boston University Medical Library, Cambridge University Library, the Folger Shakespeare Library, Glasgow University Library, Harvard University libraries, the Humanities Research Center, the Huntington, Indiana University libraries, the John Rylands Library, the Library Company of Philadelphia, the Library of Congress, the National Library of Ireland, the National Library of Medicine, the New York Academy of Medicine, Northwestern University Library, Princeton University libraries, the Public Record Office of Northern Ireland, Rutgers University Library, Saint David's University College Library, the Scottish National Portrait Gallery, Smithsonian Institution libraries, Temple University Library, Trinity College Library, Tulane University Library, University of California libraries, University of Chicago libraries, University of Essex Library, University of Illinois libraries, the University of Kentucky Library, University of Michigan libraries, University of Minnesota libraries, University of North Carolina libraries, University of Pennsylvania libraries, Washington and Lee University Library and Washington State University Library.

I would like to thank the staff at several institutions where I completed more extensive pieces of research and writing: Edinburgh University Library, the National Library of Scotland, the New York Public Library, the Scottish Record Office and the Yale University libraries.

Above all, I am grateful to the British Academy for awarding me a three-year post-doctoral research fellowship between 1989 and 1992 to write this book.

Finally, I would like to thank my family and friends — none more so than Martin Adam — for their patience and unconditional support.

A version of Chapter 4 appeared in *A Genius for Letters: Booksellers and Bookselling from the 16th to the 20th Century*, eds. Robin Myers and Michael Harris (Winchester: St Paul's Bibliographies, 1995); a section from Chapter 7 was published in *The Long Room*, 40 (1995); and parts of Chapter 10 in the *Journal of Scholarly Publishing*, 28 (April 1997).

Notes on the Text

Quotations from manuscript sources in the Murray Archive reproduce spellings as they stand, even when inaccurate. For reasons of clarity, however, small corrections have occasionally been made which would in no way alter meaning. Superscripts and other abbreviations are expanded (e.g. 'which' for wch and 'the' for y^e); missing punctuation (normally full stops) added; and the occasional upper case letter at the start of a sentence provided.

As a precaution against libel, Murray sometimes wrote a name like Johnson as 'Jo_____n'. For the sake of clarity, such a construction would appear in the text as 'Jo[hnso]n'.

The abbreviation JM has been used for John Murray, AL for Account Ledger, DB for Daybook and BB for Booksellers' Book. Other abbreviations are self-explanatory. Full citations to printed books and articles are supplied in the Bibliography.

Unless stated otherwise, documents cited are held at the John Murray Archive. To quote from this material, permission must be obtained from John Murray.

Chronology

1 Jan. 1737:	Born John McMurray in Edinburgh, only surviving son of Robert McMurray and Jean Ross.
10 May 1742:	Mother dies, aged forty.
Feb. 1752:	Attends the University of Edinburgh.
About 1754:	Enters the Royal Navy in the 34th Company of Marines.
Feb. 1763:	Treaty of Paris ends the Seven Years War. McMurray returns to the naval base Chatham.
3 Mar. 1763:	Marries Nancy Weemss (born May 1745) of Rochester in Kent, daughter of Captain William Weemss and Ann Weber. Retires from navy on half-pay.
Spring 1764:	Returns to Edinburgh to find employment.
Summer 1764:	Works as a factotum at Gordonstoun Estate near Elgin for about fourteen months.
Oct. 1765:	Returns to Edinburgh; begins to copy the letters he writes.
Mar. 1766:	Writes anonymous pamphlet, *A Letter from a Gentleman in Edinburgh, to his Friend in the Country: Occasioned by the late Theatrical Disturbances.*
Apr. 1766:	Returns to Chatham to find employment.
May 1767:	Reinstated as second lieutenant in the navy.
Nov. 1767:	Writes a fictional romance 'The History of Sir Launcelot Edgevile', published in instalments until March 1768 in the *Court Miscellany.*
Oct. 1768:	Father dies in Edinburgh; inherits £60. Changes surname to Murray. Negotiates to buy the bookselling and publishing business of William Sandby at 32 Fleet Street for £1000. Opens for business on the 20th.
c. Jan. 1770:	Illegitimate son Archie, born; mother unknown.
Oct. 1771:	Travels to Ireland to organise the sale of an estate owned by his late maternal uncle James Ross, which he and other family members have inherited.
Feb. 1774:	*Donaldson v. Becket*, the landmark case in the House of Lords, confirms a limitation on copyright. Murray testi-

fies in favour of the limitation in May when Becket and his allies appeal the decision.

Apr. 1775:	Returns to Ireland for five months to settle the estate sale. Receives £2042, his share of the inheritance.
4 July 1776:	American Colonies declare independence; war imminent.
22 Sept. 1776:	Wife, Nancy, dies.
May 1777:	Writes and publishes *A Letter to William Mason . . . concerning his Edition of Mr. Gray's Poems. And the Practices of Booksellers.*
23 Feb. 1778:	Marries Hester Weemss (born Nov. 1746), Nancy's younger sister.
27 Nov. 1778:	Son John born.
mid-Oct. 1780:	Daughter Jane born.
6 May 1782:	Suffers a stroke and is incapacitated for several months.
Jan. 1783:	Establishes the *English Review,* a monthly literary and political magazine.
July 1784:	Writes and publishes *An Author's Conduct to the Public, stated in the Behaviour of Dr. William Cullen.*
July 1785:	Visits Edinburgh to hear his case for copyright infringement against the proprietors of the *Encyclopaedia Britannica.*
May 1787	Visits Edinburgh with Hester and children.
29 Dec. 1787:	Daughter Mary Anne born.
Feb. 1790:	Writes the *Defence of Innes Munro against a Charge of Plagiarism.*
Summer 1790:	Visits Edinburgh twice to help settle estate of the bookseller Charles Elliot and purchase stock and copyrights at the Elliot sale.
Jan. 1793:	Louis XVI executed; war with France imminent.
Aug. 1793:	Incapacitated by illness.
6 Nov. 1793:	Dies in London at the age of fifty-six; interred in St Dunstan's Church.

Family Tree
The Line of John Murray

(b.=born; c.=christened; d.=died; m.=married; *=lived to adulthood)

William Murray, b. about 1625
m. Isobel Pratt, 7 Aug. 1649
  |

George Murray, b. 14 Mar. 1662
m. 1697 Lilias Lauder, b. at Lasswade, 9 Feb. 1677
  |

Robert McMurray, b. Mar. 1698 at Cockpen; d. 29 Oct. 1768 at Edinburgh
m. 1727 Jean Ross, c. 30 Dec. 1703, d. 10 May 1742
  |

1. Barbara, b. 1 Sept. 1729
2. *Elizabeth, b. 15 Mar. 1731
3. Robert, c. 28 Jan. 1732
4. *Janet, b. 30 Dec. 1732
5. James, b. 23 Jan. 1734
6. *Robina, b. 9 Oct. 1735
7. *John, b. at Edinburgh 1 Jan. 1737
8. Agnes, c. 6 Jan. 1738
9. Thomas, b. 9 March 1740

John Murray I, d. 6 Nov. 1793
m. 3 Mar. 1763 Nancy Weemss, c. in Gillingham, Kent, 27 May 1745 d.
22 Sept. 1775; no issue. Illegitimate son Archibald born about Jan. 1770.
m. 23 Feb. 1777 Hester Weemss, c. in Gillingham, Kent, 23 Nov. 1746.
    |

    1. *John Murray II, b. 27 Nov. 1778; m. Anne Elliot, 6 Mar. 1806;
        d. 27 June 1843
    2. William, b. Oct. 1779; d. soon after
    3. *Jane, c. 24 Oct. 1780; m. Rev. William Woolams Holland, Canon
        of Chichester, 30 Jan. 1809; d. 23 Mar. 1866
    4. name unknown, b. 31 Aug. 1781; d. soon after
    5. name unknown, b. about Jan. 1787

6. *Mary Anne, b. 29 Dec. 1787; m. Rev. William Cooke, Vicar at Bromyard, Herefordshire, 13 Dec. 1810; d. 17 May 1847
7. a son, b. 16 Feb. 1789, (stillborn)

John Murray III, b. 16 Apr. 1808; m. Marion Smith, 6 July 1847; d. 2 Apr. 1892
|
John Murray IV, b. 18 Dec. 1851; m. Evelyn Leslie, 4 Mar. 1878; d. 30 Nov. 1928
|
John Murray V, b. 12 June 1883; m. Lady Helen de Vere Brassey, 16 Aug. 1916; d. 6 Oct. 1967
|
John Murray VI (nephew of above), b. 22 Sept. 1909; m. 12 Apr. 1939 Diana James; d. 22 July 1993
|
John Murray VII, b. 25 June 1941; m. Virginia Lascelles; m. 3 Oct. 1970

Introduction

Today John Murray's shop at 32 Fleet Street is a branch of the Bradford and Bingley Building Society, and the rooms above, where he and his family lived, are lawyers' chambers. Little remains of the original building, described in Murray's lease with the Worshipful Company of Cordwainers down to the brass window fittings. Only a plaque — unveiled for the two hundredth anniversary of his death on 6 November 1793 — marks the location where Murray founded his business, where his son lived and worked, and where in 1808 the third John Murray was born.

In October 1768 Murray founded the publishing house which still bears his name. He had no previous publishing experience and began with capital of only £700. When he died after a twenty-five year career, his stock, shares and copyrights were valued at over £12,000, and nearly one thousand imprints included his name. Murray's son, John, who inherited the business, was to become one of the most successful publishers of the early nineteenth century, so successful indeed that he is sometimes mistakenly credited with having established the house.

In 1891 Samuel Smiles wrote an account of the second Murray, *A Publisher and his Friends*, and in 1919 the fourth Murray honoured his father with *A Brief Memoir*. There was an obvious omission.

The first Murray made his way in an exclusive and competitive business at a time when modern practices were first being introduced into the book trade. The 1710 Copyright Act, by eliminating perpetual ownership of literary property, established the principle which would ultimately lead to the author and his publisher gaining dominance in a literary world once almost entirely controlled by the bookseller. It was not until 1774, however, when the House of Lords upheld the limitation on copyright set out in this Act, that these changes began to take effect. Though it is relatively little known, this decision continues to be the basis of current copyright law.

Born in Edinburgh in 1737, Murray was one of many Scots who ventured south to make a career during the eighteenth century. An enduring affection for Scotland did not exclude equally ardent patriotism for

England, his adopted home. He felt himself in accord with the British imperial spirit, and he derived much satisfaction and profit from selling his publications throughout the Empire. A family man, he kept in close contact with his three elder sisters and managed their financial affairs until each found a husband. He himself married twice. His first wife was Nancy Weemss, whom he met at Chatham while serving in the Royal Navy. After she died in 1776, he married Nancy's sister, Hester, not long afterwards. Although Nancy did not bear him children, Murray did father an illegitimate son, Archie, during their marriage. He supported the child and afterwards established him in a naval career. By Hester he had two daughters and the son who was to carry on his business. For several reasons it is tempting to suggest that Archie's mother may have been Hester: the fact that Hester lived with her sister and brother-in-law at the time when Archie would have been conceived; the closeness of Archie to the mother and children of Murray's second marriage — even more so after Murray's death in 1793. But if this were the case, great care was taken to keep Archie's origins a secret, perhaps even unknown to Archie himself.

Happily, information about the first Murray (with certain exceptions) is plentiful. Three years before he started in business, he began to copy his letters (or extracts from them), a practice he continued until his death. This previously untapped correspondence, consisting of some five thousand letters — predominately of a business nature — forms the basis of this study. Additional information has been drawn from the replies that survive (about 500); an account ledger (AL), kept between 1768 and 1780; two daybooks (DB1 and DB2), from 1768 to 1776, in which virtually every shop transaction was recorded; a booksellers' book (BB) in which he listed his shares in certain books and the costs of producing editions of them; a diary from 1775–76; and other miscellaneous papers in the archive and elsewhere.[1] A

---

[1] An index I compiled of the letters Murray copied into ten volumes of letterbooks, as well as of the extant letters written to him, is in the Archive. The first daybook records transactions from Oct. 1768 to Dec. 1773 (428 pp.); the second continues to April 1776 (368 pp.). A further daybook from Sept. 1795 to April 1797 is extant (373 pp.). Only the first of two (or possibly three) account ledgers, covering the period from 1768 to 1780, is extant (327 pp. with an index). However, there are two ledgers from the period after Murray's death: from 1795 to 1800 (241 pp. with an index) and 1800 to 1803 (454 pp., many blank, with an index). Entries from the daybook were totalled and entered in the ledger, which contains the accounts of customers, fellow tradesmen and some accounts referring to individual publications. The booksellers' book records purchases at trade sales and shares of books between March 1776 and May 1796 (69 pp. with an index). Among those business records mentioned but which do not survive are: (1) an earlier booksellers' book; (2) a salebook, which listed book-by-book who had bought copies, in what quantity and when; (3) a receipt book, in which Murray recorded daily expenses; (4) a cash book; (5) an exchange book, in which he listed the extensive trading of stock; (6) a binders' book containing detailed accounts of

further primary resource of central importance has been more than one thousand books published between 1768 and 1795 on which the Murray name (including that of his wife and son) appears in the imprint. These are listed in the Checklist, with details of production and publication wherever they were available.

Among the hundreds of London booksellers who were active at the time, Murray left a record of his career which is, I believe, a unique survival. The archives of a handful of London printers during the eighteenth century are extant and have been productively mined.[2] Further afield, the vast records of the Société typographique de Neuchâtel are well known through the work of Robert Darnton. He describes his original study, *The Business of Enlightenment: A Publishing History of the* Encyclopédie *1775–1800* as a 'biography of a book'.[3] My study of John Murray, by contrast, offers a more traditional biography of a bookseller and publisher.

Murray's career begins to explain the ways in which someone whose primary concern is making money contributes to culture — that is culture in its widest sense. The material in the Murray Archive reveals a picture of the working life of a bookseller and publisher during a critical quarter-century in the history of the book trade. Murray responded not only to an enforceable limitation on copyright, but also to the needs of a rapidly growing reading public.

It was a time of considerable social and political change: he witnessed a protracted war with the American Colonies and watched events in France reach cataclysmic proportions. Moreover, he was keenly interested in India, the setting for so much political and economic intrigue and the source of so much wealth. During his lifetime the pace of industrial and scientific innovation accelerated, monarchical authority declined and democratic sentiment grew ever more forceful. No revolutionary, Murray supported the established order and was wary of radicalism. Yet he understood the necessity of reform. His was the attitude of a businessman who sought stability: 'A change of masters & politics', he lamented, 'makes all human affairs appear very frivolous. They naturally encourage a man's apathy.'[4]

Murray himself was anything but apathetic. Whenever an issue arose about which he felt strongly, his instinct was to write about it. Disputes

---

binding work; (7) a bankers' book in which he listed drafts and bills; and (8) a subscribing book, which presumably noted subscription orders and sales.
[2] The papers of the Strahans (1737–1857) are in the British Library (Add. MSS. 48800–48919). A considerable amount of work has been done on William Strahan, Murray's near contemporary, by Patricia Hernlund (see Bibliography). Another useful source is *The Bowyer Ledgers: the Printing Accounts of William Bowyer, Father and Son*, eds. K. Maslen and J. Lancaster (London, 1991).
[3] R. Darnton, *The Business of Enlightenment: A Publishing History of the* Encyclopédie *1775–1800* (Cambridge, MA, 1979), p. 1.
[4] JM to Rev. Alex. Murray, 13 Aug. 1771.

with authors and with fellow tradesmen over business practice occupied his pen, and on other occasions he felt moved to write on such topics as theatre riots in Edinburgh, maritime controversies and corruption in the East India Company. He also wrote a short novel before entering the book trade. His experience as a writer made him a better judge of literary merit and editor of texts — in all, a better publisher.

The agreements Murray negotiated with authors and other traders, the ways he produced and marketed his publications and the places at which he sold books show the fundamental economics of the book trade from an insider's point of view. And, perhaps more importantly, they explain something about the transmission of literary taste, scientific knowledge and political and philosophical ideas.

The publisher is at the centre of cultural history. In deciding what books he will produce, he to some extent determines the fate of ideas. An anecdote is often told of Murray's grandson, a pillar of the established church, who agreed to publish Darwin's *Origin of Species* in 1859 before he had even read the work.[5] Had this Murray been aware of its controversial nature, he probably would not have allowed it to appear. The first John Murray published no book of such significance. Nevertheless, he accomplished more than enough to perpetuate his name.

---

[5]John Murray III to Charles Darwin, 1 April 1859. Murray wrote: 'I can have no hesitation in swerving from my usual routine & in stating at once even without seeing the MS. that I shall be most happy to publish it for you . . . '.

Early Years

Kith and Kin

John Murray's father, Robert, was born in March 1698 near Dalkeith, seven miles south of Edinburgh. He was the eldest son of George Murray and Lilias Lauder.[1] The family lived at Eastmains farm on the Dalhousie estate, in the parish of Cockpen, where they were simple tenant farmers who worked the fertile tract of ground near the river Esk. After a traditional parish education, Robert enrolled at the University of Edinburgh. The Arts curriculum in the first year consisted of a class in Latin (called Humanity); in the second year Greek was studied; in the third Logic; and finally students took Natural Philosophy. Robert Murray is listed in the 1716 and 1717 rolls only.[2] On leaving university he was apprenticed to a lawyer. After training for five years, he took the oath of a notary public on 15 February 1722 and began his independent legal practice (see Plate 2a).[3]

As a solicitor, or writer as they were called in Scotland, Robert was a member of a profession which contributed much to Edinburgh's genteel identity. Scotland's distinctive legal system, largely based on Roman statute law rather than the English common law principle, was retained by an

---

[1] George and Lilias Murray produced thirteen children between the years 1698 when Robert was born and 1726 when the youngest boy, William, arrived (Old Parish Register for Dalkeith and Cockpen, Parish Record Office, Edinburgh). George Murray was born at Dalkeith on 14 March 1662. His parents, William Murray and Isobel Pratt, were married on 7 Aug. 1649 (though another parish record gives 3 April). Lilias Lauder was born at Lasswade on 9 Feb. 1677, the fourth of the six children born to Alexander Lauder (born at Lasswade about 1642) and Margaret Pursall (born at Lasswade about 1646).

[2] Robert may have continued at the university for a third year, but he did not matriculate for the final year. Two students named Robert Murray, in fact, are listed in the rolls for 1716 and 1717. However, just one continued in 1718. Throughout the eighteenth century, students at Edinburgh rarely took degrees, apart from those studying divinity or medicine ('Matriculation Rolls of the University of Edinburgh: Arts, Law, Divinity', i. 161, 165 and 169, Edinburgh University Library, Special Collections).

[3] Register of Notaries, 15 Feb. 1722, Scottish Record Office, Edinburgh.

article in the 1707 Act of Union with England. This Union of parliaments had brought an end to Scottish political autonomy, leaving elected representatives and peers of the realm to play out their politics in London. However, the law — together with Scotland's Presbyterian church and its democratic educational system — continued to be symbols, indeed expressions, of independence.

At the time Robert began to practice law he changed his surname to McMurray. Why he added the prefix is uncertain, although it was not unknown for a first-born son to do so. Perhaps he thought this distinction might set him apart from his clansmen in the competitive legal marketplace. Family tradition has it that he made this change after the failed Jacobite Rising of 1715, when one of his brothers, a colonel who fought against the Hanoverians, found himself a wanted man and was forced to take refuge in France. By altering his surname and moving to Edinburgh, Robert, so tradition has it, was attempting to distance himself from his Jacobite relations.[4] This story is doubtful as his brother Alexander was only fifteen at the time. If there was any Jacobite connection at all, it was more likely an uncle.[5]

In 1727 Robert McMurray married Jean Ross, a twenty-three-year-old woman born in Dundee who was the daughter of James Ross and Elizabeth Philips.[6] The McMurrays rented a dwelling house on the first storey of a typically warren-like tenement in Bailie Clerk's Land, a small courtyard which ran off a narrow close on the south side of Edinburgh's High Street near the Lawnmarket. At this time Edinburgh's population was about 50,000, and almost all the inhabitants were packed into the mile-long High Street running from the Castle down to the Palace of Holyroodhouse. By 1734 Robert was advancing well enough in his career that he could afford to purchase a property in Bailie Clerk's Land, which included a shop beneath their rooms.[7] Even at this date the houses in Bailie Clerk's Land were old structures, and the McMurrays often found smoke from what was then a

---

[4]Information (though inaccurate) from a late nineteenth-century paper in the Murray Archive entitled 'Tradition' — the probable source for Samuel Smiles's account in *A Publisher and his Friends*, i, 1.

[5]For years afterwards, Murray family members spoke of a gift from this Jacobite uncle, of an elegant ring, inset with diamonds, containing a picture of a savage in chains (Anne H. Murray to John Murray V, 14 March 1929). A Colonel Charles Murray was active in the failed 1715 Rising, the son of the second Duke of Atholl, who lost his right to the title for his part in the affair. But such a romantic connection, however tempting, is not supported by genealogical evidence.

[6]Jean Ross was christened 30 Dec. 1703 in Dundee. She had two siblings, an elder sister Elizabeth, christened in Jan. 1702, and a younger brother James, christened in May 1705 (*International Genealogical Index* on CD-ROM and Old Parish Register).

[7]The Sasine Record Book for Edinburgh records Robert McMurray's purchase of the property (B/22/2/26, ff. 171–3, Scottish Record Office). He received nine guineas in rent per annum for the shop.

wool shop below seeping upwards. It was a crowded urban existence, the accommodation consisting of three bedrooms, 'several closets, kitchen, cellar, and other conveniences'.[8] A band of men and women known as caddies delivered water daily, sometimes up as many as thirteen flights of stairs. Waste of all description was flung from the city's windows at designated times to the call of 'Gardyloo' (a corruption of the French *Gare de l'eau* — beware of the water). In his aptly titled poem, *Auld Reikie*, Robert Fergusson told how the inhabitants 'kindly shower Edina's roses, to quicken and regale our noses'.

On 1 January 1737, Robert McMurray waited as his wife, Jean, gave birth to a boy. This was their seventh child and the only son to survive. Of the nine children born to Jean McMurray between 1729 and 1740 only this boy, whom they named John, and three older sisters — Elizabeth, Janet and Robina (nicknamed Binny) — reached adulthood.[9] The birth of two further children undermined the constitution of Jean McMurray. Doctors diagnosed tympany, or the 'wind dropsy', which swelled her stomach and caused severe pain. She died on 10 May 1742 at the age of forty and was buried not far from Bailie Clerk's Land in Greyfriars' Churchyard.[10] Her son John was only a little more than five years old at the time.

The burden of looking after the McMurray children fell to a sister of Robert's, who moved in with the family, and to the eldest daughter, Elizabeth, who was then eleven years old. As the only son, John was given every advantage his father's means allowed. He received a classical Edinburgh training. At an early age he would have been enrolled in one of the town's private academies to receive a basic grounding in Latin, English and arithmetic. Afterwards, he took classes at the Edinburgh High School. He continued with the traditional Scottish programme of study at the University of Edinburgh, enrolling in Professor George Stuart's Humanity class from February 1752, just after his fifteenth birthday. This was an age at which students typically attended, although some were even younger.[11] McMurray spent only one year at university. He was not a bookish person; and although his father probably encouraged him to follow the legal profession, his interest lay in more active pursuits. Not long after he set up as a bookseller in 1768, he explained his very practical, businesslike view of scholarship in a letter to a friend:

[8] *Edinburgh Advertiser*, Tue. 29 Nov. 1770. Advertisement for the sale of the McMurrays' house and shop.
[9] Old Parish Register for Edinburgh, Parish Record Office, Edinburgh. Even among middle-class Scottish families more than half of the children usually died. In the *Gentleman's Magazine* for the month of Murray's birth (vii, Jan. 1737, p. 62) the 'Monthly Bill of British Mortality' reported 2296 deaths, nearly half under the age of five.
[10] Edinburgh Register of Deaths, Greyfriars' Churchyard, Parish Record Office.
[11] 'Matriculation Rolls of the University of Edinburgh: Arts, Law, Divinity', i, 229 (Edinburgh University Library, Special Collections).

Look about you and see who it is that thrives most in the world. It is the industrious and plodding no matter how illiterate not the abstracted man of sense & learning. I believe I might go farther, and assert that he whose discourse is mostly nonsense prevails infinitely better in every worldly concern, than the man who never opens his mouth without consideration and reflection.[12]

On the High Seas

At the age of fifteen or sixteen John McMurray was by no means prepared to face the mundane necessities of a professional career. He was inclined neither to the law nor to medicine, which was so popular in Edinburgh, nor was it his wish to become a cleric like his Uncle Alexander of whom he was very fond. There was an adventurous side to his character. A young man with modest finances, he wanted to break free of the confines of Edinburgh and enter the service of the Royal Marines. Tobias Smollett's picaresque hero Roderick Random may be an appropriate character with whom to compare McMurray. Like Roderick, he set off from Scotland to become a sailor, saw something of the world and embroiled himself in a series of riotous and amorous adventures. In one instance, for example, McMurray reported how, after 'I had accidently got much in liquor . . . I was beset in Chatham by 4 or 5 stout shipwrights on account of some gallantry I was foolishly showing to a girl'. So roughly was he treated that 'there were at present as many spots in my face as in the moon'.[13] Rarely one to accept fully the consequences of his folly, McMurray asked a naval friend to write an ironic article for the public papers setting forth 'the courage of four or 5 strong English men manfully bruising & breaking an unfortunate scotsman whom they catched in a corner'.[14] The victim himself penned a letter of protest to the Commissioner of the Chatham Dockyards but, upon reconsidering his embarrassing role in the affair, prudently chose not to make a formal complaint.[15]

The prospect of seeking glory and of serving his country in war against France, which had begun in the summer of 1756, excited the young Scotsman. Robert McMurray employed what influence he had to put his son on a course that would ultimately lead to a commission as a second lientenant in the 34th Company of Marines (the commission is dated 24 June 1762). Little is known of John's career at sea, what battles he fought in or where he sailed. He certainly went to Portugal and later noted with regret that his travels did not bring him to India.[16] When the Seven Years War ended in victory for Britain

[12]JM to John Cunningham, 16 Sept. 1769.
[13]JM to Wm Falconer, 23 June 1768.
[14]Ibid.
[15]JM to Thomas Hanway, 2 July 1768.
[16]JM to Capt. Wm Fraser, 28 Sept. 1779. On the subject of naval life at the time, both at

with the signing of the Treaty of Paris in February 1763, Lieutenant McMurray returned to the naval base at Chatham.

Shortly after his return to Chatham, McMurray fell in love with Nancy Weemss, the daughter of William Weemss (a retired naval captain) and his wife, Ann. It could not have been a long romance; McMurray's sea duties would have prevented their spending much time together. Nevertheless, Captain Weemss was persuaded that it was a suitable match, and on 3 March 1763 the Reverend John Jenkinson married the couple in the parish church at Chatham.[17] John was twenty-six at the time and his bride more than eight years younger.

With the war at an end, the ships laid up, McMurray retired from the marines on half-pay. Less than a guinea a week, it was a meagre subsistence for an officer accustomed to gentlemanly living. Not surprisingly, he campaigned to increase the officers' stipend. In a letter to a London newspaper he called on the government to relieve the distress of 'a Set of Men, whom every Lover of his Country must hold in Estimation'. Such a man, he continued, is 'unable in Company to afford the Expence of a common Journeyman Mechanic, and obliged to retire from Society rather than his Poverty should be discovered'.[18] McMurray's patriotic rhetoric, however, had little effect on the government which was faced with a huge national debt in the aftermath of war.

In Search of a Job

An income of less than a guinea a week offered little possibility for setting up a home with Nancy, whose dowry of £700 was closely guarded by a cautious, even suspicious father who was determined not to release the money until McMurray was settled in gainful employment. Because of these uncertain circumstances and the embarrassment it made him feel, McMurray did not publicise the fact of his marriage. To find employment, he was forced to endure an unwanted separation from his wife and return to Scotland. Nancy was left to stay with her parents and younger sister Hester at their home in Brompton, near Chatham.[19]

sea and ashore, see N. A. M. Rodgers, *The Wooden World: An Anatomy of the Georgian Navy* (London, 1986), which concentrates on the period of the Seven Years War. On the war itself as it progressed at sea, see J. S. Corbett, *England in the Seven Years War: A Study in Combined Strategy*, 2 vols. (London, 1907).

[17] Parish of Chatham Records, p. 57, entry # 219. Nancy (sometimes called Ann) was christened at St Nicholas' Church on 27 May 1745 and was probably born a matter of days or weeks before.

[18] *Public Advertiser*, Feb. 10, 1768. The article is found in JM's album of newspaper clippings and has the characteristic tick marking his authorship.

[19] Hester was christened on 23 Nov. 1746, eighteen months after her sister, at St Nicholas' Church.

Following a reunion with his family in Edinburgh, John journeyed north to work at Gordonstoun, the estate of the Gordon family near Elgin. His uncle, the Reverend Alexander Murray (Robert's younger brother) had arranged a place for him there.[20] Gordonstoun supported many tenant farmers and a large house. McMurray worked as a general dogsbody and served as a private secretary to Sir Robert (the 4th Baronet) and his son William.[21] Looking after the library at Gordonstoun, which was one of the best in Scotland, was another of his duties.[22] He also took an interest in the crops produced on the estate, suggested introducing new ones and explored the potential for creating a London export market in salted fish and pickled oysters.[23] Being in the company of worldly gentlemen was formative. And John later remarked that it was from Sir Robert 'that I acquired the small knowledge I possess of Men and things'.[24]

In October 1765, after more than a year's service, McMurray left Gordonstoun and returned to Edinburgh. To his uncle he confessed that he was 'very melancholy', and to William Gordon he told of a rash plan of 'going to London sometime next month upon chance'.[25] This hasty plan was put off, but the urgings of his wife inexorably drew him south. Her own situation was not happy. Difficulties with her parents were such that John told her she should move out, even to a boarding house, rather than 'be a minute longer under the dominion of those that used her so barbarously'.[26] Just what abuse Nancy was subjected to is unclear. But John's fears were such that he wrote to Captain Weemss asking how the man 'could use his own daughter and my wife ill'.[27] It was not long, however, before he found father-in-law and wife alike angry *at him*, both on account of his long

[20]Alexander Murray married Isobel Gordon and obtained, through the influence of her relation Sir Robert Gordon of Gordonstoun, posts in various northern parishes before becoming the minister at Duffus in 1748. Protests were made against his appointment because he was accused of having informed against distressed Jacobites after the battle of Culloden in 1746. But letters of support to Robert Gordon were sufficient to secure the post (E. D. Dunbar, *Social Life in Former Days, Chiefly in the Province of Moray*, Edinburgh, 1865, pp. 258–60; *Fasti Ecclesiasticae Scotticae*, under Murray).
[21]The earliest extant letter written by Murray is found in the Gordon Papers (National Library of Scotland, Dep. 175/75/3302) dated 13 July 1764. It concerns the building of the manse at Dunduras. For an account of the history of the Gordonstoun estate, see the early chapters of H. L. Brereton, *Gordonstoun: Ancient Estate and Modern School* (Edinburgh, 1968).
[22]This remarkable collection was formed in the early seventeenth century and is described in *A Catalogue of the Singular and Curious Library originally formed between 1610 and 1650 by Sir Robert Gordon of Gordonstoun*, Sold at Auction, London, March and April 1816. After McMurray left Gordonstoun, he added to the library with purchases at auction and in the shops.
[23]JM to Colonel Robert Gordon, 11 Oct. 1765; JM to William Brand, 11 Oct. 1765 and 17 Jan. 1766.
[24]JM to Sir Robert Gordon (5th Baronet), 19 Feb. 1774.
[25]JM to Alex. Murray, 6 Dec. 1765; to Wm Gordon, 17 Dec. 1765.
[26]JM to Nancy McMurray, 15 Oct. 1765.
[27]JM to Wm Weemss, 15 Oct. 1765.

absence and his inability to settle himself in employment. Although these accusations piqued his pride, they did not damage his genuine love and affection for Nancy. 'My intentions were suspected', he explained to her, 'but unjustly'.[28] To placate Nancy, he promised to return to Brompton as soon as possible. To placate Captain Weemss, he said that he would even agree to resuming marine service, either on a merchant ship or with a new naval commission, and a few days later he reluctantly wrote to a friend about a plan to become the purser on an Indiaman ship.[29]

McMurray had outgrown an adolescent love of change and adventure. He decided it was only a matter of time before he would 'set himself soberly down to acquire money by Industry, moderation and patience'.[30] Although far from complacent, he knew that a foolish decision at this juncture could prove disastrous. 'What I wanted', he reassured his wife (and himself), 'could not be completed in a day'.[31] But just what he did want, he genuinely did not know. At this time McMurray began to keep a record of his correspondence. These early letters are characterised by his preoccupation with an uncertain future. In desperation he asked his old university friend, Archy Paxton, to procure him an appointment as 'a superintendant over any of the new purchased lands in Grenada'. And a few weeks later he met with the 'miscarriage' of a project to get into the Duke of Gordon's service.[32]

Man of Letters

Meanwhile, McMurray mingled in Edinburgh's literary circles, often writing to his uncle in the north of Scotland with news of the latest publications. In this period the Scots were producing a remarkable number of important works in such fields as philosophy, history and science. The contributions of such men as David Hume, Adam Smith and Joseph Black, among others, have endured. McMurray knew or read the works of such men, and when he set up shop in London, his Scottish literary connections proved to be a source of opportunity.

To distract himself from the worries of unemployment and separation from his wife, McMurray diverted himself by attending the theatre, then located just up from the Palace of Holyroodhouse in Canongate. Religious controversy had often surrounded dramatic performances in Scotland, the Calvinist tenets of the Scottish church being strongly opposed to secular entertainments. Indeed, some ten years earlier in 1756, a vociferous debate

[28]JM to Nancy McMurray, 26 Dec. 1765.
[29]JM to Arch. Paxton, 28 Jan. 1766.
[30]This was how Murray later put it in a letter to his nephew, Alex. Murray, 15 March 1784.
[31]JM to Nancy McMurray, 4 Feb. 1767.
[32]JM to Arch. Paxton, 18 Oct. 1765; to Alex. Murray and to John Gordon, 28 Oct. 1765.

had arisen over the Reverend John Home's romantic tragedy *Douglas*. Many of the more zealous Presbyterians considered it improper for a minister to write plays or even for clergymen to attend performances. A pamphlet war broke out over the issue. David Hume and his enlightened ministerial friends on the side of Home were opposed by those clergymen who believed that the theatre itself was an immoral institution. The dispute was characteristic of the kind of extra-political controversy which occupied Scottish society after the Union. The outcome was a victory for Home's liberal side and more generally for the freedom of expression in Scotland.[33]

When John McMurray produced his own pamphlet on theatrical affairs in March 1766 he surely had this recent history in mind. He wrote *A Letter from a Gentleman in Edinburgh, to his Friend in the Country: Occasioned by the late Theatrical Disturbance* to make an instructive point about the need to improve the quality of performances on the Scottish stage. Authorship of this pamphlet has sometimes been mistakenly attributed to Allan Ramsay, the Scottish portrait painter.[34] Published anonymously, the piece was originally written as a private letter to his former employer William Gordon. McMurray told Gordon, somewhat disingenuously, that it was 'published in a whim' and would probably be 'the last publication I would ever attempt'.[35] In fact, he had already written a continuation, and only his departure from Edinburgh prevented him from publishing it.

The theatre was then in a state of disarray, and the public demanded better value from the managers, then Messrs Beat and Dawson. Intrigue behind the scenes between these individuals and their actresses made more compelling drama than the actual performances. McMurray described the Edinburgh theatre as an adversarial political microcosm, with these managers on one side and the public on the other. Remarkably high box office returns when the season had opened in November 1765 made the managers even more insolent. Why, McMurray asked, were they not meeting the expectations of their audiences? Why were they miscasting roles, placing comic actors in serious parts and the reverse?

> The M[anag]ers, to add to their contempt of the audience . . . have introduced Mrs. R[o]bs[o]n in preference to [Mrs. Didier]; a woman her inferior in every way: One without capacity, or genius, for any thing beyond short dialogue in low comedy . . . and who has besides the character of unchastity

---

[33]An account of the *Douglas* affair is found in R. B. Sher, *Church and University in the Scottish Enlightenment* (Edinburgh, 1985), pp. 74–92.
[34]See R. Lowe, J. E. Arnot and J. W. Robinson, *English Theatrical Literature 1559–1900: A Bibliography* (London, 1970), item 1915. Ramsay's authorship may have suggested by the title-page epigraph, a quotation from the poet and essayist William Shenstone that the profession of a player is 'like that of a painter, one of the imitative arts, whose means are pleasure, and whose end is virtue. They both alike, for a subsistence, submit themselves to public opinion' (William Shenstone, 'On Books and Writers', in *Works*, Edinburgh, 1765, ii, 193).
[35]JM to Wm Gordon, 3 Mar. 1766.

given her in a great degree. But this female it seems is in keeping of one of the M[ana]gers; (though it is confidently alledged she has already two husbands alive).[36]

It was a performance of John Gay's *Beggar's Opera* which sparked off the 'theatrical disturbance' to which the pamphlet refers. When the programmed hornpipe dance in the third act did not occur, the audience stopped the performance and demanded that the manager apologise. Upon his refusal 'the audience then imagined they were justified to proceed to extremity. They accordingly began; and scenes, sconces, boxes, and benches were quickly torn to pieces, and a deal of mischief performed.'[37] It was not the rabble who were behind the 'disturbance' but a group composed mainly of law students, some of whose fathers were judges in the Court of Session.[38] One significant consequence of these tumultuous events was an action by the government to reform and regulate the Edinburgh theatre by granting a royal licence.[39]

McMurray's pamphlet went some way towards shifting Scottish theatrical controversy from a matter of morality to one of quality. The epistolary form suited his rhetorical style and disputatious nature. The private letter made public allowed the reader a privileged view of the issue at hand, and through shared intimacy encouraged agreement with the writer's opinions. Whereas McMurray's private letters often have an air of public declamation, this published letter reads like a private complaint. Fascinated to overhear the speculations in the town on its authorship, he waited to see whether his views would have any impact.

At the beginning of April 1766 McMurray took passage on a Leith trader sailing to Great Yarmouth and from there continued to London. News that his sister-in-law Hester had contracted smallpox delayed the long-awaited reunion with his wife and an anticipated confrontation with her father. He had never had this threatening disease, nor had his wife, who for that reason had placed herself in lodgings away from the family. Already,

---

[36]*A Letter from a Gentleman in Edinburgh, to his Friend in the Country: Occasioned by the late Theatrical Disturbance*, p. 8.

[37]*A Letter*, p. 13.

[38]Ten years later Murray witnessed similar scenes in London at the Drury Lane Theatre where Garrick was acting. A riot broke out over whether the play *The Blackamour Washed White* should be performed: 'Hostilities,' Murray reported, 'began betwixt the *pros* & *cons*, and some hard knocks were given & received. But the enemies of the piece proved victorious, and Garrick's address with Mr. King's both of whom tried their rhetoric at different times with the audience proved ineffectual. After much contention 'till eleven at night the partisans of each side fled off & no entertainment was performed' (Diary, 5 Feb. 1776; compare another account of the same 'riot' in *The London Stage 1660–1800*, Carbondale, IL, 1962, Pt. 4, p. 1950).

[39]The story is told more fully in James Dibdin, *The Annals of the Edinburgh Stage* (Edinburgh, 1888), pp. 132–48. A more recent work of related interest is M. Baer, *Theatre and Disorder in Late Georgian London* (Oxford, 1991). The new Canongate Theatre Royal opened on 9 December 1767.

the girls' aunt and uncle had died in the wave of infection, and their mother was unwell. As if this cloud were not enough to taint the reunion, he himself fell ill with smallpox within a few days of his arrival. 'There is a chasm here for near 3 months', he later wrote in his letterbook in July, 'occasioned by my sickness at Brompton.'[40]

Recovery was slow, but by the middle of the autumn McMurray was well enough to be 'heartily wearied of an idle life & wished to be employed some way or other'.[41] Although actively pursuing several possibilities, he still had a considerable amount of time on his hands and therefore occupied himself with literary projects. Two of his efforts are worthy of note: the first is a fictional romance called 'The History of Sir Launcelot Edgevile' which appeared over a four-month period beginning at the end of 1767 in a periodical called the *Court Miscellany*.[42] The second is a short letter he wrote for the public newspapers on the dispute between two of the most famous literary men of the day, David Hume and Jean Jacques Rousseau.

Thousands of novels and shorter works of fiction published during the eighteenth century appeared first in magazines, especially after 1740.[43] Most of this periodical fiction has been justly consigned to oblivion, but a few works, such as Smollett's *Sir Launcelot Greaves*, are still read. A rapidly growing reading public had created a great demand for fiction in the mid-eighteenth century. Books were then costly, and subscription libraries, where one paid an annual fee for the privilege of borrowing the latest titles, were a cheaper but by no means inexpensive alternative. The magazine, circulating among families and friends, filled a gap in the market. As an aspiring author, McMurray learned something of the way this side of the trade worked. A few years later as a proprietor and editor of different periodicals, he was at the centre of these developments and knew the challenges of selling enough copies to stay afloat.

It is unlikely that McMurray was paid anything for 'Sir Launcelot'. The excitement of seeing his work in print and of sending copies to friends and relations was all the remuneration he could expect. 'Sir Launcelot' is typical of the undistinguished mass of sentimental fiction produced at the time. Certainly it is no classic. A fable-like tale of about ten thousand words, it is poorly characterised, didactic in tone, often clumsy and sometimes affected in style. It relates a few curious episodes in the life of the eponymous hero, a cosseted twenty-five-year-old who begins to make his way in a turbulent

[40]Letterbook entry for 12 July 1766.
[41]JM to Arch. Paxton, 17 Oct. 1766.
[42]The 'History of Sir Launcelot Edgevile' appeared in the *Court Miscellany*, 3 (Nov. 1767), pp. 605–6; (Dec. 1767), pp. 629–34; 4 (Jan. 1768), pp. 6–11; (Feb. 1768), pp. 78–80; and (Mar. 1768), pp. 122–4.
[43]A useful account of the subject is found in R. D. Mayo, *The English Novel in Magazines, 1740–1815*. 'Sir Launcelot' is included in Mayo's 'Catalogue of Magazine Novels and Novelettes' (item 641 of 1374), p. 525.

world. Most eighteenth-century fiction of this kind ends hastily, but 'Sir Launcelot' has no ending at all, at least not one that appeared in the *Court Miscellany*. McMurray had planned to write more of the tale, but, as he told William Gordon, he 'left it off being conscious of my inability to bring it to a conclusion'.[44] In different circumstances he might have taken it up again, but he was more a man of action than reflection and better suited to publishing and selling books than writing them.

McMurray's public letter on the affair between Hume and Rousseau was a different kind of effort altogether. It was written in the context of a mass of other related printed material about an affair which took place over the period from January 1766 to the middle of 1767 and was the literary *cause célèbre*.[45] In both Paris and London the Hume-Rousseau affair produced an amazingly large amount of public and private commentary by the main participants, from defenders and antagonists and in society at large. McMurray's letter was one of many of its kind, and coming as it did towards the end of the affair, he was concerned more with the conduct of the central players in the dispute than with its content. He hoped to have the last word. In more general terms, the strident tone of his letter suggests his desire to see an increased acceptance of publicly expressed opinion as a legitimate force for shaping and judging the outcome of events. Writing such pieces whetted an already healthy appetite for comment.

Rousseau, one of the most controversial thinkers of the age, published *Emile* and *Du Contrat Social* in 1762, texts central to his radical philosophy. Neither the State nor the Church could tolerate his politics or atheistical ideas, and under threat of arrest, the Parlement of Paris forced him into exile. Hume, who had himself suffered for his atheism, provided Rousseau with sanctuary in Britain from January 1766. Before long, Rousseau began to suspect, however unjustifiably, that Hume was colluding with Rousseau's French rivals. Private letters between the two men and to their friends began to circulate, and by gradual steps a private quarrel became a battle in the republic of letters. Hume considered his reputation to be threatened, and towards the end of 1766 resolved to clear his name by publishing his and Rousseau's correspondence.

While McMurray took Hume's side, he scorned this decision to publish, believing it was for members of the public such as himself to put forward a defence. McMurray traced the conflict to a single curious event which took place after the protagonists arrived in England: 'one night while lying in bed Rousseau heard Hume pronounce the words "Je tiens J. J. Rousseau," which

---

[44] JM to Wm Gordon, 19 May 1767.

[45] See D. Goodman, 'The Hume–Rousseau Affair: From Private *Querelle* to Public *Procès*', in *Eighteenth-Century Studies*, 25, No. 2 (1991), 171–201. The letter (preserved in Murray's album of newspaper clippings) appeared in the *Public Ledger* and is hand-dated 20 Jan. 1767. No copy of the *Public Ledger* for this period has been located.

the Frenchman conceived to portend his total destruction'. A sensible man, McMurray declared, would have regarded this 'as an omen of a gracious reception rather than an indication of a design upon his life and character'. Rousseau had fallen pray to paranoia and self-delusion.

Rousseau's emotional arguments were not altogether dismissed by the public — something which Hume had not expected. McMurray reprimanded his fellow Scotsman for taking offence at what were clearly the rantings of a madman and told him that Rousseau's 'frivolous accusations as you represent them, and as I believe them to be, merited pity and contempt, rather than a serious refutation'. McMurray found Hume's conduct out of character in one who had never before deigned to reply to his numerous adversaries, but who now 'takes the greatest pains' to answer 'a crack-brained and visionary foreigner'. McMurray asked: 'Are then the principles you have endeavoured to establish and impose upon mankind of less importance with you . . . than the character you receive from an enthusiastic opponent?' Neither McMurray nor it would seem the public understood that Hume saw an important difference between an attack on his ideas and an insult to his character. Had Hume emphasised this distinction, he would likely have won McMurray's approval.

McMurray's forays into the world of literary controversy were invaluable experience. Later, as a publisher, it was his job to deal with fractious authors and tradesmen of all descriptions. Though he might have wished to pursue a literary career, he accepted that he lacked the necessary talent, well aware that very few writers then lived comfortably from the efforts of their pen alone. In a letter to his friend Charles Gordon in Canton, China, he reflected upon his unrequited literary ambitions.

> [I] wish, dispicable as I am, that . . . I possessed a scribbling turn. For with what vanity must the reflection fill the Author to be insured of his performance being greedily perused. . . . But alas! what avails wishing but to remind us more deeply of our wants. Wishes will never bestow Riches on a Spendthrift or beauty on a Face whose Features are adverse to harmony and proportion. The dream may delude us for a moment but we awake to more acute anguish & woe! as I do when I attempt to lay aside my native dullness to sport in the gambols of wit and fancy.[46]

Living amongst those writers whose own 'wit and fancy' were earning them — some of them — fame and fortune reminded him of the ambitions he so cherished as a young man. But McMurray knew his limitations.

In the summer of 1766 McMurray gained (or rather wrested from his father-in-law) control of his wife's finances, which amounted to £700 and a farm in Kent that produced a small yearly income.[47] At the same time

[46]JM to Charles Gordon, 7 Jan. 1774.
[47]JM to Kirby & Simmons, 18 Apr. 1781 and JM to Wm Twopenny, 15 Nov. 1781. The farm was at Yelsted, and Murray kept it for many years.

Captain Weemss, who was stricken with severe gout and incapable of looking after the affairs of his daughters, entrusted him with the £500 possessed by Hester. McMurray invested her money in four per cent stocks through the agency of his Edinburgh friend Archy Paxton, who had come to London to establish himself in business. Only later did McMurray learn that Weemss strongly objected to his putting the funds jointly in his and Hester's names: 'I cheerfully conformed to their will & immediately altered it, yet it left such an impression to my prejudice, that I believe Mr Weemss had not forgot it to this day'.[48] As Nancy fell heir to her sister's fortune, McMurray considered that he had a natural right to the guardianship of Hester. When Hester stated a preference for another man to handle her affairs, McMurray bluntly explained the undesirable consequences of her behaviour, for if she were to die, it would be more difficult for Nancy to recover the money. Furthermore, he told her that 'her choice of a stranger in preference to me, would not only be a slight put upon me, but that . . . she would naturally become herself a stranger to her sister'.[49] This intimidating argument achieved the desired result, but that it should have taken place at all was unfortunate. His relationship with Hester, like that with Captain Weemss, continued to be difficult.

In June 1768 the McMurrays set up house in Love Lane at Brompton with a lease for twenty guineas a year. There, for the time being, they shared in a degree of domestic tranquillity. Although difficulties with Captain Weemss and Hester over money matters abated, they were not at an end, and Mrs Weemss, especially, continued to behave in a cool manner. Rarely one to let a matter stand unresolved, McMurray wished to know why, but she died a few months later (on 10 February 1768), before their differences could be resolved. Soon after, Captain Weemss proposed that he move into the house at Love Lane. Though McMurray acquiesced dutifully, he complained bitterly to Paxton of his father-in-law's 'continued & unaccountable hatred of me, notwithstanding the pains I had ever taken to gain [his] good opinion'.[50] Living together improved their relations, but he could never find much support or affection from Weemss. The captain and his wife had been indulgent parents. Hester was stubborn and rather coquettish, and Nancy was overly sensitive and prone to illness.[51] John was unprepared for dealing with his wife's idiosyncracies. Fortunately his sister, Binny, did not shy away from offering advice.

> The more I reflect on her behaviour . . . the more I blame you . . . for not treating her with that gentleness she deserves and giving allowance for her youth want of experience and the strange kind of people she has always

[48]JM to George Kirby, 18 Aug. 1768.
[49]JM to Arch. Paxton, 15 June 1768.
[50]Ibid.
[51]Nancy McMurray to Mrs Hawkins (Hester's schoolmistress), 17 Sept. 1768.

been amongst . . .. That you love her I have not the smallest doubt of. Why then my dear John will you not studdy to make her and yourself happy?[52]

Although there were difficulties in the first years of their marriage, McMurray matured and his wife gradually became more prudent and managed domestic affairs more sensibly. McMurray, however, did father an illegitimate son during this period. He visited prostitutes and was often out late drinking. Binny's mention of 'rustick freedoms', in the same letter likewise hints at improprieties on Nancy's part. The marriage did not seem to answer all of their needs.

Preoccupied with his own future, McMurray 'as yet was perfectly at a loss what plan of business to follow'.[53] Hopes of entering the china trade with an Edinburgh friend did not materialise and, in any case, his advisor, William Kerr, did not recommend the venture. As employment opportunities in Brompton were few, McMurray spent periods of time in London where he sought out men whose influence might be employed on his behalf. Once again separation, however brief, put further stress on his marriage. Though Nancy preferred to stay in Brompton, she travelled to London for a weekly rendezvous at the Blossoms Inn. On parting, McMurray would give her dirty shirts for laundering. Meanwhile, Captain Weemss was held at bay with veiled threats that they 'intended removing from Brompton & go to some cheaper country'.[54]

McMurray decided at last to seek reinstatement in the navy. By the end of May 1767, at the rank of second lieutenant, he was prepared to spend the rest of his days in uniform.[55] He assumed his first post on the *Yarmouth*, a guardship at Chatham, and in December 1767 he was appointed to the care of the Grenadiers Seventh Squad. His duties included presiding over Divisional Courts Martial as well as taking responsibility for dockyard and parade duty.[56] It was not long before he was employing his pen against an unpopular reform of the sea roster, recently introduced by the Lords of the Admiralty for the divisions at Portsmouth, Plymouth and Chatham. The appearance of McMurray's 'public letter' in the local press helped to achieve the desired effect, for by the beginning of 1768 he could report that 'the roster was at last settled conformable to the plan I had proposed'.[57]

In peacetime naval life could be monotonous, but a convivial band of fellow officers and a settled domestic life compensated for the absence of wartime excitement. One important friendship McMurray renewed at this

[52]Binny McMurray to JM, 8 Sept. 1770.
[53]JM to Wm Kerr, 22 Jan. 1767.
[54]JM to Wm Weemss, 2 May 1767.
[55]JM to Colonel Robert Gordon, 23 Jan. 1767; to John Stewart, 5 June 1767.
[56]Chatham Order Book, ADM 183/1B, Admiralty Archive, Public Record Office, Kew.
[57]JM to Charles Say, 3 Sept. 1767; see also to Colonel Robert Gordon, 18 Jan. 1768. The letter to which he refers has not been traced in print.

time was with William Falconer, a fellow Scotsman and mariner and a poet of considerable reputation. Falconer was a close friend who had earlier provided inspiration for McMurray's own literary efforts. His major work was the *Shipwreck*, published in 1762. Less well known, but perhaps more interesting, was Falconer's ability to compose acrostics based on the names of his shipmates' mistresses, a talent which he would demonstrate during drinking sessions.[58]

Bookseller and Stationer

Despite the security of his new commission, McMurray still considered possible business opportunities. There was, after all, £700 of his wife's money to invest. Early in October 1768 he learned that the bookselling business of William Sandby at 32 Fleet Street was for sale (see Plate 3).[59] The asking price, at £1000, was considerably more than he possessed. He consulted a number of advisors, chief among them Archy Paxton, William Kerr at Edinburgh and the London printers, William and John Richardson. On 9 October he wrote to Kerr asking for a loan of £400 to make up the difference and leave himself with some capital. While exploring this plan of finance, he also considered taking in an equal partner. His choice was William Falconer, who he knew would provide literary expertise, good sense and camaraderie. Moreover, there would be the opportunity to publish the poet's future works. On 16 October 1768 he wrote to Falconer who was then at Dover:

> Since I saw you I intend to embark in a scheme that I think will prove successful, and in the progress of which I had an eye towards your participating. Mr. Sandby Bookseller opposite St. Dunstans church has entered into company with Snow & Denne bankers. I was introduced to this gentleman about a week ago upon an advantageous offer of succeeding him in his old business, which by the advice of my friends I propose to

[58]G. Gilfillan, *The Poetical Works of Beattie, Blair, and Falconer* (New York, 1854), p. 168. When revising the third edition of the *Shipwreck*, Falconer intended to address some 'elegant and affectionate lines' to McMurray (JM to Wm Falconer, 1 Dec. 1765). The subject of the *Shipwreck* is the loss of the *Britannia*, a merchantman, bound from Alexandria to Venice, on which Falconer was once a crewman. The ship fell into a violent storm and was wrecked near Cape Colonne, with only three men surviving. Falconer's poem reveals something of what men such as he and McMurray experienced at sea.

[59]William Sandby's own career in the book trade merits a brief overview. After serving an apprenticeship under Richard Manby of Ludgate Street from 1734 until 1741, he used £150 of family money to buy into the firm of Richard Chandler and Caesar Ward (*Stationers' Company Apprentices 1701–1800*, edited by D. F. Mackenzie, Oxford, 1978, p. 222). When these London booksellers expanded their trade into the north of England in 1742, Sandby became responsible for supplying them with books from London. Their plan to sell

accept. Now altho' I have little reason to fear success by myself in this undertaking yet I think so many additional advantages would accrue to us both were your forces and mine joined, that I cannot help mentioning it to you and making you the offer of entering into company. . . . The shop has been long established in the trade. It retains a good many old customers: and I am to be ushered immediately into public notice by the sale of a new edition of Lord Lyttleton's dialogues [of the Dead], and afterwards by a like edition of his history [of King Henry II]: these I shall sell by commission upon a certain profit without risk.[60]

Falconer declined the offer, not wishing to abandon the seafaring life. The prospect of making a fortune in the East Indies was more appealing, and not long afterwards, he set sail in the frigate *Aurora*. It surely is an irony of tragic proportions that the ship and its entire crew were lost at sea at the Cape of Good Hope. Reading the *Shipwreck* would have brought McMurray little consolation.

> Down on the vale of death, with horrid cries,
> The fated wretches, trembling, cast their eyes,
> Lost to all hope: when, lo! a second shock
> Bulges the splitting vessel on the rock; . . .
> Repeated strokes her crashing ribs divide,
> She loosens parts, and spreads in ruins o'er the tide.   (Canto III)

Now McMurray had little time for anything other than planning his new career in the book trade. He resigned from naval duty and returned to half-pay. There was some prospect of retaining a full salary, but either a twinge of conscience over his short return to service or the prospect of the advantage he could gain as a bookseller from naval contacts made the difference in salary 'not . . . an object worth disputing about'. He told his

books at the equivalent London price had every prospect of success, as books traditionally cost more in the provinces. But, overextending themselves on ambitious publishing projects, they lost everything. By 1745 Chandler had committed suicide and Ward had gone bankrupt (Terry Belanger, 'Booksellers' Sales of Copyright: Aspects of the London Book Trade: 1718–1769' doctoral dissertation, Columbia University, 1970, p. 235). Sandby, however, got out unscathed by their misfortune. In fact, it benefited him. At a sale of Ward's stock and copyrights in February 1746 he bought heavily, as he had done not long before at the Chandler sale and set himself in business at 32 Fleet Street (*A Catalogue of the Remaining Bound Stock, the Books in Quires and Copies, of Mr. Caesar Ward, of York, Bookseller, Thursday, 27 February 1746*, annotated copy in the British Library).

[60]JM to Wm Falconer, 16 Oct. 1768. Sandby published the first edition of Lyttelton's *Dialogues* in 1760 and had published four editions since then. Over the course of his twenty-six-year career, Sandby published more than two hundred separate titles (*Eighteenth-Century Short-title Catalogue*). He dealt in a wide range of books typical of the day, from sermons and political pamphlets to classics and poetry. Steady sellers such as grammars and lawyers' manuals accounted for a large portion of his trade. Profitable works are not always those remembered by posterity, and it is difficult to name a contemporary author that Sandby published who is known today.

commander, 'it is Honour of belonging to the Division rather than any other advantage which I covet' — and his honour was beyond reproach.[61]

At this time he changed his surname to Murray. His friend Colonel Robert Gordon hoped that he would 'find more profit & pleasure from your new employment, than from that of the sword' and supposed that Nancy would 'not be sorry for your laying aside the Wild Highland Mac as unfashionable, & even dangerous, in the circuit of Wilk's mobs'.[62] Another friend inquired whether his unmarried sister Binny (who was visiting London at the time) would follow suit, and Murray humorously replied that 'she is not inclined to part with the mac from her Name; she would rather she says get quit of the name altogether'.[63] Of her brother's new career Binny remarked: 'I hope your Business will turn out so well as to prevent your going into the Marines again for I wish much rather to have you a Bookseller than a soldier.'[64]

In Campbell's *London Tradesman* (1757), a guide for parents selecting an occupation for their sons, the bookselling profession was scarcely recommended: 'The Trade in general is overstocked; so that considering the Expence necessary to make a real understanding Bookseller, and the Stock requisite to set him up, I cannot find much Encouragement for a Parent to design his Son to this Business'.[65] Campbell's less than enthusiastic observation was fair comment. The printing, binding and distribution of books in London had been long and largely controlled by a closely interconnected group of men. Newcomers like Murray were not altogether welcome, although outsiders clearly had to be admitted from time to time. To make one's way in the trade called for both luck and perseverance. Men had traditionally become booksellers either through inheritance, an opportunistic marriage to the daughter of a tradesman, or a seven-year apprenticeship. And if an apprentice did not have capital behind him, he could, when he gained his freedom, find himself in a position little better than that of a shop assistant. So buying an established business like Sandby's pro-

[61]JM to Captain Pitcairn, 28 Dec. 1768. When, for example, a small dispute arose with a military customer, Murray told him pointedly: 'I expected better treatment from *one officer* to another; *for an officer I must ever esteem myself tho not upon full pay*' (JM to Lieut. Atkinson, 9 June 1781). Murray in fact had resigned his commission in 1778.
[62]Colonel Robert Gordon to JM, 21 Oct. 1769. John Wilkes's anti-government activities, directed against the King and his minister, Lord Bute (a Scotsman), made it an uncomfortable time for Scotsmen in London.
[63]JM to John Cunningham, 16 Sept. 1769.
[64]Binny McMurray to JM, 13 Dec. 1770.
[65]R. Campbell, *The London Tradesman. Being a Compendious View of all the Trades, Professions, Arts . . . now Practised in the Cities of London and Westminster*, 3rd edn. (London, 1757), pp. 134–5.

vided Murray with an unusually good opportunity for entering an exclusive trade. Moreover, the £1000 he paid was a relatively small sum for the time.[66] By entering the trade through this channel, however, Murray would never become a member of the Company of Stationers, the London guild made up mainly of printers, booksellers and stationers, which had been granted a royal charter in 1557 and had, since its establishment in 1403, protected the interests of its members. Murray never seemed to regard this as any kind of bar to success. Indeed, through the latter part of the eighteenth century significant numbers entered the trade without such an affiliation or the prospect of attaining it.[67]

Confident of success, Murray bargained with one of his advisors, William Kerr, to borrow £400 (at five per cent annual interest) and made the final arrangements for buying Sandby's business.[68] At the end of October 1768 he and Nancy left Brompton and settled in at 32 Fleet Street, premises known as 'the sign of the ship opposite St Dunstan's Church' (see Plates 4 and 5).[69] John Murray's first publication — the only one to appear with his name in 1768 — was a 'fifth edition, corrected' of George Lord Lyttelton's *Dialogues of the Dead*, 'Printed for J. Murray Successor to Mr. Sandby'. The book ushered Murray into the trade in a respectable manner. Lyttelton himself asked Murray to bind presentation copies of the new edition and inscribe them 'from the author'.[70] The trade paid 2s.11d. per

[66]Compare, for example, the £1000 Murray paid in 1768 with the £2282 the first Thomas Longman had paid for a bookselling business of William Taylor forty-five years earlier (C. J. Longman, *The House of Longman 1724–1800*, London, 1936, p. 462).

[67]C. Blagden, *The Stationers' Company: A History, 1403–1959* (Cambridge, MA, 1960), pp. 246–8. The next three generations of Murrays, meeting the qualification by inheritance, became members of the Company.

[68]JM to Wm Kerr, 9 Oct. and 29 Nov. 1768; AL, pp. 17, 107. In Apr. 1769 Murray borrowed £150 more through the mediation of Kerr (Wm Kerr to JM, 7 April. 1769).

[69]Such commercial signs often passed from generation to generation and were strongly linked with the property they marked. Until the end of the eighteenth century signs rather than street numbers regularly served as addresses. Sandby had used the ship's sign since 1746, after moving his bookselling business to Fleet Street. According to Murray's second lease (3 Nov. 1790), the property was once designated 'the sign of the acorn'. Much of the long and colourful history of St Dunstan's in the West is connected with the literary figures who lived in its vicinity. John Donne, the poet, was the Rector from 1624 until his death in 1631; Izaak Walton, author of *The Compleat Angler*, held a number of church offices between 1629 and 1644; and Milton's *Paradise Lost* was published in 1677 'under St Dunstan's Church in Fleet-street'. Samuel Pepys recorded his regular attendance at St. Dunstan's, the only church left standing in Fleet Street after the Great Fire. Samuel Johnson, who lived nearby in Murray's day, also worshipped there occasionally. The enormous double-faced bracket clock of St Dunstan's was the first in London to have the minutes marked on the dial and can perhaps be credited with Murray's punctuality.

[70]I have such a copy, which is bound in blue morocco, with the inscription in Murray's hand. Lyttelton, a prominent politician, was the friend of Pope, Fielding and other literary figures of the day and was amusingly caricatured as Scragg in Smollett's novel *The Adventures of Peregrine Pickle* (1751).

copy of the *Dialogues* (provided they bought at least six), while private customers paid almost double at 5*s.*6*d.*

There are, in fact, two entirely distinct settings of Murray's 'fifth edition, corrected', both dated 1768 (see Plate 6 and Checklist items 1–2). It may have been that Murray found the first printing to be so inaccurate that he demanded another, not wishing to embarrass himself with a shoddy debut as a publisher. This would explain the delay of a few weeks in selling copies of the book, which over the next few years Murray sold steadily.[71] When the more accurate edition was gone, Murray probably began to sell the ware-housed first printing, which was reissued in 1774 with an altered title page. However, the fact that these title pages seem to be identical, apart from the date, may indicate a more complicated scenario. In any case, Murray did well out of this first publication, although the title was later taken up by other booksellers.[72]

According to the terms with Sandby, he could expect to make at least as much profit from Lyttelton's *History of Henry II*. This work in three volumes quarto sold retail for three guineas, a considerable sum which allowed a wide margin of profit to the bookseller, even though there was also a less expensive octavo edition on the market. It was an important part of the agreement Murray had struck with Sandby that he should have exclusive wholesale rights to the title. Moreover, when Lyttelton completed an intended continuation, Murray expected to retain this advantage. But he was dismayed to learn that an edition had just appeared with the name of another London bookseller, James Dodsley, on the title page. Murray complained bitterly to Sandby. The promise of an exclusive sale was, he insisted, 'one principal inducement for my closing finally with you'. Furthermore, that Sandby had not promised much made Murray 'more certainly confide in what little you did promise'.[73] Murray reacted to his first business dispute characteristically. First he tried ethical persuasion, telling Sandby: 'I always understood that the word and promise of a man of Honour was his obligation'.[74] When this approach failed, and Sandby avoided a personal meeting, Murray threatened to prosecute his claim through legal channels. However, after drawn-out negotiations with Sandby and Dodsley, Murray settled for the right to buy copies of the *History* from

[71] Sales of the *Dialogues* did not begin until 17 Nov. (DBI, p. 6), while Murray opened his doors on 20 Oct.

[72] This bibliographical conundrum is important to the extent that it determines which of the two editions dated 1768 was published (or printed) first, and which, therefore, is the first Murray book. I am preparing an article on the subject for a bibliographical journal. John Pridden issued a new edition of the *Dialogues* in 1775, the same year in which editions of Lyttelton's *Works* began to appear. Others editions of the *Dialogues* followed in 1787, 1797 and as late as 1889.

[73] JM to Wm Sandby, 10 Apr. 1769.

[74] JM to Wm Sandby, 15 Apr. 1769.

Dodsley at a price reduced enough to enable him to sell the book wholesale.[75] Still, he regretted that it was impossible for his own edition to appear. When Lyteltton's continuation was ready in 1771, Dodsley alone sold both the quarto and the new octavo sets, and Murray got nothing. In this dispute and in others which followed, Murray's threat of legal action proved to be sufficient inducement: 'I must either exact justice or distress myself,' Murray would later remark. 'I chuse the former.'[76] He was not bluffing.

In addition to the *Dialogues*, Sandby consigned to Murray bound stock valued at £330, most of the shop furnishings and the goodwill associated with a going concern. Sandby's other stock and shares in copyrights were then sold at a private booksellers' sale which took place at the Globe Tavern in Fleet Street on 15 December 1768.[77] Sandby held copyright shares in twenty-eight different titles, six of which he owned wholly. Murray did not attend the sale, which was for established members of the trade only. Nevertheless, having examined a copy of the catalogue, he used some of his remaining capital and commissioned Benjamin White, a bookseller at nearby 63 Fleet Street, to purchase on his behalf books amounting to over £46.[78]

Wholly inexperienced in buying, selling and publishing books, and lacking business knowledge of almost any kind, Murray confidently risked all. 'Many blockheads in the trade are making fortunes', he had told Falconer, 'and did we not succeed as well as these, I think it must be imputed only to ourselves.'[79] Murray's desire to succeed derived less from an exaggerated sense of self-worth than from a genuine drive to prove to himself and his family (especially to his wife and her family) that he was an industrious and self-sufficient man. With modest capital and enormous energy, a critical eye and a temperament capable of conviviality and disputation (but which was usually straightforward), he launched himself on an arduous commercial voyage that would test all his abilities. He had only to look out the window of 32 Fleet Street to see success and failure among his fellow tradesmen who lined the street. With his course charted towards success, he proceeded cautiously, well aware that any combination of false moves would shipwreck all his hopes.

[75] AL, p. 49 (James Dodsley's account); AL, p. 9 (Thomas Cadell's account). JM to Wm Sandby, 15 Apr. 1769.
[76] JM to Wm Kerr, 23 Nov. 1770.
[77] The printed catalogue for this sale is headed *Books in Quires, and Copies [copyrights] being the Genuine Stock of Mr William Sandby, which will be Sold at Auction without Reserve* (British Library copy and unfortunately without prices paid).
[78] AL, p. 36. Murray paid White in four instalments, as the money was due to Sandby, over the course of the next year.
[79] JM to Wm Falconer, 16 Oct. 1768.

2

Thirty-two Fleet Street, at the Sign of the Ship

Business as Usual

In October 1768 Murray established himself at 32 Fleet Street, a spacious four-storey house built in 1667 after the Great Fire.[1] The shop occupied the whole of the ground floor, and he and Nancy lived in rooms above. At various times they took in lodgers to offset expenses. The charge for accommodation was negotiable: most paid one guinea a week; a few as much as £1.11s.6d. Coals and candles were extras, and breakfast at three shillings a week was optional. Friendships often developed with lodgers, inclining Murray to reduce the rent by as much as half.[2] Often rooms were filled with friends and relatives visiting from Scotland and abroad.

Like Sandby before him, Murray leased the property from the Worshipful Company of Cordwainers, who had owned it since it was built. Murray paid the Company £70 a year in rent and was responsible for general maintenance and for a number of different taxes which annually amounted to about £20.[3] He also possessed a much smaller house in Falcon Court behind the Fleet Street premises, which he rented out for

[1] Behind the building is Falcon Court, accessed from the street by a narrow passage on the east side of the house and containing a number of other buildings.

[2] William Enfield lodged at Fleet Street for three weeks in May 1769 (AL, p. 37); Robert Sherriff for ten weeks from Nov. 1771 and a further nine weeks from Jan. 1772, when he paid half rate (AL, p. 71), and many other times. William Skirving lodged from 31 July 1770 to 11 Mar. 1771 (AL, p. 101).

[3] Murray listed taxes paid as well as other expenses relating to the property for 1774: land tax £10.2s.; lamp and pavement rates £4.10s.; poor rates £5; window tax £2.18s.12d; water £2; watch £1; and other occasional collections for church tythes, the common sewer and orphans (DB2, p. 365; see also AL, p. 99). The Cordwainers, a livery company of the City of London, were chartered in 1439, but had been organised since 1272, from which time they supplied the population with leather goods of all descriptions.

£24 a year.[4] Only in extreme circumstances did Murray appeal in writing to the Cordwainers to make repairs, such as when the sewers of the buildings in Falcon Court began to leak into his house. To the clerk of the Company he made this report: 'Every thing in my kitchen is destroyed by the rats, who now appear in flocks; having access thro the large breaches from the common sewer and from the waters penetrating . . . an intolerable stench arises which frequently chases customers from my shop'.[5] Temporary repairs proved ineffective, and six months later things were once again in an unhealthy state: 'I have never yet proved to be a troublesome tenant', Murray warned his landlords. The implication was obvious.[6]

Bookshops of all descriptions lined Fleet Street and the area around St Paul's Cathedral. This was the heart of the London book trade in the eighteenth century as indeed it had already been for one hundred and fifty years.[7] Murray had only to walk down a few doors to meet a fellow tradesman at his shop or in a nearby tavern to transact business. He recognised that a successful business, or its owner, needed to be widely known. When he advertised his first book, Lyttelton's *Dialogues of the Dead*, in the newspapers, for example, he alerted the public to the range of services he could provide:

> John Murray sells all new Books and Publications. Fits up Public or Private Libraries in the neatest manner with Books of the choicest Editions, the best Print, and the richest Bindings. Also, Executes East India or foreign Commissions by an assortment of Books and Stationery suited to the market or purpose for which it is destined: all at the most reasonable rates.[8]

In other advertisements Murray informed customers that 'Books may be had in all Languages, and all new Books and Publications whatso-ever'.[9] Murray also sold stationery, quills, ink, sealing wafers, calling cards, account books and diaries. And, at different times, he was happy to provide his customers with beer and wine, fever powders, Irish linen, lecture tickets, lottery tickets, even woodcocks and partridges — anything to make a profit.

[4]AL, p. 98–9. Murray let the house, designated Number One Falcon Court, to a series of tenants, including a barber named Mr Light, who shaved Murray and dressed his wigs (AL, p. 108). A bookseller named William Bingley took over the premises in April 1774 (AL, p. 73; Ian Maxted, *The London Book Trades 1775–1800. A Preliminary Checklist of Members*, p. 20), and from Sept. 1775 Mrs Mary Roper lodged there (AL, p. 280).
[5]JM to Edward Athawes, 22 Nov. 1781.
[6]JM to Edward Athawes, 6 Aug. 1782. In 1787, after twenty years' occupancy, Murray's lease was at the point of expiring. He renewed it for a further term at the same rate and laid out £300 for necessary improvements (JM to Company of Cordwainers, 4 June 1787). JM to James Cooke, 1 Feb. 1785. JM to Watson & Co, 5 Jan. 1793.
[7]See Ian Maxted, *The London Book Trades 1775–1800. A Topographical Guide* (Exeter, 1980).
[8]Murray's album of newspaper clippings.
[9]Advertisement at the end of Abbé Laugier's *History of the Negociations for the Peace at Belgrade* (1770).

Beginning on Saturday, 20 October 1768, the shop opened six days a week and twelve hours a day. Murray's first customer, the Viscount Wentworth, put him to the trouble of posting letters abroad. Somewhat inauspiciously, Wentworth neither paid Murray for the postage nor for books he purchased. The next customer was the Dean of Durham, who bought £6 worth of sermons and paid six months later. Then William Sandby, who had stood at the counter weeks before, called and, in a gesture of goodwill, bought some of the stationery he had recently sold Murray. Finally, a Mr Wall 'of the Corporation' bought a bag of sand at sixpence.[10] Murray recorded each transaction in a daybook, later transferring the information into an account ledger, where he followed the double entry or 'Italian' method of bookkeeping, a system popular since the fifteenth century. Customer accounts were carried over from year to year and from ledger to ledger (see Plates 7 and 8). From the start, Murray was willing to barter. When, for example, he sold books to Jacob Orton, the tallow chandler, a few days after he opened the shop, he acquired in exchange a year's supply of candles (about £12). He made a similar arrangement for coal (costing about £22 annually) with James Perrot.[11]

Murray employed a shopman whose most important duty was to inspect every book he had purchased for completeness and proper sequence, as the London trade usually allowed only fourteen days to claim imperfections.[12] As well as collating sheets, the shopman would pack and deliver orders and record transactions. William Weed, one of Murray's early assistants (from June 1772), received wages of sixteen guineas for his first year. Afterwards, his salary rose by two guineas.[13] Weed left in May 1776 and was followed in turn by several trained shopmen who were either serving or who had recently completed their apprenticeships: Samuel Highley, Murray's longest-serving employee, came to 32 Fleet Street in 1773; Evan Williams was employed from May 1780; and John Harding started in 1789. All three men later started successful bookselling businesses of their own.[14]

Murray presided over a lively shop. Customers asked advice about what to read and examined the latest novel or political pamphlet. Fellow tradesmen often came to make deals or to gossip. Writers, politicians and businessmen, many of them Scots, gathered to discuss the day's events or join Murray for dinner, which was served at four in the afternoon. On several occasions in the early 1770s, Murray's old navy companions came around to sample a new export beer. The club-like conviviality, so much a

[10]DB1, 20 Oct. 1768; Wentworth's account, AL, p. 3.
[11]These barter arrangements continued for several years: AL, pp. 76 and 127 (Orton); AL, pp. 26, 27, 125, 154, 248, 274, 290 (Perrot).
[12]JM to Richard Moncrieffe, 17 Nov. 1784.
[13]AL, p. 162.
[14]Other shopmen were J. Stainton from about Dec. 1780 and James Mackenzie from May 1789. See Maxted, *The London Book Trades*, for information on Highley, Williams and Harding.

feature of Edinburgh society, was transported to 32 Fleet Street. 'I have a dozen Gentlemen from Edinburgh to dine with me,' he reported in the spring of 1787.[15] It was not an unusual occurrence. Murray also socialised in town, frequenting Munday's Coffee House to read the daily newspapers, drinking Burton beer at the Peacock in Gray's Inn Lane with fellow Scotsmen, bookselling associates and navy friends.[16] He and Nancy some-times spent evenings attending the theatre and entertaining at home. In the early 1770s, however, Murray began to suffer from a gradual loss of hearing, and he described himself ruefully in 1774 as often being 'at a loss in company'.[17]

Early Publications

In 1769, Murray's first full year of business, he issued about twenty books (see Checklist). Few were original publications. There was less risk in taking books bought from Sandby, or at auction, and inserting a cancel title page with his own name.[18] The best-known title he issued in this manner was Horace Walpole's *Castle of Otranto*, first published in 1765 and generally regarded as the first true Gothic novel. Murray bought the sheets of Walpole's novel at the estate sale of William Bathoe who had published the third edition in 1766.[19] Murray's earliest 'original' publications were *The*

[15]JM to Andrew Dalzel, 3 May 1787.

[16]Munday's was a long-established coffee house located in New Round Court until about 1770 when it moved to Maiden Lane in the north-west side of the Strand (Bryant Lillywhite, *London Coffee Houses*, London, 1963, pp. 379–80). Murray and his regular Munday's 'Club' had a special annual dinner in February (JM to John Whitaker, 5 Feb. 1776).

[17]In April 1774 Murray recorded in his diary: 'Mr. Timons surgeon operator . . . after examining my ears . . . told me there was not only a probability of my being relieved, but he could ensure me of a cure. My disorder proceeded he said from a relaxation of the tympanun; and he gave me a bottle of liquid, 5 drops of which he directed me to pour into each ear every night going to bed to be secured afterwards, with a bit of wool. To take out the wool in the morning, and to repeat the operation at night. If his prognostic of relief is verified I shall not repent of the 10/6 I gave him' (Diary, 30 April 1774). Unfortunately, the treatment made matters rather worse than better.

[18]The books to which Murray affixed a cancel title page in 1769 were: (1) John Evelyn's *Sculptura*, a work about the mezzotint, first published in 1662; (2) Robert Wait's *Gospel History* (a 2nd edn.); (3) Stephen Ayde's *Treatise on Courts Martial* (first published in America); (4) *Authentic Memoirs Concerning the Portuguese Inquisition* (first published by Sandby in 1761); (5) Marquis d'Argens' *New Memoirs Establishing a True Knowledge of Mankind*; (6) Fénelon's *Demonstration of the Existence of God* (published by Sandby in 1749 and again in 1765); (7) a catalogue of the *Biblioteca Hoblyniana*, which, however, did contain some new material (see Maslen, *The Bowyer Ledgers*, item 4752); and (8) John Wood's *Description of Bath*.

[19]Murray did not purchase the copyright, which subsequently fell to James Dodsley, the publisher of many subsequent editions. See A. T. Hazen, *A Bibliography of Horace Walpole* (New Haven, 1948), p. 55. Bathoe's sale (listed under Mrs Mary Bathoe, his widow) was on 27 Jan. 1769 (AL, p. 25).

Bruciad, a much revised edition of John Harvey's 1726 poem on the life of Robert the Bruce, and an English translation of Beccaria's *Elementi di Economia Pubblica.* Both were published jointly and bore similar imprints: 'London: Printed for J. Dodsley, in Pall-mall; and J. Murray (Successor to Mr. Sandby); No. 32 Fleet-street; T. and J. Merrill, at Cambridge; and A. Kincaid and J. Bell, at Edinburgh, 1769' (Plate 31; Table 1 and Figure 1).

Murray acted merely as a selling agent for the other publications carrying his name that year. The imprint typically indicated this arrangement with the phrase 'And Sold By J. Murray at 32 Fleet Street', or something similar. Giving an agent's address was effective advertising, especially for a new trader. Agency did not involve ownership, but it normally marked an agreement to buy a considerable number of copies and sell these to both trade and public. Since there was a general understanding that the London trade fixed retail prices and offered discounts for buying in quantity, a bookseller could buy even a single book from an agent and sell it at some profit. Murray responded indignantly when a London trader refused him this discount: 'I never will be worse than porter to any Scoundrell who denies the trade their lawful profit'.[20]

In 1770 Murray issued only eight books: three were entirely his own publications; two were jointly owned; and the others were 'sold by' him. He was more ambitious the following year, publishing two new poetical works — Edmund Cartright's *Armine and Elvira* and John Langhorne's *Fables of Flora.* Both quickly sold out and went into second and third editions that year and further editions later on (see Plate 10). John Millar's *Observations concerning the Distinction of Ranks in Society,* an important study of social evolution, also sold well enough for subsequent editions to be published in 1773 and 1779. Lack of capital and fear of failure stopped Murray from investing in expensive books and prevented him from publishing all but a few new titles. While others were making and losing fortunes, he proceeded gradually. In 1771, 1773 and again in 1775, when Murray was in Ireland for extended periods sorting out a family inheritance which promised an injection of capital, little business was transacted at his shop. His wife Nancy and Murray's assistant did little more than keep the doors open. This inheritance — some £2000 from a maternal uncle — would give Murray the means to expand when it finally came through in 1775.[21] From the mid-1770s onwards the number of Murray's publications increased significantly: in 1773, for instance, he issued sixteen works, a figure which rose to nearly fifty by 1779 (see Figure 2).

Overseeing his own publications put Murray in daily contact with many London printers. Some, like William Strahan, had large printing houses with

[20]JM to Thomas Ewing, 2 Apr. 1774.
[21]The difficulties Murray surmounted to gain the inheritance are recounted in Ch. 8, pp. 133–36.

Table 1. Murray's Publishing Arrangements: number of publications per year

Year	Murray alone	Agency–Murray alone	Murray–with agency	London co-publ.	Agency–London	London syndicate
1768	2	0	0	0	0	0
1769	9	1	1	5	2	0
1770	2	0	0	3	1	0
1771	8	0	1	2	1	0
1772	5	1	0	0	0	0
1773	11	0	1	0	2	0
1774	8	0	2	2	1	0
1775	3	0	1	4	3	0
1776	9	0	1	1	2	0
1777	5	1	1	8	2	1
1778	13	1	0	2	1	10
1779	12	1	3	6	2	6
1780	6	0	0	5	1	6
1781	10	1	0	6	1	1
1782	9	3	1	7	2	7
1783	19	3	1	19	6	8
1784	22	0	1	11	7	13
1785	14	4	1	10	3	10
1786	19	4	2	6	5	14
1787	23	4	2	12	6	9
1788	19	3	1	14	6	9
1789	15	0	1	9	6	2
1790	13	1	1	7	7	14
1791	14	1	3	12	1	11
1792	13	1	1	10	6	11
1793	17	3	1	13	3	10
TOTAL	300	33	27	174	77	142
%	30.9	3.4	2.8	17.8	7.9	14.6
1794	6	0	1	11	4	4
1795	7	1	2	19	4	1

Murray alone: Murray controlled the production and distribution of the edition, although the author sometimes put up a share of the costs.

Agency: Murray had no financial interest other than in agreeing to buy a specified number of copies. In the case of **Agency–Murray alone**, the author paid all expenses and Murray organised the publication and usually shared the profits, if there were any.

Murray–with agency: Murray fully controlled the edition and appointed named traders to sell it.

London co-publishing: Murray shared the production costs and profits with other London traders.

London syndicate: titles of which Murray bought shares at the London trade sales.

Year	Edinburgh co-publ.	Agency–Edinburgh	Provincial co-publ.	Agency–provincial	Agency Totals	Stat. Comp. Reg.	Annual Totals
1768	0	0	0	0	0	0	2
1769	0	0	0	2	6	0	20
1770	0	0	2	0	1	0	8
1771	0	0	2	0	1	0	14
1772	2	0	2	2	3	0	12
1773	0	3	0	1	6	1	18
1774	2	0	1	4	2	20	
1775	2	5	1	0	8	4	19
1776	9	7	1	0	9	5	30
1777	6	0	2	0	3	7	26
1778	8	0	1	3	5	9	39
1779	9	0	3	0	3	14	42
1780	5	0	1	0	1	5	24
1781	2	1	0	1	4	6	23
1782	3	0	1	0	5	6	33
1783	2	2	1	0	11	7	61
1784	2	1	3	2	10	55	62
1785	4	1	1	0	8	4	49
1786	5	2	0	1	12	5	58
1787	5	4	0	3	17	14	68
1788	10	2	3	10	31	10	77
1789	5	1	2	2	9	3	43
1790	4	4	4	0	12	9	55
1791	6	3	1	1	6	13	53
1792	7	1	5	3	11	11	58
1793	7	1	3	2	9	14	60
	107	40	39	34	191	154	973
	11.0	4.1	4.0	3.5	20.0	15.8	
	5	1	5	0	5	1	37
	0	1	1	0	6	5	36

Edinburgh co-publishing: Murray appears in the imprint with at least one Edinburgh trader. The primary place of publication may be Edinburgh or London.

Provincial co-publishing: a work whose primary place of publication is a provincial city or town other than Edinburgh.

A separate column tallies books entered in the Stationers' Company Register.

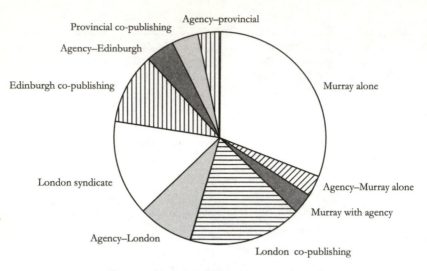

Figure 1. Murray's Publishing Arrangements, 1768–93

many presses and published books in their own right. Others limited themselves to printing on a smaller, less risky scale.[22] Murray first learned about this aspect of his trade at the printing house of William and John Richardson, who had advised him on the purchase of his business from Sandby. From their premises at nearby Salisbury Court in Fleet Street, the Richardsons (who succeeded to the business of their uncle, the novelist Samuel Richardson) not only printed several of Murray's early publications but also were partners with him in a number of these and other works such as *The Bruciad* in 1769 (which they did not print) and the *History of the Peace at Belgrade* (1770), in which they shared the copyright.[23] Furthermore, they arranged for Murray to act as a selling agent for several works they printed, such as the impressive folio volume *Registrum Roffense* (1769). The imprint reads: 'London: printed for the editor, by W. and J. Richardson: and sold by T. Longman; R. Dodsley; J. Murray; T. Smith, in Canterbury; W. Mercer, in Maidstone; and E. Baker, at Tunbridge'.

Book Production

Murray had to understand fully the technical aspects of the printing trade to ensure the product he bought was up to standard and fairly priced. A

---

[22]Very few documents detailing Murray's dealings with printers in London survive, but a sense can be gleaned from his imprints and from information in printers' archives, such as the Strahans' in the British Library.

[23]The Richardsons' printing house was a large one. In the 1750s their uncle employed more than forty workers (William M. Sale, *Samuel Richardson: Master Printer*, p. 21).

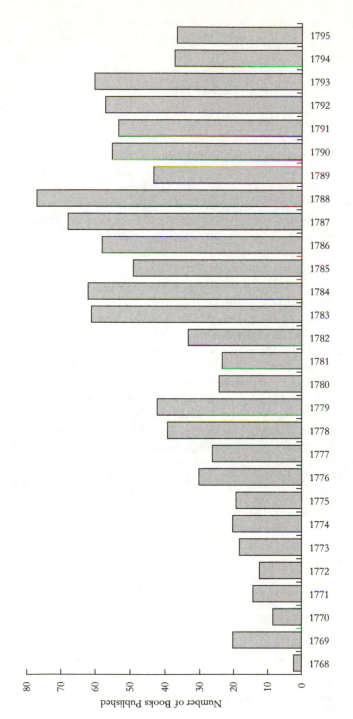

Figure 2. Murray's Publishing by Year, 1768–93

familiarity with paper, which he usually purchased from a stationer and
delivered to the printer for a given job, was also essential. Murray always
specified the size of the sheets (royal, medium, demy, crown, foolscap, or
pot) and the grade to be used (fine, second or ordinary).[24] Typically printers
charged on a per sheet basis. This figure included the composition (setting
the type) and presswork (printing the sheets), plus a small charge for
reading and correcting prior to printing. The price varied according to
the format chosen (folio, quarto, octavo or duodecimo) and the size (or
sizes) of type used. Clearly, setting the type for the sixteen pages of an
octavo sheet was normally more time-consuming than the eight pages of a
quarto sheet. All these decisions — paper, format, type size — were
Murray's alone, though he doubtless welcomed the advice of experienced
tradesmen like the Richardsons, particularly at the start of his career.

Two men worked the large wooden hand-press of Murray's day, inking
the type, setting the paper (which had been dampened to fix the ink) and
pulling the bar. Together they could print 250 impressions an hour on
average. As a rule the other side of the sheet was printed at the same
time, generally on an adjacent press, so that the paper did not dry out. The
pressroom of a large printing house was a noisy hive of industry, the
wooden frames of the presses creaking under the continual pressure of
the pressmen's arms. In the warehouse (or other rooms, depending on
space constraints) the printed sheets, stacked in groups of one or two
dozen, were then hung to dry. Afterwards, warehousemen gathered them
together in the proper order, folded them in half, pressed and baled them
up. At this stage Murray would take delivery, first deciding how many
copies to send to his binder, how many to store in sheets in his own
warehouse and how many to ship to provincial traders.

Binding was an important facet of Murray's business.[25] It was common
practice in his day to sell books either in sheets or roughly bound in boards.
Customers took these to their binders, where leathers and toolings of all
descriptions were chosen. The typical charge for an octavo volume in a
fancy morocco presentation binding was 5*s*.; for one handsomely bound in
tree calf with gilt tooling on the spine and edges about 3*s*.; and 1*s*.3*d*. for
simple full calf with a lettered label.[26] Murray offered this binding service to

---

[24]Murray purchased paper by the ream, which consisted of twenty quires of twenty-four
sheets each — or 480 sheets (Philip Gaskell, *A New Introduction of Bibliography*, chapter on
paper, pp. 57–77; the brief account of book production which follows is taken largely from
Gaskell's chapters on presswork, warehousing and binding, pp. 118–153).

[25]Murray kept a Bookbinders' Book, but it is not extant. However, the Account Ledger
supplies some of the information it contained under the names of individual binders.

[26]JM to Rev. Trist, 24 Aug. 1791. Prices would have been somewhat less at an earlier period.
On the subject generally see Mirjam M. Foot, 'Some Bookbinders' Price Lists of the
Seventeenth and Eighteenth Centuries', in *De libris compactis miscellanea*, ed. G. Colin (Studia
Bibliothecae Wittockianae, 1; Brussels, 1984), pp. 273–319.

his customers and took a small payment for his trouble. When he sold newly bound books to the trade he only charged what he himself paid for the binding.[27]

Murray employed several binders in the city and was given the standard six months' credit.[28] From November 1768 David Goodsman handled a large portion of this work. Goodsman also sold books, and often took copies of Murray's publications in lieu of payment. In the first year of trading alone Goodsman's binding charges to Murray came to nearly £100 (see Plate 11). Murray's account with James Macfarlane, who worked just down Fleet Street at Temple Bar, came to over £160 for the same period. Murray also employed James Campbell, 'Bookbinder to the King', and John Wingrave, whose shop was directly across the street.[29] A few thousand books passed between Murray and his binders each year. By 1781 he was handling enough new books to set up a bindery and employ a full-time binder. He paid this man sixteen shillings per week.[30] At busy periods journeymen binders would be hired to complete jobs.[31] The investment in the bindery, located opposite the Beaufort Buildings in the Strand, was considerable enough for Murray to insure the equipment and supplies for £500.[32]

Buying and Selling Books

From the very start of his business career Murray bought many popular titles to stock his shop — Greek and Latin classics, bibles and sermons, and practical books such as grammars, dictionaries and atlases. At Thomas Becket's trade sale in November 1768, he made modest purchases of just

[27]JM to Isaac Taylor, 2 Feb. 1777.

[28]It is estimated that there were about fifty active bookbinders in 1785. Murray's dealings with many binders at an earlier period, some of whom are not recorded in directories of the trade, suggest there may have been more (See Ellic Howe and John Child, *The London Society of Bookbinders, 1780–1951*, London, 1952, p. 22). Two examples are Abraham Dennison and Robert Burnett (AL, pp. 61, 225).

[29]AL, pp. 40, 142 (Goodsman); AL, pp. 77, 272 (Macfarlane); AL, p. 42 (Campbell); AL, p. 56 (Wingrave).

[30]In a letter to Richard Beddoes, 7 June 1785, Murray arranged to have two dozen skins sent to London from Edinburgh. The usual price for a dozen skins was fifteen shillings (JM to Mr Learmont, 16 Aug. 1786).

[31]In April 1786 Murray faced difficulties in supplying customers with bindings when the journeymen 'for some weeks past refused to work except with certain indulgencies which their masters cannot grant' (JM to Dr Forbes, 26 Apr. 1786).

[32]Sun Insurance Policy #453006 (register 299, 1781/2), Guildhall Library, London. The policy, dated 20 Dec. 1781, reads: 'John Murray at No. 32 Fleet Street Bookbinder on his Utencils, Stock & Goods in trust or on commission in the Exhibition Room facing Beaufort Buildings in the Strand Brick not exceeding Five Hundred pounds'. He paid ten shillings each term for the coverage.

over £10 (see Plate 7); at Henry Baldwin's sale in December (when Baldwin moved from Whitefriars to Fleet Street) he bought £27 worth of bibles; and at William Johnson's sale on 19 January 1769 he bought nearly £14 of general stock. The deaths and misfortunes of prominent London traders occasioned further sales: he bought £22 worth of 'books in quires' from the heirs of the printer Henry Woodfall on 15 May 1769; and he made purchases amounting to over £33 at the estate sale of Andrew Millar at the Queen's Arms on 16 April. When William Bingley was imprisoned for publishing seditious political articles and needed to raise money, he had an auction on 7 December 1769 at which Murray bought over £19 worth of stock.[33]

When books did not sell well Murray would try a number of strategies to shift his stock. He might print a new title page and reintroduce the work as a second edition, so suggesting that it was still popular. The ploy only succeeded if Murray could generate demand by advertising or if a new work by the same author should appear (Gilbert Stuart's *View of Society in Europe*, 1782, is one example). He also might advertise spurious second editions. Were a customer to call at his shop for the new edition, he merely offered a remaining copy of the first edition. When Murray printed a genuine second edition, such as the 1773 edition of John Millar's *Observations on Ranks*, he often added the phrase 'Greatly Enlarged' or 'With Corrections and Additions' to alert the public and possibly even tempt a purchaser of the first edition. Usually, only slight changes had been made, but sometimes an author had revised considerably. Indeed, a new edition of a medical work might contain important new material.

Advertising in newspapers and periodicals was expensive, but printing a list of publications on a blank page or pages at the end of a new book cost very little and offered the benefit of a potentially interested reader already at hand. A typical list of the kind included other works by the same author or on related subjects; it might also contain titles 'Soon to be Published'. In a sample list from 1769, when Murray's trade was more weighted towards the sale of publications which he did not himself commission, he advertised a number of popular works he had stocked in quantity, some at discounts. Murray's new issue of John Evelyn's *Sculptura*, for example, now sold for 3s.6d. bound, when it was formerly nine shillings. Four shillings were knocked off the original price of £1.5s. of the 'very elegant Edition' of the *Works of William Congreve*, printed by John Baskerville at Birmingham (see Plate 12). By suggesting that he was a proprietor of the Congreve edition, Murray furthered his reputation in the public eye, even though no such an edition is known to have appeared bearing his name in the imprint;

[33]AL, p. 8 (Becket); AL, p. 80 (Baldwin); AL, p. 34 (Wm Johnson); AL, p. 38 (Woodfall); AL, p. 40 (Millar); AL, p. 248 (Bingley, who later lodged at 32 Fleet Street).

he had only bought copies of the original 1761 edition.[34] The phrase 'Books printed by J. Murray', which typically heads these advertisements, is not to be taken literally. However, it is not always obvious why Murray printed cancel title pages for some works and not for others. In a list from late 1773, for example, more than a dozen of the forty-five titles seem not to have been issued in Murray's name (at least no copies are known to have been).[35]

As Murray was newly established in the trade, the terms of credit he was allowed varied. Items purchased from booksellers' sales had, as a rule, to be settled sooner than regular trade purchases. In either case the more Murray bought, the longer the terms of credit he could receive. Two to three months was usual for smaller purchases at sales. Mary Bathoe, for example, received her payment of £106.13s. in four instalments over a twelve-month period. When Murray bought stock at an established shop like that of Andrew Millar's successor, Thomas Cadell, he could get three to six months' credit.[36]

At the outset, Murray had little cash on hand, and he had to gauge carefully how quickly stock would turn over. Substantial orders (between £50 and £150) from naval contacts, ordering on their own behalf and for friends in India, reassured him he was buying wisely.[37] The ships sailed to India early in the new year and again in August. At such times Murray rushed to fill standing orders for periodicals, political pamphlets and the latest publications. As the voyage took nearly six months, he had to give unusually long terms of credit, sometimes up to two years. Nevertheless, this India trade was lucrative, and, throughout his bookselling career, it accounted for a substantial part of his retail business. Murray stood to lose money if his new publications were not ready in time for the India ships or for the opening of Parliament, when London was full of book-buying gentlemen. Similarly, he planned many of his Scottish publications to appear in May for the opening of the General Assembly of the Church

[34]The advertisement is headed 'Books just Printed for J. Murray, And Sold by him, at his Shop (No. 32.) Fleet-Street, London' and contains ten titles (copy at the Bodleian). It is possible that editions such as Congreve's *Works* (#6 in the list) did in fact appear but that no copies are presently known. The other title included in this early list which has not been found is #7, '*Plutarch's Lives*, translated by Mr. Dryden and others; a very neat Edition, in 9 vol. 18mo. with Heads. Pr. bound 18s.'

[35]A copy of this list (headed 'Books printed for J. Murray, No. 32 Fleet-Street, London.') is at the Bodleian Library (*ESTC* t185935). The titles that have not been traced, along with others of the kind, are listed at the end of the Checklist items 1047–63.

[36]AL, p. 25 (Bathoe); AL, p. 9 (Cadell).

[37]Captain Cochrane came in on 8 Dec. 1768 and bought over £75 worth in books and stationery; Captain Stokes followed on 12 Dec. with a £59 order. A discount of 2.5 per cent was standard practice for such large orders when they were paid at the time, but extra charges for packing and transporting to the wharf usually recouped the sum discounted (DB1 under the above dates).

of Scotland — a time when Edinburgh was full of clergymen. Meeting these deadlines was a source of anxiety, especially when the book's appeal was topical or a rival work was anticipated. Murray continually pressed printers and fellow tradesmen to deliver books promptly and lamented any missed opportunity for a quick sale. 'When [books] are gone', he told an Edinburgh supplier, 'gentlemen borrow from one another who would otherwise *buy*. . . . You will in vain endeavour to revive by a future supply after the novelty or first ardor is over.'[38]

Murray carried on a regular retail trade with individuals, many of them Scotsmen, in such distant places as Jamaica and China. His customers regularly asked him to select the latest literary and political works on their behalf. Although it was a difficult commission and not one he greatly relished, he knew that satisfied customers were the best assurance of further sales. As he explained to a customer in Lisbon, he chose 'to send . . . rather a few performances of some repute, than a multiplicity of trash; preferring . . . approbation to an inordinate desire of gain'.[39] A further reason for Murray's caution was that he was not inclined to accept returns, which would make accounting difficult and profits uncertain.

In the early 1770s Murray started trading in a small way with European booksellers, first shipping orders (£2 to £3 a month) to the firm of Bennett & Hake in Rotterdam. He had hoped to buy foreign books from this firm but found that the specialist dealers in London, buying in bulk, sold copies for the same or even lower prices retail than he was paying wholesale.[40] In other European cities Murray did, however, establish a modest trade. He even dealt with Messrs John Murray & Brother, booksellers at Leyden, who also published widely.[41] In Lisbon, Murray carried on a small trade with Paul Martin, and at Rouen he sold to the bookseller Justamond, but only for a short time, for when Murray refused to give a five per cent discount for immediate payment, his association with Justamond came to an abrupt end.[42] In the American Colonies, Murray traded with booksellers, merchants, academic institutions and private customers. He even had authors there. One of his first publications was a *Treatise on Courts Martial* (1769) by Stephen Payne Adye, an old Edinburgh friend who was based in Philadelphia as a first lieutenant in the Royal Regiment of Artillery. Murray bought two hundred copies of the 1769 New York edition; he then affixed a new

[38]JM to Watson & Co., 5 Jan. 1793.
[39]JM to W. H. Lyteltton, 2 Nov. 1769. To Captain West he wrote similarly on 10 Oct. 1781: 'Of *real good books* there are not two new publications in 12 months. I might indeed have put up for you a parcel of trash that issues from the press daily; but to have performed this would not in my mind have been doing my customers justice.'
[40]AL, pp. 171, 254; JM to Bennett & Hake, 24 Nov. 1773.
[41]AL, p. 238.
[42]JM to Patrick Hare (at Lisbon), 28 June 1786; JM to Justamond, 13 July 1785.

title page, distributed a handbill and advertised the work in the London papers at two shillings — considerably less than the American price. The *Treatise* sold well and Murray reprinted it the same year.[43] In 1778 he asked Adye to revise the work, and further editions came out in 1785 and 1799. Before the outbreak of the American Revolution, Murray sent books to several colonial traders, including Robert Miller, a merchant in Williamsburg, Virginia. Shipments took a number of months to arrive and lengthy credit terms had to be given. Miller ordered a typical range of books, and placed substantial orders in 1773 and 1774 (see Plate 13).[44] In February 1775, however, hostilities between Britain and the Colonies halted trade. When the war ended in 1783 Murray was able to re-establish colonial connections. In the summer of 1784, for example, the Reverend James Madison, president of the College of William and Mary, asked him to send the best new publications for the college library, but Murray doubted his own selections: 'Mens minds vary so much in their taste of books, that it is difficult for one man to chuse for another. I am however disposed to attend to your instructions.'[45] Murray continued to ship books to America for many years and encouraged Madison to promote the sale of his publications. He also penned letters of introduction to Madison for friends who had gone to America to make their fortunes.[46]

Books whose copyright Murray owned in whole or in part, or books of which he had obtained shares at auction usually produced better returns than those bought at the shops of fellow tradesmen and resold. A margin of between fifty and one hundred per cent was usual, although considerable sums had to be invested in printing and paper.[47] Murray, like other book-sellers, could expect as much as twelve to fifteen months' credit from

[43]JM to Stephen Payne Adye, 7 Dec. 1769. Rather than receive payment for his work, Adye bought books from Murray.

[44]JM to Robert Miller, 7 July 1774. One book Murray sent to Millar was Benjamin Franklin's *Experiments and Observations on Electricity*, probably the 1774 Newbery edn. Murray knew Miller personally and often saw the merchant's sisters who were then residing in London.

[45]JM to Rev. James Madison, 7 July 1784. On one occasion Madison paid in an unusual manner: Murray acted as Madison's agent for a shipment of tobacco, and only after considerable difficulty did Murray extract what he was owed from the unscrupulous merchants (JM to Madison, 17 June, 1789). At an earlier period, however, it was common to exchange books for tobacco. In the 1750s a colonial tobacco merchant could expect seven shillings' worth of books for every hundred pounds weight of tobacco he produced (See Warren McDougall, 'Scottish books for America in the mid-18th Century', in R. Meyers and M. Harris (eds.) *Spreading the Word. The Distribution Networks of Print 1550–1850* (Winchester, 1990) pp. 25–6).

[46]JM to Rev. James Madison, 25 Apr. 1792. Murray also carried on a correspondence with the Rev. T. Gates in Charleston who recommended Dr Smith, principal of Charleston College as a customer.

[47]These figures are calculated from a sample of entries in Murray's Booksellers' Book and are more or less substantiatd by entries in JM's Account Ledger.

printers but had to give trade buyers extended lines of credit.[48] Provincial booksellers generally were given eight months to pay. Some asked for books on sale-or-return, a basis which Murray discouraged if possible. In his opinion, 'the endless trouble of correspondence, expences in carriage & postage, a plague of accounts &c &c, renders it exceedingly irksome & wholly unprofitable'.[49] When a book left his shop, he liked to know it was sold.

Retailing sometimes offered high returns. For instance, Murray sold a copy of Walpole's *Castle of Otranto*, which cost him no more than one shilling, at 3s.6d. to private customers. But selling in large numbers from his shop was not easy in a competitive marketplace like Fleet Street. Wholesaling, if less profitable per unit, was more dependable. 'It is upon the trade in London', he reminded the Scottish bookseller Alexander Kincaid in 1776, 'that a Publisher relies for the consumption of an Edition of the work. Gentlemen apply to their own Booksellers for the articles they want whether the latter are Publishers of these articles or not.'[50] The London trade paid only 1s.10d. for Murray's edition of Walpole's novel, and provincial booksellers paid twopence more, provided at least six copies were bought.

In Murray's day most business was conducted through exchanging personal notes of credit. It was essential to have someone trustworthy to look after his interests outside London and make sure notes were honoured and payments made on time. Agents were also instructed to see that shipments of books were delivered and that books were advertised and sold at the agreed price. Murray was a hard negotiator and a stern creditor. But moral scruples could temper strict practice. Provided he had the money to spare, he would often extend credit terms. In turn, he would expect a creditor to give him leeway in difficult times. The law allowed a creditor to imprison his debtor without notice. Even though Murray hesitated to take such a step, the threat alone was effective when the debtor had sufficient funds. When, however, he knew the whole was unrecoverable, he often agreed to part-payment. Murray himself was no stranger to such threats, and, indeed, in 1791 he published Thomas MacDonald's *Treatise on Civil*

[48]See JM to John Millar, 10 Jan. 1780; JM to Nichol & Co. (Edinburgh printers), 2 Jan. 1784; JM to Alex. Guthrie (Edinburgh printer), 4 July 1789; JM to Hall & Elliot (Newcastle printers), 24 May 1791. Patricia Hernlund notes that 'it is a rare entry on the credit side of Strahan's ledgers which is not at least six months later than the corresponding debit' ('William Strahan's Ledgers: Standard Charges for Printing, 1738–1785' *Studies in Bibliography*, xx, 1967, p. 93).

[49]JM to James Cooke, 1 Feb. 1785. Murray's accounts with the Edinburgh booksellers Bell & Bradfute in the early 1790s show that, despite his opinion, he continued to sell on a 'return' basis (Invoice & Exchange Book No. 1, entries 156, 168, 194, 208, 215, 260, 269 and 368). These records, now in the Edinburgh City Archive, are part of a clutch of Bell & Bradfute material recently unearthed in a long-disused passage in the Edinburgh City Chambers.

[50]JM to Alex. Kincaid, 1 Sept. 1776.

Imprisonment, a work describing the unjust legal powers the law gave to creditors over the insolvent. He shared MacDonald's view that legislation was needed 'for the great ends of protecting the unfortunate; punishing the dishonest; inducing the discharge of debt; and checking the extravagance of credit'.[51]

Murray regarded himself as a generous man, although his notion of generosity was a little peculiar. When, for example, his servant, Thomas Higgs, sold a horse for him at Smithfield for £13.10s. (which had only cost £12), Murray's satisfaction was such that he gave Higgs 7s.6d. On another occasion, when about to depart from an inn, he 'scolded the waiters for want of alertness; and gave them all money'.[52] It was, however, the unexpected cheapness of the bill that prompted this gratuity.

Many of the letters Murray wrote concerned the settling of overdue accounts, which were, as for most businessmen, a constant demand on his attention and a source of considerable frustration. Prudence demanded that he pursue his debtors: 'I . . . constantly hung upon him, openly reflected upon his behaviour and after a multiplicity of promises, breaches of promise & . . . after I had resigned all expectation . . . [it] was sent to me yesterday'.[53] Anger over long-term non-payment prompted Murray to take legal action and add interest at five per cent. Despite these practices, accounts overdue for up to five years on Murray's books were not out of the ordinary. In an era of great financial uncertainty, bankruptcy was common, and Murray soon decided that new customers had to come recommended or deal with a reputable London financial house. If a bill were presented to Murray, he followed business etiquette to the letter. It was standard practice to leave the bill until the following day. If a creditor demanded payment on the spot, Murray categorically refused: 'The holder could not see the propriety of it, and would by no means leave the bill. Unwilling to humour a lump of stupidity & suspicion, after more conversation in which he attempted to be impertinent, he went away with his paper. In two days or thereabouts the Bill was brought back. . . . He left it without hesitation, received it the next day accepted and it was punctually paid when due.'[54]

Murray was exacting with fellow tradesmen and private customers alike. He watched carefully over every aspect of his joint publishing ventures, ensuring that payments were made on time and everything strictly accounted for. As a rule the largest share-owner of an edition was entitled to the handful of extra copies (called the overplus) that were normally

[51]Thomas MacDonald, *A Treatise on Civil Imprisonment* (London, 1791), p. xvi.
[52]Diary, 28 Apr. 1775.
[53]JM to Lord Torphichen, 7 July 1785. On debt and credit generally at the time see John Brewer *et al.*, *The Birth of a Consumer Society: The Commercialization of Eighteenth-Century England* (Bloomington, IN, 1982), pp. 210–11 and 229–30.
[54]JM to John Richardson, 6 Jan. 1780.

printed. This person also had a right to the leftover paper. Although Murray would use the paper only for wrapping parcels, he regularly demanded it from his printers.[55]

Murray's Correspondence

As much of his day-to-day business took place by calling at shops or by passing short notes, the vast bulk of Murray's transactions and interactions with London traders is undocumented. Important matters such as business disputes, however, required a medium to which he could subsequently refer. But there were other reasons why he turned to a letter at critical times. Fearful of reproach, or of controlling his own temper, he might be hesitant to confront in person those with whom he had fallen into misunderstanding. The letter afforded him a means of stating his case without challenge and of preserving his dignity and protecting himself. In the written medium there were no immediate winners or losers. Murray's voice in these business letters is carefully projected.[56] He tends to be formal in tone, logical in argument and emphatic in the justice of his claim, regardless of its true merits. In the majority of his personal letters humour and warmth are evident. Letters to customers are typically deferential. In Murray's public letters, which he wrote for newspapers or pamphlets, he aims to expose and embarrass his adversary, and is typically prone to exaggeration. By contrast, Murray's correspondence with tradesmen outside of London, which makes up the bulk of his extant correspondence, is predicated on the dual principles of competition and co-operation and guided by the well-established rules of the trade. Each letter is part of a dialogue, the goal of which is to produce a product and sell it at a profit.

It was expensive to post a letter in the mid-eighteenth century. The average cost was about sixpence, although a letter to London from a distant place like Aberdeen might cost as much as 2*s*.6*d*. Moreover, it was the recipient rather than the sender who had to pay. To reduce costs of a charge he grudged, Murray obtained addressed envelopes, called 'covers', from friends who were members of parliament and from post office officials (like William Kerr), who had the privilege of free postage. He gave these covers to regular correspondents and used them again and again. Occasionally, however, he worried about detection: 'Do not write to me again under Mr Dickson's cover', he warned his uncle, 'as that *member* has been dead these

---

[55]See, for example, JM to Adelard & Brown, 5 Sept. 1769; JM to Wm Creech, 21 Jan. 1777; JM to Neill & Co., 29 July 1793.
[56]A handful of letters in the copybooks are drafts in Murray's hand and include revisions that emphasise the care he took to be precise.

two years'.[57] Murray considered the postal system unfair: 'When one man writes to another upon his own business he should pay the postage of his packet. This is *my* invariable practice & ought to be every man's'.[58] By using covers he was partly able to do so. The advent of the London Penny Post opened new doors for Murray, especially for advertising. For example, when he published a work on the British peerage in 1790, he sent a handbill by this means to every peer — an early example of direct mailing.[59]

Other Ventures

From the beginning Murray was open to making money however he could. So imbued was he with a commercial spirit that he could later remark: 'Whoever affects to despise money may be certainly considered as a fool.'[60] Although he had little capital to invest in anything other than books, connections with military and mercantile men in Britain and abroad offered some relatively low risk opportunities. Among those commodities in which Murray had his hand were beer and wine, lottery tickets, medicines, replicas of antique gems, linen and even poultry.

When John Cunningham, a Glasgow brewer, asked Murray to buy some instructive books on beer making for him, Murray foresaw that he could sell Cunningham's Scottish beer in London. He also believed he could export it profitably. 'My own opinion of your beer', he told Cunningham, 'is favourable. I think it would answer for a foreign Market, I mean E. India, provided it stood the Bottle. . . . I beg to have a few dozens . . . because if I had it to show as well as to speak of, I could give you a good deal of more information in the matter.'[61]

The samples arrived and Murray invited naval officers to Fleet Street for evenings of beer tasting. He expressed pride that a Scottish product should be universally admired: 'real judges of malt liquor', he told Cunningham, 'who, at different times have tasted your beer in my house, very much approve of it, and confess that at no time have they drank any thing equal to it'.[62] Orders for cases of beer came in quickly. It was essential that the

[57]JM to Rev. Alex. Murray, 12 Apr. 1774. James Dickson, MP for Linlithgow Burghs until Nov. 1771, when he died. In 1791 Murray was getting free covers from Francis Freeling, the secretary of the London Post Office since 1787 (JM to John Whitaker, 22 Jan. 1791). In 1764 an Act of Parliament required MPs and peers to write out the addresses in their own hands (see *Scots Magazine*, 27, pp. 299–301. Further restrictions were imposed in 1784, as noted in the *Gentleman's Magazine*, 54, p. 648).
[58]JM to Henry MacNiell, 1 May 1786.
[59]JM to James Carmichael, 15 Feb. 1791. Carmichael was the editor of *Various Tracts Concerning the Peerage of Scotland*, 1790 (see Checklist item 753).
[60]JM to Archie Murray, 28 Aug. 1792.
[61]JM to John Cunningham, 16 Sept. 1769.
[62]JM to John Cunningham, 13 Feb. 1770.

shipments from Glasgow arrive in London in time for the India sailings early in the new year. Cunningham fulfilled this requirement and awaited reports of his beer's success. Murray also held tasting evenings for literary friends from whom he received private orders.[63] Something of a connoisseur, Murray gave such customers as the Reverend Crump particular serving instructions.

> Place what is first to be used upon its Bottom in a Beaufet or Closet near at Hand, and permit it to stand in this situation 14 days before it is used. If the weather is cold set it ten minutes before the fire; then Decant it in a Glass, Jug or Decanter, like wine; only in order to preserve its fineness do not go too near but Pour the last Half Pint of the Bottle into a glass or tumbler by itself. This last glass will drink as well as any of it altho it will appear to have more sediment. By no means permit a servant to shake it in the removal from carriage to Table.[64]

Initially, Murray acted for Cunningham out of friendship and received free beer for his efforts. When the brewer offered him a commission to act as his exporter, Murray suggested that they wait a year to see 'the quantity sold or likely to be sold, with all expences', adding: 'You will not find me hard to deal with'.[65] He already had laid out £10 for a warehouse at the wharf and anticipated that considerable advertising would be advantageous in promoting the beer. Above all, favourable reports from India were needed before embarking on a regular trade. By the middle of 1771 orders began to come in, and the first news from India was promising. At the end of the year Cunningham sent down an order of 729 dozen bottles for the new year's India sailings.[66] Valued at over £250, it was a substantial investment, but one which promised considerable return.

After the ships had sailed, Murray sampled bottles from this new batch held back for his London customers. To his utter dismay, he found that little of it was fit for drinking. He promptly informed the brewer of this shocking discovery: 'I am almost assured that this Disorder runs through the whole last Cargo. . . . I very much dread the consequences to its Reputation in India.'[67] With some irony, he reminded Cunningham that he had still been unable to locate a copy of a book on fermentation which the brewer had long since requested. He promised to keep searching, but it was already too late: the beer venture was over. Murray was stoical. 'It is a subject', he told Cunningham, 'that requires more attention than I can

[63]John Langhorne bought twenty-five dozen bottles; Gilbert Stuart ordered a more modest seven dozen (AL, p. 69).
[64]JM to Rev. Crump, 14 Aug. 1771.
[65]JM to John Cunningham, 3 Nov. 1770.
[66]729 is 27 squared, which gives an idea of the way the hampers of beer were packed and shipped.
[67]JM to John Cunningham, 24 July 1772.

bestow. . . . I cannot think it honest to retain the commission.'[68] Not wishing to leave the brewer without a London agent, Murray recommended someone reliable. Angered by the failure, Cunningham challenged Murray about the amount of beer he had taken for his personal use during the previous year. Murray claimed that the bottles he consumed were merely 'expended in the Service they were meant to promote' and refused to repay the brewer.[69] The rift in their friendship was hurtful because he had once looked up to Cunningham 'as a pattern for imitation'.[70] It was difficult, also, because his sisters had close social ties with the Cunningham family and even wanted to lend the brewer money to help with a debt of over £1500 which he had incurred. Conflict was averted, however, when Cunningham emigrated to North Carolina.

The unfortunate beer agency did not wholly discourage Murray from such ventures. In 1783 he offered to sell wine for William Hall, a merchant he had met at Margate while taking 'the waters' there. The tastings he conducted at Fleet Street showed it to be a good wine. However, after selling over nine dozen bottles, he reported to Hall: 'I am glad it is out of my house for indeed it has been to me very troublesome. Employ one in any thing but in the wine way.'[71] Murray himself took six bottles, paying one guinea. There was more profit in books than in wine.

Murray certainly enjoyed a glass of beer or claret, not to mention port, sherry, mountain malaga, porter, punch and, in true naval tradition, rum. A hogshead of porter (54 gallons), a weaker malt liquor of which his wife Nancy was fond, was usually on tap at Fleet Street.[72] He took an inventory of his cellar before he left for Ireland in 1775 and listed fifty-one bottles of rum on hand, and his account with the merchants Stewart & Glenny lists rum purchases of over £25 in 1772 alone.[73] He bought ten gallons at a time, costing £5. As rum was expensive and sometimes difficult to find in London, Murray was fortunate in having a close friend in Jamaica who regularly sent him 'a little good rum'.[74] It was a hard-drinking age. Evenings during which Murray and his companions drank five or six bottles of wine each were common. While in Dublin Murray recorded how on one occasion he drank six bottles of wine, which, he reported, 'intoxicated me uncommonly'. The evening did not end there: 'At twelve o'clock I went away in a chair, but broke from it in Essex street & ran after some girls.'

[68] JM to John Cunningham, 11 Mar. 1773.
[69] Ibid.
[70] JM to James Gilliland, 24 Oct. 1782.
[71] JM to Wm Hall, 3 Feb. 1783.
[72] AL, pp. 52 and 210.
[73] AL, p. 94. A loose sheet in AL (at p. 199) lists Murray's liquor orders from one merchant from Aug. 1770 to May 1772. In a single month he purchased more than two dozen bottles of port and two dozen bottles of sherry, costing him over £4.
[74] JM to Thomas Gardiner, 4 Nov. 1783.

Uncertain where he was and robbed of his gold watch, Murray 'rambled in the streets for 2 hours'. The next day, needless to say, he 'had a violent head-ake'. A visit to Achmet's Bath did little to improve his condition: 'I came home and as I still continued sick, I lay down upon the bed.'[75] Over the years these excesses undermined his health.

In other aspects of life Murray was more prudent. Indeed, he prided himself on caution and canniness. He did not lay a wager unless he was sure of winning.[76] He did not buy lottery tickets as did many of his friends and customers; instead he sold them and took a broker's commission, usually sixpence or one shilling per ticket.[77] William Kerr, who always advised Murray about financial management, was a regular lottery 'adventurer', as was one of Murray's authors, Sir David Dalrymple, a Scottish judge known for religious devotion. When his friend Lieutenant Adye lost in the lottery, Murray remarked disingenuously that 'a miscarriage of this sort is not more mortifying to the adventurer, than to the agent'.[78]

Another commodity for which Murray acted as an agent was 'fever powders'. The most popular brand of the day was 'Doctor James's Powder', first patented in 1746. The active ingredient of this type of remedy was antimony, an element which acted as a purgative. A dose of the powders reputedly saved the life of the poet Christopher Smart and temporarily lifted the insanity of George III. But a story went about that it had killed Oliver Goldsmith.[79] The proprietor of this medicine, Doctor Robert James, guarded his formula and protected his exclusive right to its manufacture. Samuel Johnson, a friend of James, had introduced him to John Newbery, a successful London bookseller who bought the patent and began to market the powders countrywide. As both books and proprietary medicines were centrally manufactured and needed national advertising and distribution, the sale of one easily complemented the sale of the other. When Newbery died in 1767, James's Powders passed into the hands of others, including

[75]Diary, 24 and 25 June 1775.

[76]In his diary Murray recorded: 'I took up a Bet with Mr. Crothers . . . that I once attended a musical entertainment at the Rotunda in some month betwixt october & april when there was *not* a Ball. Jointly subscribed a paper to this effect' (6 May 1775). 'Craig . . . gave me a card from Mr Mussenden in answer to one of mine written on Saturday to know if there had ever been an entertainment at the Rotunda betwixt the months of October & April *without a Ball*. He told me there had; this makes me winner of a wager I laid of a rump & dozen [bottles] with Mr Crothers' (15 May 1775).

[77]JM to Richard Moncrieffe, 11 Sept. 1783. Murray told the Dublin bookseller that lottery tickets could not be bought on credit because the broker's profit was small. In 1775 Murray published Henry Clark's *Considerations upon Lottery Schemes.*

[78]JM to Stephen Payne Ayde, 2 Apr. 1770. On the subject of lotteries at the time, see C. L'Estrange Ewen, *Lotteries and Sweepstakes. An Historical, Legal, and Ethical Survey of their Introduction, Suppression, and Re-Establishment in the British Isles* (London, 1932).

[79]Charles Welsh, *A Bookseller of the Last Century Being Some Account of the Life of John Newbery* (London, 1885), p. 140.

John Murray. From April 1770 he was selling it in London and sending regular orders to the Continent.

In 1772 Murray promoted the sale of a new and rival remedy called the Edinburgh Febrifuge Powder. The inventor, whose name and formula were kept secret, was Edward Galliard (see Plate 14).[80] Murray was confident that Galliard's medicine could successfully compete with Dr James's. He arranged for Galliard to present his findings to the Society of Physicians at Edinburgh in June 1772. In his address Galliard compared his remedy with several other fever medicines, condemning in particular Dr James's as 'the most irrational and improper for internal use'.[81] Galliard argued that the 'grand desideratum' of fever powders should be their solubility in water and their invariable strength. Tests had shown that his compound met these criteria, and Dr James's did not. Moreover, he claimed that the Edinburgh Powder cured (or relieved) other ailments besides fevers, including rheumatism, jaundice, smallpox, measles, pleurisy and even gout.

To establish scientific credibility and promote the sale of the powders, Murray published Galliard's findings in a pamphlet entitled *Considerations on the Use and Abuse of Antimonial Medicines*.[82] Chemists, physicians, surgeons and the public alike were encouraged to discover for themselves the 'nature, properties, and effects' of this panacea. The powders were produced under the supervision of a 'Society of Physicians at Edinburgh', and Murray was given the exclusive agency. Galliard asserted that, were a physician or surgeon to follow the directions enclosed in each packet, he would 'have few patients die of fevers'.[83] Another apparent advantage of the Edinburgh Powders was their relatively inexpensive price, selling retail in packets of four doses for three shillings, whereas a two-dose packet of Dr James's cost two and sixpence. All sales were cash only; customers could not buy on credit or wholesalers on 'sale-or-return'. Vendors' margin of profit was only fifteen per cent — their discount on the retail price when they ordered a minimum of two dozen packets.

Murray tempted Thomas Cadell (father of the London bookseller) into selling the powders 'by appointment' at Bristol and boasted that 'it is generally acknowledged to be a much better medicine than Dr James's'.[84] In Norwich he gave the agency to Abraham Brook, another bookseller.

---

[80]AL, pp. 180 and 239. Galliard lived in Carey Street, London.

[81]*Considerations on the Use and Abuse of Antimonial Medicines*, pp. 34–5.

[82]The full title of the pamphlet is *Considerations on the use and abuse of antimonial medicines in fevers, and other disorders; containing a chemical examination of all the antimonial preparations in the several Dispensatories; and a special inquiry into the nature, properties, and effects of febrifuge medicines, particularly Emetic Tartar, Dr. James's and the Edinburgh Powder. Read in a Society of Physicians and published by order of the President and Council*. Three editions of the forty-eight page pamphlet appeared in 1773.

[83]*Considerations*, p. 45.

[84]JM to Thomas Cadell Sr, 29 Dec. 1773.

Thomas Ewing sold the Powders in Dublin as did John Magee in Belfast. Ewing even reprinted the pamphlet and was given permission to include his name as the 'sole Dublin vendor'.[85] The Edinburgh Powders were selling well over Britain, and the market soon expanded to the Continent.[86] Murray's interest in periodicals like the *Medical Commentaries* — produced by the same Society of Physicians who had sanctioned the Edinburgh Powders — gave him useful advertising. Notices in the *Monthly Review*, the *Edinburgh Magazine & Review* and all the popular newspapers also increased the medicine's popularity. Through the year 1773 and into 1774 Galliard's remedy was selling in great quantities. Medical professionals and their patients hailed it as a panacea. However, midway through the year, it unaccountably lost favour. Physicians gradually discontinued their prescriptions and vendors ceased to place orders with Murray. Dr James's remedy had survived the challenge and continued to sell well.[87]

A commodity Murray sold with more lasting success were James Tassie's elegant reproductions of antique gems, seals and relief portraits of contemporary individuals. To model and cast his pieces, Tassie had invented a vitreous paste which hardened to a polished stone finish. His secret formula roused the curiosity of such men as Josiah Wedgwood, and his casts adorned library cabinets of connoisseurs in Britain, Europe and beyond. Catherine the Great even boasted a complete set of Tassie's casts.[88] As Scotsmen making their way in London, Tassie, Murray and other countrymen gathered frequently at 32 Fleet Street. From October 1771, when Tassie called there to print a business card, the two were in close association (see Plate 15).[89] Tassie's workshop was in Compton Street, Soho, where Murray was shown the impressive range of his work. Murray agreed to keep boxed sets of the gems and figures in his bookshop for sale to customers, and he directed commissions Tassie's way. Tassie in turn took on credit many expensive illustrated books from Murray, works useful in perfecting his art but somewhat beyond his means.[90] In 1775 Murray

[85]JM to Thomas Ewing, 10 Sept. 1774. No copy of the Dublin imprint of the *Considerations* has been located.
[86]In Rottterdam the bookselling firm of Bennett & Hake sold the Edinburgh Powders.
[87]Towards the end of the century all fever powders became less fashionable. The introduction of a tax (about eight per cent) on proprietary medicines in 1783, and the requirement of an annual vendors' licence fee, reduced the profit for middle men like Murray.
[88]There is a succinct study of Tassie by James Holloway, *James Tassie 1735–1799* (Edinburgh, 1986), which includes the recipe for Tassie's paste, and a more recent catalogue by John P. Smith, *James Tassie 1735–1799, Modeller in Glass. A Classical Approach* (London, 1995). See also John Gray, *James and William Tassie. A Biographical and Critical Sketch with a Catalogue of Portrait Medallions* (Edinburgh, 1894).
[89]DB1, 18 Oct. 1771. Tassie paid 12s. for the engraved plate of his calling card and 3s.6d. for 200 cards.
[90]AL, p. 211. Among the works Tassie bought were Joseph Spence's *Polymetis* (1747) and a fine large paper copy of Bernard Picard's *Religious Ceremonies of all Nations* (1733–9).

arranged for the publication of Tassie's *Catalogue of Impressions in Sulphur, of Antique and Modern Gems, from which Pastes are Made and Sold.* Printed on fine paper, with an engraved title page, two thousand copies cost Tassie nearly £50. Added to this considerable sum was advertising at five guineas and the binding of twelve copies for the author 'extra elegant'.[91] Murray took fifty copies of the *Catalogue* to sell in his shop, and when these sold, he got forty more. Prices of the items ranged from 1s.6d. for an antique seal to a few pounds for an imitation cameo.

Murray admired Tassie's pieces, but his main objective was to sell them. Typically, he bought six dozen pastes at a time, for which he received a fifteen per cent discount on the retail price of eighteen shillings per dozen. When Murray visited Dublin in 1775 he recorded a visit to Dr Henry Quin, to whom he hoped to sell a large quantity. 'The Dr is an enthusiast in Tassie's pastes. . . . I produced to him 3 gross . . . which he examined with great avidity. This operation however took him up 2 hours, during which time we drank no wine; and he would not go up stairs to coffee, and when we were ready for the latter it was cold as water.'[92] During the same visit Murray was less successful in selling Tassie's product to Thomas Craig, who 'complained of the price . . . & would not take any'.[93]

In 1791 Murray published (by subscription) Tassie's comprehensive *Descriptive Catalogue of a General Collection of Ancient and Modern Engraved Gems, Cameos as well as Intaglios.* Proposals had been issued three years before, but progress was slow. The *Catalogue* was largely the effort of Rudolph Erich Raspe, the author of *Baron Munchausen's Travels* (1786), who had taken a keen interest in Tassie's work.[94] The two volume quarto *Catalogue* — priced at £1.16s. in boards and printed in parallel French and English texts — was a lavish advertisement for the 15,000 objects it described. Tassie and Raspe attempted to reproduce every important antique gem on record, having gained access to many of 'the most celebrated cabinets in Europe', and to describe them in the *Catalogue*.[95] Raspe introduced the *Catalogue* with a history of gem engraving, from the Maori drawings discovered by Captain Cook to Wedgwood's elegant cameos. His

[91]DB2, p. 314; AL, p. 295 for an 'Account of the Delivery of Mr Tassies Catalogue' in Jan. 1775. About a year later Tassie invested nearly another £4 in binding 400 unsold catalogues in French marbled paper.

[92]Diary, 21 May 1775. Quin, the King's Professor of Physic in the School of Physic, Dublin, had helped Tassie to derive the formula for his vitreous modelling paste (John Carswell, *The Prospector Being the Life and Times of Rudolf Erich Raspe 1737–1794*, London, 1950, pp. 171–2).

[93]Diary, 18 May 1775.

[94]In 1786 Raspe had written a thirty-five page *Account of the Present State and Arrangement of Mr. James Tassie's Collection.*

[95]Some of Raspe's descriptions are especially amusing, such as item 5210: 'Cupid veiling Priapus . . . but the veil . . . is too short and does not conceal the characteristic part of the god' (i, 314). The *Catalogue* was reviewed in the *English Review*, 17 (Apr. 1791), pp. 241–9. See also Carswell, pp. 233–4.

remarks on forgeries of antique gems and on the history of coloured glass are also noteworthy. Fifty-eight etched plates illustrate the work, drawn and engraved by the Scottish artist David Allan, Tassie's friend from his student days in Glasgow at the Art Academy of Robert and Andrew Foulis. Allan also produced an elegant frontispiece engraving depicting a woman in classical dress at her gem cabinet — presumably a compliment to Catherine the Great, Tassie's foremost customer. Around the time the *Catalogue* appeared (March 1791) Tassie modelled Murray's own relief portrait. It was a gesture of thanks for seeing this elaborate publication through the press, for taking subscriptions and for subscribing to thirty copies of the work himself.[96]

Murray also traded in Irish linen for a short time. On one of his visits to Ireland he negotiated the agency for selling linen produced near his uncle's estate at Portaferry. 'I am very confident', he told James Savage, the manufacturer, 'that I can dispose of cloth that is marketable, & not overrated to as much advantage as any company in London'.[97] Savage consigned to him five boxes of linen in March 1774. Murray sold these goods quickly and took in over £470. However his commission was only £19, which for the time and trouble involved was such inadequate compensation that he adjudged it his 'misfortune' to have taken on the venture.[98]

No more successful was Murray's brief foray into woodcock and partridge dealing. When he sold a consignment of game in London for John Yeo, a bookseller in Torrington, Murray did not know what to do with what was left over:

> I can obtain no Poulterer to take the Woodcocks . . . altho' I have applied to several. And few will meddle at all with partridge, a penalty of £5 being annex'd to the sale of every bird. With much difficulty I have sold 24 brace of Woodcocks at 2/6 per brace. The poulterer refused to take the remainder on account of their staleness. I would return both them & the partridge, did I imagine you would thank me for the pains.[99]

Despite these entrepreneurial failures, Murray was not discouraged from a life in trade. Clearly, though, bookselling and publishing was itself

[96]In the Postscript to the *Catalogue* (ii, *49–50) Tassie listed Murray and other contemporary figures whose portraits he had modelled, including Captain Cook, Adam Smith, David Garrick and David Allan.

[97]JM to James Savage, 9 Apr. 1774.

[98]JM to James Savage, 18 March 1775; AL, p. 186. While in Ireland Murray recorded a visit to a cloth manufacturer in Sethlan: 'Walked to Mr Harper's who conducts an extensive manufactory for printing of chintz, muslin, cotton, linen, & wollen stuffs. His ground lying on both sides of the River Rye is finely adapted to the purpose. . . . He had . . . upon his grounds & in his warehouses 4000 pieces of cloth of various kinds which at the average price of £5 per piece makes an amount of £20,000 property, which will give the reader some idea of the extensiveness of this concern' (Diary, 5 June 1775).

[99]JM to John Yeo, 9 Nov. 1786.

a full-time occupation: 'I am keept so much employd', he told a friend in 1775, ' . . . that I have neither time to attend the House of Commons, the House of God, or any other place of public entertainment'.[100] The early 1770s, in particular, were years of financial uncertainty. The effects of the world credit crash of 1772–73 were felt by governments and small shop-keepers alike. In January 1773 Murray reported that large failures in Holland had left London 'stupified'.[101] Cash was so scarce that Murray was even compelled to ask his sister for a loan.[102] When the Ayshire bank Douglas, Heron & Company, where he and close friends had investments, was nearing insolvency, Murray contacted members of parliament, such as his close friend, Robert Mayne, and Sir John Dalrymple, to discover the likely course of events in order to protect his interests. He escaped with his money just in time.[103]

Ambitious for gain, Murray schooled himself to seek out opportunities. He wanted nothing more than to publish a steady seller like *Tom Jones* or *Robinson Crusoe*. Erudite works, whatever their contribution to the progress of mankind, rarely sold in large numbers. He knew he needed not only intelligence and determination, but luck as well. A cautious businessman, he had witnessed too many fellow tradesmen declared bankrupt to risk over-extending himself: 'I would not wish to be tempted with more adventures,' he told Thomas Beddoes. 'For the success of the best works is precarious, & copy money, expences of paper, & printing &c of those I am already engaged in, if more is added, may involve me in contracts that may be difficult on my part to fulfill'.[104]

---

[100]JM to Robert Apsley, 30 Jan. 1775.
[101]JM to Edmund Cartwright, 13 Jan. 1773.
[102]JM to Robina McMurray, 11 Jan. 1773.
[103]JM to Wm Kerr, 19 Feb. 1774. There is an entry in the Mayne & Graham account for 1777 stating £600 Ayr Bank Bonds returned (AL, p. 305). For accounts of the Ayr Bank disaster see Henry Hamilton, 'Failure of the Ayr Bank, 1772', *Economic History Review*, 8 (1956), 405–17 and Frank Brady, 'So Fast to Ruin: The Personal Element in the Collapse of Douglas, Heron, and Company' in *Collections* of the Ayshire Archaeological and Natural History Society, 11 (1973).
[104]JM to Thomas Beddoes, 21 Mar. 1785.

3

The Eighteenth-Century Book Trade

Literary Property — A Brief History

In the history of the book trade until the early eighteenth century, the author of a text had relatively little power. Printers and booksellers almost exclusively dictated the terms on which a work was reproduced. The right to make copies of a text constituted its ownership. And ownership, not authorship, decided who controlled the text as a property.[1] That a bookseller should pay a writer for his work only became common practice towards the end of the seventeenth century. Until then, most writers were either in the keeping of well-to-do patrons, or were themselves gentlemen, and so considered it beneath their station to accept payment for literary efforts. Authors freely dispensed with the ownership of their work; money was not often an issue.

The first disputed copyright, according to legend, dates from AD 567 when Saint Columba copied the psalter of his teacher, Finnian, who then claimed as his property both the original and the copy. Columba protested, and the question was brought before the King for judgement. Considering Finnian to be in the right, the King asserted: 'To every cow her calf, and accordingly to every book its copy'.[2] This judgement, however, failed to set a precedent for relations between authors and those who made and sold copies of their work. The idea of owning a copyright in England can be

[1]Philip Wittenberg, *The Law of Literary Property* (Boston, revd edn, 1978), p. 13. Parts of the following discussion on the history of the book trade follow: John Feather, *A History of British Publishing*, (London, 1988); Terry Belanger, 'Booksellers' Sales of Copyright. Aspects of the London Book Trade: 1718–1768' (doctoral dissertation, Columbia University, 1970); and Belanger, 'From Bookseller to Publisher: Changes in the London Book Trade 1750–1850', in R. Landon (ed.), *Bookselling and Book Buying. Aspects of the Nineteenth-Century British and North American Book Trade*, (Chicago, 1978), pp. 7–16.
[2]Wittenberg, p. 7.

traced to 1504 when the Crown first granted patents — exclusive rights to print certain titles. Possessing these patents allowed printers to reproduce such books as bibles and almanacks. In time, regulating these patents was left largely to the Company of Stationers. Supported by the Crown, the Company prosecuted anyone attempting to print and distribute illegal copies. In return, the Company enabled the Crown to censor printed matter, and the concentration of presses in London under the immediate direction of the Company made this censorship relatively easy to enforce. Before publication, texts were scrutinised by government or religious officials. The Company's control, however, was not absolute. Piracies — works printed without the authority of the Crown or the Stationers' Company — occasionally appeared. Usually the most popular and profitable books were reprinted, but occasionally unlicensed expressions of controversial religious and political thought were made publicly available.

A patent was always granted to an individual. But in 1585 the lucrative *ABC and Little Catechism* became jointly owned. The original owner, realising he could not wholly protect his property, decided it was more sensible to share the profits than to prosecute. Accordingly, he sold a share to the man who had been reprinting the book. This method of dealing with unauthorised reprinters became more and more common. The advantages of sharing the costs and risks of producing large editions also promoted joint ownership. As this trend accelerated, the Company of Stationers made an inventory of their patents and incorporated them into what was called the 'English Stock of the Company of Stationers'.[3] This made it more difficult for the reprinters, who now faced action not from the patent owner alone but from the much more powerful Company.

At the Restoration in 1660, Parliament passed the Licensing (or Printing) Act. This legislation was meant to control the unregulated proliferation of books, pamphlets, proclamations and broadsides which took place in the turmoil of the Civil War. The Act prescribed the places where books could be printed — London, York, Oxford and Cambridge — and shifted the balance of power from the Company of Stationers to Parliament. The greatest number of presses was located in the capital. So, to supply their customers, provincial booksellers had to establish and maintain connections with London traders. After the Licensing Act lapsed in 1695, some additional presses were set up in various provincial cities, but the end of restricted printing did not unduly divert channels of distribution. The provincial market continued to depend on the powerful London shareholders.

Around the time the Licensing Act lapsed, a group of established London booksellers, dissatisfied with the effectiveness of the Company of Stationers, formed an association to protect their valuable copyrights against opportunist booksellers. This group of about twenty individuals

[3]Feather, pp. 37–8.

became known as the 'conger' — a term alluding pejoratively to the conger eel's habit of devouring those smaller than itself.[4] Conger members pooled their copyrights and associated stock and divided their property into shares. Together they paid the expenses of production and shared the profits from wholesaling to non-conger members and retailing to the public at their shops. Sales of copyrights, stocks of books and shares in new titles took place at auctions where attendance was almost exclusively limited to conger members. By the beginning of the eighteenth century a number of congers had sprung up, specialising in such subjects as law books, foreign titles and ballads. The trade in copyrights flourished. Conger members not only invested in established works, but they also speculated on new titles whose copyrights might sell at high prices even before a single copy had been printed. Shares often changed hands. When a copyright owner died, for example, his widow or heirs often would sell a portion of the property at a private trade auction — even if they were entering the trade themselves. Sales were also occasioned by bankruptcies or simply when a bookseller wanted to raise cash. The value of blue chip titles constantly increased, so that a share in such a work could always be auctioned at profit. When a new edition of a steady seller was published, the copyright would usually drop in value in the short term, then increase again as demand for another edition grew. However, the copyright value of the latest novel, unless it were destined to become a classic, would be worth little or nothing after publication.

The earliest known printed catalogue of a trade sale of copyrights dates from 1718, although such auctions are known to have taken place earlier. A set of printed catalogues in the British Library includes over 220 of these eighteenth-century sales, where tens of thousands of copyrights changed hands.[5] The sales were also social events, held at taverns in and around Fleet Street, with dinner and, as the catalogues often note, a 'Glass of good Wine'.[6] Conger members largely controlled the supply of books. Unless an independent retail bookseller played by the conger's rules, it was difficult for him to survive. If a retailer was found to have bought unsanctioned reprints, a conger might cut off his supply. Applying this kind of pressure was less time-consuming and expensive than dealing with pirates by legal

[4]C. Knight, *Shadows of the Old Booksellers*, p. 249.
[5]The set in the British Library was collected by Thomas Longman. Another, which is in the Bodleian, was collected by Aaron and John Ward. Curiously, the last catalogue to have been collected by Longman for an eighteenth-century sale was William Sandby's in December 1768. But, unlike the others, Sandby's is not annotated with the price and buyer of each lot.
[6]For a survey of the sales see Terry Belanger, 'Booksellers' Sales of Copyright. Aspects of the London Book Trade: 1718–1768' (doctoral dissertation, Columbia University, 1970) and Richard Lutes, 'Andrew Strahan and the London Sharebook System, 1785–1825: A Study of the Strahan Printing and Publishing Records' (doctoral dissertation, Wayne State University, 1979), pp. 96–167.

means. For, even if a copyright owner was successful at law, remuneration was usually inadequate, and reprinters were not discouraged.[7] The successes of these congers were considerable, though reprinting was not completely eradicated. Those outside the congers could either buy the books at the prices set by the congers — sometimes artificially high — or take their chances with illegal supply. This system caused growing dissatisfaction, and, when sufficient numbers of booksellers rebelled, the congers sought legislation to protect their interests.

Although property and the rights and duties associated with it had long been at the centre of English life, literature was a special kind of property, less tangible than an acre of land or an oak table and, as the reprinters had shown, more easily stolen. Consequently, booksellers sought special laws to protect their rights, and they succeeded in 1710. The Copyright Act of that year was the first important legal development in the book trade since the end of licensing in 1695. Its full title was 'An Act for the Encouragement of Learning, by Vesting the Copies of Printed Books in the Authors or Purchasers of such Copies, during the Times therein mentioned'. This Act, which applied in England, Wales and Scotland but not in Ireland, put a limit on the copyright of existing works to twenty-one years and on works published after 1710 to twenty-eight years.[8] For the first time it was stated that the author had rights over his literary property. But this legal recognition was of little immediate financial benefit to an author. Indeed, a bookseller might argue that the law diminished the value of a text as it was no longer owned for all time.

Post-Restoration England witnessed the emergence of the professional writer. John Dryden stands out as one example, and Aphra Behn, as Virginia Woolf remarked, 'made, by working very hard, enough to live on'.[9] Nevertheless, writers often received only small reward for their labours, while booksellers sometimes made a considerable sum from their work. True, the copyright holder bore all the risk, but a highly organised trade protected his interests. The 'Act for the Encouragement of Learning' was by no means as progressive as it sounded. It was essentially about profit and protection, not about improving society. It also seemed impractical and difficult to enforce. The owners of valuable literary property could hardly be expected willingly to relinquish their right to publish when, under a strict interpretation of the statute, their copyright expired after twenty-one or twenty-eight years. The established holders were confident that precedents set in English common law concerning literary property would

[7]Belanger, 'Booksellers' Sales of Copyright', pp. 7–8.
[8]The Act also required that copies of each book published from that time be deposited in nine libraries across Britain. However, this did not become regular practice until a later date.
[9]Virginia Woolf, *A Room of One's Own* (London, Grafton Books, 1977), p. 70. First published in 1929.

secure their rights in perpetuity. They believed that the terms in the Act such as 'Copies' and 'Rights' were vague enough not to jeopardise the status quo.[10] Many of the most successful individuals in the eighteenth-century book trade made their profits more by the possession of copyrights than by retail bookselling. When, for example, Jacob Tonson died in 1767 his copyrights, including large shares of major classics, realised nearly £10,000 — more than any other sale of its kind had done before.[11]

The twenty-one-year limit on the protection of existing property — as set out in the 1710 Act — made what would happen in 1731 the subject of much speculation and anticipation in the trade. Long before then, however, those dealers who were not in a conger realised it might just be legally possible to reprint profitable texts. In response, members of the established trade moved to prevent reprinting altogether. The 1710 Act had been an effective deterrent against unauthorised reprinting in its first twenty-one years, and it seemed sensible to them that it should be extended. However, the London trade faced another problem whose greater urgency shifted their attention. Presses in Ireland and Scotland had been reprinting cheap editions of popular texts and cutting into the London booksellers' markets. In 1739 the London trade successfully urged Parliament to pass into law an act against the importation of those books which were reprints of books first published in Britain. They also put pressure on retailers who might consider breaking this law by threatening to terminate their supply. Moreover, the London trade worked harder to promote their wares in the provincial markets; they improved their systems of distribution; and they advertised their books so that customers would demand London editions rather than inferior, if cheaper, reprints.

Murray and the 1774 Literary Property Decision

In general, these measures proved an effective way to curtail the free trade in printed books until October 1763, when the Scotsmen Alexander Donaldson and his brother John opened up a shop in the Strand selling their own reprints of the most popular texts as the copyright elapsed or of titles that had not been entered in the Stationers' Company Register. Their right to sell was hotly contested in the courts over the next nine years. During this time the book trade continued to flourish, but uncertainties were greater than ever. The first round of legal proceedings over literary property in 1769 did not go well for the Donaldsons. The Court of King's Bench upheld the right of Andrew Millar to a perpetual copyright in James

[10]Belanger, 'Booksellers' Sales of Copyright', p. 3; Feather, pp. 76–9 and 81–2.
[11]Belanger, 'Booksellers' Sales of Copyright', p. 18.

Thomson's poem, the *Seasons*, which Donaldson had reprinted after the twenty-eight-year copyright had elapsed. Seizing the advantage, Millar obtained an injunction against the Donaldsons at Chancery.

John Murray knew the Donaldsons well and supported their cause emphatically. He believed that a decisive challenge to the principle of perpetual literary property would undermine the London monopoly and open the door to a newcomer like himself. He joined the Donaldsons' campaign to persuade the public to back the rebels. However, Murray himself did not reprint as the Donaldsons had done. Naturally cautious, he waited for a definite legal outcome. In 1770 Murray and a number of other booksellers published a pamphlet by Edmund Law, the Bishop of Carlisle, entitled *Observations concerning Literary Property* — one of many to appear on the subject. Law sided with Donaldson and argued on the utilitarian principle that the situation as it stood was disadvantageous to the majority — namely authors and readers. The only advantage in maintaining the status quo that Law could perceive was that to change it would mean certain very large works which needed major capital expenditure would be more difficult to produce. Booksellers would be less inclined to invest in publications whose returns would only be realised in the longer term. However, he concluded this was a minor drawback compared with the benefits of making the printed word more widely available.[12]

In the wake of their initial victory, the London trade sought to confirm the decision in Scotland, where the English ruling did not apply. Their aim was to strike a decisive blow at reprinting. At this point, however, they met with an unexpected difficulty. Scottish law was much more vague about the concept of literary property. In July 1773 an eleven-to-one majority in the Scottish Court of Session ruled contrary to the English decision. Property, they decided, had to be tangible to be protected.[13] Bolstered by this victory, Donaldson then appealed to the House of Lords against the original injunction.

Some books sold by Murray that summer (1773) include a two-page advertisement stating that 'New Books, Printed According to Act of

---

[12]The main publisher of the pamphlet was John Merrill of Cambridge, once an active supporter of the right of the London traders but who by 1770 had changed his views, even to the point of giving evidence against the London trade. See John Feather, *The Provincial Book Trade in Eighteenth-Century England*, pp. 8–9.

[13]Only Lord Monboddo cast a dissenting vote. James Boswell, in *The Journal of a Tour to the Hebrides*, recorded the following conversation on this topic: '[Dr Johnson] said, our judges had not gone deep in the question concerning literary property. I mentioned Lord Monboddo's opinion, that if a man could get a work by heart, he might print it. . . . — *Johnson*. 'No, sir; a man's repeating it no more makes it his property, than a man may sell a cow which he drives home.' I said, printing an abridgement of a work was allowed, which was only cutting the horns and tail off a cow. *Johnson*. 'No, sir; 'tis making the cow have a calf' (*Life of Johnson*, eds. Hill and Powell, 6 vols., Oxford, 1934–64, v, 72).

Parliament, continue to be sold as usual by John Donaldson'.[14] The advertisement compared the prices of twenty-six of the most popular books of the day bought in Donaldson's editions or at the regular London prices. The conclusion was evident: the public could save nearly fifty per cent, 'which it is hoped will induce all book-buyers to look at those CHEAP EDITIONS before they lay out their money elsewhere'. The implication was that perpetual copyright should, once and for all, come to an end.

What had come to be called 'the great question of literary property' was finally resolved in February 1774 when the House of Lords ruled in Donaldson's favour in the case of *Donaldson versus Becket*. Their decision confirmed the limitation on literary property set out in the 1710 Act. After examining whether such a practice actually 'encouraged learning', the Lords judged that books would be cheaper with limited copyright and that free trade should prevail. John Murray described their decision as 'a *magna carta*' for booksellers. Few events encouraged him as much as the Lords' decision. He was concerned, however, that his authors might not share his enthusiasm and sought to allay their fears that it would devalue literary property. To John Millar, a professor of law at Glasgow University who had published a successful book with Murray in 1771, he wrote:

> The decision of the house of Lords will perhaps have damped your ardor of writing, as you will be averse from raising a literary estate without rendering it perpetual. But . . . I am convinced that authors works will still be purchased with very little difference in price. An illegal monopoly has been justly dissolved which common or statute law never gave; and has been only an usurpation of a sett of sc[ou]n[dre]lls who instead of relief deserve punishment for the combination & oppression they have been guilty of.[15]

Not all of Murray's bookselling associates in Edinburgh rejoiced in Donaldson's victory. William Creech, John Balfour and others who had profitable connections with prominent members of the London book trade such as William Strahan, Thomas Cadell and Thomas Becket, worried about the effects of the decision on their trading relationships. It surprised Murray that Creech was fearful of selling his new forty-two-volume edition of the *British Poets* in London, despite this now being perfectly legal. In April 1774, not long after the important decision, Murray reminded Creech of their newly acquired rights:

---

[14]This advertisement comprises the final leaf of my own copy of Abbé Laugier's *History of the Negociations for the Peace at Belgrade* (1770). In June of that year the Donaldson brothers had dissolved their partnership: John remained at Arundel Street in the Strand; and Alexander opened a shop at 48 St Paul's Churchyard. One reason for this separation may have been to reduce the damage should the decision go against Alexander, but another may have been to anticipate an expansion of their business in the event of success.

[15]JM to John Millar, 19 Apr. 1774.

The London booksellers . . . have been evicted at law of usurping a property & of oppressing their brethren, which they never were legally entitled to do. And altho this decision in a particular manner must be a great relief . . . to Scotch booksellers, yet it would appear from your letters that you are willing to reinstate them in their usurpation, altho by your actions in printing you appear to be as great a pirate as the worst they complain of.[16]

Murray wrote so forcefully because the battle against the established trade was not yet over. His aim was to rouse Creech to join against the efforts of the defeated bookselling establishment to win relief for the thousands they had invested in copyrights once regarded as perpetual. The kind of compensation for the loss of their property they sought would, Murray believed, 'throw all the country booksellers in a worse state, than that from which the decision of the Lords relieved them'.[17] Murray himself gave testimony in the House of Lords. He charged that, as a newcomer, he had been excluded from the sales of stock and copyright shares regularly held by the established London trade. He also asserted that he had been put to considerable expense in defending himself against their monopolistic practices.[18]

Much to Murray's satisfaction, this appeal for monetary relief was unsuccessful. He, in fact, wanted 'to make these greedy monopolizers refund some of their illegal gains'.[19] Becket and his circle — indeed booksellers since the chartering of the Stationers' Company in 1557 — had made enough money out of a protected industry. Now others could share in the profits of the book trade. Although defeated, Becket did not give up his cause. Murray refused to be 'at all intimidated by Mr Becket who has trangress'd upon the order of the Trade' and even avoided personal business contact. When one of Murray's authors suggested Becket for a share in his book, Murray explained that he himself would be the sole publisher: 'This proceeds less from a desire to grasp the whole, than from this — Becket and Murray are disagreeable to each other'.[20] And when his trading partner in a publication sold copies to Becket, Murray was nothing less than indignant.[21] When Becket was certified a bankrupt in June 1779, Murray

[16]JM to Wm Creech, 8 Apr. 1774.
[17]Ibid.
[18]*Edinburgh Evening Courant*, 16 May 1774.
[19]JM to John Bell, 5 Apr. 1774. Just over a year later a new bill was put forward which proposed to grant Oxford and Cambridge special privileges with regard to perpetual literary property. Murray remarked that they 'are not so modest in their demands as the London Booksellers were last year. . . . I am told for certain', he added, 'that the London Booksellers will be gratified with some favourable clauses, which if the proposed Bill passes will more than gratify them for their Defeat last year' (JM to James Robertson, 18 Apr. 1775). The bill was also unsuccessful.
[20]JM to John Ogilvie, 21 Dec. 1775.
[21]JM to Mr Durham, 6 Nov. 1776; to Charles Elliot, 12 Nov. 1776.

bought heavily at the sale of his stock, copyrights and shares.[22] However, Becket's standing in the trade was such that he recovered not long afterwards and went on to hold the prestigious office of 'Bookseller to the Prince of Wales'. In time, Murray realised that there would be little harm and considerable profit in joining ventures in which Becket had a share, and in the 1780s they were partners in a handful of publications.[23]

After the Lords' decision Murray exploited the potential for reprinting. He knew it was important that his editions should appeal to the book-buying public now that the marketplace was even more competitive. He described his edition of the *Poems of Gray* (1776) as 'the most beautiful . . . ever published' (see Plates 16 and 17).[24] Two years later he published an equally attractive edition of the *Seasons* by James Thomson, the author whose work had set in motion the reform of copyright law. To enhance these editions, he commissioned lives and critical assessments of the poets and had the books embellished with engravings by leading artists.[25]

Other booksellers responded more aggressively than Murray to the Lords' decision. John Bell published an edition of Shakespeare in 1774, the *British Theatre* (1776–78) in twenty-one volumes, and then undertook his ambitious *Poets of Great Britain* in 1777, which appeared in 109 volumes over the next five years.[26] Harrison & Company tapped another market for reprints with the publication in parts of the *Novelists' Magazine* (1780–88), containing sixty popular works of fiction. These collections were characterised by their cheapness in comparison to what would have been paid before 1774 for an edition published by the established London traders. They were, in fact, the precursors of classics reprint series such as Dent's 'Everyman' editions. Murray sold many sets of works like Bell's *Poets* in his shop. Surprisingly, though, when it came to investing in the reprint market, he chose a more conservative option and purchased with more than thirty other booksellers a share of *The Works of the English Poets* (1779–80) for which Samuel Johnson wrote 'Prefaces Biographical and Critical' (see Plates 18 and 19). This multi-volume undertaking was the response of the established London trade to Bell's series. Johnson's prefaces became, perhaps, the most famous set of literary biographies ever written, and the collection itself did much to form a canon of

---

[22]BB, pp. 15–19.

[23]In the Checklist Becket and Murray are listed together in over thirty works, mainly publications with several other booksellers.

[24]JM to T. & J. Merrill, 1 Oct. 1776.

[25]Promoting the sale of his 1792 edition of Thomson's *Seasons,* Murray remarked: 'Mr [William] Sharp is the first Engraver in London & the two first Pictures for the work are in the Exhibition and much admired' (JM to John Elder, 5 May 1792).

[26]For an account of Bell's series, see Thomas Bonnell, 'John Bell's *Poets of Great Britain*: The "Little Trifling Edition" Revisited', *Modern Philology,* 85 (Nov. 1987), pp. 128–52.

literature in English.[27] Collective publishing could still generate good profits, and with less individual risk. In a relatively short period of time, Murray had moved from the outside of the trade to its centre.

Murray did not see himself abjuring his principles in shifting from radical upstart in 1774 to conger member a few years later. By supporting an end to perpetual copyright (which he would always avow) and numbering himself among the established trade, he was merely creating business opportunities for himself according to the principles he himself had asserted in the House of Lords. He had no argument against syndicate publishing, as these collective ventures are sometimes called, and he accepted the principle that his ownership in a given title was limited in time. This was still where good money was to be made, even if the stakes (i.e. the values of shares) were somewhat smaller after 1774. Rather than resenting Murray for his support of Donaldson, his fellow congerees welcomed him as a man with money to spend. He had campaigned to change the system, and, when he succeeded, he played by the new rules. The lure of even greater profits than could be had by syndicate publishing promoted ambitious individual ventures after Bell's example. In 1775, in the wake of the copyright decision, Murray explained a trend which was gradually changing the book trade.

> It is certain that the public is not fond of seeing many names to a new publication; and for this reason it will be more to the credit & advantage of the author that he dispose of it to a single person. Besides, it is a greater object to one Bookseller, who will naturally interest himself much more in the fate of it than if he enjoyed but a small share of the property. . . . And tho but the simple publisher, he is elated or depressed in the fate of his work, little short of the author himself.[28]

In Murray's analysis, the bookseller, in alliance with the author, was emerging as the 'simple publisher'. An interaction of market and political economies initiated the process; individuals regulated it. But, though Murray espoused this principle, it was left to his son to exploit it more fully in the early nineteenth century.

[27]BB, p. 11. The proprietors of the work first met at the Chapter Coffee House and as a group became known as the 'Chapter'. In the *Life of Johnson*, Boswell quoted a letter (dated 26 Sept. 1777) from Charles Dilly, one of Murray's fellow proprietors, about the origin of the *Works of the English Poets*: 'The first cause that gave rise to this undertaking, I believe, was owing to the little trifling edition of the Poets . . . sold by Bell, in London. . . . The type was found so extremely small [and] . . . the inaccuracy of the press very conspicuous. These reasons, as well as the idea of an invasion of what we call our Literary Property, induced the London Booksellers to print an elegant and accurate edition of all the English Poets of reputation, from Chaucer to the present time.' (*Life of Johnson*, eds. Hill and Powell, iii, 110). As Bonnell, op. cit., rightly points out, Bell's edition was far from 'trifling'.
[28]JM to Gilbert Stuart, 25 Sept. 1775.

Mysterious 'Murray' Imprints

Certain events surrounding the 1774 literary property dispute which relate
to Murray are intriguingly difficult to explain. In that year, for example,
editions of some of the most popular works of the day were issued with the
imprint: 'London: Printed for J. Murray in the Strand'. These include
Goldsmith's *Vicar of Wakefield*, Sterne's *Tristram Shandy* and his *Sentimental
Journey*, all of which had not yet come out of copyright and so were illegal to
reprint or sell (see Plate 20).[29] There is no record of another J. Murray
active at the time either in the Strand or elsewhere, and, although Murray
had a bindery in the Strand, no such editions are mentioned in his account
ledgers, daybooks or correspondence during this period. Moreover, in his
extensive newspaper advertising at this time these titles are not apparently
listed. If they were Murray's books, it would be unreasonable to think that
he could make enough money on their sale to justify the risk.

It has been hypothesised by Pollard, in *Dublin's Trade in Books* (1989),
that these three editions were printed in Dublin for the London market.[30] It
was not unusual for an Irish printer to fabricate a London imprint for a
piracy. But why implicate Murray? Perhaps the printer or printers who
produced the books resented Murray's small success in breaking into the
Irish market in the early 1770s (discussed in Chapter 7). Another more
speculative explanation may be that angry London traders arranged for the
editions to suggest that the end of perpetual copyright would result in a
publishing free-for-all in which even limited copyright would be unenforce-
able. Whatever the reason, these apparently spurious imprints, like others
Murray had to denounce at a later date, are indicative of the vagaries of the
dynamic trade into which he had entered.

[29]Sterne had died in 1768, Goldsmith in 1774. *Tristram Shandy* was first published 1759–67;
Vicar of Wakefield in 1766; *Sentimental Journey* in 1768. See Checklist items 79, 90 and 91.
[30]M. Pollard, *Dublin's Trade in Books*, pp. 81–2. Copies of these books are rare, but at least one
of the *Vicar of Wakefield* (which I own) is in a contemporary binding with a 1775 Dublin
imprint of Johnson's *Journey to the Western Islands*, further circumstantial evidence of an Irish
origin. Moreover, the printing of all these 'Murray' editions is rather crude and the paper of
poor quality, characteristics of some Irish reprints from the period.

4

Dealing with Authors

Judging Literary Merit

Murray would read manuscripts carefully to assess their quality and likely profitability before making an offer. After examining one book proposal, he confronted a prospective author with a realism calculated not to raise expectations: 'The explanation you have given me of your work interests me in it; but how far the public may be inclined to encourage it I am doubtful; that it will not be encouraged equal to its merit I am certain.'[1] Murray was also wary of publishing little-known authors. Even when Gilbert Stuart, a trusted advisor, suggested that Murray publish Adam Dickson's work on agriculture — which had also been highly recommended by William Robertson, one of the leading writers of the day — Murray remained circumspect: 'A Bookseller in a Purchase looks to the probability of the sale, and seizes hold of the manuscript of an author already well and successfully known to the Public in preference to another tho perhaps better, written by an author whose reputation is not so well established'.[2] Of course, successful authors usually had established links with booksellers and could commend greater payment for their works.

Once an author had been accepted by Murray and produced a profitable title for him, the author would receive every encouragement. When Sir David Dalrymple (Lord Hailes) was writing the second part of the *Annals of Scotland*, a continuation of his successful history of medieval Scotland, Murray showed himself sympathetic, even philosophical, during the three years it would take to complete the work:

> When a world was to be made, the chaos furnished materials exactly adapted to the undertaking and the maker had only the trouble of arrange-ment. Your work seems to be different: your chaos is not only defective, but

[1] JM to Sylvester O'Halloran, 5 Feb. 1776.
[2] JM to Gilbert Stuart, 11 Dec. 1775. Murray was comparing Dickson's proposed publication to Arthur Young's popular agricultural–topographical writings.

much of its materials were *improper* for your purpose yet so disguised that it
requires an uncommon share of sagacity & knowledge to distinguish
betwixt them, and your task calls upon you: not only to arrange, but to
select, to supply deficiencies, and to account for imperfections.[3]

Although Murray knew Dalrymple would overcome these difficulties, he
was pleased that the author had engaged highly competent men to assist
him: James Boswell advised on historical points; and no less a figure than
Samuel Johnson corrected Dalrymple's style.[4]

On the whole, Murray was himself an effective judge of literary works,
but he often sought the opinion of a few trusted readers. Gilbert Stuart, for
example, regularly offered frank advice, telling Murray on one occasion:
'The performance [a translation of the lives of Abelard and Eloise] is one
. . . that will bring no reputation to the Author, & no profit to the bookseller'.[5] The better to decide upon the merits of those books Murray least
understood — like medical works — he solicited the opinions of experts.
Often, however, even the most celebrated writers of the day could not
persuade him to change his views. Such caution may have allowed some
profitable titles to slip through his hands, but he understood that his chief
responsibility to himself (and perhaps to the larger culture of letters) was to
stay in business.

Murray's financial negotiations with authors were characterised by this
determination to protect his interests but also by a concern for confidenti-
ality. He had no wish to find himself bidding against other publishers,
preferring instead to buy manuscripts privately from authors. His usual
practice was to have the author name a price first. If he thought it would
allow him to publish profitably, he would agree to this figure. However, if
he considered the author's demands excessive, he would make a counter
offer. Should the author not immediately accept, he asked only that the
details of the deal not be communicated to another publisher. He hoped to
avoid a makeshift auction. Indeed, on hearing that another publisher had
offered more, he would usually refuse to add to his original figure, even
when he could afford more and still profit. But when Murray's offer was
accepted, he could be unusually generous. For example, he gave John
McArthur ten guineas more than he had originally agreed, merely because
the author had preferred him as a publisher to Thomas Cadell, the highly
successful London publisher.[6]

On rare occasions Murray would make the first offer for a book, either

---

[3]JM to David Dalrymple, 29 Apr. 1776.
[4]James Boswell to Lord Hailes, 18 and 19 April 1777, Yale MS 89, C 602–03.
[5]Gilbert Stuart to JM, 23 Aug. 1769.
[6]JM to John McArthur, 14 Apr. 1792. The work was McArthur's *Treatise of the Principles and
Practice of Naval Courts-martial* (1792). However, Murray is not included in the imprint with
Wheildon and Butterworth, partners with whom he co-published at this time. Murray had
published an edition of McArthur's *Army and Navy Gentleman's Companion* in 1784.

to an author who considered himself above mercenary matters or to one with whom he had a more than casual acquaintance. Over the matter of Dalrymple's *Annals of Scotland*, for example, Murray hesitantly named a figure through an intermediary (Gilbert Stuart):

> Altho I have always found my situation to be awkward & attended with inconveniencies in bidding for any Literary performance in the first instance, & have in general accounts avoided it, yet I trust to Lord Hailes' [Dalrymple's] candor that he will not be offended, when, to conform to his idea I make him an offer of one hundred & thirty guineas for the present edition of his Annals over & above defraying the expence of paper & print.[7]

When Murray asked Stuart himself if £150 would be acceptable for his *View of Society in Europe* (1778), he added: 'Write to me freely upon the subject, because whether I have the book or not . . . will make no alteration in my friendship for you'.[8] Stuart negotiated with John Bell, an Edinburgh trader, to receive £100 for certain and £300 more upon the sale of 1000 copies. Murray acknowledged the arrangement was 'not a bad one' but warned Stuart to 'leave nothing indefinite; for . . . Bell . . . from the peculiar turn of his mind is difficult to deal with'.[9] Murray's assessment proved to be correct: Bell did little to promote the book and reneged on the agreement, forcing Stuart to take legal action against him. Murray later bought the unsold copies from Bell and reissued them in his own name, more out of consideration for Stuart than with a profit in mind. Afterwards he urged Stuart to write a continuation of the *View of Society*, arguing that 'this work will do your reputation & pocket more service than any other you can execute'.[10] But Stuart did not heed Murray's advice.

Murray could not lay out the large sums that the most popular authors were then receiving and which others had come to expect from such well-to-do booksellers as Thomas Cadell and Thomas Longman. When he did agree to buy a work, he delayed payment for as long as possible. Part might be given upon receipt of the manuscript, if Murray were very confident or if he knew the author needed the money. As a rule, however, he did not pay until three months after publication. Sometimes settling authors' accounts was difficult. Murray was not always patient enough to explain to his authors the nature of bookselling, which ran by a logic sometimes obscure, even to highly intelligent individuals. As a result, he found some authors 'constantly suspicious of every charge which they do not understand, &

[7] JM to Gilbert Stuart, 25 Sept. 1775. In another letter written soon after, Stuart assured Murray: 'Although you would gain but little on the transaction, I would not have you scruple it. The advantage of publishing for good people is great. Think seriously, & while you calculate his Lordship's interest, do not forget your own.'
[8] JM to Gilbert Stuart, 29 July 1777.
[9] JM to Gilbert Stuart, 4 Oct. 1777.
[10] JM to Gilbert Stuart, 17 Aug. 1779.

asking explanations of it, which to a bookseller is unnecessary & never required'.[11] Through such difficulties, Murray remained determined to protect his profits, or, in the case of unsuccessful ventures, to protect himself as much as possible from substantial loss.

After agreeing to purchase a manuscript from an author, Murray would occasionally sell a share of the property to another bookseller and enter into an informal partnership. He did not always profit from selling at this stage but found compensation in the advantages of sharing production costs and using the trading partner's connections to distribute the book more widely. His partner's name was usually added to the imprint, and, as a courtesy to partners of considerable reputation, their names were sometimes placed before his. In such circumstances Murray was at pains to make the arrangement clear to the author: 'Notwithstanding this you have nothing to do with any other bookseller than myself', he wrote to one, 'I being responsible for my agreement with you.'[12] Allowing authors, who understood little of bookselling, to participate in publication arrangements only complicated matters. Indeed, as early as 1770 he found himself at odds with several authors, and even hazarded the opinion 'that authors in general however superior they may be in pointing out the nice proprieties of Behaviour which should regulate mankind . . . are not the first to set their example or to practice their own Rules'.[13] In the face of such behaviour, Murray gradually became more authoritative than conciliatory: 'My council proceeds from an Experience of 20 years in Bookselling', he told John Whitaker in 1788, '& I have your reputation as well as interest at heart'.[14] Towards the end of his career Murray told an author: 'Booksellers are more favourably treated by one another, than by those who are strangers to the business'.[15]

Modes of Publication

Should Murray believe it unwise to lay out money in advance for a manuscript, he would attempt various other strategies to secure the right to publish. Often he would share the expense of production with the author and organise the printing, distribution and advertising himself. Then, only after costs had been met, would he share subsequent profits — usually paid out every six months. He regarded the author as his partner but managed the work himself. 'An author,' he argued, 'will receive more money for one

[11]JM to Robert Robertson, 18 Mar. 1785.
[12]JM to John Millar, 28 Dec. 1786. See Checklist 1787 item 611.
[13]JM to Ralph Griffiths, 6 Dec. 1770.
[14]JM to John Whitaker, 13 Mar. 1788.
[15]JM to Benjamin Bell, 5 Apr. 1793.

half his property if his book succeeds, than he would for *the whole*, from any bookseller whatever, upon an uncertainty'.[16] Since authors typically thought highly of their books, sometimes unrealistically so, they were usually willing to accept the terms of Murray's bargain. According to trade practice, an imprint published in such a way would generally list Murray's name alone and thus not indicate a partnership. In any case, an author might not want to be seen as financing his own work.[17] Not every author was satisfied with the results of this kind of arrangement. In 1791, after publishing John Wade's *Select Evidences of Treating Fever and Dysentery in Bengal*, Murray informed the disgruntled author that expenses were not yet met: 'With all my efforts 238 copies are only sold. . . . It is difficult for me . . . to account for your anger or resentment. . . . Our agreement was to divide profits. I did not conceive that you would call for these before they existed or that I acted an ungenerous part.'[18] Murray himself was in fact anxious about his own expenditures, which he had yet to recoup.

Should Murray's funds be tied up in other expensive publications or were he less than optimistic about prospective sales, he would suggest that the author pay entirely for the paper, printing and advertising. Any profits would be shared. He preferred to deal with authors in this way when the works were topical (such as political pamphlets) and had little long-term sales potential. He also used this arrangement when publishing poetry by untried authors. The imprint of such works typically read: 'Printed for the Author, and Sold by J. Murray'. Almost every year Murray published a handful of works on these terms (see Table 2 under 'Agency–Murray Alone'). When a certain Captain Watson came to Fleet Street with his first production, the poem 'The Rhenardine', Murray told him: 'As there is not one . . . in Twenty which upon publication defrays the expences attending them, I must decline'.[19] However, the Captain persisted and eventually received a more sympathetic reply: 'Many a valuable and learned work has suffered this fate. Further, I have been so often deceived in my prognostic, that my Judgement on this point is worth but very little.'[20] However, Murray's sympathy did not extend to publishing the work on any terms. In such situations, when Murray could not agree with an author on the price or method of publication (not an infrequent occurrence), his practice was to suggest other London publishers, among them Thomas Cadell, Joseph Johnson and Thomas Longman. Of the last he told the Reverend William Lothian, who was then proffering his manuscript history of The

---

[16]JM to John Millar Jr, 7 Oct. 1786.
[17]A little more than one-third of the imprints giving Murray's name alone fit into this category, or about ten per cent of his total publications (see Table 1).
[18]JM to John Wade, 17 Mar. 1792.
[19]JM to Captain Watson, 15 May 1787.
[20]JM to Captain Watson, 17 May 1787.

Netherlands: 'There is no person in the trade, or perhaps out of it, whose character I respect more'.[21]

When Murray bought a manuscript from an author, he alone decided on the number of copies to be printed, but when an author was paying for all or part of the printing and paper, persuading him to print a modest run could be difficult. In a letter to Lothian, Murray described the predicament: 'I have constantly seen repentance follow from printing a larger number, but *never* from printing a small one. I have smarted myself several times severely from this particular. And to give a recent instance, my friend Hugo Arnot has printed 1000 copies of his [History of] Edinburgh; but which action he will repent for some years of his life.'[22] Arnot would not receive profits until the costs of the large edition were met. Indeed they never were. Typically authors wished to print large runs. However, 500 copies usually were more than enough for an edition of a new historical or poetical work, and Murray usually printed no more than 250 copies of a medical pamphlet or political tract. If a book sold out, he gladly undertook the expense of a new edition. Because printing was done by hand, the cost advantage of long runs was minimal.[23]

Another method Murray occasionally suggested, when he was not himself inclined to publish a work but wished the author to proceed, was to sell by subscription. This meant that prior to going to press, advertisements were printed in newspapers or separate proposals circulated. In one instance Murray (or the author, the Rev. William Shaw) had a subscription proposal written by no less a figure than Samuel Johnson for Shaw's 'Analysis of the Scotch Celtic Language' (see Checklist 1777 item 158). Subscribers were asked to commit themselves to a purchase and sometimes to pay part in advance. Their names were usually printed in a list of subscribers, which imparted prestige, particularly in an era when books were mainly a luxury commodity. Moreover, the subscription price was often lower than the subsequent retail price. But if few subscriptions were collected, an advertised book might not be put to press at all.[24] Subscription publishing enabled

---

[21]JM to Wm Lothian, 28 Dec. 1779. Privately Murray remarked: 'I have declined to purchase a History of the Netherlands; because, altho not without merit, it did not appear to me to be finished enough' (JM to John Whitaker, 6 July 1779). James Dodsley, not Longman, finally published Lothian's work.

[22]JM to Wm Lothian, 7 Sept. 1779. Copies of Arnot's *History* are even still relatively common.

[23]Apparently, printers' charges for very long runs were proportionally more (contrary to what one might expect) than for shorter runs, according to Patricia Hernlund ('William Strahan's Ledgers, Standard Charges for Printing, 1738–1785', *Studies in Bibliography*, xx, 1967, 105). Hernlund points out that the primary reason why printers charged more (that is, for runs well over 1000 copies) was that type had a shorter life.

[24]Two books never published were: 'Proposals for printing by subscription in one volume quarto price one guinea (half to be paid at the time of subscribing, and the other half on delivery of the book in boards) The Spirit of Commerce in three parts. . . . By Thomas Gordon. Subscriptions received by J. Murray; G. and T. Wilkie' (Murray's album of

the owner of a work — whether the bookseller, the author or both — to guarantee a sale and defray some or all of the production costs. Since the early seventeenth century books had been marketed in this way in England, but by the middle of the eighteenth century its frequency had declined considerably. Instances were not unknown in which subscription money was collected and never returned when a work did not appear. Murray remarked: 'That mode (which formerly was fashionable) is so much disliked now that the bare attempt is sufficient to throw discredit upon the performance'.[25] In all, Murray had a hand in only about twenty-five works published by subscription.

Murray encouraged Henry Boyd, an Irishman, to publish his translation of Dante's *Inferno* in this way. Boyd followed this plan, but surprised Murray in choosing Charles Dilly, another London bookseller, to sell the unsubscribed copies. Murray did not suppress his anger: 'After corresponding with me so long, putting me to the expence of much postage, and what is more taking up my time with long particular answers to your different Letters, I could not have thought that as a Gentleman or Man of Generosity or feeling you would have employed another person of the trade here to publish your Book'.[26] However genuine Murray's disappointment, the justice of his complaint was questionable. Boyd had in fact written to inquire about what progress Murray was making with the publication. Murray, who had been ill at the time, did not reply, and Boyd decided to take his manuscript elsewhere. More successful was the subscription sale of the Reverend Henry Hunter's *Sacred Biography* (1783). This work, the printed version of Hunter's lectures on the histories of the patriarchs which he had given at the Scots Church in London, proved so popular that subscriptions (which guaranteed the sale of over 400 copies) were not needed for the subsequent five volumes.

Murray sold his most profitable publication, Johann Kasper Lavater's *Essays on Physiognomy*, by subscription. This elaborate work, with over 800 engravings, appeared in parts — a mode of publication by which a numbered series came out over an extended period. Murray usually discouraged such a plan of publication, but the high costs of producing each number of the *Essays*

newspaper clippings, Checklist item 475); and David Ross's *History of the English Stage*, for which Murray circulated a broadside proposal in May 1790. The author's death in September put an end to the project. See Checklist item 789.

[25] JM to Wm Boutcher, 30 Dec. 1775. See also JM to John Imison, 27 Aug. 1784. Two of Murray's successful subscription proposals are found in the British Library: (1) 'Proposals for Printing by Subscription, an Enquiry into the Husbandry of the Ancients, by the Reverend Adam Dickson, A.M., Late Minister of Dunse', 1788; (2) 'Proposals for Printing a Descriptive Catalogue of a Collection of Pastes & Impressions of Ancient and Modern Gems Formed and Selling by James Tassie', 1788 (see Checklist items 645 and 693).

[26] JM to Henry Boyd, 26 Mar. 1785. One hundred and sixty-eight individuals subscribed for 241 sets of Boyd's two-volume translation.

— forty-one in all — necessitated it. Physiognomy, a precursor to phrenology, was a system which set out to determine the inward qualities of an individual by an examination of the outward appearance. Such was the fashion of this pseudo-science at the time that the proprietors could command a fantastic price and sell by subscription only. The first number of Lavater was published in January 1788 and the final instalment did not appear until March 1799. Priced at twelve shillings a number, the complete set of parts would cost over £24, an enormous sum for a book (see Plates 21, 22a, and 22b).[27] Subscriptions were coming in so quickly that Murray and his partners could boast that there was 'ample compensation for every expence they incur by increasing the quantity, and keeping up the quality of the future Numbers'.[28] Producing the work cost Murray and his partners over £10,000.[29] But profits were substantial.

Style Matters

In dealing with authors, Murray learnt early that the terms, especially the length of the work, had to be agreed upon and adhered to, otherwise costings and expected profits could not be calculated. Authors, however, often deviated from what had been agreed, and what Murray had been promised was not always delivered. Murray found his dealings with John Millar in 1771 particularly instructive. He had agreed to pay Millar £100 for the manuscript of his *Distinction of Ranks*, but on receiving the text he was distressed to find it about one-third shorter than he had expected. Rather than seek financial redress, he trusted to Millar's 'honour in a future bargain', but at the same time, he insisted that Millar extend the work by writing an introduction, despite the author's opinion that one would be inappropriate.[30] Although such a literary figure as David Hume took Millar's side, Murray would not listen.[31] Even with the demanded introduction, the work only amounted to 260 printed quarto pages. Murray regarded about 350 pages as an ideal length for the quarto format. Thin books looked expensive, and the public expected that philosophical works like

[27]JM to Wm Creech, 3 Dec. 1787. Murray discouraged customers from waiting until the *Essays* appeared in volumes by reminding them that early impressions of the engravings would be superior (JM to James Stewart, 1 May 1788).

[28]Quoted from the printed advertisement on the back of the original cover of the fifth part (July 1788) of the *Essays*. Even before publication the proprietors had over 200 subscribers (JM to Wm Creech, 24 Aug. 1787). The printed subscribers' list records 743 names for 748 copies.

[29]Lavater papers, Box M 10.

[30]JM to John Millar, 7 Mar. 1771.

[31]John Millar to JM, 15 Feb. 1771.

Millar's, being weighty in their subject matter, should have corresponding physical qualities.[32]

In a similar vein Murray plainly told his authors that style mattered as much as if not more than content. Even for a specialised work like Stephen Adye's *Treatise on Courts Martial*, he reminded the author, who was preparing a new edition, that '*Hume* & *Robertson*, the latter in particular . . . never would have acquired half the number of their admirers had it not been for the elegance of their style, the correctness of their language, and the judicious method in which they arrange their materials'.[33] In Murray's view these writers and a handful of others were alone worthy of emulation. But few possessed either their native talent or their determination to perfect their works: 'If a *Hume* & a *Robertson* improve their compositions in every new Edition of their books', Murray rhetorically asked Sir Robert Fletcher, 'how much more room is there for correction of yours'?[34] When confronted with Fletcher's still unsatisfactory text, Murray made the corrections himself and charged the author fifteen guineas for 'new-modelling and recomposing'.[35] If Murray sometimes angered his authors by editing their texts, he was nevertheless confident of his own judgement and usually stood up to their challenges. When John Whitaker took offence at frank criticism about the 'want of urbanity' in his style, Murray responded that his views 'however shallow, were at least well meant', and added sharply: 'I shall hardly obtrude my own opinion again upon any Literary Work that you are employed upon whatever may be my private sentiments'.[36] Of course he did. Typically, Murray recruited advisors whom he trusted to support his views. For example, when his criticisms of Arnot's *History of Edinburgh*, 'chagrined [the author] more than they should have done', he told Arnot: 'I wish I could retract my sentiments . . . & . . . punish my own folly. But the truth is the same opinion remains upon my mind, and it struck others in the same manner who perused the paper.'[37] Murray concluded his letter to Arnot in a manner typical of that used with many authors: 'I wish to behave to you as I feel myself — your friend. . . . But you must not keep me yet at a servile distance. I would be unworthy of you were it in your power to attempt it. It would be unworthy of my character, bookseller tho I am, to

---

[32] A similar situation arose when Gilbert Stuart sent Murray the manuscript of his latest work on Scottish history. After calculating production costs and the price he could charge, Murray indignantly asked Stuart how he could expect to publish 'with any degree of reputation a Quarto pamphlet under the name of a Quarto Volume and by the pompous Title too of a "History of the Reformation of Religion in Scotland"'. (JM to Gilbert Stuart, 29 Dec. 1779). Murray insisted that Stuart add a preface and an appendix. But even with its additional material Stuart's work reached only 275 pages.

[33] JM to Stephen Adye, 9 June 1771.

[34] JM to Sir Robert Fletcher, 23 Feb. 1774.

[35] JM to Sir Robert Fletcher, 4 Mar. 1774; AL, p. 226.

[36] JM to John Whitaker, 23 Apr. 1788.

[37] JM to Hugo Arnot, 19 Mar. 1779.

permit the attempt.'[38] Arnot was not won over. He summed up his opinion
of Murray not long after when he privately told William Creech, who was
looking for a London publisher for Arnot's next book: 'Speak . . . to any
bookseller on earth but John Murray'.[39]

Once the preserve of men, indeed of well-educated men, literature was
increasingly being written, bought and read by wider sections of the
population. In advising an author about the tone he should adopt, Murray
would consider the likely composition of the audience. 'To make . . . a
saleable work', he told John Whitaker, 'it should be addressed to the Mob
of Readers, to literary Amateurs, & to Smatterers in taste . . . to Slender as
well as to profound capacities: If you are able to entertain the Ladies your
business is done.'[40] Philosophical works, like John Millar's *Distinction of
Ranks*, appealed mainly to gentleman scholars. Novels, by contrast, were
read by a large and growing numbers among both sexes. In 1775 Murray's
assessment of his mediocre publishing record to date led him to remark to
one of his authors: 'Commend me . . . to a saleable Book such as the
Pilgrims progress or *Robinson Cruso* that will please the Million. What signifies a
learned and ingenious Book to me which there are not learned and ingenious men enough to buy?'[41]

Good historical writing, falling between the historical and fictional
genres, had become one of the most popular (and lucrative) literary forms.
So skilled was Hume in depicting the diverse workings of human nature
and blending instruction with entertainment in his *History of England* that
many were said to have been surprised to discover they were reading a
genuine history rather than a work of fiction. Murray studied the examples
of Hume, Robertson, Gibbon and the other leading historians of the day,
wishing for nothing less than to publish works as successful as theirs. But
paying established authors thousands of pounds was beyond his means. All
he could do was encourage the writers in his circle to adopt such literary
models: 'Gibbon is fashionable', he told an author, 'fashionable people in
their taste of books rest upon him; and fashion is all in all in London.'[42]

A case study shows Murray's efforts with one author to produce a
successful historical work. In 1782 he arranged with John Gast, the Archdeacon of Glandelagh in Ireland, for the publication of his *History of Greece*
(see Plate 24). Murray himself paid all the expenses and bargained to share
the profits with the author. To compensate Gast for declining an outright
purchase, Murray sent sixty copies of the book with a separate Irish title
page to be sold in Ireland at sixteen shillings each, all proceeds going to the

[38]JM to Hugo Arnot, 19 Mar. 1779.
[39]Hugo Arnot to Wm Creech, 27 Apr. 1780, Dalguise Muniments, RH4 26A/1–3, Scottish
Record Office.
[40]JM to John Whitaker, 6 Mar. 1783.
[41]JM to John Whitaker, 8 Apr. 1775.
[42]JM to Joseph Stock, 15 Nov. 1780.

author. While this appeared a generous gift worth as much as £48, it also lessened the likelihood of a competing Irish reprint.

Murray saw Gast as the Irish counterpart to Edward Gibbon, doing for Greece what Gibbon was doing for Rome in his *Decline and Fall of the Roman Empire* (1776–88). Murray enlisted such patrons of Irish literature as Edmund Burke and Edmond Malone to make Gast's book 'a national concern' and hold him up 'as a competitor for Literary fame in the historical walk with Gibbon and Robertson & Hume'. 'Mr Gast', Murray observed, 'writes more from the heart than any of the Historians'.[43] Murray believed that, at a time when popular taste was changing, Gast's more emotive narrative could have greater appeal than the work of either the scepticism of Gibbon, the moderation of Robertson or the irony of Hume. All the same, Murray greatly admired the historiographic methods of these writers. The novelistic dimension of their narratives — telling a story that pleased both the growing body of everyday readers and scholars alike — particularly appealed to him, and it was this he wanted Gast to emphasise. 'Affect the heart properly,' he told Gast, '& the business is accomplished . . . ' 'All our successful historical writers', Murray observed, 'interrupt not their narrations either with deep learning or profound criticism. They preserve the thread of their story from interruptions of all kinds; they heighten its interest, and carry their reader to the conclusion impatient to unwind the chain of events, and to enjoy the catastrophe.'[44]

Murray's publication expenses for Gast's *History* amounted to nearly £300 — much more than usual because Murray had to divide some £50 among four literary advisors to correct and improve the prose style.[45] Murray bluntly justified the necessity of this expense:

> The truth is that in the dress you sent it, your MS could not have been printed with the remotest prospect of success. This was not particularly my own opinion, but that of every Gentleman of learning and taste to whom it was submitted. In this situation what was to be done, the reputation of the author as well as the sale of the Book were concerned and I must either have returned your Work, or venture on the step I took — the first must have mortified you exceedingly, and the second was dangerous, as few authors chuse to have their manuscripts corrected even to their advantage.[46]

Two years after publishing the book, Murray had sold 350 of the 500 copies printed (excluding the extra sixty given to Gast). He had recouped £280

[43]JM to Joseph Stock, 24 Jan. and 6 June 1782.
[44]JM to John Gast, 11 Jan. 1781.
[45]JM to John Gast, 5 Apr. 1784. The expenses broke down as follows: paper (92 reams of very fine Demy at 21*s*.) cost £96.12*s*.; printing and corrections cost £97.19*s*.; advertising in newspapers 14 guineas; 'publishing, warehouse and interest of money' cost 10 guineas; and fifteen presentation copies cost £14.10*s*.2*d*. The historians Gilbert Stuart and James Dunbar, the orientalist John Richardson, and Robert Liston made the corrections and improvements.
[46]JM to John Gast, 5 Apr. 1784.

and was almost in profit. But now he could only expect a trickle of further
sales. Even if the remaining copies sold, profits would amount to only about
£110, a sum to be divided between the two. In fact, at Murray's death in 1793,
56 copies of Gast's *History* still remained in his stock, and as late as 1807
copies could be bought at James Lackington's London remainder shop.[47]

Gast meanwhile had asked Murray whether he should tell his readers
that the present volume was merely the first part of a longer work. Murray
strongly opposed this idea, insisting that the *History* be published as an
entity unto itself. 'To promise a continuation', he warned, 'might induce the
public to suspend making a purchase of the present portion till the history
was completed'.[48] If, however, the book met with a favourable reception,
there would be a ready-made audience for the next volume. Gast was even
hopeful of winning an advance from Murray for the continuation. But
doubtful about the likelihood of success, Murray replied in the plain
language of a man of commerce: 'Your Book has not been reprinted at
Dublin, now sixty in all were sent there. . . . If they are not sold believe not
too much in the flattering reception your book has met with. By this
statement however I mean rather to give you an honest view of your
expectations than to discourage you from finishing the entire history of
Greece.'[49]

Nothing further came of Gast's intended continuation. Murray had
another plan in mind. At the time of this exchange with Gast, he had
arranged to publish the first volume of William Mitford's *History of Greece* in
1784. It was not altogether unusual for a single firm to publish works which
might compete with one another, even if it did seem more opportunistic
than loyal. Thomas Cadell, for example, had published a handful of histories of England concurrently, and Murray himself regularly published
medical works that promoted rival theories or remedies. Murray did not
hide his disappointment when Mitford chose another (Cadell) to publish
the subsequent volumes of his history, nor did he hesitate to remind
Mitford that it was loyalty that had kept him from publishing John Gillies'
rival history of Greece, which turned out to be the most successful of the
day.[50]

[47]'A Catalogue of the Stock in Trade (with the Valuation) of Mr. J. Murray at the time of his
Decease', under Gast. My own copy records on the title page the purchase at Lackington's
shop in 1807.
[48]JM to John Gast, 28 Apr. 1782.
[49]JM to John Gast, 5 Apr. 1784. A new edition of Gast's *History* was not demanded until
1793 when the Dublin bookseller, John Exshaw, published an edition edited by Joseph
Stock. A Basil edition published by Tourneisen followed in 1797.
[50]JM to Wm Mitford, 14 Mar. 1788: 'Your right to chuse a publisher for your new Edition of
your History of Greece is unquestionable. But there are some honourable considerations
that have generally withheld authors from going to a new publisher if their old have given no
cause for just complaint. . . . I beg also to acquaint you, that relying upon your honour, I
refused, *because I was your publisher*, to be concerned in the property of Dr. Gillies's Greece.'

Murray never found an historian to write that highly successful work he often wished for. Nor is there a single author (from any genre) in his long list of original publications who produced a genuine blockbuster for him. His extensive correspondence with authors testifies to the fact that he was a man through whom the pressures of the literary marketplace were communicated — and often bluntly. Although he could be patient when necessary and generous when circumstances allowed it, patience and generosity were not the dominant features in his dealings with authors, nor in his nature. Like any publisher, there were authors with whom he worked well and whose works he sold profitably; there were also disputes and failures. In either case, Murray was typically forthright in his opinions and unwavering in his decisions. Although he had the assistance of able advisors, 32 Fleet Street was a one-man operation. Every important decision was his and his alone, as were the consequences.

Murray insisted upon clear writing, styled to the subject at hand and accessible to the reader. His own letters and published writings are evidence of this. One of his longest-running successes, William Richardson's *Analysis of Shakespeare's Remarkable Characters*, came out in over ten editions between 1774 and 1793. Brevity and simplicity were the ingredients of Richardson's success. Murray demanded them. 'Your book is a favourite with the Ladies', he informed the author. 'Whenever you tire them they infallibly lay you aside.'[51] Among his authors, Murray was fortunate to find Richardson easier than most to deal with: 'Any thing I write', Richardson told him at the outset of their association, 'is by no means in the view of profit. I find it amusing; it is my hobby horse.'[52] Richardson wanted little more than to see his writings in print; and were Murray to risk the cost of publishing, all the profits were his.[53] Like Richardson, most of the authors in Murray's list did not depend on the profits of publication for their livelihood. They held positions in the church, in academia, or in the fields of medicine or law. Few were so generous with the trade as Richardson. More often, Murray faced hard bargainers who had any number of publishers to whom they might sell their literary wares. Initially he relied on a circle of friends who were authors themselves (John Langhorne, Edmund Cartwright, Gilbert Stuart) or the associates of authors to bring in worthy manuscripts. It is no surprise that a network of naval companions and fellow Scots figure prominently in Murray's lists, not only early on but throughout his twenty-five-year career. Over dinners at 32 Fleet Street or glasses of beer at nearby taverns Murray discussed proposals, struck bargains and shared expectations of success. If

[51]JM to Wm Richardson, 18 Sept. 1779.
[52]Wm Richardson to JM, 25 Nov. 1773.
[53]Wm Richardson to JM, 6 Dec. 1772. Richardson's series on Shakespeare's characters was so successful that in 1783 Murray cheerfully paid Richardson ten guineas for a new edition (BB, p. 7).

a lack of capital and a fear of risking too much prevented him from offering the best financial inducements, he could nevertheless assure a prospective author of sound editing, attention to production, and some influence with the reviewers. By the mid-1770s authors knew he was a publisher to be reckoned, as did his fellow traders.

5

The London Trade

Co-publication

The London book trade was quite extensive and always in a state of flux. New traders constantly entered the market as others retired, died or went bankrupt. Partnerships were common, whether set up as a permanent trading arrangement or as a deal for a single publication. In 1768, when Murray opened his shop, there were about eighty active booksellers; by the end of the century there were nearly three hundred.[1] There was even another John Murray trading in London from 1783 from a shop at Princes' Street in Leicester Fields who dealt mostly in religious books. But sometimes it seemed as if competition alone motivated the trade, so much so that Murray could remark in December 1775, after an extended visit to Ireland: 'Our Trade I found here as I left it; the Professors of it over reaching one another and oppressing where they can. Self Interest is the shrine at which they sacrifice. And so earnest are they in their Devotions that the general Interest is neglected for this particular one.'[2] Most often Murray found cooperation the trade's guiding principle.

Nearly forty per cent of the one thousand titles with Murray's name in the imprint include the names of other London booksellers. A large portion of these books were published after 1776 when Murray's trade began to expand (See Table 1). Those names which appear most often alongside Murray's are Joseph Johnson and Thomas Cadell, two of the best-known and most successful booksellers of the day. Yet there were over one hundred other London booksellers with whom he occasionally published books in partnerships — sometimes with just one other in an *ad hoc* arrangement, other times in syndicates of as many as forty booksellers. Murray might be an equal shareholder, or he might act merely as a selling agent either for another bookseller or for the author.

[1] I. Maxted, *London Book Trades 1775–1800*, pp. xx–xxiv.
[2] JM to Gilbert Stuart, 11 Dec. 1775.

Murray's London co-publications divide into three general categories: (1) books he planned and financed himself and then offered to share with one or more booksellers; (2) books others had planned and then offered to Murray; and (3) books in which a number of booksellers owned shares they had bought at London trade auctions. Those titles in the first category can be regarded as Murray's publications in the fullest sense; he negotiated with the author, arranged for production, and marketed the book. An example is Thomas Beddoes' instructional novel about the dangers of drinking among the poor, the *History of Isaac Jenkins*. The imprint (excluding addresses) reads: 'London: Printed for J. Murray; and J. Johnson, 1793'. Beddoes had been translating, editing, reading and writing books for Murray since 1782. As his radical views on public health corresponded with Joseph Johnson's liberal politics Murray thought Johnson a good choice for helping to promote *Isaac Jenkins*.[3]

Imprints are not always so easily deciphered and do not always tell the whole story of ownership. Partnerships, special selling arrangements, deliberate misunderstandings, even gestures of courtesy and printing errors, cloud actual arrangements with nuances — often expressed in the subtleties of commas, semi-colons and ampersands — important to the participating names but almost impossible to unravel from the imprint alone. Moreover, printers, who were partners, often were not listed. Successful London printers like William and John Richardson and Archibald Hamilton, for instance, owned publications with Murray and other booksellers but sometimes their names were left off the imprint.

Another example of the first publication arrangement, but one not obvious from the imprint is John Millar's *Historical View of English Government*: 'London: Printed for A. Strahan, and T. Cadell; and J. Murray, 1787'. Murray sold a quarter share of the copyright to the partners Thomas Cadell and Andrew Strahan, and explained to Millar (who himself held a half share) his 'wish to extend the circulation by the aid of a partner'.[4] As a gesture of goodwill, Murray disregarded the custom of the trade and put their names before his own. He was, however, completely responsible for the negotiation with Millar, to whom he agreed to pay £150. He and Millar would share the profits after the expenses of production and marketing had been met.

An example of a book in which Murray had a stake but did little more than pay his share then sell in his shop is William Hunter's *Medical Commentaries*: 'London: Printed for S. Baker and G. Leigh; T. Cadell; D. Wilson

---

[3]Beddoes has been described as 'the finest anthropologist of cultural morbidity active in England between the death of Laurence Sterne and the emergence of Thomas Carlyle' (R. Porter, *Doctor of Society. Thomas Beddoes and the Sick Trade in Late-Enlightenment England*, London, 1992, p. 2).

[4]JM to John Millar, 28 Dec. 1786.

PLATE 1

John Murray, *c.* 1785. Oil on canvas, by an unidentified artist of the British School

PLATE 2

a. Believed to be Robert McMurray *c.* 1750. Miniature in watercolour on ivory by an unidentified artist. **b.** James Gilliland, jeweller, and his wife Elizabeth, elder sister of John Murray, *c.* 1770. Miniatures in watercolour on ivory by Henry Raeburn, who was apprenticed to Gilliland. **c.** John Murray, *c.* 1791. Miniature in watercolour on ivory, possibly by John Donaldson

PLATE 3

William Sandby's engraved trade card

PLATE 4

St Dunstan's in Fleet Street. Engraving by Thomas Malton, 1797 (Courtesy of the Yale Center for British Art, Paul Mellon Collection)

PLATE 5

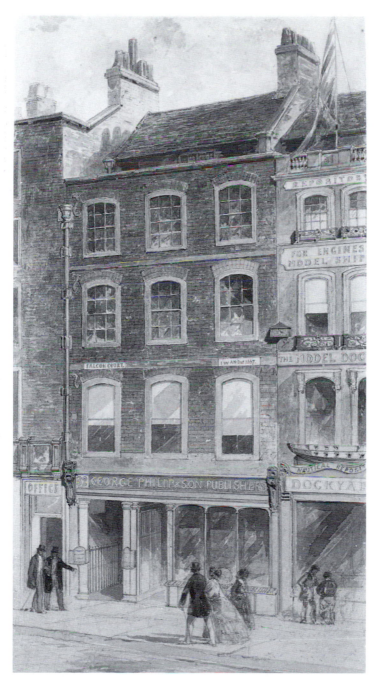

No. 32 Fleet Street in the mid-nineteenth century. Watercolour by an unidentified artist

PLATE 6

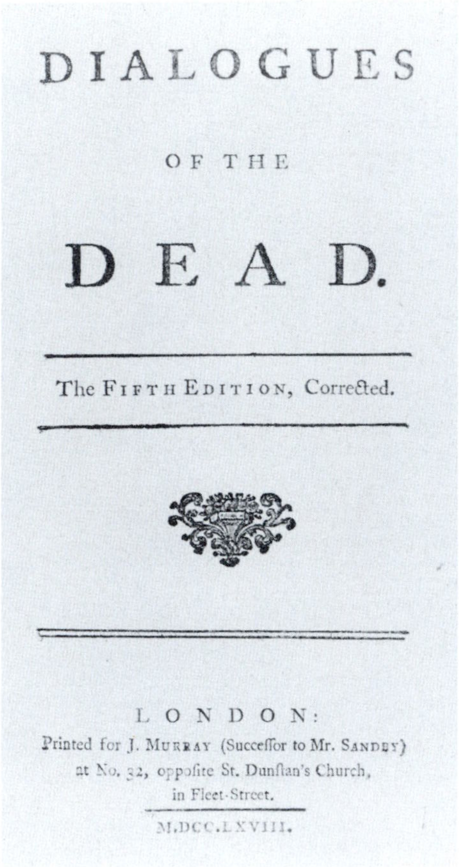
DIALOGUES

OF THE

DEAD.

The FIFTH EDITION, Corrected.

LONDON:

Printed for J. MURRAY (Succeſſor to Mr. SANDBY)

at No. 32, oppoſite St. Dunſtan's Church,

in Fleet-Street.

M.DCC.LXVIII.

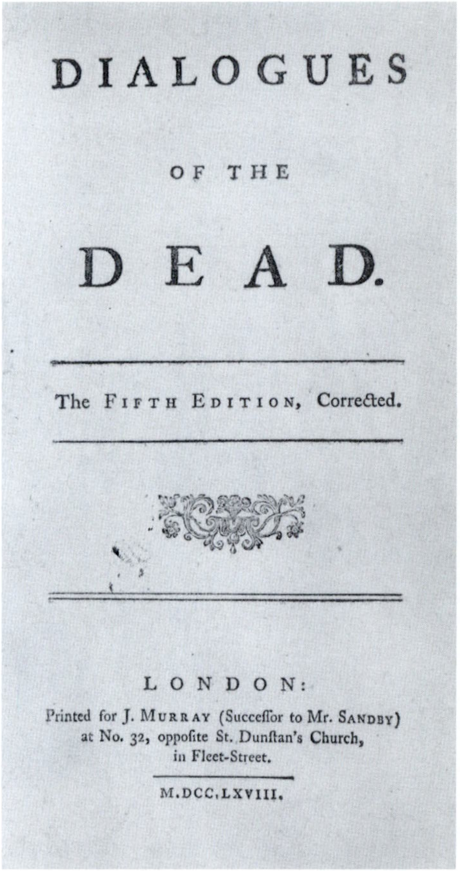
DIALOGUES

OF THE

DEAD.

The FIFTH EDITION, Corrected.

LONDON:

Printed for J. MURRAY (Succeſſor to Mr. SANDBY)

at No. 32, oppoſite St. Dunſtan's Church,

in Fleet-Street.

M.DCC.LXVIII.

Title pages of the two 1768 editions of
Lord Lyttelton's *Dialogues of the Dead*

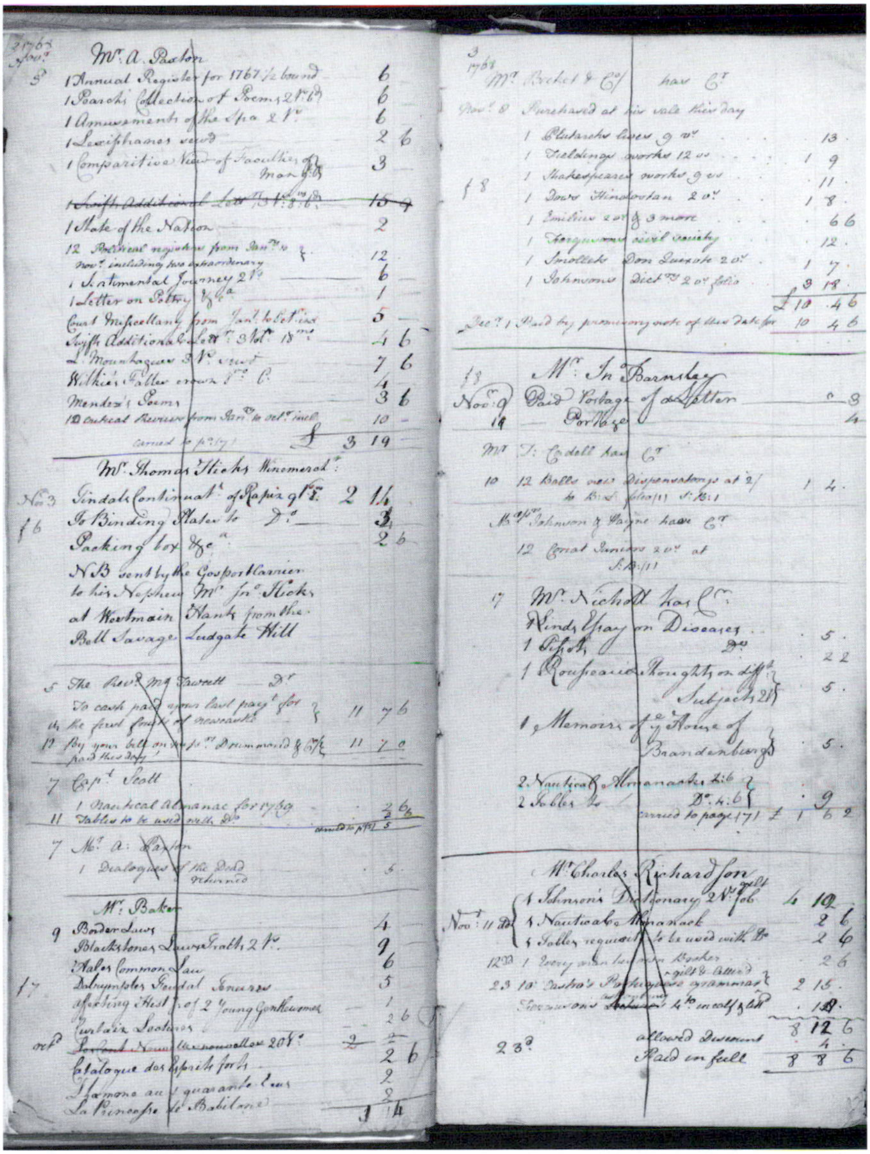

Daybook I, opened at pages 2–3

PLATE 8

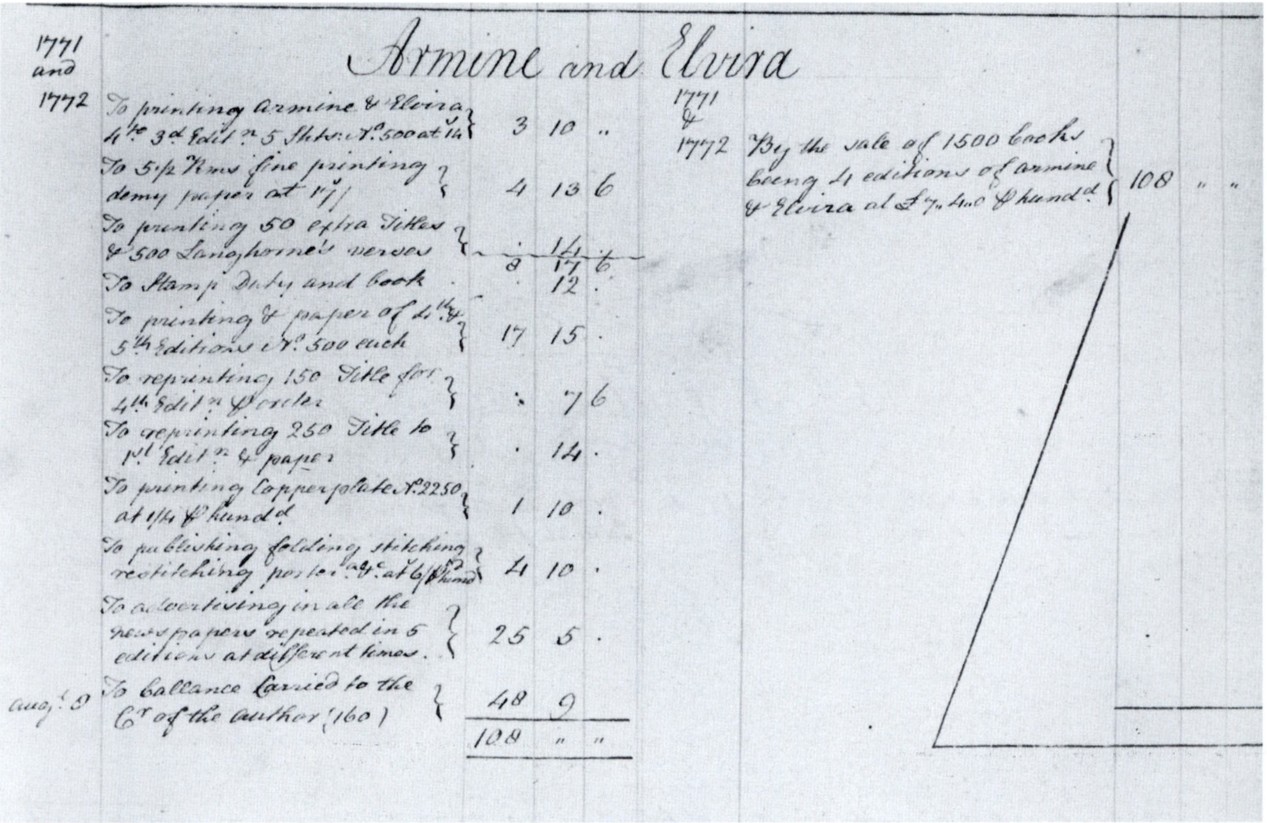

Armine and Elvira

1771
and
1772

To printing Armine & Elvira N° 3 Edit: n 5 Sheets: T. Donalds.	3	10	"
To 5½ Reams fine printing Demy paper at 14/	4	13	6
To printing 650 extra Titles		14	4
9.500 Longprimers meron	8	17	6
To Stamp Duty and book		12	.
To printing & paper of 2.13½ 3 d Edition i 1.500 each	17	15	.
To reprinting 150 Title for 4½ Edit: in J. earler	"	7	6
To reprinting 250 Title to M' Edit: 4 page	"	14	.
To printing to paper of the J.250 at 13½ J hund'd	1	10	.
To inclosing folding stitching [...]	4	10	.
To a Covering in all the [...] editions at different times	26	5	.
Aug'. 9 To Ballance carried to the C' of the author (160)	48	9	.
	109	"	"

1771
&
1772 By the sale of 1500 books being 4 editions of Armine & Elvira at 27s two Hund'd 108 " "

Account Ledger entry (p. 248) for editions of Edmund Cartwright's poem *Armine and Elvira*

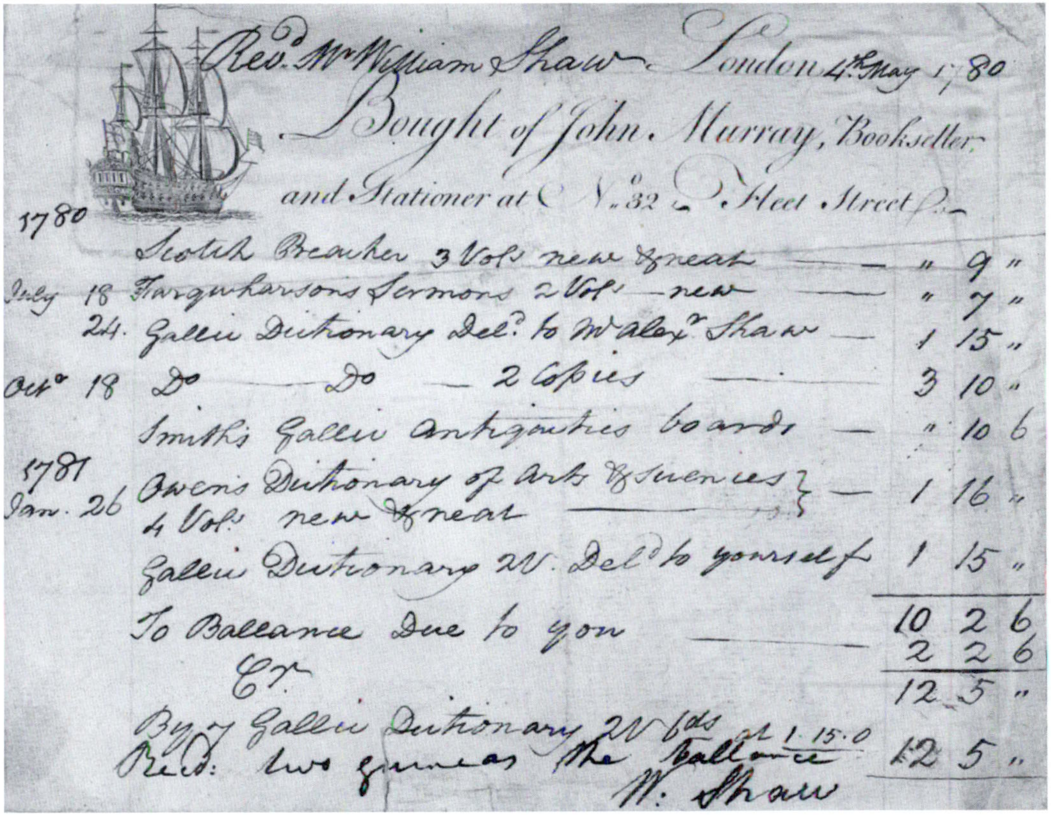

PLATE 9

1780

Rev.d Mr William Shaw
London 4.th May 1780

Bought of John. Murray, Bookseller.
and Stationer at N.o 32 à Fleet Street

	Scotch Beauties 3 Vol.s new & neat		"	9	"
July 18	Forgu[?]son Sermons 2 Vol.s new		"	7	"
24.	Gellie Dictionary del.d to Water Shaw	—	1	15	"
Oct.o 18	Do — Do — 2 Copies		3	10	"
	Smith's Galle[?] Antiquities boards		"	10	6
1781	Owens Dictionary of Arts & Sciences	—	1	16	"
Jan. 26	4 Vol.s new & neat				
	Galle[?] Dictionary 20.l del.d to yourself		1	15	"
	To Balance due to you				
	E.r				
			10	2	6
			2	2	6
			12	5	"
	B.g.t Galle[?] Dictionary 20.l del.t 1. 15. 0		£2	5	"
	Rec.d Two Guineas the Balance				
	W. Shaw				

Receipt for books bought by the Rev. William Shaw, 4 May 1780, entered on Murray's engraved stationery

PLATE 10

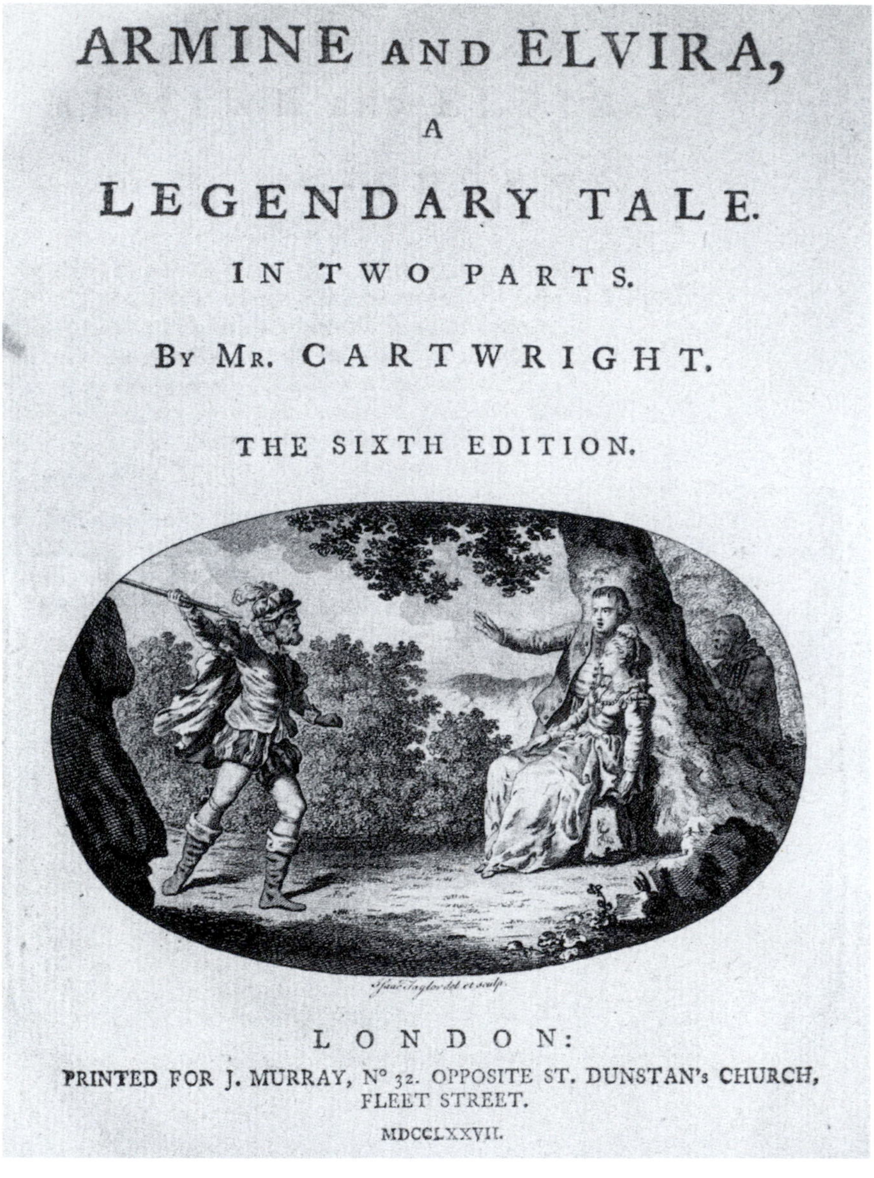

ARMINE AND ELVIRA,

A

LEGENDARY TALE.

IN TWO PARTS.

BY MR. CARTWRIGHT.

THE SIXTH EDITION.

Isaac Taylor del. et sculp.

LONDON:

PRINTED FOR J. MURRAY, N° 32. OPPOSITE ST. DUNSTAN's CHURCH, FLEET STREET.

MDCCLXXVII.

Title page of Edmund Cartwright's *Armine and Elvira*, sixth edition, 1777

PLATE II

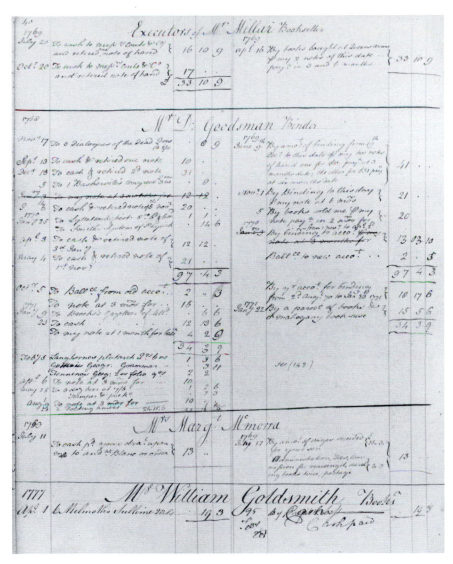

Account Ledger entry (p. 40) for David Goodsman, bookbinder

PLATE 12

BOOKS Printed for J. MURRAY,

And Sold by him, at his Shop (N° 32.) Fleet-Street, LONDON.

1. A TREATISE on COURTS MARTIAL, containing, I. Remarks on Martial Law and Courts Martial general. II. The Manner of proceeding against Offenders. To which is added, An Essay on military Punishments and Rewards. By Stephen Payne Adye, First Lieutenant in the royal Regiment of Artillery. Price 3s sewed.

2. LORD LYTTELTON's DIALOGUES OF THE DEAD, 8vo. A new Edition, being the 5th. Price 5s neatly bound.

3. THE CASTLE OF OTRANTO, 8vo. a Gothick Story, by the Hon. H. Walpole, The 3d Edition. Price 3s 6d bound.

4. AUTHENTIC MEMOIRS concerning the PORTUGUESE INQUISITION, with Reflections on ancient and modern Popery, and the Causes of its alarming Progress in this Kingdom. In a Series of Letters to a Friend, 8vo. Price 6s bound.

5. THE GOSPEL HISTORY from the Text of the FOUR EVANGELISTS, with Explanatory Notes, by Mr. ROBERT WAIT, Minister of Galston. ☞ This Work is intended to give a simple and connected View of the History of Our Saviour, as contained in the Writings of the Evangelists; and to engage Persons to read with Pleasure the Gospel History, who are apt to be disgusted with long Commentaries and Expositions.

6. A DEMONSTRATION OF THE EXISTENCE OF GOD, deduced from the Knowledge of Nature, and more particularly from that of Man, 12mo. By M. de la Mothe Fenelon, Archbishop of Cambray. A new Translation, by Sam. Boyce, A. M. Pr. 3s bound.

7. THE EPIGONIAD, a Poem, in Nine Books. By WILLIAM WILKIE, V. D. M. To which is added a Dream in the Manner of Spenser. Price 3s bound.

8. CONGREVE's WORKS, printed by Baskerville, in 3 vol. large 8vo. with Copper-plates, a very elegant Edition. Price 1l 1s bound. ☞ The original Price of this Edition of Congreve's Works is 1l 5s.

9. PLUTARCH's

An advertisement for 'Books Printed for J. Murray, And Sold by him, at his Shop'

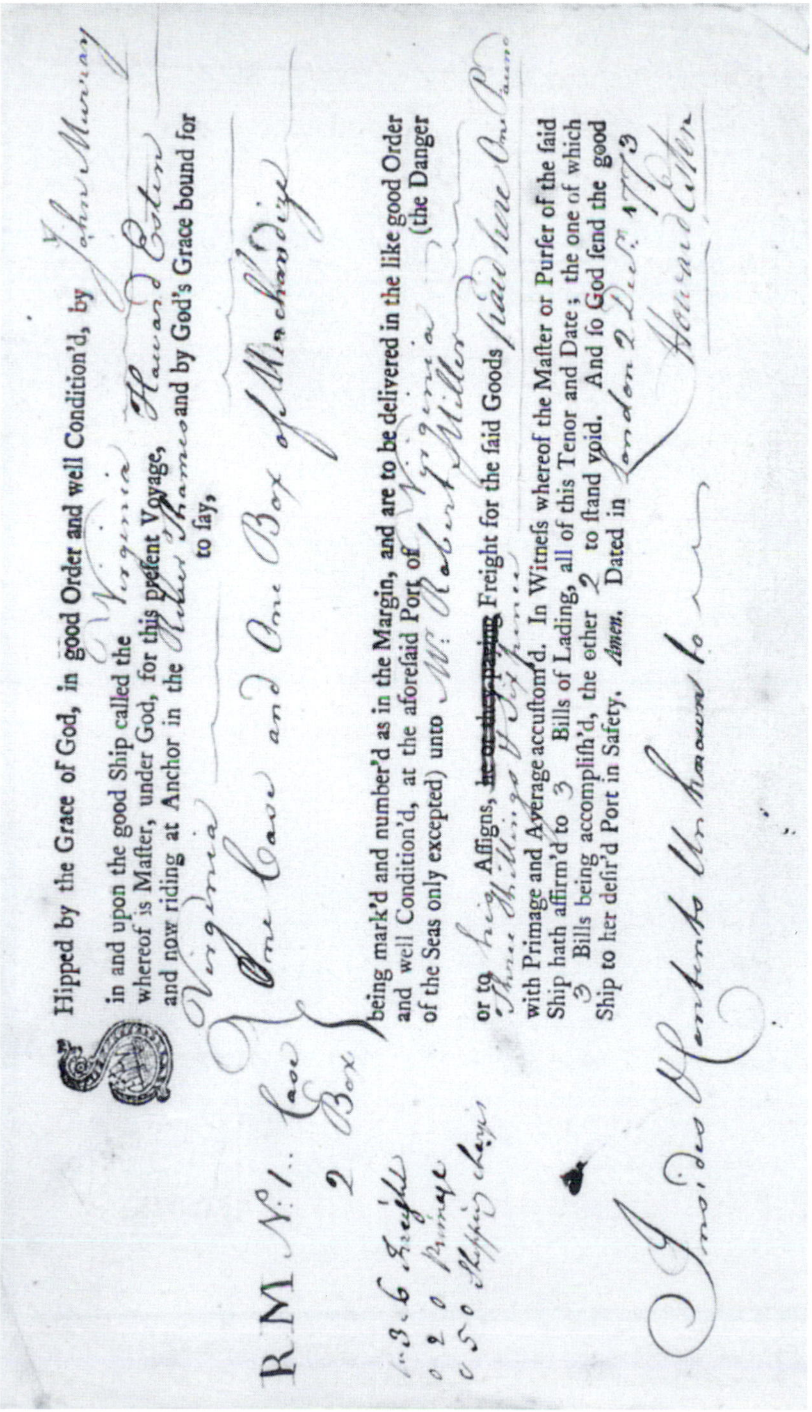

PLATE 13

Hipped by the Grace of God, in good Order and well Condition'd, by *John Murray*

in and upon the good Ship called the *Virginia* *Howard Eaton*
whereof is Master, under God, for this present Voyage,
and now riding at Anchor in the *River Thames* and by God's Grace bound for
Virginia
to say,

R M N°. 1. *One Cow* and *One Box of Merchandize*
2 Box.

being mark'd and number'd as in the Margin, and are to be delivered in the like good Order
and well Condition'd, at the aforesaid Port of *Virginia* (the Danger
of the Seas only excepted) unto *M: Robert Miller*

or to his Assigns, ~~he or they paying~~ Freight for the said Goods *paid here One Pound*
Three Shillings & Sixpence
with Primage and Average accustom'd. In Witness whereof the Master or Purser of the said
Ship hath affirm'd to 3 Bills of Lading, all of this Tenor and Date; the one of which
3 Bills being accomplish'd, the other 2 to stand void. And so God send the good
Ship to her desir'd Port in Safety. Amen. Dated in *London 2 Dec: 1773*

Howard Eaton

1. 3. 6. Freight
0. 2. 0 Primage
0. 5. 0 shipping charges

Inside Contents Unknown to me

A receipt for goods shipped to Robert Miller in Virginia, 2 December 1773

PLATE 14

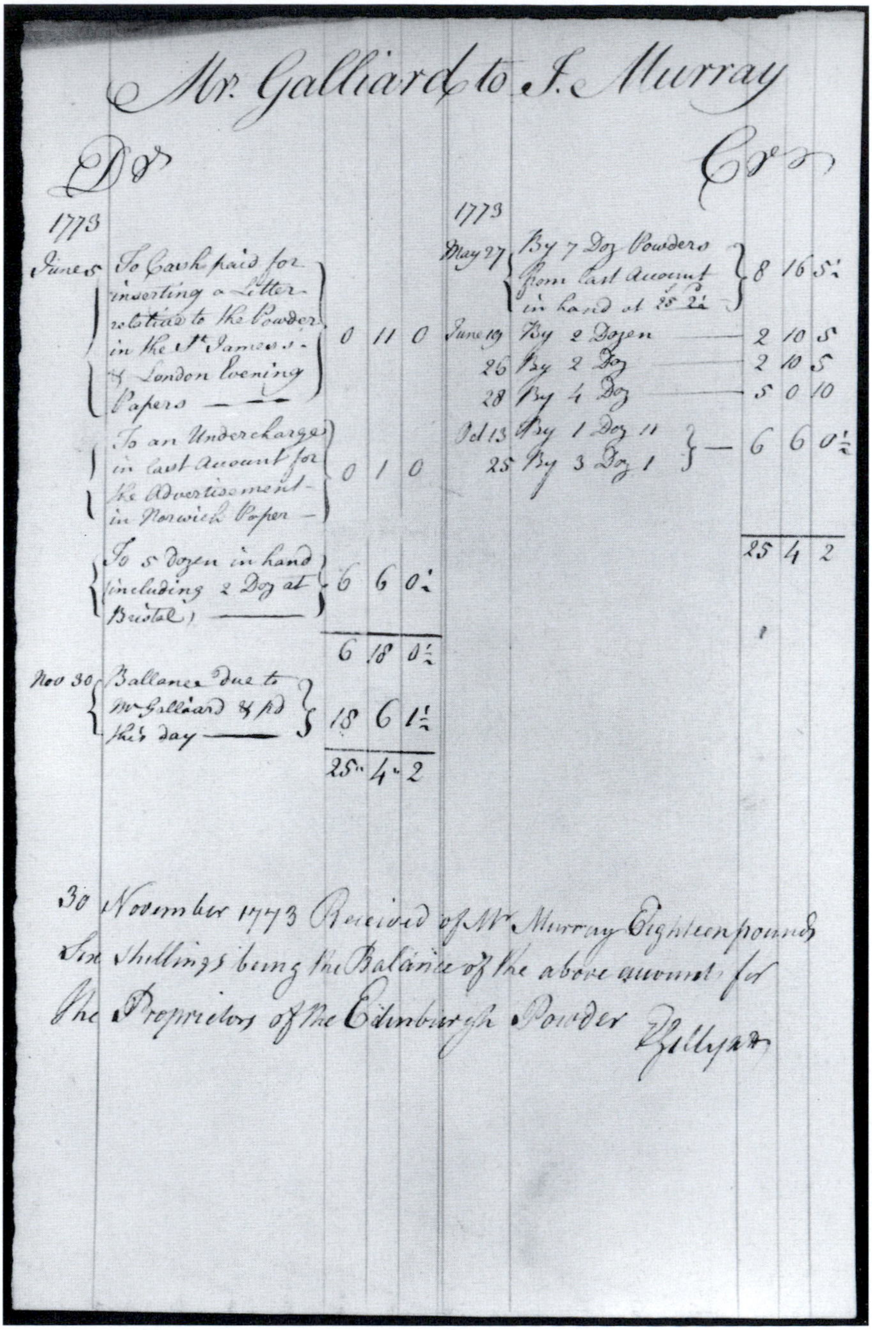

Account Ledger entry (p. 183) for Edward Galliard, formulator and proprietor of the 'Edinburgh Febrifuge Powders'

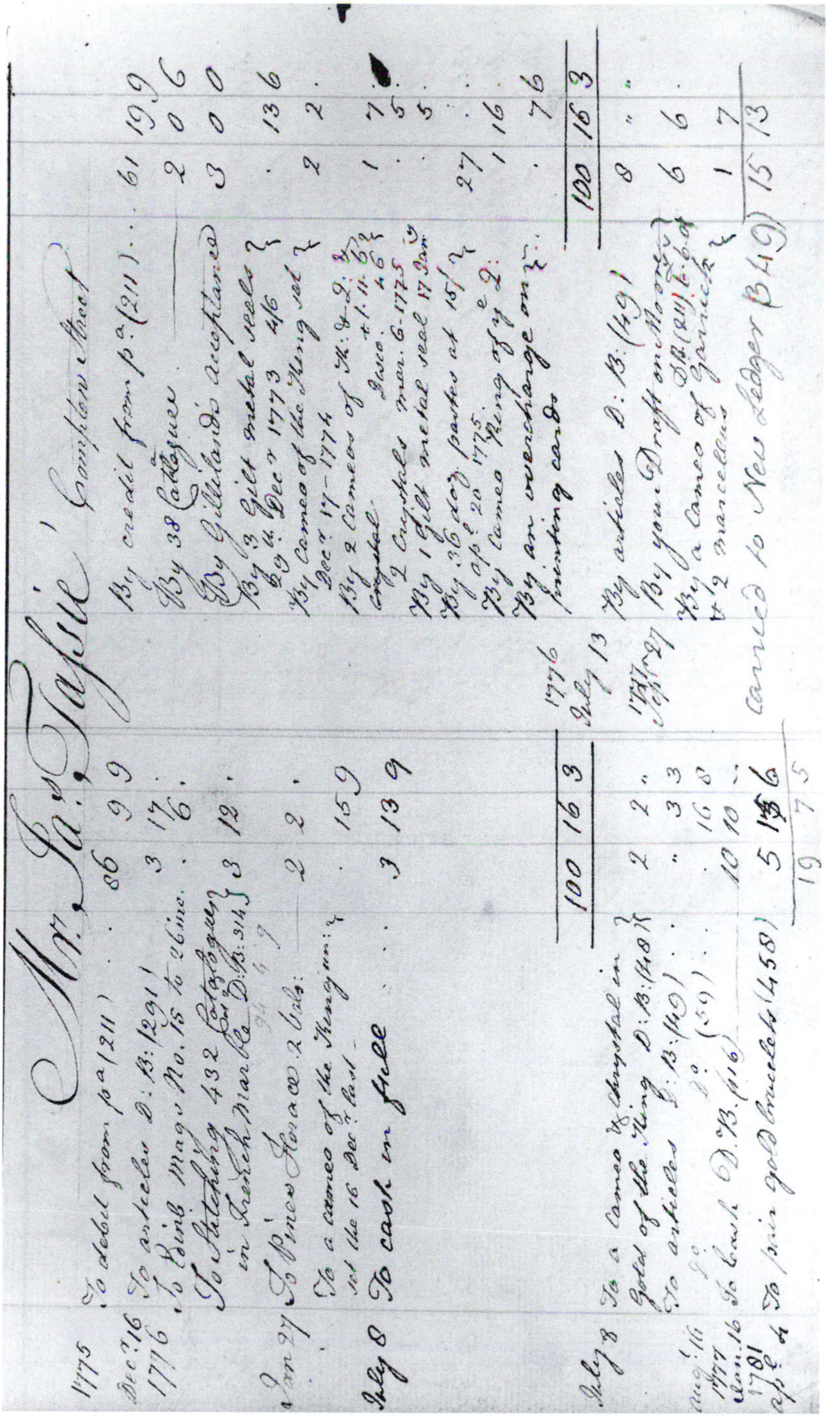

PLATE 15

Account Ledger entry (p. 295) for James Tassie, modeller in glass

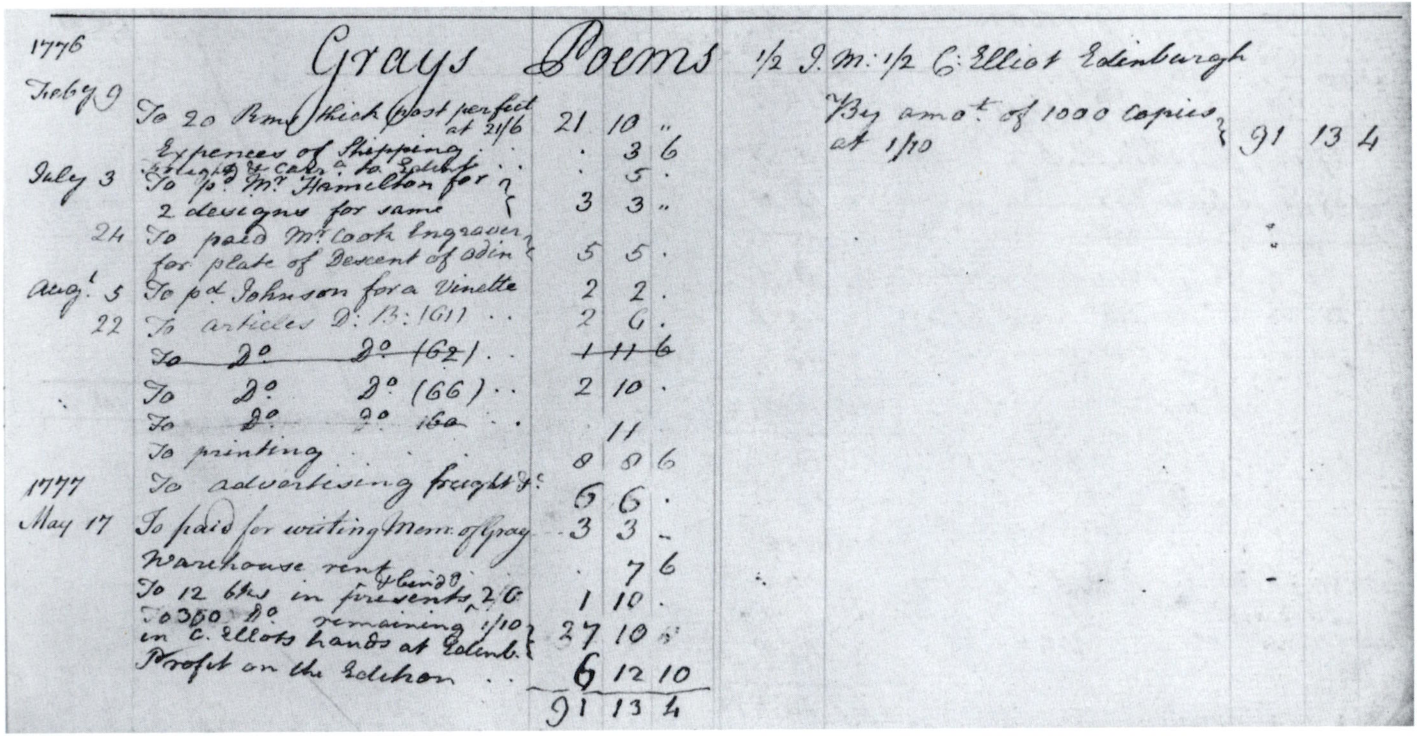

PLATE 16

Account Ledger entry (p. 41) for Murray's edition of the *Poems* by Mr. *Gray*, 1776

PLATE 17

P O E M S

BY

Mr. G R A Y,

A NEW EDITION.

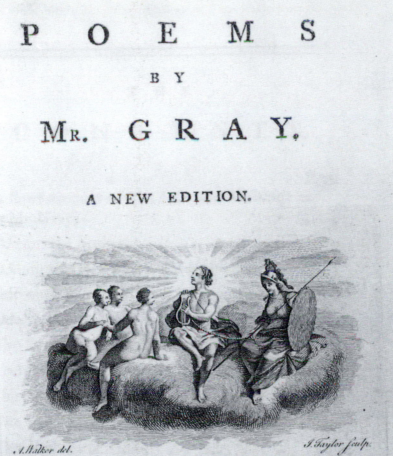

A. Walker del.   J. Taylor sculp.

L O N D O N:

PRINTED FOR J. MURRAY, NO. 32. FLEET STREET,

AND C. ELLIOT, EDINBURGH.

MDCCLXXVI.

Title page of the *Poems by Mr. Gray*, 1776

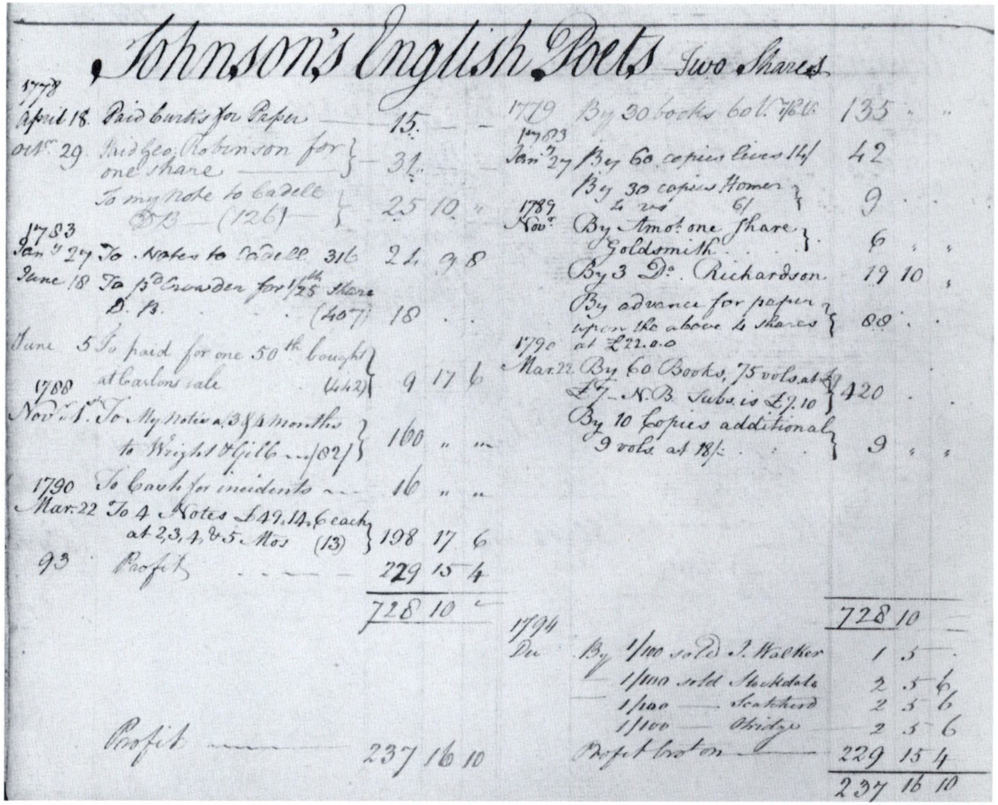

PLATE 18

Booksellers' Book entry (p. 11) for Murray's share in *The Works of the English Poets. With Prefaces, Biographical and Critical, by Samuel Johnson*, including entries for editions of Johnson's *Lives of the Poets*

PLATE 19

THE
WORKS
OF THE
ENGLISH POETS.

WITH
PREFACES,
BIOGRAPHICAL AND CRITICAL,
BY SAMUEL JOHNSON.

VOLUME THE FIRST.

LONDON:

PRINTED BY JOHN NICHOLS;

FOR J. BUCKLAND, J. RIVINGTON AND SONS, T. PAYNE AND
SONS, L. DAVIS, B. WHITE AND SON, T. LONGMAN, B. LAW,
J. DODSLEY, H. BALDWIN, J. ROBSON, C. DILLY, T. CADELL,
J. NICHOLS, J. JOHNSON, G. G. J. AND J. ROBINSON,
R. BALDWIN, H. L. GARDNER, P. ELMSLY, T. EVANS,
G. NICOL, LEIGH AND SOTHEBY, J. BEW, N. CONANT,
J. MURRAY, J. SEWELL, W. GOLDSMITH, W. RICHARDSON,
T. VERNOR, W. LOWNDES, W. BENT, W. OTRIDGE, T. AND
J. EGERTON, S. HAYES, R. FAULDER, J. EDWARDS, G. AND
T. WILKIE, W. NICOLL, OGILVY AND SPEARE, SCATCHERD
AND WHITAKER, W. FOX, C. STALKER, E. NEWBERY. 1790.

Title page of *The Works of the English Poets*, 1790 edition

PLATE 20

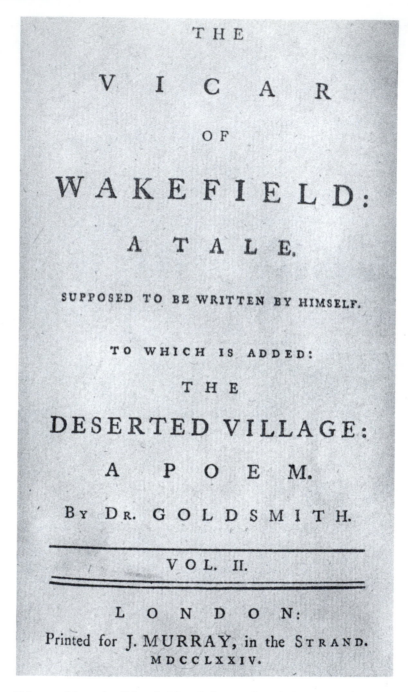

THE
VICAR
OF
WAKEFIELD:
A TALE.

SUPPOSED TO BE WRITTEN BY HIMSELF.

TO WHICH IS ADDED:

THE
DESERTED VILLAGE:
A POEM.

By Dr. GOLDSMITH.

VOL. II.

LONDON:

Printed for J. MURRAY, in the STRAND.

MDCCLXXIV.

Title page of the spurious 'Murray' edition of *The Vicar of Wakefield*, 1774, probably printed in Ireland

PLATE 21

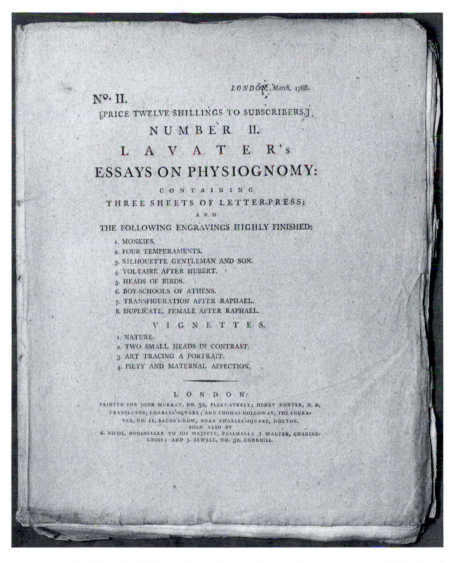

Nº. II.

LONDON, March, 1788.

[PRICE TWELVE SHILLINGS TO SUBSCRIBERS.]

NUMBER II.

LAVATER's

ESSAYS ON PHYSIOGNOMY:

CONTAINING

THREE SHEETS OF LETTER-PRESS;

AND

THE FOLLOWING ENGRAVINGS HIGHLY FINISHED:

1. MONKIES.
2. FOUR TEMPERAMENTS.
3. SILHOUETTE GENTLEMAN AND SON.
4. VOLTAIRE AFTER HUBERT.
5. HEADS OF BIRDS.
6. BOY-SCHOOLS OF ATHENS.
7. TRANSFIGURATION AFTER RAPHAEL.
8. DUPLICATE, FEMALE AFTER RAPHAEL.

VIGNETTES.

1. NATURE.
2. TWO SMALL HEADS IN CONTRAST.
3. ART TRACING A PORTRAIT.
4. PIETY AND MATERNAL AFFECTION.

LONDON:

PRINTED FOR JOHN MURRAY, NO. 32, FLEET-STREET; HENRY HUNTER, D. D.
TRANSLATOR, CHARLES-SQUARE; AND THOMAS HOLLOWAY, THE ENGRA-
VER, NO. 11, BACHE's-ROW, NEAR CHARLES-SQUARE, HOXTON.
SOLD ALSO BY
G. NICOL, BOOKSELLER TO HIS MAJESTY, PALLMALL; J WALTER, CHARING-
CROSS; AND J. SEWELL, NO. 32, CORNHILL.

21 & 22a (overleaf) Part II of Johann Kasper Lavater's *Essays on Physiognomy* in its original printed wrappers

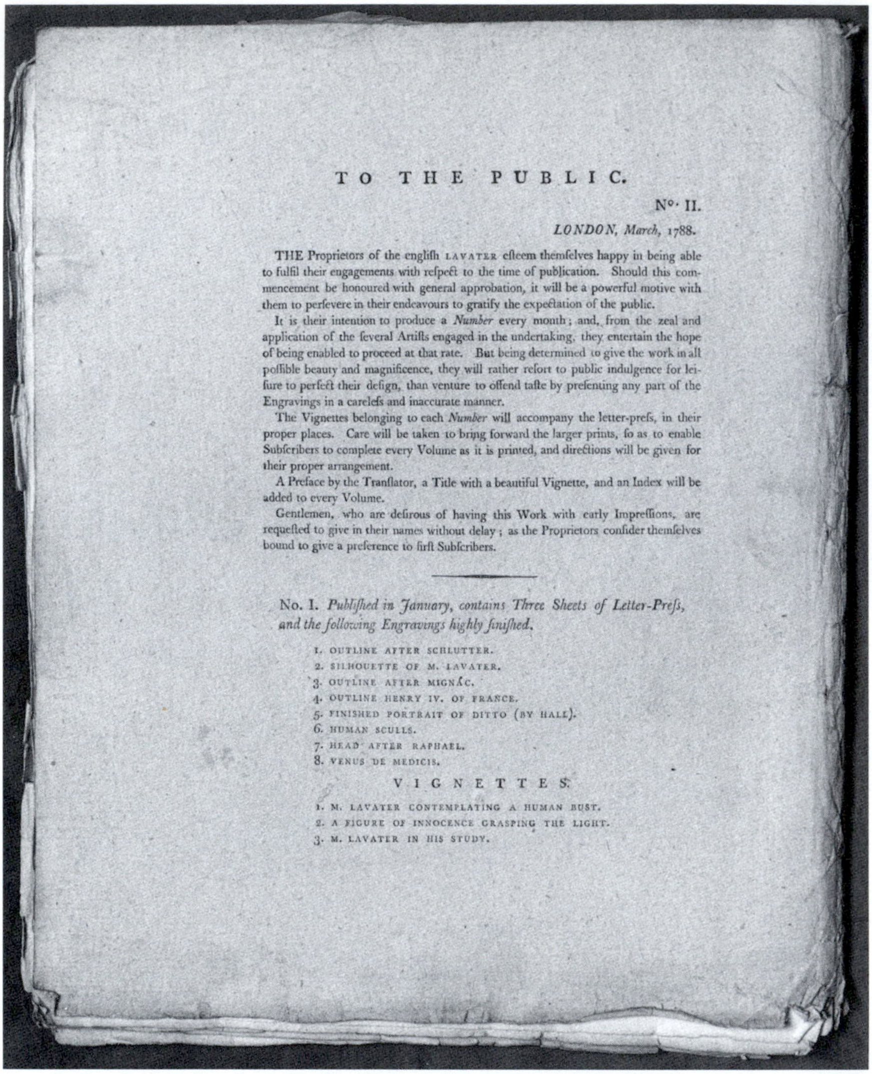

PLATE 22

TO THE PUBLIC.

Nᵒ· II.

LONDON, March, 1788.

THE Proprietors of the english LAVATER esteem themselves happy in being able to fulfil their engagements with respect to the time of publication. Should this commencement be honoured with general approbation, it will be a powerful motive with them to persevere in their endeavours to gratify the expectation of the public.

It is their intention to produce a *Number* every month; and, from the zeal and application of the several Artists engaged in the undertaking, they entertain the hope of being enabled to proceed at that rate. But being determined to give the work in all possible beauty and magnificence, they will rather resort to public indulgence for leisure to perfect their design, than venture to offend taste by presenting any part of the Engravings in a careless and inaccurate manner.

The Vignettes belonging to each *Number* will accompany the letter-press, in their proper places. Care will be taken to bring forward the larger prints, so as to enable Subscribers to complete every Volume as it is printed, and directions will be given for their proper arrangement.

A Preface by the Translator, a Title with a beautiful Vignette, and an Index will be added to every Volume.

Gentlemen, who are desirous of having this Work with early Impressions, are requested to give in their names without delay; as the Proprietors consider themselves bound to give a preference to first Subscribers.

No. I. *Published in January, contains Three Sheets of Letter-Press, and the following Engravings highly finished,*

1. OUTLINE AFTER SCHLUTTER.
2. SILHOUETTE OF M. LAVATER.
3. OUTLINE AFTER MIGNÉC.
4. OUTLINE HENRY IV. OF FRANCE.
5. FINISHED PORTRAIT OF DITTO (BY HALL).
6. HUMAN SCULLS.
7. HEAD AFTER RAPHAEL.
8. VENUS DE MEDICIS.

VIGNETTES

1. M. LAVATER CONTEMPLATING A HUMAN BUST.
2. A FIGURE OF INNOCENCE GRASPING THE LIGHT.
3. M. LAVATER IN HIS STUDY.

a.

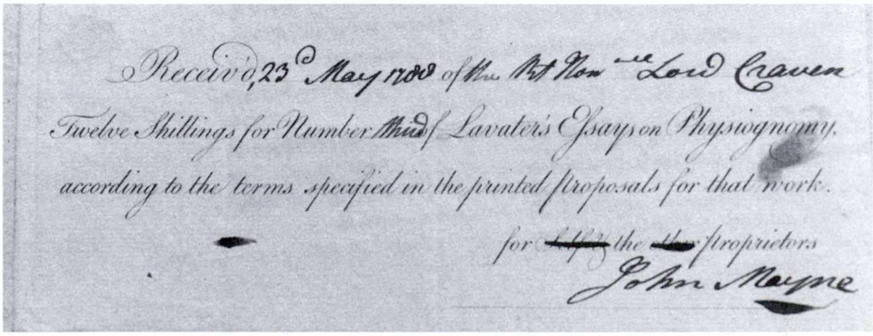

Received 23ᵈ May 1788 of the Rt Honᵇˡᵉ Lord Craven Twelve Shillings for Number third of Lavater's Essays on Physiognomy, according to the terms specified in the printed proposals for that work.

for the proprietors

John Mayne

b.

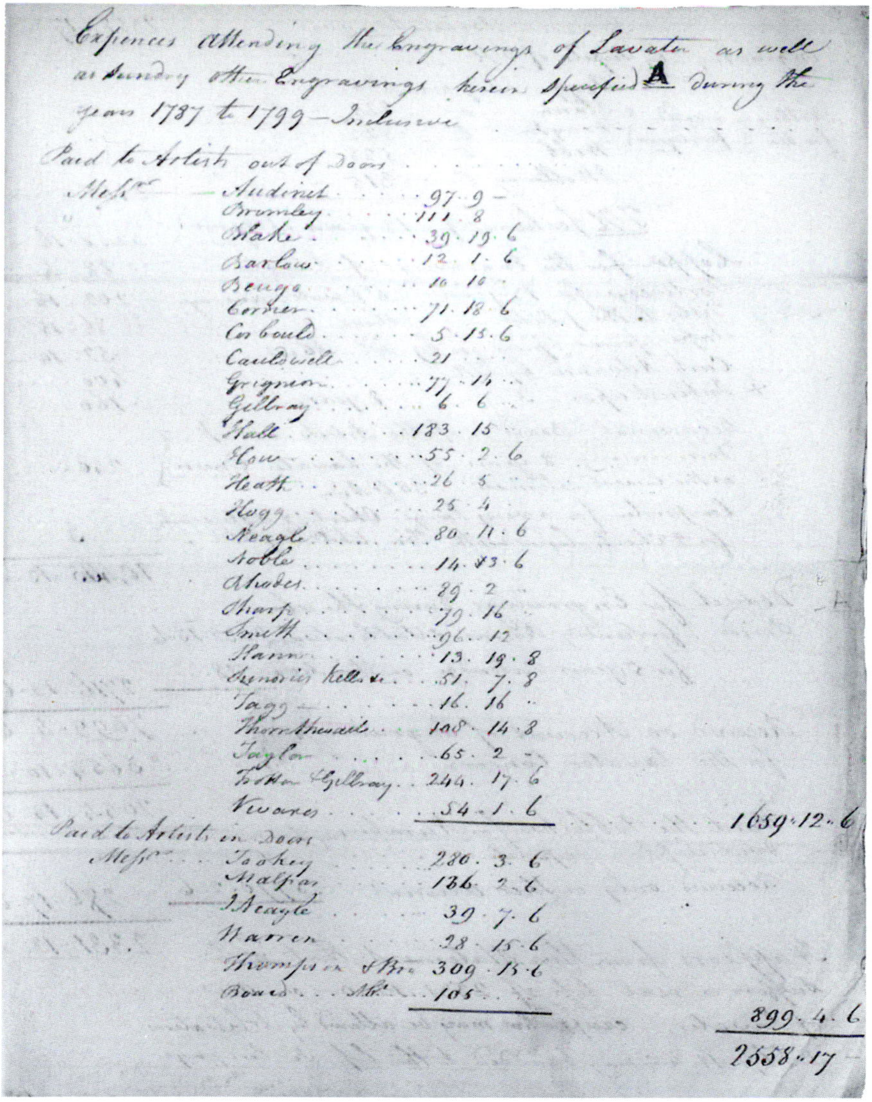

PLATE 23

Expences attending the Engravings of Lavater as well
as sundry other Engravings herein specified **A** during the
years 1787 to 1799 — Inclusive

Paid to Artists out of Doors

Mess. — Audinet	97. 9. –	
Bromley	111. 8	
Blake	39. 19. 6	
Barlow	12. 1. 6	
Beuge	16. 16	
Cromek	71. 18. 6	
Corbould	5. 13. 6	
Cauldwell	21	
Grignion	77. 14	
Gillray	6. 6	
Hall	183. 15	
How	55. 2. 6	
Heath	26. 5	
Hagg	28. 4	
Neagle	80. 11. 6	
Noble	14. 13. 6	
Rhodes	89. 2	
Sharp	79. 16	
Smith	96. 12	
Slann	13. 19. 8	
Sundries Kells &c.	51. 7. 8	
Tagg	16. 16	
Thornthwaite	108. 14. 8	
Taylor	65. 2	
Hotter Gillray	244. 17. 6	
Newares	54. 1. 6	1689. 12. 6

Paid to Artists in Doors

Mess. — Tookey	280. 3. 6	
Malpas	136. 2. 6	
Neagle	39. 7. 6	
Warren	28. 15. 6	
Thompson & Bro.	309. 15. 6	
Bones	105	
		899. 4. 6
		2588. 17. –

A list of payments made to the engravers of the *Essays on Physiognomy*, including William Blake and
James Gillray

22b (opposite) Engraved subscriber's receipt for Part III of the *Essays on Physiognomy*

PLATE 24

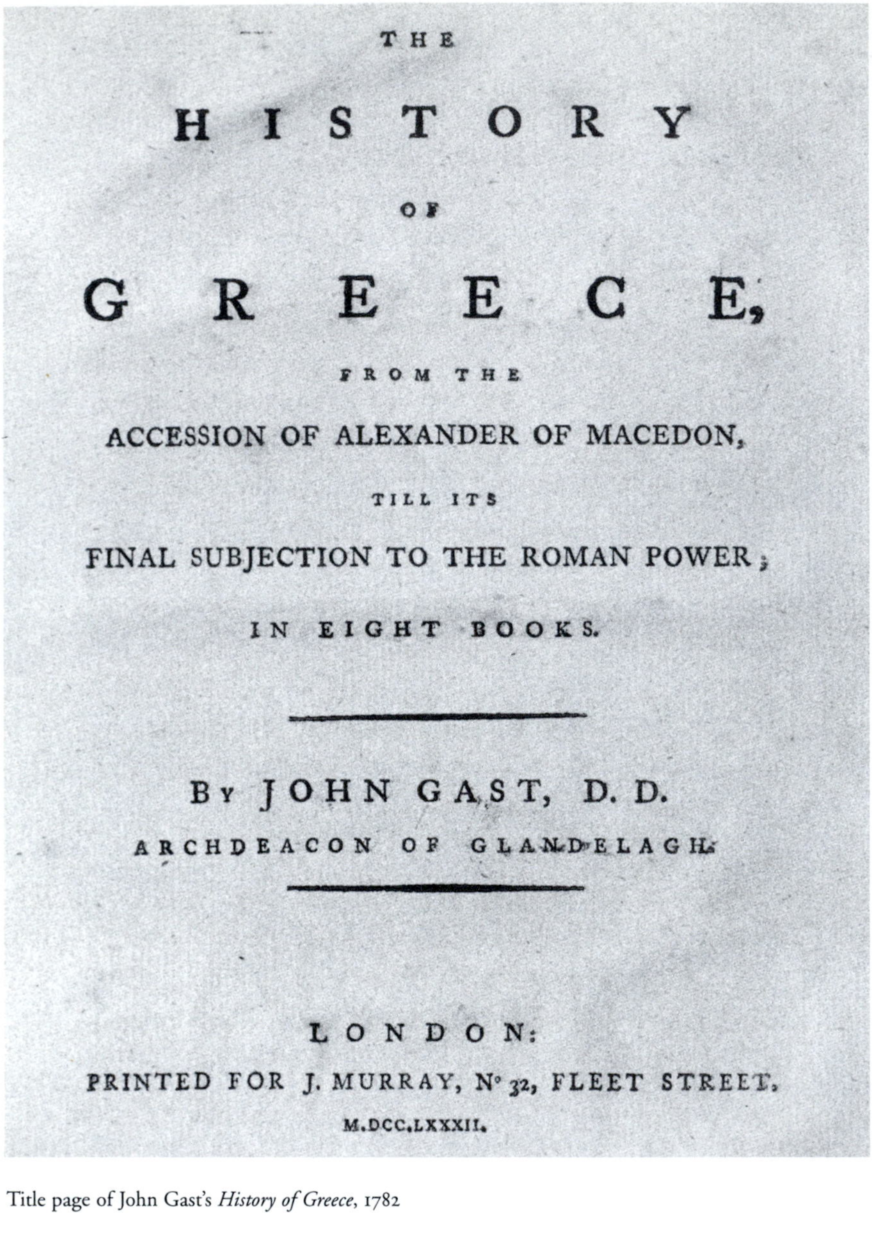

THE

HISTORY

OF

GREECE,

FROM THE

ACCESSION OF ALEXANDER OF MACEDON,

TILL ITS

FINAL SUBJECTION TO THE ROMAN POWER;

IN EIGHT BOOKS.

—————

By JOHN GAST, D.D.

ARCHDEACON OF GLANDELAGH.

—————

LONDON:

PRINTED FOR J. MURRAY, N° 32, FLEET STREET.

M.DCC.LXXXII.

Title page of John Gast's *History of Greece*, 1782

and G. Nicoll; and J. Murray, 1777'. Another example is *Lunardi's Grand Aerostatic Voyage in his Air Balloon*: 'London: Printed for J. Bew; J. Murray; Richardson and Urquhart; and R. Ryan, 1784'. On some occasions Murray would have a stake in a publication even though his name did not appear in the imprint. The beautifully illustrated edition of John Gay's *Fables*, known as 'Stockdale's edition', is one example (see Plate 25). Some thirty-five titles marked with an asterisk (*) in the Checklist indicate this kind of arrangement.

Books first published in these two ways, if they were destined to reach multiple editions, often evolved into the third category — books in which Murray had purchased shares at trade sales, or 'syndicate' publications. (Gay's *Fables* already had become one.) The proportion of this type of publication increased in his lists steadily from 1776 when he made his first notable syndicate purchases. At a gathering of booksellers at the sale of George Pearch's holdings at the Globe Tavern on 21 December 1775, Murray bought a share of Addison's *Spectator* — one of the most popular titles of the century. He paid £46 for a one-fortieth share of eight-volume editions of the work in both the octavo and duodecimo formats.[5] By dividing the expense of publishing a single title among many traders, Murray and his partners reduced the need of a large capital outlay. By including sometimes as many as forty individuals, they also decreased the likelihood of a competing edition. From 1776 onward Murray gradually built up a portfolio of shares in some of the most steadily selling books of the time: dictionaries and grammars, Shakespeare's *Works*, Dryden's *Virgil*, Pope's *Homer*, Samuel Johnson's different writings, *Robinson Crusoe*, *Don Quixote* and so on (see Plate 26). The man, who a few years before had testified in the House of Lords against the monopolistic and exclusionary tactics of the established London trade, had now joined their ranks.

Depending on the terms of the share purchase, Murray would either receive his proportion in copies of the new edition to sell in his shop or take cash at specified times as the edition sold. The latter method was the standard practice of the trade.[6] These syndicate publications yielded the most certain and often the most lucrative returns. Murray's investment of just over £200 (at different intervals) in Ephraim Chambers' popular *Cyclopedia*, for example, produced dividends approaching £1000 for several editions.[7] Nor did the limitation on the copyright of the property he was acquiring deter him. There may have been competing editions, but what

---

[5] BB, p. 4. Murray bought another fortieth share of the *Spectator* in 1777. Relative to other works in which he owned shares, he paid over the odds, and his nett profit on a £116 investment was only £24.

[6] For a work like Chambers' *Cyclopedia* (see Checklist, item 176, for details) Murray certainly received cash payments, but for the majority of titles entered in the Booksellers' Book, Murray listed the number of copies corresponding with his share and the wholesale price per copy.

[7] BB, p. 8.

were perceived to be the authorised London editions on the whole sold very well.

Sometimes, however, a book in which Murray bought a share produced no return at all. For example, he paid out £4 in September 1786 for a one-twenty-fourth share of Samuel Richardson's *Sir Charles Grandison*, but an edition never appeared, and in March 1792 he paid the considerable sum of £42 for a three-sixty-fourths share of Bacon's *Abridgement* at Rivington's sale for which no edition was to appear.[8]

At a sale of Thomas Becket's stock and shares in May 1779, Murray paid out £92 to acquire a portion of Laurence Sterne's works — shares that would enable him to profit from future editions of the novelist's most popular titles: *Tristram Shandy*, *A Sentimental Journey* and his *Letters*.[9] However, this was only the beginning of his investment. He would subsequently have to pay for producing the future editions. To recoup some of his outlay, Murray soon after sold off smaller shares in these works at some profit.[10] Buying shares of popular works of the day did not always ensure quick returns. In fact, for two years Murray realised no profits from the Sterne titles. Only when he and the other shareholders produced an edition of the *Works of Laurence Sterne* in 1780 did his investment begin to bear fruit. This ten-volume set was the first London edition of the collected works (Irish editions by Armitage had appeared in 1774 and 1779) and the first attempt at a critical edition (see Plates 27 and 28). The anonymous editor chose the texts from the most accurate editions of the individual works and annotated Sterne's letters and autobiographical memoir. He also excised certain writings which had been wrongly attributed to Sterne.[11]

Murray had to put up nearly £40 towards the cost of printing and paper for a one-fifteenth share in the *Works*, which entitled him to the profits on the sale of sixty-three sets of the 1000 printed.[12] The edition, published in 1780, was an immediate success, and he more than doubled his total investment. He was among some impressive bookselling company in the imprint: 'W. Strahan, J. Rivington and Sons, J. Dodsley, G. Kearsley, T. Lowndes, G. Robinson, T. Cadell, J. Murray, T. Becket, R.

[8]BB, p. 44 (Richardson); BB, p. 65 (Bacon). There are other examples of works in which Murray bought shares but were never published: Winslow's *Anatomy* (BB, p. 35), Ovid's *Epistles* and *Art of Love* (BB, p. 26), and Otway's *Plays* (BB, p. 25).

[9]Becket's sale was on 27 May 1779 at the Queen's Arms Tavern. Murray bought a one-eighth share in volumes four, five and six of *Tristram Shandy* for £30; a quarter share of the *Sentimental Journey* for £51; and a half share of Sterne's *Letters* for £11 (BB, p. 2, Plate 27).

[10]BB, p. 2. He was a partner in the publication of editions of the *Sentimental Journey* in 1780 and 1790, and in an edition of *Tristram Shandy* in 1782.

[11]See the Advertisement in vol. 1 of the 1780 edition and W. L. Cross, *The Life and Times of Laurence Sterne*, 2 vols. (New York, 1925), ii, 277.

[12]BB, p. 23. See Checklist under Sterne's *Works*, 1780, 1783, 1788 and 1793 (items 271, 386, 692 and 963) for the breakdown of expenses and profits.

Baldwin and T. Evans'. Further editions of the *Works* came out in 1783, 1788 and again in 1793. According to the practice of the trade, the names of the new owners were usually placed at the end of the imprint, enabling Murray to move forward with each new imprint.[13] For the 1793 edition Murray himself oversaw the touching up of the ten illustrated plates and the re-engraving of the frontispiece portrait of Sterne. These charges (£35), divided among the owners, were more than offset by the profits on the sale.[14]

Murray's Book Trade Associates

Analysis of imprints does not always give a full picture of Murray's partnerships or the arrangements behind his publications. For example, the name of one of Murray's closest associates, Archibald Hamilton, appears with his in only a handful of imprints even though Hamilton undoubtedly printed and had a share in several of Murray's publications. Hamilton's printing house was located behind 32 Fleet Street in Falcon Court, where he edited and printed the *Critical Review* — a popular monthly periodical he had founded with Tobias Smollett in 1756 to compete with Ralph Griffiths' *Monthly Review*. Murray often called on Hamilton to check the progress of works being printed for him, to place an advertisement for a forthcoming publication to be printed on the covers of the *Critical*, or to see if his latest publication would receive a favourable notice. Occasionally Murray even wrote a review for Hamilton's periodical himself.[15] A specimen sheet from Hamilton of a new book so pleased Murray that he told Gilbert Stuart, the author: 'It will make a handsomer volume than any produced from the London press for these ten years past'.[16] While Murray employed many other printers, few were more helpful or near to hand as Hamilton. As the two men worked in such close proximity, there are few written records of their dealings.

Among booksellers, Murray's most frequent partner was Joseph Johnson, whose shop in St Paul's Churchyard was just a few minutes' walk down Fleet Street. From the start his trading with Johnson went on easily, and a warm friendship developed. 'Joey Johnson & I produce wonderful

---

[13]Tracing the transfer of shares is complicated. When, for example, Thomas Evans died in 1784, his share apparently was divided by three booksellers (Bent, Wilkie and Ogilvie), while the shares of William Strahan and Thomas Lowndes passed to their sons.

[14]JM to Thomas Cadell, 5 April 1792. The charge for re-engraving Sterne's portrait was six guineas.

[15]Murray probably wrote the review of Gilbert Stuart's *History of the Reformation* in the *Critical Review* (49, March 1780, pp. 206–7) if his remark to Stuart that 'you are indebted to me for the critical' is in fact an acknowledgement of authorship (JM to Stuart, 19 June 1780).

[16]JM to Gilbert Stuart, 2 Oct. 1779.

Publications in the Winter', Murray reported in 1775 to the Reverend William Enfield.[17] In all, they shared a place in the imprints of over 150 titles. No more than a year after Murray had established himself in business, he and Johnson began trading, initially exchanging stock for retail sales and soon after embarking on joint publications. One of these was a translation of the Abbé Millot's *Elémens de l'histoire d'Angleterre* in 1771. A sum of £260 had to be advanced for translating and printing, a cost shared equally by Murray, Johnson and a third partner, the bookseller William Nicoll. Murray organised the publication but gave his partners priority in the imprint: 'London: Printed for J. Johnson, and W. Nicoll; and J. Murray, 1771' (see Plates 29 and 30). He repeated this gesture to Johnson many times.[18]

Johnson, one of the leading booksellers of the day, was at the forefront of movements for political, religious and social reform. He was the friend and publisher of such controversial and influential figures as Thomas Paine, Henry Fuseli, William Godwin, Mary Wollstonecraft, Joseph Priestley and William Wordsworth. In the 1770s he published widely, but was best known for dissenting religious works and medical texts. In the following decades his lists were largely devoted to politics, experimental science, literature and art.[19] Johnson held weekly literary dinners at which Murray was often present. The two men frequented the coffee houses and taverns in their vicinity and occasionally indulged in some less reputable activities. To the Reverend William Enfield's enquiry about the case of venereal disease Johnson was rumoured to have contracted, Murray reported: 'I hear nothing of his I[t]ch nor the bountifull Lady who bestowed it upon him'.[20]

Working together and individually, Johnson and Murray began to dominate the field of medical publishing, earning a reputation among authors and customers for fairness and reliability. From 1778 onwards, an average ten or more medical titles appeared annually with Murray's name in the imprint; Johnson's own list was even more extensive. Murray's long-standing connections with Edinburgh medical men and with physicians and surgeons who lived abroad produced publishing opportunities which he was happy to share with Johnson, who himself knew many medical authors in and around London. In 1781 Murray established the *London Medical Journal* — the first quarterly medical periodical in London. However, he handed over the proprietorship to Johnson in 1783. The two men were

[17]JM to Wm Enfield, 14 Sept. 1775. Enfield, a dissenting minister (who had lodged with Murray in 1769), was rector of the Warrington Academy, where Joseph Priestley, John Aikin and other Dissenters were tutors (see Herbert McLachlan, *Warrington Academy: Its History and Influence*, London, 1943).
[18]See, for example, Wm Richardson's *Poems, Chiefly Rural*, 1775 in Checklist item 109.
[19]G. Tyson, *Joseph Johnson: A Liberal Publisher* (Iowa City, 1979), pp. 14 and 47.
[20]JM to Wm Enfield, 14 Sept. 1775. What this information contributes to recent speculation about Johnson's homosexual orientation is open to debate (See Claire Tomalin, *The Life and Death of Mary Wollstonecraft*, rev. edn London, 1992, pp. 96–7).

on terms close enough to learn from each other's publishing experiences —
successes and failures alike. When, for instance, Johnson published his
Theological Repository in 1769 Murray saw an opportunity and began his
own *Repository: or Treasury of Politics and Literature* in 1770 (discussed in
Chapter 11). In 1783 Murray made a bold move in establishing and editing
the *English Review.* Johnson watched as the periodical gained ground in a
competitive market, and when he founded the *Analytical Review* in 1788,
Murray's example and advice enabled him to anticipate many challenges.
After Murray's death, the two periodicals merged.

One of the most ambitious and impressive publications in which
Murray offered Johnson a partnership was Lavater's *Essays on Physiognomy.*
Inspiration for their English edition came from the artist Henry Fuseli, an
intimate friend of Lavater who had come to London and attached himself
to Johnson. Such fine artists as William Blake and James Gillray, two other
figures in Johnson's circle, contributed to the project (see Plate 23).[21] At the
outset Murray confided to Johnson that 'a coalition is what I have cordially
wished for', but it was essential that their partnership 'be accomplished
upon principles of reciprocity'.[22] This was a problem initially as Johnson
had intended to publish his own translation of Lavater. However, Murray
insisted that 'competition will infallibly hurt both' and persuaded Johnson
to share equally with him.[23] Murray also divided shares equally with the
engraver Thomas Holloway and Henry Hunter, the translator. Oddly,
Johnson's name did not appear in the imprint either as a proprietor or
among other booksellers as a selling agent.[24] A work like the *Essays on
Physiognomy* — containing more than eight hundred engravings and printed
by Thomas Bensley on the finest Imperial paper in forty-one parts over a
ten-year period — was an exceptionally expensive undertaking, costing in
total more than £10,000. Johnson's financial backing and organisational
skills eased the burden. After publication of the first three numbers Murray
buoyantly reported that 'the Proprietors of Lavater have now got so many
subscribers that they tread on velvet. In other words', he added, 'the sale
already pays all charges.'[25] Johnson had no cause to regret taking up
Murray's offer. Each man must have cleared about £1,000 on Lavater's
Essays — undoubtedly Murray's most successful publication.[26]

[21] See G. E. Bentley, *Annotated Catalogue of William Blake* (Oxford, 1977), pp. 593–4.
[22] JM to Joseph Johnson, 8 Oct. 1787.
[23] Ibid.
[24] One reason why Johnson remained a silent partner in Murray's edition of Lavater may
have been that he did not want overtly to compete with an octavo edition published by the
Robinsons in 1789 and translated by Thomas Holcroft. Murray was not concerned about
this rival edition: 'The greatest service you can render us', he told Wm Creech, the
Edinburgh bookseller, 'is to let the two editions be seen at the same time' (27 July 1789).
[25] JM to Wm Creech, 16 May 1788.
[26] Papers relating to Lavater's *Essays* in Box M 10.

At booksellers' auctions Murray and Johnson often entered into private agreements: 'The best way to settle our transactions at to-days sale is this', Murray explained. 'In every lot I buy whether books or copies [i.e. shares] I shall consider you as one half concerned, if it is agreeable to you. . . . In return for this I shall consider myself in the same situation respecting the purchases you make. I shall not therefore open my mouth where you are the last bidder.'[27] By uniting their capital, the two men enlarged and diversified their publications and augmented the stock in their shops. Murray made their mutual advancement his aim and attended to Johnson's interests as if they were his own. But in 1784, when Johnson failed to respond promptly to an offer of a share in the valuable Sterne publication, Murray for a moment doubted Johnson's commitment. Rather than walk over to St Paul's Churchyard, as was his custom, he penned a frank letter.

> It is sometime since I have observed a singular reserve or distance in your Behaviour to me. This I should regret more than I do, if I either deserved it or had improper Designs upon you. But conscious of the Integrity of my Intentions respecting you at all times & the real Friendship I have borne you, independant [*sic*] of all business, my Mind sits easy with regard to my Behaviour. And if I feel concern, it is that a Man I have valued should harbour an unjust prejudice against a person, who has, as far as he recollects, never entertained a Sentiment but that of good will towards him.[28]

Murray's concern was short-lived. Whatever lay behind his uncertainty — probably no more than an oversight on Johnson's part — was removed, and Johnson took up the offer. As Murray grew older and his health declined it was typical that he should react, indeed overreact, in such situations. To those who knew him less well than Johnson, however, such an adamant defence of his own behaviour only called it into question.

Thomas Cadell was the London bookseller whose success Murray most envied. 'Publications in general are a Lottery,' Murray told William Creech in 1776, 'and most of the prizes . . . fall to the share of our friend Cadell'.[29] The son of a Bristol bookseller, Cadell had come to London in 1758, served an apprenticeship under Andrew Millar, and afterwards became Millar's partner. When Millar died in 1767, Cadell succeeded to a house that boasted many of the most popular authors. Over 4000 imprints bear Cadell's name — exceeding any other bookseller of the period.[30] In 1780 Cadell

[27]JM to Joseph Johnson, 5 June 1783. This practice was not quite the familiar auction 'ring' of the nineteenth and early twentieth centuries, where a group of buyers entered into a tacit agreement not to bid against each other and then re-auctioned the lots among themselves in what was called the 'knock out' — a practice which did not became illegal in Britain until 1927.
[28]JM to Joseph Johnson, 2 Jan. 1784.
[29]JM to Wm Creech, 24 May 1776.
[30]This figure is based on *Eighteenth-Century Short-Title Catalogue* imprint searches of the leading London booksellers.

formalised a partnership with William Strahan, a printer who had shared many best-selling titles with Millar. Their resources and reputation placed them beyond the reach of almost every competitor. Murray could only stand in amazement when he heard the news in April 1773 that 'Strahan & Cadell have paid no less than six thousand Guineas' for the copyright of John Hawkesworth's *Voyages*.[31] In 1787 Murray had hoped that his influence with prominent members of the Edinburgh literary and scientific community would make him the London bookseller to the Royal Society of Edinburgh and win him the London agency for their *Transactions*. He was disappointed to discover that Cadell, by an appeal to William Robertson (one of the founders of the Society), had gained this lucrative commission.[32]

In his dealings with Cadell, Murray, who did not have substantial assets, found co-operation the best way to proceed. He accepted lesser rewards and sought out authors who did not demand too much money. When he found a work he thought likely to do well, Cadell could usually be depended on to take a share and perhaps to reciprocate with the offer of a share in one of his own titles. In all, they appeared together in the imprints of about 150 books (about fifteen per cent of Murray's output). They began in 1772 with a short treatise on venereal disease, and in 1793 produced a splendid nine-volume illustrated edition of Buffon's *Natural History of Birds* at a cost of more than £2000.[33] Often it was left to Murray to handle their joint publications. If a problem arose, he did not hesitate to rush to their mutual defence. Murray's response to an author's premature and impolite demand for payment was typically forthright: 'The word "insidious" as applied to Mr Cadell or myself is extremely unjust and your reflections upon *my* conduct . . . I certainly did not expect because I am confident I did not merit them'.[34] When Cadell himself had not fulfilled his obligations Murray was equally forthright:

> It is extremely unpleasant to me to write to you again upon the Subject of Goldsmith's works. In the Divisions of the shares I have taken much pains. I have already written two Letters to you and must hazard a third if you should even return it as you did the first as a wrapper to a Dirty book.[35]

Usually Murray's misunderstandings with fellow tradesmen could be resolved. But occasionally a dispute ended an association. Murray's modest

[31]JM to Thomas Ewing, 25 Apr. 1773.
[32]JM to Andrew Dalzel, 11 Feb. and 17 Oct. 1786. Murray, in fact, blamed William Robertson for his failure to obtain the agency. In 1818 Murray's son (in partnership with Cadell's son) became the London agent for the Society's *Transactions*.
[33]The medical book was Andrew Duncan's *Observations on the Operation and Use of Mercury in the Venereal Disease* (Edinburgh: Printed for A. Kincaid and W. Creech; and for T. Cadell and J. Murray, London, 1772). The translation of Buffon was wholly organised by Murray. The imprint — 'Printed for A. Strahan, and T. Cadell; and J. Murray, 1793' — is another instance where Murray gave his partners priority of place.
[34]JM to John Skinner, 13 Jan. 1792.
[35]JM to Thomas Cadell, 15 July 1786.

but lucrative trade with George Kearsley, his neighbour at 46 Fleet Street, ended abruptly after Kearlsey publicly insulted Murray: 'You have in your advertizement in this days Herald said, that "you do not pretend to be equal to Mr. Murray at *misrepresentation*." The expression is in a high degree illiberal & justifies me in dropping the little connexion I have with you. We will therefore, if you please, deal in future as strangers.'[36] There were others Murray deliberately avoided whenever possible, including such prominent tradesmen as Thomas Becket, Charles and Edward Dilly and James Dodsley. His coolness towards Becket dated from the 1774 copyright dispute. Regarding his personal dislike of the Dillys he remarked to an Edinburgh bookseller: 'As my affection to Mr Dilly is equal to yours for Mr Bell I shall sell but few of his books'.[37]

Advertising

Advertising was an essential though expensive means of promoting publications which Murray regarded as a priority in the competitive London marketplace. He lavished substantial sums on timely advertising and insisted that his partners share equally in the charges. Provincial traders, in particular, often complained of the expense, as London advertising costs were far greater than anywhere else. 'The article of advertising', Murray told members of the Edinburgh trade, 'which gives a London Bookseller the greatest trouble and upon which he bestows the most pains, is what is least understood in the Country, and for which the agent receives the smallest thanks'.[38]

Authors often lamented that advertising swallowed their anticipated profits, but Murray asserted that with the majority of publications 'when the advertising is at an end so is the sale'.[39] Typically, fifteen to thirty per cent of the total cost of production might be put towards advertising. The successful *Medical Commentaries*, which Murray published quarterly from 1773 to 1786, was allotted ten guineas in advertising for each number (paper cost ten guineas; printing seven guineas; copy money to the editor £15). If all the copies printed were sold, Murray's profit would come to only ten guineas.[40] So

---

[36] JM to Kearsley, 29 Oct. 1786. This article has not been traced.
[37] JM to Wm Gordon, 7 Dec. 1782. Murray's antipathy towards Dodsley is noted in Ch. 10, pp. 186–87.
[38] JM to Wm Creech, Charles Elliot and Wm Smellie, 17 Aug. 1776.
[39] JM to Andrew Duncan, 29 Aug. 1774. Another author met with a similar assertion: 'Booksellers in London have no profit by advertisements. They suffer sometimes loss, and are always sure to have much trouble' (JM to John Aitken, 14 Feb. 1780).
[40] JM to Andrew Duncan, 29 Aug. 1774. It should be noted that Murray probably put these figures on the *Medical Commentaries* in the most unfavourable light possible as he was attempting to show Duncan that he could not pay him any more than £15 for editing each number.

meticulous was he about advertising that he even collected many of his newspaper and magazine advertisements and pasted them in an album (see Plate 31). The *Morning Chronicle* and the *Public Advertiser* were two London papers in which he regularly placed notices. He also used the *St. James's Chronicle* and the *General Evening Post*, the two evening papers with the largest circulation not only in London but throughout England.[41] Murray was a co-proprietor in the *Morning Chronicle* from 1772 and afterwards had a share in other newspapers. This entitled him to discounted advertising. The savings, as was customary in the trade, were rarely passed on to the author.

Periodical works Murray published, such as the *Medical Commentaries* and *English Review*, were issued in blue wrappers (also called covers) on which he regularly printed advertisements for his publications. This was a cheap way to promote books and focus on a specialised market. When Andrew Duncan, the editor of the *Commentaries*, attempted to interfere with the advertising on the wrappers, Murray did not hesitate to assert his authority.

> I always conceived that the cover of any periodical publication was the Bookseller's, and all persons of good sense will esteem it so; altho I know that there are fools enough that will take such opportunities. . . . If you . . . insist that no advertisement whatever shall be printed upon the cover but what is first submitted to your perusal and approbation, I cannot agree to it. At first sight you will perceive the impropriety of such a request, which not only fetters me inconveniently . . . but which denotes your want of faith in me.[42]

It may have been that Duncan objected to an advertisement for a medical remedy, the use of which his readers might mistakenly believe he recommended.

Catalogues

Turnover was essential in any business — more so in one with a bulky commodity like books. Murray's operation quickly grew beyond the space of the Fleet Street house, and he had to lease a warehouse.[43] To reduce his stock, widen his market and better publicise his books he issued occasional catalogues. Sale by catalogue had long been a common feature of the trade.[44] From the start Murray produced lists for the public and fellow

---

[41] JM to Gordon & Murray, 7 Sept. 1780.
[42] JM to Andrew Duncan, 17 May 1777.
[43] On the front pastedown of DB2 Murray wrote: 'Saturday, May 7 1774 entered Mr Scotts warehouse at £3 per annum'. In Apr. 1775 Murray moved into a larger warehouse for which he paid five guineas annually. This is probably the warehouse 'in Fleet Street' recorded in 'A Catalogue of the Stock in Trade (with the Valuation) of Mr. J. Murray at the time of his Decease'.
[44] See on the subject generally, Graham Pollard and Albert Ehrman, *The Distribution of Books by Catalogue from the Invention of Printing to A.D. 1800* (Roxburghe Club, 1965).

booksellers alike. Advertising individual titles in newspapers was expensive, though for new or struggling publications it was absolutely necessary. The catalogue approach, a far cheaper alternative, had the additional advantage of targeting potential customers — particularly those who lived outside London. Typically, the trade received a discount on catalogue sales and could arrange easy credit terms. Private customers, whose orders tended to be small, usually had to pay immediately.

At the outset of his career one of Murray's prime objectives was to make himself known as a bookseller who could supply any book. The first catalogue he issued in May 1769 contained over thirteen hundred items — mainly stock left over after the India ships had sailed and the London 'season' had come to an end but also individual copies of second-hand titles (see Checklist item 13 and Plate 31). A considerable number of orders were received, and on the whole this first venture into cataloging was a success. He was embarrassed, however, that in more than one instance he could not supply books at the stated prices, or even at all. Apologetically he told a customer: 'I am hopefull that the next [catalogue] I publish will be more worthy your Perusal'.[45]

In 1774 Murray issued a *Catalogue of Several Thousand Volumes: the Whole Making a Large Assortment of Valuable Books, in Most Languages, Arts, and Sciences.* He was keen to accumulate ready capital at a time when the book trade seemed to be entering a new phase after the 1774 copyright decision. This densely printed eighty-two page list was a statement that he was a dealer of means. Nearly three thousand items are listed, arranged by language, subject and size. The diverse selection of topics includes law, medicine and anti-quarian (including a run of 'curious tracts' on the Civil War). Murray was confident enough to charge sixpence, and he arranged to sell the *Catalogue* at several London shops and outside London at T. & J. Merrill's in Cambridge, John Bell's and William Creech's shops in Edinburgh, and Thomas Ewing's in Dublin. While primarily a selling venture, the *Catalogue* also gave Murray an opportunity to announce his interest in purchasing 'any Library or Parcel of Books'. In November 1779 he issued another miscellany on a similar plan, but almost twice the size of the 1774 one. This, apparently, was Murray's last general catalogue. The advent of an annual trade sale proved more expedi-tious for selling off stock and raising capital. Murray told Benjamin Bell in 1793 that 'booksellers . . . at their Sales . . . can have the best books. . . . I sell my books in this manner once a year.'[46]

When Murray began to focus on publishing medical works in the late 1770s, he issued several catalogues aimed at physicians, surgeons, hospitals

---

[45]JM to Rev. Crump, 24 May 1769. See also JM to T. & J. Merrill, 13 June 1769. No copy of Murray's first catalogue is extant. However, an advertisement for the work is found in Murray's album of newspaper clippings.
[46]JM to Benjamin Bell, 6 Apr. 1793.

and medical societies. Around 1778 he issued the first in a series *Murray's Catalogue of Books in Medicine, Surgery, Anatomy, Natural History for the Use of the Faculty, and Practitioners in General*. (see Plate 32).[47] The fourth one, published in 1784, lists some 1300 medical works and even includes a selection of manuscripts, mainly of notes from the lectures by prominent physicians and surgeons. In 1787 Murray produced an even larger medical catalogue, containing nearly 2000 different publications and claiming to be 'the most numerous of any extant, of the kind, in this country'. Murray saw these *Catalogues* as 'a repository, where a large collection of such [medical] tracts might always be kept in readiness for demand'.[48] His *Catalogue of Medical Books, chiefly those upon the Diseases of Seamen, as well as those Incident to Hot Climates and in Long Voyages* was an attempt to combine two related areas in which he specialised. This catalogue and others of its kind — usually from four to ten pages long and listing one hundred or so books — did well.[49]

The Antiquarian Book Trade

Murray's customers occasionally asked him to find out-of-print or antiquarian books. He took pride in being able to secure almost any title, and when this proved impossible, he bluntly told a dissatisfied customer: 'Whenever I have occasion to say that a book cannot be got, I do not mean barely that *I* have it not, but that it is not to be got in London'.[50] It was important to offer this service, but the search could take considerable time, and profits were usually small. 'My method', he told a customer who complained of the high price of a rare book, 'is to pick them up for my customers as reasonable as I can by myself or my servants and to lay a moderate charge upon the same for my own trouble' — usually five to ten per cent.[51]

Murray also sought to buy private libraries when the opportunity arose. His usual method was to ask the seller his price rather than first make an offer. He believed this approach would be 'the means of bringing matters to a conclusion much sooner'.[52] The real advantage, however, was that he

[47] No copies of numbers one to three of Murray's occasional medical catalogue are extant. Number Four exists in a single copy (see Checklist, item 437). The medical catalogue Murray published in Sept. 1778 is either Number One or Two (JM to John Whitaker, 11 Sept. 1778); the one from 1783, containing 'most modern books and a good many ancient ones', is probably the Number Three (JM to Patrick Hair, 9 July 1783).
[48] The *Catalogue* (for which Murray charged 3*d.*) was noticed in the *English Review* (9, Feb. 1787, 148). A copy has recently come to light (see Checklist 1787, item 612).
[49] Another catalogue was called *For Gentlemen Going to India. Books Printed for J. Murray and Recommended by the Honourable Court of Directors*.
[50] JM to Charles Kite, 19 Sept. 1787.
[51] JM to John Whitaker, 17 July 1777.
[52] JM to Rev. Quickie, 22 Aug. 1776.

knew the value of the books and that the seller often did not. More than anything, he detested his offer being played off against those of other bidders. So when he proposed thirty guineas for a collection and was told that another bookseller had offered fifty he responded in characteristic fashion: 'To pay 50 Guineas for what I only offered 30 would give me a worse opinion of myself than I entertain; and you ought to have no further dealings with a man capable of such Behaviour. From my offer I see no reason to depart; and with respect to the trouble you have given me I am subjected to it from my profession.'[53] Murray meant what he said, but calling the bluff of an opportunist was no small incentive to adopting this ethical pose. This time the deal fell through. At the next opportunity to purchase a collection he adopted a strategy more certain to yield some return. Having fixed a value on the library, but unsure whether his offer would be accepted, he asked for a guinea and a half payment in advance for his time, agreeing to deduct the fee if his bid was accepted. In another instance Murray was led to expect that his offer of £150 would be accepted and took the books away, refusing to return them until a five per cent commission for his valuation was paid.[54] Clearly he had no inclination to be taken advantage of, but his overly cautious approach gained him few libraries.

By the late 1770s, less than a decade after he established himself at 32 Fleet Street, Murray was a force to be reckoned with in the London trade. He had a considerable customer base, both in the town, in provincial cities and more particularly in foreign lands. He had built up his own list of publications, advertising them in newspapers and selling them in his own catalogues. And he had forged links with the great booksellers and printers of the day by exchanging publications and owning with them shares of valuable syndicate titles. When in 1777 an author complained of slow sales and asserted that Murray was not '*a first rate Bookseller*', he had no scruples in asserting: 'I esteem my name to be much higher in professional repute than any Bookseller you ever employed in London before, except [George] Robinson & with him it is equal'.[55] In the 1780s Murray continued to build upon his successes, putting the profits he made back into the business and pushing himself to work harder in every department.

[53] JM to Wm Morris, 2 Oct. 1784.
[54] JM to Mr Arrow, 24 Apr. 1792.
[55] JM to John Ogilvie, 21 Apr. 1777.

— 6 —

Trade Outside London

Edinburgh

Early in 1769 Murray began to establish connections with booksellers in Scotland, Ireland, and England's provincial cities. He had four main trading objectives: to sell his own publications directly to agents in these places; to enter into joint publication deals; to manage the wholesale distribution in London of new books printed outside the capital; and to acquaint himself with local authors and publish their works. Murray called his provincial bookselling associates 'correspondents', and he wrote frequently to these men and women to make sure trading went smoothly. The main cities in which he did business were Edinburgh and Dublin, but he also established worthwhile associations in Glasgow, Birmingham, Warrington, Newcastle and Belfast, and carried on a smaller trade in several other markets.

By the time Murray left Edinburgh in 1766, the city had the thriving book trade of an enlightened cultural centre. Scotland's three distinctive institutions — the Court, the Church and the College — were generating a considerable amount of printed matter. Still, the book trade in Edinburgh was small compared to the trade in London. The first-rate Scottish authors (such as David Hume and William Robertson) often brought their manuscripts south where fellow countrymen such as Andrew Millar and William Strahan paid their authors well and printed and published impressive books. A London imprint carried greater prestige and brought advantages that only a thriving metropolis could offer. Still, booksellers in Edinburgh carried on such an ample and expanding trade that Murray could not neglect the potential for profit.[1] His Scottish interests kept him

[1] The papers in the Murray Archive of the Edinburgh bookseller and publisher Charles Elliot, consisting mainly of letters Elliot wrote and his account books, may be the single best source for information about the Scottish trade between 1770 and 1790. Elliot's daughter Anne married Murray's son, which explains how these documents ended up at the Murray Archive. Another important source is the archive of the Edinburgh firm of Bell & Bradfute

in close contact with a country for which he always held a warm regard. The associations he formed gave him an excuse to visit there regularly and to entertain Scottish booksellers and authors when they were in London. Of his feeling for his native land, Murray remarked in 1770: 'I am not like many Scotsmen, who abate in affection to their country according to the times or distance they happen to be removed from it'.[2] The large proportion of Scottish authors in his lists, and the number of letters to Scots in his copybooks is further evidence of this regard.

Murray dealt directly with his Edinburgh correspondents, but was fortunate in having two trusted friends helping him to look after his deals, not only with fellow tradesmen but with customers and authors. James Gilliland was a prosperous jeweller who had married Murray's sister Elizabeth in February 1769 (Plate 2b). One of Gilliland's principal tasks was to call on Murray's customers who had not paid their bills. When Murray issued catalogues, Gilliland hired the city's water caddies to deliver them to likely purchasers.[3] He regularly took instruction from Murray over transactions with other booksellers, often negotiating important deals. So considerable was Gilliland's involvement that Murray told him good humouredly: 'I have made half a Bookseller of you'.[4] In return for these efforts Murray regularly handled the London side of Gilliland's jewellery dealings.[5] Gilliland was a useful intermediary when Murray's relationships with individuals in the Edinburgh trade became so troubled that he could not resolve disputes by letter, or, indeed, when correspondence had ceased altogether. In one instance Murray implored: 'I pray God you may extricate me from this vexatious & most perverse mistake'.[6] The diplomacy of Gilliland and the regard in which he was held among Edinburgh merchants and tradesmen enabled him to assist Murray in many essential ways. But Gilliland himself sometimes found Murray's peculiarly unremitting attention to detail annoying and once remarked to his wife that Murray was 'a very exact man to remember so many trifles'.[7]

The role of William Kerr, who had already lent Murray money to establish his business, was no less important. Kerr served as his banker and helped him to establish trade connections in Edinburgh. Moreover, as an official at the Post Office, he was in a position to facilitate the distribution of Murray's publications, especially periodicals and newspapers which the Post Office carried as part of the mail. Where Gilliland settled day-to-day

(established in 1789). Some of their papers are in the National Library of Scotland; others were discovered in August 1996 and are now in the Edinburgh City Archive.
[2] JM to John Cunningham, 13 Feb. 1770.
[3] JM to James Gilliland, 5 Feb. 1785.
[4] JM to James Gilliland, 14 Apr. 1775.
[5] James Gilliland to JM, 6 Apr. 1775.
[6] JM to James Gilliland, 11 July 1782.
[7] Eliz. Gilliland to JM, 24 Aug. 1772.

matters for Murray, Kerr advised him more generally. In 1769, not long after Murray opened his doors, Kerr told him:

> You are now in Business that requires judgement and excepting when you want to indulge the fancy of pleasing yourself as a private man, you must lay down the generall Rule to put a proper value on your time, and lay it out only in proportion as you apprehend it will return payment.[8]

Kerr suggested Alexander Kincaid as Murray's first Edinburgh correspondent. Kincaid was long established in the book trade, having started in business in the early 1730s. Since 1744 he had held the post of King's Printer and Stationer for Scotland, giving him exclusive rights to print bibles and government papers. His bookselling premises were located opposite St Giles' Cathedral in buildings known as the Luckenbooths — where the poet Allan Ramsay had established Britain's first circulating library in 1726. Kincaid's printing business was profitable, and he did equally well selling popular London publications, in many of which he held shares (with Andrew Millar and William Strahan) of the copyrights. Such was his success that around 1760 he took his relation, John Bell, into the bookselling firm to assist him. When Kincaid was in London in the spring of 1769, he and Murray had an opportunity to discuss the terms of an association. In July, Murray offered to put the names of Kincaid and Bell as agents to a work called the *Bruciad*, a half share of whose copyright he had recently purchased.[9] This was a much-revised edition of John Harvey's epic poem on the life of the Scottish patriot, Robert the Bruce. John Cumming, the editor, had reworked the 'poetical and political language', toning down anti-English passages to accommodate the pro-Union sentiment of the day.[10] Murray persuaded Kincaid to take 150 copies at 2s.6d. each.[11] To widen his market, he also made the Cambridge booksellers T. and J. Merrill wholesalers of the book and included their name in the imprint. In exchange the Merrills agreed to put Murray's name on the title page of one of their new publications. At the same time he struck a similar bargain with Kincaid over a new translation of Cesare Beccaria's *Elementi di Economia Pubblica*. He was glad to be trading with Kincaid but found him inattentive to their mutual affairs. 'I am not surprised that you have had no return from Kincaid,' Gilbert Stuart told Murray. 'His business is carried on in the most negligent manner.'[12] Murray had to urge Kincaid to meet

[8]Wm Kerr to JM, 9 Apr. 1769. After Kerr's death in 1782 his son, William, who followed his father's vocation as a post office official, looked after Murray's Edinburgh financial affairs.
[9]Murray bought the copyright from William Chapman for £15. The other half was held by the printers William and John Richardson (AL, p. 42; JM to Alex. Kincaid, 1 July 1769).
[10]The work had first appeared in 1726 and was reprinted as recently as 1768. See John Cuming's preface to the *Bruciad* for a further account of his emendations.
[11]AL, pp. 39, 41–42. See Checklist item 9.
[12]Gilbert Stuart to JM, 15 Sept. 1769.

deadlines and settle accounts, and encourage him to take on joint ventures. In the years to come Murray and Kincaid joined together in a number of successful Edinburgh medical publications, including Andrew Duncan's *Observations on the Use of Mercury in the Venereal Disease* (1772) and the *Medical and Philosophical Commentaries*, the serial founded by Murray (and edited by Duncan), which first appeared in 1773 and continued for many years.

In 1771 Murray informed Kincaid that William Cullen, an eminent physician in Edinburgh, had recommended 'me as a fit Person to be joined with you in the Publication of what he may hence forward write'.[13] The list of Cullen's publications with Murray began with his *Synopsis Nosologiae Methodicae*, published under the imprint: 'Edinburgh: A. Kincaid & W. Creech; London, T. Cadell, J. Murray and E. & C. Dilly, 1772'. Murray owned part of the property, but he had to share the London sale with other booksellers. He had hoped for the exclusive London agency, but Kincaid was not inclined to desert his established associates.[14] Kincaid's firm dealt directly with the author and organised production. When the first volume of Cullen's most important work, *First Lines of the Practice of Physic*, was ready for the press towards the end of 1776, Murray wrote to Kincaid to tell him: 'I had agreed to take one half of [Cullen's] Intended publication upon the terms he should settle with you'.[15] These terms, however, turned out to be so disadvantageous — only a potential profit of sixteen shillings on an investment of £182.10s. — that Murray insisted Kincaid renegotiate with the author, either reducing the sum paid to Cullen (which was £100) or increasing the number of copies printed, but Cullen 'turned a deaf ear to all remonstrances' and refused to alter the bargain Kincaid had made.[16] Murray was compelled to accept a deal, 'the hardest ever made by an author with a bookseller'. However, he was hopeful that for the next volume of the *First Lines*, Cullen would be more inclined 'to make us a living allowance'.[17]

In May 1771 Kincaid had taken William Creech, who was formerly his apprentice, into the firm as a partner. By 1774 he was leaving much of the everyday running of the bookselling business to Creech and devoting himself to his printing concern and to city politics. When Kincaid suddenly died in 1777, Creech took over completely. The shop became a centre for the literary activity of the city. Creech published the works of many important Scottish authors, including Adam Smith and Robert Burns,

---

[13]JM to Alex. Kincaid, 18 Mar. 1771.
[14]Another issue of this edn. of Cullen's *Synopsis* even included a further London bookseller, W. Johnston, in the imprint (Checklist 1772, item 49).
[15]JM to Alex. Kincaid, 1 Sept. 1776.
[16]John Murray, *An Author's Conduct to the Public, Stated in the Behaviour of Dr William Cullen*, p. 4. A related and more complicated dispute with Cullen (the subject of this pamphlet) is discussed in Ch. 10.
[17]JM to Wm Cullen, 1 Apr. 1777.

and dabbled in literary pursuits himself. In his *Letters to Sir John Sinclair*, a work describing recent improvements in Scottish society, Creech compared the value of literary property in 1763, when 'authors acquiring money by their writings, was hardly known', to 1783, when 'the value of literary property has been carried higher by the Scots than ever was known among any people'.[18] Murray looked to Creech, as he had to Kincaid, for a share of the profits from such a development. Soon the two men worked out acceptable ways to do business. It was natural that Murray would continue as a partner with Creech in those Scottish medical writers he had shared with Kincaid. When Murray began to publish English and Continental medical authors, Creech was an obvious choice for the Scottish agency, or, indeed, for a partnership.

Murray bargained more successfully with Creech to be his sole London publisher than he had with Kincaid. Creech even complied, however grudgingly, with his demands for money to advertise joint publications in the London papers, although the expense was considerable. In turn, Murray employed his influence with the editors of such important London literary journals as the *Monthly Review* and the *Critical Review* to get favourable notices for their publications. When his own periodical, the *English Review*, was gaining a national reputation months after its launch in 1783, Murray put Creech's name to it and later offered him a share in the proprietorship 'upon fair terms'.[19] Over a twenty-five-year period they were partners in some manner in about one hundred books — more than ten per cent of all Murray's publications. Hundreds of other titles passed between them by stock exchanges and catalogue orders. Their annual accounts ranged upwards of £500 and, at the height of their trading in the mid 1780s, approached £1000. Nevertheless, it was an inauspicious start, Kerr advising in 1774 to 'get as well tho slowly. . . out with him [Creech] as you can'.[20] At first Murray's lack of respect for Creech was evident. Privately he remarked to Gilbert Stuart in 1774: 'I am sorry that C[ree]ch the dancing master bookseller was not made a Constable. His wielding of his staff of office would have exhibited a grotesque piece of distress which would have afforded entertainment. If you can draw a character of a non-entity, draw this creature's.'[21] Over time Murray's opinion of Creech improved enough to develop their trading. The extent of their mutual interest was such that Creech put his reputation at risk by allowing Murray to print his private letter in a pamphlet Murray wrote in 1784 about a dispute between himself and William Cullen, when Cullen refused to supply the fourth volume of his *First Lines of the Practice of Physic* to purchasers of the other three,

[18]Reprinted in William Creech, *Edinburgh Fugitive Pieces* (Edinburgh, 1791), p. 67.
[19]JM to Wm Creech, 25 July 1787.
[20]Wm Kerr to JM, 22 Feb. 1774.
[21]JM to Gilbert Stuart, 21 Mar. 1774.

claiming he had changed the three volumes so materially as to render them useless. Creech told Murray: 'It was a duty I owed to myself to stand vindicated to the public, from what must have appeared to them base and unbecoming a gentleman'.[22] Murray told Creech that he was surprised that Cullen 'would deal with you after the appearance of your printed letter!' and was grateful to Creech for his support and the successful resolution of the dispute.[23]

Creech and Murray also promoted many non-medical publications. Murray, for example, put Creech's name to a number of editions of his successful *Philosophical Analysis and Illustration of some of Shakespeare's Remarkable Characters*, begun in 1774; and Creech gave him an interest in the chemist Joseph Black's *Experiments upon Magnesia Alba* (1777). They exchanged shares in many other works — poetical, political and historical — which sold well in each city. Creech, however, did not depend on Murray alone for the London side of his business. Indeed, he had a number of other and more important associates there, above all William Strahan and Thomas Cadell. When preparing the London edition of Burns' *Poems Chiefly in the Scottish Dialect* in 1787, it was Strahan and Cadell whom he made his partners, not Murray. Moreover, Murray soon discovered that he was paying more than other London traders for copies of Burns' book, and, rather than promote Creech's works for little profit, threatened to return them.[24] In another instance, Creech deliberately suppressed the Scottish sale of one of Murray's books, apparently at the insistence of a London bookseller more powerful than Murray. 'It is my opinion', Murray ruefully remarked, 'you did not mean it to succeed'.[25]

Murray found Creech difficult to deal with and often asked Kerr or Gilliland to call by the Luckenbooths to resolve disputes. 'Thank you for the trouble you have taken with Creech,' Murray told Kerr. 'He has just behaved as I expected like a fool & an Idiot.'[26] On one occasion Creech resisted settling an account outstanding for five years. On another occasion Murray challenged the probity of Creech's accounting practice: 'Altho' I never was bred a bookseller; yet I could not vary an account were I ever so much disposed to do it. And were I even dead, my people could not vary any account betwixt us *one iota*.'[27] It was no wonder that Creech did not always reply to Murray's demands: 'Answer my last ten letters!' implored Murray, who, despite his frustration, was still 'unwilling to break with you or any man with whom I can do business . . . to mutual advantage'.[28] The

[22]Creech's letter to Murray, printed in *An Author's Conduct to the Public*, pp. 39–40.
[23]JM to Wm Creech, 28 Mar. 1785. This subject is discussed further on pp. 191–95.
[24]JM to Wm Creech, 8 Oct. 1787.
[25]JM to William Creech, 27 July 1779. The work was Gilbert Stuart's controversial *Observations concerning the Public Law of Scotland* (1779), which attacked Wm Robertson.
[26]JM to Wm Kerr, 5 March 1774.
[27]JM to Wm Creech, 24 Aug. 1787.
[28]JM to Wm Creech, 1 Apr. 1784.

distance between Edinburgh and London made business between the two men more difficult, but when they were able to meet, they usually managed to resolve their differences — at least for a time: 'I may be mistaken, and I may be hasty, but I shall never continue obstinate', Murray told Creech.[29] Too often it seemed as if one were trying to get the better of the other. Indeed, such was their disharmony as early on as March 1774 that Murray could revel in an idle rumour that Creech was about to lose his shop through insolvency.[30] In turn, some months later Murray himself had to contradict 'the report of Mr Creech concerning my intention of leaving off business'.[31] Despite such petty exchanges, they grew to depend upon each too much to allow their association to lapse. As time passed, they were able to understand each other's business practice, and something approaching a friendship evolved. When Murray and his family visited Edinburgh in the summer of 1790, Creech treated them with such 'unbounded civilities' that Murray felt himself greatly in his debt.[32]

Apart from Kincaid and Creech, Murray carried on an extensive trade with several other Edinburgh booksellers and printers. Foremost among them were John Balfour, William Smellie, Charles Elliot and John Bell.[33] John Balfour was a well-established Scottish bookseller when Murray entered the trade in 1768. At that time he was a partner with William Smellie in a printing establishment, although he carried on an extensive independent bookselling business in his own name.[34] He and Murray began exchanging copies of their publications in May 1771. By 1773 they had begun to take shares in their respective publications. Theirs was also a relationship in which one continually tried to get the better of the other. For example, when Balfour insisted that Murray buy from his paper mill for printing in Edinburgh, Murray initially resisted as he usually shipped paper from London where it was considerably cheaper. However, he then told

[29] JM to Wm Creech, 25 July 1787.
[30] JM to Wm Kerr, 5 Mar. 1774.
[31] JM to Wm Kerr, 5 Mar. 1774; JM to John Gillies, 14 Jan. 1775; see also John Gillies to JM, 10 Jan. 1775.
[32] JM to Wm Creech, 4 Oct. 1790.
[33] Other Edinburgh booksellers and printers with whom Murray corresponded were Robert Allan, Charles Cowan, James Dickson, William Drummond (and his widow), John Elder, John Fairbairn, Robert Fleming, Robert Gordon, William Gordon, Alexander Guthrie, Peter Hill, James Hunter, Alexander Kincaid Jr, Laurie & Symington, George Mundie, Robert Murray, Adam Neill, John Oliphant, John and James Robertson, Walter Ruddiman, James Sibbald, and James Watson.
[34] In 1739 Balfour became partners with Gavin Hamilton, with whom he published many important works of the period, including editions of Pope and Swift and philosophical writings by David Hume. After the partnership was dissolved in 1762 Balfour joined the printing firm of Auld and Smellie for a short time (see Warren McDougall, 'Gavin Hamilton, John Balfour and Patrick Neill: a Study of Publishing in Edinburgh in the Eighteenth Century', doctoral dissertation, Edinburgh University, 1975).

Balfour he would be willing to take the paper if Balfour would buy more copies of his publications.[35]

Balfour and Smellie dissolved their partnership in 1783, but Murray continued to trade with both men individually. 'You will observe', he told Balfour, 'that I have not delayed settling either your partnership account of printing, or your own for Books, with any Illiberal or shuffling design'.[36] Afterwards, in October 1784, he told him frankly that 'altho' I always found you keen yet you never evaded facts and . . . I have been able to settle accounts with you to my satisfaction which is more than I have been able to accomplish with some of your neighbours'.[37] Murray also purchased by proxy a modest amount of stock at a sale Balfour held two months later in December.[38] A year before Murray had expressed concern to Balfour about a rumour that Smellie and Creech were about to form a partnership. He already had enough difficulty dealing with each individually, and he speculated privately that the combination would result in bankruptcy 'before 3 years are at an end'.[39] However, the rumour proved unfounded.

Balfour and Smellie, and afterwards Smellie alone, printed a number of Murray's books, especially those with a large Scottish market. As Murray had several Scottish authors in his lists, it usually made sense to print in Scotland where proof-reading the sheets and making corrections was more easily accomplished.[40] The drawback was that Murray occasionally found the job not done properly, yet by the time copies had arrived in London, it was too late to reprint. When printing outside of London, Murray had to calculate carefully the costs and risks of transportation. Bales of books sent by sea — his usual way of shipping — took time, and there was the danger of wreck or of capture by enemies or pirates; transport over land was quicker but far more expensive. Murray found it difficult to work with Smellie, whose literary and scientific interests limited the time he could give to his printing business.[41] He complained bitterly that Smellie often neglected their mutual ventures: 'You can write fully in a magazine or in a newspaper;

[35]JM to Wm Smellie, 31 Dec. 1774.
[36]JM to John Balfour, 3 June 1783.
[37]JM to John Balfour, 9 Oct. 1784.
[38]JM to John Balfour, 11 Dec. 1784.
[39]JM to John Balfour, 10 Nov. 1783.
[40]One example is David Dalrymple's *Annals of Scotland* (Edinburgh: Printed by Balfour & Smellie, for J. Murray, London, 1776). A second volume appeared in 1779 under the same imprint.
[41]Smellie edited the first *Encyclopaedia Britannica* (1768–71) and wrote many of its scientific articles; he translated Buffon's *Natural History* (1780) and wrote the *Philosophy of Natural History* (1790–99) as well as works in a variety of other fields. He also lectured in Edinburgh on scientific topics. See Robert Kerr, *Memoirs of the Life, Writings and Correspondence of William Smellie*, 2 vols. (London, 1811).

But to a correspondent, who by the bye is of most importance to your interest, it is below you to attend.'[42]

As frustrated and angry as Murray might become with his Scottish 'correspondents', he was loath to sever potentially profitable ties. Dispute and controversy were inevitable features of the book trade, exacerbated by the distance between Murray and his partners. His association with Charles Elliot began in 1775 and followed both the productive and disruptive patterns Murray had established with other members of the Edinburgh trade. The two men collaborated on over fifty publications between 1774 and 1790. Murray actively promoted the sale of these works through advertising and through his influence in London literary and publishing circles. Elliot received the same exclusive distribution rights in Edinburgh for several of Murray's most important publications, including his edition of Gray's *Poems* (1776) and John Millar's *Historical View of English Government* (1787).

One of the first books Elliot offered Murray was a new edition of Robert Simson's *Elements of Conic Sections* (1775), which Elliot was keen for Murray to get 'introduced to the different Schools' in and around London.[43] In March 1776 Murray heard a rumour that one of Elliot's main London associates, Thomas Cadell, was quitting the trade after his warehouse had burned down. He relished the opportunity of becoming Elliot's primary correspondent, stipulating only that Elliot would settle accounts every nine months.[44] The news proved false, for Cadell had sufficient capital to carry on despite his misfortune, and Murray had to rest satisfied with just a share in Elliot's wide range of new publications. Some of these, pamphlets in particular, Murray had great difficulty in selling. In May 1778 he told Elliot: 'No apology is requisite for any Books you may give to Mr Cadell to publish for you. I only wish you to give him some of your pamphlets also. The publication of these being always attended with more trouble than profit.'[45]

The competitive side of their partnership occasionally caused disagreements. Murray always tried to get the best deal possible. When offering what he considered to be favourable terms, he did not hesitate to announce his generosity, nor was he always above what he himself had termed 'illiberal or shuffling design'. Elliot was aware of Murray's tactics and occasionally caught him out: 'You should take the advice you give', he told Murray, 'and send your books only to one person'.[46] Murray did not

[42]JM to Wm Smellie, 29 May 1777. Earlier Murray had told Smellie: 'You tell me you cannot bear to write Letters. I answer if you are averse to giving satisfaction . . . you ought to give up business' (JM to Wm Smellie, 28 Mar. 1775).
[43]Charles Elliot to JM, 11 Mar. 1775.
[44]JM to Charles Elliot, 26 Mar. 1776.
[45]JM to Charles Elliot, 30 May 1778.
[46]Charles Elliot to JM, 2 Aug. 1781.

readily accept criticism, and when Elliot challenged him for offering a meagre list of books in exchange for one of Elliot's new publications, Murray became indignant:

> If you had stated your dissatisfaction to the list in a cool and temperate manner it might have been altered and made agreeable. But I have receivd a letter . . . so coarse and so ignorant that it would disgrace a man of common civility to reply to it as it deserves. . . . Not being used to receive favours from Mr Elliot, it is natural for me to suspect every thing tendered in the way of kindness from that quarter for I have not forgot his attention in compelling me to receive and pay for goods which I never ordered and this too all in the way of kindness — and these acts will infallibly make an impression upon a mind gratefull like mine.[47]

James Gilliland attempted to heal the widening rift between the two booksellers, pointing out that their affairs were so intertwined that a rupture would be disadvantageous to both. Murray knew it was not in his interest to quarrel, but he was not inclined to be mistreated: 'Insolence equal to his I would hardly receive quietly from a much greater man', he told Gilliland in July 1783.[48] Elliot then turned to the attack, and Murray now refused to answer letters. By April 1784 an opportunity for a reconciliation arose and trading resumed, if on a more cautious footing. 'I envy no man his publications,' he told Elliot. 'There is room enough in the world for all of us, and I wish to go on quietly.'[49] When Murray heard of the large sums Elliot had begun to pay authors in the late 1780s, he remarked to Creech: 'The temptation held out . . . by Elliot was irresistible. . . . I nevertheless can only admire Elliot without proposing his conduct for imitation.'[50] Elliot had seen too many Scottish writers sell their works to the London trade for high prices and gain their booksellers huge profits. He risked hundreds, even thousands of pounds, on single titles, and he did well. He even opened a shop in London at the end of 1786 in partnership with Thomas Kay, who was his brother-in-law, and James Mackenzie, who had been his manager at Edinburgh.[51]

When Elliot died in 1790 (leaving an estate worth over £30,000), Murray offered to assist the trustees in the dispersal of stock and copyrights. He made two separate visits to Edinburgh on this account: the first to clarify the extent of Elliot's property; the second to buy nearly £1000 of stock and copyrights at the sale itself. He had also hoped to 'treat privately' with the

---

[47]JM to Charles Elliot, 24 June 1783.
[48]JM to James Gilliland, 4 July 1783.
[49]JM to Charles Elliot, 1 Apr. 1784.
[50]JM to Wm Creech, 24 Aug. 1787. Murray noted that Elliot had paid £300 for James Gregory's *Conspectus Medicinae Theoreticae*, 2 vols., 1788, and 1000 guineas for William Smellie's *Philosophy of Natural History*, 1790–99.
[51]*Edinburgh Evening Courant*, 28 Dec. 1786 and 25 Jan. 1787. The shop was located in the Strand (No. 332) opposite Somerset House.

trustees for one of the more valuable properties, but this was not permitted.[52] Before the sale Murray had joined forces with the Robinsons (London booksellers) and with John Bell and his partner (Bradfute) in Edinburgh to gain an advantage and maximise the returns of the sale. Murray's dissatisfaction with his share was exacerbated when Elliot's trustees demanded a small sum still outstanding from an earlier arrangement, even adding interest which it was not the practice of the trade to charge in such circumstances: 'I am of opinion', he told one of the trustees, 'that I rendered the estate of C. E. more service at Edinburgh than all the interest twice told, without being able to celebrate the treatment we received in return, in all its parts as either the most generous or honourable'.[53] Afterwards, Murray continued to trade with Elliot's nephew Cornelius, who carried on in bookselling.

Long before Elliot's sale, Murray had been involved in over thirty joint publishing ventures with John Bell.[54] Late in 1773 Murray made it known he was keen to do business, and the following year he reminded Bell: 'A publisher you must have in London and I shall serve you as well as any other person'.[55] However, as usual, Murray wanted the London market exclusively, and reminded Bell that 'his publications might be an object to one bookseller here & to no more'.[56] As Bell had many popular books in his lists and was generally co-operative in this way, Murray benefited considerably from selling editions of works by important writers of the Scottish Enlightenment. Although most of their deals went smoothly, some were fraught with complications and deceptions. At one point in 1778, when Murray discovered that the books sent by Bell were defective, he told Elliot: 'I decline having any concern with J. Bell. . . . His articles were so exceedingly disordered & erroneous that it was a months work to make them perfect.'[57] Like Creech, Bell hindered the sale of certain publications under pressure from Murray's London rivals. When Murray finally bargained to buy back the unwanted copies, he was distressed to meet with unexplainable delays. 'It will be strange indeed', Murray said of Bell privately, 'if his tergiversation is so complete as to induce him to deny his hand writing. . . . If he keeps the copies . . . the [work] is totally ruined.'[58]

[52]JM to James Hunter, 26 Apr. 1790. Many uncatalogued documents relating to Elliot's estate are located in the Murray Archive.

[53]JM to Adam Bruce, 8 Aug. 1792; and see JM to James Hunter, 26 Apr. 1790; Elliot folder, Box M8 for details of Elliot's estate settlement.

[54]Bell traded alone after his partnership with Kincaid ended in 1771 until 1790 when he took in as a partner his nephew, John Bradfute. He is not the John Bell who published the *British Poets*. For an account of his career see the *Edinburgh Evening Courant*, 11 Oct. 1806.

[55]JM to John Bell, 11 July 1774.

[56]JM to John Bell, 17 Jan. 1775.

[57]JM to Charles Elliot, 9 May 1778.

[58]JM to Gilbert Stuart, 1 Nov. 1781. Murray was referring to Stuart's *View of Society*.

Although Murray was growing angrier, he told Bell: 'I wish to compose grievances not to aggravate them. My disposition is to be friendly with you, & indeed it hurts me to be out of temper with any man.'[59] The accounts of the two men were another source of difficulty, complicated by allowing each other to return unsold books after long periods.[60] Murray, in fact, returned far greater numbers.

A colourful range of booksellers and printers — including Bell, Elliot, Smellie, Balfour, Creech and Kincaid — met Murray's basic needs for the Edinburgh side of his business. As his friendships with these men fluctuated and his own publications lists diversified, he sought out others in the trade there and on the whole did well. In moments of frustration, however, Murray would lament the extent of his Scottish connections, and implore Gilliland, as he did in July 1782, 'to relieve me from all further trouble with the booksellers at Edinburgh. . . . With Creech I can come to no settlement. I have an unsettled account with Balfour, with the others I have no account at all and desire none.'[61] Ten years later he told an Edinburgh bookseller: 'The times are bad. I can get no money from your city.'[62]

In 1770 Murray became the London agent for the Advocates' Library in Edinburgh.[63] William Wilson, a friend who was prominent in Edinburgh legal circles, influenced Robert Cullen — the acting curator of the library (and son of Dr William Cullen) — to propose Murray to the Advocates.[64] The appointment of Alexander Brown as librarian in 1771 initiated a regular programme of acquisition. Brown held the post for most of the period Murray was in business, and the two men worked closely together to build up the collection. As the library had not retained a London agent for a number of years, there was a considerable backlog, particularly of periodicals and state papers which Murray promptly acquired. One of Murray's regular functions was to forward books entered at Stationers' Hall. During the eighteenth century only a small number of titles were afforded this additional copyright protection, mainly because some publishers (or authors) grudged giving over the mandatory nine copies, even though

---

[59]JM to John Bell, 15 Mar. 1785.
[60]See AL, pp. 198 and 284; and DB2, p. 267.
[61]JM to James Gilliland, 10 July 1782.
[62]JM to James Sibbald, 15 July 1793. In a similar vein Murray told Adam Neill: 'From the trade in your city I cannot draw a shilling after giving three years credit, which is the reason why I cannot pay you prompt as I will to do' (JM to Adam Neill, 15 July 1793).
[63]For records of Murray's dealings with the Advocates see Curators' Minutes, FR 119 and 120 at the National Library of Scotland. Before Murray, Andrew Bell had been the Library's London agent, though there are no curators' minutes between 1763 and 1771.
[64]JM to Wm Wilson, 5 Oct. 1770. Wilson, a Writer to the Signet, is the same man who gave James Boswell his first legal fee as an advocate (*Boswell for the Defence, 1769–1774*, eds. Wm Wimsatt and F. A. Pottle, p. 30, 14 Mar. 1772).

registration brought the book within the 1710 Copyright Act.[65] Murray also regularly supplied the Advocates with works published on the Continent and often was left to select new British books for the Library.

When auctions of important collections were held in London, he acted on behalf of the Advocates. One of the more notable was the sale of the books of Joseph Smith, formerly the British Consul in Venice and one of the greatest collectors of the age. The auction took place in the Spring of 1773 and lasted many days. Over ten years before, the King had bought books from Smith's collection to form an important part of his great library (now the British Library). Smith then amassed a second collection in the years before his death. Murray's remit from the Advocates was to buy the books they had marked in the Catalogue 'provided they are in good preservation and can be bought at reasonable prices'.[66] Such discretion did not altogether appeal to Murray as he ran the risk of bidding too little for important books and too much for others. At the sale the King's heavy buying raised prices, and the Advocates' Library came away with less than it had hoped.[67]

Commission work of this kind was prestigious although not altogether profitable. Murray charged a guinea a year for his services, but forgot to bill the Library eight years running. When he finally demanded the money the treasurer objected, but Murray persisted, and finally the Advocates agreed to pay rather than risk losing their agent.[68]

Glasgow

In September 1769 Murray started promoting his business in Glasgow. As he knew no booksellers there, he entrusted John Cunningham, the brewer, to find a correspondent who wanted a London agent, and 'who is besides accurate, honest and to be depended upon'.[69] Murray also relied on John Moore — a Glasgow doctor who wrote popular fiction and travel accounts.[70]

[65] Of all Murray's publications about 15 per cent (160) were entered in the Stationers' Company Register.

[66] JM to Robert Cullen, 25 Jan. 1773. AL, pp. 146 and 278, DB1, pp. 334, 336, 340. See *Biblioteca Smithiana. A Catalogue of the remaining part of the curious and valuable library of Joseph Smith*, Sold by James Robson, New Bond Street [London, 1773]; Stuart Morrison, 'Records of a Bibliophile: The Catalogues of Consul Joseph Smith and some Aspects of his Collecting', *The Book Collector*, 43 (Spring, 1994), 27–58.

[67] Murray bought 130 of the 2000 marked lots for the sum of £112. He also bought for the Advocates at the West sale in Apr. 1773, but again the King dominated the sale. At the sale of the library of Topham Beauclerk in the spring of 1781 Murray spent over £240 for the Advocates (See JM to Alex. Brown, 5 and 20 June 1781).

[68] Murray told Gilliland: 'It is a fair charge . . . I do not yet give it up as lost' (26 Sept. 1780; also JM to Alex. Brown, 14 Nov. 1780).

[69] JM to John Cunningham, 16 Sept. 1769.

[70] John Moore to JM, 23 July 1771; and letters following both to and from.

They had met in London, and Moore then introduced him to Glasgow
literary men, such as John Millar and William Richardson, professors at the
University, whose works Murray went on to publish. Millar and Richardson
in turn recommended Murray's appointment in 1775 as the London bookseller to Glasgow University Library, where he dealt mainly with Archibald
Arthur, a philosophy professor and the University Librarian.[71] He sent the
library the latest publications, newspapers and periodicals, charging one
guinea a year in much the same manner as he had the Advocates' Library.
And he performed other services for the University: advertising courses in
the London newspapers before term-time, and finding rare and out-of-
print books for professors.[72]

In the early 1770s Murray was introduced to Robert and Andrew Foulis,
the printers to the University. Their finely printed and scholarly editions of
Greek and Latin texts — published from the 1740s to the 1770s — had
brought their press international fame and earned them the title of 'the
Elzevirs of Britain', after the renowned seventeenth-century Dutch printers.
Their pocket editions of English authors put them at the centre of the
copyright disputes of the 1760s and 1770s.[73] Although their positions on
this important issue were similar, Murray found dealing with them difficult.
In 1773, for instance, William Richardson asked Murray to publish his *Poems*
in a new edition, the first of which had been printed by the Foulis brothers.
However, when Richardson found them 'extremely averse to part with the
Poems', he suggested a joint publication.[74] Foulis rejected the proposal.
And only when Richardson persisted and Murray offered six guineas for
the copyright did the printers acquiesce. Later Richardson remarked that
Murray's edition was 'printed more elegantly'[75] (see Checklist item 109).

Murray was encouraged to trade with the Foulis brothers by some of his
Scottish friends in London who had trained in Glasgow at the Foulis
brothers' Academy for the Fine Arts. Most prominent among these men
were James Tassie, John Donaldson (who drew portraits of Murray's

---

[71]Thomas Reid, founder of the 'Common Sense' school of philosophy, held the office of
librarian for a short time in 1781 (JM to Reid, 16 Nov. 1781).
[72]'It is long since I sold Hume's treatise on Human Nature', Murray told John Millar. 'I shall
look out for another copy; the book however is very scarce' (JM to Millar, 24 Jan. 1782).
[73]When London booksellers petitioned against the Lords' 1774 decision, Robert Foulis
responded with a *Memorial of the Printers and Booksellers of Glasgow to the House of Commons*
(dated 24 Apr. 1774): 'It is not the reprinting of books', he wrote, 'that any way sensibly
hurts the London trade; on the contrary, they . . . diminish their own trade by endeavouring
to bind the hands of their brethren all over the kingdom, who, if free and independent,
would be able to trade with them more extensively, and on more equitable terms' (*Memorial*,
p. 6).
[74]Wm Richardson to JM, 25 Nov. 1773.
[75]Wm Richardson to JM, 7 Oct. 1774. Murray sent Foulis fifty copies on 3 May 1774 (DB2,
p. 179 and AL, p. 257). For the Foulis' original edition, see Philip Gaskell, *Bibliography of the
Foulis Press* (2nd edn., 1986), item 588.

authors for frontispieces to their books) and John Paxton (who apparently had painted Murray's wife in 1769 and attained a measure of celebrity as an artist before his premature death in India in 1780).[76] The Academy was established in 1756 and was Scotland's first dedicated art school. The cost to the brothers for supporting the school was considerable, and they were distracted from their printing concern. Insurmountable debt forced Robert to sell the Academy's valuable collection of classical master works. Murray, who wished Foulis to profit fully from the sale of the paintings, suggested he 'consign them to . . . myself, and to your two old pupils, James Tassie and John Paxton, to manage for your interest and advantage, by exhibition (for there are plenty of rooms in London) or by sale according to your instructions'.[77] Foulis did not take up Murray's offer. Nor did he listen to the advice of James Christie, the auctioneer, to wait until the London season before selling the collection. Foulis was so distraught over the meagre prices realised at the sale that he died on the journey back to Glasgow.[78] Upon hearing this news, Murray was interested to know from John Millar 'in what manner the Stock of the late R & A Foulis is to be disposed of' and asked the Glasgow booksellers Dunlop & Wilson if they would join him in making purchases, which they did.[79] Robert Foulis' son, Andrew, continued the business, producing several handsome books but generally failing to maintain the high standards of his father and uncle. In one instance Murray was compelled to return copies of Foulis' edition of Isaac Watts' *Hymns and Spiritual Songs* because it was 'printed on paper so coarse and bad that I could not hazard my reputation by exposing the book to sale'.[80]

Despite grave misgivings, Murray succumbed to John Millar's suggestion in 1779 that Andrew Foulis should print the much revised third edition of Millar's book, newly entitled *The Origin and Progress of Ranks*. Millar was keen to help Foulis by bringing work to his press, but Murray was unhappy

---

[76]Attribution of a portrait of Murray by John Donaldson is suggested in a letter from Wm Kerr: 'As to your request to sitt for Donaldson we will settle that . . . have not I the same right to ask you to sitt for yours. . . . I am fond of Pictures, and was thinking of asking Tassie who is in this country just now to take my lovely visage off in a bust . . . that I may give impressions off by Dozens to my innumerable friends' (Wm Kerr to JM, 14 Sept. 1775). For an account of John Donaldson's career, see W. H. Tapp, 'John Donaldson: Enameller, Miniaturist and Ceramic Artist', *Apollo*, 36 (Aug. and Dec. 1942), 39–42, 55; 37 (Jan. 1943), 4–7, 22. In Nov. 1774 Murray paid £17.10s. for Donaldson's London lodgings, a sum possibly put towards his portrait. Murray also alludes to a portrait of his wife Nancy in a letter to his sister-in-law, Hester Weemss, 9 Mar. 1769, but neither work is known.
[77]JM to Robert and Andrew Foulis, 24 Dec. 1774.
[78]D. Murray, *Robert & Andrew Foulis and the Glasgow Press with some Account of the Glasgow Academy of Fine Arts* (Glasgow, 1913), pp. 99–100.
[79]JM to John Millar, 20 Sept. 1776; to Dunlop & Wilson, 21 Sept. 1776.
[80]JM to Andrew Foulis, 15 Nov. 1784. The book is listed as 'not seen' in Gaskell, *Bibliography of the Foulis Press*, item 674.

about printing a work that would be both more expensive and more difficult to supervise than if Murray himself were to produce the work in London: 'The difference betwixt [Foulis'] price and the London price is by no means so small as you seem to imagine', he complained to Millar, and insisted that the book be 'printed exactly similar to the last Edition. For Mr Foulis's Taste will not make a handsomer page'.[81] To save money and assert his authority, Murray shipped high-quality paper from London. When printing was complete, Foulis refused to send copies to Murray until he was paid. Outraged at this behaviour, Murray told Millar:

> I employed him at the London price, from my then favourable opinion of him, and at your very earnest solicitations, and I mean certainly to pay him as I do other printers. I must add that his Father or his uncle had they been alive would not have embraced his conduct; nor has my behaviour, or my reputation in my profession merited it. . . . The Delay he has already made is of moment & the consequences of carrying his design into execution will not be pleasant . . .. The session of Parliament will now be over, the India ships sailed, & the Town empty before your book can be brought to market.[82]

To Millar's assertion that Foulis could legally demand payment, Murray indignantly told him that, although 'I know no law to prevent a printer . . . from arresting his employer at the conclusion of his work . . . the reverse is use & practice. . . . Glasgow', he continued, 'will not over rule the practice of every other place.'[83] Nevertheless, Murray was so anxious to get copies of the book that he agreed to pay Foulis in seven rather than twelve months. Although disinclined to deal any further with Foulis, Murray yielded to the entreaties of mutual associates. They were partners in an elegant edition of Allan Ramsay's *Gentle Shepherd* (1787), with twelve aquatint illustrations by David Allan — another artist trained at the Academy of Fine Arts.[84] Still, relations with Foulis were never easy: one seemingly straightforward exchange of books took three years to settle.[85]

Other Cities

Like the Foulis brothers, John Baskerville of Birmingham was renowned for typographical excellence. Murray held Baskerville in high regard and

[81]JM to John Millar, 5 Aug. 1779. William and John Richardson had printed the 1st and 2nd edns.
[82]JM to John Millar, 10 Jan. 1780.
[83]Ibid.
[84]Allan's aquatints for the *Gentle Shepherd* blended Enlightenment refinement with native Scottish simplicity. He also painted the portrait of Murray for which Murray apparently paid £40 (AL, p. 226; see frontispiece).
[85]JM to Andrew Foulis, 10 June 1783.

bought books from him on good terms.[86] When ten of the printer's elegant bibles arrived at Fleet Street, priced at the bargain rate of 18s.9d. each, Baskerville reminded Murray he expected 'on the strictist Honour you will keep this a secret from the Trade'.[87] Otherwise, other London booksellers would demand the same price. Murray was also fortunate to be one of the London agents for the sale of Baskerville's edition of William Hunter's *Anatomy of the Gravid Uterus* (1774). This elephant folio, containing thirty-four finely engraved plates (some printed at the Foulis Academy), sold for six guineas, and was among the more spectacular and expensive books of the century. It brought Murray prestige among his fellow traders at an early stage in his bookselling career, even though the profit was minimal.

Murray was, on the whole, particular about the typography of his publications. However distant the press, he insisted that specimens should be sent to Fleet Street for approval. He knew that an aesthetically pleasing page mattered to discerning readers — even more so after 1774 when many editions of a work were competing in the marketplace: 'We must have something to give it a preference', he told his partner in a publication, '& *that*, must be in the print & paper'.[88] Murray therefore spared no expense over his 1778 edition of Thomson's *Seasons* and hailed it as 'the handsomest edition of the Book yet Printed'.[89] At considerable cost, he commissioned a set of engravings (some by David Allan) and engaged John Aikin to write 'an essay on the plan and character of the poem'. The work was printed at Warrington by William Eyres, a man who, Murray remarked, could 'join elegance, correctness and good press-work together'.[90] Murray had met Eyres through the Reverend William Enfield, the rector of Warrington Academy and a writer who had lodged at 32 Fleet Street in 1769. Enfield often supervised the progress of Murray's publications at Eyres' press, the most handsome being his 1778 edition of Thomson's *Seasons* (see Checklist 1778, item 206).

William Charnley, the Newcastle bookseller, was Murray's first provincial associate. As Murray had few of his own publications at the outset of his career, his wholesale trade with Charnley was not very profitable.[91] However, Murray took a stake in several of Charnley's publications, notably

[86]Josiah Ruston (executor to Baskerville's estate) to JM, c. 21 Mar. 1775, in which Murray was told: 'You say you had a great regard for the personage and character of the late Mr Baskerville; therefore, I hope you will pay a decent attention to the just demands of his Executor'. Murray paid his account on 13 Apr. (DB2, p. 220). See also AL, p. 182 (Baskerville's account) and DB1, p. 319 (Murray's orders).
[87]John Baskerville to JM, 10 Jan. 1774.
[88]JM to John Bell, 24 Feb. 1787.
[89]JM to John Aikin, 14 Apr. 1778. Murray published seven editions of the *Seasons*, the last appearing in 1794, just after his death. Each time he improved the work, touching up and adding new engravings, using higher grades of paper or resetting with new type.
[90]JM to John Aikin, 6 June 1777.
[91]JM to Wm Charnley, 21 July 1769.

John Rotheram's *Philosophical Inquiry into Water* in 1770 and the *Complete System of Land-Surveying* by Thomas Breaks in 1771. Rotheram's book — Murray's first essay into the field of medical publishing — had a limited sale despite efforts to have it reviewed in the London journals and considerable sums spent on advertising. Murray took the work on a 'sale or return' basis and, after three years, shipped many copies back to Newcastle at Charnley's expense. Breaks' book, which originally sold in parts, was somewhat more successful, although some numbers were returned.[92] With the remainder Murray printed a new title page and advertised a 'second edition' in 1778.

An analysis of imprints in which Murray's name appears alongside those of traders in Britain's provincial cities and towns is of limited use in determining the nature of his activities as a whole in these places. Quantitatively, the titles which involve either a co-publication or an agency arrangement with a provincial trader amount to less than twenty per cent of his total known output (see Table 1 and Figure 1). This does not suggest, however, either that Murray's own publications were difficult to obtain outside of London or that provincial titles were not on the shelves at 32 Fleet Street. They undoubtedly were available or promptly ordered. The long lists of books appended to much of Murray's correspondence with provincial traders, along with corresponding references in his daybooks and account ledger, indicate the extent of his dealings outside of London. How profitable this side of Murray's business was is another matter, one that is also difficult to determine. Only a handful of accounts survive, and these only in the early part of Murray's career. However, the letters he wrote to the provinces, when taken together, document a steady flow of books and money in both directions. They also represent a considerable time commitment. Murray would not have continued, or indeed have cultivated these associations were they not beneficial to his business. There was little out of the ordinary in Murray's trade in Scotland or in England's provincial towns, though he did benefit from personal links in Edinburgh in a way that set him apart from all but the more important London dealers such as Strahan and Cadell. In Ireland, the topic of the next chapter, Murray was more of a maverick.

[92] AL, p. 109; Checklist items 29, 31, and 173.

— 7 —

The Irish Trade

Getting a Foot in the Door

Irish trading links were harder for Murray to establish than Scottish ones. The Irish book trade had its own character and operated on different principles from those governing either the English or the Scottish trades.[1] For example, in England and Scotland, Crown patents were limited to bibles, prayer books, almanacs and government publications; in Ireland, from 1551 when the first book was printed there, the holder's grant — and there was only one holder — included printing of every kind. Under such a monopoly virtually no other commercial trade in books could develop in Ireland, apart from selling imported books. However, at the end of the seventeenth century, the King's Printer in Ireland lost his exclusive privilege, and over the next hundred years trade began to expand.

The 1710 Copyright Act did not extend to Ireland, where there was still hardly any competitive trade to regulate. During the course of the century, however, Irish printers and booksellers made the most of there being no legal concept of literary property. On the one hand, they were forced to by necessity because Irish writers were inclined to publish their works with London publishers, who recognized a property in and thus would pay a price for their writings. On the other hand, the Irish trade profited considerably by reprinting books first published in London, where they could choose from the most popular publications. Without the costs of purchasing manuscripts from authors or of competing for shares in steady sellers at trade sales, they could produce and sell books for less than the London trade. Most Irish book buyers bought these editions, though they were often less elegant and less accurate, and greater status could be had by owning London editions. London booksellers often complained that large

---

[1] The best study of the eighteenth-century Irish book trade is M. Pollard, *Dublin's Trade in Books 1550–1800* (Oxford, 1989). The following background information depends largely on this work.

numbers of these reprints found their way into Britain and cut into the sales
of their editions. However, this trade was smaller than they made out; the
real issue was losing a large part of the Irish market. So the 1739 Importation Act, which prohibited the importation of any book printed abroad that
was written and printed in Britain, neither greatly benefited the London
trade nor affected the majority of Irish booksellers and printers.[2] Only a
few Irish traders depended on selling reprints in the British market: the
Importation Act forced some to give up; the others continued trading as
'pirates'.[3]

For their own part, the Irish trade had their own complaints against
monopolistic London booksellers, forcefully expressed in 1736 by no less a
literary figure than Jonathan Swift in a letter to Benjamin Motte, his
London bookseller: 'You send what books you please hither, and Booksellers here can send nothing to you that is written here. . . . This is
absolute Oppression.'[4] Swift, like most Irish authors, usually published
his works in London. Only a handful of books (usually of Irish interest)
were first printed in Ireland. Swift was exceptional in making separate deals
with his Dublin bookseller for Irish editions of his works. In the absence of
copyright legislation, self-regulating systems developed to control the reprint market and divide the profits equitably. The trade generally acknowledged the proprietary right of the first bookseller who advertised a work or
who posted the newly printed sheets on his door. Co-operation and prin-
cipled competition characterised the trade as the Irish book-buying public
grew and new markets, especially in America, opened up.

This was how things stood when Murray first ventured into the Irish
market. He wanted to form an alliance with a Dublin trader who believed
that a London correspondent could be a valuable asset. He also knew that
he could benefit by publishing London editions of books newly printed in
Dublin. In February 1770 Murray asked a Scottish friend who was visiting
Dublin to attempt to procure such works, and he explained to him the way
the trade worked:

> In Ireland the booksellers without ceremony reprint upon the English; and
> the English have the privilege in their turn to reprint upon the Irish. The
> former however come off with the Loss as it is in London only where the
> most esteemed English books are first printed. Be this as it will, the book in
> question . . . is not printed here. . . . I wish you would see and speak with
> [the author] upon the subject. Acquaint him with the hazard he runs, of his
> book being printed here even without his consent, & that it will be better

[2]Pollard, p. 71.
[3]Pollard, ch. 3, 'The Implications of the Copyright Act: Dublin's Relations with London',
esp. pp. 79–95.
[4]Swift to Benjamin Motte, 25 May 1736. *The Correspondence of Jonathan Swift*, ed. Harold
Williams, 5 vols (Oxford, 1963–5) iv, 493; quoted in Pollard, *Dublin's Trade in Books*, p. 75.
Swift made these remarks three years before the Importation Act.

for him to accept of a small matter for his assignment of the copy right to a Bookseller here.[5]

Murray offered the author five guineas, although he was fully aware that the assignment of the copyright by the author did not make it a property at law as it already had been printed in Ireland. His offer only morally obliged the author not to sell to another London bookseller. A work that had first appeared in Ireland could be reprinted by any London bookseller. Indeed, this might have happened if there had been a widespread expectation of considerable gains.

This first attempt of Murray's failed.[6] However, in December 1770 he tried another approach: when a Quaker friend, Thomas Cumming, went to Dublin, Murray asked him to show the leading booksellers one of his publications that was about to appear in London (John Langhorne's *Fables of Flora*) and tempt one of them into paying for a pre-publication copy to gain the advantage of being the first to offer it to the Irish public. Cumming made this report to Murray:

> I instantly applied to Alderman [George] Faulkner . . . but he told me he would not give a shilling for any Original Copy whatever; as there is no Law, or even Custom, to secure any Property in Books in this Kingdom. From him I went directly to [William] Smith, afterwards to [Abraham] Bradley, &c. &c. They all gave me the same answer to my Proposal. The last mentioned of these, told me that he had once gave a Sum of Money for a London Copy, and some of his Brothers in Trade came modestly to him and demanded a share in the Sale but absolutely declined being a Farthing Sharers in the Money he gave for the Copy! *Look ye here,* said they, *as you gave so many Guineas for it you must sell it at _____ or you must be a Loser; but as we shall immediately advertise that we shall publish and sell it at _____, you know the Publick will wait till ours comes out; yours will lie on your Hands, and ours will go off, and we, who paid nothing but for Paper and printing, must get Money.*[7]

Cumming doubted whether Murray would find a bookseller he might do business with. The trade was intractable; nor could he see much future for Murray even were he to establish a contact. Dublin, he concluded, was 'not a reading, but a hard drinking City'.

Murray did not succumb despite this discouragement. He asked Cumming to approach Thomas Ewing, a successful bookseller and printer

[5] JM to John Cunningham, 13 Feb. 1770. The author was Bennett Cuthbertson whose *System for the Compleat Interior Management and Oeconomy of a Batallion of Infantry* had been published at Dublin by Boulter Grierson in 1769.

[6] British editions of Cuthbertson's work appeared in 1776 (Bristol) and 1779 (London).

[7] Thomas Cumming to JM, 13 Dec. 1770. Cumming, a London merchant and a friend of Dr Johnson, was known as the 'fighting Quaker' because he 'persuaded the Government to allow him to lead an armed expedition into Senegal, which drove out the French and established British trading supremacy there' (*Boswell in Search of a Wife 1766–1769*, eds. F. Brady and F. A. Pottle, 1957, p. 172n.).

whose family had long been in the trade. Rather than offer the *Fables of Flora*, Cumming showed Ewing Murray's two latest historical publications — a translation of the Abbé Millot's *Elémens de l'Histoire d'Angleterre* and John Millar's *Observations concerning the Distinction of Ranks in Society*. Murray had paid out over two hundred guineas for these works and hoped that an Irish trader would pay at least twenty guineas for pre-publication copies. He told Cumming to point out that the whole of Millar's work 'has been revised by David Hume and the public have great Expectation from it'.[8] Ewing seemed to be interested, but he wanted Murray to pay half the expenses of the Dublin edition. Murray insisted upon an outright return, however small, on his substantial investment. Ewing finally consented to paying fifteen guineas for Millar's work and quickly published an edition. After this successful beginning, Murray then sold him Langhorne's *Fables of Flora* and Edmund Cartwright's *Armine and Elvira* for an undisclosed sum, and these texts appeared in a single volume in 1772, published by Ewing.

Murray did well to persuade Ewing to pay for what might have been his for nothing. Ewing's edition of the *Distinction of Ranks* was not a piracy but the product of a legitimate bargain. The secrecy of their arrangement prevented the Dublin trade from quickly publishing a less expensive edition of the work.[9] A serious difficulty remained, however: copies of Ewing's cheap octavo edition might make their way to Britain and compete with the sale of Murray's more expensive quarto edition. In that event Ewing's payment would provide little compensation for the loss of sales. To stop this, Ewing had to agree that he would sell only in Ireland. Murray had the Importation Act on his side but thought it better to depend on Ewing's word rather than go to court. When John Millar, the author of the work, drew Murray's attention to Ewing's edition, Murray had to feign surprise: 'They have printed I find a near Edition of it in Ireland. You will oblige me by discountenancing the Sale . . . in Glasgow.'[10] When a book did well, like the *Distinction of Ranks*, a few rogue copies would not matter much. Ewing even took fifty copies of the London edition for Irish customers who might prefer the larger quarto format.[11] Millar's book sold out, and Murray published new editions in 1773 and 1779.

When Murray visited Dublin in October 1771, he formed a warm friendship with Ewing. He also modified their way of doing business: 'You may assure yourself', he told the Irishman, 'that I shall introduce

[8]JM to Thomas Cumming, [no date] March 1771. Murray later reminded Ewing himself that the historian William Robertson also had a hand in the revision (JM to Thomas Ewing, 22 Mar. 1771). JM to John Millar, 9 Aug. 1771.
[9]James Williams, who regularly reprinted new London publications, produced an edition of the Millot translation in 1771. Ewing may have made a deal with Williams, but equally, he may have not been able to stop him from printing. Murray never mentioned Williams' edition.
[10]JM to John Millar, 9 Aug. 1771.
[11]DB1, p. 205.

your name wherever I can in my Publications and you may put my name to any thing new that you produce'.[12] In 1772 Murray published Stephen Adye's *Considerations on the Act for Punishing Mutiny and Desertion* under the imprint: 'London: printed for J. Murray; Kincaid & Creech, Edinburgh; and T. Ewing, Dublin'. In the same year there appeared an edition of a work which Ewing had originally published in 1771, John Curry's *Observations on the Popery Laws*, under the imprint: 'London: printed for J. Murray, and T. Ewing, Dublin'. Two periodical publications in which Murray had a share (the *Medical and Philosophical Commentaries* and the *Edinburgh Magazine and Review*) also named Ewing in the imprint (see Plate 33). By including Ewing's name on the title page, he reduced the likelihood of a reprint, or worse a piracy, and guaranteed himself a large share of the Irish market. Moreover, when Ewing published a new work, Murray would control the London sale. As part of their arrangement, Murray also supplied Ewing with a general stock of the standard works of the day. It was essential to provide this service, although it brought little profit. In all, Murray's account with Ewing ranged upwards of £200 annually.[13] He visited Dublin three times between 1771 and 1775, and Ewing not only treated him cordially but introduced him to other Irish booksellers.

Murray would have liked to trade with Ewing as he did with booksellers in Edinburgh and in the provincial cities, exchanging publications for mutual advantage. Unfortunately, not all of his publications had an Irish market, and there were not enough new Irish titles to make regular exchange a standard practice. Moreover, Ewing was naturally unwilling to set precedents that would greatly upset the way his fellow Irish traders did business. Irish reprinting and pirating continued and this harmed Murray's business. When Alexander Hamilton, one of Murray's most successful authors, enquired about the Irish sale of his *Elements of the Practice of Midwifery*, Murray told him: 'At Dublin the Booksellers reprint every new book without regarding literary property, so that there is no chance of disposing of your edition in that Kingdom'.[14]

At other times, however, Murray turned Irish trade practices to his advantage. When John Bell broke an agreement to put Murray's name to the title page of a new (the sixth) edition of the *Edinburgh Pharmacopoeia* (1774), and refused to send him copies to sell in London, Murray retaliated by obtaining a pre-publication copy through 'clandestine Methods' — probably corrupt workers in the printing house. He had Ewing reprint and export copies to Britain.[15] When Bell finally sent copies to Murray, but at

[12] JM to Thomas Ewing, 6 Apr. 1772.
[13] AL, p. 255.
[14] JM to Alex. Hamilton, 25 Oct. 1777.
[15] JM to Thomas Ewing, 27 Aug. 1774. The influence of the *Edinburgh Pharmacopoeia* for drug prescribing continued (through seven further editions) until 1864, when it was replaced

too high a price, Murray indignantly told him: 'You have ruined the sale of the Edinburgh Pharmacopoeia at my *House* by permitting Dilly [a London bookseller] to . . . sell it to the Trade at one penny per Book cheaper than you charged it to me'.[16]

Another better-known book that Murray sent in advance to Ewing was Samuel Johnson's *Journey to the Western Islands of Scotland* (1775). Strahan and Cadell published the London edition on 18 January, and Murray managed to get Ewing the printed sheets '2 days before the trade had it here', so that Ewing might be first off the mark with a Dublin reprint.[17] Murray's 'premium' (as he called it) for this service is not recorded. Afterwards he sent Johnson's pamphlet *Taxation no Tyranny* to Ewing together with other important works (such as Thomas Warton's *History of English Poetry*), through such 'clandestine' channels.[18] Although some-what apprehensive, he even tried to get a pre-publication copy of Hawkesworth's *Voyages*, a work for which Strahan and Cadell were said to have paid Hawkesworth six thousand guineas.[19] Supplying the Dublin trade with pre-publication copies was not in itself illegal, but the methods Murray employed might very well have been. He did not engage in genuine subterfuge very often. Such acts might be discovered and bring upon him the wrath of powerful London traders with whom he regularly dealt and on whom he largely depended. Murray's main goal was to create an Irish market for his own publications. However, he occasionally had to offer inducements.

In January 1774 Caleb Jenkin, another prominent Dublin bookseller, made overtures to Murray to establish a trading connection. Cautious, even suspicious, of the Dublin trade, Murray asked Ewing for a 'Character of this Gentleman'.[20] A few months later the two men met in Dublin: 'Being left alone with Mr. Jenkin . . . I explained to him the nature of our business with country customers, and acquainted him that I should be glad to deal . . . with such good men as himself provided I could draw for value at the

---

by the British Pharmacopoeia (*William Cullen and the Eighteenth Century Medical World*, eds. Doig, *et al.*, Edinburgh, 1993, p. 65).

[16] JM to John Bell, 31 Mar. 1775. A pharmacopoeia, as the name suggests, is a guide for druggists and apothecaries on dispensing.

[17] JM to Thomas Ewing, 14 Jan. 1775. Johnson's *Journey* was entered in the Stationers' Company Register on 13 Jan., half shares assigned by the author to Strahan and Cadell. As many as three Dublin editions of the work appeared in 1775. Indeed, Ewing may also have been associated with a pirate Irish edition intended for the London market under the fictitious imprint, 'London: Printed for J. Pope' (Pollard, p. 82). See also William B. Todd, 'The Printing of Johnson's *Journey*', in *Studies in Bibliography*, 6 (1954), pp. 247–54.

[18] JM to Thomas Ewing, 11 Mar. 1775. Murray received ten guineas for sending Ewing an edition of Johnson's *Dictionary* from which Ewing printed his 1775 quarto edition.

[19] JM to Thomas Ewing, 25 Apr. 1773 and 17 June 1774.

[20] JM to Thomas Ewing, 8 Feb. 1774.

end of every six months.'[21] Jenkin became one of Murray's regular and trusted correspondents, and this association led to others.

On a visit to Dublin in May 1775, Murray found Ewing in a poor state of health — 'so bad indeed that he had come to the resolution of selling off his stock & retiring. He is much emaciated,' added Murray, 'and when I leave Ireland I never expect to see him again.'[22] When Ewing died, Lawrence Flin assisted Murray in purchasing stock at Ewing's sale, and afterwards the two men regularly traded.[23] Gradually Murray had worked his way into the inner circles of the Dublin trade. Amongst those with whom he dealt regularly through the 1770s and 1780s were Thomas Armitage, John Exshaw, William Gilbert, Greuber & McAlister, William Halhead, James Hoey, M. Lynch, J. and William Porter, and Luke White. Even a member of the old guard like George Faulkner (and afterwards his nephew T. T. Faulkner) dealt with Murray. On one occasion Faulkner invited him to a Sunday meal so elegant that it included nine different dishes and four wines. Gazing upon the portraits of Dean Swift, Alexander Pope and Lord Chesterfield — men Faulkner had known personally — Murray drew this picture of his host in May 1775, just four months before Faulkner's death:

> Alderman Faulkner is past 60, of a diminutive size, and having a cork leg with which he rather hobbles than walks he appears shorter than he is. He is generous in his disposition, attentive to his guests, & hospitable at his table. In his transactions he is fair, and his reputation as far as I ever heard unblemished. He is possess'd of some information & his company by no means unentertaining. He has some blemishes which hardly arise to be faults. His manner is affected, which by the force of habit cannot now be laid aside. His acquaintance with Pope & Swift he is fond to remember; and desires you should believe he was of great importance with them. He seldom tells a story or relates an incident wherein Lord Chesterfield, the Duke of Bedford or other high characters with *himself* are not the heros in it, and he affects the tone & manners of a man of fashion.[24]

Other booksellers entertained Murray, if less grandly. He enjoyed the

[21]Diary, 12 May 1775.
[22]Diary, 2 May 1775.
[23]JM to Lawrence Flin, 16 Sept. 1776. The auction of Ewing's stock took place on 23 Sept. 1776. Among the books Murray requested Flin to get were forty copies of the quarto edition of Thomas Parnell's *Poems* (1773), twenty-five sets of Ewing's twelve-volume *Plays of Shakespeare* (1771), and twenty copies of Ewing's beautiful edition of John Ball's *Odes* (1772). Murray got copies of all but the *Odes* for just over £36 (JM to Lawrence Flin, 1 Oct. 1776).
[24]Diary, 7 May 1775. Faulkner invited Murray to other events, including a dinner for one hundred prominent civic men called the 'Sheriffs' Feast'. Richard Cumberland described a similar occasion in his *Memoirs* (London, 1808), p. 174, quoted in R. E. Ward, *Prince of Dublin Printers. The Letters of George Faulkner* (Lexington, Kentucky, 1972), pp. 29–30.

generosity of the Irish and was struck by the differences of national character and custom:

> Their hospitality to strangers is notoriously known; and their freedom with the bottle was in former times unbounded; and even now is under little restraint. In this they depart a little from the fashion of London, where a stranger in general is permitted to drink as he pleases. Not so at Dublin, where if a person is not careful Bumper after bumper is pressed upon him, 'till before he is aware he finds his head turn round. Nor can a liberal man find fault with a custom meant to shew hospitality & to promote Society.[25]

The 'Dublin Cartel'

When the Society of Dublin Booksellers was formed in January 1776, Murray became their London agent. The purpose of the Society, which he called the 'Dublin Cartel', was to regulate the supply of new London publications entering Ireland and, more generally, to protect and further the trade interests of its members.[26] For a yearly commission of seven guineas, Murray shipped orders on demand. An additional stipulation was of considerable importance: he charged the retail price for each book, or as he put it, 'Gentleman's prices'.[27] When Murray received the Society's first order, he promptly sent a parcel of novels and dramatic works amounting to nearly £32. Another order for over £26 followed a week later.[28] Before long Murray was sending new publications to individual members by every post, often sending parcels free of postage — a saving to the Irish trade — but as he charged 'Gentleman's prices', books had to be marked up accordingly in Dublin to make a profit. When the Dublin bookseller James Hoey applied to Murray independently for books in March 1776, he was told to join the Society if he wanted to be supplied.[29]

By June 1776 complaints about the expense of the articles compelled Murray to respond with a more acceptable arrangement. Keen to continue his agency and knowing that the Society had approached other London

---

[25]Diary, 13 July 1775.
[26]JM to Lawrence Flin, 15 Feb. 1776. A Society of Edinburgh Booksellers established itself in the same year (1776). John Bell, Charles Elliot, Creech and a number of Murray's other associates were original members. The Society was incorporated by a City Charter in 1792 and continues to this day. Its papers are deposited in the National Library of Scotland. See Richard B. Sher, 'Corporatism and Consensus in the Late Eighteenth-Century Book Trade: The Edinburgh Booksellers' Society in Comparative Perspective', in J. Rose (ed.), *Book History* (University Park, PA, 1998).
[27]JM to an unnamed correspondent, 25 Jan. 1776. Caleb Jenkin mediated the negotiation to retain Murray on these terms.
[28]JM to Caleb Jenkin, 10 Feb. 1776. AL, p. 228 (under Jenkin's account); DB2, p. 327 lists the entire first order.
[29]JM to James Hoey, 8 Apr. 1776.

booksellers, he presented a radically different plan. He offered to do all the business for 7.5 per cent of the prime (or wholesale) cost. For example, he would sell at 4s.4d. a book which would retail for 7s., provided the trader took at least six copies. If fewer were taken, the price rose to 4s.7d. — or a forty-five per cent discount for six or more copies and slightly less for fewer. Murray would, however, send books by ordinary means of trans-portation. Should the members of the Society require books to be sent by post (a far quicker method) the charge would remain at 'Gentleman's prices'. He also promised to be 'very punctual & faithful to their Interest, and, scrupulous to give them satisfaction', indicated that the 7.5 per cent commission was negotiable.[30] Murray set out these terms in his 'ostensible letter' to the Society. In a private letter to Jenkin he reiterated his genuine desire to continue his agency, adding: 'I hardly think they will be better supplied by another'. In closing, he reminded Jenkin: 'I should endeavour at all times to save them the expence of postage, as I think I have interest enough always to procure a sufficient number of covers for their use'.[31] Murray's plan, however, did not meet with the Society's approval, and, in August 1776, the Baldwins assumed the London agency. Letters from Dublin associates expressed concern about offending Murray, but he reas-sured them of his continued friendly regard. In fact he had made little profit relative to the effort invested on their behalf. The Baldwins' agency did not last. After them, John Wallis began to fill the Society's orders. But when Wallis went bankrupt in August 1778 Murray renewed his interest in providing for the Society. He sent a copy of his original 'Prime Cost' proposal, having determined that 'I can make no fairer one, to make me active in your business'.[32] This proposal was rejected yet again.

By November 1778, however, Murray was writing to a number of Dublin booksellers having heard 'that every bookseller in Dublin is now permitted to deal with his own correspondent'.[33] The 'Dublin Cartel' was no longer a collective purchasing body, and Murray readied himself to supply the Irish trade with individual orders for London publications, as he had done before. He also continued to publish jointly with Dublin booksellers. In 1779, for example, he and Luke White reissued three books about music that had recently been published: English translations of J. J. Rousseau's *Dictionnaire de musique* and Rameau's *Traité de l'harmonie*; and an abridgement of Alexander Malcolm's *Treatise of Musick*, which had first appeared in 1721.

Despite his reliable correspondents, Murray's Irish trade was rarely

[30]JM to Caleb Jenkin, 24 June 1776.
[31]JM to Caleb Jenkin, 24 June 1776 (second letter). Murray's friend at the Irish Post Office was Thomas Bond, who supplied him with free covers.
[32]JM to Caleb Jenkin, 14 Aug. 1778.
[33]JM to Luke White, 3 Nov. 1778.

straightforward and not always profitable. Booksellers typically settled
accounts by exchange of stock, but the Irish trade published little to sell
(at least legally) in the London market. Stocking a piracy in his shop would
anger the London bookseller who held the copyright. 'You will admit', he
informed Luke White, 'that you have sent me some books that I cannot
consistently either with Justice or my own safety expose to sale.'[34] He did,
however, sell many sets of White's Dublin edition of Gibbon's *Decline and
Fall*. Customs duties were another hazard. 'Formerly we escaped payment',
he told White, but when a parcel was charged duty of £2.5s. Murray had to
absorb the loss.[35] Further problems arose over Murray's 1792 edition of
Alexander Dow's *History of Hindostan*: 'The Commissioners have siezed
upon them entirely for a wrong entry. This transaction has cost me
much trouble; and more loss and I know not where to apply for relief'.[36]
Murray petitioned the Commissioners three times to return the books but
was refused. White, however, had agreed to 'run all risks and . . . land them
safe in Fleetstreet'.[37] The majority of Murray's trade with Ireland was
conducted legally. However, that shipments had been confiscated, whether
justly or not, suggests that there were others which had been smuggled in.[38]

Not all of Murray's Dublin correspondents were satisfied with his
efforts on their behalf, and Murray tried to answer their complaints: 'It
gives me pain that my method of supplying you should occasion your
murmuring. The truth is that trade admits little profit upon any books . . .
and I really think you should charge the freight & expences you pay to your
customers.'[39] Nor were all his Irish ventures profitable. The bankruptcies of
Flin and Halhead in 1781 left him considerably out of pocket. When
Richard Moncrieffe decided to cease trading with Murray in 1792 and
delayed settling an outstanding account, Murray responded with a mixture
of threats, supplication and self-righteous indignation:

> You will oblige me much and not permit a man who in acting by your own
> orders endeavoured what he could to serve you to be injured. . . . I request
> you only to do by me as you would be done by. After living with you . . . so
> long upon a friendly footing it would hurt me exceedingly to have this

[34]JM to Luke White, 13 Nov. 1783.
[35]Ibid.
[36]JM to Luke White, 22 June 1793.
[37]Samuel Highley to Luke White, 6 Jan. 1796. The matter was not resolved until 1796, after
Murray's death, when a foreign duty was paid and the books released.
[38]Murray discovered how difficult the customs' officers could be upon his return from
Ireland in Aug. 1775. When the ship docked at Holyhead, he refused to allow Customs'
officers to take away his belongings and demanded that the bags be searched in his presence.
Consequently, he and the other passengers were obliged to remain on board until the
following morning when they were summoned to the Customs' House (Diary, 27 Aug.
1775).
[39]JM to M. Lynch, 23 Mar. 1776.

correspondence interrupted. And as you are yourself a magistrate, you will I flatter myself act in your own person, as it is your duty & I hope your practice to inculcate upon others.[40]

Murray had told Moncrieffe that he 'would do every thing rather than come to extremities', but there was no room for compromise. This was the end of a twelve-year correspondence.

Instead of cash, Murray sometimes received books or other items from his Irish traders. Occasionally he accepted copies which he already had in stock or those which he claimed were 'good for little or nothing'. Rather than return them, he proposed a ten per cent reduction and told Caleb Jenkin, 'I offer this principally with a view of serving you, as I protest I would rather want them than have them'.[41] To make up for disadvantages of this kind, Murray exchanged books for other commodities. Dublin booksellers were then making huge profits selling Irish lottery tickets — some much more, in fact, than they made from books. Each ticket cost about £10, but shares of one sixty-forth were commonly bought and sold. Murray made a considerable amount of money as an agent, selling tickets in London and Edinburgh. He also supplied Irish booksellers with tickets for English lotteries, for which he demanded immediate payment, as credit could not be had either from the Lottery Office or from a broker.[42]

By the mid-1770s Murray was deeply enough involved in the Irish trade to need a representative in Dublin to handle his business affairs. This man was John Ormiston, a Scot from Kelso who had introduced the first iron foundry to Ireland.[43] When Ormiston visited Scotland in the summer of 1776, he met Murray's sister, Robina. After a short courtship they married on 1 September 1776 and went to Dublin to live with Ormiston's two sons from a previous marriage. Murray hesitated to trouble the industrialist with the everyday tasks of bookselling, but Ormiston seemed happy to oblige, and before long he was assisting with some of the more complicated

[40]JM to Richard Moncrieffe, 16 June 1792.
[41]JM to Caleb Jenkin, 9 Dec. 1776.
[42]JM to Richard Moncrieffe, 11 Sept. 1783. Luke White, the most successful of all the Irish lottery ticket sellers, entered upon a new scheme and sent tickets to London for Murray to sell. But as there were already a number of different lotteries in England, this one did not meet with public approval (JM to Luke White, 17 Nov. 1784). In 1780 State Lotteries had been instituted in Ireland, drawing on average £200,000 each year in prizes (C. L'Estrange Ewen, *Lotteries and Sweepstakes*, pp. 337–44).
[43]JM to John Ormiston, 11 Dec. 1786. Ormiston and his partners were granted a royal patent to protect their substantial investment. Impressed with Ormiston's ingenuity, Murray remarked that he 'has been the means of saving to the country that article of importation and of employing many idle hands' (Diary, 5 June 1775). Ormiston's success was such that he sought Murray's assistance to establish an export market in Britain. However, Murray guessed rightly that the high duty charged would 'be equal to a prohibition' (ibid.). For a contemporary account of the topic see William Gibbons, *A Reply to Sir Lucius O'Brien, Bart. . . . [on] the present state of the Iron Trade between England and Ireland is considered* (Bristol, 1785).

negotiations with the Irish trade. However, in the mid-1780s, Ormiston ran into financial difficulties at his foundry which so preoccupied him that he turned over responsibility for Murray's affairs to his son, Archibald.

Publishing Irish Authors

While in Dublin Murray became acquainted with a number of authors and not long after began to publish editions of their works. Michael Kearney, the Professor of History at Trinity College, told his bookseller, William Halhead, that he wanted Murray to publish the London edition of his *Lectures concerning History* (1776).[44] Murray wanted to be sure that the London edition of a work appeared before the Irish one, as a book first printed in Ireland, under copyright law, became common property in Britain. Any London bookseller might then put out a rival edition. And none knew better than Murray that secrecy was essential to prevent copies of the printed sheets being sent surreptitiously to London.

From the mid-1770s Murray successfully published the works of other Irish writers: medical books by William Dease, Charles Quin, George Renny, Edmund Cullen and Robert Scott; Gerald Fitzgerald's poem, the *Injured Islanders*, Gast's *History of Greece*; Sylvester O'Halloran's *History of Ireland*; Felix O'Gallagher's scientific and philosophical works; and Joseph Stock's formative biography of George Berkeley. When the distance between Murray and his authors led to complications, he was able to call on the assistance of Irish booksellers: 'Submit my proposition to some person versed in such business', Murray told Edward Cullen during a disagreement over fair payment. 'Luke White . . . is esteemed a Gentleman of knowledge in his profession, and were it convenient for you to consult him I am confident he would give you his sentiments without reserve.'[45] Disputes inevitably arose, but on the whole Murray worked well with Irish authors, profited from the sale of their works and gave them satisfaction.

In Belfast the book trade was much smaller than in Dublin. Nevertheless, Murray established connections there from 1773. He dealt with John Magee not only in books, but also in lottery tickets and other commodities. However, their dealings were not especially profitable.[46] Even less remunerative was his trade with John Hay, who did not settle his bill in full.[47]

[44]JM to Wm Halhead, 15 and 17 Feb. 1776. When Murray was in Dublin in 1775 he met Kearney at his apartments in Trinity College and described him as a man 'who is equally agreeable for his extensive learning and mildness of manners' (Diary, 17 June 1775).
[45]JM to Edmund Cullen, 6 Nov. 1788.
[46]JM to John Magee, 18 Jan. 1774, and many letters following; AL, pp. 205 and 257.
[47]JM to John Hay, 18 Jan. 1774 and 20 Jan. 1776; AL, pp. 78, 88 and 119.

Murray's friend, Robert Apsley, a surgeon in Belfast, did his best to ensure what little trade he had there ran smoothly.[48]

By various means — some legitimate, others less so — Murray found a worthwhile trading niche in Ireland. He came to mutually advantageous terms with members of the trade, both individually and, for a time, collectively as the London agent for the Society of Dublin Booksellers. He also published a number of Irish authors in a range of fields. There is little evidence that cheap Irish reprints of his works were sold in any considerable numbers in Britain, but there were many occasions when Irish reprints affected the sales of his exported London editions.

Murray's trade in Ireland was smaller and less profitable than his business in Scotland, but it was less fraught with difficulties. He shared publications with Creech, Elliot, Bell and others, but he also had to compete with them for authors. Murray regarded these men primarily as rivals — despite partnerships in many publications. He was determined to outsmart his fellow countrymen. It was not an easy formula for doing business, but he believed it was necessary. In Ireland Murray faced a different set of problems. He needed to understand the way Irish book-sellers worked and find ways to entice them to do business with him. He had everything to gain and little to lose. Different laws and a wholly different notion of literary property worked to his advantage. In 1772 Murray published Stephen Adye's *Considerations on the Act for Punishing Mutiny and Desertion*, his first book to include both a Dublin and Edinburgh correspondent in the imprint — the ideal publishing arrangement since it maximised provincial sales and minimised the risk of an unauthorised reprint. The imprint reads: 'London: printed for J. Murray; Kincaid & Creech, Edinburgh; and T. Ewing, Dublin'. This was the usual imprint for his early catalogues and for periodical works such as the *Medical Commentaries* and the *Edinburgh Magazine and Review*, but for no others. More often Murray's arrangements with Irish traders can not be discerned from an imprint.

Murray presumably fared better than most London booksellers of the day in tapping into the growing Irish trade, though there is very little documentation for such an assessment. The arrangements he made, and the prosperity of Irish booksellers generally, was relatively short-lived; the extension of the Copyright Act to Ireland in 1801, after the Act of Union, removed the autonomy the Irish booksellers had enjoyed. The reprint became illegal — a radical change reducing the Irish trade to doing little more than selling imported books.

[48]JM to Robert Apsley, 8 Jan. 1776.

— 8 —

Family Matters

Nancy

The thirteen-year marriage between Nancy Weemss and John Murray was passionate and tumultuous, characterised more by stressful periods of separation than by scenes of domestic tranquillity. Murray described his wedding anniversary (the third of March) as 'my Thraldom day', and indeed their marriage sometimes felt more like a bond of slavery than of love.[1] Moreover, they were unable to produce children, and this must have been a cause of frustration and regret. Murray had frequent dealings with prostitutes in London and other cities. He also fathered an illegitimate child, named Archibald, whose existence he did not hide from Nancy and whom he supported and regularly visited. Murray even alluded to this when he told the Reverend William Enfield: 'I pray for your success in begetting all Legitimate Children. I would not be churlish tho unsuccessfull my self.'[2] When this son had come of age, Murray, advising him about the ways of the world and of married life in particular, remarked: 'A woman of sagacity keeps up the flame of desire in her husband; whenever *that* is extinguished she is considered with indifference and her society little coveted'.[3]

The first period of unavoidable separation between John and Nancy (when Murray went to Scotland for eighteen months in 1764) set an unfortunate precedent. He kept promising to return, and she built upon these hopes only to be cast down by his innumerable delays. Extended journeys to Ireland in the early 1770s caused Nancy further unhappiness: 'A few weeks may be past by one self but months will never do', she told him. 'Had I the least grain of sense, or prudence I should have thought so before

---

[1] JM to Wm Paxton, 25 Dec. 1774.
[2] JM to Wm Enfield, 14 Sept. 1775. If Murray, like many of his contemporaries, had contracted venereal disease, he would have known medical men to whom he might discreetly apply for a cure. And as the publisher of works on the subject, he was well placed to study the latest remedies.
[3] JM to Archie Murray, 7 Sept. 1791.

you left me but I flatter'd my self your stay would not exceed six weeks.'[4] He, on the other hand, seemed to enjoy himself on these trips: 'How come you go to the Theatre at Dublin twice', she demanded, 'when you will not allow your self to go to the one here with the greatest entreaties?'[5]

The playhouse was not Murray's only entertainment. While visiting Belfast in the autumn of 1771 he had a more than casual flirtation, and even wrote to Nancy about his affection for one Jane Ann Burgess. Nancy was inconsolable, and their friend Archy Paxton was appalled at Murray's extremely frank account of his behaviour. Although Paxton hesitated to involve himself in 'the Quarrels of Man and Wife', he charged Murray with unfeeling audacity for suggesting the young woman come back with him to London: 'You have acted cruelly not only by her [Nancy] but also by the young Lady. How absurd! to think that Mrs Murray could possibly be happy with having a person in the house, who had formerly and still seems to make an impression on your heart.'[6] The visit was cancelled, but a flirtatious correspondence continued: 'Had somethings you wrote' Jane Ann told him, ' . . . come from the pen of an unmarried gentelman I should certainly rally him for it, but from the person who wrote me I must not take that Liberty'.[7] Nancy's outrage over this flirtation manifested itself in illness, so serious at one stage that the doctors were called in to apply a 'blister'. Paxton impressed upon Murray the importance of returning soon, not only for the sake of his marriage but to prevent losing 'what little Business you have'. Few customers were visiting the shop while he was away. Paxton demanded further to know why Murray had not employed an agent to handle the sale of the Irish estate. During his absences, Nancy helped to manage the shop, and their assistants worked diligently, but she reported that 'we take but little'.[8] To occupy herself and, perhaps, to hasten his return by incurring expenses, Nancy had the shop redecorated, and made 'very handsome'.[9]

Although Murray's London business suffered from his frequent visits to Ireland in the early 1770s, he did establish profitable associations with members of the book trade there. Nor did he wholly forget his wife. While lying in the bed of his Dublin lodgings one night, pining after her, he composed 'a little song . . . in honour of my dear Mrs M'.

> A zone of flowers I fondly placed,
> Around my Nancy's Beauteous waste! [*sic*]
> But by her cruel hands unbound
> Sudden she threw it to the ground.

[4] Nancy Murray to JM, 18 June 1775.
[5] Ibid.
[6] Arch. Paxton to JM, 13 Dec. 1771.
[7] Jane Ann Burgess to JM, [no date] Nov. 1772.
[8] Nancy Murray to JM, 10 June 1775.
[9] Nancy Murray to JM, 21 Oct. 1775.

With bracelets next I strove to move
The precious fair one to my love.
The ornaments she turned around
And dropped the baubles on the ground.

. . .

'Ah cruel fair'! But here she cried
'My mind no more I'll strive to hide
'No gifts of gold to me impart
'The gift I love's my Husband's heart.'[10]

Murray admired his poetical effort. He even sent the verses to a friend,
adding the humorous remark that their applicability to any woman 'with the
change of a couple of words' makes them more valuable 'as a medicine is,
whose efficacy extends to all disorders, and can be prescribed with equal
success in a Diabetes or a Dropsy'.[11] It was not the most romantic simile,
but such was the economy of Murray's love. The poem was perhaps more a
reflection of his wishes than of the actions of Nancy, who would have liked
'gifts of gold' as well as her husband's love and fidelity.

Murray struggled to resist temptation. Yet, while Nancy was ill, lonely
and, without her husband, much restricted in her socialising, he was
indulging in pleasures of all kinds in Dublin. In a diary he kept during
these travels, he recorded an evening's activities:

> Had a fine dinner, consisting of boiled chickens, boiled neck of mutton,
> roast ducks, quarter of lamb, ham sallad, pease & asparagus, for which we
> were charged 2/6 each. Drank about six bottles claret . . . and before I went
> home had a frolic of my own which if not attended with ugly consequences
> I shall be happy.[12]

The next morning Murray repented having drunk too much and 'resolved
not to drive so hard'. It was not long, however, before another evening of
debauchery produced some unexpected and 'ugly consequences':

> Drank six bottles wine, which it seems intoxicated me uncommonly. At
> twelve o'clock I went away in a chair, but broke from it in Essex street &
> ran after some girls in Crampton Court. . . . I rambled in the streets for 2
> hours, at which time I discovered that my watch was gone. This event
> brought me a little to my senses. But I had no remembrance where I lost it.
> I went into no house. So that in all probability it was picked from my pocket
> on my first sally into Crampton Court (see Plate 34).[13]

Murray recalled little of his frolic, but was fortunate enough to recover his
watch. A soldier who visited the prostitute the same night was suspicious

---

[10]Diary, 1 May 1775. The other stanzas of Murray's poem merely expand upon the theme.
[11]JM to Robert Apsley, 20 Jan. 1776.
[12]Diary, 27 May 1775.
[13]Diary, 24 June 1775.

and took it from her. Murray's advertisement in the papers the following day alerted the soldier to its owner. Though embarrassed to have put himself in such a position, there was no suggestion that it effected any reform. Suspicions that Nancy was herself flirting prompted Murray to write in the harshest terms. She responded boldly to his accusations: 'Good god your ungenerous Letter kills me, & strikes deep to the heart that never yet deceived you or was since your absence otherwise employed than in my attention to your shop & house'.[14] But Nancy was in reality so upset, her nerves so agitated, that she wished to put an end to her 'miserable existence'.[15] The longer he was away the worse matters became. Their reunions, however, did not always realise expectations of happiness.

Frequent and often extended visits from Nancy's sister Hester provided companionship during Murray's absences and, when they were all together, a happy family atmosphere usually prevailed. At Christmas time, especially, there were jovial scenes at 32 Fleet Street in the company of the Paxtons and other old friends. Writing in a jolly mood to Thomas Gardiner, a friend in Jamaica, Murray reported at the end of 1774: 'My Nancy and her sister . . . bid me to tell you that Miss Weemss remains unmarried and Mrs. Murray says that whenever you come home again and make decent, that is proper, proposals for her sister you shall be entitled to her best interest. Miss W[eemss] at this turns her nose up & exclaims "Lard, Mr. M[urray] you are very odd, what will Mr G[ardine]r think now."'[16]

During Murray's second visit to Ireland in the summer of 1772, Nancy visited his sisters in Edinburgh. She was unwell for much of the time and complained of pain in her side. William Cullen, the most eminent physician in Edinburgh, was called in to attend her. Although the results of the examination were not an immediate cause for alarm, Cullen did diagnose 'some tendency to a consumption'.[17] The doctor advised horseback riding, which Nancy enjoyed and from which she seemed to benefit. However, after a further consultation, Cullen's opinion was less favourable: 'He thought her always delicate but thinks her more so now,' Elizabeth Gilliland told her brother in September 1772.[18] Cullen advised Nancy to leave Edinburgh before the damp weather set in. 'We was vexed at this', Elizabeth added, 'because you wanted her to stay.' Nancy could be a demanding guest and a fretful patient. Binny McMurray, who was unwell herself, wrote frankly to her brother in Ireland to complain about her sister-in-law: 'Poor Scotland gets the blame for every thing that now ails her'; and added, 'you know very well her temper.'[19]

---

[14]Nancy Murray to JM, 26 Aug. 1775.
[15]Ibid. Nancy signed the letter 'the most unhappy woman that breathes'.
[16]JM to Thomas Gardiner, 26 Dec. 1774.
[17]Eliz. Gilliland to JM, 29 Aug. 1772.
[18]Eliz. Gilliland to JM, 17 Sept. 1772.
[19]Binny McMurray to JM, 24 Oct. 1772.

Accustomed by her upbringing to attention and indulgence, Nancy had gradually to adjust to the responsibilities of being a tradesman's wife. Her fondness for finery, especially clothing, was restrained by her modest circumstances. Rather than apportion her an allowance, Murray gave her money on demand. She ran the house and satisfied her own personal wants on about 125 guineas a year — a relatively modest sum for the time.[20] On one occasion, when Murray was in Ireland, Nancy displayed good sense and uncommon courage. In the course of a ride with friends in the countryside the coach was overtaken by robbers:

> I can assure you I have highly entertain'd every one at the trick I play'd the highwayman. They all say I had great presence of mind. . . . The moment the highwayman presented his pistol in the coach, and whilst the rest delivered their money — I untied my purse, took out my guineas and put in its place a halfpenny then tied it in two hard nots & gave it him, he asked if he had got all we had. I told him yes & to go away as the Lady . . . was much frightened. . . . As soon as Mr & Mrs Whitaker and the other gentleman was recover'd from their fright they all laught very much at my coolness and thought.[21]

However much such an event lifted her spirits, Murray's absence still depressed her. She even went so far as to tell him: 'I positively believe these frequent journeys to Ireland . . . will in the end prove the destruction of my Health if not my life'.[22]

When Murray finally returned in September 1775 after several months' absence, he found his wife much weakened. Although Nancy struggled through a particularly damp and cold winter, in the spring her consumptive condition worsened. In July Murray took the desperate measure of transporting her to Rochester for the fresher country air. There she showed no sign of improvement, and by the middle of August it was clear she would not recover. She lingered for another month, often in a fevered and delirious state, until 22 September, when Murray recorded in his diary: 'At a quarter before nine o'clock at night my virtuous and innocent wife expired'. Five days later she was interred, as she had requested, in the same grave as her mother, at the churchyard of St Mary Magdalen, the Gillingham parish church, near Brompton. Murray and seven other mourners attended the service. Nancy's father and sister, Hester, were too distraught to be there. Two days later Murray left Rochester with his sister-in-law, and, after passing the night at Dartford, arrived in London. Friends and associates came to Fleet Street to offer their condolences. One even wrote a commemorative

---

[20]Nancy was given five guineas each fortnight (AL, loose sheet at p. 131 for the account of Arch. Paxton, from whom she received money while JM was away).

[21]Nancy Murray to JM, 19 May 1775. Whitaker, a lawyer, was the brother of John, the historian.

[22]Nancy Murray to JM, 18 June 1775.

Latin inscription for the gravestone reflecting on the timeless beauty of Nancy, which Murray 'perused . . . with melancholy pleasure': 'Quicquid denique agebat / Subsequebatur Decor' (Whatever she undertook, finally, beauty followed her).[23]

The death of Nancy, in spite of all their trials, was a severe blow — a loss which, he believed, 'I can never repair'.[24] He became despondent about bookselling, but it was impossible to avoid pressing responsibilities: 'I am fatigued from morning to night', he wrote some months later, 'about twopenny matters, if any of which is forgot I am complained of as a man who minds not his business. I pray heaven for a lazy & lucrative office, & then I shall with alacrity turn my shop out of the window.'[25] But by throwing himself into work, Murray began to recover. And the company of Hester, just eighteen months younger than Nancy, rekindled his appetite for living.

Sisters

Murray was very fond of two of his three sisters — Elizabeth and Binny. His relationship with Jenny, by contrast, was difficult and often argumentative. The distance between Edinburgh and London prevented his seeing them often, but he corresponded with Elizabeth and Binny regularly, and with Jenny when necessary. After the death of their father in October 1768, the burden of family financial affairs fell largely upon Murray's shoulders, even if the day-to-day matters could be handled by William Kerr, his dependable Edinburgh associate.[26] Robert had divided his small estate equally among his unmarried daughters, each inheriting a few hundred pounds and a share in the property at Bailie Clerk's Land. John received just £60, with the rather threatening proviso that he either renounce any further claim or lose that sum entirely. Rather more generously Robert added, 'in case the said John McMurray shall behave in an affectionate & brotherly manner to his sisters, I recommend to them to give him forty pounds more'.[27] John was satisfied with the settlement, and told Kerr that if his sisters' proportion did not turn out considerably larger than his own, he would relinquish all claim to the additional £40.[28]

[23]Quoted in JM to Gilbert Stuart, 12 Oct. [misdated Sept.] 1776. George Stuart, Gilbert's father, wrote the Latin inscription and Gilbert translated it into English verse (JM to George Stuart, 12 Oct. 1776). Apart from these lines, the inscription is not known.
[24]JM to General Robert Gordon, 27 Oct. 1776.
[25]Ibid.
[26]Robert McMurray died of a palsy on 29 Oct. 1768 in his seventy-first year. He was buried beside his wife near the west window of Greyfriars' kirk, Edinburgh (Old Parish Records, Edinburgh).
[27]Robert McMurray's will, Scottish Record Office, CC8/8/121/1, registered 30 March 1769.
[28]JM to Wm Kerr, 29 Nov. 1768.

Murray's sisters were all independent-minded unmarried women who were living comfortably on the modest means left to them by their father. Even though Murray was not overly concerned about their situation, he was pleased to learn not long after their father's death that Elizabeth, the eldest, had become engaged to James Gilliland, the well-to-do Edinburgh jeweller (see Plate 2b). On 5 February 1769, just a few weeks before her thirty-eighth birthday, they were married.[29] Murray sent the couple an elaborate Delft china service, with a letter containing flattering remarks about his sister. Thanking him, she remarked: 'You have drawn a character so much above all I can deserve that I must sit down in despair of ever coming near it'.[30] However, Elizabeth could read between the lines of her brother's compliments and tell him: 'You have a very delicate way of giving advice & by telling a person what they are you very genteely insinuate what they ought to be'.[31] Murray also held Gilliland in high esteem, more so because this new brother-in-law could be depended upon to manage some of his Edinburgh bookselling activities. 'There are few men', he told Gilliland, 'I wish to live longer than you, both for your own sake & that of your family.'[32]

When Elizabeth moved out, quarrels which had been simmering between Binny and Jenny exploded. Murray was called upon to referee. His immediate concern, however, was for Binny's health, which had always been uncertain and since the death of her father had grown worse. My leaving her', Elizabeth reflected, 'has unfortunately added to it. You know there was always much more friendship betwixt her & me than what subsisted betwixt J[enny] & any of us. . . . They do not think you interest yourself so much about them & there [*sic*] affairs as they cou'd wish. You will say this is being captious. But you must remember they have nobody except you.'[33] Murray wrote mollifying letters, but to little effect: Binny's health worsened and Jenny, unhappy as a maiden, continued to behave selfishly. If he had not appreciated the degree of their mutual antipathy, a letter from Elizabeth in April 1769 removed any doubt: 'They are soon to part now; & we never must permit them to go together again if we have not a mind to lose Binny'.[34]

---

[29]In a letter to Murray dated 4 Feb. 1769, Binny reported the marriage settlement between Elizabeth and James Gilliland: 'Mr G gets . . . one hundred and fifty pounds sterling of my sisters mon[e]y to which he obldges himself to add three hundred pounds to be laid out to the best advantage for my sister in liferent and the children of the marriage'. This arrangement was intended to protect Elizabeth in the event of Gilliland's death, at which time his entire estate would pass on to a daughter by a previous marriage named Kitty. However, the young girl died two years later in March 1771.
[30]Eliz. Gilliland to JM, 8 Mar. 1769.
[31]Ibid.
[32]JM to James Gilliland, 15 May 1783.
[33]Eliz. Gilliland to JM, 8 Mar. 1769.
[34]Eliz. Gilliland to JM, 6 Apr. 1769.

Meanwhile Jenny went to the west of Scotland to find a husband. She stayed with John Cunningham, the brewer, and his wife but moved elsewhere when it was discovered that this woman was having an affair with Cunningham's brother. Unlucky in her own search for a partner, she penned critical remarks to her brother about the Glaswegian company she was keeping:

> Affability and Politeness, I assure you, constitutes no part of the Glasgow Peoples character, at least if I may judge from those I have seen of them, but their money makes up all the defects of that kind. Grand houses, rich furniture & expensive cloths are just the thing in this part of the world, without either taste or elegance. In short I'm quite disgusted with finery, a lucky disgust you may say for me.[35]

While in the west of Scotland, Jenny visited her aunt and cousins at Maybole, where she learnt the news that the only son of her wealthy uncle, James Ross, had died.[36] His nieces and nephews were now heirs to a valuable estate in Ireland believed to be worth more than £10,000. Moreover, their uncle was infirm and could not be expected to live many more years.

The prospect of an inheritance alone improved the standard of living and lifted the marital hopes of Jenny and Binny. By February 1772 they were sufficiently reconciled to move together to a large flat in Edinburgh's splendid New Town. Murray cautioned against this extravagance; the annual rent of £22 was more than they could afford before the sale of the Irish estate was certain. But his sisters' enthusiasm was uncontainable: 'Next time you come to Scotland', Binny told him, 'we will have an apartment for you. And in the place where all the great people stay.'[37] Once Binny and Jenny settled into the fashionable part of town, and the rumour went out that they were to be heiresses, suitors appeared at their door. Jenny was hasty in her choice of James Finlay for a husband. He and his brother John had grown up with the MacMurray family, but all was not well with the Finlay brothers.[38] In 1771 Murray had counselled John to 'overcome your inclinations for liquor', telling him 'this curs'd vice that has hitherto pursued you like a demon to your ruin.'[39] Finlay's troubles were such that he ultimately had to flee Britain. Nor did Murray realise when he approved the marriage (which took place on 28 October 1773), that James likewise had his share of troubles. Binny had also expressed her approval,

[35]Jenny McMurray to JM, 9 Aug. 1769.
[36]Eliz. Gilliland to JM, 10 Oct. 1769.
[37]Binny McMurray to JM, 1 Feb. 1771. The flat was in Princes Street.
[38]Murray had remarked in 1767 that Finlay's father, James Sr, was 'a disinterested friend to my father and his family' (JM to James Finlay Sr, 8 Aug. 1767).
[39]JM to John Finlay, 18 Mar. 1771.

believing Jenny 'would be one of the happiest of women as there was no man I had a better oppinion than . . . Mr Finlay'.[40]

James Finlay was a widower with a son and daughters. His dominating children took an immediate dislike to their quick-tempered stepmother. He was also impatient over the delay in settling the Irish estate, expecting to receive about £100 a year in interest on Jenny's share. Before two years were out he openly told his wife 'that he ought not to have married at all'.[41] Elizabeth described him as 'a low spirit'd & . . . foolish man', and Binny added that 'I shall never forgive myself for pressing her to it'.[42] William Kerr's reports to Murray were even more alarming: '[Finlay] provoked her to get out of bed at 5 in the morning two different times. . . . And besides she is troubled with a peculiar disorder — she lately passed some live worms.'[43] Murray did not hesitate to intervene as the affair reached a crisis: 'Whether F[inlay] is mad, or, whether more unhappily for my Sister, he had laid a deep and infernal design to prove her health by continued and unremitted cruelty, is one and the same thing. It is time', he told Kerr, '. . . some spirited measures [are] taken for the relief of our sister.' Murray recommended that Jenny get witnesses to her husband's 'acts of tyranny', asserting that 'the Laws of her Country will afford her proper redress: if Scotland will not, she is certain of relief here'.[44] Plans were made to draw up a new marriage contract — a legal bond formalising a separation and ensuring that neither Finlay nor his children could touch Jenny's anticipated Irish inheritance. By the time Murray arrived in Edinburgh to negotiate the terms, he could only lament that little was to be expected and a great deal to be feared from Finlay. At this time Jenny was in a suicidal condition.[45]

By the terms of the new settlement Finlay kept control of the money he was given at their marriage, and agreed to allow Jenny £30 each year, which Murray sardonically referred to as 'pin-money'.[46] It was a disadvantageous arrangement, but Murray saw no other way to extricate his sister from her misery. Publicly he appeared satisfied, but privately he was indignant over the paltry sum and told Kerr so: 'For heaven sake what would he allow a mistress? or a servant were he to keep either of these in her place'.[47] Jenny's immediate troubles were alleviated, but she could only remarry if Finlay were to die. Her Irish inheritance, when it came through, gave her enviable financial security, but this was all. There had never been much warmth between Jenny and her brother. The Finlay affair only made matters worse.

[40]Binny McMurray to JM, 25 Feb. 1774.
[41]Eliz. Gilliland to JM, 28 May 1774.
[42]Eliz. Gilliland to JM, 16 Feb. 1774; Binny McMurray to JM, 25 Feb. 1774.
[43]Wm Kerr to JM, 10 Dec. 1774.
[44]JM to Wm Kerr, 15 Dec. 1774.
[45]Eliz. Gilliland to JM, 28 May 1774.
[46]JM to Wm Kerr, 15 Dec. 1774.
[47]Ibid.

A few years later he reflected on their relationship: 'She has behaved to me for sometime past without either affection, or almost common civility. But this I regard less than settling her fortune for her advantage.'[48] Jenny had not lost her spirit of independence and insisted on controlling her finances. Although still wary of James Finlay claiming the money, Murray reluctantly turned over the funds in August 1779. In 1786, seven years later, he unburdened himself of accumulated resentment after Jenny had drawn upon him for money without his permission and at a time when she knew he was short of funds: 'Your behaviour to *me* has for some years been pointedly unnatural, & is confirmed by your present intention of distressing me'. And he wrote in a letter to her — which he did not send — telling her with no small degree of irony to remit the bills at Edinburgh and free her mind 'from the alarm it must have suffered . . . from your fears of my insolvency'.[49] From this time there was little affection, indeed communication, between them.

Murray's relationship with Binny, grounded in love, good humour and shared interests, was markedly warmer. Where Elizabeth was maternal and Jenny competitive, Binny was, as she said herself, a 'sincere friend & affectionate sister'.[50] When Murray had been badly bitten by a dog in a London street, and was confined to his bed, he remarked: 'To make Biny easy tell her I have not yet begun to bark'.[51] None took more of an interest in Murray's literary efforts than Binny, who offered opinions on works like 'Sir Launcelot Edgevile' and encouraged him to write more: 'Pray, has not your fertile imagination produced nothing this winter', she asked in December 1770. 'I should be glad to know whether you have consulted the Comick or Tragick muse and likewise to see any of your performances. But none of your polliticks for I hate them.'[52] Murray regularly sent her the latest publications from London and she commented on them by way of thanks.[53]

Binny could also be depended upon to handle business matters diplomatically. In 1773, for instance, she met with William Wilson to arrange for a letter of introduction to the physician William Hunter. Binny told her brother how to win over Hunter and offered to help: 'I have got for you six old coins all Scottish', she reported to her brother, 'and have showed them to Mr Wilson . . . who says a present of them will have more effect on Doctor Hunter than any letter whatever. These coins I got some weeks ago thinking they might be of service to you in this very way.'[54] Binny's strategy

[48]JM to Wm Kerr, 29 June 1779.
[49]JM to Jenny Finlay, 31 May 1786.
[50]Binny's usual salutation.
[51]JM to John Ormiston, 27 Dec. 1784. It was a serious wound which greatly impaired his ability to walk and took over five months to heal.
[52]Binny McMurray to JM, 13 Dec. 1770.
[53]Binny McMurray to JM, 26 Jan. 1771.
[54]Binny McMurray to JM, 24 May 1773.

worked. Not only did Murray become one of the few London booksellers
to sell Hunter's landmark publication, the *Anatomy of the Gravid Uterus* in
1774, but he later co-published Hunter's own *Medical Commentaries* in 1777
and even the impressive catalogue of Hunter's coin collection in 1782.

The only occasions for friction between Murray and his sister Binny were
over romantic matters. First, there had been Murray's troubles with Nancy,
who had confided in Binny during a visit to London in 1770. Binny insisted
on having a private correspondence with her sister-in-law to discuss the
situation freely. And she was equally frank when she wrote to her brother:

> My dear John you must excuse me but I must repeat what I told you befor
> in person that many of these disagreable disputes which I have seen I
> generaly thought more owing to you than to her (Not that I think she
> was not sometimes to blame) but had you behaved to her with that respect
> and tenderness and esteem every husband ought to a wife it would have
> prevented these rustick freedoms which always leave a sting behind.[55]

Although it hurt Murray to be confronted, he knew his sister had his
interest at heart. It piqued his pride, but not so much that Binny regretted
her peacemaking: 'I am extremely sory any thing I have wrote should
offend you so much as you seem to be in your last. Indeed from it I
have reason to think your anger prevented you either from reading or from
seeing what you did read.'[56] Binny urged her brother to meet his responsibilities, and he listened.

When her own personal situation was at issue, she was equally forceful
in her views. In 1775, for example, her sisters were pressuring her to accept
the offer of marriage by a certain 'Mr B' and had even enlisted the support
of their brother. Her health suffering under what she termed 'cruel' treatment, Binny told her brother why she had refused to acquiesce.

> It is me not them that is to live with the person and while (I thank God) I
> can live independent I will marrie no man but what is agreeable to me. . . . I
> give you my promise never to marrie any man whatever without first
> informing you of it, but at same time I wont promise to be entirely
> determined by your opinion.[57]

Binny's decision to marry John Ormiston the following year pleased Murray
who, after all, had made the introduction after meeting Ormiston in Dublin:
'She has advertured in the matrimonial Lottery', Murray told their cousin,
'and if she has drawn a prize her friends will receive pleasure for her sake'.[58]

[55] Binny McMurray to JM, 8 Sept. 1770.
[56] Ibid. When Binny wrote the original letter (quoted in part above) she concluded it: 'I know
you will be very angry with me and even curse and damn and very likely wish I had never
come to London' (8 Sept. 1770).
[57] Binny McMurray to JM, 12 Jan. 1775.
[58] JM to Eliz. Crawford, 16 Jan. 1777.

Ormiston already had two sons and a daughter by a previous marriage, and Murray later used his connections to start the boys in careers with the East India Company. The birth of Binny's son — named Robert Murray Ormiston after 'my late worthy father' — and afterwards of a daughter, were occasions of great joy.[59] Reunions were infrequent after Binny moved to Dublin.[60] Nevertheless, Murray and his sister wrote regularly. When she fell a letter in arrears, he remarked to her husband: 'Tell Binny that her intentions of writing to me by a private hand who disappointed her is no excuse for silence whilst the post office is open.'[61]

The Irish Inheritance

The inheritance of their uncle's estate in Ireland was an event of unparalleled importance in the lives of Murray and his sisters. There were five other heirs — an aunt and four first cousins. The burden of settling this complex and time-consuming affair fell to Murray, the only male among the nine heirs. He was assisted by William Kerr, in whom he had absolute trust, and by an assortment of Irish, Scottish and English lawyers whose probity was suspect and whose services were expensive.

When James Ross died in 1769 Murray began the long process of selling the Mount Ross estate.[62] Located about twenty miles south-east of Belfast near the town of Portaferry, it was a beautiful freehold, set on the coast, with an abundance of harvestable seaweed and peat together with acres of arable land rented by tenant farmers. Proximity to the principal trading towns and a deep harbour were other notable selling points.[63] The transfer of such a substantial property presented many legal problems, and Murray, unfamiliar with Irish law and responsible to eight anxious heirs, faced many challenges in the three years it took to complete the sale. First, he had to be appointed receiver of the rents by the Irish Court of Exchequer; then arrangements had to be made to collect and divide this income, which amounted to over £500 a year.[64] At an early stage James Savage, the son of a man who had owned Mount Ross before Murray's uncle, made a claim to

[59]JM to John Ormiston, 4 June 1777. On 21 June 1783 Binny had a girl named Emmy.
[60]In response to an invitation from Binny to visit her Dublin home, Murray lamented: 'My situation here will not permit me to accept' (JM to Jenny Finlay, 23 June 1781). On another occasion a visit of the Ormistons to London had to be cancelled.
[61]JM to John Ormiston, 1 Mar. 1785.
[62]James Ross, the brother of Murray's mother, Jean, had bought the estate in 1748. According to a document in the Public Record Office of Northern Ireland (D.552/b/3/2/193), it included the towns and lands of Ballyfuneragh, Balycam, Corrage; one quarter of the town and lands of Ballbranigan, of Berry, Ballgarvigan, Ballyhendry, Bally Harley, and the Mill of Ballyharley; all in the Barony of Ards and County of Down.
[63]JM to Wm Gallway, 19 Apr. 1773.
[64]JM to Hellen Kennedy, after 10 Nov. 1772.

the property. Murray was assured that Savage's claim was unfounded, but there was no avoiding the additional legal fees a refutation of his claim would involve.[65] Moreover, there was fear that a pending Irish land tax bill would considerably reduce the sale price. This bill did not become law, but it did cause delay.[66] Murray's sisters knew he was working hard on the sale, but his aunt and cousins were often impatient. To William Gallway, a friend of their late uncle who lived in Portaferry and helped with the sale, Murray explained the pressures under which he worked: 'Mr Rosses Heirs had begun to want money and to complain of the delay made as if I had some private views in putting off the sale; and Individuals of them had got married and the rest I suppose were impatient to be so'.[67] At one point his aunt even hired lawyers to ensure that Murray was acting fairly — an affront which he did not take lightly. Nor was he pleased when they refused to let him see the lawyer's report which he was told 'she got . . . for her own privet satisfaction'.[68]

More than any of the heirs, Murray himself had reason to settle matters quickly: he was neglecting both a newly established bookselling business and an unwell wife. The three visits he made to Ireland were a considerable hardship, even if he received £300 (plus expenses) for his trouble — a sum grudgingly approved by his aunts and cousins.[69] He began the first journey on 21 October 1771, travelling initially to Edinburgh then on to Belfast and Dublin and returning to London three months later (a gruelling thousand miles). The following September he and William Kerr repeated this journey, adding two separate visits to the estate itself. Murray returned home on 29 December 1772, worn out from the cold weather and bumped and bruised from a number of carriage overturns. When the estate was about to be put on the market, Murray sent specific instructions to William Gallway as to the advertisement: 'It is allowable in Trade to speak of your commodity in terms higher than it deserves. And as this custom is generally understood by the buyer, the Merchant would actually undervalue his Merchandize did he not *over value* it.'[70] The result was an offer by Lord Bangour to purchase the estate for £14,000.[71] However the 'subterfuge', as Murray called it, of his lawyer complicated matters. 'Duplicity of conduct appears evident',

[65]JM to Robert Carson, 31 July 1772.
[66]JM to Wm Gallway, 18 Mar. 1774.
[67]JM to Wm Gallway, 30 July 1774.
[68]Robina Kennedy to Wm Kerr, 18 May 1774. Enclosed in Kerr's letter to JM. Murray's aunt had engaged two of the most prominent lawyers of the day (Alexander Wedderburn and James Thurlow) to prepare an opinion on Murray's handling of the sale.
[69]Accounts relating to the sale of the estate are found in AL, pp. 143, 250.
[70]JM to Wm Gallway, 19 Apr. 1773.
[71]JM to Wm Kerr, 15 June 1773. This sum is Irish currency, which was approximately £13,000 sterling. Lord Bangour (Bernard Ward, 1719–81) was MP for County Down 1745–70, when he was created Baron Bangour of Castle Ward; from Jan. 1781 Viscount Bangour.

Murray lamented, 'but how far our agent may benefit himself by this conduct I am ignorant.'[72] This complication was enough to dissuade Lord Bangour from progressing with the sale. Legal expenses alone during the two journeys had totalled £550, and still Murray was no nearer to finding a buyer.[73]

A year and a half later Murray concluded a verbal agreement for the purchase of the estate. The new buyer was John Camack, a gentleman of Lurgan who had made a fortune in India. He had agreed to pay 17,000 Irish pounds for the property.[74] His agent for the purchase was William Burgess (the father of Jane Ann), a Belfast lawyer with whom Murray regularly dealt from this time forward. Reporting the good news to Kerr, Murray remarked: 'I flatter myself the Parties will give me some small credit for the additional £1000 I have got added to the price.'[75] A few years later in a letter to his aunt he reflected with satisfaction on the figure: 'We should console ourselves . . . when we consider that our estate would not fetch within £5000 of the money we sold it for, were it this day in the market'.[76] At the end of April 1775 Murray made one final journey to conclude the sale. He was gone for more than four months, and nothing went smoothly. On his arrival in Dublin he learnt that his attorney had just died. Another was recommended but Murray recorded disconsolately that 'this event happening at the critical juncture . . . renders the loss to be more severely felt'.[77] However, he retained a new lawyer, briefed him on the negotiation and met with Burgess to prepare the conveyancing documents. A further difficulty arose when Burgess began to make unreasonable demands. Surrounded by greedy lawyers (including his own), Murray struggled to hold his ground:

> Not contented with being paid by one side he [Burgess] insists upon being paid by both. And in all probability we must submit to the imposition unless we chuse to suffer difficulty & delay in closing the transaction. My own attorney however from my behaviour thinks I will never be brought to agree to such a demand. I have spoken violently against it, and altho I perceive that Mr Hamilton thinks it will be better to submit to the extortion in order to get matters expedited yet he is afraid directly to advise me to it.[78]

[72] JM to Wm Gallway, 19 Apr. 1773.

[73] AL, p. 143. Murray's personal expenses for the first journey were £72; £150 for the second journey. He rode a horse during the first, but on the second hired a post chaise costing £50 (one shilling for each of the 1000 miles) for himself and Kerr.

[74] Or £15,700 sterling. See Camack's account, AL, p. 292.

[75] JM to Kerr, 25 July 1774. It is not clear why Murray said £1000 when the difference would seem to be £3000.

[76] JM to Hellen Kennedy, 19 June 1778.

[77] Diary, 2 May 1775.

[78] Diary, 1 July 1775.

Murray took the less troublesome route and agreed to pay Burgess the 'exorbitant' fee of £100 for accompanying him to Scotland to conclude the sale.[79] Murray's personal expenses amounted to £250, while legal fees for this phase were an additional £727 (£1,276 in total). After a speedy journey to Edinburgh, stopping for hardly more time than was necessary to gather the signatures of the heirs, he and Burgess returned to Ireland. Camack then paid £7000 in cash and was given a mortgage by the heirs for £10,000 for which he annually paid five per cent interest.[80] The money from the sale, after expenses were deducted, was divided according to the proportions set out in James Ross's will: Murray and his sisters each received £2042; a cousin, Miss Betty Crawford, received £2749; an aunt, Mrs Hellen Kennedy, received £2184; and her unmarried daughters (Margaret, Robina and Jennet) each received £819.[81]

Murray invested his share conservatively.[82] He used the interest on his investments and some of the principal to develop his business, mainly by purchasing shares of books at London trade sales. He also purchased different commercial and residential properties in London over the next few years, which generated about £150 in income annually.[83] The inheritance did not remove all of his financial worries, however. And many times during the 1780s he was in difficulties, more because assets were tied up in publishing ventures than because the inheritance had been squandered.

[79]Diary, 26 July 1775.

[80]Camack paid interest on the £10,000 from 13 July 1775 until 5 Nov. 1778, a total of £1688.10s. At that time he produced £6942.17s.5d. in cash. The balance of the mortgage, £3057.2s.7d. had interest paid at 6 per cent until 23 Sept. 1779 (AL, p. 292). Murray and his sisters' share of this figure was £1150.

[81]AL, pp. 283–6.

[82]In Apr. 1776 he purchased a five year 'Bond of Annuity' upon General Mackay's Life and by December he had made £79 at which time he redeemed it (AL, p. 324). Between May and July 1777 he invested £700 with Archibald Stuart & Co., which produced a short-term (less than six months) yield of nearly £20 (AL, p. 301). He also invested £500 at 4 per cent with the banking firm Allen & Marler (AL, p. 324). In June 1777 he lent £461 to Alexander Cockburn (a surgeon at Grenada who had married one of his Kennedy cousins) which produced an annual return of £23, or 5 per cent interest (AL, p. 84). He also lent to his good friend Archy Paxton, (AL, p. 239).

[83]Murray owned a house at 38 New Bond Street which he rented annually for £45.7s.9d.; a house in Bream's Buildings was let for £37.8s.6d. (to the Bishop of Chichester); a house in Mills' Buildings, Knightsbridge, rented for £12.7s.9d (to a Mr Welch and before that to a Mr Cowley, apparently for £18; JM to Cowley, 28 Sept. 1791) and a house at 28 Queen's Row, Pimlico, rented for £39.9s.3d. (to a grocer named Henry Hughes and afterwards to a Mr Edwards). He also received rent from buildings at 32 Fleet Street amounting to £37.5s. These figures are based on the rents in 1797 and were probably somewhat less at earlier dates. The house at Mills' Buildings was sold at auction at Garroway's Coffee House on 1 Mar. 1799 (Donald Grant and Arch. Paxton to Henry Paget, 2 May 1797 — letter reviewing the financial history of Murray's estate — and Samuel Highley to Henry Paget, 19 Feb. 1799).

The Irish Jaunt

Murray's stay in Ireland was not wholly a battle with lawyers. Hardly a day or evening passed when he was not in company, either dining, drinking, or attending some form of entertainment. He knew many booksellers and paid regular visits to their shops. Friends took him to interesting places in and around Dublin — from the races at the Curragh to Lord Charlemont's fabulous library — where, Murray remarked, 'the spectator must be destitute of feeling if he is not delighted'.[84] He also made general observations on the customs and manners of the Irish. Activities like head shaving ('I was rather scalped than shaved') and shoe polishing were recorded in his diary alongside such grave topics as poverty and child murder:[85]

> An incident occurred that was really horrid, and which marks in a particular manner the barbarity of the lower people of this kingdom. By the road side a little box in the shape of a coffin was observed which contained a new born child which had been evidently murdered. The owner it seems did not imagine there was any necessity for concealing it in the earth but left it loose & the box open. Nor did this matter draw such a crowd round it as it would have done in England or Scotland . . . . The perpetrators of this crime are doubly guilty at or near Dublin, as there is an hospital in this city appropriated for receiving without reserve or publication of the parents all new born children that are brought to it.[86]

On the condition of Dublin's poor Murray had this to say:

> The lower people are slothful, deceitful, & barbarous. Acts of cruelty that shock humanity are committed by them. . . . And in this city it is no unusual sight to meet gentlemen walking the streets with drawn swords for their defence after ten at night. . . . Till within these two years the streets of Dublin were infested with beggars. . . . All Dean Swift's wit & strength of reasoning were in vain bestowed in his time with the legislature or the magistrates to remove this nuisance by making a provision for these miserable wretches amongst whom many idle & healthy vagrants sheltered themselves. It was not 'till within these 2 years that poor houses were erected and the streets of Dublin cleared of these vermin. But altho beggary expressly is not now permitted there, yet you are still plagued with it in another shape. Those who before made a good trade of it are unwilling to leave it off, and therefore practise it under the mark of vendors of small wares.[87]

[84]Diary, 1–2 July 1775.
[85]Diary, 13 July 1775.
[86]Diary, 18 June 1775.
[87]Murray had more to say about the dangers of Dublin, especially those inflicted by the students at Trinity College: 'The outrages of Collegians too has risen to such a height that unless they are speedily suppressed Dublin will be unsafe to live in. Permitted for a series of years to practise their wantonness with impunity they do not believe they are governed

In almost every respect Murray found Irish society more violent and more corrupt than that of England — innkeeper, lawyer, beggar and minister of state alike: 'Patriots bluster here indeed as well as at other places. But I am yet to know an instance of one of them resisting the lure of a pension or a ribband.'[88]

Wherever he travelled, Murray was on his guard at all times. He feared being duped, not only by lawyers but by anyone with whom he transacted business. His complaints about the high cost of food, lodging and particularly transportation went beyond a scrupulous frugality. Even more than bad value, he objected to the bad treatment he often met with on his travels. While progressing from Stranraer to Edinburgh, for example, he and William Burgess stopped the night at an inn near Glasgow. Upon arrival Murray recorded in his diary that they suffered 'considerable insults from our Ayr [horse] hirer, for not submitting to be imposed upon by him, and in which insults he was abetted by the ostler [of the inn] and his assistants'.[89] So outraged was Murray that he published a letter in an Edinburgh newspaper, the *Caledonian Mercury*, addressed 'To the Lord Provost and Magistrates of Glasgow', complaining about 'acts of barbarity, that would disgrace the humanity of savages'. The attempt by the horseman to extricate an extra four shillings and the failure of the innkeeper to lend them assistance took on vividly imagined proportions in print:

> The ruffian . . . came armed and prepared into the stable-yard, in order to attack the gentlemen. . . . He seized their luggage as soon as it appeared, and struck one of the strangers with such violence, with a bludgeon . . . that, had he not retreated, he must, in all probability, have been murdered. . . . The strangers retreated precipitately from . . . this slaughter-house, glad to put up with the injuries they had sustained, rather than risk the loss of their lives entirely.[90]

The diary Murray diligently kept while in Ireland was as much a literary exercise as an account of his activities concerning the sale of the estate. The leisure to record his observations revived literary aspirations. But Murray knew that the diary as it stood was wholly unfit for publication and after returning home confessed: 'I want genius to make a Book of [it].'[91] Such reflections on his own literary shortcomings enabled him at this time to pass on advice to a prospective travel writer: 'You will find your account more I think in observing manners and customs than in giving insipid

in the same laws with other citizens. . . . These desperate Boys in frolic sometimes resolve to stab the first man they meet' (Diary, 13 July 1775).
[88]Diary, 7 May 1775.
[89]Diary, 19 July 1775.
[90]*Caledonian Mercury*, 26 July 1775. One consequence of this public letter was the threat of a law suit from Mrs Graham, the proprietor of the inn (Wm Kerr to JM, 29 Dec. 1775).
[91]JM to Wm Enfield, 14 Sept. 1775.

details of Pictures and Buildings. I own the latter should not be entirely neglected; but your work . . . will be so much the more valuable if you illustrate the former. This too gives more scope to Genius and Philosophy.'[92]

Archie

Murray concealed the identity of his illegitimate son's mother. It is possible that this woman was a prostitute. But a prostitute would not have been able to prove the father's identity and would probably be versed in abortion methods. It is more likely the woman was his kept mistress or possibly his sister-in-law Hester, who lived with Murray and her sister around the time Archie would have been conceived. Whether Murray's relationship continued after the boy's birth is not known. However, extra-marital activities certainly did. For his errant behaviour, Murray accepted full responsibility. Social custom, as well as moral compulsion, dictated that he would support the boy, but from a distance. When he learned that others did not do their duty in similar situations, he was indignant: 'Can you . . . think of abandoning such a Woman & her Infants to the bitter blasts of a rude & unfeeling World?' he rhetorically asked a friend whose son had abandoned his family. 'Human nature would cry aloud against you even if your own conscience were silent.'[93]

From July 1770 Archie, then just a few months old, was put into the care of Mr and Mrs Furnival, a couple living in London, with whom he remained until the age of nine. Who these people were, and what association, if any, they had with the boy's mother is not known. Murray paid them a guinea a month for board; clothing and medicines were extra.[94] Sometimes Archie's guardians came to Fleet Street to collect payment and to report on his well being, and two or three times a year (more frequently as Archie grew up) Murray visited the Furnivals, spending part of the day with his son. In the summer of 1779 the date of Archie's departure for school approached. He was fitted out in a smart blue suit with 'solid gilt anchor buttons' that would suggest Murray had already destined his son for a career at sea (see Plate 35a).[95] First, Archie had to be properly, if economically, educated. 'I wish the Boy to be proficient in the knowledge of history Antient & Modern', Murray told the master of the Academy at Halifax, adding that, 'without understanding both Geography and Chronology this can never happen'.[96] Archie remained at the school for two years. He would

---

[92]JM to John Gillies, 30 Sept. 1775.
[93]JM to Alex. Dallas, 28 Mar. 1778.
[94]AL, pp. 94 and 200 (Mrs Furnival's account).
[95]AL, loose sheet at p. 200.
[96]JM to Rev. Hudson, 3 Nov. 1779.

have continued there longer had not concern over ill-health forced his removal to a school where he could take 'Salt Water' treatments and relieve a mild respiratory disorder.[97] Between schools, Archie stayed briefly with his father at Fleet Street, where he had usually visited at Christmas and other celebrations. While residing there Murray put Archie to work copying letters and keeping account ledgers up to date.[98] Early in 1783 the boy was sent to the academy at Brighthelmstone, a seaside town, where he continued to study Latin, French, writing and accounting, and began classes in Greek and drawing. He was a quick learner with a gift for languages. Murray remarked that his son had 'an excellent character for Docility, Quietness and Capacity', but he was also aware of a tendency to laziness, in which trait Murray, surprisingly, saw something of himself.[99]

He wrote regularly while his son was at school and afterwards when he went to sea, counselling him in the general rules for his 'good government and welfare' with an affectionate firmness, and often reminding him of the importance of 'cleanlyness in your person' (see Plate 35b). Consideration of others and the cultivation of their good opinion were essential, but, he added: 'Remember that every thing depends principally upon yourself; and that disappointment in more instances than one, will not justify impatience, far less despair'.[100] Although Murray doubted how far the lessons of his own experience might be imparted, he continued to impress upon his son the outlook of a middle-class tradesman, namely to 'Push your advancement in life by every fair and honourable means.'[101]

After Archie's formal education was complete, Murray used his connections at the Admiralty Office to get him employment. Murray knew first-hand the pitfalls of naval life and so advised caution and moderation: 'As you are going upon a station, & into scenes that will be new to you; permit me to entreat that you guard against too much indulgence. Pleasure is fascinating, but excess counteracts it. . . . Health should be prized & promoted above every other earthly object; all our enjoyments proceed from it, and without it we can enjoy nothing.'[102] Murray's advice was especially detailed over the matter of drinking: 'Be careful how you fill your glass', he advised:

> Observe what others do, and be below their lowest mark. But were all the company to set in for drinking and to fill bumpers upon a penalty, fill one also; but effect an immediate escape. For it is much better to risk giving

[97]JM to Rev. Sutcliffe, 11 June 1781.
[98]From 10 Aug. for a short period, the letters are in Archie's hand.
[99]JM to Hugh Cameron, Schoolmaster, 24 Feb. [mis-written Jan.] 1783. Murray's remark that, 'the youth whom I wish to place at a good Academy, is about the Age of 14', gives an idea of Archie's date of birth for which no record has been found.
[100]JM to Archie Murray, 14 June 1791.
[101]JM to Archie Murray, 7 Sept. 1791.
[102]Ibid.

offence than to convert your self into a Bachanal. For he who is enraged at such conduct when drunk will approve of it when he is sober.[103]

After leaving school Archie was first put under the direction of Murray's old navy friend George Noble to learn the skills he would have to perform at sea. At the age of twenty-one Archie gained an appointment as one of the secretaries to Captain John Inglefield, aboard the warship *Medusa*. Inglefield was another of his father's friends and an author on military affairs.[104] But if Archie expected special treatment, he was sorely mistaken. Letters complaining of his commander's severity poured into Fleet Street. Though sympathetic to his son's situation, Murray resolutely asserted the importance of pleasing Inglefield, for he alone controlled Archie's future: 'Preserve good humour . . . and in short bear every thing'.[105] In a remark which perhaps says more about Murray's own strategies for dealing with those in positions of authority, he told Archie: 'It is necessary in these days (perhaps it was so at all times) for a dependent to be a sycophant to his patron or patrons, and to *effect* to be governed by their sentiments if in reality he is not'.[106] Gradually Archie came to respect Inglefield and even discovered him to be a friend. Murray marked this development in a report to Noble with paternalistic pleasure: 'Archie has weathered it out & returned in the Medusa well spoken of by his Captain'.[107]

Murray continually advised enterprising ways for Archie to get ahead. In one instance he encouraged him to prepare a paper for Captain Inglefield to introduce a printing press at sea for the Royal Navy. 'Collect every argument respecting the danger, impropriety & inconvenience of this scheme; and overturn these by showing the use & superior advantages of a printing press'.[108] The plan met with approval, and in the years to come Archie played an active role in writing and publishing newspapers at sea. A skilful reporter, Archie provides a unique account of the naval campaign against France in the first decade of the nineteenth century.[109]

[103] Ibid.
[104] In 1783 Murray had published Inglefield's *Narrative concerning the Loss of the Centaur*, a short work that was popular for a time and which Byron later used to write the shipwreck sequence in *Don Juan* (see *Boswell: The Applause of the Jury, 1782–1785*, eds. I. S. Lustig and F. A. Pottle, London, 1981, pp. 130–4, for a portrait of Inglefield). In 1787 Inglefield was involved in a case against his wife in the Ecclesiastical Court. She charged him with desertion and he countered with an allegation of adultery. Murray published a series of pamphlets on the affair which were noticed in the *English Review*, 12 (Nov. 1788), 395–6.
[105] JM to Archie Murray, 19 Oct. 1991.
[106] JM to Archie Murray, 20 Jan. 1793.
[107] JM to George Noble, 24 Sept. 1792.
[108] JM to Archie Murray, 14 June 1791.
[109] The names of the newspapers Archie Murray had a large hand in were: the *Triton Chronicle* (1809), the *Omnibus* (1832) and the *Defiance* (1834), manuscript copies of which are preserved in the Archive.

For five years Archie acted as Inglefield's secretary on various ships, sailing in the Mediterranean and as far west as Jamaica. Afterwards, he served under Inglefield's son, Samuel Hood Inglefield, as a purser, in which office he continued under other commanders for many years. Archie's knowledge of French and especially Spanish made him indispensable in important negotiations. He saw action in several battles in the Channel and elsewhere. Although he served with distinction, promotions and financial recompense came all too slowly.[110] Wherever his ship docked, Archie met his filial duty by enquiring at the shops of respectable booksellers for orders of his father's publications, copies of which he had on hand to show.[111] On more than one occasion, however, he angered his father by charging goods to his name without permission.[112] Murray responded with a severity reserved for his worst customers: 'I now repeat for the last time that I never will honour any bill you draw upon me were it but for a shilling'.[113] Murray knew that at the time Archie's pay alone could not meet his basic needs, and told him to 'enquire what perquisites . . . belonged *legally* to your office'.[114] Financial independence was essential. Without it, he told his son, 'no virtue or genius nor abilities meet with regard'.[115] Like debt, scandal was always to be avoided. When William Kerr's son committed misdeeds so heinous that he was forced to flee to Virginia, Murray remarked to the miscreant's brother: 'If my own Son should ever equal his behaviour I hoped that some friendly person would shoot him thro the head'.[116] Archie, by contrast, was a dutiful son and a responsible individual, whose naval career, had Murray lived to witness more of its progress, would have made him proud.

Hester and Family

The remarriage of Captain Weemss in 1772 had left his daughter Hester little option but to shift her dependence and allegiance to Nancy and John. 'Now he has got a wife', she told her brother-in-law, 'he cares very little what becomes of his poor Daughter Hester'.[117] All that the girl had said against Murray in the past, all her suspicions that he was after her money,

---

[110]Archie's experience at sea is well, if sporadically, documented. There is a series of letters from Archie to his half-brother, John, between 1814 and 1840 describing his struggles for promotion and, indeed, employment, which was difficult to retain in peacetime.
[111]JM to Archie Murray, 10 July 1791.
[112]JM to Archie Murray, 12 Sept. 1792.
[113]JM to Archie Murray, 4 Apr. 1793.
[114]JM to Archie Murray, 28 Sept. 1792.
[115]JM to Archie Murray, 28 Aug. 1792.
[116]JM to Wm Kerr Jr, 26 Sept. 1785.
[117]Hester Weemss to JM, 12 Mar. 1772.

were forgotten — or at least excused on account of her youth and inexperience. And Hester herself could remark: 'I . . . am happy I find a Friend in Mr Murray who once I thought my enemy'.[118] From 1773 Hester stayed at 32 Fleet Street for extended periods. Murray controlled her finances, keeping a detailed account of her rather extravagant purchases of dress cloth. He even charged her room and board.[119] In a letter to a family friend Murray described the activities which occupied Nancy and Hester: 'sometimes they go to a Play & sometimes to a Preaching; sometimes they give way to the heavenly dictates of Charity & relieve the distressed; & sometimes they indulge in the Diabolical passion of scandal. These . . . employments, discordant & contradictory as they are, are yet in human nature.'[120]

When Murray first went to Ireland, his sisters encouraged Nancy to visit Edinburgh, but they were not pleased that Hester had planned to accompany her. Binny, who always spoke her mind, told her brother why she objected to Hester: 'She is young and I think handsom[e] and were she to come here and make a foolish marriage as many do it realy would have vexed me greatly'.[121] John's opinion of Hester had gradually improved, but Binny continued to harbour suspicions and probably wished to protect her own interests in the marriage market. Excuses were made and Hester was shipped off to friends in Kent, while Nancy went to Scotland.

After Nancy's death in September 1776 (perhaps even before) the platonic affection between Murray and Hester became romantic. Some might have questioned the propriety of an unmarried woman living under the same roof with her widowed brother-in-law. But where was Hester to go? Living together caused emotional and sexual bonds to develop, and on 23 February 1778, seventeen months after Nancy's death, they were married across the road at St Dunstan's Church. Their union simplified economic matters; moreover, Hester's £500 was a welcome addition, as money for a growing business was always in demand.[122] There were precedents for marrying a deceased wife's sister. However, proscriptions against such a union on religious grounds were frequently heard. Although the practice had been permitted by English civil law since the days of Cromwell, orthodox clergymen, appealing to the Levitical prohibition, had always regarded it as 'incestuous fornication'.[123] In Murray's day marriages within

---

[118]Ibid.

[119]Hester was charged at the higher rate of £1.16s.9d. a week (AL, p. 121 and 227).

[120]JM to Wm Paxton, 25 Dec. 1775.

[121]Binny McMurray to JM, 4 Apr. 1772.

[122]Hester also held the mortgage on two tenement houses in Brompton (AL, p. 227). When the interest had not been paid for two years, she wrote to Mr Twopenny, her attorney (20 Aug. 1777) at Murray's advice to foreclose or 'dispose of it altogether'.

[123]See F. W. Puller, *Marriage with a Deceased Wife's Sister Forbidden* (London, 1912), p. 139. The relevant biblical passages are found in *Leviticus*, 18, xvi. See the Act of 1835 (5 and 6

this 'degree of affinity' regularly occurred, but by the end of the eighteenth century, under the greater influence of the Church, they became rare.

Murray's second marriage was far less turbulent than his first. It began under better economic circumstances and on a more mature basis. Hester was less strong-willed than Nancy and more eager to please: she 'proves one of the best of wives', Murray told Thomas Gardiner, who himself had been a candidate for Hester's hand, 'and I must do her the justice to say that if I am not perfectly happy it is not her fault.'[124] Usually one to blame others, Murray was bestowing no offhand compliment. Hester, like her sister, helped out in the shop, serving customers and copying letters and accounts. Hester was also fond of Archie. Murray encouraged this relationship, and later reminded Archie that 'When I am no more, transfer your regard and affection to Mrs. Murray and her children who have readily seconded & approved the assistance you have repeatedly received from me altho it might have been thought to have militated against their own interest'.[125]

The children Murray and Hester quickly produced were a source of mutual joy, attention and entertainment. Writing to John Paxton in India in July 1780, Murray remarked: 'We have now been married above two years and I have no reason to repent of my choice. I have one boy near 20 months old who is thriving; there is an appearance of another to be coming.'[126] John and Hester's first son was born on 27 November 1778, nine months and four days after their marriage. After a christening at St Dunstan's, the proud father wrote to his old navy friend John Samuel with the good news: 'My good woman brought me a son . . . whom I have named, as I told you I would, John Samuel Murray. And the last accounts I had from the little fellow, who is at Enfield at nurse, are that he is finely. Should you therefore never see me, I have left to you a token of my friendship & remembrance.'[127] Naming his son after Samuel was a mark

William IV, ch. 54), called Lord Lyndhurst's Act. In the mid-nineteenth century the movement to reform the law was central to the Liberal Party's election platform and a frequent object of public attention, as is evident from W. S. Gilbert's couplet in *Iolanthe*: 'He shall prick that annual blister/Marriage with deceased wife's sister'. In 1907 Parliament passed the 'Deceased Wife's Sister Marriage Act', which removed the power of the Church to influence people against it.

[124] JM to Thomas Gardiner, 4 Nov. 1783.

[125] JM to Archie Murray, 7 Sept. 1791. This remark is further circumstantial evidence that Archie was in fact the child of Hester.

[126] JM to John Paxton, 7 July 1780.

[127] JM to John Samuel, 11 Feb. 1779. Samuel was then stationed at Rhode Island as a purser aboard the *Rainbow*. He had lodged at 32 Fleet Street from 1 Oct. 1774 to 19 Apr. 1775, and for a further period in 1776. He and Murray had travelled together to Ireland in 1775. Such was their closeness at the time that Murray remarked when Samuel went to the country for a few days: 'I am deprived of the company of a friend whom I love' (Diary, 7 May 1775).

of a warm attachment. But nine years later their friendship ended abruptly when they fell out over money.[128]

The infant remained with his wet nurse for five months at Enfield, a town in Middlesex about an hour's ride from London. His parents visited him regularly, and when they heard that he had cut a tooth, brought him back to Fleet Street. Once again Hester became pregnant, and in October 1779, eleven months after John's birth, another boy arrived: 'The mother & child are as well as their friends can wish them', Murray told John Ormiston, his brother-in-law.[129] They named the child Willie after their friend William Paxton, who had gone out to India. But within four weeks — before the letter to Paxton had arrived with the news — the baby had died. Before the next year passed Hester had produced another, a girl named Jane (called Jenny), christened on 24 October 1780. She was healthy at birth and grew stronger day by day. Her brother, Johnny, Murray informed his own sister Elizabeth, was 'Jealous of the notice taken of her'.[130] At the age of two John was inoculated for smallpox, then an uncertain method of preventing the dreadful disease which killed and disfigured so many. Murray was greatly relieved to report to the Gillilands that the boy was 'perfectly recovered'.[131] Only a year before Murray had published *A Letter . . . upon General Inoculation* (1779) in support of the controversial treatment. But when his little girl was inoculated, and developed measles at the same time, she was so ill that Murray doubted the risk. He and Hester fretted until she was out of danger.[132]

The arrival of another child on 31 August 1781 was met with concern, and, after struggling against a catalogue of ailments, the infant died less than a month later. Such a loss, however frequent an occurrence in Georgian England, struck hard. Murray and Hester shared their grief and, taking stock of their two healthy children — one 'a lusty stout fellow', the other 'a pretty little creature' — still counted themselves thankful.[133]

[128]In 1781 Samuel retired from the navy and sold furniture in London. Murray reported that Samuel's 'behaviour bordered very much upon insanity' (JM to John Ormiston, 8 June 1787). £1500 was at stake.

[129]JM to John Ormiston, 30 Oct. 1779.

[130]JM to James Gilliland, 23 Dec. 1780. Jane later married the Rev. Wm Holland, Canon of Chichester.

[131]JM to James Gilliland, 19 Dec. 1780. In the same letter Murray thanked his relations for a parcel of Scotch bannocks, relished by all the family—especially his son. The practice of inoculation had gradually spread from China and India and was described in the *Transactions of the Royal Society* in 1714 and 1716. In the 1760s less invasive methods of inoculation were introduced in Britain by Robert and Daniel Sutton, but it was not until Jenner's experiments in 1798 that the safer cowpox vaccination was introduced (See Donald R. Hopkins, *Princes and Peasants: Smallpox in History*, 1983, pp. 12, 59; Peter Razzell, *The Conquest of Smallpox*, 1977).

[132]JM to James Gilliland, 4 July 1783. Murray also published the anonymous *Letters and Essays on the Small-pox and Inoculation* (1778) and Robert Walker's *Inquiry into the Small-pox, Medical and Political* (1790).

[133]JM to Geo. Tilsley, 10 June 1782.

Murray did not like being apart from his wife. And when she went to the country for a week, he reflected: 'I live unharmonious by myself'.[134] Though his days of debauchery and revelry were nearly at an end, he still jokingly warned a friend of Hester's at the time of her absence that 'if any thing wrong happens', she will have herself 'to blame for the mischief'.[135] Such remarks were indicative of domestic contentment rather than of unrequited desire. Scenes of happiness did not last for long. In February 1782 both husband and wife became seriously ill with influenza, which was then raging through London. Murray in particular was 'seized . . . in a worse manner than other people' and unwell for many months.[136] Their children had to be moved out of Fleet Street to avoid infection. When he and Hester began to recover, family members were reunited, but Murray continued to suffer: 'I write in pain, & have been confined with a severe rheumatism in my head for these five weeks which has thrown my own affairs behind hand'.[137] Illness hit at the busiest time: the India fleet was about to sail, and Parliament had opened. The great quantities of medicines Murray was taking, rather than alleviating his pain, made him irritable and lethargic.[138] Nor was this all.

At midday on 6 May 1782, while working at the counter of his shop, he felt a peculiar swimming feeling in his head and a numbness along the left side of his body. Believing it to be the return of a neuralgic rheumatism, he took large doses of medicine to dampen the pain in his face and eyes and then put himself to bed. Murray did not realise at the time that he had suffered a stroke. Through the night and for much of the next day he was violently ill.[139] Fearful for his life, Hester called in their physician, David Pitcairn, who, observing that Murray had almost completely lost control of his left side, confirmed the diagnosis. The prognosis for recovery was not wholly unfavourable. Pitcairn told Murray of cases where stroke victims much older than himself (he was forty-five at the time) had fully recovered. Murray, however, was utterly despondent: 'These things in my favour I hear with a stragling hope', he told his brother-in-law Gilliland, 'but without foolishly flattering myself that I shall ever be a man again'. The sight of his wife and young children at his bedside (John not yet four and Jenny not yet two) rallied him somewhat: 'To bewail my calamity . . . is fruitless. . . . It is better . . . to bear it with fortitude, & to conduct my business with patience & attention for the benefit of my family; for it is of moment now that I lose as little time as possible.'[140] At the first sign of improvement, the doctors recom-

---

[134]JM to Mrs Faulkner, 14 May 1778.
[135]Ibid.
[136]JM to Geo. Tilsley, 10 June 1782.
[137]JM to Andrew Blane, 6 Mar. 1782.
[138]JM to John Ormiston, 12 Oct. 1782.
[139]JM to James Gilliland, 27 May 1782; and to John Ormiston, 13 June 1782.
[140]JM to James Gilliland, 27 May 1782.

mended that Murray go to Brighton or Margate to take salt water baths. The considerable expense of these health resorts deterred him; in his opinion both were 'very extravagant places'.[141] However, in August 1782 he decided on Margate. Although his condition gradually improved, he was still gloomy, and remarked to his brother-in-law that 'this winter will prove what I have to rely upon respecting my health'.[142]

In November 1782 Murray and his family moved from Fleet Street to a small house at Peckham, four miles from London. The children thrived on the fresher country air and he continued to make a slow recovery.[143] Murray enjoyed the hour's walk to his shop, though he was far from his former robust self. If he was to see his young children grow up, his days of excess must end altogether. But taking proper care of himself was another matter; and he confided to John Ormiston that 'nothing is easier in theory, in practice it is too little attended to'.[144]

Ill-health and the unexpected death of close friends like William Kerr and Jenny Paxton (the sister of Archy, William and John) were stark reminders of his own mortality. Kerr, in particular, had been indispensable as a business and family advisor and was sorely missed. In a letter of condolence to Kerr's son, Murray expressed his hope 'that I should be able to live, lame as I was, till I had showed my sense of . . . kindness'.[145] His letter to Jenny Paxton's brother stirred other equally powerful emotions: 'She has made a vacancy in the world and we 'poor fools of Nature' are left to moralize upon the occasion. . . . Life has nothing in it substantial. . . . The cause of our existence is unknown to us.'[146] When an aunt to whom he was close died in 1786, he reflected: 'I have no person now that stands in the same relation to me' — another sober reminder, if it were needed.[147]

Murray recovered enough to resume the day-in and day-out tasks of bookselling and publishing. Indeed, even when ill, he conducted business from his bedside, giving orders to assistants and receiving visits from authors and tradesmen. He was short-tempered and sensitive to the least hint that others might be taking advantage of him. Tolerating little and demanding much, he was difficult to deal with. Nor was he as attentive as

[141]JM to Wm Cullen, 27 July 1782.
[142]JM to John Ormiston, 12 Oct. 1782. Murray paid several other visits to Margate and other health spots in the next decade. He also published books on 'the waters', including James Playfair's 'do-it-yourself *Method of Constructing Vapor Baths . . . in Private Families* (1783), Richard Kentish's *Essay on Sea-Bathing, and the Internal Use of Sea-Water* (1787) and an anonymous pamphlet: *An Analysis of the Medicinal Waters of Tunbridge Wells* (1792).
[143]The rent for what Murray called at different times a 'cabin' and a 'hovel' was £15 a year (JM to James Gilliland, 11 Jan. 1783).
[144]JM to John Ormiston, 2 June 1783.
[145]JM to Wm Kerr, Jr, 28 Jan. 1783.
[146]JM to Wm Paxton, 15 Mar. 1784.
[147]JM to Andrew Blane, 9 June 1787.

he had been: 'I have committed a blunder . . . ' he told John Balfour, the Edinburgh bookseller. 'When I accepted of your bargain . . . I [was] never in my senses.'[148]

After a few months the family left the house at Peckham and returned to Fleet Street. In the following decade illness and depression plagued Murray. 'The stroke by which I suffered . . . is only suspended,' he told his son Archie. 'It *will* be repeated, and I must fall in the contest.'[149] Lame and somewhat accident prone, he once fell on some steps and dislocated his left shoulder.[150] In early 1790 there was another more serious scare: 'I was siezed . . . with a fit of illness that had nearly terminated my career in this world. I am now however unexpectedly restored to my ordinary state of health.'[151]

Hester herself was not free from worrying complaints. The series of pregnancies had worn her down, and more children would follow. 'Mrs M. & myself have both been ill', Murray told Ormiston early in 1787. 'She has suffered by a miscarriage, from the effects of which she has not recovered; and I am ill with an ugly rheumatism.'[152] Eleven months later (in December 1787) Hester produced another child, Mary Anne, who struggled through the dangerous illnesses of infancy and childhood.[153] Just over a year afterwards, Hester was pregnant again. However, a persistent cough in the fifth month was thought serious enough to send her to Bath for treatment. She returned after three weeks 'in good spirits, but her cough tho better has not left her'.[154] A few weeks later, on 16 February 1789, she delivered their seventh child, a son stillborn.[155] For another year Hester was unwell.

The health of the couple was not so poor as to render them unable to lead active lives. In fact they travelled considerably in the 1780s. In July 1785 the family journeyed to Edinburgh, where the children met their father's relatives for the first time. They all returned to Scotland in May 1787 and again in the summer of 1790. In attending to the running of his shop and coping with illness, Murray did not neglect other important obligations. Foremost was the education of his son and heir (see Plate 36).[156] Such was his and Hester's attachment to the boy that they hesitated to send him off

---

[148]JM to John Balfour, 4 Dec. 1783.
[149]JM to Archie Murray, 7 Sept. 1791.
[150]JM to Wm Kerr, 16 July 1787.
[151]JM to John Millar, 20 Jan. 1790.
[152]JM to John Ormiston, 12 Feb. 1787.
[153]'Mrs Murray . . . is upon the point of bringing me an accession to my family', Murray told Robert Liston in a letter dated 18 Dec. 1787. Mary Anne was born on 29 Dec. 1787. She later married the Rev. William Cooke, who became Vicar of Bromyard in Herefordshire and subsequently Canon of Hereford, and with whom she had several children.
[154]JM to Wm Kerr Jr, 27 Jan. 1789.
[155]JM to to Wm MacCormick, 25 Feb. 1789.
[156]The education of Murray's daughters was a more informal matter — assisted, perhaps, by books he published such as: the Rev. John Moir's *Female Tuition; or, an Address to mothers, on the*

to school as was customary for an eight-year-old: 'The little fellow has made himself so agreeable . . .' Murray told a prospective tutor, the Reverend John Trusler, 'we are . . . loth to think of parting with him, altho perhaps it is proper even for *his* advantage'.[157] Hester continued to resist but finally consented 'to give over the little oriental'. Trusler, a Murray author, was entrusted with this important charge: 'I have the less regret in doing it to you,' Murray confided, 'as I rely upon your tenderness & that he will be taught to read & write. You may therefore have him at your pleasure; and I can assure you, that you will find him an innocent & good boy.'[158]

For five months the child lived with Trusler and learned the rudiments of reading and writing. Afterwards Murray sent his son to the academy at Uxbridge, where the master was the Reverend William Rutherford. Murray had an odd association with Rutherford: since 1777 he had been sending the clergyman books for his school, and had even published Rutherford's *Elements of Latin Grammar* in May 1787.[159] But Rutherford had never, or had rarely, settled his account. Sending John to the Academy (which had a good reputation) in September 1787 was one way of recouping outstanding money. After a term, however, Murray removed his son from Uxbridge and threatened Rutherford with arrest for debt: 'I am now directed to take out a writ against you', he warned. 'Considering your character as a clergyman and as an arrest may do you irrepairable mischief at Uxbridge, I shall ward it off till the afternoon of thursday.'[160] Fortunately the dispute was settled. The following year Murray published Rutherford's *View of Antient History* ('Printed for the Author'), but the failure of the work to sell as well as the author expected fuelled an already heated association.[161]

From Uxbridge Murray enrolled his nine-year-old son in the 'second class' at the Edinburgh High School, where he himself had attended thirty years before.[162] Murray was anxious for an account of his son's academic progress: 'Pray tell me what report there is of my son's opening appearance at the high school . . . ', he asked William Kerr Jr Murray did not expect brilliant examination results, but he hoped the boy would not feel

---

Education of Daughters (1784, 2nd edn. in 1786); and John Burton's *Lectures on Female Education and Manners* (1793, 2nd edn same year).

[157] JM to John Trusler, 29 Mar. 1786.

[158] JM to John Trusler, 8 Apr., 1786.

[159] The favourable notice Rutherford's *Grammar* received in the *English Review*, 9 (May 1788), 388, was good advertising for the Academy at Uxbridge.

[160] JM to Wm Rutherford, 6 Feb. 1787. See also JM to Mr. Harvey (his attorney), 4 Feb. 1789.

[161] A second volume of Rutherford's *History* appeared in 1791. For an outline of the history course he gave at Uxbridge Academy, see Rutherford's *Heads of a Course of Lectures on History* (1783), favourably reviewed in the *English Review*, 2 (Aug. 1783), 143. Murray probably published it for Rutherford, although there is no name given in the imprint.

[162] JM to John Ormiston, 19 July 1787. The boy journeyed north with his mother and lodged with his aunt and uncle, the Gillilands.

despondent. In the event, Murray relied on Kerr to present him with a prize 'in order to keep him in countenance'.[163] But the results revealed reasons for concern about John's ability. Murray accepted that 'it would be folly to attempt to combat the opinion', and decided that 'no time should be lost . . . to put him again under Dr. Rutherford'.[164] Over the 1787–8 academic year John progressed well at Uxbridge. But in the spring he suffered an injury while playing with the other boys: 'My poor Son Johnny . . . met with an accident upon his head at School from a brick bat.' The wound itself was not serious, but a persistent fever was worrying: 'We think him one way indeed better, for he is chearfull,' Murray told Kerr, 'but a headach & weakness of his limbs prevents him from sitting up; nor does he show any inclination to sit up'.[165] The boy slowly recovered his health, but fearful that side effects associated with the accident might recur, Hester and John did not return their son to Uxbridge. Instead they sent him to the Reverend Charles Wells' academy at Margate where he could take restorative baths. In 1785 Murray had published Wells' *Brief Account of the Seminary of Learning, established at Margate in Kent, for the Reception of Twelve Young Gentlemen.* 'The school is not the best', he told the boy's half-brother, Archie, 'but . . . his health leaves no alternative'.[166]

During the two years John remained at Margate he made considerable academic progress. Whatever concern Murray might have had at Edinburgh was allayed, or almost: 'He writes a good hand', his father observed, 'is fond of figures, & is coming forward both in latin & french. . . . His appearance, open, modest, & manly, is much in his favour.'[167] Yet Murray was concerned to discover that his son was somewhat indolent and short-tempered — traits to which he himself admitted. When Archie was at Margate to visit his half-brother, Murray had him follow up on a report from the master that John, now thirteen, was a poor speller: 'Pray, take an opportunity to examine him', he enjoined, 'and make a report'.[168]

From Margate John moved on to Dr Burney's school at Gosport. There, however, a freak accident happened which left the boy completely

---

[163]JM to Wm Kerr Jr, 25 July 1787.

[164]JM to Wm Kerr Jr, 4 Aug. 1787.

[165]JM to Wm Kerr Jr, 17 June 1788.

[166]JM to Archie Murray, 21 July 1791. In 1785 Murray had taken out advertisements in the London newspapers for 'A beneficed Clergyman taking in pupils for Bathing and Private Tuition' at Margate. 'Applications', the advertisement stated, 'may be made to Mr Murray' (album of newspaper clippings). No copy of the pamphlet Murray published is extant, but it was reviewed in the *English Review,* 5 (May 1785), 391. Wells, according to the review, followed the plan of education recommended by Vicesimus Knox in his *Liberal Education: or a Practical Treatise on Polite Learning* (1781). Murray also published Wells' *Sermon Preached . . . before the Free Masons of Kent* (1787).

[167]JM to Archie Murray, 23 July 1791. From June 1792, the boy copied letters for his father in books with ruled lines until 29 July.

[168]JM to Archie Murray, 19 Sept. 1792.

blind in his right eye. A book had dropped off his desk while the writing master was examining his paper; and when John stood up, the master's knife (used to sharpen student's quills), went into his eye.[169] The shocking news so disturbed Murray that he thought of nothing else and could not sleep for days. Hester was already nervous about her son's health; and Murray, reporting the tragedy to Archie, confided that 'she is yet ignorant of it & I dare not tell her'.[170] After John was out of immediate danger, he was brought to London. Murray sought out the most qualified specialists in the vain hope of restoring the boy's lost sight. He reported to the attending surgeon at Gosport that Mr Ware, 'an eminent occulist' in London had 'some expectation that . . . it may in some degree be recovered'.[171] Hopeful of improvement, yet fearful of raising his, and particularly Hester's, expectations, Murray was cautious.[172] Eventually it became clear that the cornea had been irreparably damaged and the essential fluids lost.

As the boy began to adjust to his handicap, Murray considered two further possibilities for his education: either John would study at Edinburgh University under the care of Robert Kerr, an eminent scientist; or he would attend the Loughborough House School, whose headmaster was the Reverend Roberts. Kerr outlined the first option: 'Should you still continue in the mind to have your son educated for a year at Edinburgh, and chuse to put him under my direction, you may send him directly to my house. . . . I shall charge you ten guineas a quarter for his board and lodging. . . . I must have minute instructions, as to his education, expences of various kinds, and pocket money.'[173] Fear of their son living at such a distance after his accident convinced the Murrays to opt for Loughborough, and Murray wrote to accept the place: 'I commit to you the charge of my Son; & . . . I agree to the [annual] terms of fifty G[uinea]s. . . . The youth has been hitherto well spoken of, by the Gentlemen he has been under. You will find him sensible & candid . . . & if you are kind enough to bestow pains upon him, the obligation on my part will be lasting.' Murray listed those subjects — deferring to Roberts' 'superior judgement' — at which he wished his son to become proficient: 'Latin, French, arithmetic, Merchants accounts, Elocution, History, Geography, Geometry, astronomy, the globes, mathematics, Philosophy, Drawing, and martial exercise'.[174]

Murray knew that education was essential for advancement. As Archie

[169]Samuel Smiles, *A Publisher and his Friends*, i, 22.
[170]JM to Archie Murray, 19 Mar. 1793.
[171]JM to Mr Sempil, 9 May 1793.
[172]Curiously, over ten years before, Murray had remarked when he learnt that a friend had lost not only his wife but his eye: 'The first loss [his wife] he has borne better than expected. The second [his eye] he must always feel' (JM to John Henderson, 7 July 1780).
[173]Robert Kerr to JM, 18 Mar. 1793.
[174]JM to Rev. Roberts, 30 July 1793.

was trained to his father's original career, so John was groomed for the second, more enduring one. During visits home, even when he was not fully recovered from his illnesses, the boy was put to work, transcribing letters and, under the direction of his father and of the shop assistants, learning the trade.[175]

[175]From June to Aug. 1792 young John copied letters for his father on pages ruled in pencil.

9

Diversity and Specialisation

Novels

Of Murray's publications only a handful were new novels — about two per cent of his total output.[1] Not one is remembered today and only a few sold well. If a manuscript destined to become a classic did arrive on his desk, he must have returned it to the author. Murray was reluctant to pay the copyright for a novel; if he paid at all it was a paltry sum: John Heriot received £10 for the *Sorrows of the Heart* (1787) and Jane Timbury just £5 for the *Male Coquet* (1788).[2] The problem was that Murray found it difficult to know what would appeal to the novel-reading public. His own opinion, he acknowledged to an author in 1774, was not always a sure guide: 'We often consider our own Taste to be that of the community, and are certain that what pleases our selves must be as favourably received by the public at large; repeated experience to the contrary teaches us to be more circumspect & modest in our conclusions.'[3] The market for fiction — subject to the whims of fashion more than most literary forms, and in Murray's day a relatively new genre — was even more problematic. The capital outlay for a novel that might be a complete failure was too considerable for Murray often to take such a risk. So Murray usually left this line of publishing to other booksellers such as William Lane, the proprietor of the Minerva Press. However, he was usually willing to publish at the author's expense and was sometimes surprised at a good sale.

When the second edition of the Reverend John Trusler's *Modern Times, or the Adventures of Gabriel Outcast* (1785) had nearly sold out, Murray invited the author around to 'eat a bit of dinner . . . & take the money'. Over a bottle of wine he suggested improvements for the third edition: 'That the work

---

[1] Murray published just over fifty novels: about twenty were editions of new works; about thirty were reprints of classics, or translations — approximately 5.5 per cent of his output (See Table 2 and Figure 3, pp. 158–61).
[2] BB, pp. 66, 43.
[3] JM to Andrew Duncan, 29 Aug. 1774.

has *some* merit is undoubted. But it is rather a collection of detached characters than a fable of any interest.'[4] Murray advised Trusler to consider the comments in the *English Review* on the first edition, and warned him against lengthening the novel beyond three volumes. Trusler himself wrote a short notice of the second edition for the *English Review* and then was bold enough to send the publisher a bill for the piece.[5] Murray, surprisingly, paid him, but retorted: '*I* ought rather to be paid by you for that article'.[6]

The *English Review*, when Murray launched it in 1783, was a useful medium for promoting novels and other publications, and Murray did not scruple to serve himself and his authors in this way. Occasionally such tactics were exposed. An advertisement for the publication of the fictional *Adventures of George Maitland* (1786) met with the strictures of 'Detector', who told the public that the novel was 'word for word the same as the *Adventures of James Ramble, Esq* which we have all read twenty years ago'.[7] In reply, 'Terrier' (Murray's friend Gilbert Stuart) asked why Murray 'should be held up to public notice for what may be his misfortune more than his crime?' 'Terrier' then explained that with redundancies 'lopped off', the tale 'possessed merit superior to nineteen in twenty of the novels in vogue'. Finally, he reminded 'Detector': 'from an illiterate bookseller you had no literary danger to apprehend'.[8] Murray presumably sanctioned this reply, confident that more publicity would only improve the sale.[9] Any kind of notice, even if it was controversial, drew attention to Murray's product, in this case at no cost. Indeed, the *Adventures of George*

---

[4] JM to John Trusler, 9 July 1785.

[5] JM to John Trusler, 29 March and 8 Apr. 1786. *English Review*, 5 (April 1785), 274–7. The review, which may have been written by Murray himself, digressed onto the subject of bookselling and noted some writers who 'have united the character of bookseller with that of author', including Trusler, whose 'voluminous productions . . . have been ushered into the world in the same way, not unprofitable to *himself*' (p. 276).

[6] JM to John Trusler, 6 Oct. 1786. *English Review*, 8 (July 1786), pp. 66–7. Trusler began the article: 'We are happy to find that the author of this ingenious novel has fallen in with our ideas respecting some little improprieties that stood in the first edition . . . particularly that of placing the hero . . . in a less conspicuous character than that of prime-minister of this country'. He concluded by asserting that the novel '*will most likely* be reprinted again and again'. A third edition did follow in 1786 (Checklist item 556).

[7] *Whitehall Evening Post*, 27 Dec. 1785. The *Life and Adventures of James Ramble*, a tale of the 1715 Jacobite Rising, was the anonymous work of Edward Kimber, first published in 1755 and reprinted by Newbery in 1770. 'Detector' was Charles Butler, whose work, *The Continuation of Mr. Hargrave's Edition of Lord Coke's Commentary of Littleton*, had been unfavourably reviewed by Gilbert Stuart ('Terrier') in the *English Review*, 6 (Oct. 1785), 275–8.

[8] *Whitehall Evening Post*, 31 Dec. 1785.

[9] In an article in the *English Review* for Jan. 1786 the republication was admitted, but it was asserted that the *Adventures of George Maitland* is better than 'nine-tenths of our modern novels' (*English Review*, 7, 56).

Maitland turned out to be very profitable: on a £100 outlay Murray more than doubled his investment.[10]

Some novels Murray published were intended for purposes other than entertainment. In 1783 Murray published a political satire by William Thomson called *The Man in the Moon*, whose characters are easily identified with political figures of the day. Then in 1789 he published Pollingrove Robinson's *Cometilla; or Views of Nature*, which indeed was no novel at all but an astronomy text book, got up as a romance. Thomas Beddoes' short tale, the *History of Isaac Jenkins* (1793), sought to impart the lessons of healthy and abstemious living to Britain's poor.[11] His radical views on social matters were sufficiently provocative to create an almost immediate demand for a second edition.

The real money Murray made from novels came more from buying shares in and reprinting the classics of English literature than from publishing new titles. Here, the steady sale of books was virtually guaranteed. The works of Fielding, Sterne, and Smollett all appeared in his lists — even Defoe's *Robinson Crusoe*. Murray purchased a one-sixteenth share in 1783 and published in syndicate the sixteenth edition of the novel the following year.[12] It eventually sold out, and a seventeenth edition appeared in 1791 (see Plate 37 and Murray's remark about Defoe's novel on p. 72).

Poetry

Murray was fortunate that William Falconer, before his untimely death, had introduced him to fellow poets Edmund Cartwright and John Langhorne. These men — together with Thomas Nugent (the editor of Milton's works) and Abraham Portal (another poet) — were among Murray's first circle of London literary associates.[13] Over beefsteaks and punch at the Peacock Tavern in Gray's Inn Lane, both Cartwright and Langhorne granted him the right to publish their next poetical efforts. Langhorne's *Fables of Flora*, published by Murray in 1771, went into three editions in that year alone. A handsome quarto production, it included a title page vignette drawn by Murray's boyhood friend John Paxton.[14] When Langhorne sold the copyright to Thomas Becket the following year and Becket paraded into the

[10]BB, p. 38. Murray netted £125 on the *Adventures of George Maitland*, of which just over 750 copies (priced at 6s.) were printed.
[11]R. Porter, *Doctor of Society. Thomas Beddoes and the Sick Trade in Late-Enlightenment England* (London, 1992), pp. 58 and 170.
[12]Murray bought his share of the two-volume edition of *Robinson Crusoe* for £4.10s. (BB, p. 33 and Checklist under DeFoe. 1784, item 408, and 1791, item 814).
[13]Another member of the circle was Thomas Cumming. See Cumming to JM, 17 July 1772, on their convivial group.
[14]Paxton did the drawing gratis; Thomas Simpson engraved it for five guineas (AL, p. 199).

shop to announce his purchase, Murray told Langhorne that he felt 'a sensible mortification not to possess the Property . . . of which I was so fond and for whose author I inherited a very uncommon share of Friendship and Regard'.[15] Nor did Murray's hopes to publish further works by Langhorne materialise. However, when Becket's property was auctioned at a bankruptcy sale in May 1779, Murray bought the whole of the copyright of the *Fables of Flora* for £5.3s. Profit could scarcely have been his motive since there was no demand for a new edition.[16] Langhorne, a cleric by profession, wrote poetry as a pastime. 'As to literary matters', he told Murray, 'I am good for nothing when I am married for I mind nothing but my wife. I peruse the contents of no volume but hers, and I think of no Production but what may issue from *that Press*.'[17] Sadly, Langhorne's wife died in childbirth in 1777 — the second of his wives to meet such a fate. Murray, by then a widower himself, tried unsuccessfully to draw Langhorne into town to lift his spirits, but Langhorne, never fully recovered from the calamity, took to drink and died in 1779.

Murray's relationship with Edmund Cartwright was happier and longer lasting. A cleric and poet like Langhorne, Cartwright was also a talented inventor whose chief contributions to the industrial revolution were the power loom and a wool-combing machine. But, despite this mechanical aptitude, he was a failed investor, and fell deep into debt. The sale of Cartwright's poetry, though considerable, did little to offset these losses. Cartwright's first effort, *Armine and Elvira*, went into three editions in 1771, two further in 1772 and another in 1777. In all, two thousand copies of the poem were printed, making it one of Murray's better selling publications.[18] Murray commissioned Isaac Taylor, a prominent artist, to draw and engrave a title page vignette for the work, but the illustration so displeased Cartwright that he asked Murray to retouch Armine who, he remarked, 'looks more like a butcher's boy than the son of an earl in disguise'.[19] Cartwright's literary innovation in *Armine and Elvira*, the tale of a would-be shepherd who falls in love with a girl of superior rank, was to take this popular romantic formula and cast it into narrative verse. He chose the ballad form for his composition, a genre popularised by Thomas Percy, the editor of the *Reliques of Ancient English Poetry* (1765), though he enhanced this traditional form with the more affected poetic language typical of the day. Through most of the poem Armine laments the injustice of his plight, but happily he

---

[15]JM to John Langhorne, 25 Aug. 1772.
[16]AL, p. 199; BB, p. 20. Twelve years later, at the sale of Murray's own shares and copyrights, Charles Dilly bought the property of the *Fables* for a mere 10s.6d. and afterwards anthologised the poem.
[17]John Langhorne to JM, 15 June 1772.
[18]Murray had some copies of *Armine and Elvira* printed by Jackson in Oxford and others by John and William Richardson (full details in AL, pp. 160, 163, 248; Plates 8 and 10; Checklist).
[19]Edmund Cartwright to JM, 24 May 1771.

discovers himself to be of noble birth, and wins his girl. Cartwright was apprehensive about how such a poem would be received, and apologised to Murray for 'the paternal Anxiety that a man must unavoidably feel for the first Brat that he publicly owns'.[20] In the *Monthly Review* John Langhorne (writing anonymously) praised the composition for its skilful blend of ancient simplicity without having resort to 'rudeness of nature'.[21] Cartwright was duly grateful and added a dedicatory verse to Langhorne in the third edition of the poem.

Although *Armine and Elvira* earned its author notoriety in the literary world and its publisher recognition in the trade, it did not make either man rich. Total profits were under £100.[22] By 1777 the vogue for the poem had passed, and Murray accepted ten guineas from a bookseller for the copyright. Murray's other publications of Cartwright's work were less successful. Even the topical *Prince of Peace* (1779), a poem deploring the American War, did not win public praise. Equally unprofitable was a poem by the Dubliner, Gerald Fitzgerald, entitled the *Injured Islanders; or, the Influence of Art upon the Happiness of Nature* (1779) (see Plates 38–40). Murray was extremely fond of the poem, which has some continuing interest as an early sociological study of Tahitian natives. He spent nine guineas on an unusual engraved vignette for the title page and printed five hundred copies. However, less than half of these sold.[23]

In the mid-1770s it was fashionable to publish longer poems in parts. Two popular titles published in this manner were William Mason's *English Garden* (1772–81), published by Dodsley and Cadell in four books, and James Beattie's *Minstrel* (1771–4), by the Dillys and Creech in two books. Murray was keen to try this method with a new poem by the Aberdeen divine John Ogilvie: 'I mean to usher *Rona* into the World this way. . . . [It] will be less apt to tire the Public, as a part will be read easier than the whole nor will the Expence of the Purchase be felt so heavily.'[24] This was not Murray's only consideration. The expense of publication, while it would not be less, would be spread out over a longer period, allowing the profits of the first part, should it be successful, to pay for the production cost of those that would follow.

Murray continued to publish a handful of new poems each year, but he did not deliver a single poetic masterpiece into the world. He profited from

---

[20] Ibid.

[21] *Monthly Review*, 45 (Aug. 1771), 103. Walter Scott later noted the beauties of *Armine and Elvira* in his introduction to the *Minstrelsy of the Scottish Border* (1802).

[22] Profits on *Armine and Elvira* were £108, but expenses came to over £60. Murray laid out over £25 on advertising *each* edition in the newspapers. His profit was in the difference between the £7.4s. he had agreed to pay Cartwright for each hundred. So selling copies retail (at 2s.) he could make only £10 (AL, pp. 163, 195).

[23] W. Hamilton drew the picture and Isaac Taylor engraved it. See Checklist item 220.

[24] JM to John Ogilvie, 21 Dec. 1775.

Table 2. Murray's Publishing Subjects: number of publications per year

Year	Agric.	Arts	Biog.	Drama	Econ.	Educ.	Fiction
1768	0	0	0	0	0	0	0
1769	0	1	0	0	1	0	1
1770	0	0	0	0	0	0	0
1771	0	0	0	0	0	0	0
1772	0	0	0	1	1	0	0
1773	0	0	0	0	0	1	0
1774	0	0	0	0	1	0	5
1775	1	1	0	0	2	0	0
1776	0	0	1	0	3	1	2
1777	0	0	2	0	0	0	1
1778	1	1	2	2	1	0	0
1779	0	0	2	0	1	0	0
1780	0	0	0	0	2	0	4
1781	0	0	1	1	0	1	1
1782	0	0	0	0	0	1	6
1783	0	0	1	0	1	1	4
1784	2	0	2	1	1	2	2
1785	1	0	2	4	1	1	2
1786	0	1	1	8	1	1	3
1787	1	0	2	3	0	4	3
1788	2	1	2	4	0	2	4
1789	0	0	2	0	2	2	1
1790	0	0	1	3	1	1	3
1791	1	1	0	4	1	4	3
1792	0	0	1	0	0	1	6
1793	0	0	2	1	1	3	3
TOTAL	9	6	24	32	21	26	54
%	0.9	0.6	2.5	3.3	2.2	2.7	5.6
1794	0	0	0	0	1	2	1
1795	1	0	1	0	2	1	0

publishing cheap and attractive editions of the poems of long-established favourites such as Thomas Gray and James Thomson, (made available by the 1774 copyright decision). He also bought shares in poetical works at trade sales, among them Homer, Virgil, Horace, Ovid, John Milton, John Gay, Oliver Goldsmith and Samuel Johnson.[25] In all, he produced over one hundred poetical titles (eleven per cent of the total), making it a publishing category second only to medical works (see Table 2 and Figure 3).

[25] BB, p. 32 (Homer); p. 73 (Dryden's Virgil); p. 8 (Horace); p. 26 (Ovid); pp. 9 and 58 (Gay's *Poems* and *Fables*); p. 74 (Milton's *Paradise Lost*); pp. 38 and 64 (Goldsmith); p. 43 (Johnson).

Year	Hist.	Lang.	Law	Lit. Crit.	Med.	Milit.	Misc.
1768	0	0	0	0	0	0	0
1769	0	0	0	0	1	1	3
1770	2	0	2	0	0	0	0
1771	2	0	0	0	0	0	0
1772	2	0	0	0	2	1	0
1773	4	1	0	1	5	0	1
1774	0	0	0	2	4	0	2
1775	2	2	0	1	4	0	1
1776	4	2	0	0	5	0	1
1777	0	3	1	0	8	0	2
1778	3	5	0	0	8	1	2
1779	6	0	1	0	12	2	5
1780	2	1	1	1	10	0	0
1781	3	0	0	1	9	0	1
1782	3	1	1	1	11	1	1
1783	3	4	0	0	15	3	3
1784	4	1	2	5	17	3	5
1785	1	2	2	4	12	2	3
1786	3	2	2	2	16	1	5
1787	4	4	4	1	19	1	5
1788	3	1	3	2	12	3	7
1789	5	2	2	1	7	0	5
1790	3	3	1	0	9	2	4
1791	2	3	2	1	3	0	4
1792	2	4	1	1	15	1	6
1793	4	2	2	3	11	2	4
TOTAL	67	43	27	27	225	24	70
%	6.9	4.4	2.8	2.8	23.2	2.4	7.2
1794	1	2	0	1	14	1	5
1795	0	1	0	1	14	0	3

cont.

In 1778 Murray acquired a one-twenty-fifth share of the *Works of the English Poets*, edited by Samuel Johnson. This ambitious undertaking of the London trade — published in various multi-volume forms — was presented to the public as the definitive edition of the English canon and set out to compete with John Bell's popular (and less expensive) series.[26] Few writers brought the London trade more profit than Johnson. Nor did any man of the day so dominate literary London. Murray's direct contact with Johnson was limited to occasional meetings among mutual friends and less frequent

[26] BB, p. 11; see Checklist under *Works* 1779, item 250, and 1790, item 801.

Table 2. *(cont.)*

Year	Phil.	Poetry	Polit.	Relig.	Sci.	Trav.–Top.	Annual Totals
1768	2	0	0	0	0	0	2
1769	0	3	0	7	0	2	20
1770	0	0	3	0	1	0	8
1771	0	8	1	2	1	0	14
1772	0	4	0	1	0	0	12
1773	0	2	2	0	0	1	18
1774	1	4	1	0	0	0	20
1775	0	2	1	1	1	0	19
1776	3	4	1	2	1	0	30
1777	1	2	0	3	2	1	26
1778	0	5	3	1	2	2	39
1779	0	5	1	3	3	1	42
1780	0	1	0	1	0	1	24
1781	1	0	2	2	0	0	23
1782	0	2	1	1	1	2	33
1783	0	5	6	8	4	3	61
1784	0	5	2	2	4	2	62
1785	0	2	1	2	4	2	48
1786	0	2	2	3	4	1	58
1787	0	5	3	5	4	0	68
1788	0	10	10	5	4	2	77
1789	0	8	1	2	2	1	43
1790	0	10	5	4	2	3	55
1791	2	2	1	3	1	5	53
1792	0	6	5	4	4	1	58
1793	0	6	8	5	1	2	60
TOTAL	10	103	60	66	46	32	973
%	1.0	10.6	6.1	6.8	4.7	3.3	
1794	0	1	2	4	2	0	37
1795	0	0	9	2	0	1	36

exchanges over literary matters (see below, under 'Translations' p. 172). His profits on Johnson's literary efforts — including shares in editions of the *English Poets*, the *Dictionary*, the *Rambler* and the *Works of Johnson* — were more enduring.[27]

[27]Investments and profits of the *English Poets*, BB, p. 11; the *Dictionary*, BB, pp. 10 and 23; *Rambler*, BB. p. 28; Johnson's *Works*, BB, p. 43.

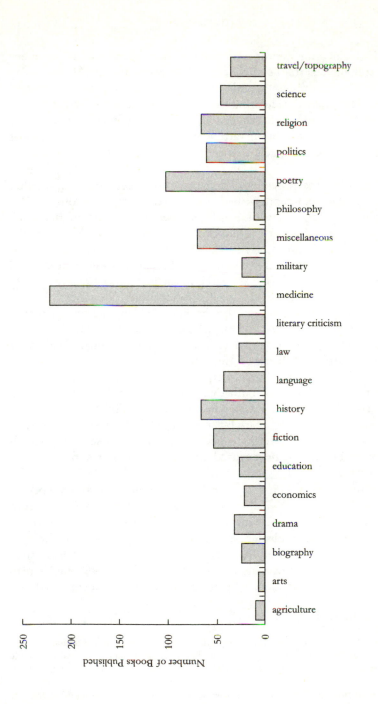

Figure 3. Murray's Publishing Subjects, 1768–93

Sermons

In the early eighteenth century the clergy had been the pre-eminent profession and their sermons the best-selling literature. In Murray's day the shift from the devotional towards the historical and fictional — a trend that reflected the gradual secularisation of British society — created new opportunities for a publisher. Nevertheless, he lived in what was still a profoundly religious age: church attendance was high; and the rise of Methodism and other evangelical movements was making its mark on British society.

William Sandby (the previous occupant of 32 Fleet Street) and other booksellers of the mid-century had published many religious works. Although Murray bought few of Sandby's titles at the sale of his stock and copyrights, he did inherit a handful of clerical authors and many religiously-minded customers. Even if Murray asserted that 'Divinity is not the most saleable article in the world', he remained aware that it could still bring profit.[28] Murray's name appeared in the imprints of nearly seventy religious titles (some seven per cent of his publications). In general, he was more inclined to publish moderate books like William Laurence Brown's *Essay on the Folly of Scepticism* (1788), which aimed at finding a proper medium between religious dogmatism and scepticism, than radical tracts that did not support the Church of England. Murray himself was less than devout. Though a regular churchgoer, religion was not central to his existence. Such was his lack of faith that his sister, Binny, when speaking of a zealous friend, remarked: 'I wish you only had what he could spare. I'm sure you would be a better man by a great deal.'[29] In truth, Murray's religious sentiments were rarely stirred. Even when chosen as a parish overseer for St Dunstan's, he excused himself by paying a fine of £10 rather than serve.[30]

One of Murray's first ventures into religious publications was a work by Donald Grant, a vicar in Yorkshire who was an old family friend from Edinburgh. In 1771 Grant gave Murray his *Two Dissertations on Popish Persecution*. Neither author nor publisher was sanguine about the sale of the 500-copy edition — a rare situation that said more about their friendship than about financial considerations. Grant even remarked that 'it will only be read by a few clerical People, or those who are counted equally queer'.[31] After a

---

[28]JM to John Whitaker, 19 July 1781.

[29]Binny McMurray to JM, 4 Dec. 1771.

[30]Parish Records of St Dunstan's in the West, Vestry Minutes 1749–89 (Guildhall Library, MS 3016, vol. 4), 29 Mar. and 7 Apr. 1780. Murray had also been elected a parish constable on 16 Dec. 1777, but he similary paid a fine of £12 and was excused. His attendance is not listed at a single parish meeting.

[31]Donald Grant to JM, 30 July 1771. Grant's work was a response to James Ussher's *Free Examination of the Common Methods Employed to Prevent the Growth of Popery* (1766–8).

modest sale, the work lay virtually untouched in Murray's warehouse until 1779 when he took advantage of the recent establishment of Protestant Associations (and in particular of anti-Catholic rioting in Scotland) to reissue the work with a new title page. Grant added a prefatory 'Contrast between the popish oath of allegiance and the principles of popery'.[32]

When the Reverend Jacob Duché of Philadelphia wrote in 1769 in the hope of finding a publisher, Murray reflected on the rise of secularism in society and offered the author hints for success:

> I confess that the spirit of dissipation & diversion prevails too much in the present age for any one to expect that a work of such a serious Nature as yours will be generally read. There are nevertheless some people, degenerate as the present times are, who think of these things. For this reason you have my advice to finish one volume or two; which when I see, you shall have my candid opinion.[33]

It was important to adapt to the changing tastes of the age without sacrificing devotional propriety. So Murray urged Duché to keep his essays short and write in the manner of Addison's *Spectator* or Johnson's *Rambler*. As a further improvement, he suggested introducing each essay with a Latin or Greek motto instead of a scripture text. And, wary of offending, Murray added that his remarks related only to 'the craft of book-selling'. Frankness did not win Murray the London publication of Duché's works, which were successfully sold by Cadell and other London booksellers.[34]

When Murray published the Reverend William Craig's *Discourses on Various Subjects* in January 1775 he had reason for guarded optimism. William Richardson, one of Murray's more successful authors, had a particular affinity for his fellow Glaswegian and told Murray: 'If any sermons sell . . . Dr Craig's will. They are elegantly and correctly written.'[35] But after a month of disappointing sales Murray, who was not inclined to offer consolation, told Craig: 'The Discourses would have been more fashionable had they been much shorter'.[36] Despite these failures early in his career,

---

[32]The list of stock at Murray's death surprisingly records no copies of Grant's *Dissertations*. It may be that the second edition of 1779 (Checklist items 224–25) sold well.

[33]JM to Jacob Duché, 10 Aug. 1769. In the same letter Murray, typically, solicited potential authors and customers in Duché's colonial circle. Duché was the minister of the United Churches of Christ Church and St Peter's in Philadelphia, Pennsylvania. An ardent supporter of the American cause, he became first chaplain of the Continental Congress, but after the Declaration of Independence, he wrote to George Washington predicting defeat. Cursed as a traitor, he fled to England in 1777 (*Dictionary of American Biography*, ii, 476–77).

[34]Duché's two-volume *Discourses* appeared in 1779 and went into a second edition the following year. An earlier work, *The Duty of Standing Fast*, was first published in Philadelphia and reprinted in London by Thomas Evans in 1775.

[35]Wm Richardson to JM, 1 Dec. 1774.

[36]JM to Wm Craig, 2 Feb. 1775.

Murray published the sermons of other Presbyterian divines, a number of whom preached in England. Henry Hunter, minister of the Scots Church at the London Wall, was the most prolific of all Murray's clerical authors. His *Sacred Biography, or the History of the Patriarchs* first appeared in 1783 and continued to be expanded and reissued into the nineteenth century.

Drama

Murray rarely published plays. Of his thirty-odd dramatic titles, only a handful were new works; the majority were reprints of classics. The first play Murray published was *Valentia; or, the Fatal Birthday*, written in 1772 by Thomas Stewart, a hairdresser turned dramatist. Murray was unwilling to risk anything on the work and charged all expenses to the author. Described as 'a dull Tragedy', *Valentia* was never acted.[37] Murray also published John Hough's *Second Thought is Best*, a two-act opera performed at the Theatre Royal in Drury Lane in March 1778. For the tragedy *Vimonda* (1788), he paid Andrew McDonald thirty guineas, but sales never came close to breaking even.[38] Later, he took unsold copies and appended them to an edition of McDonald's *Miscellaneous Works* (1791). It was the only way to dispose of unwanted copies of an unpopular play. Murray found there could be a more certain profit in publishing works about theatrical controversy, such as the censorship dispute described in William Taylor's *Concise Statement of Transactions respecting the King's Theatre, in the Haymarket* (1791).

Murray regularly reprinted popular dramatic works. In June 1783, for instance, he purchased a twelfth share in the plays of Henry Fielding. Thomas Cadell and George Robinson were among the other owners, and all parties just about doubled their investment.[39] At a London trade sale in 1778 Murray bought an eightieth share in the Samuel Johnson–George Steevens edition of the *Plays of William Shakspeare* [*sic*] (and an additional eightieth in 1783). This was both a prestigious property and a profitable one, so much so that in 1790 he invested in a large share of Edmond Malone's new edition of Shakespeare.[40] As a co-owner (one of over thirty),

---

[37] *Some Account of the English Stage from the Restoration in 1660 to 1830*, ed. John Genest (Bath, 1832, New York repr.), x, 155. Checklist item 56.
[38] JM to Wm Richardson, 14 Sept. 1792; BB, p. 69. *Vimonda* was scheduled for performance on 5 Sept. 1792 at Haymarket but was never acted (*Some Account of the English Stage*, vi, 455). The success of a new dramatic publication largely depended on how well the performance itself was received. Copies were usually made available at the theatre.
[39] Murray bought the Fielding shares at the sale of Thomas Caslon (5 June 1782) for £4.12s. See BB, p. 31, Checklist 1783, item 346, and 1784, item 414.
[40] BB, pp. 12 and 67. JM to James Sibbald, 4 Dec. 1790, where Murray noted two editions of Malone's edition of Shakespeare: one in eleven vols. large octavo and another less expensive one in seven vols. duodecimo.

Murray also had a hand in the publication of individual Shakespeare plays. In all, Murray's name appeared on over twenty-five Shakespeare titles between 1778 and 1793 (see Plates 41 and 42).[41]

Histories and Historians

When David Hume remarked to his bookseller William Strahan, 'I believe this is the historical Age and this the historical Nation', he was alluding to the predominance of historical writing as a literary genre in Britain.[42] More than ever before booksellers were paying historians substantial sums for their manuscripts and making large profits. Murray, as a publisher of new historical works, had a share of success, although neither a Hume, a Robertson nor a Gibbon was in his lists. Such topics as the rise and fall of republics, the reign of Mary Queen of Scots, the Commonwealth, and the history of America interested the public at large as never before, a public growing increasingly literate and ever more conscious of its own history. Murray would not have used the phrase 'the beginnings of modern histor-iography', but that was the intellectual domain he was determined to enter as a publisher. He encouraged his authors to take up subjects relevant to 'the people' and to write about the controversies which engaged the successful historians of the day.

One of Murray's first original historical publications was John Millar's *Distinction of Ranks* (1771), an important work in the socio-historical, or 'conjectural' tradition that was popular in Scotland. The book went into three editions in Murray's day and is currently in print. Afterwards Murray published Millar's *Historical View of English Government* (1787). Some of Murray's other historical titles are Millot's *Elements of the History of England* (1771), David Dalrymple's *Annals of Scotland* (1776–79), Michael Kearney's *Lectures concerning History* (1776), Hugo Arnot's *History of Edinburgh* (1779), Gilbert Stuart's *History of Mary Queen of Scots* (1782), histories of Greece by John Gast (1782) and William Mitford (1784), John Whitaker's *Mary Queen of Scots Vindicated* (1787), and a number of military histories. Murray also bought shares in such popular historical works as Oliver Goldsmith's histories of England and Rome (in both complete and abridged forms) and the sixty-volume *Universal History* (1779–84). These syndicate publica-tions proved to be profitable investments.[43]

---

[41]On Shakespeare editions of the period, see Colin Franklin, *Shakespeare Domesticated. The Eighteenth-Century Editions* (Aldershot, 1991).
[42]David Hume to Wm Strahan, [Aug. 1770], *The Letters of David Hume*, 2 vols., ed. J. T. Grieg (Oxford, repr. 1969), ii, 230.
[43]BB, p. 13. See Checklist (Goldsmith) items 223, 418, 586, 762, 938 and 940; *Universal History* items 248 and 260.

Gilbert Stuart and John Whitaker were two historians, well known in their day, who published their works with Murray and played important roles in his bookselling career. Stuart was one of his closest friends and most trusted advisors; Whitaker was the recipient of some of Murray's most thoughtful remarks on the literary scene. Both men had a taste for controversy, which Murray, being similarly disposed, encouraged. Though impressed by their acute intellects, he did not always judge accurately the public appetite for their contentious modes of historical literature.

Stuart and Murray had both arrived in London from Edinburgh in 1768 to make careers for themselves. Stuart — a scholar by inclination and Grub Street writer by necessity — was at 32 Fleet Street almost every day planning projects that might increase Murray's business and his own income. The conversations continued over the daily newspapers at Munday's Coffee House and, afterwards, over supper (usually punch and beefsteaks) at the Peacock in Gray's Inn Lane.[44] Stuart kept irregular hours, and Murray, who had the responsibility of running a business and the obligations of a husband, could not always keep up with his friend's dissolute pace. But he tried.

No man — Archy Paxton excepted — was fonder of Murray or more interested in his advancement in the book trade than Stuart. When an opportunity in Edinburgh compelled Stuart to leave London in September 1773 without bidding a proper farewell, Murray wrote an affectionate letter of complaint. Stuart apologised, but reminded him: 'We are too well acquainted to stand on ceremony with one another, or to vie in that formal impertinence, which the world terms complaisance, good-breeding, or politeness'.[45] Murray was equally forward in offering advice. He marvelled at the effortless and speedy manner in which Stuart wrote, but he knew that Stuart tended to misdirect his tremendous energies. When Murray saw the promise of Stuart's *Edinburgh Magazine and Review* begin to fade under his careless management and controversial digressions, he wrote in the strongest terms:

> For Heavens sake know your self better than squander your precious time to such an unprofitable purpose. Or does the gratification of your spleen and resentment . . . recompence you for the odium and poverty you sustain in conducting the work? . . . I am serious in what I write to you, and your conduct becomes the more absurd the more I reflect upon it — so that I drop the subject now for fear of growing angry upon it. But I beseech you seriously to lay to heart my remonstrances which my regard for you alone dictate.[46]

---

[44]For an account of their gatherings see T. Somerville, *My Own Life and Times, 1741–1814,* (Edinburgh, [1861]), p. 149. For a general biography of Stuart see W. Zachs, *Without Regard to Good Manners. A Biography of Gilbert Stuart 1743–1786* (Edinburgh, 1992). This section, rather than repeating what I have already said about Stuart, looks at his career from a point of view relevant to a study of Murray.
[45]Gilbert Stuart to JM, 1 Sept. 1773.
[46]JM to Gilbert Stuart, 22 Nov. 1774.

After the failure of the periodical Stuart returned to historical writing. Although Murray did not always make the highest offer for Stuart's manuscripts, he always managed the London sale of the works and used his influence with the proprietors of reviews and newspapers to procure favourable notices. In one work, however, Stuart had launched such a severe attack on the character of William Robertson, one of the most popular historians of the day, that Murray found himself the object of a covert challenge by Robertson's booksellers (Strahan and Cadell). 'It is impossible', he adamantly told Stuart, 'to select men fonder of their interest . . . than the proprietors in question. . . . Those persons who wish to damn you as an author, have it next at heart to ruin me as a publisher.'[47]

By 1779 Stuart had become *persona non grata* in the literary world, but Murray stood by him and joined the challenge against some formidable adversaries. In 1780 Murray paid Stuart just £60 for his *History of the Reformation in Scotland*. It was certainly a small sum — much less than Stuart expected. Only half of the 750 copies sold. So two years later, when Stuart had completed another work — a history of Mary Queen of Scots — Murray offered Stuart two options for the publication: either accept £50 for a first edition of 500 copies plus £20 more if they all sold; or, take £60 regardless of the sale. Although Murray was apologetic about the offer, he had to protect his financial interests. He urged Stuart — whoever he chose as his publisher — to retain the right to renegotiate on the second edition, and added that, 'I have never yet given you interested, or even erroneous counsel, and this consideration I think entitles me to your confidence. From this however do not infer that I mean you should prefer my offer. I desire no more than that you should dispose of your work upon the principles I have mentioned.'[48] Stuart had few publishers to whom he could turn and so accepted the £60. Murray produced an elegant edition in two quarto volumes in 1782. Hopeful of success, he advertised Stuart's earlier works (many copies of which he had on hand) on the final leaf of the *History*. The first edition sold out within a year and was followed by a second in the less expensive octavo format. Stuart's portrait of the Queen of Scots as a tragic heroine had captured the public imagination. Critics hailed the work as the definitive account of sixteenth-century Scottish history, and the *Encyclopedia Britannica* (second edition) reprinted most of the work along with Stuart's *History of the Reformation*.[49]

Stuart, who had been living in Scotland for several years, returned to London late in 1782 in the wake of his new-found celebrity. Murray had

[47]JM to Gilbert Stuart, 11 March 1779. The work in question was Stuart's *Observations concerning the Public Law, and the Constitutional History of Scotland*.
[48]JM to Gilbert Stuart, 22 Nov. 1781.
[49]*Encyclopaedia Britannica*, 10 vols. (Edinburgh, 1778–83), ix, 6988–7174 [misnumbered 8074]. Murray initiated a law suit which is discussed in Chapter 10, pp. 189–91.

asked him to assist with the *English Review* which he was about to establish. Under Murray's editorial supervision, Stuart and other talented writers produced a periodical to rival the leading London literary reviews. Murray sometimes had to check Stuart's extremism — his hyperbolic praise of some writers and unaccountably scathing attacks on others — but he was confident enough to entrust Stuart with the management of the *Review* when he had to be out of town.[50]

After two years' service, Stuart was offered the editorship of a radical journal — the *Political Herald* — sponsored by the leaders of the Opposition party.[51] Murray was reluctant to part with his right-hand man, but there was no question that Stuart should seize the opportunity and the financial rewards that came with it. Murray could still count on him for the occasional review and for his regular company at the Peacock. Stuart's success was short-lived. In the spring of 1786, less than a year after he became editor of the *Herald*, illness forced him to retire. Jaundice, dropsy and asthma had been brought on by years of dissipated living. Stuart's hasty departure for Scotland prevented Murray from seeing his friend one last time. In a note Murray reflected on their long friendship: 'If you are able to favour me with a line . . . you will greatly oblige a man who since the commencement of our acquaintance always had your reputation and real welfare at heart'.[52] Writing to John Millar in September 1786, a month after Stuart's death, Murray remarked: 'Dr. Stuart . . . was the greatest enemy to himself. He could not endure to be thought subject to human infirmities; he was confident to the last in his constitution; and this confidence killed him, for he would take no care of himself.'[53] Murray, though himself somewhat more prudent and responsible, nevertheless understood that Stuart's limitations as a man were, paradoxically, his virtues as a writer. That same excess of passion in his day-to-day life animated the pages of his historical and critical works. Murray's admiration was mixed with regret. More than any other man, he guided Stuart, profited from his labours, appreciated his peculiar genius, and defended his character.[54]

John Whitaker was a Church of England vicar who met Murray in the early 1770s at Munday's Coffee House. Born in Manchester, he lived for a time in London before obtaining a post at Ruan in Cornwall. In 1773 Murray published two books by Whitaker: a much revised edition of his

[50]*Gentleman's Magazine*, 57 (Apr. 1787), 296.

[51]The leaders of the Opposition in 1785 were Edmund Burke, Charles James Fox and Richard Brinsley Sheridan. The head of Government was William Pitt.

[52]JM to Gilbert Stuart, 5 Aug. 1786. Stuart died on 13 Aug. 1786 at the age of forty-three.

[53]JM to John Millar, 7 Sept. 1786.

[54]After his death Stuart came under attack in the public press, and Murray (together with William Thomson) came to his defence (*Gentleman's Magazine*, 56, Dec. 1786, 1128). 'I have lately been employed in defending his memory from the attacks of [John] Pinkerton . . . in the Gentleman's Magazine', Murray told Andrew Dalzel on 4 Apr. 1787.

History of Manchester, and a second edition of the *Genuine History of the Britons Asserted*. Whitaker had published at his own expense the first edition of these titles in 1771 and 1772 respectively. After meeting Murray in London, he transferred their management to him and began an association that continued for over twenty years.[55]

The plan of the *History of Manchester* appealed to Murray because, more than providing an account of a provincial town, Whitaker had encompassed a general view of British history in his work. He had planned a comprehensive four-book study: the first on the Roman and Romano-British period; the second concerning Saxon times; and two further volumes bringing events to the modern era. While Whitaker was at work on the Saxon volume, Murray encouraged him to emphasise his opposition to historians like David Hume: 'Your work will acquire more eclat from your strictures on . . . Hume [who] is alive & in the zenith of his Reputation. Spare him not therefore but wield your weapons like a Gentleman.'[56] Murray solicited a glowing review of the *History* from Gilbert Stuart, who afterwards told Murray:

> I am perfectly in admiration of the whole work; and I . . . may be tempted to offend the nationality of our countrymen by saying of it what it deserves. I am only afraid, that I should irritate *you* beyond measure. I know your admiration of Hume & Robertson; and if I should venture . . . to assign the palm of history to Mr Whitaker, you would never forgive me.[57]

Murray admired Hume and Robertson because their historical works were written for a wide audience and sold well. Stuart admired Whitaker because, like himself, he was an historian of an antiquarian and controversial bent. Concerned about Whitaker's overly learned manner, but not wishing him to err on the side of simplicity, Murray advised him to direct his writing 'not indeed to the capacities of old women; but to such common capacities as my own'. It mattered little to Murray if Whitaker gained a reputation 'amongst antiquaries and the mere learned', of whom he added, 'in general I have not the highest opinion.'[58] (Indeed, on a visit to Manchester in 1775

---

[55]The imprints of the first editions of the *History of Manchester* and the *Genuine History of the Britons* list Dodsley and Cadell among other London booksellers as the selling agents. However a loose sheet (in AL) headed an 'Account of Mr. Whitakers Books' states that the copies were delivered from George Nicoll, a bookseller not included in the imprints. It may be that Nicoll bought them from Robert Dodsley who had died in 1771. Murray also managed the sale of the *Principal Corrections made in the History of Manchester* (1773), which was given to those who had bought the first quarto edition as the revised second edition was in the octavo format.

[56]JM to John Whitaker, 24 Aug. 1774.

[57]Gilbert Stuart to JM, 2 Mar. 1775, Hughenden Papers G/1/936, Bodleian Library. Stuart's review of the *History of Manchester*, Book 2 appeared in the *Edinburgh Magazine and Review*, iii, 259. He had also reviewed the first book in the same periodical (ii, 490).

[58]JM to John Whitaker, 8 Apr. 1775.

Murray politely suffered Whitaker's long, guided tour of the local antiquities but later recorded in his diary that he could remember 'nothing . . . so averse is my taste from the study'.[59]) Murray's 'common capacity' was representative of the active lay reader of his day — the body of people who bought books.

The poor sale of the first two books of the *History of Manchester* discouraged Murray from publishing any more. Neither favourable reviews nor any amount of advertising could extend the sale much beyond Manchester, and he described surplus copies of this 'unfortunate adventure' as 'little better than waste paper'.[60] Despite this failure, Murray did not lose interest in Whitaker's literary projects. Still, steering his author in more profitable directions proved arduous. Whitaker often lost interest in the work at hand, preoccupied as he was with clerical duties and the responsibilities of a farm and family. Among the works Murray had hoped to publish were a pamphlet against Dr Johnson favouring the authenticity of Ossian's poems, a 'new English dictionary in opposition to Johnson's', and a volume of sermons.[61] But none of these ever materialised.

Whitaker did write two books published under the Murray imprint which did achieve some notoriety: *Mary Queen of Scots Vindicated* (1787) and *Gibbon's History of the Decline and Fall Reviewed* (1791). If Whitaker could not write like Gibbon (in 1775 Murray had encouraged him to write a history of Rome), he could successfully criticise the historian of Rome as an infidel. Whitaker's attack (on the last three volumes of Gibbon's work) had first appeared in Murray's *English Review* in several instalments and was popular enough for Murray to plan a separate publication. 'Mr. Gibbon', Whitaker wrote, 'comes forward with all the rancour of a renegado, against Christianity. He tramples upon it at first, with the cloven-foot of Heathenism. He dungs upon it at last, from the dirty tail of Mohametanism.'[62] Whitaker was only one of Gibbon's many detractors (though among the more vituperative) who fell away as the *Decline and Fall* became a classic.

Whitaker's investigation into the story of Mary Queen of Scots grew out

[59]Diary, 25 Apr. 1775.
[60]JM to John Whitaker, 20 Mar. 1775. Whitaker appears to have made some progress on the third volume, the Danish and Norman-Danish periods. The *Dictionary of National Biography* notes the existence of a manuscript in the Chetham Library, Manchester.
[61]On Whitaker's Ossian pamphlet see JM to John Whitaker, 8 Apr. 1775. Murray had second thoughts on the work: 'Altho I dare believe it will be well executed yet I could wish the author to let it alone as I am apt to believe that the learned *Bear* [Johnson] is right in that argument' (JM to Robert Cullen, 28 May 1775). On the proposed dictionary, see Whitaker to JM, 4 Apr. 1775. On Whitaker's sermons, see JM to Whitaker, 19 July 1781. Whitaker's *Course of Sermons, upon Death, Judgment, Heaven, and Hell* was in fact published in 1783 by Charles Dilly.
[62]Whitaker, *Gibbon's History of the Decline and Fall Reviewed*, p. 256. Murray said of the review: 'There is no instance of so long an account of any publication since Journals called Reviews commenced in England; and the size of the work & reputation of its author are our only apology' (JM to John Whitaker, 2 Feb. 1789).

of the renewed interest that Gilbert Stuart's *History* had raised on the subject. Murray had done well by Stuart's work, but ultimately it had not supplanted William Robertson's more enduring account of the Queen. Whitaker had more to say, but Murray was not altogether optimistic about the prospect of a good sale. He acknowledged that Whitaker's new research on the Queen would please 'the partizans of that unfortunate Princess', but he was convinced 'that like the Knight errants of old, the action must be its own reward, for there are not readers enough interested to make the sale a suitable reward for the author'.[63] Whitaker wanted £200 for the two-volume book — a large sum. Murray explained that he would willingly give £400 were he 'indemnified against loss', and proceeded to offer just £40. Finally the two men settled on £50.[64] Before publication, Whitaker added material extending the *Vindication* to a third volume, so Murray agreed to give him £60 in total. By way of apology he remarked: 'Had it been a regular history, an additional volume would have been of additional value. I am afraid that in works of controversy this sentiment will not hold.'[65] When Whitaker asked for money before the date of publication, Murray reminded him that booksellers in general never pay for at least three months. But he allowed Whitaker to draw £25 in a month's time.[66]

Murray himself took a special interest in the historical period which Whitaker (like Stuart before him) had investigated. As a Scot he was sympathetic to the injustice of Mary's imprisonment by her cousin Queen Elizabeth. The intrigue of late sixteenth-century politics fascinated him, and he encouraged Whitaker to recreate vividly the historical drama.

> Elizabeth . . . was every thing but humane, virtuous, or generous. Nevertheless she was a princess of firmness & prowess. . . . And after all it must be admitted that she lived in critical times; not only her Crown but her life became the forfeit of the least piece of political inattention or negligence. Yet under these circumstances would a heroic mind have put to death a princess altho' a Rival who by invitation claimed her protection?[67]

Whitaker's *Vindication* met with initial success. Murray planned the date of publication in May 1787 to coincide with a new edition of Robertson's history of the queen (it was also the two hundredth anniversary of Mary's death). The public bought Whitaker's book, and Murray issued a revised second edition in 1788. Robertson, Murray told Whitaker, 'shelters himself under your *manner*, which he has declared in company is *scurrilous*, to

[63] JM to John Whitaker, 6 Oct. 1785.
[64] JM to John Whitaker, 16 Aug. 1786.
[65] JM to John Whitaker, 7 May 1787.
[66] JM to John Whitaker, 7 Oct. 1786.
[67] JM to John Whitaker, 23 Apr. 1788.

insinuate that you are not entitled to a reply from his pen'.[68] According to Murray, Whitaker's overzealous manner had hurt the reception of the *Vindication*. The author took this criticism so badly that Murray temporarily retreated. He did not want to fall out with Whitaker since their relations on the whole had been long-lived and profitable. The rift over Whitaker's style was healed and their correspondence resumed. In October 1790 he told Whitaker, 'I should consider the smallest interruption to our antient friendship as a real disaster', and the two continued to plan literary projects until the final weeks of Murray's life.[69]

Translations

Publishing English translations of popular foreign works could be profitable. No copyright money had to be paid either to the author or the original publisher. Just as Dublin booksellers reprinted London publications, so booksellers like Murray freely translated and published new foreign works. Between 1768 and 1778 Murray published fifteen translations, and afterwards some seventy-five more — about eight per cent of his total output. French works, including those of Voltaire, predominated, but German, Italian, Latin, Greek, Sanskrit and even Hebrew titles were also in his lists.[70] In his first year of business Murray issued editions of two translations long since popular in Britain: the Marquis d'Agens' *New Memoirs Establishing a True Knowledge of Mankind* (first translated in 1747); and Fénelon's *Demonstration of the Existence of God* (1713). Murray did not own the copyright to these translations. He had merely bought enough copies of the previous editions to warrant his printing a new title page (Checklist items 4 and 8).

New translations did, however, involve expense and risk. Translators had to be paid, and their fees were not small. Moreover, another bookseller might publish a competing translation. Whoever produced his edition first was usually the most likely to succeed. So, when Murray was preparing a multi-volume translation, his strategy was sometimes to print the first volume and make it available to the public and thus stake his claim. Other times, he might offer a share in his edition to a competitor. 'We are sorry', he told George Robinson, 'that there are likely to be two translations of Volney's Travels. Our translation is in reality advanced, the paper ordered

---

[68]Ibid. Murray added of Robertson: 'If he had not this apology he would find some other. He is a man of the World who loves money, and knows that controversy is unprofitable & laborious withal to an author'.
[69]JM to John Whitaker, 2 Oct. 1790.
[70]The Hebrew translation was the *Travels of Rabbi Benjamin of Tudela* (Checklist 1783, item 332, and 1784, item 394).

for printing, and the plates engraving. In order however to prevent any competition or rivalship, we are willing to join forces.'[71]

Murray engaged competent literary men — often in the early stages of their careers — to prepare his translations. Thomas Beddoes, who later became a prominent figure in the medical world, translated Torbern Bergman's *Essay on the Usefulness of Chemistry* (1783); William Godwin translated the *Memoirs of Simon Lord Lovat* (1785); and the scientist John Leslie translated Buffon's *Natural History of Birds* (1792).[72]

In 1771 Murray published his first translation from scratch — a two-volume edition of the Abbé Millot's *Elémens de l'Histoire d'Angleterre* (1769). Millot's work, containing the basic 'elements' of English history from Roman times to the reign of George II, was an abridgement designed for readers who lacked the time or inclination to read much longer histories of England by Clarendon, Rapin, Hume or Smollett. The title page credited the miscellaneous writer William Kenrick with the translation, but Murray in fact had commissioned Gilbert Stuart and John Langhorne each to complete a quarter of the work. The translation was done freely rather than word for word. Langhorne, summing up their approach, told Murray: 'You will find the work concluded with proper spirit, tho, God knows, it is in many places the very reverse of what the Popish Frenchman has alledged'.[73] In an era when anti-French and anti-Catholic sentiment ran high, authorial intention mattered less than a favourable reception. Translating alone cost over £100, and printing and paper for one thousand copies amounted to £160. Murray paid Stuart an additional five guineas to correct the stylistic inconsistencies that were inevitable when different hands had been at work on the translation. An index, extensive advertising (over £24), and other miscellaneous expenses raised the total to nearly £260 — a considerable sum, and more than Murray might venture for the copyright of an original work in English (see Plates 29 and 30).[74] But it was a gamble encouraged by the popularity of the French edition.

Murray anticipated a good sale, but, unwilling to risk the entire cost himself, he brought in two equal partners — William Nicoll and Joseph Johnson. As publication day neared, he met with an unexpected setback: a rival translation by the novelist Frances Brooke, published by Dodsley and Cadell, went on sale. It was now clearly too late to ward off competition, so strong advertising and favourable notices were essential. Murray's publication

---

[71]JM to Geo. Robinson, 6 June 1787. The work was C. F. Volney, *Travels through Syria and Egypt* (London: G. G. J. and J. Robinson, 1787). A 2nd edn. followed in 1788. Just what arrangement Murray made with Robinson, if any, is not recorded. He may have been paid a sum to discontinue his translation, or more probably he was given copies of Robinson's edition at a reduced price.

[72]JM to John Leslie, 13 Aug. 1790.

[73]John Langhorne to JM, 2 Apr. 1771.

[74]AL, p. 123, and the loose sheet at this page.

got the upper hand when Gilbert Stuart anonymously reviewed the two translations together in an article in the *Monthly Review*. Although well qualified to judge the work, Stuart clearly had reason to be prejudiced about their merits: 'Ease and freedom, and the dignity of historical narration have been aimed at by the one. The . . . other is faithful but feeble', he told the public.[75] Less influence could be wielded in the rival *Critical Review*, which printed separate and equally favourable reviews of the two translations.[76] The publication that year of Oliver Goldsmith's *History of England*, which covered the same period as Millot's history, brought further challenges. Stuart volunteered to write the review in the *Monthly*, and, in his hands, Goldsmith was condemned on political and literary grounds.[77] Nor was this all: Stuart (or Murray) wrote a piece in the *Middlesex Journal* comparing Goldsmith to Millot and instructing the public which book to buy: 'The Frenchman has entered profoundly into the state of parties, and was possessed of much political sagacity. The Irishman, destitute of penetration, was totally incapable of making a proper estimate of the actions and the views of statesmen.'[78] Murray profited from his translation of Millot. But Goldsmith's *History* sold well — so well that Murray even bought a share in 1778.[79] The work appeared in many editions and remained popular well into the nineteenth century.

Murray published other translations of French accounts of English history. The most successful was J. L. DeLolme's *Constitution of England; or an Account of English Government*. George Kearsley was the main proprietor of the work, but in 1773 Murray arranged for Gilbert Stuart to translate it for thirty guineas. DeLolme, who was then in London and had begun a translation himself, made the final corrections.[80] In 1785 Murray produced a revised French edition to which DeLolme added introductory remarks reflecting on the constitutional implications of recent events in America. In all, Murray published seven editions — more than 2000 copies. His profit from the work, selling copies as well as shares of the copyright to other booksellers, was nearly £300.[81]

Not all of Murray's translations were so successful. And some never appeared. In July 1772 Immanuel Johann Scheller, a struggling German writer, came to 32 Fleet Street to consult Murray about publishing a

[75] *Monthly Review*, 45 (Nov. 1771), 269.
[76] *Critical Review*, 32 (July 1771), 56–61 (Brooke's trans.); (Nov. 1771), 337–40 (Kenrick *et al.*).
[77] *Monthly Review*, 45 (Dec. 1771), 436–44. Stuart wrote of Goldsmith's 'insipid langour and the tawdry pettiness of romance' (p. 444).
[78] *Middlesex Journal*, 9 Apr. 1772.
[79] BB, p. 13.
[80] The imprint of the first English edition of DeLolme reads: 'London: George Kearsley, 1775'. The first French edn. was published in Amsterdam in 1771. Stuart also reviewed the work (*Edinburgh Magazine and Review*, iv, 595).
[81] BB, pp. 24 and 68.

translation he was preparing of Isaak Iselin's *Geschichte der Menschheit* (1764), or the 'History of Mankind'.[82] Scheller had even obtained the promise from Samuel Johnson to inspect his English translation. He had already purchased (on credit) a set of Johnson's *Dictionary* from Murray to aid him with the translation, and, on the strength of the money Scheller expected to receive for the translation, borrowed a few guineas from the bookseller.[83] When Murray received the manuscript, he was less than pleased with the translation. Rather than confront Scheller, he asked Dr Johnson to rework the translation, which he judged unpublishable in its present form.

> It would be required in many places to be taken to pieces; the english idiom to be preserved a great number of the periods to be transposed & harmonized and the author's meaning to be renderd every where clear and distinct. This is a Task which I never considered that your promise of barely looking over the English implied. But unless it is performed I cannot think of printing the Book.[84]

Murray told Johnson to name the terms for his editorial services, but nothing ever came of this suggestion. Johnson was evidently not inclined to do more than had been originally agreed. Murray might even have done the editing himself or found someone else to improve the translation, but he did not. Scheller, whose hopes rested on the project, already owed him over £14 and was compelled to return his copy of Johnson's *Dictionary*. Only six years later did he settle his account.

Medical Works

In 1770 William Wilson, a family friend from Edinburgh who had taken an interest in the success of Murray's business, recommended him to William Cullen, the eminent medical professor at Edinburgh University.[85] Murray and the Edinburgh trade began to publish Cullen's works in 1772 and continued to the end of the century. Cullen was such a tough negotiator

---

[82]Immanuel J. G. Scheller (1735–1803), the son of Johan Gerhard Scheller, was a philologist and pedagogue and was well known on the Continent as an author of instructional books for Latin, Greek and Hebrew. Isaak Iselin, together with a group of German intellectuals, founded a society — the Europäische Aufmunterungsgesellschaft — to consider legal and moral issues. To further their programme, they contacted such men as Rousseau, Helvetius, Diderot, Algarotti, Kames, Hume, and Adam Smith (see Ulrich Im Hof, *Isaak Iselin und die Spätaufklärung*, Bern und München, 1967).

[83]AL, p. 166.

[84]JM to Samuel Johnson, 31 Jan. 1773.

[85]JM to Wm Wilson, 5 Oct. 1770. In his lectures and in a long list of published works Cullen influenced a generation of research and practice by emphasising the chemical basis of medicine and by categorising diseases systematically (nosology). See *William Cullen and the Eighteenth Century Medical World*, eds. Passmore and Doig (Edinburgh, 1993).

that Murray initially reaped only a small profit (see p. 94). However, a connection with one prominent member of the medical community cleared the way for other more profitable publishing opportunities.

In the space of a decade Murray became one of the leading medical publishers in Britain. Scottish, English and Continental physicians and surgeons all had a place in his lists. Over 220 titles — almost one quarter of his publications — were on medical topics, by far his largest area of specialisation (Figures 3 and 4). From the late 1770s to the time of his death in 1793 Murray was known among medical authors for reliable and expert dealing. In no other sphere was his reputation as high. Fellow tradesmen recognised his ability to cultivate the leading practitioners and theorists and promote their works. Although more dependent on the advice of experts to determine the value of a work, he was fortunate in his circle of highly qualified readers.

At first Murray was somewhat prudish in his choice of medical publications. When Charles Elliot offered him the London sale of a cure for syphilis in 1774, he explained: 'I must refuse it as the nature of it might affect with modest people the character of my shop'.[86] This caution soon gave way to the realisation that there was profit in selling such books and no cause for embarrassment. From the mid-1770s Murray published many titles on venereal disease and other 'sensitive' afflictions. Some of his publications could even be classed more as sexual curiosities than as scientific studies: for example, Thomas Brand's *Case of a Boy, who had been Mistaken for a Girl; with Three Anatomical Views of the Parts, before and after the Operation and Cure* (1787); or Richard Griffith's *Singular Case of Reproduction of the Sphincter Ani* (1792).[87]

The number of medical publications was increasing every year, and new discoveries were changing the science. Where a literary work like *Robinson Crusoe* might remain ever popular, medical books usually had a more limited shelf-life and a narrower audience. By printing to meet demand, by dealing firmly with authors and other booksellers, by sensible marketing, and, indeed, by promoting controversy, Murray made money.[88] During the eighteenth century in Britain there had been a gradual shift from the use of Latin to English in medical and other scientific works. Murray urged his authors to write in English to maximise sales. No longer was it the scholar-practitioner alone who wrote, or read, treatises on disease; nor were lectures

---

[86]JM to Charles Elliot, 10 Dec. 1774.
[87]Brand's operation was a success and 'the child, who could before make water only in a sitting posture, performed this function in the manner of any other boy' (as noted in the *English Review*, 11, Jan. 1788, 70).
[88]On the subject of medical controversy generally, see David Harley, 'Honor and Property: the Structure of Professional Disputes in Eighteenth-Century English Medicine', in A. Cunningham and R. French (eds.), *The Medical Enlightenment of the Eighteenth Century* (Cambridge, 1990), pp. 139–64.

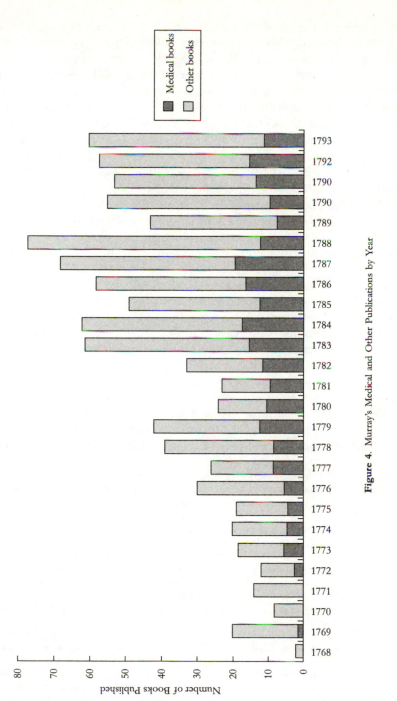

Figure 4. Murray's Medical and Other Publications by Year

by members of medical faculties delivered in Latin. 'The most eminent medical people in England', Murray remarked in 1772, 'altho they can read latin upon occasion are fonder of English.'[89] Similar trends among European medical authors opened a market for English translations of the most important foreign texts. Murray planned and published many of these.[90] He also published the *Foreign Medical Review* in 1779 and 1780. As well as medical titles, the editor (François Xaviar Swediaur) included accounts and extracts of new books on natural history, botany and chemistry. The public was informed that it would be possible 'to procure speedily all Books that may be desired' and 'any new invented chirurgical or obstetrical instruments or drawings of them'.[91]

In the last part of the eighteenth century the public had begun to regard medicine less as a mysterious art and more as a rational science which they could practise at home according to simple principles. The market was increasing rapidly for such works as George Motherby's *New Medical Dictionary; or the General Repository of Physic* (first published by Joseph Johnson in 1775 and afterwards by Murray and others in 1785 and 1791) and Bryan Cornwell's *Domestic Physician* (first published by Murray and others in 1784 and again in 1787 and 1788), which pointed out 'in the most familiar manner, the symptoms of every disorder . . . together with their gradual progress and method of cure'. These authors may have sometimes been at odds with the medical establishment for their democratising efforts, but for Murray the sale of their works generated income.[92] Thomas Beddoes, who came to be known as one of the leading promoters of public health, virtually began his career at 32 Fleet Street. Initially, he translated medical and other scientific works for Murray; afterwards, Murray published some of Beddoes' original medical and social inquiries.[93] Of Beddoes' talents

[89]JM to Thomas Cumming, 3 July 1772. Murray added that 'many belonging to the faculty can read no latin. On these accounts I am unwilling to risk expence upon such a large work' (i.e. a work in Latin by the Irish physician John Rutty). He did, however, publish a few medical works in Latin, such as Cullen's *Synopsis nosologia methodica*, 1772, 1780, 1785; Wm Smellie's *Thesaurus medicus*, 1778–79; and Joannis Nathanael Lieberkühn's *Dissertationes quatuor*, 1782.
[90]Some examples are Torbern Bergman's *Essay on the Usefulness of Chemistry*, 1783 (and other works by Bergman); Friedrich Hoffmann's *System of the Practice of Medicine*, 1783; Felix Fontana's *Treatise on the Venom of the Viper* (1787); the Académie Royale des Sciences' *Cases, Medical, Chirurgical, and Anatomical* (1788); J. L. Baudelocque's *System of Midwifery*, 1790; and A. G. Richter's *Treatise on the Extraction of the Cataract* (1791).
[91]Preface to Part I, *Foreign Medical Review*, pp. v–vi. For an account of Swediaur's career, see *Dictionnaire biographie française*.
[92]On the social ideology behind the 'Family Physic' texts of the late eighteenth century see: Roy Porter, *Doctor of Society. Thomas Beddoes and the Sick Trade in Late-Enlightenment England*, pp. 157–164.
[93]Beddoes translated Lazzaro Spallanzani's *Dissertations relative to the Natural History of Animals and Vegetables* (1784), Torbern Bergman's *Dissertation on Elective Attractions* (1785), C. W. Scheele's *Chemical Essays* (1786) and in the non-medical line, C. A. Musaeus's *Popular Tales of the Germans* (1791). Murray had a share in most of Thomas Beddoes' early original

Murray remarked: 'His manners are agreeable without ostentation, his thirst of Knowledge ardent, his reading great both in the dead & living languages and his views liberal & comprehensive'.[94] During their ten-year acquaintance he brought Beddoes into contact with prominent medical men both in London and Edinburgh, relied on his advice for publishing decisions, and employed him as a reviewer.

One of Murray's most successful medical projects was the *Medical and Philosophical Commentaries*. This quarterly began publication in 1773 and continued for more than twenty years. It remained under Murray's management until 1786 (excluding 1780–82), when another publisher (Charles Elliot) took it over. The work went into a number of editions; it was translated into German and reprinted in America.[95] The guiding force behind the *Commentaries* was Andrew Duncan, a physician at Edinburgh whose *Elements of Therapeutics* (1770) had established his medical reputation. The *Commentaries* was not the first work of its kind; as early as 1733 the Edinburgh medical community had produced a multi-volume series called the *Medical Essays and Observations* (1733–44). Also, a periodical published in Leipzig, *Commentarii de rebus in scientia naturali et medicina gestis*, 1752–98, was a model for Duncan. Like these works, the *Commentaries* aimed to publicise the latest discoveries and improvements in medicine and, as Duncan remarked, to alleviate 'the calamities of mankind'.[96]

Duncan divided the work into four sections: (1) a review of new publications; (2) original cases communicated by attending physicians and surgeons for publication; (3) accounts of recent medical discoveries and general news; and (4) a catalogue of recent medical publications, foreign and domestic. Duncan was largely responsible for selecting the content of the work, although the title page gave 'A Society of Physicians' as the authors. Murray engaged William Smellie to print 1000 copies of each number (which averaged 115 pages) and arranged with agents in various cities to sell the work.[97] The price to the trade for a single copy was 1s.1d, while the public paid 1s.6d. Murray agreed to pay Duncan £15

---

works: *Alexander's Expedition Down the Hydaspes* (1792); *The History of Isaac Jenkins* (1793); *A Letter to Erasmus Darwin on a New Method of Treating Pulmonary Consumption* ([1793]); *Observations on the Nature and Cure of Calculus, Sea Scurvy, Consumption, Catarrh, and Fever* (1793); and *A Guide for Self-preservation, and Parental Affection* ([1793]).

[94] JM to Andrew Duncan, 2 Nov. 1784.

[95] Benjamin Rush, the Philadelphian doctor, later published his own *Medical Inquiries and Observations* on the model of Murray's publication.

[96] *Commentaries*, vii, 14. Each yearly volume contained a preface by Duncan soliciting the support of contributors and quite often apologising for the delayed appearance of the work.

[97] Murray also sent Smellie the paper from London, where it was then less expensive and of a better quality, to print the *Commentaries* (AL, p. 246; BB, p. 66). At first the Edinburgh agents were Kincaid & Creech and Wm Drummond, and Ewing in Dublin (until 1777). Elliot and others were added over the years (see Checklist, items 60, 76, 102, 122, 152, 219, 468 and 518).

for editing each issue.[98] When it was clear, after about eighteen months, that the work was selling well, Duncan asked for more copy money. Even though Murray had already printed second and third editions of the first volume, he justified his refusal:

> I would willingly offer you more . . . did the state of matters admit it. . . . The truth is my offer at first (considering the Work was to be established and that all the Risk was mine) was too much. . . . Had the Commentaries died in their infant state, I must have been a considerable loser.[99]

Murray's profit on each issue at first averaged about £10, but afterwards the return was considerably larger. Concern that Duncan might change publishers led him to give the editor a dozen free copies, and in August 1778, five years into the project, Murray agreed to increase Duncan's fee to £20. It continued to be a difficult relationship, however. In 1779, when Murray began to publish the *Foreign Medical Review* (see Plate 43), Duncan regarded this an encroachment on the *Medical Commentaries*, and Murray temporarily lost favour and 'hundreds out of my pocket'.[100] Charles Dilly, the London bookseller, took over publication of the 1780 issues and the following year turned the work into an annual publication. Murray reassumed the proprietorship in 1783 and continued the new format.

A reviewer of the ninth volume of the *Medical Commentaries* in June 1786 marked out the importance of the work: 'Were it not for this periodical vehicle of extraordinary occurrences in medical practice . . . how many observations of great importance, might never have made their progress beyond the narrow boundaries of a single practitioner in medicine!'[101] At this time, however, Murray found that sales had slackened considerably; only five hundred of the 1250 copies of the *Commentaries* he was then printing were selling, a figure that produced no profit. Murray proposed a new basis for publication: Duncan would pay for printing and profits would be split equally.[102] But Duncan struck a better bargain with Charles Elliot, who then assumed the publication until his death in 1791, after which it continued until 1795.[103]

To further the aim of publicising the ever-growing amount of medical information, Murray planned the *Medical Register* in 1779 and engaged Samuel Foart Simmons, a prominent London physician, as editor. Set out in the

---

[98]Murray calculated the fee to Duncan based on the figure of two guineas per sheet (sixteen printed octavo pages), which was the going rate for review articles in London literary periodicals in the mid-1770s.
[99]JM to Andrew Duncan, 29 Aug. 1774.
[100]JM to Thomas Beddoes, 15 Apr. 1785.
[101]*English Review,* 7 (June 1785), 433.
[102]JM to Andrew Duncan, 17 Aug, 1786.
[103]In 1791 Peter Hill in Edinburgh and G. G. J. and J. Robinson in London became the publishers, and in 1795 (the final year for the *Medical Commentaries*) George Mundie in Edinburgh and the Robinsons and Joseph Johnson in London took over.

manner of a directory, the annual work listed the members of the various academies, hospitals, societies, dispensaries and military establishments active in England, Ireland, Scotland and in foreign countries. A second section catalogued recently published medical books (Murray's publications among them), while a further part listed medical prizes and the deaths of prominent medical men. Murray published only the first issue of the work, turning it over after one year to the bookselling firm of Fielding and Walker when only 450 of the 1000 copies he printed sold.[104] In 1780 Murray published a number of works by Simmons, including his *Anatomy of the Human Body* (for which he paid Simmons £52 10s.), *Observations on the Cure for Gonorrhoea*, and *Practical Observations on the Treatment of Consumptions*.[105] Murray acted only as the selling agent for these last two works, which were pamphlets. In 1781 he agreed to Simmons' idea of establishing a London-based periodical on the plan of the *Medical Commentaries*, and in February of that year the *London Medical Journal* first appeared — published 'for the Editor and Sold by John Murray'. Having initially conceived this as a monthly periodical, Simmons more realistically shifted to quarterly publication. In the preface he explained that the journal would 'contain an account of new medical books, and useful discoveries in physic, and at the same time be a repository for original essays'. Murray reaped the benefit of prominent notices for his publications, but after six months he turned over the agency to John Walker. He had found it impossible to work alongside Simmons — a man 'I contemn & dislike exceedingly'.[106] When Walker was declared bankrupt in 1782, Joseph Johnson took over the *London Medical Journal* and continued it successfully (with Simmons as editor) for many years.

By the early 1780s Murray was so widely known as a medical publisher that 32 Fleet Street became a centre for important news in the field. When, for example, William Hawes, the founder of the Humane Society, was lecturing on the 'Theory and Practice of Restoring Animation to the Human Body', tickets could be had at Murray's shop.[107] Murray's catalogues of medical books enabled individual practitioners and institutions to acquire the latest and most important publications from Britain and abroad (see Chapter 5, pp. 88–89). The medical authors in his lists rivalled any other bookseller in London — even Joseph Johnson. Gilbert Blane's *Observations on the Diseases Incident to Seamen* (1785) became a medical classic. Blane, the Physician to the Fleet, was instrumental in introducing wine and fresh fruit into the naval diet to prevent scurvy.[108] In 1786 Murray published Thomas

[104]BB, p. 18. This produced a nett loss of £3.18s. Simmons received £21 for editing the work.
[105]BB, p. 22.
[106]JM to Alex. Hamilton, 11 Jan. 1783.
[107]Hawes' lecture was on 5 Feb. 1780. The printed advertisement is found in Murray's album of newspaper clippings.
[108]For a more detailed account see Kenneth J. Carpenter, *The History of Scurvy and Vitamin C* (Cambridge, 1986), pp. 91–7. Murray also published Blane's *Lecture on Muscular Motion*,

Skeete's *Experiments on Quilled and Red Peruvian Bark* which showed that quinine (the active ingredient of the bark) prevented malaria. Other important Murray medical publications were by the surgeon C. B. Trye, who advanced theories that decreased post-natal mortality, and James Wood, who wrote on the nature and cure of typhus.[109]

Edinburgh and London were the main centres for medical practice, education and publication, and Murray reaped the benefits of a burgeoning field in both cities. However, when opportunities arose elsewhere, he was not inclined to miss them. Dublin was also contributing to the advancement of medicine. The bookselling associations Murray had developed there generated a number of medical publications. In 1780 Murray issued the first volume of the Dublin professor William Dease's *Introduction to the Theory and Practice of Surgery*. He was not willing to pay Dease anything in advance, but he did offer to print at his own expense, pay for the engraved plates and advertise to the sum of twenty guineas. The profits would be shared. Anticipating that the author might be disappointed with the arrangement, Murray explained: 'The public professors in Surgery & Anatomy at Edinburgh & London have got into such vogue, that performances whatever may be their merit, of which they are not the authors, are not at first so well received by practitioners & students in this place. It requires more industry & expence to push them.'[110]

Murray also looked beyond the British Isles for markets. Long-standing naval associations, like that with Gilbert Blane, enabled him to capitalise on medical developments throughout the Empire. Many who went to distant lands to seek their fortunes fell ill; among them were some of Murray's closest friends. It was imperative to conquer tropical disease and reduce the human cost of material gain. In 1778 Murray bought the copyright of John Clark's *Observations on the Diseases in Long Voyages to Hot Countries*, which he published in three further editions; he also published James Lind's *Essay on Preserving the Health of Seamen* — a steady seller.[111] In 1791 Murray published a significant number of useful books for the foreign market: John Peter Wade's *Method of Treating Fever and Dysentery in Bengal*; Robert Jackson's *Treatise on the Fevers of Jamaica*; and John Bell's *Inquiry into Diseases among British Officers, Soldiers, and Others in the West Indies*. The following year he

---

1788, which Blane had read at the Royal Society in Nov. 1788. Blane and his brothers Andrew and William were old friends from Edinburgh.

[109]Two of Trye's most important works were *A Review of Jesse Foote's Observations on the New Opinions of John Hunter in his late Treatise on the Venereal Disease* (1787) and *An Essay on the Swelling of the Lower Extremities, Indicent to Lying-in Women* (1792). Wood's notable work was *Thoughts on the Effects of the Application and Abstraction of Stimuli on the Human Body; with a Particular View to Explain the Nature and Cure of Typhus* (1793).

[110]JM to Wm Dease, 12 May 1779.

[111]Both works had been published earlier: Lind's *Essay* in 1757 by Andrew Millar and others; and Clark's *Observations* by David Wilson and George Nicol in 1773.

published Wade's *Nature and Effect of Emetics, Purgatives, Mercurials, and Low Diet, in Disorders of Bengal and Similar Latitudes* and Robert Robertson's *Observations on Fevers, and other Diseases, which Occur on Voyages to Africa and the West Indies.*

Throughout the 1780s and into the 1790s Murray published ever more medical works. These titles, together with a diverse portfolio of shares in syndicate publications (medical and otherwise), widened his financial base. Even if cash almost always seemed short (much of his capital was in fact tied up in ongoing publications), Murray was consistently expanding his lists and spreading his reputation. When a doctor inquired about Murray's plan for marketing his new book, Murray confidently told him: 'My being chiefly in the medical branch in my profession, makes this service more in my way'.[112]

[112]JM to Wm Dease, 12 May 1779.

10

A Litigious and
Disputatious Nature

Murray versus Mason, 1777

In February 1777 Murray found himself the defendant in a legal battle at the Court of Chancery. The Reverend William Mason, a poet of considerable reputation, had obtained an injunction to prevent Murray from selling a new edition of the poems of Thomas Gray. Mason claimed as his property three poems in the collection, these having been bequeathed to him by the late poet and first published in his *Poems of Mr Gray; to which are prefixed Memoirs of his Life and Writings* (1775).[1]

Murray had published his edition of Gray in March 1776. Priced at three shillings, the book was both a cheaper alternative to Mason's book (which cost fifteen shillings) and more elegant than other reprints. He commissioned four engravings to accompany the work and asked Gilbert Stuart to write a short 'Life' of the poet. It was, he boasted, 'the most beautiful small edition of *Gray's poems* ever published, and I flatter myself it wants only to be shown to be purchased'.[2] To offset production costs, he offered a half share to the Edinburgh bookseller Charles Elliot, who agreed to oversee the printing at Edinburgh.[3] The edition was selling extremely well in London when Murray learned of Mason's injunction. He was surprised because other editions published after Mason's, although they contained the three poems under contention, had appeared unchallenged. At the same time, Murray knew that his collection was affecting the sales of Mason's edition more than any other.

Mason did not entrust his cause entirely to his capable team of lawyers. In April 1777 he attacked Murray as a literary pirate in the Advertisement to

[1] By the terms of Gray's will Mason inherited all of his 'books, manuscripts, coins, music . . . and papers of all kinds, to preserve or destroy at his own discretion' (quoted in Murray's edition of the *Poems by Mr. Gray*, 1784, p. xxx).
[2] JM to T. & J. Merrill, 1 Oct. 1776.
[3] The printers were Murray & Cochrane, who ran off 1000 copies (Checklist item 126).

the second book of his poem the *English Garden*. Murray in anger read Mason's complaint about 'the fraudulent practices of certain Booksellers' and the assertion that the 1710 Copyright Act, 'though it encourages an injured Author to prosecute, seems not (as it now stands) to give him damages . . . adequate to the injury he may sustain'.[4] Mason wanted to set a legal precedent for greater compensation. As it stood, a proven literary pirate was accountable only for the profits he had acquired from the sale of the material in question. Mason's action was in part prompted by his discontent with the 1774 House of Lords ruling. In his view a limit on copyright decreased the value of an author's property.[5]

Murray did not let Mason's remarks in the *English Garden* pass unanswered. In May 1777 he wrote *A Letter to W. Mason, concerning his Edition of Mr. Gray's Poems and the Practices of Booksellers* (see Plate 44). Before publishing it, however, he sent Mason a copy 'to give you time to put me right in any fact you may discover me to have unintendedly mistated'.[6] Receiving no reply, he paid Mason a visit, intent on offering compensation and avoiding a costly and time-consuming legal battle. In the *Letter* Murray recorded (or rather recreated) what they had said to one another:

> [Murray] 'It is my opinion that you can receive no *legal redress* for the trifling matter betwixt us. . . . But in order to shew that my intention was never to injure you . . . *permit me to ask what satisfaction it is that you require. Name your terms. I dare say I shall agree to them*'. These last words I repeated more than once. Mason hesitated, muttered, and gave evident marks of confusion. But . . . gave no direct reply.[7]

Murray surely did not expect Mason to respond favourably to what amounted to libel. Indeed, many parts of his *Letter* read more like satirical harangues than reasoned arguments: 'What degree of lenity, though living example of Christian charity, have those persons to expect, who injure you *wilfully*, when you exhibit such priestly rancour and revenge against the author of an *oversight*, which, taken even in your own malevolent point of view, you are conscious, can harm you in no degree?'[8]

In the *Letter* Murray censured Mason's *Memoir* as a makeshift publication

---

[4]Murray quoted Mason's Advertisement to the second book of the *English Garden* in his *Letter to W. Mason, concerning his Edition of Mr. Gray's Poems and the Practices of Booksellers*, p. 7.
[5]James Beattie, a fellow poet, had remarked to Mrs Montagu in 1774 that Mason 'is tempted to throw his *Life of Mr Gray* (which is now finished, or nearly so) into the fire, so much is he dissatisfied with the late decision on literary property' (William Forbes, *An Account of the Life and Writings of James Beattie*, 2nd edn., 3 vols., Edinburgh, 1807, ii, 70).
[6]JM to Wm Mason, 9 May 1777. In a presentation copy of the *Letter* (at Yale University) Murray told Lord Chief Justice De Grey: 'A copy of this Pamphlet was transmitted to Mr. Mason 3 weeks before publication, and every reasonable expedient used by the author to suppress it, but without success'.
[7]*Letter*, pp. 38–9.
[8]*Letter*, p. 34.

which sacrificed the reputation of Gray to the prospect of financial gain. The public, Murray believed, wanted Gray's poems alone and not the additional four hundred pages of biographical material Mason had collected. Two years before, however, Murray's opinion of the *Memoir* was rather more favourable: 'Mason . . . has acted faithfully . . . ' he told John Millar. 'Gray, in his hands, acquires an addition of reputation rather than suffers a diminution of it.'[9] But this was conveniently forgotten in the heat of the dispute.

As well as visiting Mason, Murray wrote to James Dodsley, the publisher of Mason's *Memoir* and of other popular editions of Gray's poems which had appeared before Murray's. He suspected Dodsley was behind the 'very illiberal treatment' he had received.[10] Murray brought Dodsley into the dispute to make a legal point: there was no difference between the fifty lines he took from Mason's edition of Gray and the extracts of poetry and prose Dodsley regularly took from new publications for his *Annual Register*, a compendium of politics and literature. In the *Letter* Murray declared: 'I have not acted like the barefaced Dodsley, in committing depredations upon every literary performance of merit, to the manifest prejudice of the proprietors, for my own particular emolument'.[11] Although he was adamant about the justice of his argument, Murray could not have been insensible to the insults he had written. After reading the *Letter*, Dodsley refused to do business with Murray, who then wrote to Dodsley in a tone even more ironic and insulting:

> How you will reconcile your conduct to your professions I know not, for I am certain of the truth of what I advanced . . . that you are the greatest literary pirate without exception in these kingdoms.
>
> Your behaviour . . . respecting *me* might have been expected from the capacity of a child; but if your understanding had profited either from experience or observation you would . . . deal with every person able to pay for your goods . . . . You was never however if I am rightly informed much celebrated for superior apprehension or sagacity. And if Robert Dodsley had not existed James Dodsley would never have emerged beyond a Hall or a Ballad Shop.
>
> You ought however to be more watchful over your own interest. For if you discover wisdom in all your proceedings equall to that which you have exhibited in your transaction with me, I shall flatter myself with the prospect of acquiring even the Reverend Mr Mason for my customer in

[9]JM to John Millar, 14 Apr. 1775. Boswell admired Mason's *Memoir*, which served to some extent as a model for the *Life of Johnson*. Johnson, however, thought the work 'mighty dull' and written in a style 'fit for the second table' (*Life of Johnson*, eds. Hill and Powell, iii, 31).
[10]JM to James Dodsley, 26 May 1777. In 1775 Dodsley had published the lavish *Designs by Mr R. Bentley, for Six Poems by Mr. T. Gray*.
[11]*Letter*, pp. 29–30. Large portions of Murray's own publications (such as *Armine and Elvira* and the *Fables of Flora*) had been reprinted by Dodsley in the *Annual Register*.

preference to you. Other gentlemen also will leave off frequenting your house whenever they discover (which I hope they will never do) that excellence of your character is comprised more in possessing money than brains.[12]

If Mason won his case, Murray claimed, then reprinting extracts — indeed reprinting a single line — would, strictly speaking, be illegal. Murray noted that Mason himself had included in his *Memoir* an account of Gray first published in the *London Magazine* in March 1772.[13] He compared the number of words it contained with those in the three poems and concluded, 'Mason is the greatest reputed pirate'.[14] Originally Murray had planned to use Mason's edition as the text for his own, but, apprehensive about this, he told Charles Elliot: 'I think it will be judicious to print the poems *alone that are in Donaldson's edition,* because this edition being published we tread on safe ground with regard to the proprietor; if there is one'.[15] This caution, as it turned out, served no purpose.

At the end of his *Letter,* Murray invoked Gray himself to chastise Mason: 'Impelled by the sordid love of gain', Gray asked Mason rhetorically, 'have you attempted to stop the circulation of an edition [i.e. Murray's] of my works, calculated to reflect credit on my name? . . . Does this edition retail childish and ill-written letters, the publication of which I would sooner have died than have consented to? . . . Has this edition been swelled into an immoderate size, for the purpose of gratifying a rapacious editor with inordinate profits?'[16] This was both an attack on Mason and an advertisement for Murray's own edition. Murray was confident that the publication of his *Letter* would enhance his case. Mason thought otherwise, and told Horace Walpole so: 'I have got by it what Job wished for, when he said, "O that my adversary had written a book, surely I would . . . bind it as a crown to me," for the abuse is so gross and illiberal that I think it will tend greatly to give a right issue to the cause, and lead to the end for which I first instituted it, which you know was to procure an act in favour of authors, and prevent the piracy of booksellers.'[17]

In May 1777 the case was heard at Lincoln's Inn Hall before the Lord Chancellor. Murray first filed a demurrer to dissolve the injunction. Even if Mason's facts were true, he claimed, there was no cause for legal action. His

[12]JM to James Dodsley, 19 Dec. 1778. Robert Dodsley had died in 1771.
[13]Murray reprinted this extract, written by William Temple, in an appendix to the *Letter.* For the attribution, see *Boswell for the Defence 1769–1774,* eds. F. A. Pottle and W. K. Wimsatt (London, 1960), p. 21.
[14]*Letter,* p. 62. In the 1787 edition of the *Letter* Murray removed the word 'reputed' (p. 32).
[15]JM to Charles Elliot, 26 Mar. 1776. Alexander Donaldson's edition had appeared the year before in 1775.
[16]*Letter,* pp. 53–5.
[17]Wm Mason to Horace Walpole, 26 May 1777, in the *Correspondence of Horace Walpole,* ed. W. S. Lewis, xxviii (1955), 310.

lawyers told him the demurrer would 'infallibly be sustained', but the Lord Chancellor overruled it on the grounds that Murray had not shown the literary property of the poems to be his own rather than Mason's.[18] Another setback followed when the court moved to charge Murray with breaching the injunction for reprinting the three poems in his *Letter*. However, this charge was not sustained. During the case regular reports appeared in the London newspapers. Both men were confident of victory. 'Tis quite a pleasure', Mason told Walpole in July, 'to see one's name so public. My lawyers give me a pleasant account of my Lord Chancellor's decision.'[19] In September Murray rather less sanguinely reported: 'The cause is not ended; on the contrary it is hardly begun'.[20] *Mason versus Murray* was the talk of literary London. In the *Life of Johnson*, Boswell recorded a conversation on the topic:

> Somebody mentioned the Reverend Mr. Mason's prosecution of Mr. Murray, the bookseller, for having inserted in a collection of 'Gray's Poems,' only fifty lines, of which Mr. Mason had still the exclusive property, under the statute of Queen Anne [the 1710 Copyright Act]; and that Mr. Mason had persevered, notwithstanding his being requested to name his own terms of compensation. Johnson signified his displeasure at Mr. Mason's conduct very strongly; but added, by way of shewing that he was not surprized at it, 'Mason's a Whig.' MRS KNOWLES, (not hearing distinctly:) 'What! a Prig, Sir?' JOHNSON. 'Worse, Madam; a Whig! But he is both.'[21]

Early in 1778, before the final decree was reached, Murray brought out another edition of Gray's poems, leaving off the three contested poems but adding four additional engravings. He was intent on showing Mason that regardless of the outcome he would 'persist in selling Gray's poems'.[22] He also prefixed an Advertisement to the edition, reiterating the arguments in the *Letter*. Mason and Dodsley countered by publishing a cheaper four-volume edition of the *Memoirs*, reminding the public that, unlike their edition, Murray's did 'not contain either those Poems for which the Editor obtained an Injunction in Chancery, or any of Mr Gray's Latin Poetry, Letters or finished Fragments'.[23]

---

[18]JM to Wm Kerr, 28 May 1777. The Lord Chancellor was Henry Earl Bathurst. The extensive papers relating to *Mason v. Murray* are located in the Public Record Office: Chancery 442/21 IND/1829/1776B/152, 297, 467,472 and 484; C33/448/383, 390, 396, 488, 498–99, 507–8; 444/23 IND/1831/1777B/126; C33/450/314 and 501; 446/25/IND 1833/1778B/77, 186,197–8, 252, 307; C33/452/486; C12/1643/16; C12/1648/19.

[19]Wm Mason to Horace Walpole, 27 July 1777, in *The Correspondence of Horace Walpole*, xxi, 322. A review of the *Letter* appeared in the *Gentleman's Magazine*, which asserted that Murray's 'illiberally endeavouring to prejudice the public . . . must operate very differently from what he intended' (47, July 1777, 332).

[20]JM to John Ogilvie, 20 Sept. 1777.

[21]*Life of Johnson* (15 Apr. 1778), eds. Hill and Powell, iii, 294.

[22]JM to Charles Elliot, 6 Dec. 1777.

[23]Advertisement to Mason's *Memoirs* in Murray's album of newspaper clippings.

The final decree in *Mason versus Murray* was granted on 13 July 1779. Mason's ownership of the copyright of the three poems was confirmed — a judgement which established an important point in copyright law.[24] 'The whole thing', Murray reported, '. . . hinged upon *a proof of his property*'.[25] Mason had shown the property in the three poems to be his and the Court ordered Murray to just pay £3, adjudged to be his profit from printing the poems. However, his legal expenses amounted to over £200.[26] 'Controversy is unprofitable', Murray reflected after the decision.[27] Eight years later, still smarting from the affair, he reprinted the *Letter* with a few minor corrections. He also continued to include the disputatious Advertisement when he published new editions of Gray's poems in 1786 and 1790.[28]

Murray versus the *Encyclopaedia Britannica*, 1783

In the spring of 1783 Murray was himself the victim of what seemed — to him at least — a case of literary piracy, and one far more egregious than taking three poems from Mason. The article on 'Scotland' in the second edition of the *Encyclopaedia Britannica* reprinted verbatim large portions of two works by Gilbert Stuart that he had recently published: the *History of the Scottish Reformation* (1780) and the *History of Mary Queen of Scots* (1782).[29] As Murray had paid substantial sums for these properties, he sought compensation for the loss of sales and threatened a legal suit in the Scottish Court of Session against the proprietors of the *Encyclopaedia* if his demands were not met. In a private letter to the proprietors Murray reflected on his own recent experience in the courts: 'Mason's prosecution . . . was no doubt illiberal, but I do not imitate his example. . . . I do not prosecute for a piracy . . . of 50 lines but perhaps for one of 5000.'[30] The absence of a

[24]See *English Reports*, xxi, 378–9 and xxix, 47.
[25]JM to Andrew Blane, 7 Aug. 1783.
[26]JM to Andrew Blane, 9 Aug. 1783. Murray tried to get Charles Elliot, his partner in the edition, to pay part of the legal bill and even considered legal proceedings against Elliot when he refused.
[27]JM to Wm Richardson, 24 July 1779.
[28]Murray also renewed his attack on Mason in the *English Review* in a review of Mason's translation of Du Fresnoy's *Art of Painting*: 'This unnecessary addition [of 'scraps from the works of Pope and Dryden'] makes up near one half of this very dear eight shilling pamphlet. — Besides, the London Booksellers consider the writings of the last two authors as property, and their works are bought and sold at their sales every day. The Reverend Poet should not have done unto others what he wished not to be done to himself — he should not have invaded the rights of the trade. Or had he forgotten the striking instance he gave of his own tenaciousness of literary property a few years ago?' (*English Review*, 1, Apr. 1783, 281–2). Murray reprinted this passage in an extended form in the second editon of his *Letter*.
[29]*Encyclopaedia Britannica*, 10 vols. ix, 6988–7174 (misnumbered 8074) (Edinburgh, 1778–83).
[30]JM to Colin Macfarquar, Andrew Bell and John Hutton, 26 Aug. 1783.

genuine offer of compensation left him no alternative but to sue for damages.

In July 1783 he hired Andrew Blane, an Edinburgh lawyer and long-time friend, to manage the affair. Blane first retained as counsel the Lord Advocate (Ilay Campbell) as well as Robert Blair, another eminent legal figure. Murray was confident that he had a just complaint, but he knew that legal proceedings were expensive and unpredictable. He told Blane to bring the suit against all those listed in the imprint of the *Encyclopaedia*, among whom were many long-time associates, including John Balfour, John Bell, Charles Elliot and William Creech. However, upon reflection, he charged only the actual owners of the work: Colin Macfarquar, the printer; Andrew Bell, the engraver; and John Hutton, the stationer. First, Murray applied to the Court for an injunction (called an interdict in the Scottish court) to stop the sale of the volume. When this failed, he suspected that 'some policy is at the Bottom of it, as . . . Dr. S[tuart] is not agreeable to Lord M[onboddo]', one of the Court of Session judges.[31] Eight years earlier Stuart had written scathing reviews of Monboddo's works.[32] The setback did not deter Murray, but eighteen months passed before the case finally came to court.

In July 1785 he travelled to Edinburgh to hear the proceedings. The defendants argued that they had only taken an abridgement from Stuart's works amounting to one-sixth of the original. Reading the 'Scotland' article in the *Encyclopaedia* would, they claimed, encourage rather than hinder the sale of Murray's publications. Moreover, 'no person would purchase a book of twelve guineas price [the price of the *Encyclopaedia*], for the sake of one that might be had for twelve shillings' [the price of Stuart's *History of Mary Queen of Scots*].[33] They pointed out further that Murray himself regularly printed extracts from publications in periodicals and newspapers. Recalling how little such an argument had helped against Mason, Murray instructed Blane to emphasise that his own 'conduct is not before the court, but the piratical conduct of defenders'.[34] Murray's lawyers had little difficulty countering the defendants' arguments. It was claimed that more than a third of Stuart's works had been 'pillaged' — a figure far closer to fact — so a person who had read the *Britannica* article would have little need of the originals. Moreover, they charged that Stuart was nowhere mentioned as the

[31]JM to Andrew Blane, 5 Jan. 1784.
[32]Stuart's attacks on Monboddo and his *Origin and Progress of Language* in the *Edinburgh Magazine and Review* in 1775 (v, 80 *et seq.*) were themselves the cause of legal proceedings against William Smellie, the printer of the periodical.
[33]The case was reported in the *Edinburgh Evening Courant*, Sat., 25 June 1785. A notice also appeared in the *Daily Universal Register* (afterwards *The Times*) on 30 June 1785. See also *Decisions of the Court of Session 1785*, pp. 340–41 and William Maxwell Morison, *The Decisions of the Court of Session*, xxx, 8209–10 (Edinburgh, 1805).
[34]JM to Andrew Blane, 14 July 1785.

author of the lengthy extracts.[35] They cited *Mason versus Murray*, among other cases, in support of their argument, emphasising that neither in that case nor in others on record 'was there a greater infringement of literary property than . . . in the present case'.[36] After considering the arguments, the Court found for Murray. Though satisfied with the decision, he was anxious about the legal expenses and about the compensation he would receive. He accepted twenty-five copies of the *Encyclopaedia* — a retail value of £300.[37] After celebrating with friends and family he returned to London, where other disputes over literary property awaited him.

Murray versus Cullen, 1784

In the history of the eighteenth-century book trade, authors typically took up their pens to complain about booksellers: Grub Street hacks cursed their servitude; and aspiring writers, turned out of bookshops, manuscripts in hand, lamented their rejection. It was unusual, however, for a bookseller to complain in public about an author. In 1784 Murray considered himself to have a just complaint against William Cullen — eminent physician and successful author. Unable to compromise with Cullen privately, Murray published a forceful attack called *An Author's Conduct to the Public, Stated in the Behaviour of Dr. William Cullen* (see Plate 45). He selected a series of letters between himself and the Doctor documenting their dispute, to which he added editorial remarks on the affair along with a letter from the bookseller William Creech supporting his side. Murray's purpose in publishing a private correspondence was to lay an objective account before the public and to embarrass Cullen into making restitution.

The dispute was over Cullen's *First Lines of the Practice of Physic*, which had appeared in four volumes between 1777 and 1784 and was to become 'a leading text book on the practice of medicine for more than fifty years'.[38] When the fourth volume came out, Cullen insisted on selling it only with revised editions of the first three. This left Murray with incomplete sets of earlier editions in stock. His customers also stood to suffer, as their only

[35]The only reference to Stuart's works in the *Britannica* article is in a footnote (vol. ix, 8039), where his *History of Scotland* is referred to as 'a performance masterly in the highest degree, and exhibiting the most consistant and interesting view that has hitherto been given of the affairs of this eventful period'. These remarks would, however, suggest to the reader that the article itself was not written by Stuart.

[36]*Decisions of the Court of Session* 1785, p. 341.

[37]When the dispute first arose Murray had implied that fifty copies would be adequate compensation (JM to Andrew Blane, 14 Aug. 1783).

[38]*William Cullen and the Eighteenth Century Medical World*, Passmore and Doig (eds.) (Edinburgh, 1993), p. 37. Vol. 1 of the *First Lines* was published in 1777; vol. 2 in 1779; vol. 3 in 1783; and vol. 4 in 1784.

option was to buy the four new volumes. Murray offered Cullen three
options for a settlement: (1) to complete the sets in Murray's stock with the
additional fourth volume; (2) to exchange Murray's sets of volumes 1–3 for
revised ones; or (3) to be compensated by Cullen for the value of the
obsolete stock. Just £16 would have settled the dispute, but Cullen challenged Murray's demand. Their disagreement brought an acrimonious end
to a productive fourteen-year association.

Murray first began to sell Cullen's works in 1772. Although it was prestigious to have such an author in his lists, he made little profit. Nevertheless,
he was hopeful in future deals to augment his purse as well as his reputation.
In a reply to Cullen's inquiry for the news from London in 1774, Murray had
displayed an almost obsequious regard for the doctor's own reputation.

> I know of nothing new here either in medicine or in politics. It would
> appear indeed that Lord North [the Prime Minister] is at the head of the
> latter as you preside over the former. Nor is his reputation more extensive
> as a great minister than yours as a great physician. That you may both reach
> the summit of Fame, if you have not attained it already: and both continue
> very long to flourish for the benefit of the countries which gave your birth
> is [my] very sincere wish.[39]

Cullen kept a tight rein on the production and sale of his works. Although
well remunerated by his private practice and from lecture subscriptions at
Edinburgh University, he relied on the revenue from his publications to
help support a large family. By retaining the copyrights of his works, he was
able to renegotiate favourably when new editions were called for. Moreover,
Cullen was exceptional among authors in being allowed to make separate
deals with Edinburgh and London booksellers. He also reserved the right
to sell copies himself.[40] In 1777 Murray published volume one of the *First
Lines* in partnership with William Creech. Cullen had driven such a hard
bargain that Murray gained little, despite a quick sale of one thousand
copies. Murray reported his dissatisfaction to Charles Elliot: 'I have no
Cullen's practice left; nor do I expect to be concerned in another edition, the
Doctor's terms being so hard that his booksellers have incurred a loss; and
as long as I have a house & servants to maintain I cannot afford to slave for
nothing'.[41] Murray refused to meet Cullen's price for two further editions

[39]JM to Wm Cullen, 10 Dec. 1774.
[40]When Cullen was preparing a revised edition of his *Nosology*, Murray did not apply to
Creech (the Edinburgh publisher) for an expected new edition, but to the author himself
from whom he could buy at a better price. Murray paid Cullen 3s. while Creech charged him
3s.9d. Murray, however, asked Cullen 'to exchange the Old for the New Edition should any
copies of the former be left when the latter is published' and was confident the Doctor
'would not permit me to be a loser by any remains'. As it turned out, the old edition had sold
out by the time the new one arrived in London. But it was on the issue of returns that the
dispute with Cullen arose in 1784 (JM to Andrew Duncan, 10 and 31 Mar. 1775).
[41]JM to Charles Elliot, 28 Aug. 1777.

of the first volume and acted only as the London agent. However, he successfully negotiated to publish the second volume in 1779 on terms which, if hard, left him a profit. Although he did not secure publication of the third volume at the end of 1783, he was able to purchase individual copies for his customers. He also bought sets with the revised edition of the first two volumes (see Checklist items 150, 178, 217 and 278).

When Cullen completed the *First Lines* in 1784 he offered Murray the copyright of the whole four-volume property for £1500. It was an extraordinarily large sum, but Cullen placed a high value on his work and enlisted their mutual friend Gilbert Stuart 'in support of my opinion and demand'.[42] Even though Cullen was at the summit of his fame and the book certain to sell well, £1500 was more than Murray could afford. In the meantime Cullen persuaded Charles Elliot to pay £1200. Murray still wanted a share and asked a friend to 'sound Elliot as to a partner for a 1/3 or 1/4 without mentioning [my] name'.[43] He was subsequently annoyed to learn that Elliot had already sold Thomas Cadell half of the copyright. To protect his interest, Murray quietly asked friends to 'pick up for me at Edinburgh every copy you can procure of Cullens Lines Vols 2 & 3 either separately or together. I have 40 copies of the Vol 1 and if I do not perfect them as well as I am able I find I must be left in the Lurch.'[44] Murray was even willing to pay the full retail price. Unfortunately, this strategy only made matters worse: Cullen had instructed Elliot not to sell the fourth volume separately. Elliot, however, had grave doubts about this plan as it was long the practice of the trade to enable purchasers to complete their sets. 'They will abjure us', he told Thomas Cadell, '& I think justly.'[45] Cullen, however, justified his position in a letter to Murray, where he claimed that the improvements he had made to the earlier volumes would make it 'an imposition on the public, and a piece of knavery' to sell the final volume separately. 'I have been very averse', he added, 'from any person's trusting to my former edition, who desired to know the true state of my doctrine'.[46] Murray saw greed rather than medical ethics as motivating Cullen. Creech likewise thought the alterations were 'not so material, as to render the first volumes . . . useless'.[47] There

---

[42]Wm Cullen to Gilbert Stuart, 16 Aug. 1783, Royal College of Physicians, Edinburgh, MS Cullen C 32, vol. 3.

[43]JM to Andrew Duncan, 21 Oct. 1783. After the first complete edition of 1784 sold out, Elliot published the *First Lines* again in 1786, 1787, 1788, and 1789 — a very profitable investment.

[44]JM to Andrew Duncan, 21 Oct. 1783.

[45]Charles Elliot to Thomas Cadell, 11 May 1784. When Elliot died in 1790, Murray took this letter as proof that he had acted justly in demanding a separately published fourth volume. The original is in the Murray Archive.

[46]*Author's Conduct*, p. 18.

[47]Wm Creech to JM, 10 June 1784, printed in *Author's Conduct*, p. 41. That Cullen did in fact make considerable changes to his work is evident from his heavily annotated copy (interleaved with corrections) at the Royal College of Physicians, Edinburgh.

was another problem resulting from Cullen's revisions: the contents of volume four, as published, did not follow logically from volume three.

Murray was reluctant to involve himself in a public dispute with a famous man. What he wanted was £16, but Cullen was unyielding. Hopeful that the threat of publicising their dispute would bring Cullen around, Murray sent him a pre-publication copy of the first part of the pamphlet and even threatened to bind it up with the new sets of the *First Lines*. Towards the end of 1783 Murray also quietly purchased copies of the Dublin edition of the *First Lines* and other Cullen titles to sell in Britain.[48] At this stage an ally of Cullen's (a fellow physician named Maxwell Garthshore) intervened, a move which only fuelled Murray's anger: 'I am not affraid of a public rupture with Dr Cullen or any person who uses me so grossly ill as he has done and what ever way the business terminates, I am confident I shall never have the benefit of his friendship'.[49] Argument quickly turned to insult. In a letter afterwards published by Murray in *An Author's Conduct* Cullen told Murray, 'I despise your malice', and alluded to reasons why he had dropped him as his publisher that reflected unfavourably on Murray's character.[50] Murray then aimed a blow at Cullen's professionalism: 'It is to be hoped . . . that he maintains the doctrines contained in his First Lines upon firmer grounds, than he does the honour of his conduct'.[51] But this was not all: 'Throughout the whole business', Murray added, 'he has exhibited much meanness, equivocation, and contradiction; and all to retain a little sordid pelf. . . . His conduct indeed affords a striking instance of human weakness; and it is to be lamented, that a person who is so eminent in his line . . . should degrade his character.'[52]

The publication of *An Author's Conduct*, together with the opinion of the book trade and the public that Murray's complaint was on the whole just, had the effect Murray desired.[53] Cullen finally agreed to sell the fourth volume of the *First Lines* separately. It was a vindication of sorts: 'To these pages alone', Murray wrote of his pamphlet, 'the public is indebted for a separate publication of his 4th volume'.[54] But months later he was still reeling: 'If I was ever swindled out of a shilling', he told John Balfour privately, 'Dr. C. has swindled me out of £16 which from every consideration was shamefull in him, and my exposing him as I have done is by no

[48]JM to Luke White, 17 Nov. 1783.
[49]JM to Maxwell Garthshore, 28 June 1784.
[50]*Author's Conduct*, pp. 20–21.
[51]*Author's Conduct*, p. 29.
[52]*Author's Conduct*, pp. 37–8.
[53]A review of the Murray pamphlet in the *Gentleman's Magazine* (54, Dec. 1784, 926–7) supported Murray's side but reflected that he 'is unlucky in his transactions with authors, having been engaged, a few years ago, in a disagreeable controversy with another celebrated writer, Mr. Mason'.
[54]*Author's Conduct*, p. 38.

means sufficient punishment'.[55] Murray eventually displaced his anger and recouped his loss by other means. In 1790, not long before Cullen's death, he acquired a one-sixth share of the *First Lines* and in 1791 published a new edition edited 'with practical and explanatory notes' by Dr John Rotheram. Murray probably bought his share at the Edinburgh estate sale of Charles Elliot's stock in the spring of 1790, along with Creech, Bell & Bradfute and the Robinsons, although his name did not appear with these traders in the imprint of their 1790 edition, possibly because Cullen was still alive. Cullen's work was still the definitive medical text book, and Murray made hundreds of pounds in profit from its sale.[56]

Murray versus Captain Innes Munro, 1788–90

Murray's inclination to argue publicly did not abate as he grew older; if anything, it grew stronger. Although he usually did not provoke a dispute, he was always alert to the first sign of an adversarial situation. Confident of his own integrity, he defended the legal and moral high ground against every assault. 'With all your doubts of my conduct, which . . . in the end you will find unfounded, you will admit that I do not shrink from a scrutiny' — so he told a would-be rival in 1787.[57] Murray always believed victory was obtainable, though what strategy he employed varied according to the situation. As the proprietor of magazines and newspapers such as the *English Review* and the *Evening Star*, and as the friend of many editors and owners of periodicals, he was in an advantageous position when it came to a public argument.

The range of Murray's literary artillery was never more evident than in his encounter with Innes Munro from 1788. Munro, a retired Captain in the East Indian service, was the author of the *Narrative of the Military Operations on the Coromandel Coast* (published April 1789). Murray charged Munro with plagiarising from two works which he had published: *Travels in Europe, Asia, and Africa* (an anonymous work published April 1782 and though attributed to William Macintosh, largely the work of William Thomson) and Thomson's own *Memoirs of the Late War in Asia* (published January 1788).[58] Munro countered by accusing Thomson of plagiarising from him first. This was a dramatic turn of events, for Murray had been about to publish Munro's

[55]JM to John Balfour, 9 Oct. 1784.

[56]See Checklist 1791, item 812; BB, p. 54. That Cullen had considered writing a fifth volume of the *First Lines* is noted in a letter to Cullen from Charles Elliot dated 3 Apr. 1789. However, Elliot would not undertake the project on the terms proposed (see J. Thomson, *An Account of the Life, Letters and Writings of William Cullen*, ii. 650).

[57]JM to Colonel Watson, 22 Jan. 1787.

[58]Some of the letters in the *Travels in Europe* are 'addressed to J____ M____, Esq. London', presumably Murray himself.

Narrative when the altercation arose.[59] The dispute was first publicised in the London newspapers, where advocates from both sides, writing under pseudonyms as well as in their own names, argued the case. Afterwards, Murray collected these pieces and compiled the *Defence of Innes Munro against a Charge of Plagiarism from the Works of William Thomson*, which appeared in February 1790, over two years after the dispute had begun (see Plate 46).[60] 'My time has been taken up unremittingly these last 8 days in preparing an answer to Captain Innes Munro, a weak but an obstinate and designing man who has attacked me', he wrote to William Kerr Jr. 'I am averse to this business; but I am told it is necessary; and if truth prevails my victory must be decisive.'[61]

Over two-thirds of the sixty-page pamphlet — more aptly titled the 'Indictment of Munro' — contains Murray's own 'defence' of himself. He used heavy irony to emphasise the impossibility of Munro's being defended at all. To keep up an appearance of impartiality Murray even had James Ridgeway, a fellow bookseller, publish the pamphlet for him. The private disagreement between Murray and Munro first became a public quarrel when William Thomson had reviewed Munro's *Narrative* in the *English Review* for May 1789 and accused him of plagiarism.[62] Munro's associate, Lieutenant John Heriot, came to his defence by attacking Thomson and Murray. Quarrelling with these men, whom Murray had once regarded as friends, was a matter of regret. A former military man himself, Murray hesitated to cast a fellow officer in an unfavourable light, but defending his reputation took precedence.[63] Moreover, as the employer of literary men like Thomson, he felt insulted by his adversary's remarks.

> Mr. Munro . . . looks down, with a mixture of pity and contempt, on the necessitous situation of authors by profession — The profession of writing will become miserable indeed, if gentlemen of the army, beating their swords into pen-knives, are to seize whatever they think proper in the works of poor authors, and publishing their plunder by subscription, rest the merit of their productions on pre-established circulation.[64]

[59]Munro's *Narrative* was ultimately published by subscription under the imprint, 'Printed for Author, by T. Bensley, and sold by G. Nicol'.
[60]A presentation copy of the *Defence* (to Alexander Fraser Tytler) in the National Library of Scotland contains Murray's identification of the pseudonymous authors.
[61]JM to Wm Kerr Jr, 1 Sept. 1789.
[62]*English Review*, 13 (May 1789), 372–82. 'The plagiarism alleged against this young man [Munro] is not confined to facts and phrases, but extends to observations and sentiments, and above all, to that order or arrangement, the most difficult part of historical composition, by which his guide, the author of *The Memoirs of the War in Asia*, is distinguished (p. 373).' Thomson's *Memoirs* had been reviewed (though not altogether favourably) in the *English Review* 11 (Mar. 1788), 198–206.
[63]John Heriot had written an anonymous novel called the *Sorrows of the Heart*, published by Murray in 1787.
[64]*Defence*, p. 17.

Munro believed Murray had delayed the publication of the *Narrative* to prevent competition with the sale of Thomson's *Memoir*. Murray denied the charge, asserting first, that the manuscript had required extensive revision and second, that the illustrations had taken considerable time to engrave. He also argued that there was no impropriety in publishing two works on the same subject and referred to the two histories of Greece (Gast's and Mitford's) he had sold 'without jealousy or censure'.[65] In fact, he asserted, it was a common practice of the trade. The irony was that Murray himself had given Munro copies of Thomson's works to assist him with the revisions.

Munro did not hestitate to allude to Murray's litigious reputation. 'I had seen,' he related, ' . . . publick controversies in the daily papers, between Mr. Murray and persons who had confided in him'.[66] More contentiously, Munro referred to 'that violence of passion by which this unhappy man is so notoriously characterised', to his '*wicked* and distracted brain', '*scurrilous scribbles*' and 'illiberal attacks of disappointed malice'.[67] Murray did not take these insults lightly. On the contrary, this personal attack gave him the freedom to respond with a catalogue of Munro's own apparently reprehensible behaviour.

> Into such ridiculous situations do weak men bring themselves whenever they affect to be *cunning* and depart in any instance one *iota* from the truth. The picture is full and complete. It is drawn from Mr. Munro's own materials. And the Captain himself stands the principal figure on the canvas. There let him stand![68]

In three long letters, reprinted in the *Defence*, Murray refuted, virtually sentence by sentence, Monro's accusations. But however forcefully he argued, there remain points in the *Defence* where his integrity is open to doubt. He had, for example, no scruples about praising his own pseudonymous contributions (written under the name Themistocles), yet he was quick to attack his opponent for hiding behind a pseudonym.[69] Towards the end of the pamphlet Murray's restrained legalistic tone gave way. Mockingly, he lamented the predicament in which Munro had put him.

> All, all conspired against me; and the best opportunity he could wish for, now occurred to the Captain for dismissing with disgrace, a man who had distinguished himself by *controversies in the newspapers*. Under this impending

---

[65] *Defence*, p. 39.

[66] *Defence*, p. 16.

[67] *Defence*, pp. 19, 22, and 24.

[68] *Defence*, p. 47.

[69] Murray had referred to Themistocles (and his famous phrase, 'I have you') over twenty years before in his public letter on the Hume–Rousseau affair (Chapter 1, pp. 15–16). The implication in the present context was that he now 'had' Munro.

storm . . . *broad blown, and flush as May*, aggravated also with all the eloquence for which this literary Officer is so highly celebrated — I am ashamed to divulge the sequel — I blush for Captain Innes Munro![70]

Others might well have 'blushed' for Murray. He acknowledged that the details of the dispute were tedious, but it was many pages before he laid down his pen, and with some regret at that.[71] Having the last word in the dispute, Murray seemed to come off the winner. How he might have fared in a court of law was another matter. Too many points turned on the word of one man against the other. Moreover, going to court would have served little purpose: there was almost nothing to gain financially from exposing Munro—except perhaps £6 owed him, and this likewise was a debt under dispute. Murray considered his honour to be at stake, and that motivated him to engage his adversary.

Murray versus _____

Controversy invigorated Murray. On the printed page he could argue a train of logic without interruption. If he could justify himself before the public — the final arbiters in all disputes — little else mattered. Mason might have won his case in Chancery, but his actions were still reprehensible. Cullen might have refused to pay £16 compensation, but his avarice was evident. Munro's *Narrative* might have sold well, but he was exposed as a plagiarist. There were other times in Murray's career — too many to record — when he took up his pen to assert (or defend) his integrity before the public. He even collected clippings from the newspapers in which such articles appeared — evidence in print of a litigious and disputatious nature.[72]

Sometimes Murray even fabricated controversy to gain free publicity. The publication of his *Historian's Pocket Dictionary* in 1789 led to a case at the King's Bench (1 Dec. 1789) in which the Reverend John Trusler charged that Murray's book was a piracy of his *Chronology, or the Historian's Vade Mecum* (1768). Murray had even reprinted Trusler's obvious errors. His only defence was that both works had been taken from a third. The press reported the case, but one newspaper saw through the 'farcical dispute'

---

[70]*Defence*, p. 46.

[71]'The reader is tired, and I have fatigued myself. I shall therefore as speedily as possible draw to a conclusion' *(Defence*, p. 47).

[72]In 1787 Murray was threatened with a prosecution by John Imison, the author of the *School of Arts* (1785), who alleged that Murray (who published the work) was selling a pirated edition. However, Murray claimed that Imison had reneged on their agreement and refused to supply him with 600 copies which he had printed. Imison died before the dispute could be settled (See *Morning Post*, c. 2 Aug. 1787 and JM to Imison, 30 Aug. 1786; to Colonel Watson, 22 Jan. 1787; and to Edmund Wood, 1 Sept. 1788).

and exposed Murray (Master Calves-skin) and Trusler (Doctor Sapscull) in an article headed:

Puffing. A Dialogue

Doctor Sapscull. Well, Master Calves-skin, how does your Chronology sell?
Calves-skin. Very badly indeed, notwithstanding it is so close a copy of your's. How does your's [*sic*] go off?
Sapscull. As slow as my Sermons — Something must be done. Suppose I commence an action against you for pirating my edition. It will make a noise, and be much better than any thing I can write by way of puff.
Calves-skin. I like the idea, and am only afraid that the public papers will smoke our plan . . . .
Sapscull. . . . If we don't take this step both Chronologies will be a drug: for, between you and me, there is . . . a much better than either in print — the very one from which I stole all that is good in mine.[73]

Despite the catalogue of disputes in which Murray involved himself during his career as a bookseller (indeed, before it), he found it possible towards the end of his life to see himself as a man who generally avoided controversy. To his son Archie, he remarked that 'it is incumbent . . . upon small men in our situation, altho we inherit an opinion, not to *dispute*, but to retain it silently'.[74] The contentious persona Murray developed in some degree reflected the man he really was, but in some other ways it was heightened for effect. The competitive marketplace promoted this attitude, and Murray's fellow tradesmen, on the whole, imbibed it themselves. Even after Murray's death, challenges and litigation were not at an end. In 1795 his former partners in the successful publication of Lavater's *Essays on Physiognomy* threatened an action against his estate to recoup money they believed was theirs. (The affair is described in Chapter 13.) When arbiters finally decided against the Murray estate, the executors had to pay out the substantial sum of £3900.[75]

[73] *Daily Universal Register* (later *The Times*), 8 Dec. 1789. See also 2 Dec. for a report of the case itself and a 7 Dec. article headed 'A CARD' for further exposures of Trusler and Murray. The *London Chronicle* also reported the case on 3 Dec. 1789.
[74] JM to Archie Murray, 20 Jan. 1793.
[75] Samuel Highley to Henry Paget, 15 Jan. 1802. Documents relating to the Lavater dispute are in the 'Lavater' folder in Box M10

Periodical Publications

Early Periodical Ventures

In the summer of 1769 Gilbert Stuart offered Murray some sound advice: 'You ought to connect yourself with . . . some review or periodical work. . . . The advantage of such things to a bookseller is inconceivable. Let me hear that you have done some thing of this kind. Even a newspaper would be useful.'[1] At this time Murray had only been in business for ten months, and he had little money to spare. An opportunity to buy the *Court Miscellany* in the summer of 1769 had already been missed, and Stuart reminded him that it had sold for very little.[2] Purchasing a well-established newspaper or magazine could be expensive.[3] Starting a new one was risky, as most folded after a few issues. In August 1769 Murray went some way towards following Stuart's advice and bought a twentieth share of the *Morning Chronicle and London Advertiser*, a daily newspaper first published in June of that year by William Woodfall. It was a relatively large investment: for four months Murray was obliged to pay Thomas Evans, the printer, a subscription of £10; afterwards, he had to pay out £5 at irregular intervals.[4] For ten months Murray paid his share and looked on as the *Chronicle* struggled to establish

---

[1] Gilbert Stuart to JM, 23 Aug. 1769.
[2] Gilbert Stuart to JM, 23 Aug. 1769. The *Court Miscellany* was the magazine in which Murray's romance 'Sir Launcelot Edgevile' had appeared a few years before. Although it is not certain who, if anyone, purchased the *Court Miscellany*, which was printed by Richardson & Urquhart, it has been noted that by July 1769 the periodical's 'focus had changed once more', though its editor, Hugh Kelly, remained unchanged (*British Literary Magazines. The Augustan Age and the Age of Johnson, 1698–1788*, Alvin Sullivan (ed.) (Westport, CT, 1983), under 'Court Miscellany'.
[3] For example, in 1761 the bookseller Robert Collins bought a quarter share of Ralph Griffiths' *Monthly Review* for just over £755 (Charles Welsh, *A Bookseller of the Last Century*, London, 1885, p. 19).
[4] AL, p. 55. For an account of the general workings of an eighteenth-century newspaper, see H. R. F. Bourne, *English Newspapers. Chapters in the History of Journalism*, 2 vols. (New York, 1966), i, 195–6. For a list of the proprietors of the *Morning Chronicle* see Charles Mackay, *Through the Long Day. Memorials of a Literary Life* (London, 1887), i, 66.

itself. In June 1770, in need of cash and fearful that the paper would fail, he sold half of his share to John Bell (the London bookseller) at a small profit.[5] Since the paper was still not making money, he was lucky to persuade Bell to take the share (for £31.10s.). Soon after, the proprietors were fined for publishing parliamentary debates, which were then illegal to print. Murray's sister Binny, who had heard of the paper's troubles, told him:

> We are very uneasy at seeing in the news paper that the publisher of the morning Chronicle [William Woodfall] has been brought befor the House of Commons . . . and that he was to be fined £100 besides imprisonment for a month. Now as we dont know of any paper that the[y] call the morning chronicle but yours we are affraid you may be brought to some trouble about it. . . . They say it will make your paper sell the better. But I dont like that way of selling. For my part I love you to be slow and sure.[6]

Not long afterwards, Murray sold his remaining share, though it was worth little, and entered a £48 loss in his books.[7] The *Chronicle*, however, survived its initial difficulties and became one of the leading papers of the day, ceasing publication only in 1862.

This poor start did not discourage Murray. In the autumn of 1771 he planned a newspaper with William Strahan, the wealthy London printer. He also met with Edward and Charles Dilly to discuss the publication of a literary review. In December, proposals for the newspaper were sent out, subscriptions taken, and the first issue announced for the new year.[8] At this critical stage Murray had to be away from London for three months in Ireland. He left the management of these nascent projects to Gilbert Stuart, who subsequently had to pass on the unexpected news that 'Dilly has dropped all thoughts of his Review: And your [newspaper] scheme, I find, must also drop'.[9] In Murray's absence a new newspaper had been established by the printer John Wheble, but the levying of a prohibitive stamp tax — which the government put on each printed sheet — made it increasingly difficult to publish profitably.[10] Two years later Stuart was still

---

[5]AL, p. 55.

[6]Binny McMurray to JM, 30 Mar. 1771. These daily parliamentary reports by Woodfall were something new and became very popular.

[7]AL, p. 55.

[8]Gilbert Stuart to JM, 9 Dec. 1771. A copy of the proposal has not been located. John Moore told Murray on 1 Oct. 1771: 'When the Proposals for your weekly Review & News Paper are Published you may send me a few, and I shall endeavour to procure you ten or a Dozen Subscriptions. . . . Every body can compile News. The Reputation & success of your Paper will depend upon the Review. I hope therefore you have engaged some good pens for it.'

[9]Gilbert Stuart to JM, no date but probably early in 1772.

[10]John Wheble was a bookseller and printer at nearby 22 Fleet Street. In 1772 he published the short-lived *Morning Post*, most likely the paper to which Stuart referred. Wheble also published the *Middlesex Journal* and the *Lady's Magazine* from 1769 until 1772 when he was declared bankrupt (Maxted, *London Book Trades*, p. 243).

hopeful that Murray might join with Dilly as the co-proprietor of a literary journal. Writing to Murray in June 1774 he reported: 'Dilly I find is still determined to have a Review. . . . He has money & is indefatigable. Whitaker would do you noble critiques. . . . I will also come to your assistance.'[11] But, once again, the plans failed to materialise.

One of the difficulties in establishing any kind of periodical publication at this time (especially a newspaper) was the stamp tax, levied mainly to curtail the spread of radical political views. When the radical politician John Wilkes challenged governmental authority in 1763 in the periodical, the *North Briton*, a controversy erupted over what liberties the press should have. The tension between Britain and her colonies in America — the subject of almost daily pamphlets and newspaper articles — together with the attacks on the government by the pseudonymous 'Junius', author of a series of provocative letters, also quickened the debate. More generally, the evolving notion of public opinion as a political force was being discussed in print. Amidst these changing circumstances, Murray and other London publishers saw dangers, but they also saw profit-making opportunities.

In January 1770 Murray founded the *Repository: or Treasury of Politics and Literature*, a monthly periodical composed of 'the best letters . . . and essays from the daily papers'. Unlike Joseph Johnson's recently established *Theological Repository*, which was 'calculated to promote religious knowledge', Murray aimed to enable the public 'to arrive at the truth of those Transactions and Events which have so much agitated the present times'.[12] At a vital period in British politics, he believed there was a need for a well-chosen, non-partisan account of the most important happenings. Murray hoped his periodical would be 'extreamly well calculated for country gentlemen' as well as Londoners.[13] At a cost of one shilling per issue, the *Repository* was an inexpensive way of keeping abreast of national events.

Murray combed the newspapers and clipped the best political articles. Each month he pasted twenty or so in an album which was sent to the printer, George Scott, to be set up in type (on average seventy-five pages) and run off. As editor, Murray occasionally added brief notes to help the reader distinguish what he referred to in the *Repository* as 'the heat of Party-zeal . . . from candid reasoning'.[14] For a time Murray was assisted by Gilbert Stuart, who was then among those rumoured to be the acclaimed (or notorious) 'Junius', whose controversial letters were featured in the early issues of the *Repository*.[15] Murray requested letters from his readers and included these at the beginning of some issues. Public opinion made good

[11]Gilbert Stuart to JM, 17 June 1774.
[12]*Repository*, 2 vols. (London, 1771), 'Editors to the Reader'. Johnson's *Theological Repository* (first published in 1769) was edited by Joseph Priestley and continued until 1788.
[13]JM to Wm Kerr, 13 Feb. 1770.
[14]*Repository*, 'Editors to the Reader'.
[15]Stuart was paid nine guineas to edit the *Repository* for six months (AL, pp. 92 and 102).

copy. Although Murray claimed to be impartial (the running title was the 'Impartial Compendium'), he regularly expressed approval of political reform through his selection of articles and in the notes which occasionally accompanied them. Tories such as Samuel Johnson and the jurist William Blackstone were treated severely.[16] From August 1770 onwards, as the intensity of the political debate diminished somewhat, the content of the issues shifted to literary and social topics.

At the outset Murray calculated that the costs of producing each number would be more than he was willing to manage himself, so he took in three partners.[17] When all the expenses of a year's publication were paid — paper, printing, advertising (very heavy), editing, indexing and the stamp tax — Murray tallied a net loss of £32.15*s*.[18] Many sets of the work still stood on Murray's shelves yet to be bound, let alone be sold at twelve shillings, so he decided to discontinue the venture.

When Gilbert Stuart returned to Scotland late in 1773 to establish the *Edinburgh Magazine and Review,* Murray lost immediate contact with an able writer and trusted advisor. However, he gained access to a powerful outlet for the promotion of his publications.[19] More important, he had the opportunity to learn from the inside how to run a monthly periodical — or, as it turned out, how *not* to run one. Stuart and William Smellie, the Edinburgh printer and sometime writer, were the literary forces behind the periodical, and each owned a one-third share. The other third was divided equally between William Creech and Charles Elliot.[20] Murray provided the editors with both a regular supply of new London books for review and with newspapers and magazines from which they extracted articles and information. He also sent original poems that he had solicited from John Langhorne, Edmund Cartwright and William Jones.[21] Each month Murray advertised the work extensively in the London papers and distributed it to booksellers in Ireland, India, Europe and America.[22]

---

[16]Johnson and his pamphlet on American affairs, *False Alarm*, were attacked (*Repository*, i, 216–20) as was Blackstone (ii, 94).

[17]Murray's partners were the London booksellers, John Bell and Samuel Bladon, and Christopher Etherington, who sold the *Repository* in and around York. The work was printed in London by George Scott.

[18]AL, p. 92.

[19]Murray also advertised such products as the Edinburgh Fever Powders and books like the *Medical Commentaries* on the covers of the *Edinburgh Magazine and Review* (JM to Wm Smellie, 2 Dec. 1773). No copies in covers are extant. This five-volume periodical was reprinted in 1998 by Thoemmes Press, Bristol.

[20]Stuart to JM, 1 Sept. 1773, Bodleian Library, Hughenden Papers, G/1/919, for a discussion of the division of ownership.

[21]JM to Wm Creech, Charles Elliot and Wm Smellie, 17 Aug. 1776.

[22]Thomas Ewing was the Dublin agent for the *Edinbugh Magazine and Review,* and his name, like Murray's, appeared in the imprint. Continental sales: JM to Bennet and Hake

There was a genuine demand for the kind of periodical Stuart and Smellie had conceived, and the *Edinburgh Magazine and Review* met with initial success. Its best reviews offered readers a new type of criticism, one that made the article itself an object of literary entertainment rather than merely a vehicle to summarise and judge new works. Before long, however, an increasingly contentious tone and provincial tendency led to a decline in sales. 'There are complaints', Murray told Stuart, 'that you pay too many compliments to Scotch authors. You ought to be more general.'[23] From the start Murray had tried to temper Stuart's vituperative critical style and often biased political reports, but at a distance is was difficult to reason with him. For example, when Stuart mercilessly attacked John Leland's *History of Ireland* (1773), Murray implored him to 'take the first opportunity of making it up with the Irish'. Sales in Ireland had fallen off with this single unfavourable review.[24]

When Stuart and Smellie's hopes for success did not materialise, they proposed a complete revamping of the project. Murray wrote to express his interest, even to purchase a share, but insisted he must know the details if the new plan was to be a genuine improvement. It was essential, he told them, 'to guard against every foreseen & even unforseen contingence', and know 'the number of shares that it was divided into; the names of the proprietors; an estimate of paper & printing; the price proposed to be paid per sheet to Reviewers; what sum was agreed upon to be laid out on advertising; at what time it was proposed to advertise . . . and the particular departments Mr Creech, you, and my self were to occupy; the money to be subscribed in order to insist upon the publication for some months . . . should it not prove successfull at the first starting.'[25] Murray never received answers to these important questions. He grew angry with Stuart and Smellie, and the appearance of subsequent issues made him embarrassed to have his name on the work. 'Indolence and carelessness seems to have siezed the whole', he told Stuart scornfully, 'and by a continuence of this management the work must perish in a very little time nor leave a wreck behind'.[26] The editors did introduce some minor changes. But these, rather than improve the *Edinburgh Magazine and Review,* only made it less burdensome for Stuart and Smellie to produce. As the work continued, sales declined and debts increased. The loss of a lawsuit brought by an angry author whose book had been scathingly reviewed, and the unanticipated

Booksellers in Amsterdam, 24 Nov. 1773. American sales: JM to Robert Miller, Bookseller in Williamsburg, Virginia, 5 Dec. 1773.

[23]JM to Gilbert Stuart, 21 Mar. 1774.

[24]Ibid. Murray also had it in mind to 'make it up' with the publishers of Leland's book, his fellow tradesmen John Norse, Thomas Longman, George Robinson and Joseph Johnson.

[25]JM to Wm Smellie, 13 Sept. 1774.

[26]JM to Gilbert Stuart, 24 Nov. 1774.

demand for payments of a stamp tax further exacerbated the difficulties.[27] In August 1776 publication stopped.

Murray had put over £125 towards advertising the periodical in the London papers. Had it done well, his profits would have more than covered the expenditure. But as things stood, he refused to be out of pocket for a collective expense. He wrote to the proprietors demanding payment, and, receiving an ineffectual reply, threatened legal action.[28] To show the justice of his demands, he requested four London booksellers to state in writing the amount of money necessary to establish a new magazine in England for the first year.[29] An extended argument ensued, and now both sides threatened legal proceedings. Finally, convinced of Murray's serious intentions, the proprietors paid him what he demanded.[30]

While Murray was witnessing the fall of the *Edinburgh Magazine and Review*, he was enjoying the success of the *Medical Commentaries*, the quarterly review of the publications and developments in the field of medicine, edited by Andrew Duncan. Smellie, who printed both works, always had to be pressed to keep to schedule. However, the parallels between the two periodicals were few. A literary magazine had to establish itself in a competitive market, while a medical compendium catered to a specialised audience and was at the time virtually unique.

The failure of Stuart's periodical did not discourage Murray from attempting one himself. In mid-1778 he planned a new work to resemble the *Annual Register*, the popular collection containing accounts of national and international events, essays in natural history and antiquities, poetry and literary reviews.[31] The *Annual Register* was sometimes overtly factional in its politics and did not always appear on time.[32] Murray judged that an impartial and promptly published competitor might succeed. By October 1778 the project was far enough advanced that Murray began printing the first sheets. However, he was still uncertain of a title and wrote to Gilbert

[27]On the law suit with Lord Monboddo, Murray wrote: 'I am sorry to learn that Mr Smellie has lost his cause, but it will serve to make the authors of the *Edinb Mag* more cautious in their strictures of living characters' (JM to Balfour, 25 June 1776). The stamp tax was two shillings per sheet (JM to Wm Smellie, 25 Sept. 1775).
[28]JM to Creech, Elliot and Smellie, 17 Aug. 1776.
[29]JM to Thomas Evans, before 7 Aug. 1776. Murray also wrote to George Robinson, George Kearsley and John Wheble.
[30]AL, p. 306.
[31]The Dodsleys published the *Annual Register* 1758–1800, and Edmund Burke edited it for many years. The contents varied but the typical categories of the work were 'History of Europe', 'Chronicle' (a day-by-day account of important events), 'State Papers', 'Characters', 'Natural History', 'Useful Projects', 'Antiquities', 'Miscellaneous Essays', 'Poetry', and 'Account of Books'.
[32]This opinion of the *Annual Register* was expressed in a review in the *English Review*, 5 (Feb. 1785) 124. Murray may not have written the review, but he undoubtedly concurred in the opinion.

Stuart in Scotland for a suggestion. He also asked Stuart to 'furnish early as you can any matter . . . which you are inclined to give me'. Murray specifically requested reviews of recent publications, an account of the General Assembly of the Church of Scotland and 'a good character of David Hume', the Scottish historian and philosopher who had died two years before.[33] Even though production had begun and Murray had paid out substantial sums for copy and printing, he suddenly dropped the project for no apparent reason. To Stuart — who had not supplied the requested articles — he explained only that 'the new annual register has miscarried. The story of this abortion is full of Particulars, but none of them sufficiently important to Dwell upon.'[34]

At this time Murray invested considerable sums to become one of the proprietors of the *General Advertiser, or Morning Intelligencer*. Early in 1778 he purchased a one-thirty-second share for £102. And, confident that the newspaper would do well, he bought two additional sixty-fourth shares in May 1779 (for £51) and in November 1780 (for £48). In July 1779 he received a dividend of £15 and in December ten guineas more and had expectations of making money. However, the following year he was called upon for £60 to support the struggling newspaper. In all he now had £235 invested, a sum he would never recoup.[35]

Early in 1781, two years after his failed attempts to establish an annual compendium, Murray finally met with somewhat more success when he published the *London Mercury; Containing the History, Politics, and Literature of England, for the Year* 1780. Murray engaged as its editor William Thomson, a Scottish minister from Perthshire who had come to London to begin a literary career. He was glad to have the ten guineas Murray was willing to pay him to write the original parts of the work and compile the sections extracted from other publications.[36] In the Advertisement to the *Mercury*, Thomson (under the supervision of Murray) compared this new work with other established periodicals, declaring that there was not one 'which records National Events with Impartiality, or delineates Public Characters with Candor'. He appealed to the independent spirit of his readers: 'If there be yet in the Country such a Thing as a Public, distinct from all political Parties, a Performance of this Kind will not want Encouragement'. Though a standard feature of even the most factional publication, the appeal to impartiality meant something more after the most important political event of 1780 — rioting in London over proposed Catholic relief legislation that had brought home the fear of how volatile popular politics could be.[37]

---

[33]JM to Gilbert Stuart, 3 Oct. 1778.
[34]JM to Gilbert Stuart, 18 Feb. 1779.
[35]BB, p. 4.
[36]BB, p. 27.
[37]The so-called 'Gordon Riots' were discussed in many sections of the *London Mercury*. They are further analysed in Ch. 12, pp. 226–28.

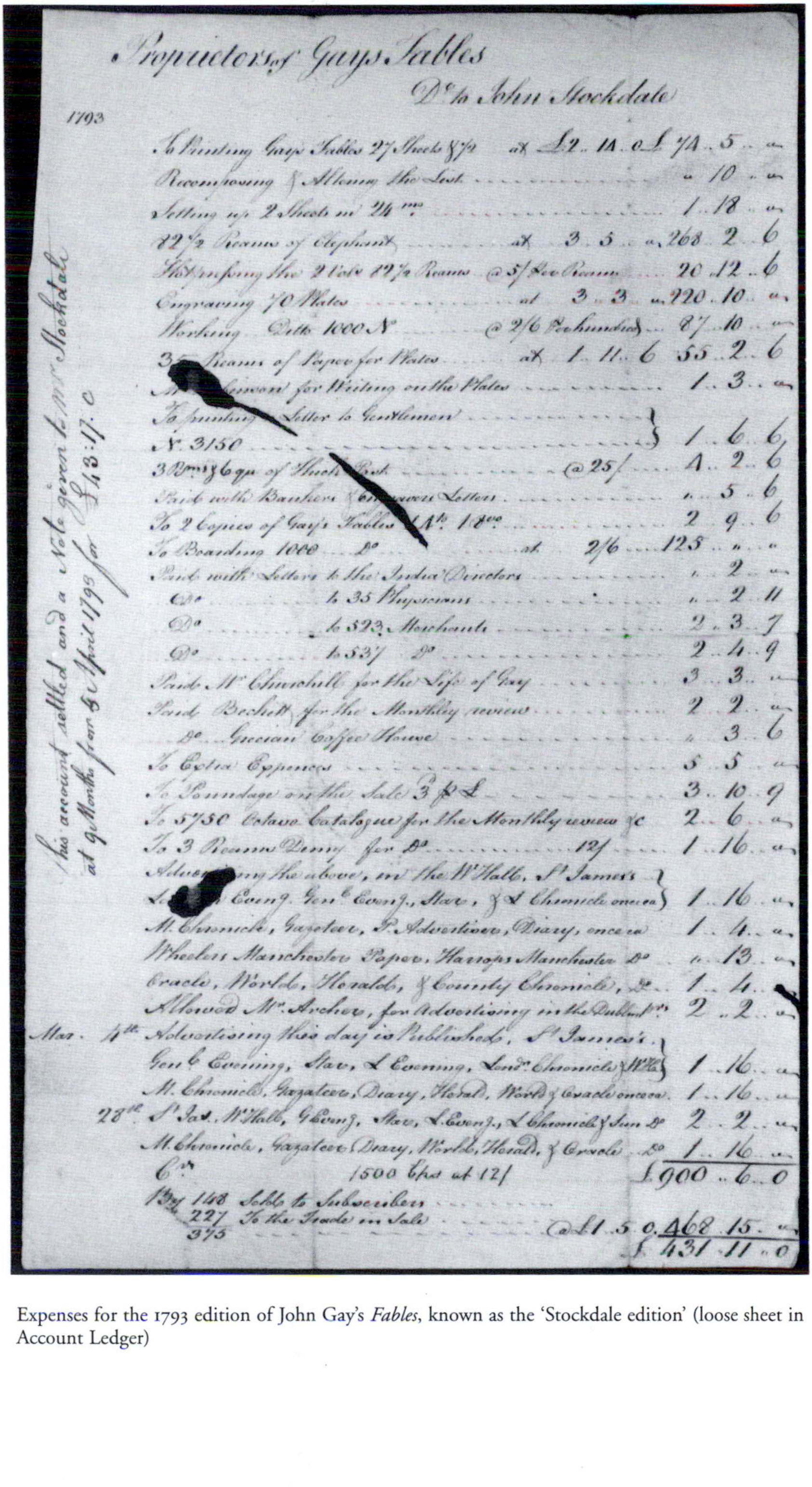

PLATE 25

Expenses for the 1793 edition of John Gay's *Fables*, known as the 'Stockdale edition' (loose sheet in Account Ledger)

PLATE 26

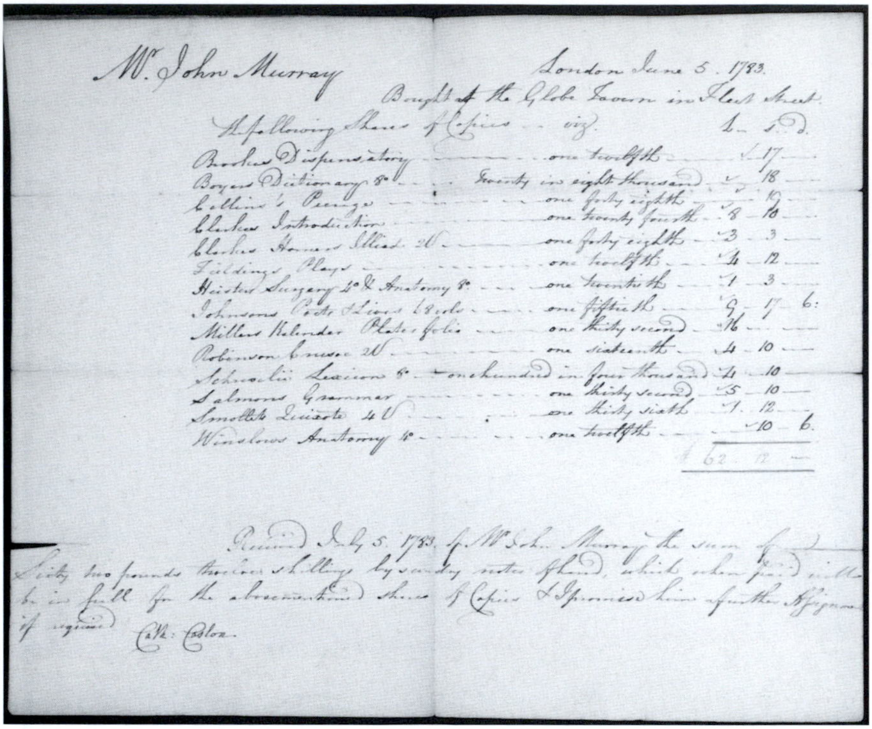
Mr. John Murray London June 5. 1783.

Bought at the Globe Tavern in Fleet Street the following Shares of Copies viz.

		£	s	d
Brookes Dispensatory	one twelfth	–	17	–
Boyers Dictionary 8°	twenty in eight thousand	–	18	–
Collins's Peerage	one forty eighth	–	19	–
Clarkes Introduction	one twenty fourth	8	18	–
Clarkes Homers Illiad 2 V	one forty eighth	3	3	–
Fieldings Plays	one twelfth	4	12	–
Heisters Surgery 4° & Anatomy 8°	one twentieth	1	3	–
Johnsons Poets & Lives 68 vols	one fiftieth	9	17	6
Millers Kalendar Plates folio	one thirty second	16	–	–
Robinson Crusoe 2 V	one sixteenth	4	10	–
Schrevelii Lexicon 8°	one hundred in four thousand	4	10	–
Salmons Grammar	one thirty second	5	10	–
Smolletts Quixote 4 V	one thirty sixth	1	12	–
Winslows Anatomy 4°	one twelfth	–	10	6
		£ 62	12	–

Received July 5. 1783. of Mr John Murray the sum of Sixty two pounds twelve shillings by sundry notes of hand, which when paid will be in full for the abovementioned shares of Copies & I promised him a further Assignment if required Cath: Caslon.

Receipts for Murray's 'syndicate' purchases in shares of fourteen titles, Globe Tavern, 5 June 1783 (loose sheet in the Booksellers' Book)

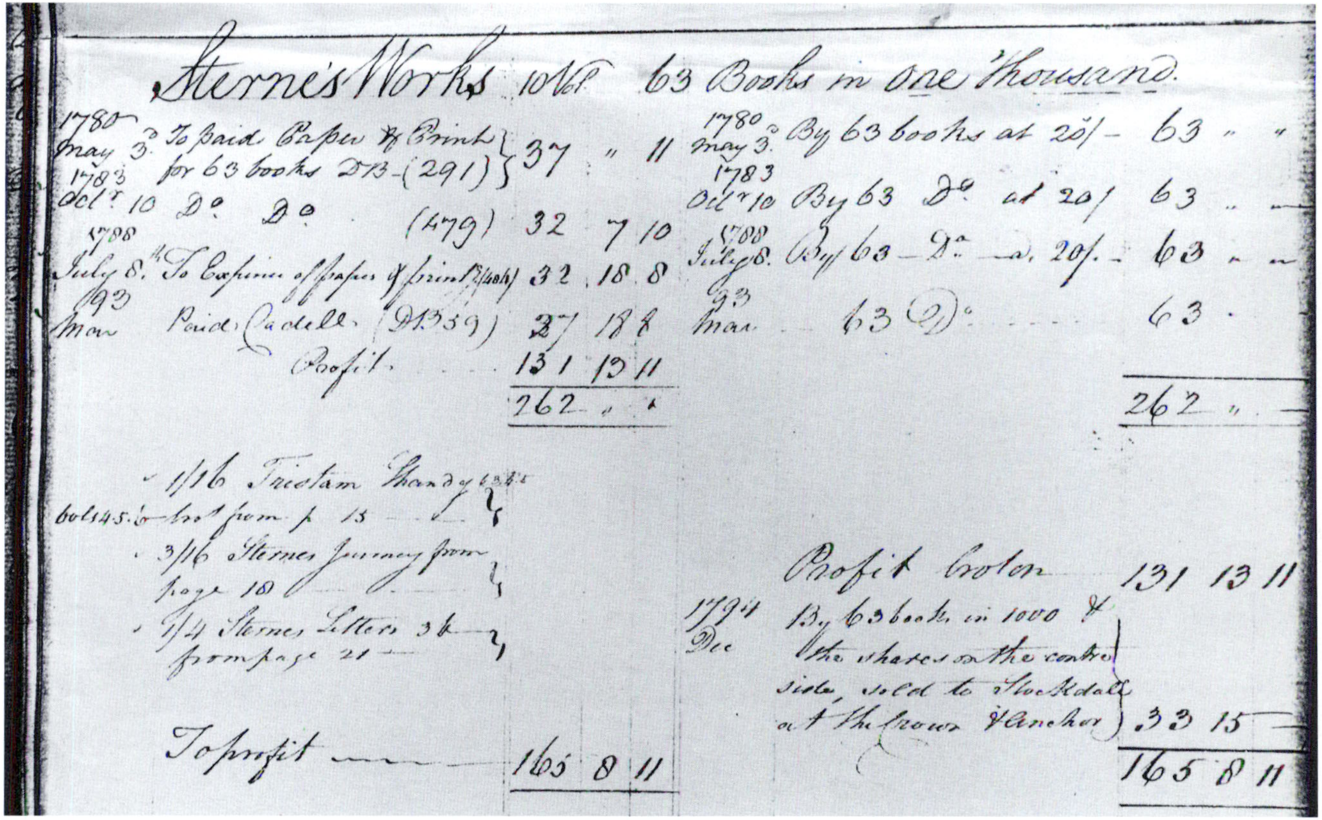

PLATE 27

Booksellers' Book entry (p. 23) for Murray's share in *The Works of Laurence Sterne*

PLATE 28

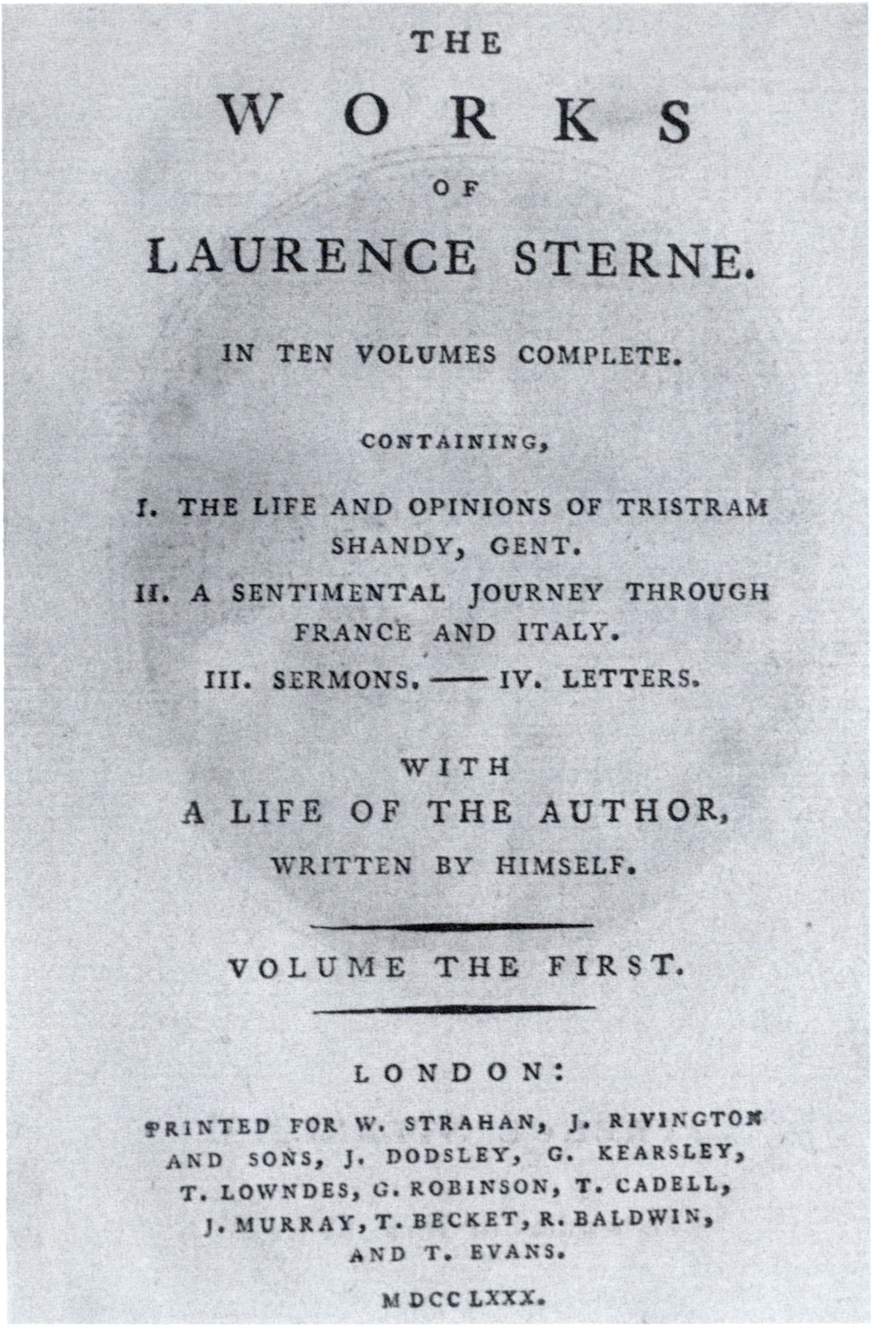

THE
W O R K S
OF
LAURENCE STERNE.

IN TEN VOLUMES COMPLETE.

CONTAINING,

I. THE LIFE AND OPINIONS OF TRISTRAM
SHANDY, GENT.

II. A SENTIMENTAL JOURNEY THROUGH
FRANCE AND ITALY.

III. SERMONS. —— IV. LETTERS.

WITH
A LIFE OF THE AUTHOR,
WRITTEN BY HIMSELF.

_____

VOLUME THE FIRST.

_____

LONDON:
PRINTED FOR W. STRAHAN, J. RIVINGTON
AND SONS, J. DODSLEY, G. KEARSLEY,
T. LOWNDES, G. ROBINSON, T. CADELL,
J. MURRAY, T. BECKET, R. BALDWIN,
AND T. EVANS.

M DCC LXXX.

Title page to *The Works of Laurence Sterne*, 1780

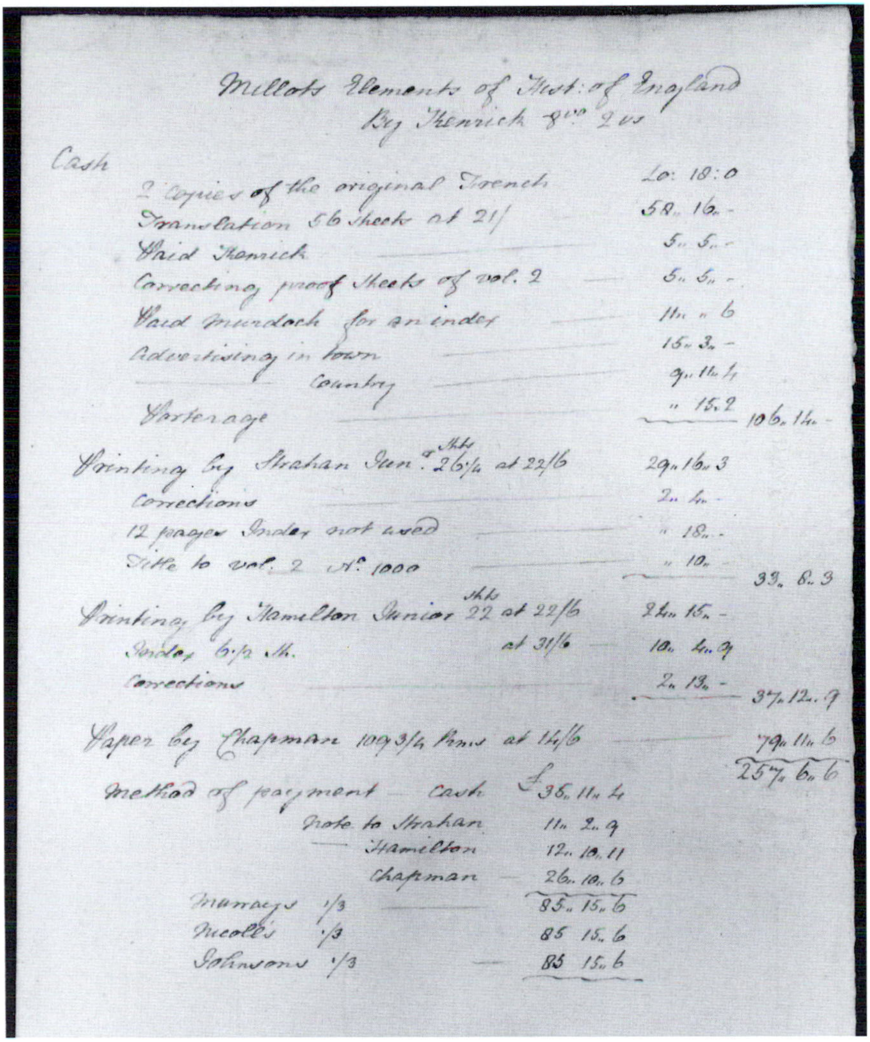

PLATE 29

Millots Elements of Hist: of England
By Kenrick 8vo 2 vs

Cash

2 Copies of the original French	Lo: 18: 0
Translation 56 Sheets at 21/	58. 16. -
Paid Kenrick	5. 5. -
Correcting proof Sheets of vol. 2	5. 5. -
Paid Murdoch for an index	11. - 6
Advertising in town	15. 3. -
—————— Country	9. 14. 4
Porterage	" 15. 2
	106. 14. -

Printing by Strahan Jun.r 26/4 at 22/6	29. 16. 3
Corrections	2. 4. -
12 pages Index not used	" 18. -
Title to vol. 2 N.o 1000	" 10. -
	33. 8. 3

Printing by Hamelton Junior 22 at 22/6	24. 15. -
Index 6½ Sh. at 31/6	10. 4. 9
Corrections	2. 13. -
	37. 12. 9

Paper by Chapman 109 3/4 Rms at 14/6	79. 11. 6
	257. 6. 6

method of payment — cash	£35. 11. 4
note to Strahan	11. 2. 9
——— Hamelton	12. 10. 11
Chapman	26. 10. 6
	85. 15. 6
Murrays 1/3	85 15. 6
Nicolls 1/3	85 15. 6
Johnsons 1/3	85 15. 6

Expenses for Millot's *Elements of the History of England* (loose sheet in Account Ledger, p. 123)

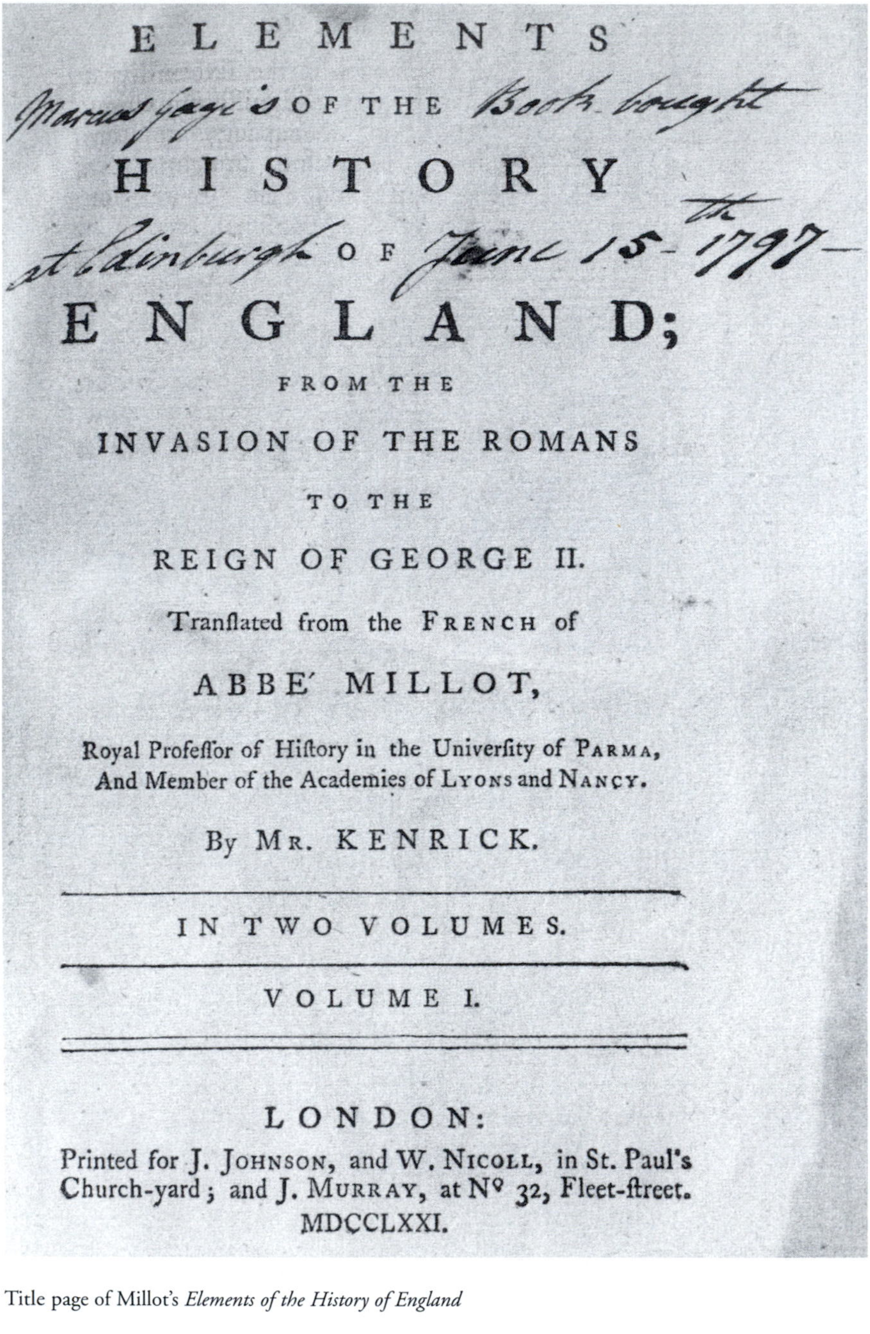

PLATE 30

Marius Gage's [handwritten annotation] *Book bought*

at Edinburgh [handwritten] *June 15th 1797* [handwritten]

E L E M E N T S
OF THE

H I S T O R Y
OF

E N G L A N D;

FROM THE

INVASION OF THE ROMANS

TO THE

REIGN OF GEORGE II.

Tranflated from the FRENCH of

ABBE' MILLOT,

Royal Profeffor of Hiftory in the Univerfity of PARMA,
And Member of the Academies of LYONS and NANCY.

By MR. KENRICK.

IN TWO VOLUMES.

VOLUME I.

LONDON:

Printed for J. JOHNSON, and W. NICOLL, in St. Paul's
Church-yard; and J. MURRAY, at Nº 32, Fleet-ftreet.
MDCCLXXI.

Title page of Millot's *Elements of the History of England*

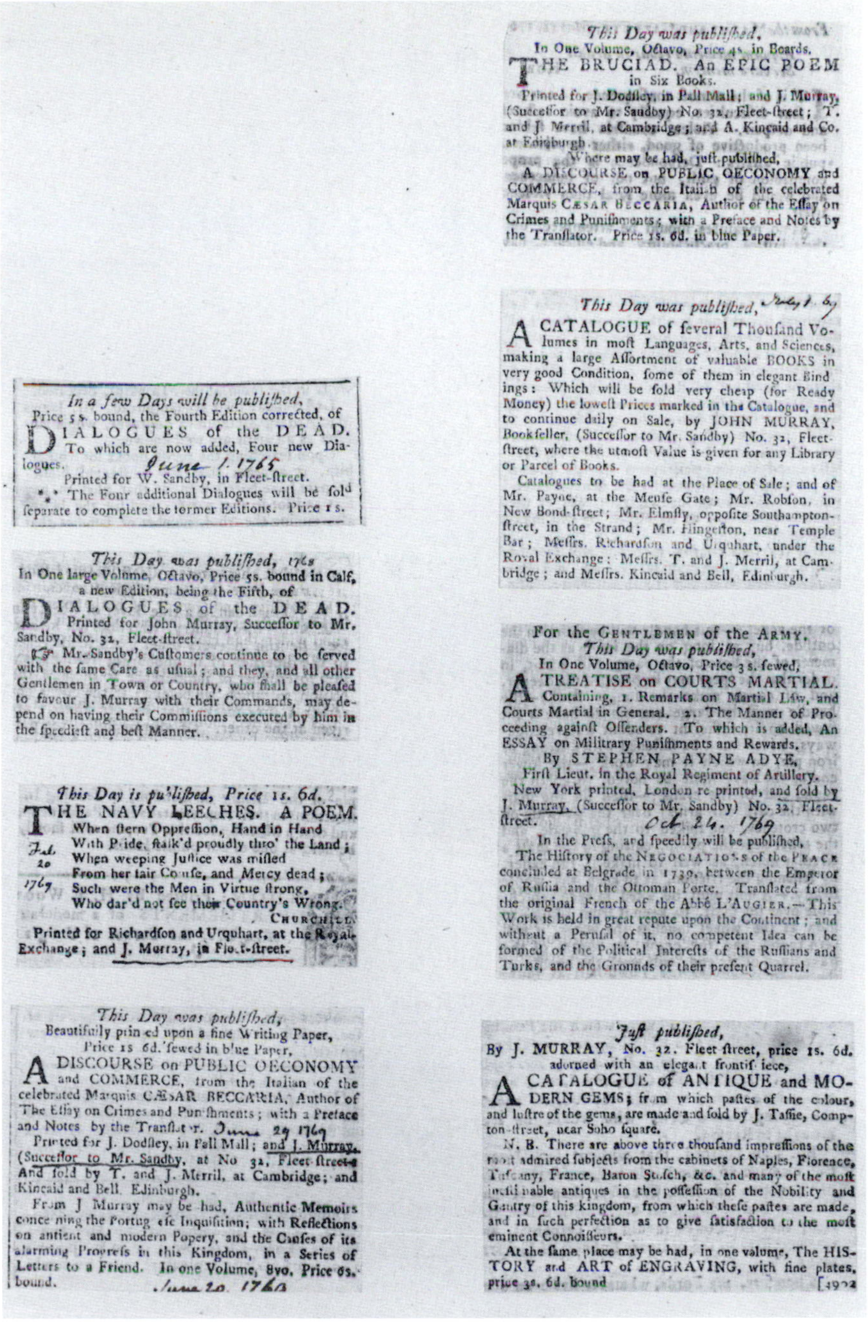

PLATE 31

Advertisements for Murray's publications, some dated in his hand, from his newspaper clipping album

PLATE 32

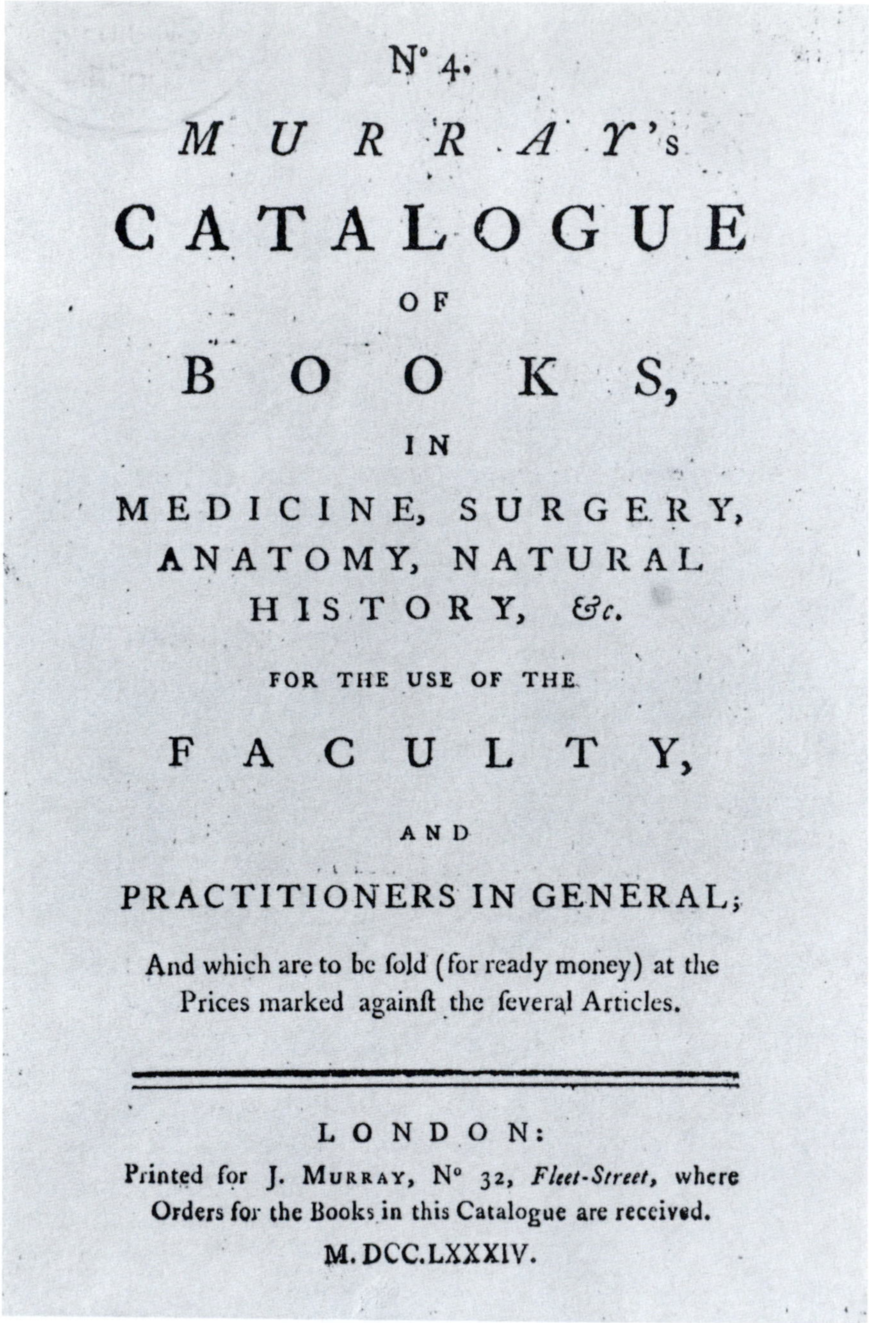

Nº 4.

M U R R A Y's

CATALOGUE

OF

B O O K S,

IN

MEDICINE, SURGERY,
ANATOMY, NATURAL
HISTORY, &c.

FOR THE USE OF THE

FACULTY,

AND

PRACTITIONERS IN GENERAL;

And which are to be fold (for ready money) at the
Prices marked againft the feveral Articles.

———————————

LONDON:

Printed for J. MURRAY, Nº 32, *Fleet-Street*, where
Orders for the Books in this Catalogue are received.

M. DCC.LXXXIV.

Title page of *Murray's Catalogue of Books in Medicine, Surgery, Anatomy, Natural History for the Use of the Faculty, and Practitioners in General*, 1784 (Courtesy of the Logan Clendening History of Medicine Library, University of Kansas)

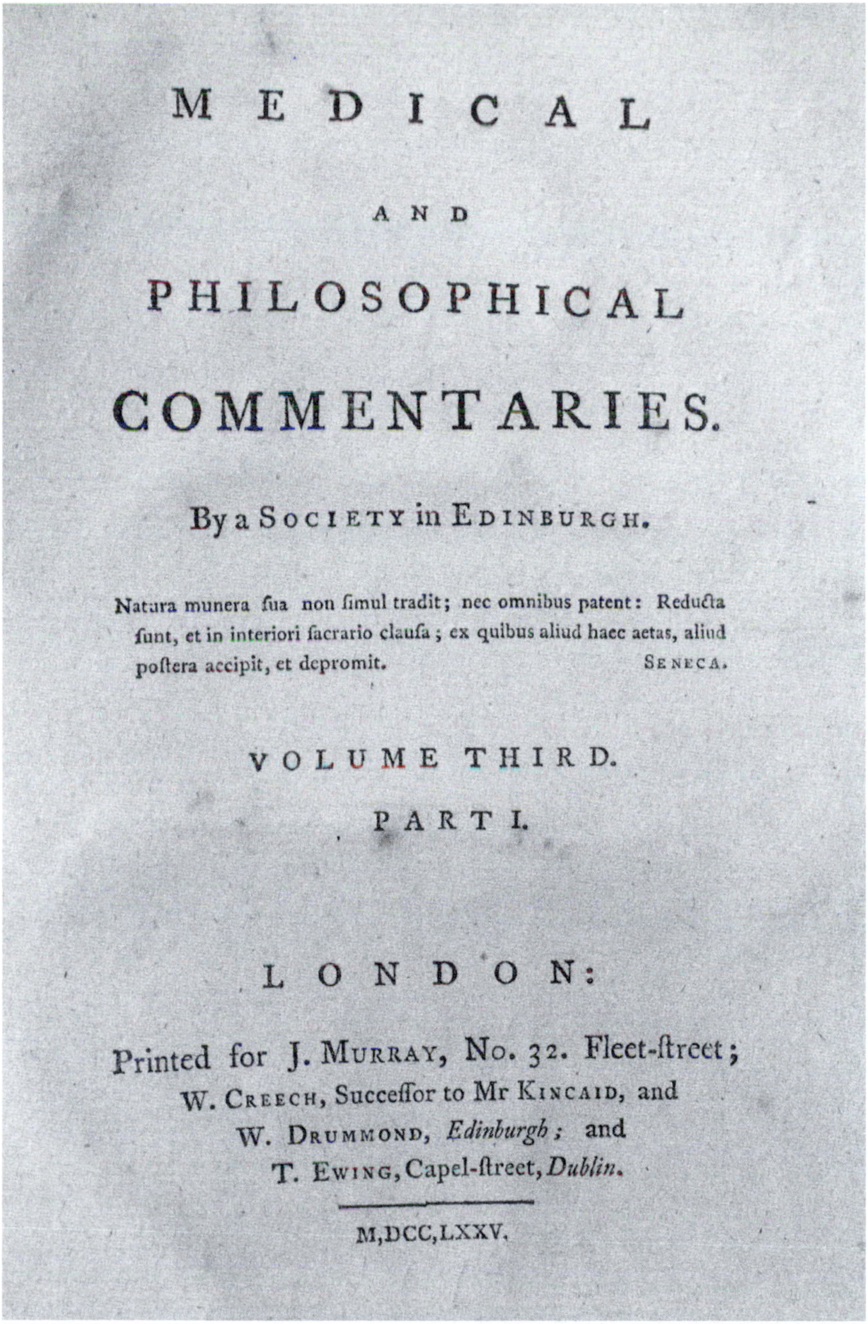

PLATE 33

M E D I C A L

A N D

PHILOSOPHICAL

COMMENTARIES.

By a SOCIETY in EDINBURGH.

Natura munera fua non fimul tradit; nec omnibus patent: Reducta
funt, et in interiori facrario claufa; ex quibus aliud haec aetas, aliud
poftera accipit, et depromit.   SENECA.

VOLUME THIRD.

PART I.

L O N D O N:

Printed for J. MURRAY, No. 32. Fleet-ftreet;
W. CREECH, Succeffor to Mr KINCAID, and
W. DRUMMOND, *Edinburgh;* and
T. EWING, Capel-ftreet, *Dublin.*

M,DCC,LXXV.

Title page of the *Medical and Philosophical Commentaries,* 1774

PLATE 34

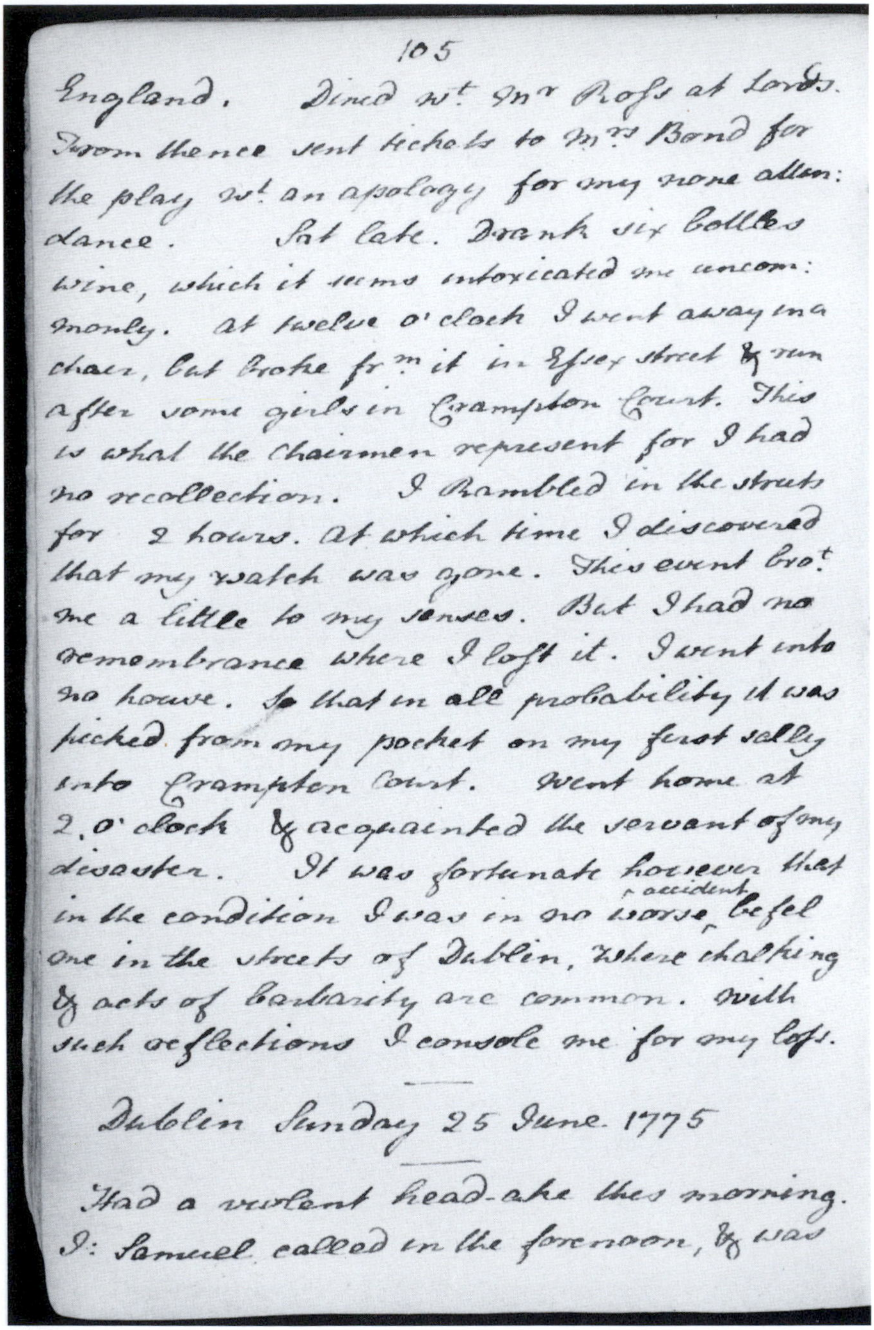

105

England.   Dined wt. Mr. Ross at Lords.
From thence sent tickets to Mrs. Bond for
the play wt. an apology for my non atten:
dance.   Sat late. Drank six bottles
wine, which it seems intoxicated me uncom:
monly.   At twelve o'clock I went away in a
chair, but broke frm. it in Essex street & run
after some girls in Crampton Court. This
is what the chairmen represent for I had
no recollection.   I Rambled in the streets
for 2 hours. At which time I discovered
that my watch was gone. This event bro.t
me a little to my senses. But I had no
remembrance where I lost it. I went into
no house. So that in all probability it was
picked from my pocket on my first sally
into Crampton Court.   Went home at
2 o'clock & acquainted the servant of my
disaster.   It was fortunate however that
in the condition I was in no worse, accident befel
me in the streets of Dublin, where chalking
& acts of barbarity are common. With
such reflections I console me for my loss.

———

Dublin Sunday 25 June. 1775

———

Had a violent head-ake this morning.
I: Samuel called in the forenoon, & was

An entry from Murray's Irish diary for 24 June 1775, describing an evening of debauchery

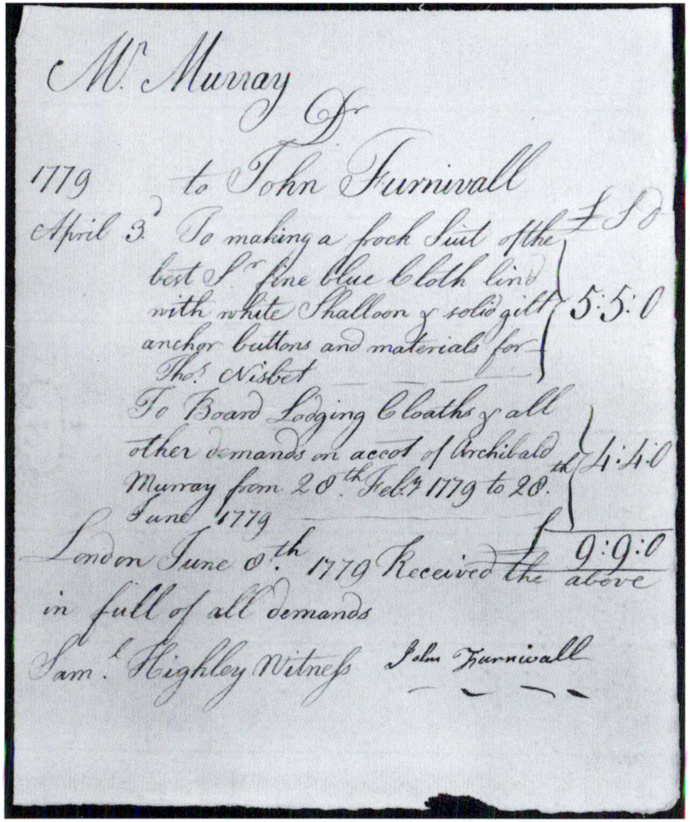

PLATE 35

b. A letter written by Murray to Archie, 10 May 1791

a. Bill listing clothing and boarding charges for Murray's illegitimate son Archie, 8 June 1779 (loose sheet in Account Ledger, p. 200)

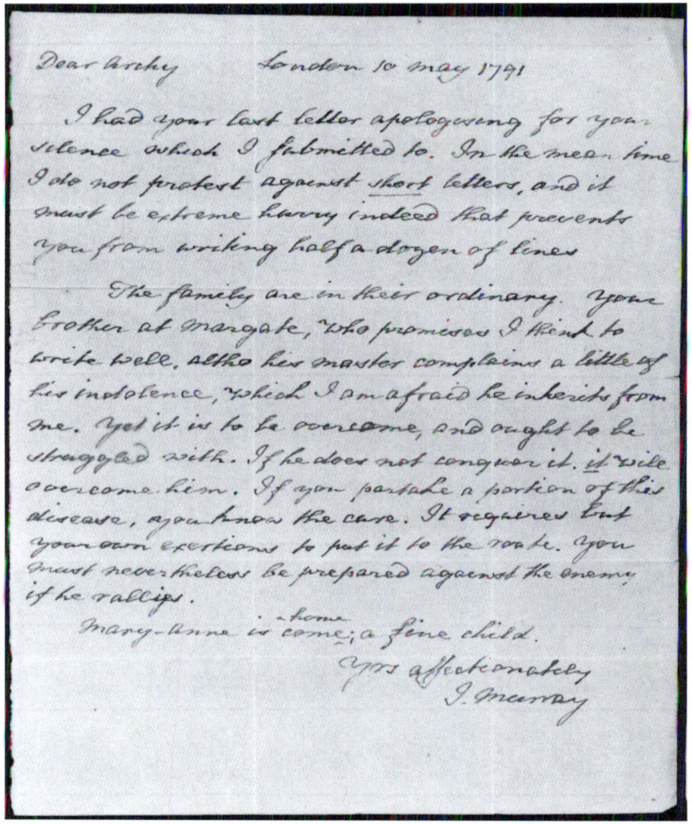

PLATE 36

John Murray II (born 17 November 1778) about the age of five. Crayon drawing on paper by an unidentified artist

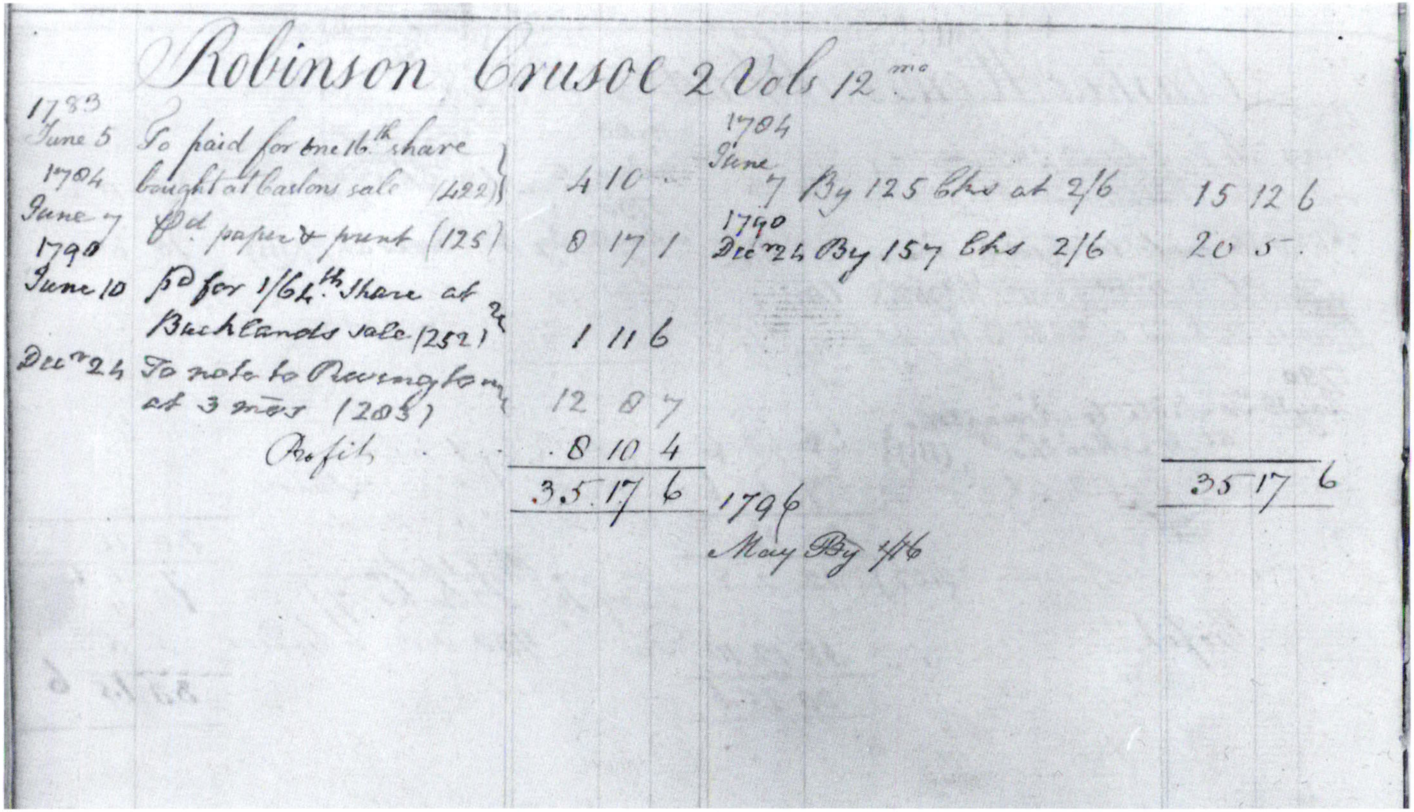

PLATE 37

Booksellers' Book entry (p. 33) for Murray's share in *Robinson Crusoe*, 1784 and 1791 editions

PLATE 38

Title page of Abraham Portal's *Nuptial Elegies*, 1774

PLATE 39

Title page of Edmund Cartwright's *The Prince of Peace*, 1779

PLATE 40

THE

INJURED ISLANDERS;

OR,

THE INFLUENCE OF ART

UPON

THE HAPPINESS OF NATURE.

New wonder rose, when ranged around for Thee,
Attendant Virgins danc'd the TIMRODEE.

LONDON,

PRINTED FOR J. MURRAY, No. 32, OPPOSITE ST. DUNSTAN'S CHURCH,
FLEET-STREET.

MDCCLXXIX.

Title page of Gerald Fitzgerald's *The Injured Islanders,* 1779

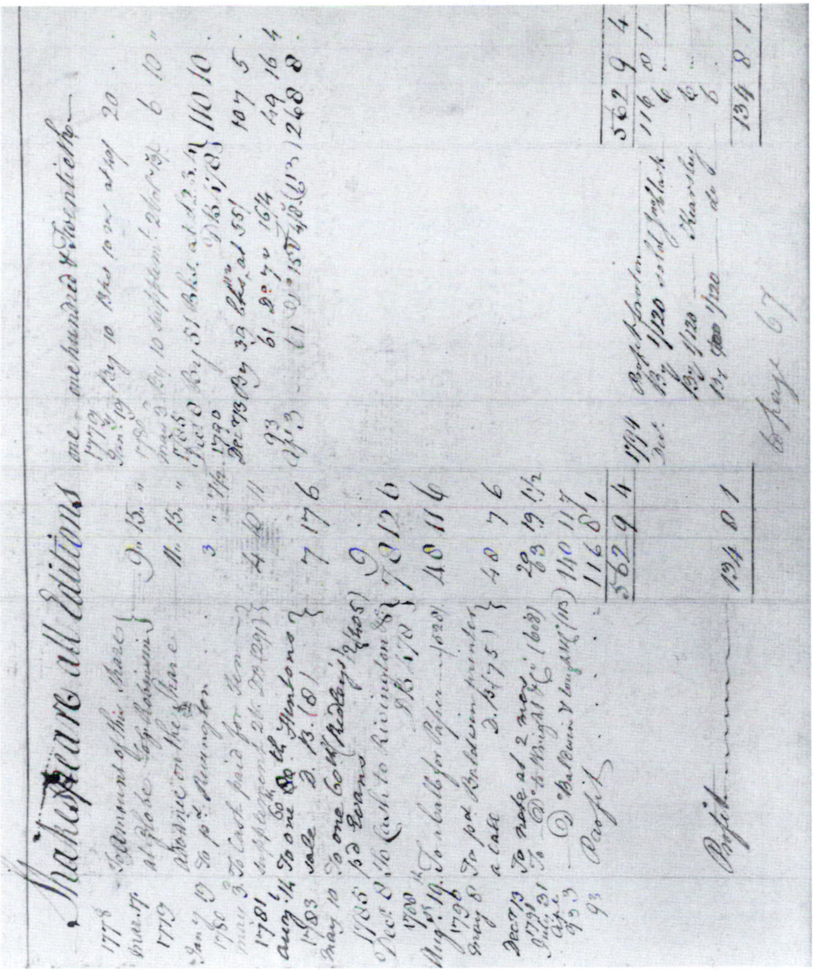

PLATE 41

Booksellers' Book entry (p. 12) for Murray's share in *The Plays of William Shakespeare*

PLATE 42

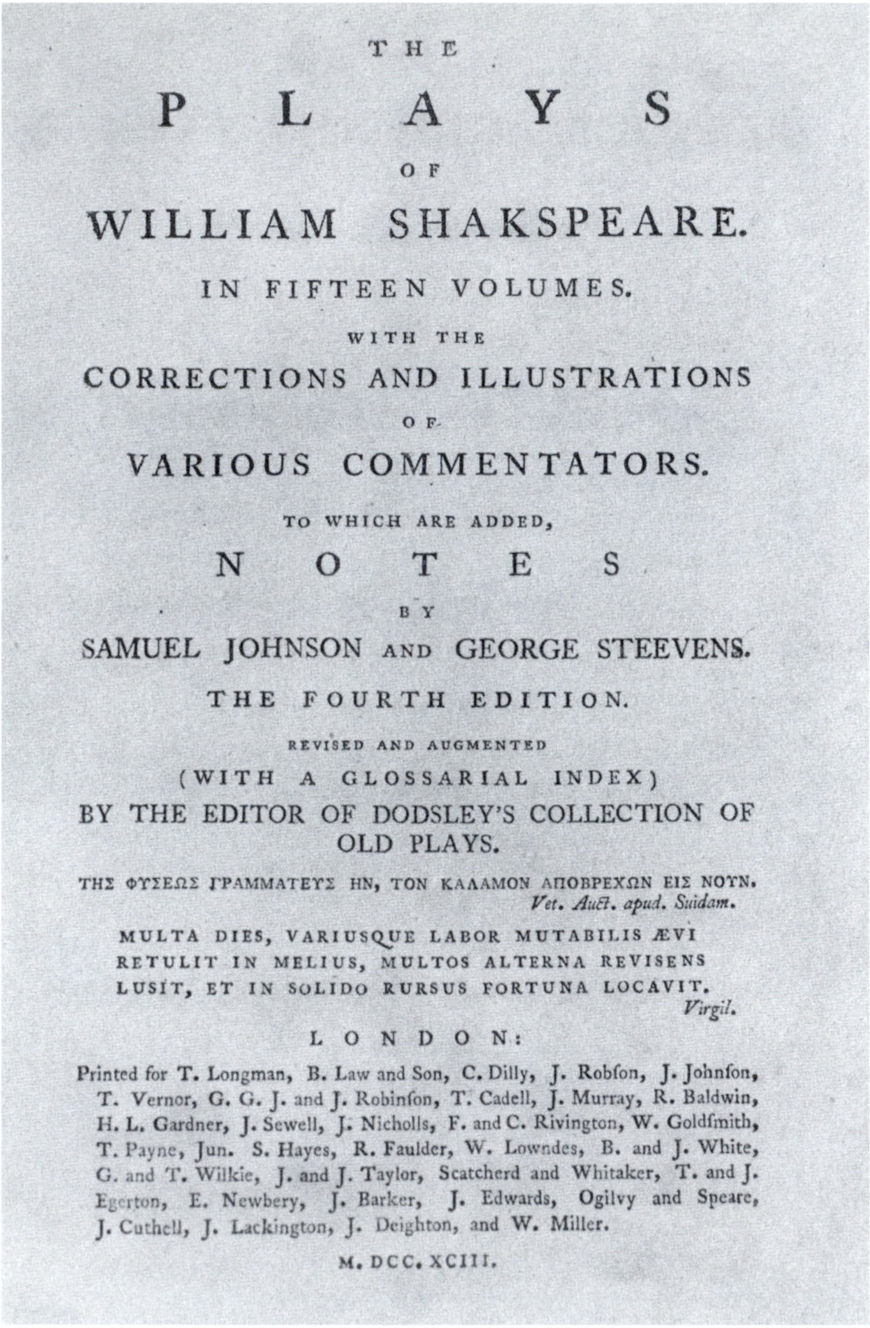

THE
PLAYS

OF

WILLIAM SHAKSPEARE.

IN FIFTEEN VOLUMES.

WITH THE

CORRECTIONS AND ILLUSTRATIONS

OF

VARIOUS COMMENTATORS.

TO WHICH ARE ADDED,

NOTES

BY

SAMUEL JOHNSON AND GEORGE STEEVENS.

THE FOURTH EDITION.

REVISED AND AUGMENTED

(WITH A GLOSSARIAL INDEX)

BY THE EDITOR OF DODSLEY'S COLLECTION OF OLD PLAYS.

ΤΗΣ ΦΥΣΕΩΣ ΓΡΑΜΜΑΤΕΥΣ ΗΝ, ΤΟΝ ΚΑΛΑΜΟΝ ΑΠΟΒΡΕΧΩΝ ΕΙΣ ΝΟΥΝ.
Vet. Auct. apud. Suidam.

MULTA DIES, VARIUSQUE LABOR MUTABILIS ÆVI
RETULIT IN MELIUS, MULTOS ALTERNA REVISENS
LUSIT, ET IN SOLIDO RURSUS FORTUNA LOCAVIT.
Virgil.

LONDON:

Printed for T. Longman, B. Law and Son, C. Dilly, J. Robfon, J. Johnfon, T. Vernor, G. G. J. and J. Robinfon, T. Cadell, J. Murray, R. Baldwin, H. L. Gardner, J. Sewell, J. Nicholls, F. and C. Rivington, W. Goldfmith, T. Payne, Jun. S. Hayes, R. Faulder, W. Lowndes, B. and J. White, G. and T. Wilkie, J. and J. Taylor, Scatcherd and Whitaker, T. and J. Egerton, E. Newbery, J. Barker, J. Edwards, Ogilvy and Speare, J. Cuthell, J. Lackington, J. Deighton, and W. Miller.

M.DCC.XCIII.

Title page of *The Plays of William Shakspeare,* 1793 edition

PLATE 43

FOREIGN
MEDICAL REVIEW:

CONTAINING

An ACCOUNT with EXTRACTS

OF ALL THE

NEW BOOKS

PUBLISHED ON

NATURAL HISTORY,	SURGERY,
BOTANY,	MIDWIFERY,
MATERIA MEDICA,	AND THE
CHEMISTRY,	PRACTICE OF
ANATOMY,	PHYSIC,

In every Part of the Continent of EUROPE.

TOGETHER WITH

INTELLIGENCE OF NEW AND INTERESTING
DISCOVERIES.

VOL. I. PART I.

LONDON,

PRINTED FOR J. MURRAY, Nº 32, FLEET-STREET.

MDCCLXXIX.

Title page of the *Foreign Medical Review*, 1779

PLATE 44

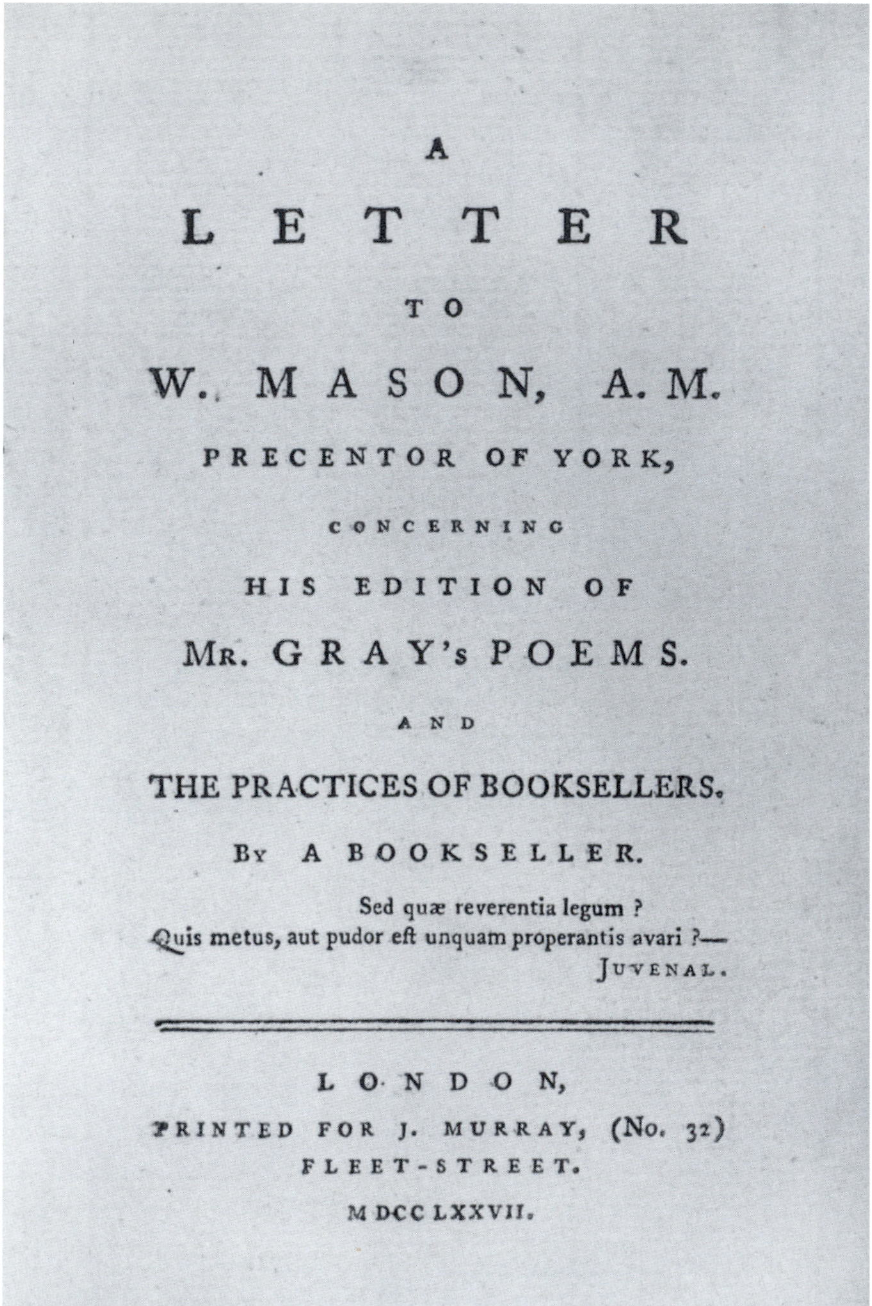

A

L E T T E R

T O

W. M A S O N, A. M.

PRECENTOR OF YORK,

CONCERNING

HIS EDITION OF

MR. G R A Y's P O E M S.

AND

THE PRACTICES OF BOOKSELLERS.

BY A BOOKSELLER.

Sed quæ reverentia legum ?
Quis metus, aut pudor eft unquam properantis avari ?—
JUVENAL.

L O N D O N,
PRINTED FOR J. MURRAY, (No. 32)
FLEET-STREET.
M DCC LXXVII.

Title page of *A Letter to W. Mason, concerning his Edition of Mr. Gray's Poems and the Practices of Booksellers*, 1777

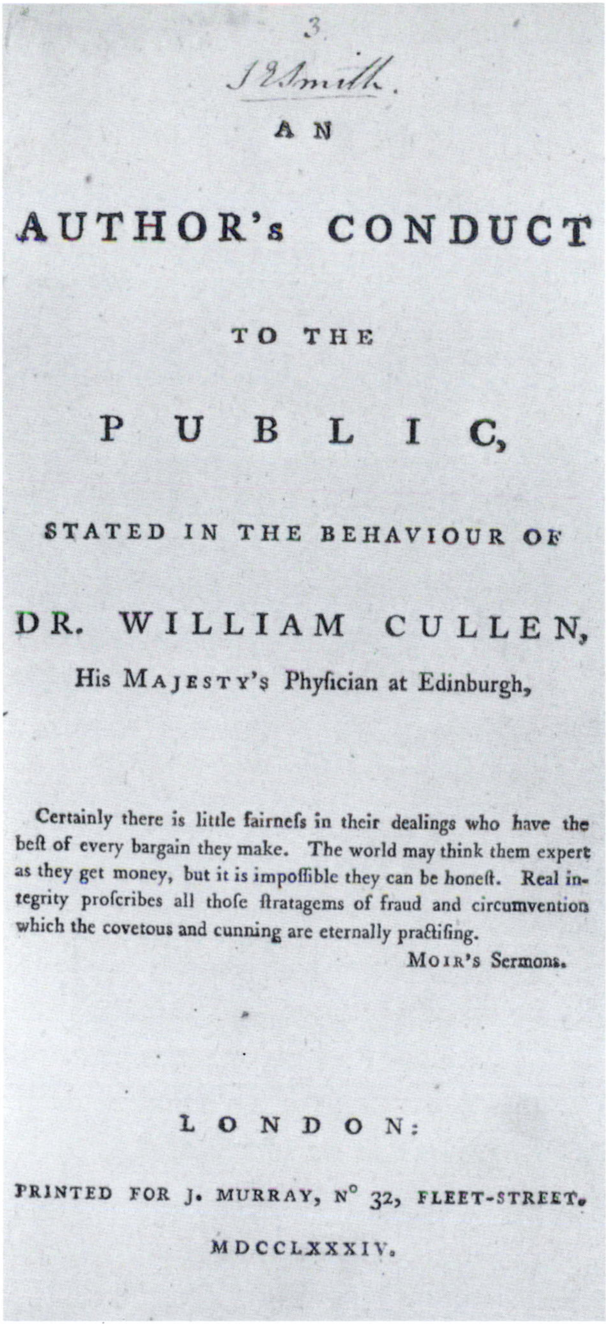

PLATE 45

3.

J E Smith.

A N

AUTHOR's CONDUCT

TO THE

PUBLIC,

STATED IN THE BEHAVIOUR OF

DR. WILLIAM CULLEN,

His MAJESTY's Physician at Edinburgh,

Certainly there is little fairnefs in their dealings who have the beft of every bargain they make. The world may think them expert as they get money, but it is impoffible they can be honeft. Real integrity profcribes all thofe ftratagems of fraud and circumvention which the covetous and cunning are eternally practifing.

MOIR's Sermons.

LONDON:

PRINTED FOR J. MURRAY, N° 32, FLEET-STREET.

MDCCLXXXIV.

Title page of *An Author's Conduct to the Public*, 1784, Murray's attack on Dr William Cullen

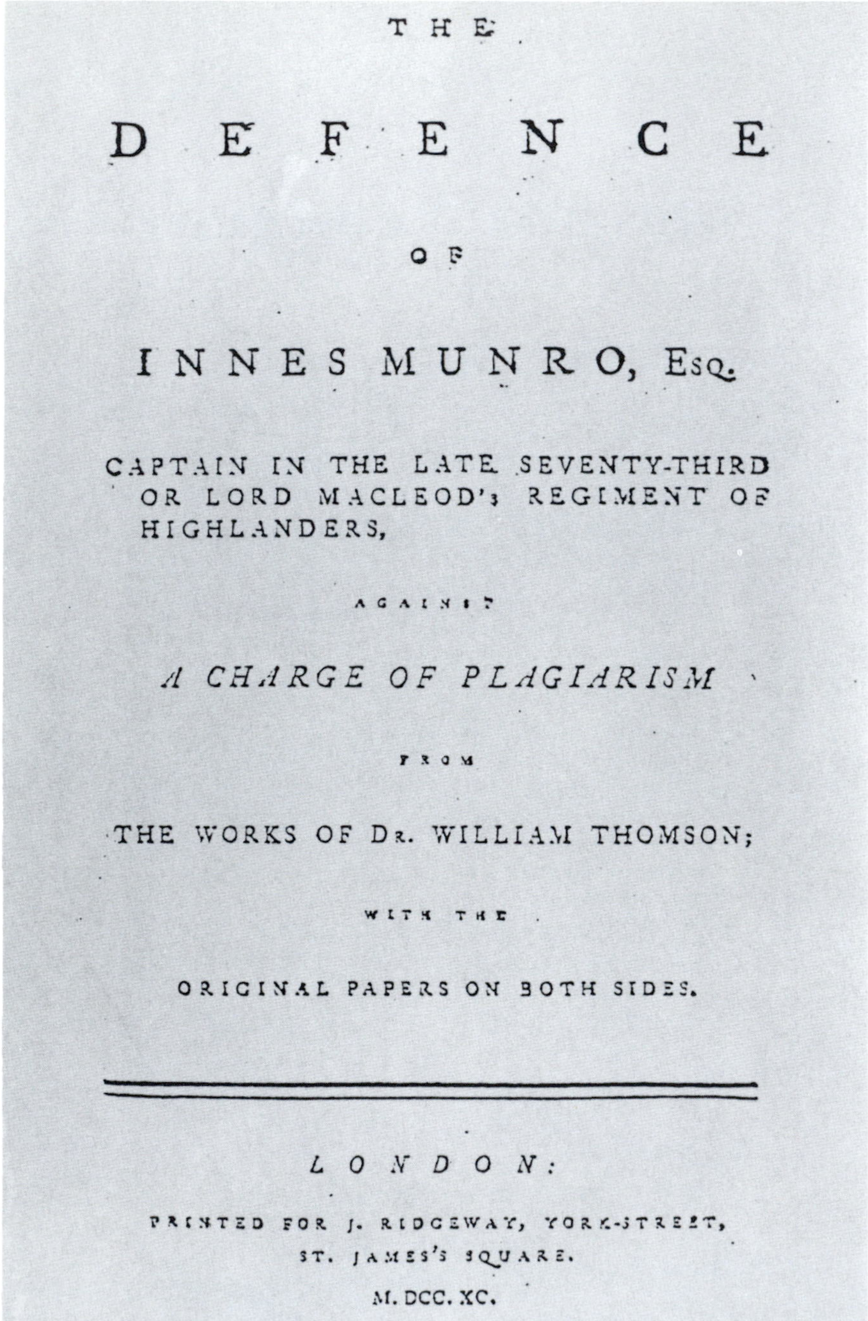

PLATE 46

THE

DEFENCE

OF

INNES MUNRO, Esq.

CAPTAIN IN THE LATE SEVENTY-THIRD
OR LORD MACLEOD's REGIMENT OF
HIGHLANDERS,

AGAINST

A CHARGE OF PLAGIARISM

FROM

THE WORKS OF Dr. WILLIAM THOMSON;

WITH THE

ORIGINAL PAPERS ON BOTH SIDES.

LONDON:

PRINTED FOR J. RIDGEWAY, YORK-STREET,
ST. JAMES'S SQUARE.
M. DCC. XC.

Title page of *The Defence of Innes Munro*, 1790

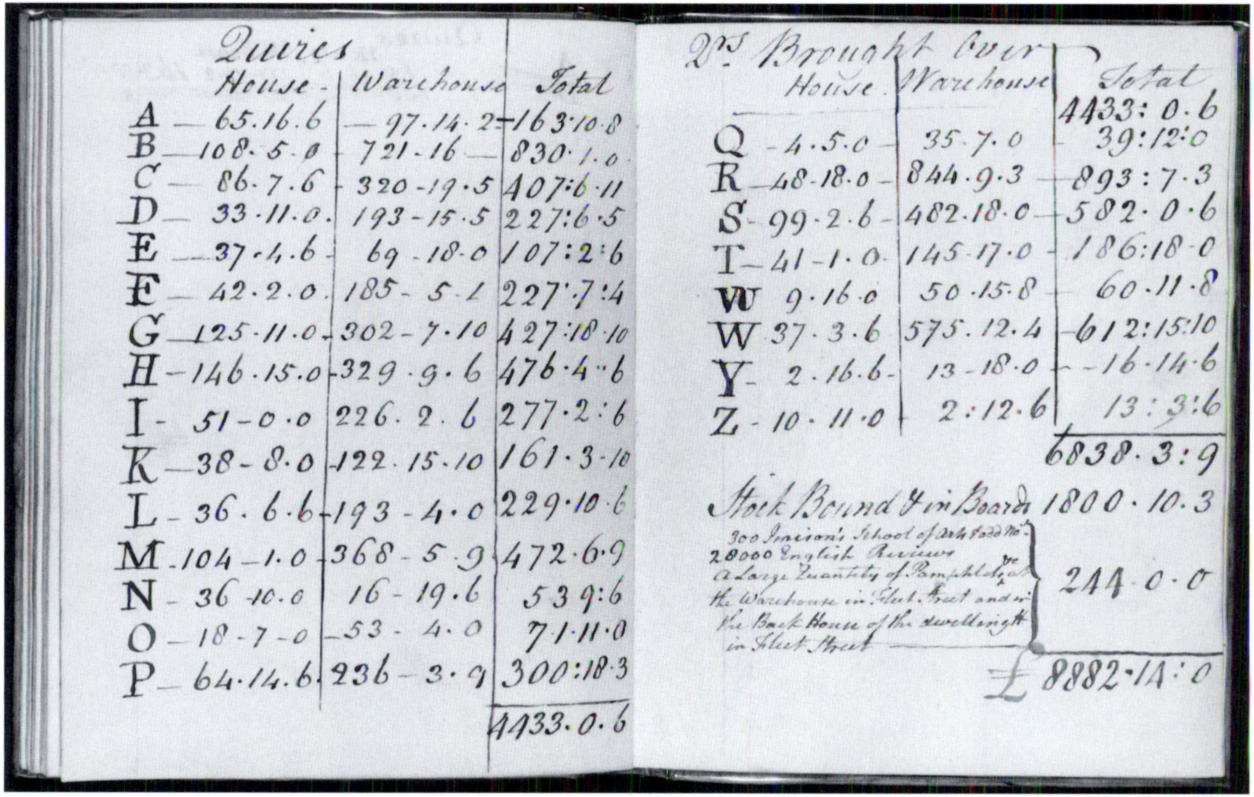

PLATE 47

Queries	House	Warehouse	Total
A	65.16.6	97.14.2	163.10.8
B	108.5.0	721.16	830.1.0
C	86.7.6	320.19.5	407.6.11
D	33.11.0	193.15.5	227.6.5
E	37.4.6	69.18.0	107.2.6
F	42.2.0	185.5.4	227.7.4
G	125.11.0	302.7.10	427.10.10
H	146.15.0	329.9.6	476.4.6
I	51.0.0	226.2.6	277.2.6
K	38.8.0	122.15.10	161.3.10
L	36.6.6	193.4.0	229.10.6
M	104.1.0	368.5.9	472.6.9
N	36.10.0	16.19.6	53.9.6
O	18.7.0	53.4.0	71.11.0
P	64.14.6	236.3.9	300.18.3
			4433.0.6

Dr. Brought over	House	Warehouse	Total
			4433.0.6
Q	4.5.0	35.7.0	39.12.0
R	48.18.0	844.9.3	893.7.3
S	99.2.6	482.18.0	582.0.6
T	41.1.0	145.17.0	186.18.0
V	9.16.0	50.15.8	60.11.8
W	37.3.6	575.12.4	612.15.10
Y	2.16.6	13.18.0	16.14.6
Z	10.11.0	2.12.6	13.3.6
			6838.3.9

Stock Bound & in Boards 1800.10.3

300 Ancient Sheet of 2445322.
28000 English Ancient
a Large Quantity of Pamphlets
the Warehouse in Lett. Part also
the Back House & the dwelling
in Fleet Street
} 244.0.0

£ 8882.14.0

'Catalogue of the Stock in Trade (with the Valuation) of Mr. J. Murray at the time of his Decease'. The letters of the alphabet refer to the listing of books in the catalogue by the authors' surnames

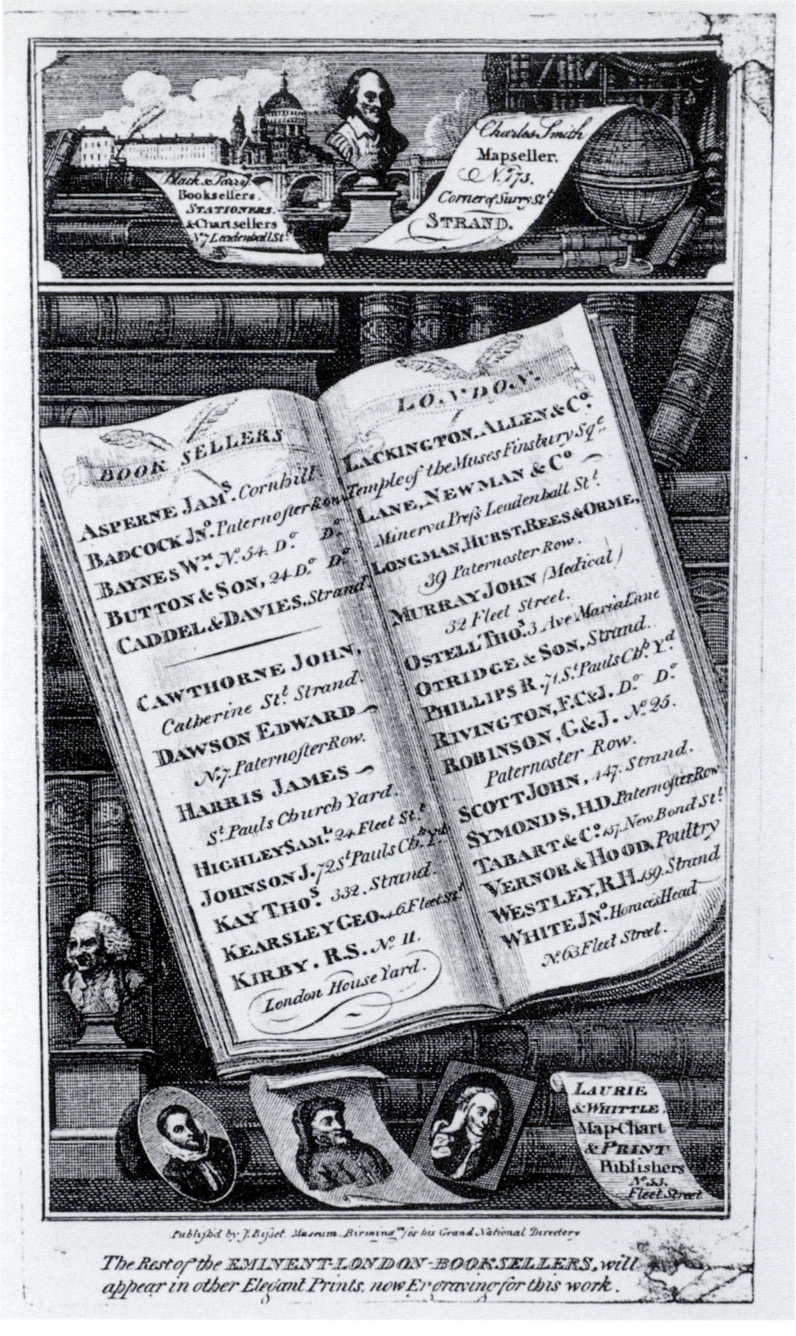

PLATE 48

London Booksellers' trade card about 1800, listing John Murray II as a medical publisher (By permission of the Bodleian Library, John Johnson Collection)

Murray knew that an original summary of the leading political events during the past year would be of primary interest. In fourteen chapters, each about eight pages long, Thomson recounted what had happened in 1780: the American war; the Protestant Association (established to protest the passage of pro-Catholic legislation); the Yorkshire Association (established to reform parliament); and affairs in India. Also included were more general articles, such as a 'contrast between Asia and America' and 'the prospect of Great Britain at the present moment'. The literary section of the *Mercury* included poetry (34 pages) and a 'Review of Books', including Gilbert Stuart's *History of the Reformation* and the current volume of Edward Gibbon's *Decline and Fall*. Just over one-third of the 540-page annual was original writing, the greater part being made up of extracts from new publications and from parliamentary papers. The sale of the first volume of the *Mercury* was sufficient for Murray to contemplate a continuation 'for the year 1781'. In July of that year he wrote to Gilbert Stuart for 'a short Chapter upon the present state of Literature in Scotland; or characters of the Judges of the Court of Session; or a Review of one or two Books; or any thing else that may be of use'.[38] Murray's aim was to increase the Scottish sale, having heard from William Creech that literary men in Scotland had disapproved of the work — information Charles Elliot confirmed when he told Murray in November 1781: 'The London Mercury has not answered here'.[39] Others, to Murray's surprise, had found Thomson's political views 'antiministerial', but Murray still believed he had published a good and impartial compendium, and rather defensively told Creech: 'It was not published for those that disapprove of it. By its own merit it must sink or swim, and there let it rest.'[40]

Pride might have motivated Murray to continue the publication, but common sense dictated otherwise. The first volume of the *Mercury* had not made a profit; nor was it certain that sales would improve. The work had to compete not only with Dodsley's *Annual Register* but with the *New Annual Register*, organised on a similar plan to the *Mercury* and published by the Robinsons (booksellers for whom Murray had considerable respect). George Robinson had enlisted talented men like William Godwin and Andrew Kippis to write for the whiggish *Register*.[41] So Murray let the *Mercury* 'sink', (as he put it), and, when he saw how successful the Robinsons' periodical had in fact become, he offered £50 for a quarter-share and tempted Robinson with the promise that 'the assistance I should give to the sale would, I think, make up in the end a considerable addition to the

---

[38] JM to Gilbert Stuart, 7 July 1781.

[39] JM to William Creech, 5 Oct. 1781; Charles Elliot to JM, 22 Nov. 1781. Elliot added: 'I think you have not put half enough in it'.

[40] JM to William Creech, 5 Oct. 1781.

[41] William St Clair, *The Godwins and the Shelleys* (London, 1989), p. 32. See a review of the *New Annual Register* in the *English Review*, 5 (Feb. 1785), 124–9.

profits of the publication'.[42] The offer, less than what Robinson was willing to accept, was declined, and Murray looked for other ways to enter the potentially lucrative periodical market.

The *English Review*

When Murray established the *English Review* in January 1783, he put to use his varied experience of periodical publications, and at long last he succeeded. The full title of this monthly journal was the *English Review, or an Abstract of English and Foreign Literature*. Although conceived to make money, it was also a creative enterprise, reflecting Murray's literary and political ideas more than any other single thing he published. After months of planning, the first issue (dated January 1783) appeared on the first of February. Like most literary monthlies, it was priced at one shilling. Murray appointed John Balfour and James Dickson to be the Scottish publishers of the work, while Richard Moncrieffe agreed to take Irish subscriptions and sell the periodical in his Dublin shop. He put the names and addresses of these booksellers on the cover and insisted that they advertise the periodical in the local newspapers.[43] Though uncertain of success, Murray was quietly determined. At the outset he remarked to James Gilliland: 'I mean to lose £200 before it is relinquished'.[44]

Murray edited and published the *English Review* for nearly eleven years. What with all his other publishing and bookselling activities, it was a major undertaking. Each month some eighty pages of copy had to be produced: books were chosen for review, writers assigned, deadlines met, printing, advertising and distribution organised. 'No article', he told a reviewer, 'should be very long, & they should be rendered as general as possible in order to furnish instruction & entertainment to a common capacity, in some degree at least as well as to men of learning & science'.[45] In the pages of the *English Review* Murray could publicise his own books at will and serve the interests of friends in the trade. But he had to be careful to preserve at

---

[42]JM to George Robinson, 25 July 1782.
[43]JM to James Gilliland, 11 Jan. 1783; to Richard Moncrieffe, 14 Jan. 1783 and 25 Jan. 1783. In Nov. 1786 Murray offered to make James Sibbald the sole Edinburgh publisher of the *English Review* (JM to Sibbald, 4 Nov. 1786), but in July 1787 Creech became the Scottish agent (JM to Wm Creech, 25 July 1787). No copies with original covers have been located but newspaper advertisements (in the Archive) give information about changes in agency. For example, the Jan. 1785 cover imprint reads: 'London: J. Murray; E. Balfour, W. Gordon, and J. Dickson, Edinburgh; L. White, Dublin. And to be had of all other Booksellers in Town & Country'.
[44]JM to James Gilliland, 11 Jan. 1783.
[45]JM to John Hellins, 31 Jan. 1785.

least an air of impartiality. 'Too great a panegyric', he told an author who had not expected criticism, 'is always suspicious'.[46]

For many decades two London literary reviews had dominated the market: the *Monthly Review*, run by Ralph Griffiths since 1749; and the *Critical Review*, established in 1756 by Archibald Hamilton and Tobias Smollett. Murray's aim was to produce a work which was not so readily associated with political ideology, as the earlier reviews were perceived to be (the *Monthly* being Whiggish, the *Critical* being Tory).[47] He planned a periodical that was more a reflection of the new literary trends — more modern — and that answered the needs of a new body of readers. It is 'a matter of surprize', he wrote in the Preface to the *English Review*, 'that two publications only of the critical kind should have been able to establish themselves in England. That another should start for the public approbation cannot justly be a subject of wonder.' Rather than criticise the established Reviews, Murray intended only to compete with them and attract readers to a journal which would 'ascertain the progressive improvement, as well as the reigning follies of mankind'.[48] He proposed to give an account of every book and pamphlet published in England, Scotland, Ireland, and America. Although the *Monthly* and *Critical* noticed American publications, the *English* looked to be the first to give comprehensive coverage. Murray also planned to include occasional accounts of new literature in Europe. His was to be an eclectic and cosmopolitan journal which avoided specialisation, partisanship and provincialism. Though essentially a literary review (rather than a miscellany like the long-running *Gentleman's Magazine*), Murray proposed to include other features: short biographical memoirs designed to highlight the 'connexion between eminent men and their writings'; an 'arts' (or theatre) section in which 'the performances of great masters . . . enlighten our history'; and a political article — essential in an era when, as he put it, 'there is a reciprocal action of government on literature, and of literature on Government'.[49] Murray believed that

[46]JM to Benjamin Bell, 6 July 1793. One Murray publication less than favourably reviewed was Helenus Scott's *Adventures of a Rupee*, which had 'nothing to recommend [it] either from incident, fancy, or character' (*English Review* 1, Feb. 1783, 159).

[47]The extent to which either the *Monthly* or *Critical* adhered to, or could be characterised by, these opposing political ideologies is debatable, and too much should not be made of such labels in this context. Dr Johnson characterised the reviews as follows: 'The Monthly Reviewers (said he) are not Diests; but they are Christians with as little christianity as may be; and are for pulling down all establishments. The Critical Reviewers are for supporting the constitution, both in church and state' (James Boswell, *Life of Johnson*, eds. Hill and Powell, iii, 33).

[48]The Preface was first distributed as a proposal for the *English Review* in handbill form, though no copy is extant. An excellent study of the state of the literary review in the late eighteenth century (frequently mentioning the *English Review*) is Derek Roper, *Reviewing before the* Edinburgh *1788–1802* (London, 1978).

[49]Preface. In the political article for April 1787 (*English Review* 9, 313–18) this premise was discussed on a more theoretical basis under the heading 'On the Reciprocal Influence of Literature, Liberty, Government, and Manners'.

in the pages of the *English Review* public opinion would make itself heard and would influence the course of affairs.

To ensure success Murray recruited able writers. Many, but by no means all, were Scots. Gilbert Stuart, who had returned to London, was a close advisor in the project's planning stages. Afterwards he regularly contributed reviews of historical works. Stuart's involvement was such that he was even falsely rumoured to be 'the despotic ruler of the English Review'.[50] Under Murray's close guidance, Stuart's journalistic talents were productively channelled and the acrimony, though not the vitality, of his opinions restrained. Although Murray and Stuart were themselves deeply interested in publications from Scotland and in Scottish affairs generally, it was still thought necessary to employ an able writer for these matters. Murray solicited John Logan — a minister at Leith who had written poetry and published a work on the philosophy of history — to 'furnish . . . an account of literary news, & of every thing relating to literature or the arts &c in Scotland'.[51] He also asked William Richardson for reviews of publications and news from Glasgow.[52] Murray then asked an old Edinburgh friend, Robert Liston, a diplomat living in Italy, to write reviews of foreign books, and 'a paper now & then of literary news, discoveries in arts, sciences & manufacture'.[53] He intended to pay Liston 'higher than . . . any other person', ensuring anonymity and promising that the choice of books would be left to him.[54] This 'Foreign Literature' section was among the most appealing and well written parts of the *Review.* Murray recruited many others with proven literary skills. Among clerics (besides those mentioned) he received assistance from John Whitaker, John Ogilvie, Joseph Stock, Jeremiah Trist, John Trusler, and William Thomson. He also enlisted quality medical and scientific writers — Thomas Beddoes, Alexander Hamilton, John Hellins, John Leslie and Thomas Dancer. Others who wrote for the *Review* were John Moore, James Anderson, James Currie, John Richardson, John Justamond, John Skinner, William Roberts, Thomas Holcroft and William Godwin.[55] Reviewers usually received two guineas per sheet (six-

[50]*Gentleman's Magazine*, 57 (April 1787), 296. In JM to Andrew Blane, 14 July 1785 Murray denied that 'Dr. Stuart conducts the E. Review'.

[51]JM to John Logan, *c.* 7 Dec. 1782. Murray also asked for an article on 'the present state of Church politics'. In another letter (7 Jan. 1783) he asked Logan to write 'a Life of the late Lord Kaims' containing 'not only serious matter concerning him but also his oddities'.

[52]JM to Wm Richardson, 30 Oct. 1783.

[53]JM to Robert Liston, 8 Nov. 1782.

[54]JM to Robert Liston, 8 Nov. 1782. In the early 1770s Liston had translated French works for Murray (Gilbert Stuart to JM, 5 March 1773, Bodleian Library, Hughenden Papers, G/1/912).

[55]JM to John Whitaker, 11 June 1784; to John Ogilvie, 21 July 1787; to Joseph Stock, 12 Nov. 1782; to Jeremiah Trist, 8 Oct. 1793; to John Trusler, 29 Mar. 1786; to Wm Thomson, 27 June 1785; to Thomas Beddoes, 25 Dec. 1783 ('The best articles . . . I frankly ascribe to you'); to Alexander Hamilton, 11 Jan. 1783; to John Hellins, 31 Jan. 1785; John Leslie to JM, 14 Feb. 1792; to Thomas Dancer, 1 June 1791; to James Anderson, 11 June 1787; to John

teen pages) for reviews of English books, more for foreign ones, and up to four guineas per sheet for original articles. Sometimes Murray would accept a review in lieu of money owed to him.[56] The average review contained long extracts. However, Murray insisted that these 'must not be disproportioned to the original strictures furnished, but rather be illustrative of these strictures'.[57]

Murray initially planned issues of eighty-eight pages, (or five and a half sheets), but after five months (May 1783) an eighty-page format was fixed.[58] The main section contained from ten to fifteen reviews of important new publications and ran to around sixty pages. The foreign literature section, which appeared most months, came next and was followed by the 'Monthly Catalogue', containing twenty to thirty short notices of the latest books and pamphlets. Murray divided this 'Catalogue' roughly by genre: fiction, poetry, politics, divinity, medicine and so forth — in all about ten pages. The theatrical and political articles appeared in the last quarter of each issue. Thomas Holcroft, the dramatist and novelist, wrote the theatre piece and received four guineas each month. His lively accounts of London plays and players attracted many readers. But in June 1783, when Holcroft left for Paris, the theatre article was discontinued. However, Murray encouraged him to send articles, offering him three guineas per sheet and reminding him that was 'as high as any review in London pays'.[59]

The article on 'National Affairs', which ran from four to ten pages, was another popular feature of the *English Review*. In the January article the leading events of the last year were usually reviewed and speculations

Skinner, 28 June 1788; to Wm Roberts, 25 May 1789; to Thomas Holcroft, 10 June 1783; to Wm Godwin, 30 Nov. 1786. For others see Derek Roper, *Reviewing before the* Edinburgh, p. 22. Among these writers some had already published, and others would later publish, their own works with Murray.

[56] JM to John Skinner, 13 Jan. 1792.

[57] JM to James Anderson, 26 May 1787.

[58] The first five issues (Jan. to May 1783) were five and a half sheets (eighty-eight pages), except for Feb. which was six sheets (ninety-six pages). From June onwards the eighty-page (five sheet) format was strictly followed. Every six months readers bound up their copies when Murray supplied a volume title page, table of contents and index. Murray first engaged James Fleming to print the *English Review*, then switched to John Walter for a short time in 1787, after which he turned the presswork over to an unidentified printer. Walter may have printed the work 'logographically' as he did the *Daily Universal Register* and other works at this time.

[59] JM to Thomas Holcroft, 10 June 1783. Holcroft's first theatre article was called 'A State of the London Stage, during the last Season. With an Account of the new Tragedies, Comedies, Operas, and Farces . . . at the Theatres Royal of Drury Lane and Covent Garden from September 1781 to May 1782'. The other topics on which he wrote were: 'A View of the Performers, Tragic and Comic, of the London Theatres, and of their respective Powers and Abilities' (Feb.); 'Some sketches of the theatrical talents of Mrs. Siddons' (Mar.); 'The principal comic [actors] of Drury-lane' (Apr.); and 'The principal comic actresses belonging to Drury Lane' (May).

offered about the future. Those living outside of London found this section especially informative as political news was more difficult to come by in the country.[60] Murray demanded that all articles, but this one especially, 'should be done with the utmost impartiality'.[61] The public, he believed, were already inundated by divisive political writing. Clearly stated facts and judicious analysis were needed to reduce factionalism. Murray believed that, to be read and regarded, he must adhere to a strict editorial position and 'avoid violence & party spirit in my publication'.[62] This policy, however, did 'not preclude disinterested praise or censure where they are merited'.[63] Indeed, the political article was no mere chronology, but a cogent and sometimes audacious analysis of affairs. In response to a reader's letter in the April 1783 issue challenging the *English Review's* impartiality, Murray reiterated the principles on which he published the political article: the *Review* 'aims at exhibiting a picture of the Political Speculations of the Month, and tracing some connections between the events that happen in that limited period, and others that have preceded, or are likely to follow them'.[64] The founding of the *English Review* coincided with the formation of the coalition government of Charles Fox and Lord North. Fox, the radical, and North, the pillar of authoritarian government, were censured as a self-interested combination. Their fall less than a year later in December 1783 and the subsequent rise of William Pitt to power was portrayed as a moment of great political significance, for it marked the rise of 'a party . . . different from King, Lords, and the House of Commons' — the people — who were now the arbitors in disputes between the different branches of government'.[65] Alongside this, the assertion of a collective political authority, the political article 'hailed the virtues of a free press'.[66]

A number of different men wrote the political article for Murray, including William Godwin and William Thomson. Godwin's articles had attracted considerable attention, but by the end of 1786 Murray could no longer tolerate his radical views. In a letter of dismissal he told Godwin:

From the trial I have experienced I am apprehensive that our Ideas will

[60]JM to John Yeo (at Torrington), 17 Dec. 1785.
[61]JM to John Logan, *c.* 7 Dec. 1782. Some of the more important issues in the political article are considered in Chapter 12.
[62]JM to John Logan, *c.* 4 Dec. 1782.
[63]JM to James Anderson, 26 May 1787.
[64]*English Review,* 1, Apr. 1783, 360.
[65]*English Review* 2 (Dec. 1783), 476. The political significance of the 'National Article' is discussed further in J. A. W. Gunn, *Beyond Liberty and Property. The Process of Self-Recognition in Eighteenth-Century Political Thought* (Kingston and Montreal, 1983), pp. 86–8 and 284–8. Gunn describes the *English Review* as the 'most sophisticated of the periodicals in terms of its sensitivity to changing political vocabulary' (p. 254).
[66]Gunn, *Beyond Liberty and Property,* p. 286.

never meet respecting the political Article. As sole proprietor of the English
Review and as responsible for what it contains, I cannot admit matter foreign
to my sentiments. Your principles on the contrary are as unbinding, and no
doubt you will think it impertinent in an illiterate fellow of a bookseller to
attempt in any shape to control or to dictate in these matters.[67]

Murray nevertheless recognised Godwin's talent, and in his very next letter
extolled the merit of the article.[68] Indeed, at this time the political article
began to be pirated in newspapers and magazines across Britain.[69] Despite
such popularity, he fired Godwin, one of the most profound thinkers of the
era, and hired William Thomson. Murray made it his business (as he told
Thomson) 'firmly to maintain a controul over my own property'.[70] Before
long, however, he had to dismiss Thomson for having 'prostituted the
National Article'. Enraged over Thomson's disregard for his authority,
Murray reminded his employee who was in charge:

> The Article in question was *mine*; and that, for the best of all reasons,
> because I paid for it. . . . The *idea* of it was new, and that is mine. I
> employed you to carry it into execution; if you had declined it, there was
> a possibility of getting some other person. If it is alledged that you did it
> better than another would have done the greater praise is due to me for my
> choice of a proper instrument.[71]

Murray read and corrected every word of the *English Review.* Many
articles he received 'frequently required the pruning knife'.[72] Writing to
John Whitaker, for example, he justified cutting out a large part of a review
of Gibbon's *Decline and Fall*: 'The abuse in it upon Mr G. is not liberal &
extremely long. Every reader of sentiment will be disgusted, & turn from
the perusal. It will be seen that you are angry, and your harshness will recoil
upon the Reviewer.' Other discarded parts of Whitaker's review were 'so
extremely violent' that Murray feared prosecution.[73] On matters of religion
Murray was equally adamant. When William Godwin contemplated an
explicit assertion of his Socinian beliefs (that is, denying the divinity of
Christ), he knew that he would be 'restrained . . . by the character of the

[67]JM to Wm Godwin, 30 Nov. 1786.
[68]JM to Geo. Eden, 30 Nov. 1786.
[69]Murray warned: 'In order to put a stop to such piracy and unfair conduct . . . every
number of the English Review is regularly entered in Stationer's-Hall, according to Act of
Parliament' (*English Review* 8, Oct. 1786, 315). When an Aberdeen magazine editor reprinted
the article, Murray made a deal to get free advertising for the *English Review,* and insisted that
the source be acknowledged (JM to James Dunbar, 23 Apr. 1787).
[70]JM to Wm Thomson, 27 June 1785.
[71]JM to Wm Thomson, 28 Aug. 1786.
[72]Ibid.
[73]JM to John Whitaker, 8 July 1789. However, Murray thought enough of the lengthy article
to publish it separately (Checklist item 855). Roper (*Reviewing before the* Edinburgh, pp. 227–37)
discusses Whitaker in his analysis of the contemporary reviews of Gibbon's work.

review', and by its editor, who supported the established church.[74] At least for the time Godwin was compelled to accept Murray's view that 'the immediate business of the reviewer is not . . . to make himself a party, but to represent candidly the arguments of both sides'.[75]

To fill the allotted space and achieve a balance of subject matter Murray chose each month from a pool of reviews he had commissioned. But some months it was difficult to find enough publications to review. To Thomas Beddoes he wrote in November 1783: 'Any articles you could furnish for the E[nglish] Review I should be doubly grateful for, as the dearth of books at this Instant is so great that I really know not where to provide for that publication'.[76] More often, however, Murray could not review every new book. Indeed, some of his own publications were not even noticed. Murray depended on his writers to produce copy on time, especially for the regular features. He demanded the political article on the twenty-fifth of each month — time enough to include the latest news but also early enough to publish on the first of the following month. 'My mind is kept in a constant state of anxiety', he explained to Thomson, who had been on a drinking binge when he should have been writing for Murray.[77] When Thomson failed to meet this deadline, John Logan was solicited 'with strong cries and tears'.[78] And when Thomson sobered up, Murray sternly reminded him: 'I have more at stake than you have, & you should consider that one hour's delay shipwrecks the Review'.[79]

Murray struggled to produce a periodical that would command respect and sell well. At the outset, however, few expected the *English Review* to compete successfully against the *Monthly* or the *Critical*. In April 1783 Boswell recorded Dr Johnson's opinion of the work: 'He [Johnson] had before him [the] *English Review*, which he called "an irregular review" (in opposition to the regular established ones). Doubted if it could be established. The others, he said, were done well.'[80] But Murray did succeed,

---

[74]Wm Godwin to Joseph Priestley, before 9 Feb. 1785 (the date of Priestley's reply), quoted in Wm St Clair, *The Godwins and the Shelleys*, (London, 1989), p. 35. Godwin had written reviews of three responses to Priestley's *History of the Corruptions of Christianity* (*English Review*, 5, Feb. 1785, 105–24).

[75]Ibid.

[76]JM to Thomas Beddoes, 25 Nov. 1783.

[77]JM to Wm Thomson, 27 June 1785.

[78]John Logan to Alex. Carlyle, 12 Apr. 1786, Edinburgh University Library, MS La. II, 419/8. As well as Logan, Murray later asked John Whitaker to write the political article (JM to Whitaker, 2 Feb. 1789).

[79]JM to Wm Thomson, 27 June 1785.

[80]The conversation continued: '[Boswell] mentioned writers in them being well paid; Shebbeare's getting six guineas a sheet. "He might," said he, "get six guineas for a particular sheet. But not *communibus sheetibus*." I asked, "What is meant by a sheet?" He (hastily). "Why, don't you know what a sheet is?" and was going to show me. "I mean," said I, "is it a sheet all of the writer's own composition? Are extracts deducted?" "No, Sir," said he. "It is a sheet,

though modestly at first. Subscriptions arrived, and after some months revenues from sales met, and soon exceeded, costs of production. To make money Murray had to sell about 750 copies.[81] 'The English Review', Murray reported to John Whitaker in July 1784, 'has already acquired reputation, and I hope will bear a comparison with any other printed in London'.[82] In 1786 the anonymous author of a poem called the *Patriad* placed the *English Review* beside the so-called 'regular established ones':

> The *Monthly* — whisper: on my life
> Is wrote by Griffiths, and his wife.
> The *Critical*, it is well known,
> Is scribbled all by Hamilton.
> As for the *English*, all its stock
> Of knowledge issues from the Loch.[83]

The suggestion that Scots were the main contributors to the *English Review* was something of a moot point. In January 1784, more than two years earlier, Murray had the novel idea of naming some of the regular contributors to the *Review* on its covers and in advertisements in the London newspapers. He listed Dr William Thomson, J. O. Justamond and 'other Gentlemen who have applied to the Cultivation of Literature and the Sciences'.[84] Even though the writers of individual articles were not revealed, naming regular contributors reflected Murray's idea of an impartial and public-minded enterprise — at least to a point, as he told Thomas Beddoes: 'The ostensible authors have no more responsibility than they had from the beginning. . . . The sole direction & property rests as before with me.'[85]

To further the perception of a journal 'for the people' Murray solicited articles and letters from the public at large. Typically correspondents complained that certain books had been neglected or others unfairly reviewed. Sometimes, however, he received articles on literary matters or unsolicited reviews, which, if deemed worthy, were included under the heading 'For the English Review'.[86] Murray occasionally addressed his

---

no matter of what." I objected. . . . He said, "A man would easier write a sheet of his own than read an octavo volume to get extracts." (Here I fancy he was not quite right).' *Boswell: Applause of the Jury 1782–1785*, eds. I. S. Lustig and F. A. Pottle (London, 1981), pp. 119–20 (28 Apr. 1783).

[81] There are no records for the circulation of the *English Review*. But estimating that Murray printed either 1000 or 1500 copies of each issue (a figure based on known printing runs of the *Edinburgh Magazine and Review*), and taking into account a stock inventory after his death that about 200 of each number were unsold, it would appear that 800–1200 were sold each month.

[82] JM to John Whitaker, 11 June 1784.

[83] [John Berkenhout], *The Patriad, an Heroic Poem* (London, 1786), pp. 30–31.

[84] *Morning Chronicle*, 27 Jan. 1784.

[85] JM to Thomas Beddoes, 22 Jan. 1784.

[86] Murray insisted that those who submitted articles or letters should reveal their names, but these were not made public. One of the more bizarre letters asserted that Goethe's *Sorrows of Werter* was written by James MacPherson, of Ossian fame (*English Review* 10, Aug. 1787, 160) — an opinion refuted the following month (p. 240).

readers to thank them for 'their very liberal Encouragement' of the *Review* or to dismiss 'every hostile attempt . . . both open and concealed . . . to injure it in their estimation'.[87] One writer (Innes Munro), who had been severely reviewed, wrote a public letter to expose the editor's motives:

> Mr. Murray's last resource for the gratification of his unjust and unmanly revenge, has been to traduce myself, as well as my work, in his periodical publications. . . . In place of hurting, he has essentially served my work, as I have observed that those books which the English Review most virulently condemns, are not, unfrequently, the best received by a candid and discerning publick.[88]

But this same discerning public had, on the whole, approved of Murray's periodical and were not put off by the assertions of one antagonist. In an era when publications were proliferating for a rapidly expanding reading public, the *English Review* met a demand for well-written and carefully edited criticism. There were readers enough not only for Murray's *Review* and the 'regular' reviews but for others like Joseph Johnson's *Analytical Review*, established in May 1788. If, as the years went by, Murray grew more sceptical about the beneficial role literature could have on society, he always understood the need for sound critical opinions. Speaking on behalf of the writers of the *English Review*, Murray remarked in June 1788:

> It is from an honest, and they hope an unbiased, regard to Truth, as well as a sense of Duty, that they are constrained occasionally to expose Ignorance and Dullness, Puerility, Absurdity, and Nonsense, which seem to increase upon us daily. But they have at all times endeavoured to guard against Illiberality and Rudeness in their strictures; and have generally preferred the exercise of Lenity to Severity, when the smallest Dawnings of Genius, Learning, or Judgment, offered themselves to their consideration.[89]

The services the *English Review* rendered Murray as a publisher were beyond measure, and the regard it gave him among authors and among fellow tradesmen was enviable. Nowhere else did he have such an unencumbered opportunity to sell his wares or express his views. As an editor, indeed as a writer of parts of the work, he gave the public a monthly picture of literature and politics — his picture.

Other Periodical Ventures

After the successful establishment of the *English Review*, Murray interested himself financially in several other periodicals. One of these was the

---

[87] *English Review* 11 (June 1788), 480.
[88] Reprinted in Murray's *Defence of Innes Munro*, p. 23.
[89] *English Review* 12 (June 1788), 480.

monthly *Political Magazine and Parliamentary, Naval, Military, and Literary Journal*. This work was established in 1780 by Robert Butters, a printer at 79 Fleet Street. Butters published the work until 1785 when Murray took over the publication. Murray printed two thousand copies of the *Political Magazine* and paid an editor six guineas a month to compile the different sections noted in the full title.[90] Over a four-and-a-half-year period he produced eight volumes. But as the periodical made little profit, Murray grew anxious to rid himself of a time-consuming project. 'Such an Adventure', he told John Trusler as early as 1786, 'would suit your press & bring you more profit than it does me as you would save the Editorship & also a good deal of the Printing'.[91] Trusler did not take up the offer. Finally, in 1789 Butters reassumed the proprietorship, and two years later the magazine folded.

Murray was one of a handful of proprietors of the annual *London Calendar, or Court and City Register for England, Scotland, Ireland and America*, first published in 1782. He bought a share in 1783 which he held for several years. The proprietors, including John Stockdale and Alexander Donaldson, met annually at the Chapter Coffee House to divide charges and delegate responsibilities.[92] Another periodical work in which Murray had a share was the *Looker-On*, a publication written in the essayist tradition of Addison's *Spectator* and Johnson's *Rambler* by William Roberts, whose *nom de plume* was the Reverend Simon Olive-Branch. The work came out in eighty-six numbers in the year 1792. Murray hoped that it would succeed as had the *Spectator* and the *Rambler*, or (more recently) as Henry Mackenzie's *Mirror* (1779–80) and *Lounger* (1785–7) had done, but this did not happen.[93] New publications were always a gamble, and the safer bet was to buy shares of established favourites at trade sales. Murray had in fact bought into the *Spectator* as early as 1775 and the *Rambler* in 1781, each work coming out in a number of profitable editions in the course of his career.[94]

[90]JM to John Trusler, 6 Oct. 1786.

[91]Ibid.

[92]On 20 Oct. 1783 (the date of the annual meeting for the proprietors of the *London Calendar*) Murray wrote to John Wallis: 'Your not attending the meeting upon the business of the London Kalendar . . . makes the Proprietors conclude that you have relinquished the concern. I have therefore to acquaint you by their direction that you are not considered any longer as a partner'. Wallis's name did not appear in the 1784 imprint.

[93]Multi-volume editions of the *Looker-On* did come out after Murray's death: in 1794 (printed for J. Evans) and in 1797 (for the Robinsons) and continued to be published until 1856.

[94]Murray had bought a fortieth share of the *Spectator* at George Pearch's Sale on 21 Dec. 1775 — both the octavo and duodecimo editions. He paid Joseph Johnson initially £46 and more afterwards for production costs. He bought another fortieth share in 1777 (BB, p. 28). Murray bought a thirty-second share (126 copies) in the four–vol. edn. of the *Rambler*, on 14 Aug. 1781 at John Hinton's sale (BB, p. 28). Editions of the work were published in 1784, 1789 and 1793 (see Checklist, items 425, 726 and 948).

Murray was one of twelve original owners of the *Star and Evening Advertiser*, which began publication on 3 May 1788 and was the first every-evening journal in Britain. Published at three o'clock each afternoon, it was distributed in London and sent swiftly by the post coach to provincial cities. Peter Stuart, who held a share, printed and edited the newspaper from his shop at 31 Exeter Street in the Strand. The expense of producing a daily paper was considerable, especially the purchase of stamped paper and the employment of over a dozen men in the print house. Murray initially laid out £40, but, concerned about the additional money he knew would be regularly demanded, he quickly sold half of his share to the bookseller Luke White at Dublin. Three weeks into production he informed White: 'The Star still goes on, & most of the Proprietors are very sanguine in their hopes of it'.[95] The chief advantage Murray and the other bookselling proprietors sought from the newspaper was a reliable medium for placing advertisements for their latest publications. In the first number they offered advertising space to merchants and tradesmen, promising speedy service and even offering to have 'advertisements drawn up *gratis*, by a gentleman properly qualified'.[96]

During the first months the circulation of the *Star* gradually increased, but it continued to operate in the red. This, Murray remarked to White, 'proceeds from want of ready money advertisements; and part perhaps from bad management'.[97] At a proprietors' meeting in June 1788, Murray stated his dissatisfaction with Peter Stuart, the printer, but was suprised to find himself challenged for having appropriated over £50 out of the newspaper's advertising revenues. Insulted at this affront, he stormed off, refusing to return until the 'wretched & unmannerly insult' was withdrawn.[98] An even more serious allegation was voiced that Murray had been attempting to impose his political views in the paper by compelling Stuart to support the Prime Minister, William Pitt, and to attack the rival party of the Prince of Wales, with whom Stuart and his friends were apparently aligned.[99] Murray had hoped that the paper's rising circulation might prompt a purchase by the Treasury, so he persuaded the proprietors at a meeting in December 1788 to adopt a pro-Government position. Stuart, however, refused and instead published articles supporting the Prince and abusing Pitt. On 12 February 1789 the proprietors dismissed Stuart. Murray quickly organised compositors and printers, found an able

[95] JM to Luke White, 27 May 1788.
[96] *Star*, 3 May 1788. For a more general account of the paper, see Lucyle Werkmeister, *The London Daily Press 1772–1792* (University of Nebraska Press, 1963), pp. 219–62. JM to Luke White, 23 Dec. 1788.
[97] JM to Luke White, 23 Dec. 1788
[98] JM to the *Star* Proprietors, 25 June 1788.
[99] *Stuart's Star*, 13 Feb. 1789, the newspaper where Peter Stuart's side of the controversy was afterwards explained. *Star*, 14 Feb. 1789.

editor and succeeded in publishing as usual.[100] Stuart, wasting no time, produced a new paper also called the *Star*, the following day.

In the first 'spurious' *Star*, Stuart explained his 'Reasons for abandoning the Exeter-street Star' and initiated an attack on Murray, whose 'Epicurean Intrigue' had not only 'duped' him but also others — in particular, Murray's authors.[101] The following day (14 February) Murray and the other proprietors gave their side of the argument and took 'leave of the friendship and services of Mr. Peter Stuart for ever'. Attacks continued on both sides. Stuart, for example, referred to Murray and William Lane (another proprietor) as 'two paltry Booksellers, who never yet gained a friend whom they did not deceive'. They were made the object of a parody of the reports on the mental health of the King, whose 'madness' was the leading daily news item.[102] 'Mr. MURRAY *had a very restless night — has been much disturbed — and is irritable . . . this morning.*' And even more scurrilous: 'Dr. Lane yesterday *walked* JOHN MURRAY round St. Dunstan's. The MANIAC knocked down a *dustman*, bit the finger of a *sweep*, and overturned some mad oxen in Fleet-market. Dr. Lane was obliged to put on the *strait-jacket*.'[103]

Under the direction of Murray and Lane the original *Star* continued to appear. Circulation, however, had slipped to between 600 and 650 and the proprietors still were paying out money every week to keep the paper afloat. In April 1789 Murray had the satisfaction of seeing Stuart's *Star* fold (although it reappeared afterwards as the *Morning Star*). Despite this apparent victory, the financial problems of the original *Star* were not yet over. In October 1789 eight of the original proprietors withdrew, considerably raising the burden of payment. Murray immediately dunned Luke White for £90 and explained that although 'well furnished with advertisements' the paper was still losing between £3 and £5 a week. Murray was

---

[100]Murray engaged the Scots poet John Mayne, who had earlier served as a selling agent for subscriptions for Lavater's *Essays*, to print and edit the *Star* (JM to John Mayne, 11 June 1792).

[101]*Star*, 14 Feb. 1789.

[102]The public had been reading daily reports of George III's illness. His temporary recovery in March 1789, Murray wrote, 'happily prevents a scene of anarchys, confusions & disorder that much in all probability have attended the administration of the Prince of Wales as Regent' (JM to Wm Blane, 4 Mar. 1789). In Jan. 1789 he had published the *Report from the Committee Appointed to Examine the Physicians who have Attended His Majesty, during his Illness* (Checklist item 738).

[103]*Stuart's Star*, 18 Feb. 1789, quoted in Werkmeister, p. 245. The 'paltry Booksellers' quotation is from 27 Feb. 1789. In another attack a few months later reference was made to Murray's former naval career when he was called a 'swabber in a man of war' (*Stuart's Star*, 30 April 1789). When some of these attacks were reprinted in the Edinburgh newspaper the *Caledonian Mercury*, Murray wrote to the printer, John Robertson, that 'from regard to an old School fellow who has occasionally endeavoured to serve you, I thought you would not have admitted [them] into your print without at least first conselling him' (JM to John Robertson, 2 July 1789).

optimistic that the redistribution of shares 'will prove more beneficial'. Given an earlier opportunity, he confided to White, he would have gotten out, but having invested so much, Murray advised that they should hold on.[104] A few weeks later, however, Murray changed his mind and asked for what little he could recover for himself and White. Disappointed, but by no means apologetic, he told White: 'Any loss . . . you will not impute to my management for I am a fellow sufferer'.[105] The *Star* survived these difficulties and continued to be profitably managed by John Mayne for many years.[106]

[104]JM to Luke White, 5 Oct. 1789.
[105]JM to Luke White, 31 Oct. 1789.
[106]The *Star* was published until 1831 when it was absorbed by *The Albion*. See Stanley Morison, *The English Newspaper* (Cambridge, 1932), p. 193; also an obituary of John Mayne in the *Gentleman's Magazine*, May 1836, pp. 556–7.

12

The Politics of a Bookseller

The American Revolution

Murray was keenly interested in politics, both national and international. His service in the Royal Navy had made him feel a part of the British imperial tradition.[1] There he had formed enduring friendships (as he had before in Scotland) with men who were living and travelling throughout the world. He corresponded regularly with these men, transmitting and receiving the latest news about events in Europe, America and India. Living in London from 1768, he was at the centre of political activity. Among his customers and associates were Peers of the Realm, Members of Parliament and political journalists. Moreover, as the owner of newspapers and periodicals, he was in the business of selling political information at a time when the press was emerging as the 'fourth estate'. Although he would tell an associate that 'I am a bad politician & I always enter upon the subject of national affairs with aversion and constraint', he would in fact often write letters, public or private, and debate political issues when he had an opinion to express.[2]

Preoccupied with running a business, Murray was not inclined towards philosophical contemplation. Nevertheless, such abstract political concepts as liberty and property had real meaning for him. They were the foundation of British society — a society which, for all its corruption and injustice, was in his view better and freer than any other. Upon his return from Ireland in August 1775, a detention at the Customs House in Holyhead prompted him to reflect on his status as a Briton:

[1] Murray always took pride in the uniform he had worn. One time, when he saw a company of guards, he remarked: 'This is a truly martial sight and must give pleasure to every spectator. The men made a fine appearance. They were clean, young, rigorous & alert; and seemed to be perfect in their manoeuvres & manual exercise. Troops thus disciplined & thus commanded, cannot fail giving a good account of their enemies should ever they have the misfortune to be led against them' (Diary, 8 May 1775).
[2] JM to Capt. Wm Fraser, 28 Sept. 1779.

It is unreasonable to think that the interruption we met with was legal; or that the officers at this port could justify their conduct in detaining the King's subjects from their honest pursuits & business. This however is more or less practised at every port in the Kingdom. And little men cannot redress themselves. . . . The expences & delay of obtaining justice would be more grievous than the hardships complained of. Thus it is in this free country that in some instances we suffer oppression & restraints upon our natural liberty, that the subjects of arbitrary government know nothing of.[3]

Murray opened his shop at a dynamic political moment. In 1769 a series of public letters by the pseudonymous 'Junius' were rekindling the radical flame ignited by John Wilkes in 1763 when he attacked the King and Lord Bute in the *North Briton*. Charges of seditious libel against the printer of the newspaper in which Junius' letters had appeared and the return of Wilkes from exile in France further heightened the tension. Murray favoured political reform but abhorred the uncontrolled violence of the Wilkite mobs, some of which was directed at Scotsmen living in London. When his old navy friend William Falconer criticised Wilkes in June 1768, Murray took a more liberal stance.[4] He could see that an important consequence of Wilkes' challenges was a freer press.[5] Murray was no radical, but publishing the *Repository* in 1770 carried the risk of prosecution, even if it was mainly a compilation. Also, a political pamphlet he published the same year, including a letter by 'Junius', was so contentious that he told a friend he 'dare not advertise' it in the London papers.[6]

Alongside Wilkes and 'Junius', the political conflict of greatest consequence in the late 1760s and 1770s concerned the American Colonies. Murray's boyhood friend Stephen Adye, who was stationed in Philadelphia as an officer in the Royal Artillery, regularly sent him accounts.[7] As the situation became more serious, Murray was compelled to form an opinion. Although he did not condone oppression or the arbitrary power of government, he did agree that strong measures should be taken to punish the 'fomenters of sedition'. In March 1775, writing to General Robert Gordon in India, he remarked further that 'all good Citizens think that the honour and prosperity of the British Empire depend in some measure upon a reasonable submission of its Colonies to good order and government. And

[3]Diary, 27 Aug. 1775.
[4]JM to Wm Falconer, 23 June 1768. Murray, however, 'forgave the warmth [Falconer] discovered against that man [Wilkes] on account of . . . loyalty to his king & affection to his country'.
[5]On the subject see J. Brewer *et al.*, *The Birth of a Consumer Society. The Commercialization of Eighteenth-Century England* (Bloomington, 1982), pp. 253–60.
[6]JM to Wm Kerr, 13 Feb. 1770. The pamphlet was Charles Fearne's *Impartial Answer to the Doctrine Delivered in a Letter under the Signature Junius*. Murray had printed 500 copies but sold fewer than 130 (DB1, p. 38; Checklist item 25).
[7]Murray sometimes placed Adye's accounts in the London newspapers (JM to Stephen Payne Adye, 10 Oct. 1769).

this at present has every appearance of being soon consumated.'[8] Before the Americans declared their independence in 1776, many Britons had strongly supported their cause. They saw the issue in the more general context of a debate about political liberty and good government, and, like Murray, agreed that the power of the Crown had grown too great. 'The K[ing]', he remarked in September 1779, 'is his own minister.'[9] Nevertheless, he supported the firm measures adopted by Lord North's government. While travelling in Ireland in 1775 Murray often discussed American affairs and usually found himself defending Great Britain against more radical points of view. Of a meeting with a twenty-year-old 'genius from Philadelphia' named 'Duffel', who had come to Edinburgh to study medicine and was travelling in Ireland, he remarked:

> His patriotism was glowing. The Americans were arrived by this modest account at perfection in arts manufactures & commerce; and would perish every man of them before they would submit to the coutroul of the mother country. . . . Being asked when he meant to return home, he replied that he had not intended it for 4 or 5 years . . . ; but the war being now begun & his country in danger it became necessary for him to go back as his assistance would be wanted.[10]

By the summer of 1776 political arguments gave way to open hostilities. In September, Murray told a friend in Belfast: 'Our politicians on this side wait for tidings of the fate of N[ew] York with anxious eyes & lengthened visages'.[11] As late as December, he remained confident that the measures taken by the Government would quell the Americans, provided neither France nor Spain came to their aid. Interested though these countries might be, Murray believed 'the terrors of our Navy (from which they are by no means recovered) will probably keep them quiet'.[12]

Murray's trade with America, though never substantial, stopped altogether in 1776. As ships on which he transported goods either to Scotland or farther afield to Europe and India ran the risk of capture by pirates, he had to pay high insurance premiums.[13] Sailing heavily armed and in convoy did not altogether eliminate the danger. These worries, compounded by an

---

[8]JM to General Robert Gordon, 10 Mar. 1775.

[9]JM to Capt. Wm Fraser, 28 Sept. 1779.

[10]Diary, 21 May 1775. The 'Duffel' Murray (who suffered from poor hearing) met was in fact Benjamin Duffield (1759–99), whose father, Edward, a clockmaker from Philadelphia, was a close friend of Benjamin Franklin. See a letter from Franklin to Lord Kames, 14 Mar. 1775, introducing the younger Duffield (*The Papers of Benjamin Franklin*, xxi, 268–9 and 523–4).

[11]JM to Robert Apsley, 19 Aug. 1776.

[12]JM to John Burges, 19 Dec. 1776. Murray added, 'The Americans too are such dastardly rascals that any ally would be ashamed'.

[13]Charles Elliot to JM, 1 May 1781; JM to Mrs Wm Drummond, 3 June 1783; and to John Richardson, 31 Aug. 1780. Murray told General Robert Gordon on 25 July 1777: 'French privateers under provincial colours annoy our trade materially'.

escalating war, increased his antipathy towards the Americans and their allies. When an attempt was made to burn Portsmouth Dock and the warehouses at Bristol early in 1777 Murray asserted: 'These villains must be Americans, for I hardly think the french or Spaniards would countenance such a diabolical design'.[14] As hostilities with America continued, and other countries became involved, there were few occasions for celebration. In October 1779 Murray lamented that 'a Revolution has taken place much to the prejudice of our business. . . . This, added to the defection of America, & a french and Spanish war, has not made matters better.'[15] And in July 1777 he reported to General Gordon in India: 'The *Howes* are much blamed at home for protracting the war & being slow in their operations. This campaign will certainly give a new face to our expectations.'[16] The failure to achieve a quick and decisive victory made tradesmen like Murray despondent. 'Wiser heads than mine', he reflected, 'must determine how long it will last.'[17] By the autumn of 1778 Murray could only contemplate some vague radical solution to the country's troubles: 'The British empire . . . declines, & without some internal Revolution happens in its favour, which I cannot now fore see, our Glory, at present in its declination, is likely to set altogether'.[18]

By the spring of 1779 the financing of a war had slowed Britain's internal economy considerably. Murray would take few risks. For instance, even though he held a high opinion of William Lothian's new history of the Netherlands, he declined publishing it: 'A Spanish war, with the American trade totally shut, have struck me with such timidity, that I find myself incapable of offering for your book any thing like what you might expect'.[19] Two years before, he had offered Gilbert Stuart £150 for a work, and now £60 was all he felt able to venture for one more likely to succeed. Apologetically, he explained to Stuart:

> The ardor of the booksellers here for purchasing copies is surprisingly abated from what it was. Dodsley, a few days since refused a respectable historical work well recommended without ever seeing it, with the answer 'that the times were adverse to Literary business'. And they are really so; the bookselling trade falling off daily & greatly. . . . The French have taken

[14]JM to John Richardson, 18 Jan. 1777.
[15]JM to Wm Richardson, 15 Oct. 1779.
[16]JM to Gen. Robert Gordon, 25 July 1777. Sir Wm Howe had been the British Commander-in-Chief in the Colonies since Oct. 1776, a post in which he served until May 1778. Blame for his actions and those of his brother, Admiral Lord Howe, was such that a House of Commons committee made an official inquiry in early 1779 but found no grounds.
[17]JM to Charles Gordon (in Canton, China), 25 Dec. 1775.
[18]JM to Capt. Wm Fraser, 28 Sept. 1779.
[19]JM to Wm Lothian, 29 June 1779.

Grenada by Storm, Déstain has beaten Barrington, who, is come home wounded. . . . These accidents hurt Literary business.[20]

Other worrying financial problems were on the horizon. The death of a naval associate, to whom he had lent money, left him out of pocket over £200.[21] Moreover, the banking business of Murray's close associate Robert Mayne was precariously close to failing. Murray had substantial sums invested. But, privy to news of a collapse, he got his money out in July 1782, just before Mayne and his partners were declared bankrupt. A financial scandal was uncovered. And Mayne, a member of parliament, suddenly killed himself. It was a devastating turn of events which Murray could hardly believe. 'Send no more of Mr. Mayne's franks' (free postal envelopes), he told his brother-in-law John Ormiston, 'for he is dead'.[22]

Although the war depressed business, adding duties and restrictions on trade and increasing taxes, it could also generate opportunities. When Joseph Atkins wrote in October 1777 in search of a publisher for his 'Historical Memoirs of the Civil & Military Transactions in America', Murray guessed that the work might have 'a great sale', but he was only interested in publishing 'a good narrative of the *whole rebellion*' not just of the first six months.[23] Instead, he published shorter works, including Alexander Carlyle's sermon *The Justice and Necessity of the War with our American Colonies Examined* in 1777, and in 1779 Edmund Cartwright's poem the *Prince of Peace*.

> Ungenerous Britons, spare your country's shame!
> Your injur'd country's faded glory spare.[24]

Cartwright's sentiments struck a popular chord — one frequently echoed by Murray in the early 1780s: 'Our Politics here are in a wretched state. There seems to be a fatality attending all our measures against America for they have hitherto uniformly failed.'[25]

Some of Murray's family and friends were directly involved in the war. When he learnt that his first cousin Archibald Murray had been captured by the Spaniards in 1780, he wrote a letter to his aunt reassuring her that her

[20]JM to Gilbert Stuart, 7 Sept. 1779. For an account of the battle, which began on 6 July, and of the individuals involved (Comte D'Estaing, Vice-Admiral De Croy and Hon. Samuel Barrington, Vice-Admiral of the Blue) see Captain W. M. James, *The British Navy in Adversity. A Study of the War of American Independence* (London, 1926), 146–52 and 434–5.

[21]AL, p. 321 (account of Captain Samuel Hough).

[22]JM to John Ormiston, 12 Oct. 1782. At the time Mayne was an influential government contractor, supplying the army in America. He killed himself on 5 Aug. 1782 (See *The House of Commons, 1754–1790*, Namier and Brooke (eds.), 3 vols., 1964, under Mayne).

[23]JM to Joseph Atkins, 25 Oct. 1777. Atkins' work, if it was published, has not been located. In 1794 Murray published Charles Stedman's *History of the Origin, Progress, and Termination of the American War*.

[24]Edmund Cartwright, *Prince of Peace*, p. 15.

[25]JM to Lieut. Col. McClellan, 13 May 1780.

son, though a prisoner, would be well treated.[26] Murray was also 'anxious for the fate' of Gilbert Blane, a senior physician under the command of Admiral Rodney, from whose fleet, he regretted, 'no news has been received for some time past'.[27]

An election in 1780 did little to improve affairs at home or abroad. Murray was downcast and told Blane: 'Candidates make large promises to their constituents, but regard them very little after their point is gained'.[28] In the summer of 1782 enemy fleets were in the Channel and all the country was 'in great suspence'.[29] When news finally came towards the end of 1782 that peace was near, Murray could only lament to his cousin that 'it will not be the best one for this country'.[30] In the first number of the *English Review* (published 1 February 1783) the state of Britain twenty years earlier was recalled, when the Treaty of Paris, ending the Seven Years War, had confirmed the British accession of all of North America east of the Mississippi, and the prosperity and greatness of Britain seemed to be secure.

> In February 1783, another treaty separates the North American Colonies from the Mother-country for ever; and thereby undermines the foundations of British opulence and grandeur. History does not afford an instance of such a rapid declension. In no other empire has humiliation so quickly succeeded to glory.[31]

The disappointing outcome of the American war, the illness Murray suffered in the early 1780s, and financial worries all combined to sour his former optimism: 'Our political contests are merely contests for places & power, & public virtue amongst our great men is greatly decayed'.[32] But if disenchantment coloured his view of politics, it did not diminish his interest. He had a business to run and a family to support.

National Affairs

During the 1770s and 1780s British domestic affairs were also in a volatile state. In June 1780 what came to be known as the Gordon Riots brought

[26]JM to Isobel Murray, 2 Oct. 1780. Archibald was later released, and he went on to pursue a career in India.
[27]JM to Thomas Gardiner, 5 Sept. 1780. From 1779 Admiral George Rodney had been commanding a large fleet on the Leeward Islands station. In March 1780 an attempt to capture the French fleet near Martinique had apparently failed because of poor communication with his captains (*Dictionary of National Biography* under 'Rodney').
[28]JM to Gilbert Blane, 5 Sept. 1780.
[29]JM to Wm Blane (brother of Gilbert), 18 July 1782.
[30]JM to Arch. Murray (his cousin), 2 Jan. 1783.
[31]*English Review*, 1 (Jan. 1783), 82.
[32]JM to Wm Blane, 2 Jan. 1783.

chaos to London.[33] Mobs took to the streets to protest at a recent Act of Parliament which had removed religious and legal restrictions on Catholics in England. Anti-Catholic laws had prohibited priests from saying mass and heirs from inheriting property; they also disallowed entrance into public office or military service. The need to raise troops from the Catholic population for the American campaign had brought about their repeal.

For many people, Murray amongst them, the opposition to Catholic relief was seen as a part of the general movement for political reform — a movement to make public opinion a force in the parliamentary process — rather than an overt display of religious intolerance.[34] Murray was himself a member of the Protestant Association, and Lord George Gordon, their charismatic leader, was one of his customers.[35] Murray knew that the violence, which occurred on the day the Association's petition was delivered to the Commons, would only injure their cause. When similar rioting had erupted in Glasgow some months before, Murray told a Scottish friend, 'I admire your Mob'.[36] However, days after the London riot he reported to Gilbert Stuart: 'The late Confusion of this great City has been superior to any thing you can conceive. Nor is it yet over. In such times . . . business is materially hurt.'[37] Murray had just published Stuart's *History of the Reformation in Scotland*, a work resonating with Protestant propaganda. He sent a presentation copy to Lord Gordon, although he told Stuart 'from the Protestant Association I expect nothing. Nor do I like to publish a book that has occasion for any artifice to push it'.[38] Nevertheless, he saw an opportunity to capitalise on a volatile public issue and so encouraged Stuart to address himself 'to the capacity of the multitude', adding, however, that he should do this 'without forfeiting the attention of men of sense and learning'.[39] Many months after the London riot, when Lord George Gordon was on trial, Murray wrote a public letter denying that Gordon should be held personally responsible for the violence. He blamed the disaster on the ineffectual handling of the original instigators and asserted

[33]The riots were named after Lord George Gordon, leader of the Protestant Association. See C. Hibbert, *King Mob. The Story of Lord George Gordon and the Gordon Riots* (London, 1958).
[34]Of religious differences, Murray remarked in his Irish diary on 18 June 1775: 'Sunday is not equally reverenced here as in the other 2 kingdoms. . . . After mass is performed Sunday is over with the Catholics. And those actions on the Lord's day which would strike horror, & be considered as opening a gate to his everlasting damnation by a rigid presbyterian, is considered not only as innocent but even as laudable by a Catholic. Thus different are our minds affected from our different education. Both parties are certain that their form of worship & practice is the right one and anathematize their opponents. And thus will it ever be as the world is never likely to be inhabited by a majority of philosophers or rational thinking men.'
[35]JM to Lord George Gordon, 8 July 1791.
[36]JM to Wm Richardson, 26 Feb. 1779.
[37]JM to Gilbert Stuart, 19 June 1780.
[38]JM to Gilbert Stuart, 1 Jan. 1780.
[39]JM to Gilbert Stuart, 2 Oct. 1779.

that 'had they been made immediate examples of, the horrid scenes that ensued would have had no existence.'[40]

Despite the dire consequences of the Protestant Association's objectives, Murray still held to the view that public opinion and a free press were not only expressions of political liberty but also integral features of good government. Disgusted with factionalism and private interest, he remarked in March 1784: 'The present Session of Parliament has been totally taken up by the contest betwixt Mr Fox and Mr Pitt to the great Joy of our Enemies and to the detriment of the Nation'.[41] Murray's views gradually grew more conservative. Ever mindful of the conditions which promoted business, he could tell a would-be subscriber to the *English Review* in 1788 that he, like the periodical, 'wishes to support the establishment in Church & State'.[42]

The mid-1780s, after the conclusion of the American war, were years of profit and growth for Murray. He had gained a considerable reputation as a medical publisher, ran an influential review and held shares in many popular works. During this period he also published many political pamphlets. In association with John Debrett, a leading publisher of official parliamentary papers, and others he acquired an interest in this profitable line of the trade (see Table 2). For example, when an issue such as the abolition of slavery preoccupied the British public (as it did in the spring of 1788), Murray published on the subject and devoted parts of the *English Review* to both sides of the debate.[43]

The French Revolution

The news in July 1789 of a revolution in France — the Bastille captured and an ancient government overthrown — greatly interested Murray. He must

[40]The article is dated 5 Feb 1781; a copy is in Murray's album of newspaper clippings. Many years later Murray wrote to Gordon to settle an account: 'I send you an account of Long Standing, which the various turns of your life has obliterated from your memory; and which the hardships you have suffered has hitherto prevented me from bringing forward to yourself. If it is convenient for your Lordship to discharge the same it will confer a favour upon a man who has so long entertained a high Respect for you' (JM to Lord George Gordon, 8 July 1791).
[41]JM to Major Lumisdane, 15 March 1784.
[42]JM to Thomas Harwood, 15 Dec. 1788.
[43]In 1788 he published Hollingsworth's *Dissertation on the Manners, Governments, and Spirit of Africa*, which included observations on the bill in Parliament to abolish slavery in the British West Indies, and *Poems on Slavery* by Maria and Harriet Falconar. The following year he published *An Inquiry into the Origin, Progress and Present State of Slavery* and a poem by John Jamieson called the *Sorrows of Slavery*. He also published on the other side of the debate, namely two pamphlets, both by West Indian merchants: William Innes' answer to William Wilberforce's speech against slavery on 13 May 1789; and an anonymous address to Members of Parliament who favoured the abolition of the slave trade.

have wondered whether the radical political and philosophical ideas of Rousseau, Voltaire and Helvétius had actually been realised? In the political article of the *English Review* for July, the significance of the Revolution 'in the annals of history' was digested, though some surprise was expressed that 'the French monarchy could die . . . without more violent pain and convulsion'.[44] Dining often at the home of the bookseller Joseph Johnson, in the company of political theorists and recent visitors to France, Murray heard first-hand reports of the unfolding drama there and speculations about the impact it might have in Britain. Radicals, asserting the rights of the people, could claim that Britons, despite their own Glorious Revolution one hundred years before, now had fewer liberties than the French.[45] Reform was in the air, and Murray played his part, buying up copies of the English edition of Rousseau's *Treatise on the Social Compact* and reissuing them in 1791 with a cancel title page.[46] Others reiterated the conservative sentiments of Edmund Burke, who warned that the theories of Rousseau were not relevant to British society. A public debate ensued in which scores of books and pamphlets were published, the most notable of which were Burke's *Reflections on the Revolution in France* (1789–90) and Thomas Paine's *Rights of Man* (1791–2). Writing to John Richardson in Calcutta in October 1792, Murray observed: 'French affairs & the rights of Man engross all attention'.[47]

Murray's thoughts on the capture of Louis XVI as he attempted to flee Paris in June 1791 and stage a counter-revolution were characteristically logical and non-committal. He knew that the capture had prevented 'the effusion of much blood', and he was critical of those who sympathised with the King, 'as if one man should be gratified in a whim at the expence of the civil liberty of 25 millions of people'. But Murray was himself uncertain what should be done with the monarch and was concerned about the clamour the debate had spawned: 'Parties upon this business begin to run high', he told his son Archie; 'and the most violent are generally ignorant. It becomes a sensible man therefore to take no part in the dispute,

[44]*English Review* 14 (July 1789), 75. The national article had been reporting on France for some months. Although the actual fall of the monarchy had not been predicted, various conjectures had been made, and it was asserted that 'matters cannot long remain in their present state' (13, June 1789, 474).

[45]One main point of political debate at the time was over the bill to repeal the Test and Corporation Acts (requiring religious oaths for government jobs), which had narrowly failed in 1787. Another point was over legislation to redress an imbalance between taxation and parliamentary representation. The city of Manchester, for example, had no parliamentary representatives.

[46]A manuscript note in the British Library copy of Murray's edition of Rousseau indicates the reactionary turn of events in the 1790s: 'This book fell by lot to me from the Shrewsbury Library; in consequence of a resolution . . . May 4th 1798 that [it] should be expelled from the Society'.

[47]JM to John Richardson, 6 Oct. 1792.

or to abandon the question whenever he finds heat to be intruded for argument.'[48] A year and a half later (January 1793) when he heard the news that the King had been executed, Murray could only express disbelief and was so filled with 'melancholy mixed emotions' that he was at a loss for words.[49] Such cataclysmic events and political controversies could lend themselves to publishing opportunities, even within the constraints imposed by the Royal Proclamation of May 1792 against seditious writings.[50] In this year Murray acted as the London agent for John Jones' pamphlet, *The Reason of Man: with Strictures of Rights of Man*, which went into three editions and was followed by a second part in 1793. He also published François Pictet's *Letter on the Present Situation of France* (1793) and acted as an agent for Joseph Trapp's *Proceedings of the French National Convention on the Trial of Louis XVI* (1793). Among Murray's publications at this time there was none that might be deemed (as *The Times* put it) 'tending to alienate the affections of his Majesty's subject, and, to disturb the peace, order, and tranquility of the State'.[51] There is no record that Murray joined any organisation promoting Jacobin or republican principles (such as the London Corresponding Society, founded in January 1792), or, for that matter, that he participated directly in the conservative reaction leading up to what came to be known as 'The Terror'.[52]

Murray's greatest concern as 1792 drew to a close was not about selling pamphlets or about the political debate between reactionaries in Burke's camp and radicals in Paine's: he was worried about the prospect of another unwanted — and, in his view, unnecessary — war. 'The die is not yet cast', he told a friend in Bombay, 'but a very little time will decide it.'[53] In January 1793, one month before the outbreak of war, Murray reflected on what was at stake:

> England has every thing to lose & nothing to gain. If the people murmur in times of peace & wealth; will their dissatisfaction cease in the days of scarcity and war? A dearth of money already prevails, which is not likely to be removed by a rupture with any foreign power. Our commerce is most extensive and flourishing. The British flag is respected over the Globe. Our territories in India exceed in wealth and extent any thing upon record. Wherefore then should we disturb such scenes of prosperity?[54]

[48]JM to Archie Murray, 23 July 1791.
[49]JM to Archie Murray, 20 Jan. 1793.
[50]For background information about this period see H. T. Dickinson, *British Radicalism and the French Revolution* (Oxford, 1985).
[51]*The Times*, 21 May 1792, the day the Royal Proclamation was issued.
[52]Had Murray been a member of the Stationers' Company he probably would have signed their declaration of loyalty, issued on 12 Dec. 1792 (the signatory roll of Association is in the Company Archive; the declaration itself is found in British Library Add. MS 16,930, fol. 60ʳ).
[53]JM to Robert Taylor, 29 Dec. 1792.
[54]JM to Archie Murray, 20 Jan. 1793.

Tradesmen like Murray — indeed the average man in the street — did not want war. Of course, he had seen enough to know that public opinion mattered little. 'The aristocracy is alarmed,' he told his son Archie. 'And a crusade of the princes of Europe will be undertaken against france; however it may be disguised under different pretences.'[55]

While the war continued, Murray faced many of the same problems as during the American war. In March 1793, an author from Scotland told him that his volume was ready and would be sent 'as soon as a regular convoy is established between Leith and London; for much as I respect the French, I am not at all disposed to favour them with any of my labours gratis'.[56] As a further precaution, shipments were divided and dispatched separately. By the spring of 1793 bankruptcies in Britain became far more common, and by July Murray had lost nearly £600 through bad debt, a large sum and more than he could afford.[57] This and other bad news made him so despondent it undermined his health.

India

During Murray's career at sea he had (as he wrote) 'the misfortune never to have taken one trip to India' — the scene of so much trade and military activity.[58] Nevertheless, this vast subcontinent was the source of many important bookselling connections. Twice-yearly shipments of books and stationery supplies guaranteed him a certain if long-delayed income. He published books about India, from grammars and dictionaries of eastern languages to medical tracts on tropical diseases, and he served as the London agent for the Society of East India Commanders, organising their monthly meetings and managing their Nominees' Fund.[59]

An opportunity to 'shake the pagoda tree' drew many ambitious Britons, Scotsmen especially, east. Some of those who acquired a fortune — they were called 'Nabobs' — returned home to buy country estates and parliamentary seats. Murray observed how infrequently such a plan succeeded: 'Gentlemen upon their arrival here from India are generally disappointed. The Novelty of seeing England and their friends soon wears off and dissatisfaction and disgust succeed.'[60] For his own part, Murray looked on as fortunes were made and lives lost in the service of the East

[55]JM to Archie Murray, 20 Jan. 1793.
[56]Robert Kerr to JM, 18 Mar. 1793.
[57]JM to Dr Dancer, 26 June 1793; JM to Thomas Cadell, 15 July 1793. JM wrote to John Richardson (22 June 1793): 'Bankruptcies . . . continue, & war does not tend in its operations to diminish them'.
[58]JM to Capt. Wm Fraser, 28 Sept. 1779.
[59]AL, pp. 19, 51, 177 and 317.
[60]JM to Major Lumisdane, 23 Oct. 1783.

India Company. Established for trade in the early seventeenth century, the Company had gradually assumed a governmental role, conquering regions and extracting vast wealth. Seeking to regulate its activities was a major preoccupation of British governments in Murray's day. Lord North's Regulating Act of 1773, by which Parliament established a court of justice (headed by Sir Elijah Impey) and board of governors (headed by Warren Hastings, the first Governor General), imposed more orderly rule in India but did not altogether eliminate corruption. Fox's East India Bill of 1783 was a matter of extensive debate, though it failed and brought down his coalition government with Lord North. Soon after, William Pitt's successful India Act of 1784 introduced an important realignment of power between the Company and the British government.[61]

As Murray owned shares in the capital stock of the East India Company from as early as 1769, he took more than a passing interest in its affairs.[62] 'Proprietors' of India Stock were permitted to attend the meetings of the General Court (held at East India House in Leadenhall Street) and to vote on important matters. At the time there were about two thousand Proprietors, who, together with a board of twenty-four Directors, ran a vast commercial and military establishment. Until Pitt's 1784 Act, the Proprietors could reverse decisions of the Directors. Even after their power was reduced, they remained the clearest expression of public opinion in matters which concerned the operation of the Company.[63]

On several occasions Murray involved himself in Company politics. In 1774, for example, he helped to win the command of Company forces in Bombay for Colonel Robert Gordon, the illegitimate son of his one-time patron Sir Robert Gordon of Gordonstoun. Stationed in Bombay, Gordon needed advocates in London to support his nomination. Murray organised the campaign and applied himself as a public letter writer and political lobbyist.[64] 'What I wrote upon the occasion', Murray told his uncle, 'would make a small volume. . . . I should have had no notion of being capable of what I performed'.[65] This tireless effort to defeat Gordon's rival, Colonel

[61]For a detailed study of Anglo-Indian politics see L. S. Sutherland, *The East India Company in Eighteenth-Century Politics* (Oxford, repr. 1962) and C. H. Philips, *The East India Company 1784–1834* (Manchester, repr. 1968).
[62]British Library, East India Company records, L/AG/14/7/1, L AG/14/5/19. Murray owned shares from 1769. In 1784 the return on Company stock was fixed at eight per cent (Phillips, *The East India Company*, p. 2).
[63]Phillips, *The East India Company*, pp. 2–3.
[64]DB2, p. 28 for a list of the letters Murray wrote. The letters appeared mainly in the *Public Advertiser* and the *Morning Chronicle* between 8 Dec. 1773 and 2 Feb. 1774 (see Murray's album of newspaper cliippings for some of the texts). For a nearly contemporary history of Bombay about the time of Gordon's command see *An Historical Account of the Settlement and Possession of Bombay* (London, 1781).
[65]JM to Rev. Alex. Murray, 12 Apr. 1774. Murray related Gordon's history in the same letter: 'Colonel Gordon was a captain in the service of the E[ast] India Company in the year 1747

James Stuart, earned him praise and respect with Company officials and with the public. Gordon was promoted to the rank of General and gained a seat on the Council of the Company.[66] He himself bore testimony to Murray's contribution:

> It must have cost you great labour to find out & digest so many materials for your publication, to which, & to the uncommon zeal and attention of those other friends you mention, may be ascrib'd the entire success of my cause. Your publication not only maintain'd my character & claim to my just rights, but also to great honour to yourself from the sense & spirit of your productions, which must commend you to the world as well as your dilligence & attachment for those you wish to serve.[67]

No event had ever given Murray more satisfaction. Falsely modest, he remarked to Gilbert Stuart: 'My reputation with ignorant people, of which you know the bulk of mankind consists, is very much exalted'.[68] Murray and his wife Nancy received valuable gifts from Gordon, but there were greater advantages in having such a powerful friend — gaining for friends and relations jobs in the Company and increasing his trade. On both fronts Murray benefited, if for a shorter time than he had expected. In 1777 Murray again supported Gordon when his command in India was challenged by another rival.[69] Writing public letters and employing his influence with Company Directors, Proprietors and members of parliament, Murray anticipated victory. But the tide turned against Gordon. Relaying this news to India, he could only add philosophically:

> We live not in the most generous & honest times. . . . Ministerial influence carries every measure right or wrong; and this influence unfortunately we were not possessed of. . . . You will reflect that disappointments try the virtue & steadiness of men, & that your character will rise in estimation according to the equanimity with which you bear accidents of this sort.[70]

Though ardent in his pursuits, Murray was stoical in defeat and concluded his account with the reflection that 'it is more glorious to die in battle than to be assassinated'. Only later did he learn that Gordon had himself died of a tropical illness before this letter would arrive. When Murray received this

when he rais'd & carried with him the compleatest and best disciplin'd independent company that went at that time to India, for which he receiv'd the particular thanks of the officers appointed to review those troops; that he serv'd in India until the peace, particularly at Pondicherry, where his brother officers being sick or disabl'd he led on three attacks in one day'.

[66] JM to Gen. Robert Gordon, *c*. Feb. 1774, a long and detailed letter explaining the complex events surrounding Gordon's appointment.

[67] Gen. Robert Gordon to JM, 20 Aug. 1774.

[68] JM to Gilbert Stuart, 21 Mar. 1774.

[69] Murray assisted Gordon on other occasions in smaller ways (see JM to Wm Paxton, 25 Dec. 1774; and to Gen. Robert Gordon, 10 and 13 Mar. 1775 and 27 Oct. 1776).

[70] JM to Gen. Robert Gordon, 7 July 1777.

news, though saddened, he was disgusted that Gordon had not taken 'the smallest notice in his *will*, of those friends . . . to whose joint endeavours he was chiefly indebted for his commission of Brigadier General & the emoluments flowing from it'.[71] Gordon had left his vast fortune to his estranged brother Sir William, with whom Murray had a long-standing difference.[72] In a moment of recrimination, Murray bitterly remarked: 'A man of another country, an Englishmen for example or an Irishman, would have hardly thought they could ever have recompensed such services'.[73]

Although Murray's hopes of gain were not fully realised before or after Gordon's death, his interest in Indian politics did not diminish. During the 1780s and early 1790s he continued to campaign on behalf of himself, his friends and relatives. He wrote public letters and pamphlets and met with influential men in the Company and in government.[74] To his friend Robert Taylor at Bombay he remarked in December 1790: 'I know not what success has attended your application to the Court of Directors, but I strengthened it with the little interest I possessed, and I have no doubt but your success will soon enable you to return home & to rival your Friend Mr.

[71]JM to Wm Paxton, 8 Feb. 1778.
[72]In 1770 Murray had supported Sir Robert Gordon in his unsuccessful claim to the Sutherland Peerage — the oldest and one of the richest titles in Scotland. The four-year case turned on a complex point of Scots law relating to female succession, the other claimant being the late earl's daughter. Murray was engaged by William Gordon to print the important papers relating to the case — chief among them the *Supplemental Case of Sir Robert Gordon* — and to write letters in the public papers. In one (written under the pseudonym 'Junius Asiaticus') Murray asserted that their opponent's case was 'hollow and deceitful' (*Morning Chronicle*, 21 Mar. 1771). However, the House of Lords found in favour of the late earl's daughter. The Gordons had spent thousands of pounds on the case and Murray found himself over £50 out of pocket for printing bills which William Gordon refused to pay. Murray had to call in arbiters and ultimately lost more than £32 for his efforts (AL, 69). To his uncle, he poured out complaints against Wm Gordon, 'a creature devoid of a soul' (JM to Rev. Alex. Murray, *c.* 13 Aug. 1771 (See also Colonel Robert Gordon to JM, 23 Dec. 1771).
[73]JM to Wm Paxton, 17 Feb. 1778.
[74]In March 1780 Murray unsuccessfully opposed the election of Sir George Wombwell (a supporter of the Ministry) to the Court of Directors. 'It was', wrote Murray, 'with difficulty & after a hard struggle that Sir Geo: Wombwell obtained his Election. I am told the opposition his behaviour created has made him more reasonable & modest than he used to be' (JM to Lt. Col. Maclellan, 13 May 1780). Murray's letters appeared in the *Morning Chronicle*, 27 Mar. 1780 and in the *Public Advertiser*, 1 Apr. 1780. For a fuller account of Wombwell's election, see Sutherland, *The East India Company*, p. 346. Murray is credited with having written in 1786 *Considerations on the Freight and Shipping of the East India Company* (H. Curwen, *A History of Booksellers. The Old and the New*, London, 1873, p. 165). But the only pamphlets on the subject recorded from that year are the anonymous *Serious Address . . . on the Subject of the Present Disputes relative to the Company's Shipping* and what was presumably a reply to it by Alexander Dalrymple, *A Fair State of the Case between the East India Company, and the Owners of Ships now in their Service. To which are added Considerations on Mr. Brough's Pamphlet, concerning the East India Company's Shipping.* Brough was probably the author of the *Serious Address.*

Scott in parliament.'[75] From 1786 Murray defended Warren Hastings when a debate about his impeachment for 'high crimes and misdemeanors' began in the House of Commons, and was ultimately heard in the House of Lords. Lasting some seven years, it was 'one of the great political trials in British History'.[76] In the *English Review* for April 1786 Murray himself wrote a balanced account, acknowledging the former Governor General's important contribution to stability and progress in India but urging 'that no violent opinions should be prematurely entertained on either side'. More to the point of his agenda, Murray asserted that even if the charges against Hastings were proven, 'was he not empowered with the sole right of pronouncing on the state of affairs thus submitted to his management'.[77] In the June issue Murray wrote a much longer and more adamant defence, arguing against Burke and Pitt — Hastings' 'two most powerful adversaries' — and reminding the public that Hastings' 'chief object' was not, like most Indian officials, to amass a fortune, but to secure 'the prosperity of the India Company and the glory of the British empire'.[78] Murray was proud of 'a polite letter from Mr Hastings for the able manner in which it [the *English Review*] has defended him'.[79]

Murray had already published a number of Hastings' most important accounts of his command, including the authorised version of his *Memoirs relative to the State of India* in 1786.[80] Murray may have been the anonymous editor mentioned in the preface, who with the benefit of information sent from India, was able to 'place some subjects in a clearer light and to state as facts what were probabilities only, when Mr. Hastings resigned his government'. When the actual impeachment trial finally began in 1788, Murray was no less active co-publishing Hastings' answers to the charges and reporting the case regularly in the *English Review.* Dining at the Commanders' Club, Murray heard the latest news of the trial.[81] It was not until 1795, however, that the House of Lords dismissed the charges against Hastings, whose

[75]JM to Robert Taylor, 24 Dec. 1790. John Scott (then MP for Stockbridge) was Warren Hastings' special agent in London (*The Parliamentary History of England*, eds. Namier and Brooke, 3 vols, under 'Scott'). Taylor did not succeed.

[76]*The Impeachment of Warren Hastings*, G. Carnall and C. Nicholson, eds, (Edinburgh, 1989), p. 1.

[77]*English Review* 7 (Apr. 1786), 317–18. It can be inferred that Murray wrote the article from comments in a letter from John Logan to Alex. Carlyle, 12 Apr. 1786 (Edinburgh University Library, MS La. II, 419/8), stating that, except for the Hastings section, Logan had written the political article in the March *English Review.*

[78]*English Review,* 7 (June 1786), 477. Although Hastings was not himself a Scot, he had been instrumental in placing Scots (among them friends of Murray) in positions of power. See J. Reddy, 'Warren Hastings: Scotland's Benefactor', in *The Impeachment of Warren Hastings*, op. cit.

[79]JM to John Millar, 27 July 1786.

[80]There were in fact five issues (at least) of the work, the first with twenty-two additional pages (see Checklist 1786 items 527–8, and 1787, 589–90).

[81]JM to John Richardson, 22 June 1793.

modest fortune had been exhausted by this long defence — an event Murray would not live to witness.

One of Hastings' most significant extra-political contributions was to convince Indian scholars (both Hindu and Muslim) to introduce westerners to their languages and cultures.[82] By founding educational institutions, he fostered an appreciation of Indian society in Britain and among East India Company officers and traders. Murray understood the importance of Hastings' efforts, particularly in sponsoring the publication in print of Indian culture. But he did not believe enough was being done. It was no coincidence that the first article in the *English Review* was on Nathaniel Halhed's *Grammar of the Bengal Language* and that Hastings should be complimented: 'There have been times', the author wrote, 'when the labours of a Jones [the author of a Persian grammar], a Richardson [the author of an Arabic grammar] and a Halhed, would, as well on account of their political utility, as of their literary merit, have engaged the notice of men in power. But this is not the age. The genius of a Hastings does not shine in the councils of St. James's or Leadenhall-street.'[83] Murray himself published important works by John Richardson other than the *Grammar of the Arabick Language* (1776), most notably a *Dictionary of Persian, Arabic, and English* (1777–80). This impressive two volume folio publication (printed at the Clarendon Press and priced at five guineas) included a 'Dissertation on the languages, literature, and manners of Eastern Nations', which Murray published separately in 1778. Initially, he had only agreed to sell the work as an agent, but in May 1785 he gave £1130 for the copyright — the largest sum recorded that he paid for a book and one which he was concerned 'for some time will press upon my funds'.[84] The *Dictionary* sold well and appeared in revised editions during the nineteenth century. Although Richardson was not the most renowned orientalist of the day, he did provide Murray with a scholarly link to Indian culture. While at Oxford, and afterwards in Calcutta, Richardson regularly wrote for the *English Review* and served as a reader for books relating to India which Murray had been offered. Thomas Beddoes also assisted in this department, and in 1792 Murray sold his poem *Alexander's Expedition down the Hydaspes & Indus*, which contained voluminous notes on Indian history and culture. In 1792 Murray published selections from the first two volumes of the *Asiatick Miscellany* (Calcutta printed: London, reprinted for J. Murray, 1792). This periodical, edited by Francis Gladwin and published quarterly in Calcutta from 1785, brought almost wholly unknown literatures into print for the first time.

---

[82]On this subject see J. L. Brockington, 'Warren Hastings and Orientalism', in *The Impeachment of Warren Hastings,* op. cit. pp. 91–108.

[83]*English Review* 1 (Jan. 1783), 13–14. Murray published the 3rd edition. of Jones' *Grammar of the Persian Language* in 1783.

[84]JM to Thomas Beddoes, 28 May 1785.

Murray's volumes contained the best works of native Indian writers and well known British orientalists.[85]

Through the 1770s, 1780s and 1790s Murray published pamphlets on Indian affairs, military accounts, histories, reports of trials, and even a novel — Helenus Scott's *Adventures of a Rupee* (1782).[86] He could count on sending a substantial number of copies of all these to India and could anticipate a more general sale in Britain. In all, his successful trade in India, where British imperialism was flourishing, contrasted with his failures in America. Murray had a fair (but not effortless) shake of the pagoda tree. He had earned it.

[85]See G. Shaw, *Printing in Calcutta to* 1800 (London, 1981) items 52, 64 100, 112 and 134. Another Calcutta publication Murray reprinted was the *Narrative of the Sufferings of James Bristow, during Ten Years captivity with Hyder Ally and Tippoo Saheb* (1793).
[86]In 1792 Murray published Alexander Dow's translation from the Persian of Firishtah's *History of Hindostan*; in 1793 *The Trial of Avadaumum Pupiah Bramin . . . against David Haliburton.*

13

Later Years

Decline and Fall

For twenty-five years Murray worked hard selling and publishing books. His approach — in theory at any rate — was simple: 'Undertake only what you can perform, and perform it well'.[1] On the whole, he ran a multi-faceted enterprise professionally and profitably. It was better to please customers (as he said) 'by pains & a moderate charge, than to disgust by . . . exaction.'[2] Sometimes his way of doing business got him into difficulty, and the gap between expectations and results seemed discouragingly wide. A hard negotiator and tireless worker, Murray tried to get as much and give as little as possible. This was a basic business principle — however generous he might have been at times. When challenged about a prompt demand for an account settlement, he was indignant: 'Can you believe I am able to discharge a heavy rent, aggravated by oppressive taxes, & maintain a family besides of 9 people by sloth & negligence?'[3] And when an author complained about unrealised profits, Murray forthrightly charged him to 'examine my conduct or let whom you please do it'.[4] The shop at 32 Fleet Street was essentially a one-man operation. However, Murray would not have done as well, or as much, without the help of competent and obedient assistants. Although their jobs were neither easy nor very well paid, shop-men like Evan Williams, Samuel Highley and John Harding received a thorough training and could hope some day to have their own bookselling businesses.[5]

[1]JM to Wm Thomson, 28 Aug. 1786.
[2]Ibid.
[3]JM to Daniel Keith, 22 June 1785. The nine people in his 'family' were Hester, Archie, John, Jenny, Mary Anne, Highley, Harding, a house servant and himself.
[4]JM to John Peter Wade, 17 Mar. 1792. The work was Wade's *Nature and Effects of Emetics* (1792).
[5]Williams began trading for himself in 1787, Highley in 1803 and Harding in 1799 (Maxted, *The London Book Trades 1775–1800*, pp. 101, 110 and 248).

The advances Murray had made in the 1780s were not matched in the first years of the next decade, even though his lists of new publications and shares of syndicate publications continued to increase (Table 1; Figure 2). War with France had slowed the book trade; indeed the whole British economy was straining under new burdens and restrictions. At the end of 1791, after twenty-three years of business, Murray tersely summed up the state of his finances when he told a friend: 'I am much distressed for money'.[6] Regarding his state of mind, he had remarked some months before: 'I continue to vegetate, wishing to retire but not able to accomplish it'.[7] Murray was fifty-four at this time (see Plate 2c).

The steady supply of income from a successful work like Lavater's *Essays on Physiognomy* was small relative to the expenditures on other publications. Murray urged Thomas Holloway, the chief engraver of the *Essays* and a partner in the undertaking, to work faster, yet at the same time told Holloway he could not pay for work already completed.[8] Matters were further complicated when a selling agent cheated Murray of subscription fees.[9] There were other successes, if on a more modest scale. One of Murray's new authors, Isaac D'Israeli, offered him a work called the *Curiosities of Literature* in 1791. The public soon bought all the copies, and a second edition was issued, after which a continuation and several further editions appeared. A warm friendship developed between the two men and plans were made for future projects. More and more, Murray asked his authors to share the expense of publishing their works, or to bear it all. In January 1791 he declined a new book John Whitaker had offered gratis. During the past year, he explained, the cost of paper had greatly increased and advertising had doubled. Typically, six months or even a year's credit was given for paper and printing, but in the stagnant economy of the early 1790s only three months, or a little more, was usually held out.[10] While production costs were higher, wholesale and retail prices, especially for reprints of standard classics, were declining.

On paper Murray was in profit; the problem was his customers — the trade in particular — were not paying. Time and again he wrote angry letters of demand, some so severe that he thought better and redrafted more tactful ones.[11] When customers complained of the interest he added to

---

[6]JM to James Ogilvie (brother of the author John), 17 Nov. 1791.
[7]JM to John Richardson, 17 Mar. 1791.
[8]JM to Thomas Holloway, 16 Sept. 1791. Publication of the *Essays* became more and more irregular. Originally the proprietors intended to 'produce a *Number* every month' (No. I, Jan. 1788), but this proved difficult. For example, after the July 1792 number (24), the next was not issued until Dec. 1792. See Checklist item 727.
[9]JM to John Mayne, 11, 13 and 15 June 1792; and 22 Apr. 1793.
[10]JM to John Whitaker, 22 Jan. 1791.
[11]See, for example, JM to Patrick Hare, 13 and 14 Jan. 1791; and to Mrs Urquhart, 14 Apr. 1791.

overdue accounts — five per cent a year was standard practice — they met
with the retort that 'no interest . . . can compensate for the want of
punctual payment to men in business'.[12] One bookseller who surprised
Murray by non-payment was told that his behaviour was 'destroying faith
between Tradesmen that ought to be inviolable'.[13] Murray prided himself
on keeping exact records. On one occasion it so irked him to be found in
error that, along with a corrected account, he sharply remarked to the
customer: 'It can be no desire of mine to impose extra expences upon my
correspondents which so far from serving myself exposes me to double
trouble without benefit'.[14] Though under considerable pressure, he was
determined to honour his own notes and protect his reputation as a
businessman. When John Stockdale, a partner in many ventures, did not
press for payment, Murray resisted the concession, insisting that, 'altho my
affairs have suffered some derangement lately, you have with-held favouring me with your account of printing notwithstanding my earnest entreaties'.[15] During 1792 and 1793 matters grew even worse. All around him
businesses were failing. To Thomas Cadell's just demand for the settlement
of a debt, Murray could only attempt to explain his late and partial payment:
'From Edinburgh I cannot obtain 6*d* and some bankruptcies here [in
London] have affected me to the amount of between £500 & £600'.[16]
These sums, or the greater part of them, would never be recovered, and
more bad debts would follow. 'The times are bad', he lamented. 'I can get
no money'.[17] Politically, the French war was (in Murray's words) 'unnecessary'; economically, it was doing irreparable harm.[18]

On top of these concerns, Murray was not feeling well.[19] Since his
stroke in 1782, he had taken better care of himself and avoided a recur-
rence, but he was plagued by rheumatism and often accidentally injured
himself. He was now in his mid-fifties and wishing to slow down at a time
of greatest demand. Two visits to Edinburgh in 1790 seemed to have had
little or no adverse effect on his health. Upon his return to London he
knew there could be no let-up. By September 1792, however, he was feeling
so poorly that his doctors advised a visit to Margate to take the waters.
Murray was worried, not only about himself but about Hester's persistent

[12]JM to Mr Butterworth, 18 Oct. 1791.
[13]JM to Robert Faulder, 15 Aug. 1793.
[14]JM to Watson & Co., 24 May 1792.
[15]JM to John Stockdale, 21 Dec. 1789. John Stockdale replied (on 23 Dec. 1789): 'I am really
sorry for any derangement in your affairs, but I am very certain they are only of a temporary
nature; I, for one, will give you credit to any amount you may think proper to order of my
Publications'.
[16]JM to Cadell & Co., 15 July 1793.
[17]JM to James Sibbald, 15 July 1793.
[18]JM to John Peter Wade, 22 June 1793.
[19]JM to John Stockdale, 20 Jan. 1790.

cough and his children's various complaints. At the end of August 1793 he was overcome with severe pain, and doctors ordered him to bed. Incapacitated but oppressed with business worries, he called his assistant, Highley, to his bedside for reports. When demands came for money (from Thomas Cadell, for example), Highley explained that 'Mr Murray . . . is sorry that he finds himself at this time less capable of paying you the remainder . . . proceeding from a severe fit of illness . . . and also to the late failures at Edinburgh which has much distressed him'.[20] Murray suffered. London's leading physicians and surgeons were, for the most part, either his customers or his authors, yet they could do little. For short intervals he was able to dictate letters, direct Highley and see people, but the burden of running the shop fell to Highley as the senior assistant. Articles for the *English Review* still had to be collected and edited each month. Fortunately, William Thomson was on hand to take charge, while John Whitaker and others supplied much-needed copy for the autumn issues.

Word travelled through the London trade that Murray was gravely ill. Several booksellers called by to report on joint affairs and judge his condition for themselves. Archy Paxton, who had the closest knowledge of Murray's finances, visited regularly and took care of essential business. Faced with grim reports from his medical advisors, Murray made out a will in the middle of September. Through October his condition worsened and the pain increased. There was no hope of recovery. After discussing the matter, Hester agreed to take charge of the business on behalf of herself and their children. On 6 November 1793, a Wednesday, John Murray died at the age of fifty-six. The newspapers the following day carried the news:

> Died yesterday Morning, after a long and painful illness, Mr. John Murray, Bookseller, Fleet-street.[21]

Three days later he was interred in the north vault at St Dunstan's Church, a site reserved for well-to-do gentlemen of the parish.[22]

Hester, his wife of fifteen years, was forty-seven at the time. Their son, John, was not yet fifteen; Jenny was thirteen and Mary Anne just six years old. At this time arrangements were made to send Mary Anne to live in Dublin with her aunt and uncle, the Ormistons, to whom boarding fees and expenses were paid. John and Jenny stayed at Fleet Street with their mother.

---

[20]JM to Cadell and Co., 25 Sept. 1793. Insistent demands continued from creditors like Thomas Cadell. After years of trading, Murray expected to be treated better: 'I request explicitly', he wrote to Cadell on 11 June 1793 to 'never attempt to draw upon me without permission'. Murray arranged to pay part of the account and signed a new note on the balance for September.
[21]*The Times*, 7 Nov. 1793; *St. James's Chronicle*, 5–7 Nov.
[22]Burial Register for St Dunstan's in the West (Guildhall Library, M/F 10356/1).

In his will Murray appointed three of his oldest friends as executors: Archy Paxton, the Reverend Donald Grant and George Noble. These men were to serve as trustees to administer his estate for the benefit of Hester and her family, and were likewise appointed guardians of the children. Hester was also named an executrix. In standard fashion, Murray set out that one half of the yearly income from his estate would go to his three lawful children, the other half to Hester in her lifetime, with the proviso that 'should she marry again . . . she should be entitled only to one third of the said interest'. In separate bequests Hester received £200 in cash; Archie Murray, £50; his sister Binny, twenty-five guineas; Donald Grant, twenty guineas and an 'ivory figure of Prometheus'; George Noble 'my metal horizontal stop watch; and Samuel Highley, his 'faithful shopman', £10. If all the principal beneficiaries were to die without issue, Murray set out that one half of his estate would go to Robert Murray Ormiston, his sister Binny's son, and the other half to his 'natural son' Archie or the heirs of these men.[23] Hester was also given the rights to one half of the rent from the property Murray owned — three houses in London.[24]

At Murray's death the value of his stock *alone* was nearly £9000; syndicate shares and other property were worth an additional £3300.[25] Each month he had bills to discharge of about £500; so, since he was not in debt, his annual turnover exceeded £6000.[26] These figures were modest compared with those of other London publishers such as William Strahan, who was worth nearly £100,000 when he died in 1785, or Thomas Cadell who retired in 1793 with a substantial fortune, though somewhat less than Strahan's.[27] But Murray, who started in business with little, did better than most.

'Printed for H. Murray'

It was not unusual for the widow of a bookseller to take up her husband's trade, even if her practical experience was limited or she had little genuine interest in the business. Hester's course was determined by the youth of her

[23]The will was dated 17 Sept. 1793 (Middlesex Deeds Registers 1799, vol. 2, piece 27, Greater London Record Office).
[24]See p. 136n for details of the properties.
[25]In a letter from Arch. Paxton and Donald Grant to Hester Paget (her remarried name), the value of 'Mr Murray's Property at the time of his death' was calculated conservatively at £12,348.2s.
[26]JM to John Elder, 12 Aug. 1793. Although Murray's accounts after 1777 are not extant, it is possible from occasional references in his correspondence to reconstruct the general state of his finances.
[27]J. A. Cochrane, *Doctor Johnson's Printer. The Life of William Strahan* (London, 1964), p. 206. Murray's close associate in Edinburgh, Charles Elliot, who died in 1791, left an estate valued at over £30,000 (Elliot folder, Box M8).

son (who was the natural successor), Murray's deathbed wishes, and sheer necessity. Guided by the trustees, she directed Highley to continue managing the day-to-day running of the business, as he had since Murray fell ill. At this time young John was indentured as an apprentice to Highley for the usual term of seven years.[28]

The executors' two principal aims were to settle Murray's estate and to keep the business going. Murray himself had laid down the plan before his death. All accounts were called in — authors, tradesmen and retail customers alike. In principle, customers were told that 'the Executors cannot . . . deliver any more on credit', but in practice four months was given for orders over £10.[29] It was not a climate for easy collection, as war with France continued to hinder business. Even Murray's once dependable trade to India did not have 'so good an appearance as formerly'.[30] One customer who owed money even attempted to flee Britain. He was apprehended, but recouping the debt was another matter.[31] Writing to the Dublin bookseller Luke White in the middle of 1794 for an account of nearly £600 unpaid since 1789, Hester reminded him that she was 'much pressed for Money at this juncture'.[32] William Creech, who had always been lax, took five years to settle.[33] Moreover, Highley's strict adherence to the instructions of the executors sometimes caused friction with long-time associates like John Whitaker, who was warned by Highley to 'consider well the affair before you take any step to the prejudice of [a] Man who you say was your friend'.[34]

Several authors, having heard that their publisher was dead, inquired about the status of their works. William Brown, for instance, hoped to buy the copyright and unsold copies (605 out of 750 printed) of his *Essay on the Folly of Scepticism* (1788), but he was surprised to learn that he would first have to pay £21, the debt still outstanding from the production costs which Murray had been offsetting against profits.[35] Others who might have wished to forget their debt were reminded that 'the want of success cannot be imputed to any neglect on the part of the Bookseller'.[36]

[28]The indenture is dated 3 Dec. 1793 (Box M15).
[29]Samuel Highley to an unidentified customer, 7 Dec. 1793 (this letter is found at the end of Murray's album of newspaper clippings). See also Hester Murray to Henry Hunter, 25 Mar. 1795. For the time even India accounts had to be prepaid (Hester Murray to John Peter Wade, 22 March 1794).
[30]Hester Murray to Robert Allan, 9 Dec. 1793.
[31]Hester Murray to Robert Taylor, 12 May 1794.
[32]Hester Murray to Luke White, 9 May and 14 July 1794.
[33]Samuel Highley to Wm Creech, 28 June 1798. Even then there was a dispute when Creech tried to put some second-hand books towards the debt.
[34]Samuel Highley to John Whitaker, 11 July 1794.
[35]Hester Murray to Wm Brown, 21 Feb. 1794. Hester also wrote to Marie Élisabeth de La Fite, author of *Reponses à Démeler* (1790), regretting the poor sale and demanding the money Murray had put up against anticipated profits (8 Mar. 1794).
[36]Samuel Highley to John Peter Wade, 22 Mar. 1794.

From the start Hester began to publish, using 'H. Murray' and 'Mrs. Murray' in her imprints. In 1794 alone she issued upwards of forty books, though few, if any, were noteworthy. About ten were in the press when Murray died and so bore his name. Conservatism was, as it had always been, the guiding principle; nor would the watchful eyes of the trustees have approved any risky ventures. Hester published editions of steady sellers like Thomson's *Seasons*, books by 'house' authors such as Thomas Beddoes and Isaac D'Israeli, medical works, pamphlets on the India trade, and the usual round of syndicate publications. In 1795 the numbers rose modestly. One aspect of Murray's business Hester could not manage was the *English Review*. At the end of 1793 she was advised to accept William Thomson's offer that he become the proprietor. Her name continued to appear in the imprint, and she received a portion of the profits.[37] In a 'Prospectus' to the January 1794 issue (volume 24) Thomson outlined a plan 'gradually to transform the English Review', proposing to introduce the novel practice of allowing authors to review their own books and deciding to drop the 'Monthly Catalogue'.[38]

In March 1794 the first step was taken to turn Murray's assets into cash when two London booksellers took an inventory and valued the stock in his shop (mainly bound books) and in his warehouses (books in sheets). Altogether, the estimated wholesale value was just under £9000 (see Plate 47).[39] Murray also owned freehold property and leases valued at over £1600.[40] If these, together with his stock and copyrights (estimated at over £1400) were sold, Hester could expect some £360 a year as her half share of the interest.[41]

Hester, who was now forty-eight, was not content to live out her days as the widow of John Murray. No more than a few months after her husband's death she formed a friendship with Henry Paget, a retired army captain from Shropshire. In the autumn of 1794, one year after Murray's death, she accepted his proposal of marriage and became Mrs Paget

[37]Samuel Highley to Laurie & Symington, 25 Jan. 1794. For Thomson's role see the *Annual Biography and Obituary*, 2 (1818), 101–2.

[38]Thomson's preface (*English Review*, 24, Jan. 1794) is an interesting document in the history of the literary review.

[39]The exact sum was £8882.14*s*. In the shop itself were bound books (in leather and boards) totalling £1800; in the storehouse in Falcon Court were books in quires valued at £1250; and in a warehouse elsewhere in Fleet Street were books in quires valued at £5600. 'A large quantity of pamphlets' and 28,000 unsold numbers of the *English Review* were valued at £244 (A Catalogue of the Stock in Trade (with the Valuation) of Mr. J. Murray. Richard Banister and David Walker, both London booksellers, received fifty guineas for the valuation). The unsold *English Reviews* were not so many as they may seem: on average just over 200 per number.

[40]Arch. Paxton and Donald Grant to Henry Paget, 2 May 1797 (a letter reviewing the financial history of Murray's estate).

[41]In 1794 the highest interest rate was 6 per cent (Hester Paget to Arch. Paxton, 9 Mar. 1797).

shortly before Christmas.[42] At this time she announced her intention of quitting the book trade and urged the executors to sell the remaining stock and settle accounts. During Hester's year-long proprietorship, house expenses had come to about £720. Profits covered this figure but with little to spare.[43]

In December 1794 at the Crown & Anchor the first of three trade sales was held to dispose of a portion of Murray's stock, shares and copyrights. All the leading booksellers were on hand. Longman, Kearsley and Stockdale were among the heavier buyers.[44] Early in the new year of 1795 the trustees formally appointed Samuel Highley as their agent. Then in April, Hester moved out of 32 Fleet Street and, with daughter Jenny and her new husband, settled at Bridgnorth in Shropshire.[45] John was just sixteen at the time, his future largely left to the benevolent yet autocratic dictates of his guardian, Archy Paxton. His father was dead; his mother had left London with his sister; and he was unhappy, as he confessed to his half-brother Archie at the end of April 1795:

> I am no farther advanced with regard to my settlement than when you left me, from which it would appear, that Paxton has not a very good conscience, or I am sure it would have pricked him on ere this, so as to have established his most humble, & dutiful ward in some eligible situation; and God knows it is not every Guardian that is blessed with such a ward, but patience is a virtue which, as [I] think I may still have occasion for I shall the very first opportunity take a good dose of.[46]

In the absence of a more 'eligible situation', John continued in the shop. His indenture left him little choice, however much he hoped otherwise.

In May 1795 the second sale took place. John hardly had a moment to write to his brother, his time 'so entirely taken up in consequence of a sale we have lately had'.[47] Together, the two sales realised nearly £10,000. However, it would be more than two years before accounts were due in full.[48] Hester was anxious to begin collecting interest, and she and her new husband wrote frequently to the executors demanding a settlement. The

[42]Paget had formerly been a lieutenant in the West Norfolk Militia. He lived at Cann Hall in Bridgnorth, Shropshire.
[43]Arch. Paxton and Donald Grant to Henry Paget, 2 May 1797.
[44]The prices paid for the syndicate publications (as well as a few others) are recorded in BB after each book entry and noted individually in the Checklist. Details of the stock purchases are found in the account ledger kept between 1795 and 1800.
[45]At this time the bulk of the furniture was sold for over £800 (Samuel Highley to Hester Paget, 5 Mar. 1797).
[46]JM2 to Archie Murray, 21 Apr. 1795.
[47]JM2 to Archie Murray, 14 May 1795.
[48]The exact total was £9899 (Samuel Highley to Hester Paget, 5 Mar. 1797). On the long term of credit see Arch. Paxton and Donald Grant to Henry Paget, 2 May 1797. Details of the purchases are recorded in the 1795–1800 account ledger.

dispute turned on whether she was entitled to interest on the estate from the time of Murray's death or only after the value of the estate was realised. The executors explained that they were 'not warranted to pay . . . out of the Principal that share which by the Will is ordered to be paid out of the Interest or annual income'.[49] However, in May 1797 she succeeded in getting about £140 in addition to the annual sum of £205.16s. The executors believed this was treating her 'in a very liberal manner', and on the whole a potentially volatile situation was amicably resolved.[50] Hester also arranged to have Jenny's annual allowance increased from thirty to seventy guineas — an amount paid out of the estate before the net income was divided.[51]

One substantial account from Murray's estate remained to be settled — the *Essays on Physiognomy*. But the final number was not issued until March 1799. A settlement with Murray's co-proprietors (Thomas Holloway, Henry Hunter and Joseph Johnson) was a matter of serious contention and not settled until January 1802, when arbiters determined that the estate owed a staggering £2900 plus an additional £1000 in interest (eight years) accrued on the debt since his death. One arbiter objected, but the majority opinion conferred the award.[52] According to the partners' original contract (signed on 15 January 1788), it had been agreed that upon the death of a partner his share would devolve to the others, who would then be obliged to pay the estate of the deceased for its value (in November 1793 Murray's share was calculated at a mere £150). Murray's executors had, however, continued to receive their share (totalling £2900) from the sale, to which, strictly, they were not entitled. The decision was a serious blow to the beneficiaries of the estate, even if thousands of pounds still remained. The executors took legal advice as to whether they might succeed in reversing the decision in the courts, but the opinion was unfavourable.[53]

'J. Murray and S. Highley (Successors to the Late Mr. Murray)'

On 14 November 1795 a co-partnership agreement for a term of six years was signed. It set out that when John reached the age of twenty-one (on 27

[49]Arch. Paxton and Donald Grant to Henry Paget, 2 May 1797.
[50]Ibid.
[51]George Noble to Henry Paget, 12 May 1797.
[52]Samuel Highley to Henry Paget, 15 Jan. 1802. The executors reported that the decision was 'as little to their satisfaction as it can possibly be to yours'. The arbiters were three book-sellers: George Nicol, Charles Rivington and George Wilkie. Holloway and Hunter received £958 each, Johnson, £2,134. Nicol refused to sign the deed of arbitration on two grounds: first, that interest should not have been charged as the partners had not given Murray's executors their account when requested; and second, the partners' accounts greatly exceeded the original contract (papers relating to the arbitration Box M 10).
[53]'The Opinion of Mr A. Piggott, 25 Jan. 1802' (Box M 10).

November 1799) he would, having completed the term of his apprentice-ship, become a full partner. In the meantime, Highley would remain directly answerable to the trustees. He continued to keep accounts for the estate and also opened new ledgers and letter books for the partnership. In May 1796 the final sale of stock, shares and copyrights was held. The partnership of Murray and Highley bought parts of many copyrights at the fair market value.[54]

Highley conducted business as he had been taught. The deals he made, the kinds of books he published, even the authoritative tone of his corre-spondence all recalled the practices of his master. The firm began to build their lists, focusing on medical works and printing new editions of past successes such as William Jones' *Persian Grammar* (a fourth edition in 1797) and Gilbert Blane's *Observations on the Diseases Incident to Seamen* (a third edition in 1799). New literary works were not wholly neglected — for instance, Thomas Frognall Dibdin's *Poems* (1797) and Isaac D'Israeli's *Vaurien: or, Sketches of the Times* (1797). Like the first Murray, the partners interested themselves in periodicals. They published successfully the *London Medical Review* and resumed the proprietorship of the *English Review,* which in 1796 (volume 27) William Thomson had renamed the *English Review of Literature, Science, Discoveries, Inventions, and Practical Controversies and Contests.*[55] The following year, however, it merged with Joseph Johnson's *Analytical Review* to become the *English Analytical Review.*

Each year, on average, the business of the partnership grew. From September 1795 to the following September receipts from sales came to £3171, which after expenses left a profit of £400, divided between Murray and Highley. By 1799 receipts had risen to £5122, and profits to over £540.[56] By the year 1800 Murray & Highley had amassed over £2300 in capital stock, shares and copyrights.[57] John by now had passed his twenty-first birthday and become a full partner. In March the co-partnership agreement was about to expire and decisions about the future had to be made. At this time he and his sister Jenny initiated a proceeding in Chancery to gain control from the trustees of their share of the principal of their father's residuary estate (amounting to several hundred pounds). The trustees were willing to allow this; they only insisted upon an indem-nity from the court in the event of a claim on the sum from Robert Ormiston or Archie Murray, who would be the beneficiaries were John and Jane to die without issue. The court, however, was of the opinion that

[54]BB lists the purchasers after each entry. More detailed accounts are listed in the 1795–1800 ledger.
[55]The only significant difference in format was the addition of a new section, 'A Retrospect of the Active World; or, A General Review of Discoveries, Inventions, and Practical Controversies and Contests', placed before the 'National Affairs' article.
[56]1775–1800 Account Ledger, p. 226.
[57]Articles of Co-partnership, dated 25 Mar. 1800. The exact sum was £2328.

their claim should not be allowed, and this failure prevented Murray's children from gaining even a small share of independence.[58]

John had learned to run a shop and publish books, but it had been an unpleasant five years. The arrangement was awkward. Highley had worked at the shop since 1773 — five years before John was even born. And, though accustomed to Highley from childhood, John had formed no close bond with him. Confiding to his half-brother, Archie, over his 'connection with Highley', he remarked that 'so many disagreeable remembrances crouch upon me that [I] think myself very unlucky, nay often very unhappy'.[59] Young Murray was in a difficult situation: 'I know not well how to . . . determine upon a subject so important as my future prospects in life. And this is not for want of endeavouring at it either. But so unprotected, so unpatronised, so unadvised, I am so fearful. . . . Indeed I wish my Father was alive.'[60] Uncertain of what else to do, however, Murray accepted Paxton's practical advice and renewed terms with Highley for a further eight years. The articles of co-partnership (dated 25 March 1800) stipulated that all important deals had to be agreed upon by both men and that accounts would be settled once a year. Serious disputes, should they arise, would be brought to arbitration. There was a further clause that the partnership could be dissolved in six years by either partner if six months' notice were given.[61]

Things did not go well. From the start the two men disagreed on too many important matters to work together effectively or live happily in the same house. After struggling for eighteen months, a decision was made in September 1802 'suddenly to resolve upon a dissolution of their partnership'. On 17 December their case went to arbitration, and on 24 March 1803 Murray and Highley formally separated.[62] By the agreement, Highley received £1032.10s. in cash — calculated to be his share of the value of the business itself and the lease at Fleet Street. The figure was somewhat less than half the value assigned to the business two years before, but apparently it was enough to satisfy Highley. A notice was put in the newspapers announcing their split and noting that 'All Debts due to the Firm are hereby requested to be paid'.[63]

[58]Document headed 'In Chancery Murray vs. Paxton' (Box M8).
[59]JM2 to Archie Murray, 14 May 1795.
[60]JM2 to Archie Murray, 30 July 1800.
[61]Deed of Partnership (Box M15).
[62]JM2 to Edward DuBois, 15 Sept. 1802; JM2 to Samuel Highley, 19 Nov. 1802. The arbiters were George Nichol for Murray, Richard March for Highley, and James Watson as the umpire. The papers relating to the partnership are found in Box M15.
[63]*London Gazette*, 29 Mar. 1803.

Highley moved to premises a few doors down at 24 Fleet Street. He began selling books and stationery supplies and issuing new publications almost immediately.[64] A notice in his *Catalogue of Medical Books* published on 28 April 1803 clarified his status:

> Samuel Highley, Apprentice and Shopman to the late Mr John Murray, for Nineteen Years, and afterwards his Successor, in all a period of Twenty Seven Years; begs leave to acquaint his Friends and the Public in general, that the Partnership . . . was dissolved on the 25th day of March last; that he has removed to No. 24, of the same Street, a few doors nearer to Temple Bar, as he is resolved to sell all new Medical Books as soon as published on the most moderate terms for Ready Money.[65]

Over the next few years Highley established himself as a successful independent trader. Shortly after Murray moved to 50 Albemarle Street in 1812, Highley returned to 32 Fleet Street — the house he knew so well. In 1815 his son became a partner in the business, and through the nineteenth century the firm of Highley continued to prosper as publishers of medical and scientific books, with agents in all the major British cities and in Europe, America and India.[66]

The Second John Murray

Rather more enterprising than Highley, and certainly more interested in the literary side of publishing, the second Murray effectively used his share of the capital from his father's estate to build up his own lists. However, he did not by any means abandon medical publishing or other profitable fields his father and Highley had cultivated (see Plate 48). In 1809, for example, he

---

[64]Curiously, Highley's name had appeared separately on at least two books even before the first Murray's death: a new edition of the *Supplement to the Life of David Hume* (1789) and an *Additional Volume to the Works of Samuel Johnson* (1792). The *Supplement* first appeared in 1777, at which time Murray, who sold large quantities of the work, wrote: 'The thing is not printed for me; but I . . . am desirous of obliging the publisher' (JM to Charles Elliot, 10 May 1777).

[65]A copy of Highley's *Catalogue* is in the Murray Archive.

[66]Affixed to a Highley publication from 1854 is a lengthy catalogue of 'Medical and Scientific Works published by Mr. S. Highley', as well as a list of the firm's periodical scientific publications, a notice for 'Highley's Library of Science & Art', a list of books on 'Photography in its application to Science', and an advertisement for 'Medical and Microscopical Apparatus', including 'Highley's Microscope Camera', priced eight guineas. The *Catalogue* is found in John Cockle, *Clinical Handbook of Auscultation and Percussion* (London, 1854). The periodicals Highley published at the time were *The Scientific Book Circular*, the *Medico-Chirurgical Review*, *The Alysum Journal* and *The Dublin Hospital Gazette*. On the title page to Cockle's book is the Samuel Highley monogram, incorporating the year 1773 (when he began his bookselling career) and the year 1667 (when 32 Fleet Street was built). In all, the sign of a long-established firm. As late as 1875 Highley's descendant was corresponding with JM3 (See letter 27 May 1875 in Box M15).

issued his own *Medical Catalogue*. He published books on Indian affairs, and he issued navy lists. Like his father, Murray used his influence at the Admiralty and Naval Board to get employment for friends and relatives — including his half-brother Archie.[67] He had considerable influence with the Edinburgh trade, and so acquired (among many other more profitable publications) the agency for the *Transactions of the Royal Society of Edinburgh*, which had eluded his father.

More than with any other author, the second Murray's name will always be associated with that of Lord Byron. Yet Walter Scott, Jane Austen and other enduring writers of the early nineteenth century were in his lists and brought him large profits — not to mention such endeavours as the *Quarterly Review*. In 1812 he followed the trend of well-to-do Londoners as they moved from the City to fashionable districts in the West End. The purchase of the house at 50 Albemarle Street and of the copyrights of William Miller (a successful bookseller at that address for several years) helped to establish Murray as the leading literary publisher of the day. Rather than stand behind a counter as his father had done, he began to concentrate almost entirely on wholesale publishing. He made deals with other traders, but more and more began to finance publications himself. He was responding to a shift in the trade towards specialisation; indeed, he was an innovator in this respect. The age of the bookselling publisher, in which his father had advanced so stalwartly, had almost come to an end. But the house of Murray would endure.

---

[67]Archie Murray to JM2, 15 June 1817 and 2 July 1830.

A Checklist of Murray Publications
1768–1795

A Checklist of Murray Publications
1768–1795

Introductory Notes

Titles are listed by year, and within each year they are arranged alphabetically. Variant *issues* of a single edition in a given year are listed but not as separate entries (see item 21,Wilkie). Subsequent *editions* in a given year are, however, listed separately, though to avoid repetition only additional facts are supplied. Information has been extracted mainly from the *Eighteenth-Century Short-title Catalogue* (on-line as of July 1997). Relevant additions to *ESTC* entries, such as pagination of multi-volume works (in ten or fewer volumes) and a complete list of names in the imprint where only 'others' were noted, have been taken from available copies. Addresses of the imprint are not recorded. *ESTC* identification numbers beginning with 't' refer to locations in Britain or Europe; those with 'n' to North America. A primary location (referred to by *ESTC*'s standard library code) and shelf mark (where available) follow each identification number. If a work is not listed in *ESTC*, such as a periodical, I have cited the copy consulted.

References to Murray's letterbooks give the name of the recipient and the date of the letter only (for example, item 31, Breaks). The abbreviation JM has been used for John Murray, AL for Account Ledger, DB for Daybook and BB for Booksellers' Book. Other abbreviations are self-explanatory. See note 1 of the Introduction (p. 2) for descriptions of these sources. Monetary units are in standard form (e.g. £2.8s.6d); 'gn' is a guinea. References to published bibliographical sources are cited by author, with the full citation given in the Bibliography. Periodical publications are listed annually, even though they may have been issued more frequently (e.g. monthly or quarterly), as noted. Subsequent editions of individual parts are listed under the original year of publication (see, for example, item 60, Duncan, *Medical and Philosophical Commentaries*). Murray's newspaper publications (as described in Chapter 10) are not listed. Book prices (where noted) are taken from contemporary reviews, newspaper advertisements, Murray's catalogues, and sources in the Archive.

'Stock' refers to information found in the manuscript 'Catalogue of the Stock in Trade (with the Valuation) of Mr. J. Murray at the time of his Decease'. The figures are divided according to the stock in Murray's house (H) at 32 Fleet Street, and in his warehouses (W), one behind the house and the other at an unrecorded location in Fleet Street. When uncertainty has arisen about which edition is listed in Murray's 'Stock in Trade' (the edition date is not usually recorded in the 'Catalogue'), I have cited the one published nearest to his death (Nov. 1793).

(*) An asterisk indicates that a contemporary source, such as Murray's *English Review,* the *Monthly Review,* the *Critical Review,* the Stationers' Company Register, or a newspaper advertisement, lists Murray as the publisher or selling agent, but that copies of the book do not list Murray in the imprint (see item 19 — Daniel Watson). Thirty-five such titles are noted below. Titles listed in publishers' advertisements as 'Books printed for J. Murray' which fall into this category are listed separately at the end of this Checklist when there was not significant external evidence of Murray's involvement.

(**) Two asterisks indicate that a contemporary source lists Murray as the publisher or selling agent although no copy is recorded in *ESTC,* the *National Union Catalog,* or elsewhere, as far as I have discovered (see item 13 — Murray). The number of books in this category, sometimes described as 'lost' books, has been gradually reduced as more titles are entered into *ESTC* and other catalogues. Twenty-five titles are noted below.

(***) Three asterisks indicate a spurious 'Murray' publication, that is, a book in which his name appears in the imprint but with which he apparently had no involvement of any kind (see item 79 — Goldsmith). Only six titles fall into this category.

Each entry has been assigned a single subject category: agriculture, arts, biography, drama, economics, education, fiction, history, language, law, literary criticism, medicine, military, miscellaneous, philosophy, poetry, politics, religion, science, or travel–topography. This information has been compiled in Table 2 and Figure 3 (pp. 158–61) and is discussed for the most part in Chapter 9. Each entry has also been assigned a publishing category based either upon the imprint or, where applicable, upon documentation in the Archive, in newspapers or reviews, or in other relevant sources. The different arrangements Murray came to with authors and fellow tradesmen are described in Chapters 3–6 and compiled in Table 1 and Figure 1 (pp. 31–2).

There is no sense in which this Checklist can be regarded as complete. *ESTC* alone generates a handful of new Murray imprints every year, or reduces the number of 'No copy located' entries, and I continually find additions in other places.

An index of Murray's publications by author or if anonymous by title, giving the year (or years) of publication, follows on p. 410.

1768

1. [Lyttelton, George Lyttelton, Baron, 1709–1773.]
Dialogues of the dead. The fifth edition, corrected. London, printed for J. Murray (successor to Mr. Sandby) at No. 32, opposite St. Dunstan's Church, in Fleet-Street, 1768.
[2],xv,[1],406p., 8vo. Price: 5s. bound.
The text, pagination and signature follow Wm Sandby's fourth edn. published 1 June 1765, incorporating its errata list. However, the press figures, which begin iv–2, [xi]–2, 6–3, 16–3, 25–5, are entirely different. The final three dialogues are by Elizabeth Robinson Montagu.
ESTC t111533: L, 716.f.1.
Philosophy. Murray alone.

2. Another edition.
The text, while also following Sandby's fourth edn., is completely reset from the one above; press figures begin 9–6, 28–6, 41–6. An analysis of the textual and typographical differences between these editions in relation to the fourth edition, as well as evidence of bindings, provenance of copies consulted and circumstances surrounding publication suggest that priority should be assigned to the edition above (see Ch. 1, p. 22–3 and Plate 6).
Philosophy. Murray alone.

1769

3. Adye, Stephen Payne, d. 1794.
A treatise on courts martial. . . . To which is added, An essay, on military punishments and rewards. By Stephen Payne Adye, . . . [London], New-York, printed, London, re-printed, and sold by J. Murray, (successor to Mr. Sandby), 1769.
[2],ii,iv,139,[9]p., 8vo. With a list of subscribers at the end and a final errata leaf. Price: 2s. sewed.
A reissue of the New York edition of 1769, printed by H. Gaine; published 24 Oct. 1769. Murray had 200 copies shipped and printed a cancel title page for which he charged Adye 5s. He also printed a handbill to advertise the work (JM to Stephen Payne Adye, 7 Dec. 1769.)
ESTC t083270: L, 228.e.31
Military. Agency–Murray alone.

4. Argens, marquis d' [Jean Baptiste de Boyer], 1704–1771.

New memoirs establishing a true knowledge of mankind, by discovering the affections of the heart, and the operations of the understanding, in the various scenes of Life: being a critical inquiry into the nature of friendship and happiness. And essays on other important subjects. By the Marquis d'Argens, . . . with letters from the Baron de Spon, . . . and two novels, Spanish and French; . . . with thoughts on the art of beautifying the face. By Mademoiselle Cochois, . . . The second edition. In two volumes. London, printed for J. Murray, 1769.
Vol. 1: [1],vii,[15],261,[1]p.; vol. 2: [1],[12],274p., plate, 12mo. Price: 6s.
A translation of *Nouveaux mémoires pour servir à l'histoire de l'esprit et du cour*, with the sheets of the 1747 London edition published by D. Browne. The final leaf of vol. 1 advertises books by Argens published by Browne and press figures follow this edition.
ESTC n041697: IU, x844Ar2.L1769.
Miscellaneous. Murray alone.

5. Authentic memoirs concerning the Portuguese Inquisition, never before published: . . . Also, reflections on ancient and modern Popery, and the causes of its present alarming progress in this kingdom. To which are added, several striking facts relating to the Portuguese Jesuits, . . . In a series of letters to a friend. London, printed for John Murray (successor to Mr. Sandby), 1769.
xv,[1],528p., 8vo. Price: 6s. bound.
ESTC n004467: NjP, WIT 5457.136.
Religion. Murray alone.

6. Beccaria, Cesare, marchese di, 1738–1794.
A discourse on public oeconomy and commerce. By the Marquis Casar Beccaria Bonesaria, . . . Translated from the Italian. London, printed for J. Dodsley; and J. Murray (successor to Mr. Sandby); and sold by T. and J. Merrill, Cambridge; and Messrs. Kincaid and Co. at Edinburgh, 1769.
[4],vi,47,[5]p., 8vo. With a half-title and two final advertisement leaves. Price: 1s.6d. in wrappers.
A translation of *Elementi di economia pubblica* with a preface and notes by the unidentified translator; published 20 June 1769.
ESTC n008843: MH-H, Econ 302.1.5* Tr2360*
Economics. London co-publishing.

7. Evelyn, John, 1620–1706.
Sculptura; or, the history and art of chalcography, and engraving in copper: with an ample enumeration of the most renowned masters and their works. To which is annexed, a new manner of engraving, or mezzotinto, communicated by His Highness Prince Rupert to the author of this treatise, John Evelyn, Esq;. The second edition. Containing some corrections and additions . . . London, printed for J. Murray, (successor to Mr. Sandby), 1769.
[4],xxxvi,140p., plates, port., 8vo. Price: 3s.6d.
A reissue of the second edition of 1755, with a cancel title page; first published in 1662. See Geoffrey Keynes, *John Evelyn. A Study in Bibliophily*, 1968, item 37.
ESTC t134297: L, 1651/17.
Arts. Murray alone.

8. Fénelon, François de Salignac de la Mothe-, 1651–1715.
A demonstration of the existence of God: deduced from the knowledge of nature, . . . By M. de la Mothe Fenelon, Archbishop of Cambray. Translated from the French, by Samuel Boyse, A.M. Second edition. London, printed for John Murray, successor to Mr. Sandby, 1769.
xxiii,[1],279,[1]p., 8vo. Price: 3s. bound.
A translation of *Démonstration de l'existence de Dieu*. Wm Sandby had published editions in 1749 and 1765. Murray took the remaining sheets of the 1765 edition and printed a cancel title page. The final page advertises two Sandby publications by Lord Lyttelton, the *History of King Henry* and the *Dialogues of the Dead* (fourth edn). Stock: 12 (H).
ESTC n028834: NNC, 193sp4.FF6.
Religion. Murray alone.

9. Harvey, John, 1702–29?
The Bruciad, an epic poem, in six books. London, printed for J. Dodsley; and J. Murray (Successor to Mr. Sandby); T. and J. Merril, at Cambridge; and A. Kincaid and J. Bell, at Edinburgh, 1769.
xiv,[2],237,[1]p., 8vo. Price: 2s.6d.
A new edition of the *Life of Robert the Bruce* by John Harvey (first published Edinburgh, 1726), edited by John Cumming (a reprint of the original edition had appeared in 1768). Murray bought the copyright from Wm Chapman for

£15. His partners were W. and J. Richardson (AL, pp. 39, 41–2; DB1, p. 290). Adelard & Brown printed 750 copies at Edinburgh.
ESTC t125271: L, 11632.f.7.
Poetry. London co-publishing.

10. Hoblyn, Robert, 1710–1756.
Bibliotheca Hoblyniana: sive, catalogus librorum, juxta exemplar, quod manu suâ maximâ ex parte descriptum reliquit Robertus Hoblyn, armiger, de Nanswhyden, in comitatu Cornubia. Londini, prostant apud J. Murray, 1769.
vi,[2],337,[2],338–650p., plate, 8vo. Price: 10s.
250 copies printed by Wm Bowyer, delivered 7 Mar. 1769 (Maslen, 4705). Apparently a reissue of the 1768 London edition (imprint: London, 1768) with a new title page, reset contents section, and an additional errata leaf. John Quicke (who married Hoblyn's widow in 1759) was the editor (AL, p. 28). The collection was auctioned in 1778.
ESTC t009580: L, 821.i.16.
Miscellaneous. Murray alone.

11. A letter from a lady to the Bishop of London. London, printed for J. Brown; and sold by J. Murdoch, and T. Noteman; J. Murray; G. Kearsly; J. Wilkie; and W. Davenhill, and H. Parker, [1769?].
60p., 8vo. With a final advertisement leaf.
Signed: Prudentia Christiania, a pseudonym. Addressed to Richard Terrick on the subject of justification by faith.
ESTC t102227: L, 4105.aa.3.
Religion. Agency–London.

12. A letter to Mr. Dale Ingram. In which the arguments he has advanced in his Enquiry into the cause of Mr. Clarke's death, are confuted. By Chururgicus. J. Murray, 1749 [1769].
36p., 8vo. Price: 1s. With a half-title.
A reply to Ingram's *The blow; or, an enquiry into the causes of the late Mr. Clarke's death,* London, printed for Messrs. Richardson and Urquhart, 1769 (*ESTC* t079398).
ESTC n061268: Ds, Widdess room, 13A1.
Medicine. Murray alone.

**13. Murray, John, 1737–1793
A catalogue of several thousand volumes in most languages, arts and sciences, making a

large assortment of valuable books in very good condition, some of them in elegant bindings: which will be sold very cheap (for ready money) the lowest prices marked in the catalogue, and to continue daily on sale, by John Murray, bookseller, (successor to Mr. Sandby) No. 32 Fleetstreet, where the utmost values is given for any library or parcel of books. Catalogues to be had at the place of sale; and of Mr. Payne, at the Meuse Gate; Mr. Robson, in New Bond-Street; Mr. Elmsly, opposite Southampton-street, in the Strand; Mr. Hingerton, near Temple Bar; Messrs. Richardson and Urquhart, under the Royal Exchange; Messrs. T. and J. Merril, at Cambridge; and Messrs. Kincaid and Bell, Edinburgh, [1769].
No copy known. An advertisement in Murray's newspaper clipping album stating 'this day published' is hand-dated 1 July 1769 (see Plate 31). Miscellaneous. Murray–with Agency.

**14. The navy leeches. A poem. Printed for Richardson and Urquhurt, at the Royal-Exchange; and J. Murray, in Fleet-street, [1769]. 4to. Price: 1s.6d.
No copy known. An advertisement in Murray's newspaper clipping album and hand-dated 20 Feb. 1769 lists this work with the imprint as above (see Plate 31). Sales of the poem begin in DB1 from 24 Feb. It was noticed in the *Critical Review*, 27 (Mar. 1769), 154, listing only Richardson and Urquhurt: 'This performance is calculated entirely for the meridian of Wapping. The author's intention seems to be to lash the abuses practised in certain offices within the marine department' (see also *Monthly*, 40 (Mar. 1769), 176).
Poetry. London co-publishing.

15. Registrum Roffense: or, a collection of antient records, charters, and instruments of divers kinds, necessary for illustrating the ecclesiastical history and antiquities of the diocese and cathedral Church of Rochester. Transcribed from the originals by John Thorpe, . . . and published by his son John Thorpe, . . . Together with the monumental inscriptions in the several churches and chapels within the diocese. London, printed for the editor, by W. and J. Richardson: and sold by T. Longman; R. Dodsley; J. Murray; T. Smith, in Canterbury; W.

Mercer, in Maidstone; and E. Baker, at Tunbridge, 1769.
[4],vi,[2],697,[5],701–1056,[16]p., plate, port.,ill., Fo. With a list of subscribers. Price: £1.18s.
ESTC t098287: L, 206.g.10.
Travel-Topography. Agency–London.

16. [Sharpe, Gregory, 1713–1771.]
A letter to the Right Reverend the Lord Bishop of Oxford, from the Master of the Temple. Containing remarks upon some strictures made by His Grace the late Archbishop of Canterbury, in the Revd. Mr. Merrick's annotations on the Psalms. London, printed by W. Richardson; and sold by T. Longman; J. Dodsley; R. Dymott; and J. Murray, 1769.
[2],62p., 8vo.
Signed at end: Gregory Sharpe, and dated: Jan. 2, 1769.
ESTC t004918: L, T.1022(4).
Religion. London co-publishing.

17. Wait, Robert, d. 1777.
The gospel-history, from the text of the four Evangelists. With explanatory notes. In five books. To which are subjoined, tables . . . The second edition. By Mr. Robert Wait, minister of Galston. London, printed for J. Murray, (successor to Mr Sandby), 1769.
[2],xii,543,[1]p., 8vo. Price: 6s. bound.
The first edition of 1768, with a cancel title page. Stock: 3 (H).
ESTC t205510: C, C-9–37–17.
Religion. Murray alone.

18. Walpole, Horace, 1717–1797.
The castle of Otranto. A Gothic story. The third edition. London, printed for John Murray, successor to Mr. Sandby, 1769.
xxiv,200p., 8vo. With a half-title. Price: 3s.6d. bound.
Murray bought the remaining sheets of Wm Bathoe's third edition and printed a cancel title page. Reference: Hazen, *Walpole*, p. 55.
ESTC t063196: L, 12614.bb.19.
Fiction. Murray alone.

*19. Watson, Daniel.
An historical catechism: or, short discourses on the progress of revealed religion; . . . and the principles of Christianity. By Daniel Watson,

. . . Newcastle, printed by J. White and T. Saint; and sold by W. Charnley, [1769].
[2],x,130p., 12mo. With a half-title. Price: 1s.6d. The dedication is dated Oct. 15, 1768. *Monthly Review* 41 (Sept. 1769), 224: Newcastle. printed by White & and sold by Murray, in London. Murray took 200 copies and in May 1773 returned 25 to Charnley (DB1, p. 370).
ESTC t101607: L, 4016.aa.56.
Religion. Agency–Provincial.

20. Watson, Richard, 1737–1816.
Christianity consistent with every social duty. A sermon preached at the University Church in Cambridge, at the assizes, before the Honourable Sir Richard Adams, . . . on Thursday, March 9, 1769. By Richard Watson, . . . Cambridge, printed by J. Archdeacon; for T. & J. Merrill in Cambridge; sold by J. Johnson & Co. B. White, J. Robson, and J. Murray, in London, 1769.
[4],16p., 4to. Price: 6d.
ESTC t009255: L, 694.i.12(1).
Religion. Agency–Provincial.

21. Wilkie, William, 1721–1772.
The epigoniad. A poem. In nine books. By William Wilkie, V.D.M. The second edition, carefully corrected and improved. To which is added, A dream. In the manner of Spenser . . ..
London, printed for Wilson and Nicol; and J. Murray, 1769.
xlviii,228p., 12mo. Price: 3s.6d. bound.
First published Edinburgh, 1757; this edition is the 1759 London edition (A. Millar; and A. Kincaid and J. Bell, Edinburgh) with a cancel title page. See DB1, p. 155 for 3s.3d. charge for printing new title. Stock: 275 (W).
ESTC n006617: ICIU, 182368.
Another issue: London, printed for J. Murray. And Wilson and Nicol, 1769.
ESTC t090252: L, 993.g.40.
Poetry. London co-publishing.

22. Wood, John, 1705?–1754.
A description of Bath, . . . By John Wood, Esq; the second edition, corrected and enlarged. In two volumes. London, printed for .J [*sic*] Murray, (successor to Mr. Sandby), 1769.
[8],456,[4]p., plates, maps, 8vo. Price: 11s. With a leaf of postscript, and a final leaf of directions to the binder.

First published in 1742 as *An essay towards a description of the city of Bath*. Stock: 4 (H).
ESTC t164717: E, A.47.e.31–2.
Travel–Topography. Murray alone.

1770

23. Caylus, Madame de, (Marthe-Marguerite), 1673–1729.
Memoirs, anecdotes, and characters of the court of Lewis XIV. Translated from Les souvenirs, or recollections of Madame de Caylus, . . . By the translator of the life and writings of Ninon de l'Enclos. In two volumes. . . . [London], Printed for the editor; and sold by J. Dodsley; J. Murray; and Richardson and Urquhart, 1770.
Vol. 1: [iii]–viii,183,[1]p.; vol. 2: [4],190p., 8vo. Price: 5s. sewed.
Translation by Elizabeth Griffith of *Souvenirs*.
ESTC t110524: L, 10662.b.2
History. Agency–London.

24. A dialogue of the dead: betwixt Lord Eglinton and Mungo Campbell. To which is added a genuine abstract of the trial of Mungo Campbell, late officer of excise at Saltcoats, for the killing of the Earl of Eglinton, before the Court of Justiciary in Scotland, on Monday the 26th of February, 1770. London, printed for J. Murray, 1770.
42,2p., 8vo. With a half-title and final advertisement leaf. Price: 1s.
ESTC t061591: L, T.1612(6).
Another issue: London, printed for J. Murray, (successor to Mr. Sandby), 1770.
ESTC t061592: L, 113.h.10.
Law. Murray alone.

25. Fearne, Charles, 1742–1794.
An impartial answer to the doctrine delivered in a letter, which appeared in the Public Advertiser, on the 19th of December 1769, under the signature Junius. By Charles Fearne, . . . London, printed for J. Murray (successor to Mr. Sandby), 1770.
iv,43,[1]p., 8vo. Price: 1s.
500 copies printed, but Murray sold fewer than 130. Published in Jan. (DB1, p. 38).
ESTC n007621: MH-H, *EC75.F3116 770i.
Politics. Murray alone.

26. [Langhorne, John, 1735–1779.]
The crisis. In answer to The false alarm. London,

printed for J. Murray and Richardson and Urquhart, 1770.
31,[1]p., 8vo. Price: 1s.
Langhorne's account (AL, p. 80) confirms authorship, though the pamphlet is sometimes attributed to Philip Rosenhagen. *The false alarm* is by Samuel Johnson.
ESTC n027870: PPL, U Eng Cris 1773.O.3.
Politics. London co-publishing.

27. Laugier, Marc-Antoine, 1711–1769.
The history of the negociations for the peace concluded at Belgrade September 18, 1739. between the emperor, Russia, and the Ottoman Porte, . . . Translated from the French of M. l'abbé Laugier. London, printed by W. and J. Richardson; for J. Murray (successor to Mr. Sandby), 1770.
xx,534,[2]p., plate, map, 8vo. With a final advertisement leaf. Price: 6s. in boards.
A translation of *Histoire des négociations pour la paix*. Murray paid J. Ellis £6.12s. to engrave the map; the printing and paper of the map cost 30s (AL, p. 39). The Richardsons had a half share of the copyright (AL, p. 39). Stock: 1 (H); 9 (W).
ESTC t128728: L, 121.c.13.
History. London co-publishing.

28. [Law, Edmund, 1703–1787.]
Observations occasioned by the contest about literary property. Cambridge, printed by J. Archdeacon. Sold by T. & J. Merrill, in Cambridge; and by J. Johnson & J. Payne, B. White, T. Cadell, J. Robson, and J. Murray, in London; J. Fletcher and D. Prince, at Oxford, 1770.
[4],20p., 8vo. With a half-title.
ESTC t013046: L, 1651/137.
Law. Provincial co-publishing.

29. Rotheram, John, 1751–1804.
A philosophical inquiry into the nature and properties of water. With elegant copper-plate figures of the several salts. By J. Rotheram, M.D. Newcastle upon Tyne, printed by I. Thompson, Esq; and sold by J. Murray, London; and by W. Charnley and T. Slack, in Newcastle, [1770].
[8],132p., plate, 8vo. Price: 2s.6d.
ESTC t085497: L, 8775.b.28.
Science. Provincial co-publishing.

*30. Two remarkable letters of Junius and the

Freeholder, addressed to the K—. With answers and strictures. London, printed, and sold by all the booksellers, 1770.
[4],51,[1]p., 8vo. Price: 1s. With a half-title.
An advertisement leaf in *A dialogue of the dead: betwixt Lord Eglinton and Mungo Campbell* (item 24) lists this title as 'published and sold' by Murray.
ESTC n046994: IU, x836.42.K77p 1768.
Politics. London co-publishing.

1771

31. Breaks, Thomas.
A complete system of land-surveying, both in theory and practice, containing the best, the most accurate, and commodious methods of surveying and planning of ground by all the instruments now in use; . . . To this work is annexed, a true and correct table of the logarithms of all numbers, . . . By Thomas Breaks. Newcastle upon Tyne, printed by T. Saint for W. Charnley, and J. Murray in London, 1771.
[2],ii,593,[1]p., plates, 8vo. Price: 7s.6d.
Published in 15 (?) parts; Murray took 200 copies of each part, (DB1, p. 370), having received 500 proposals from Charnley to distribute in London (To Wm Charnley, 22 June 1769).
ESTC t112950: L, 529.d.22.
Science. Provincial co-publishing.

32. [Cartwright, Edmund, 1743–1823.]
Armine and Elvira, a legendary tale. In two parts. London, printed for J. Murray, 1771.
38p., 4to. With a half-title. Price: 2s.
ESTC t004703: L, 11631.g.53.
Poetry. Murray alone.

33. The second edition. Oxford, printed for J. Murray, London, 1771.
ESTC t126035: L, 11661.t.1.
Poetry. Murray alone.

34. The third edition. Oxford, printed for J. Murray, London, 1771.
500 copies printed (AL, p. 248; see Plate 8).
ESTC t133723: L, 11661.t.18.
Poetry. Murray alone.

35. [Cary, Patrick, fl. 1651.]
Poems, from a manuscript, written in the time of Oliver Cromwell. London, printed for J. Murray, 1771.

35,[1]p., 4to. Price: 1s.6d.
The poems are from a maunscript collection in
the possession of Pierrepoint Cromp (a Murray
correspondent).
ESTC t101642: L, 79.k.22.
Poetry. Murray alone.

36. The second edition. London, printed for J.
Murray, 1771.
[2],35,[1]p., 4to. Price: 1s.6d.
ESTC t173368: E, [Al].1/1.13(1).
Poetry. Murray alone.

37. Grant, Donald.
Two dissertations on Popish persecution and
breach of faith. In answer to a book, intitled,
'A free-examination of the common methods
employed to prevent the growth of popery'. . . .
By D. Grant, . . . London, printed for J. Murray;
and sold by Kincaid and Creech, Edinburgh,
1771.
[8],206,[2]p., 8vo. With a half-title and final
errata leaf. Price: 2s.6d.
500 copies printed. *A free examination*, 1766–68,
is by James Ussher (Grant to JM, 30 July 1771).
ESTC t028393: L, 3940.h.5(2).
Religion. Murray–with agency.

38. Langhorne, John, 1735–1779.
The fables of flora. By Dr. Langhorne. London,
printed for J. Murray, 1771.
65,[3]p., 4to. With a half-title and final leaf of
advertisements. Price: 3s.
Murray paid £7.4s. for paper (9 reams at 16s.
each) and £6.7s.6d. for printing (8½ sheets at
15s. each); 5 gns paid to Simpson to engrave the
title vignette (AL, p. 199). Murray purchased the
copyright on 27 May 1799 at Thomas Becket's
sale at the Queen's Arms for 5s.3d. However, he
never published a new edition. The copyright
was sold 23 Dec. 1794 to Dilly for 10s.6d. (BB, p.
20).
ESTC t061575: L, 11602.gg.26(2).
Poetry. Murray alone.

39. The second edition. London, printed for J.
Murray, 1771.
65,[3]p., 4to. With a half-title, a leaf of advertisement and errata following the dedication,
and a final leaf of advertisements. Price: 3s.
ESTC n031619: KU-S, Poems 47.
Poetry. Murray alone.

40. The third edition. London, printed for J.
Murray, 1771.
65,[3]p., 4to. With a half-title and a final adver-
tisement leaf. Price: 3s.
Stock: 198 (W).
ESTC t074919: L, 1490.ee.9.
Poetry. Murray alone.

41. Millar, John, 1735–1801.
Observations concerning the distinction of
ranks in society. By John Millar, . . . London,
printed by W. and J. Richardson, for John Murray,
1771.
[4],xv,[3],242,[2]p., 4to. With a half-title and a
final advertisement leaf. Price: 9s.
750 copies printed in partnership with the
Richardsons. Cost: £184.13s.6d., deducting £15
for 'Irish copy money' from Ewing (AL, p. 39).
Millar was paid £100 for the copyright, and
£16.14s was spent on advertising (AL, p. 122).
Stock: 183 (W).
ESTC t100408: L, 30.e.20.
History. London co-publishing.

42. Millot, abbé, (Claude François Xavier),
1726–1785.
Elements of the history of England; from the
invasion of the Romans to the reign of George
II. Translated from the French of Abbé Millot,
. . . By Mr. Kenrick. In two volumes. . . .
London, printed for J. Johnson, and W. Nicoll;
and J. Murray, 1771.
Vol. 1: xxxii, 388p.; vol. 2: 456p., 8vo. Price: 10s.
bound.
First published in 1769 as *Élémens de l'histoire
d'Angleterre*. Partly translated by John Langhorne
and Gilbert Stuart as well as Wm Kenrick. 1000
copies printed by Wm Strahan (who charged
£33.8s.3d) and by Alex. Hamilton (who charged
£37.12s.9d); paper supplied by Chapman for
£79.1s.6d. It cost £257.6s.6d in all to produce
the work, a sum split three ways by Murray and
his partners (Al, p. 123 and separate sheet; see
Plates 29 and 30).
ESTC n031650: MWA, J430.M656.E771 (1).
History. London co-publishing

43. The repository: or treasury of politics and
literature, for MDCCLXX. Being a complete
collection of the best letters (including those
of Junius) and essays from the daily papers; . . .

London, printed for J. Murray; J. Bell; S. Bladon; and C. Etherington, at York, 1771. Vol. 1: iv,556p.; vol. 2: [ii], 464p., 8vo. Price: 1s. each monthly number; 10s. the set.
ESTC t111539: L, 713.d.5,6.
Politics. Provincial co-publishing.

44. A review of the history of Job; wherein the principal characters, transactions, and incidents in that book are considered with attention; . . . With an appendix; containing remarks on that generally misapplied passage, ch. xii ver. 12. By a private gentleman. London, printed for the author; and sold by J. Buckland; J. Murray; and J. Towers, 1771.
xii,94p., 8vo.
ESTC t063278: L, 4372.f.5(5).
Religion. Agency–London.

1772

45. Adye, Stephen Payne, d. 1794.
Considerations on the Act for punishing mutiny and desertion; and the rules and articles for the government of His Majesty's land forces. London, printed for J. Murray; Kincaid and Creech, Edinburgh; and T. Ewing, Dublin, 1772.
[2],53,[3]p., 8vo. Price: 1s.6d.
Forms the second section of Adye's *Treatise on courts martial*, 1769. Stock: 87 (W). Published Feb. 1772.
ESTC t087683: L, 103.e.64.
Military. Provincial co-publishing.

46. [Cartwright, Edmund, 1743–1823.]
Armine and Elvira, a legendary tale. In two parts. By Edmund Cartwright, . . . The third edition. Oxford, printed for J. Murray, London, 1772.
[7],6–38p., 4to. With a half-title. Price: 2s.
500 copies printed. With the addition of a poem to the author by John Langhorne (see Plate 8).
ESTC t133724: L, 11660.c.7.
Poetry. Murray alone.

47. The fourth edition.
[2],38p., 4to. With a half-title. Price: 2s.
ESTC t022417: L, 1500/221.
500 copies printed.
Poetry. Murray alone.

48. The fifth edition.
ESTC t133725: L, 161.l.20.

500 copies printed.
Poetry. Murray alone.

49. Cullen, William, 1710–1790.
Synopsis nosologia methodica. In usum studiosorum. Editio altera. In quarta parte emendata; et adjectis morborum speciebus aucta. A Gulielmo Cullen, . . . Edinburgi, apud A. Kincaid & W. Creech: Londini, apud T. Cadell, J. Murray, et E. & C. Dilly, 1772.
iv,220–227,[6],228–232,241–414p., 8vo. Price: 6s.
ESTC n024539: MnU-B, B616.01.C897 1772.
Another issue: Edinburgi, apud A. Kincaid & W. Creech: Londini, apud W. Johnston, T. Cadell, J. Murray, et E. & C. Dilly, 1772.
iv,220,[4],[221]-227,[3],228–232,241–414p., 8vo. Price: 6s.
ESTC n023214: MBCo, RC96.C89 1772.
Medicine. Edinburgh co-publishing.

50. [Curry, John and Charles O'Conor]
Observations on the popery laws. London, printed for J. Murray, and T. Ewing, Dublin, 1772.
[4],iii,[1],72p., 8vo. With a half-title. Price: 1s.6d.
Ewing had published an edition in 1771 (*ESTC* t094012) and again in 1774 (*ESTC* t185918). Stock: 297 (W). This edition published June 1772.
ESTC t041838: L, 518.k.10(3).
Religion. Provincial co-publishing.

51. Duncan, Andrew, 1744–1828.
Observations on the operation and use of mercury in the venereal disease. By Andrew Duncan, M.D. . . . Edinburgh printed for A. Kincaid and W. Creech; and for T. Cadell, and J. Murray, London, 1772.
viii,175,[1]p., 8vo. Price: 2s.6d. in boards. With a half-title.
ESTC t026908: L, T.451 (1).
Medicine. Edinburgh co-publishing.

**52. The new topic of conversation; or, dialogues on the abuse or excess of credit in trade. Adapted to the present times. Second edition. [Newcastle, 1772].
8vo. Price: 1s.6d.
No copy located. *Critical Review* 34 (Sept. 1772), 238. 'Murray'. 'The revival of a pamphlet which was published in the year 1766, and certainly

merits attention.' Murray returned 82 copies to Hilton at Newcastle in July 1774 (AL, p. 153). Economics. Agency–provincial.

53. O'Halloran, Sylvester, 1728–1807.
An introduction to the study of the history and antiquities of Ireland: ... By Sylvester O Halloran. London, printed for J. Murray, 1772. [8],xx,[2],384p., plates, 4to. Price: 12s. in boards. 750 copies printed. The Dublin edition with an altered imprint. Cambridge report [12],xx,384p., with a list of subscribers.
ESTC t056429: L, 185.b.15.
History. Murray alone.

54. A sketch of the secret history of Europe since the peace of Paris; with observations on the present critical state of Great Britain. London, printed for J. Murray, 1772. [4],8,13–39,[1]p., 8vo. With a half-title. Price: 1s. Possibly by a man named Richardson to whom Murray sent '6 of His Sketch' on 25 Sept. 1772 'at Lord Cathcart's St James Street' (DB1, p. 305); also listed in DB1, p. 304 (21 Sept. 1772); Murray paid an extra 3s. to the printer 'for Expedition'.
ESTC t053813: L, 1093.e.84.
History. Murray alone.

*55. Spencer, John, of Newcastle.
Hermas, or, the Acarian shepherds: a poem. In sixteen books. The author, John Spencer. ... Newcastle upon Tyne, printed by T. Saint, 1772. [2],xiv,274p., 8vo. Price: 8s.
Monthly Review 47 (July 1772) 69: 'Newcastle printed. Sold by Murray in London.' Murray returned 56 copies to Wm Hilton (the editor) at Newcastle in Dec. 1773 (AL, p. 153). This is a different setting from the 2-vol. 1772 edition (*ESTC* t101978).
ESTC n043556: CaOLU, SpC PR3699.S5H3.
Poetry. Agency–provincial.

56. Stewart, Thomas, Hairdresser.
Valentia; or, the fatal birthday: a tragedy. By Thomas Stewart. London, printed for the author; and sold by him; and by J. Murray, 1772. vi,[2],83,[1]p., 8vo.
The cost of printing and publishing, paid by Stewart, came to £8.9s.6d.—£5.8s for printing 6 sheets at 18s./sheet; £2.9s.6d. for 3 reams

Demy at 16s.6d./ream; 9s. for corrections; and 3s. for 'printing and publishing' (AL, p. 164). *ESTC* t108049: L, 11777.b.80.
Drama. Agency–Murray alone.

1773

57. [Bannerman, Patrick, 1715–1790.]
Letters containing a plan of education for rural academies. London, printed for J. Murray, 1773. [4],iv,130p., 12mo. Price: 1s.7d.
ESTC n034244: PPL, Ia Lett 728.D.
Education. Murray alone.

58. Brown, John, 1715–1766.
A dissertation on the rise, union, and power, the progressions, separations, and corruptions, of poetry and music. To which is prefixed, the cure of Saul. A sacred ode. Written by Dr. Brown. The second edition. London, printed for J. Murray, 1773.
iv,[5]–19,[20–22],[xxiii]–xxiv,25–248p. [p. 248 misnum. 244], 4to, Price: 8s. in boards.
The contents, collation, and press figures match the 1763 first edition, of which 1000 copies were printed by Wm Bowyer for L. Davis and C. Reymers. Murray printed a new title page (Donald D. Eddy, *A Bibliography of John Brown*, #77.
ESTC n64328: TxU Ak.B813.763db.
Literary Criticism. Murray alone.

59. Duncan, Andrew, 1744–1828.
Elements of therapeutics: or, first principles of the practice of physic. By Andrew Duncan, M.D. The second edition, in two volumes. ... London, published by J. Murray, 1773.
Vol. 1: xvi,[2],192p.; vol. 2: [4],225p., 8vo. Price: 4s. in boards.
Another issue published the same year under the imprint 'Edinburgh, W. Drummond'.
ESTC n001406: MBCo, Alpha Green Book 6856, 6852.
Medicine. Murray alone.

60. Duncan, Andrew, 1744–1828, editor.
Medical and philosophical commentaries. By a society in Edinburgh. Volume First ... London, printed for J. Murray; Kincaid & Creech, and W. Drummond, Edinburgh; and T. Ewing, Dublin, 1773.
iv,[5]–458p., 8vo. Pp.113–128 misprinted 1–16.

With an index. Price: 1s.6d. each part, or 6s. a vol.

Issued in four parts with separate title pages. 1000 copies printed by Balfour and Smellie at Edinburgh on paper Murray shipped from London. Each part cost Murray £7.7s. (7¼ sheets at £1/sheet). Murray lost the publication to Charles Dilly 1780–82, at which time the work began to be issued annually. Some volumes (as well as individual parts) went into subsequent editions, as listed below. Vols. 7–10, dated 1780, 1783, 1785 and 1786 respectively, are entitled *Medical commentaries*. Charles Elliot published a second series of the *Commentaries*, 1787–95.

Pts 1–4 The second edition; same imprint and pp. (misnumbering corrected), 1774.

Pts 2–4: The second edition, corrected; same imprint, 1784.

Pt 1–3: The third edition, corrected; same imprint, 1780.

Sets consulted at Eu, L, Roy. Col. of Phys. Edin.

Medicine. Murray–with agency.

61. The Edinburgh Magazine and Review. Volume I. Edinburgh, Printed for W. Creech, successor to Mr Kincaid, and W. Smellie, printer; and sold by all the booksellers in Scotland; by J. Murray, London; and by T. Ewing, Dublin, 1773.

392p., plates. 8vo. Price: 1s. per monthly part. Edited by Gilbert Stuart and Wm Smellie, who printed it. Six parts (Nov. 1773–May 1774). However, some copies begin with an Oct. issue (Gu); others have two initial Nov. issues (L, E); still others begin with a Nov. followed by two Dec. issues (Eu).

Primary location: E, R.B. 1535.

Miscellaneous. Agency–Edinburgh.

*62. Fergusson, Robert, 1750–1774.

Poems by Robert Fergusson. Edinburgh, printed by Walter & Thomas Ruddiman, 1773.

[2],iii,[1],132p., 12mo. Price: 2s.6d.

Monthly Review 51 (Dec. 1774), 483: 'Edinburgh printed, sold by Murray in London'. *Critical Review* 39 (Feb. 1775), 160–61, 'Murray'. In April 1775 Murray received 89 copies from Wm Drummond, the Edinburgh bookseller, (68 in sheets; 17 in boards; and 4 bound) at 1s.6d. each, plus 2s.10d. for the boarding and 2s.8d. for the binding: total £6.19s. (DBII, p. 218).

ESTC t075316: L, C.28.c.4.

Poetry. Agency–Edinburgh.

63. [Galliard, Edward.]

Considerations on the use and abuse of antimonial medicines in fevers, and other disorders; . . . Read in a society of physicians, and published by order of the president and council. London, printed for John Murray, 1773.

[4],iii,[1],48p., 8vo. Price: 1s.

See Galliard's account for evidence of authorship (AL, p. 183).

ESTC n014962: DNLM, 18th c.coll.

Medicine. Murray alone.

64. The second edition.

ESTC t148921: GOT, 80Phil.VI,4920(5).

Medicine. Murray alone.

65. The third edition.

ESTC t165238: Dt, FF.m.15 no.2.

Medicine. Murray alone.

66. [Hilton, William.]

Happiness: characteristic poem. [Newcastle], Printed by Isaac Thompson, Esq. And sold for the author, by J. Murray, London; and D. Akenhead, in Newcastle upon Tyne, 1773.

31,[1]p., 4to. Price: 1s.

Murray returned 91 copies to Hilton at Newcastle in July 1774 (AL, p. 153).

ESTC t097835: L, 11633.bb.52(1).

Another issue: 'Happiness: a characteristic poem'.

ESTC t166688: C, Syn.7.77.37.12.

Poetry. Agency–Provincial.

67. A letter to Sir Richard Hotham, Knight, in answer to his Reflections upon East India shipping. London, printed for J. Murray, 1773.

[2],58p., 8vo. Price: 1s.

Letter signed: Huron, but possibly by Sir Robert Fletcher (see To Fletcher, 23 Feb. 1774)

ESTC t187872: L, IOL T12300(2).

Politics. Murray alone.

68. The second edition.

ESTC n019920: CSmH, 216050.

Politics. Murray alone.

69. Mair, John, 1702 or 3–1769.

The tyro's dictionary, Latin and English.

Comprehending the more usual primitives of the Latin tongue, digested alphabetically, . . . The third edition. By John Mair, A.M. Edinburgh, printed for A. Kincaid & W. Creech and J. Bell. Sold, in London, by W. Johnston, S. Crowder, R. Baldwin, E. & C. Dilly, T. Cadell, and J. Murray, 1773.
vii,[1],444p., 8vo.
ESTC n013390: CaBVaU, PA2365.E5M35 1773.
Language. Agency–Edinburgh.

70. Millar, John, 1735–1801.
Observations concerning the distinction of ranks in society. . . . By John Millar, . . . The second edition, greatly enlarged. London, printed for J. Murray, 1773.
[4],xxii,312p., 8vo. Price: 5s.
750 copies printed by W. and J. Richardson, with whom Murray shared the copyright (AL, p.39).
ESTC t113111: L, 521.g.7.
History. Murray alone.

71. Parkinson, Sydney, 1745?–1771.
A journal of a voyage to the South Seas, in his Majesty's ship, the Endeavour. Faithfully transcribed from the papers of the late Sydney Parkinson, . . . Embellished with views and designs, . . . London, printed for Stanfield Parkinson, the editor: and sold by Messrs. Richardson and Urquhart; Evans; Hooper; Murray; Leacroft; and Riley, 1773.
xxiii,[1],212,[2]p., plates, 4to. With a final errata leaf. Price: 1 gn. in boards.
Entered in the Stationers' Company Register, 10 June 1773, 'Sydney Parkinson, The Whole'. The editor's preface signed: Stanfield Parkinson; in fact by William Kenrick. This work was reissued in 1777 with the addition of 'Explanatory remarks on the preface to Sydney Parkinson's journal . . . By John Fothergill' (item 162).
ESTC t147793: L, L.R.294.c.3.
Travel–Topography. Agency–London.

72. Whitaker, John, 1735–1808.
The genuine history of the Britons asserted against Mr. Macpherson. The second edition, corrected. By the Rev. Mr. Whitaker, . . . London, printed for J. Murray, 1773.
[4],313,[1]p., 8vo. Price: 4s.6d. in boards.
500 copies printed by Wm Bowyer and delivered 7 Jan. 1773 (DBII, p. 209; Maslen, 4972). To this edition are added Macpherson's reply

and two observations upon it originally printed separately and given to the purchasers of the first edition of 1772. Stock: 259 (W).
ESTC t082463: L, 9510.dd.13.
History. Murray alone.

73. Whitaker, John, 1735–1808.
The history of Manchester. In four books. By the Rev. Mr. Whitaker. The second edition corrected. London, printed for J. Murray, 1773.
Vol. 1: xvi,385p.; vol. 2: [ii],428p., ill., 8vo. Price: 10s.6d. in boards.
A new edition of the 1771 one-vol. quarto edition comprising the Roman and Romano-British period. No more published. Wm Bowyer printed 1000 copies, delivered 8 March 1773 (DB2, p. 124, 209; Maslen, 4981). Stock: 2 (H); 361 (W).
ESTC t139691: L, 578.c.4,5.
History. Murray alone.

*74. Whitaker, John, 1735–1808.
The principal corrections made in the History of Manchester, book the first, on republishing it in octavo. [London], sold by White, Lowndes, Dodsley, Payne, Baker and Leigh, Evans; Davis, Holbourne, and Newton; Clarke, and Harrop, Manchester, 1773.
[4],186p., ill., 4to., Price: 3s.
Vol.1 was published by Dodsley et al. in 1771. This supplement, printed for those who had purchased the original editon, contains some additional minor corrections not found in the octavo second editon (above), 'as they did not occur to the author before that edition was printed off' (p. [2]).
ESTC t099382: L, G.3244(1).
History. Agency–London.

1774
75. Catullus, Gaius Valerius.
Catulli Tibulli Propertii opera. Londini, typis J. Brindley, sumptibus J. Murray, 1774.
Vol. 1: [3],132p.; vol. 2: 120p., 12mo. Price: 3s.
First published by Brindley in 1749, this new edition was edited by Edward Harwood. See item 1062 below. Stock: 500 (H).
ESTC t101092: L, 1485.aaa.18.
Poetry. Murray alone.

76. Duncan, Andrew, 1744–1828, editor.
Medical and philosophical commentaries. By a

Society of Physicians in Edinburgh. Volume second. London, printed for J. Murray, W. Creech, successor to Mr Kincaid, and W. Drummond, Edinburgh; and T. Ewing, Dublin, 1774.
468p., 8vo. Price: 1s.6d. each number, or 6s. per vol.
Issued in four parts, with separate title pages. 1000 copies printed by Balfour and Smellie at Edinburgh. Each part cost Murray £7.7s. (7¼ sheets at £1/sheet).
Pt 1: The second edition, corrected, same imprint, 1774; another edition, London, printed for J. Murray, 1784.
Pt 2: The second edition, corrected, same imprint, 1774; third edition corrected. Printed for J. Murray, 1786.
Pts 3–4: The second edition, London, printed for J. Murray; W. Creech, and W. Drummond, Edinburgh; and T. Ewing, Dublin, 1775.
Sets consulted at Eu, L, Roy. Col. of Phys. Edin.
Medicine. Murray–with Agency.

77. The Edinburgh Magazine and Review. Volume II. Edinburgh, Printed for W. Creech, successor to Mr Kincaid, C. Elliot, and W. Smellie, printer; by J. Murray, London; and by T. Ewing, Dublin, 1774.
[ii],395–786,[6]p., plates. 8vo. Price: 1s. per monthly part.
Six parts (June-Dec.). Edited by Gilbert Stuart and Wm Smellie, who printed it.
Primary location: E, R.B. 1535.
Miscellaneous. Agency–Edinburgh.

78. Fordyce, Sir William, 1724–1792.
A new inquiry into the causes, symptoms, and cure, of putrid and inflammatory fevers; with an appendix on the hectic fever, and on the ulcerated and malignant sore throat. By William Fordyce, . . . The second edition. London, printed for T. Cadell; J. Murray; and W. Davenhill, 1774.
xvi,228p., 8vo. Price: 3s.
First edition entered in Stationers' Company Register, 5 Feb. 1773, 'The Author, The Whole'.
ESTC t069560: L, 1485.p.17.
Medicine. London co-publishing.

***79. [Goldsmith, Oliver, 1728–1774.]
The vicar of Wakefield: a tale. Supposed to be written by himself. To which is added: The

deserted village: a poem. By Dr. Goldsmith. . . . London, printed for J. Murray, in the Strand, 1774.
Vol. 1: [iv],111p.; vol. 2: 124p., 12mo.
Possibly a Dublin piracy. There is no record of Murray advertising or selling this edition; however in his stock (W) are listed 93 copies of a 2–vol. 12mo edn. Apparently this 1774 edition is the earliest to include *The deserted village* with the text of *The Vicar of Wakefield*. See Plate 20.
ESTC t181364: O. Vet.A5f.1904.
Another issue: vol. 1 dated 1775, vol. 2, 1774.
ESTC t177074: C, S727.d.77.28/1,2.
Fiction. Murray alone.

80. Hunter, William, 1718–1783.
Anatomia uteri humani gravidi tabulis illustrata, auctore Gulielmo Hunter, . . . The anatomy of the human gravid uterus exhibited in figures, by William Hunter . . . Birmingham, by John Baskerville, 1774. Sold in London by S. Baker and G. Leigh; T. Cadell; D. Wilson and G. Nicol; and J. Murray, 1774.
[42]p., 34 plates, 10. Price: 6 gns.
Published in Dec. 1774. Murray bought copies in cash from the author at £5.7s. in boards and sold them wholesale at £5.18s. Parallel; Gaskell, *Baskerville*, 56). Some plates had a later engraved statement: Pub: Nov. 15. 1774, by Dr. Hunter.
ESTC t137584: L, 3 Tab.9.
Medicine. Agency–London.

81. Lyttelton, George Lyttelton, Baron, 1709–1773.
Dialogues of the dead. The fifth edition, corrected. London, printed for J. Murray (successor to Mr. Sandby), 1774.
xv,[1],406p., 8vo.
This is item 2 above with a cancel title page, and to date a unique copy.
ESTC n066455: CSmH, 342446.
Philosophy. Murray alone.

82. [Mercer, Thomas, b. 1709.]
Poems. By the author of The sentimental sailor. Edinburgh, printed for the author. Sold by W. Creech, Edinburgh; and by E. & C. Dilly, and J. Murray, London, 1774.
viii,[2],115,[1]p., 4to. Price: 3s.6d.
ESTC t080575: L, 1501/32(2).
Another issue: London, printed for the author.

Sold by E. & C. Dilly, and J. Murray, London; and by W. Creech, Edinburgh, 1774.
ESTC t054022: L, 11633.i.7.
Poetry. Agency–Edinburgh.

83. Murray, John 1737–1793.
Catalogue of several thousand volumes: the whole making a large assortment of valuable books, in most languages, arts, and sciences, in very good condition; some of them in elegant bindings . . . which will be sold very cheap, the lowest prices marked in the catalogue, and to continue daily on sale . . . by John Murray, opposite St. Dunstan's Church, No. 32, Fleetstreet London, where the utmost value is given for any library or parcel of books. Catalogues to be had at the place of sale; of Mr. Elmsly; Mess. Richardson and Urquhart; Mess. T. and J. Merrill, at Cambridge; J. Bell and W. Creech, Edinburgh; and T. Ewing, Dublin. [London, 1774].
81p., 8vo.
Primary location: Murray Archive.
Miscellaneous. Murray–with Agency.

*84. Pharmacopoeia Collegii Regii medicorum Edinburgensis. Edinburgh, apud G. Drummond et J. Bell, 1774.
xviii,[2],184,[16]p., 8vo. Price: 5s. bound.
This is the sixth edn. of the Edinburgh Pharmacopoeia. The Edinburgh Magazine and Review (ii. 780) lists Murray as a publisher with Bell, who had reneged on his promise to include Murray in the title page (JM to John Bell, 31 March 1775). Murray obtained 350 copies (at 2s.3d. each) from the Edinburgh bookseller Wm Drummond in Sept. 1774 (AL, p. 159), which he sold wholesale for £1.10s.—a 3d. profit per book.
ESTC t136796: L, 44.f.24.
Medicine. Edinburgh co-publishing.

85. Perry, William, lecturer in the Academy at Kelso.
The man of business, and gentleman's assistant: containing a treatise of practical arithmetic, . . . book-keeping by single and double entry, the former upon an entire new plan, . . . Together with an essay on English grammar. Adapted to the use of gentlemen, merchants, traders, and schools, By W. Perry, . . . Edinburgh, printed for the author, by David Willison: and sold by J.

Murray, London; J. Bell, Edinburgh; D. Baxter, Glasgow; T. Slack and W. Charnley, Newcastle; A. Graham, Alnwick; J. Richardson, Berwick; and G. Elliot, Kelso, 1774.
xiv,[2],184,12,18,70,27,[24],332–371,9,7,[2],8,"8" [=16],59,[1]p., 5 plates, 8vo. With a list of subscribers. Price: 7s. bound.
The bookkeeping examples are separately paginated, sometimes in parallel. Reference: Alston iii. 315.
ESTC t087434: L, 1029.i.5.
Economics. Agency-Provincial.

86. [Portal, Abraham, fl. 1758–1796.]
Nuptial elegies. London, printed for G. Kearsly, and J. Murray, 1774.
viii,31,[1]p., 4to. Price: 2s.
See title page illustrated on Plate 38.
ESTC t092952: L, 163.l.51.
Poetry. London co-publishing.

87. Richardson, William, 1743–1814.
A philosophical analysis and illustration of some of Shakespeare's remarkable characters. Edinburgh, printed for W. Creech; and J. Murray, London, 1774.
[4],224p., 8vo. Price: 2s.6d.
Printed by Balfour & Smellie, Edinburgh for £9.1s.4d. (14¼ sheets at 12s.8d./sheet). Entered in the Stationers' Company Register, 11 April 1774, 'John Murray. The Whole'.
ESTC t118923: L, 1607/1802.
Another issue: London, printed for J. Murray; and W. Creech, at Edinburgh, 1774.
ESTC t139828: L, 642.b.31.
Literary criticism. Edinburgh co-publishing.

88. The second edition, corrected.
London, printed for J. Murray; and W. Creech, at Edinburgh, 1774.
[4],203,[1]p., 8vo.
'Young [Andrew] Strahan' printed 750 copies (To Wm Creech, 13 Aug. 1774).
ESTC t136685: L, G.18558(1).
Literary Criticism. Edinburgh co-publishing.

89. Smollett, Tobias George, 1721–1771.
Independence: an ode. By the late T. Smollet, M.D. London, printed for J. Murray, 1774.
18,[2]p., 4to. With a half-title and a final advertisement leaf. Price: 6d.
The Foulis brothers published a Glasgow

edition in 1773. This edition includes a transcription of the Latin inscription by John Armstrong on Smollett's monument near Leghorn but excludes the 'Observations' on lyric poetry in the Foulis' edition probably written by Wm Richardson. Stock: 44 (H). Entered in the Stationers' Company Register but not found.
ESTC t004600: L, 11630.f.59.
Poetry. Murray alone.

***90. [Sterne, Laurence, 1713–1768.]
The life and opinions of Tristram Shandy, gentleman. In three volumes. London, printed for J. Murray, in the Strand, 1774.
Vol. 1: 204p.; vol. 2: 227p.; vol. 3: [2],286p., plates, port., 12mo. With half-titles.
Possibly a Dublin piracy. There is no record of Murray advertising or selling this edition.
ESTC t014818: L, 012611.e.19.
Fiction. Murray alone.

***91. [Sterne, Laurence, 1713–1768.]
A sentimental journey through France and Italy. By Mr. Yorick in two volumes. The sixth edition. London, printed for J. Murray, in the Strand, 1774.
240p (continuous pagination), plate, 12mo.
Possibly a Dublin piracy. There is no record of Murray advertising or selling this edition.
ESTC t207321: C, Oates.282.
Fiction. Murray alone.

92. [Stuart, Gilbert, 1743–1786.]
Considerations on the management of George Heriot's hospital. Dedicated to the most impudent man alive. Edinburgh, printed for C. Elliot; and Cadell, Dodsley, and Murray, London, [1774].
20p., 4to. Price: 1s.
Dedication signed: Lucius Junius Brutus. Gilbert Laurie, the Lord Provost of Edinburgh is the 'most impudent man alive.' First published in 1773 as *An address to the citizens of Edinburgh*.
ESTC t009483: L, 1303.k.17(1).
Politics. Edinburgh co-publishing.

93. Voltaire, Francois Marie Arouet de, 1694–1778.
Le taureau blanc: or, the white bull. From the French. Translated from the Syriac, by M. de Voltaire. London, printed for J. Murray, 1774. 75,[1]p., 8vo. Price: 1s.6d.
The translation is attributed to Jeremy Bentham. Another English edition also was published in 1774, London, printed for J. Bew.
ESTC n021547: ICU, PQ2083.T21.
Fiction. Murray alone.

94. The second edition.
ESTC t068094: L, T.198(8).
Fiction. Murray alone.

1775

95. Bell, W., A.B.
A new compendious grammar of the Greek tongue: wherein the elements of the language are plainly and briefly comprized in English, for the use of schools and private gentlemen, whether they have been taught Latin or not. By W. Bell, A.B. London, printed for the author; sold by J. Murray; and G. Burnet, 1775. iv,102p., 12mo. With an errata slip pasted to the blank leaf after p. 102. Price: 2s.
Published 18 Jan. 1776.
ESTC t099656: L, 121.e.2.
Language. Agency–London.

*96. Borthwick, George, Surgeon of the 14th Regiment of Dragoons.
A treatise upon the extraction of the crystalline lens. By George Borthwick, . . . Edinburgh, printed for Charles Elliot, 1775.
viii,30p., 8vo. Price: 1s.
Monthly Review 56 (March 1777), 229: 'Edinburgh. 1775. Sold by Murray in London'.
ESTC t026210: L, 7306.c.1(1).
Medicine. Agency–Edinburgh.

97. Boutcher, William, Nursery-man, at Comely-Garden, Edinburgh.
A treatise on forest-trees: containing not only the best methods of their culture hitherto practised, but . . . new and useful discoveries, . . . as also, plain directions for removing . . . forest-trees, . . . and, . . . for transplanting hedges . . . to which are added, directions for the disposition, planting, and culture of hedges, . . . By William Boutcher, . . . Edinburgh, printed by R. Fleming, and sold by the author, by J. Murray, London, and the other booksellers in Great Britain, 1775.

4,xlviii,259,[5]p., 4to. With a list of subscribers and a postscript; additional title page, engraved. Price: 15*s*. in boards.
Published Oct. 1775.
ESTC t101306: L, 33.e.18.
Agriculture. Agency-Edinburgh.

98. Buc'hoz, Pierre-Joseph, 1731–1807.
The toilet of Flora; or, a collection of the most simple and approved methods of preparing baths, essences, pomatums, . . . with receipts for cosmetics of every kind, . . . A new edition improved. London, printed for J. Murray, and W. Nicoll, 1775.
[16],272p., 12mo. Price: 3*s*. bound.
A translation, with alterations, of *La toilette de Flore*.
ESTC t027164: L, 1037.e.46.
Medicine. London co-publishing.

99. Clark, Samuel, teacher of mathematics.
Considerations upon lottery schemes in general; containing a minute investigation of the real and eventual profits arising to lottery offices, . . . By Samuel Clark. London, printed for the author; and sold by J. Murray; T. Axtell; G. Laidler and by the author, at his house, 1775.
[2],iii,[1],54p., 8vo.
ESTC t103145: L, 104.c.63.
Economics. Agency–London.

100. Craig, William, 1709–1783.
Twenty discourses on various subjects. By William Craig, . . . In three volumes. . . . London, printed for J. Murray, 1775.
Vol. 1: vii,214,[2]p.; vol. 2: vii,210,[6]p.; vol. 3: viii,271,[1]p., 8vo. With half-titles and advertisements in all volumes. Price: 9*s*. bound.
Published 4 Mar. 1775. Stock: 18 (W). Murray owned a half share (BB p. 6).
ESTC t135523: L, 694.b.9–11.
Religion. Murray alone.

**101. Curry, John, d. 1780.
An historical and critical review of the civil wars in Ireland, from the reign of Queen Elizabeth, to the Settlement under King William. With the state of the Irish Catholics, Dublin, 1775.
2v., 8vo. Price: 13*s*.
No copy located: *Monthly Review* 55 (Dec. 1776), 444–53: 'Dublin printed, and sold by Murray in London, 1775.' A one vol. quarto edition also

was published in 1775: Dublin, printed and sold by J. Hoey, and T. T. Faulkner; G. Burnet; and J. Morris (*ESTC* t064962). Murray took 50 copies of the Dublin edition and sold 40 at 10*s*. each (To James Hoey, 13 March 1777; see Curry 1786, item 515).
History. Provincial co-publishing.

102. Duncan, Andrew, 1744–1828, editor.
Medical and philosophical commentaries. By a Society of Physicians in Edinburgh. Volume third. London, printed for J. Murray, W. Creech, and W. Drummond, Edinburgh; and T. Ewing, Dublin, 1775–6.
468p., 8vo. Price: 1*s*.6*d*. each number, or 6*s*. per vol.
Issued in four parts, with separate title pages. Pt. 4 dated 1776. 1500 copies printed by Balfour and Smellie at Edinburgh on paper Murray shipped from London. Each part cost on average £8.17*s*. (7¼ sheets at £1.4*s*./sheet). Pt 1 entered in the Stationers' Company Register, 1 Feb. 1775, 'J. Murray. The Whole' (see title page illustrated on Plate 33).
Pts. 1–3: second edition corrected. London, printed for J. Murray, 1784.
Pt. 4: a new edition, London, printed for J. Murray, 1786.
Sets consulted at Eu, L, Roy. Col. of Phys. Edin.
Medicine. Murray–with Agency.

103. The Edinburgh Magazine and Review. . . . Edinburgh, printed for W. Creech, successor to Mr Kincaid, C. Elliot, and W. Smellie, printer; by J. Murray, London; and by T. Ewing, Dublin, 1775.
Vol 3: 392p.; vol 4: 393–784p. 8vo. Price: 1*s*. per monthly part.
Vol. 3, Jan.-July; vol 4, Aug.-Feb. 1776. Edited by Gilbert Stuart and Wm Smellie, who printed it.
Primary location: E, R.B. 1535.
Miscellaneous. Agency–Edinburgh.

104. Hamilton, Alexander, 1739–1802.
Elements of the practice of midwifery. By Alexander Hamilton . . . London, printed for J. Murray, 1775.
[4],vii,[1],xii,293,[1],11,[1]p., 8vo. Price: 5*s*.
Entered in the Stationers' Company Register, 24 Nov. 1776, 'J. Murray. The Whole'.

ESTC t032603: L, 1177.h.13(1).
Medicine. Murray alone.

*105. Ode to the British empire. London, printed for T. Evans, 1775.
[3],6–15,[1]p., 4to. Price: 1s.
250 copies printed by Wm Richardson 'for Mr. Murray'. Printing cost £1.8s. Murray also arranged for the printing (by Richardson) of an octavo Dublin edition (*ESTC* n010508) of 250 copies for Thomas Ewing. Ewing, like Evans, was charged all expenses, including 3s. for a copy 'elegant' bound delivered to Edmund Burke (AL, p. 248 and loose sheet; DB2, pp. 226, 229, 263).
ESTC t099696: L, 164.n.34.
Politics. Agency–London.

106. Perry, William, lecturer in the Academy at Edinburgh.
The royal standard English dictionary: in which the words are not only rationally divided into syllables, accurately accented, their part of speech properly distinguished, and their various significations arranged in one line; but likewise by a key to this work, . . . By W. Perry, . . . Edinburgh, printed for the author, by David Willison; and sold by J. Wilkie, T. Evans, and J. Murray, London; J. Bell, W. Creech, J. Dickson, C. Elliot, R. Jamieson, Edinburgh; Charnley, Newcastle; Etherington, York; Norton, Bristol; Frederick, Bath; and by the author, 1775.
liv,427,[5]p., oblong 12mo. With five final pages of errata and advertisements. Price: 3s. bound. Entered in the Stationers' Company Register, 30 Nov. 1775, 'Wm Perry. The Whole'. The final advertisement describes Perry's academy at Taylors' Hall, Edinburgh.
ESTC t087431: L, 1212.b.1.
Language. Agency–Edinburgh.

107. Portal, Abraham, fl. 1758–1796.
Nuptial elegies: the third edition. To which is added, a second edition of War, an ode. By the same author. London, printed for G. Kearsly, and J. Murray, 1775.
viii,47,[1]p., 4to. Price: 2s.
ESTC n011105: OCU, PR1215.A62 v.19 RB.
Poetry. London co-publishing.

108. Richardson, William, 1743–1814.
A philosophical analysis and illustration of some of Shakespeare's remarkable characters. By Wm. Richardson, . . . The second edition, corrected. London, printed for J. Murray; and W. Creech, at Edinburgh, 1775.
[4],203,[1]p., 8vo. Price: 2s.6d. boards.
ESTC n020611: PU, Furness C81.3.R39P.2.
Literary criticism. Edinburgh co-publishing.

109. Richardson, William, 1743–1814.
Poems, chiefly rural. By Mr. Richardson, . . . The third edition, corrected. London, printed for J. Murray, 1775.
[8],155,[5]p., 8vo. With a half-title and two final advertisement leaves. Price: 2s.6d. boards.
1000 copies printed (both issues). Murray and Joseph Johnson were equal partners. Johnson's half share of expenses broke down as follows: for printing eleven sheets at 22s., £6.1s.; for paper (eleven reams thick writing at £1), £11; half copy money to Foulis (the Glasgow printer who first issued the work) was three guineas (DB2, p. 179 and AL, p. 257; Gaskell, *Foulis*, 588).
ESTC n021047: MnU, Y824.R395 OP.
Another issue: London, printed for J. Johnson and J. Murray, 1775.
ESTC t042605: L, 11642.bb.52.
Poetry. London co-publishing.

110. Simson, Robert, 1687–1768.
Elements of the conic sections, by the late Dr Robert Simson, . . . The first three books, translated from the Latin original. . . . Edinburgh, printed for Charles Elliot. Sold, in London, by T. Cadell, and J. Murray, 1775.
[6],255,[1]p., plates, 8vo. Price: 4s.6d.
Translated by John Hill. Entered in the Stationers' Company Register, 4 Mar. 1775, 'Charles Elliot. The Whole'.
ESTC t113192: L, 529.e.6.
Science. Agency–Edinburgh.

111. Tassie, James, 1735–1799.
A catalogue, of impressions in sulphur, of antique and modern gems from which pastes are made and sold, by J. Tassie . . . London, printed for J. Murray, 1775.
vii,[1],99,[1]p., 8vo. The title page is engraved. With a half-title. Price: 1s.
ESTC t121009: L, 1608/5058.
2000 copies printed by Wm Bowyer. Printing cost £16.9s. (7 sheets at 47s. sheet); paper cost

£28 (28 reams thin writing Demy); plus 3 gns for 'corrections and close reading proof shts'. 432 were stitched in 'French marble' for £3.12s. or 2d. each. (DB2, p. 179; AL, p. 211, 295; Maslen, 5075).
Arts. Murray alone.

112. Thomson, John, 1733?–1807.
Tables of interest, at 4, 4½, and 5 per cent. The usual rates at which money is lent, from 1 to 365 days, . . . Also, tables of exchange and commission, . . . The second edition, with considerable additions. By John Thomson, . . . London, printed for T. Cadell, and J. Murray; and W. Creech, Edinburgh, 1775.
[8],400p., 12mo. Price: 3s.6d.
2000 copies printed. Murray took 750 copies at 1s.6d. total: £56.5s. (AL, 197) and dealt directly with the author (AL, p. 272). A note in 1775 advertisement for this work states that 'No copy of this Book is warranted genuine or correct, but what is signd by the Author'.
ESTC t172979: E, NG.1201.c.2(2).
Economics. Edinburgh co-publishing.

113. Whitaker, John, 1735–1808.
The history of Manchester. In four books. Volume two. Book the Second. By John Whitaker . . . London, printed for Joseph Johnson. And J. Murray, 1775.
594,[24],[1]p., plates, maps, 4to. With a half-title and adverts. Price: 1 gn.
Wm Boyer printed 500 copies, delivered on 14 Sept. 1774 (DB2, p. 209; Maslen, 5044). Murray and Johnson paid Whitaker £130 for the copyright (AL, p. 252). No more published. Vol. 1 was published by Dodsley *et al.* in 1771. Stock: 83 (W).
ESTC t145509: L, 189.a.23–24.
History. London co-publishing.

1776

*114. Account of the martyrs at Smyrna and Lyons, in the second century. With explanatory notes. Edinburgh, printed by A. Murray and J. Cochran, 1776.
vi,210p., 8vo.
Monthly Review 57 (Oct. 1777), 334: 'Sold by Murray in London.' A translation of *Ecclesiae Smyrnensis de martyrio S. Polycarpi epistola circularis* and of *Ecclesiarum Viennensis et Lugdunensis epistola de martyrio S. Pothini episcopi et aliorum pluri-*

morum, edited by Sir David Dalrymple, Lord Hailes.
ESTC t028263: L,1372.a.1(1).
Religion. Agency–Edinburgh.

115. [Arnot, Hugo, 1749–1786.]
An essay on nothing. A discourse delivered in a society. London, printed for J. Murray; and C. Elliot, Edinburgh, 1776.
[2],vi,[1],5–100,[2]p., 8vo (in fours). With a final advertisement leaf. Price: 1s.6d.
ESTC t091222: L, 112.a.18.
Philosophy. Edinburgh co-publishing.

116. The second edition.
vii, 104p., 8vo. Price: 1s.6d.
ESTC ID: n009343: WU-M, WZ260.A764E.
Philosophy. Edinburgh co-publishing.

117. Another edition, completely reset, with Arnot's name on the title page.
viii,5–100p., 8vo (in fours). Price: 1s.6d.
ESTC n056128: CSmH, 333162.
Philosophy. Edinburgh co-publishing.

*118. [Arnot, Hugo, 1749–1786.]
The XLV. chapter of the prophecies of Thomas the Rhymer, in verse; with notes and illustrations. Dedicated to Doctor Silverspoon, preacher of sedition in America. Edinburgh, printed for C. Elliot, 1776.
19,[1]p., 4to. Price: 6d.
Dr Silverspoon is John Witherspoon. Reference: Adams 76–9.1. *Monthly Review* 54 (June 1776), 490: 'Edinburgh printed, and sold by Murray in London'.
ESTC t006507: L, 11630.b.8(15)
Politics. Agency-Edinburgh.

119. Clarke, Henry, 1743–1818.
Practical perspective. Being a course of lessons, exhibiting easy and concise rules for drawing justly all sorts of objects. . . . By H. Clarke. In two volumes. vol. 1. London, printed for the author, and sold by Mr. Nourse, and Mr. Murray, 1776.
xv,[6],18–113,[7]p., plates, 8vo. Price: 4s.4d.
No more published (but see Clarke 1794, item 982). The last 3 leaves contain advertisements for H. Clarke's publications, and the Commercial and mathematical school, in Salford, Manchester.

ESTC t101235: L, 60.c.21.
Education. Agency–London.

120. Cullen, William, 1710–1790.
A letter to Lord Cathcart, President of the Board of Police in Scotland, concerning the recovery of persons drowned and seemingly dead. By Dr. William Cullen, . . . London, printed for J. Murray, 1776.
[4],45,[3]p., 8vo. With a half-title and a final leaf of advertisements. Price: 1*s*.6*d*.
The 1774 edition: Edinburgh, C. Elliot. Stock: 105 (W).
ESTC t056706: L, 116.l.28.
Medicine. Murray alone.

121. Dalrymple, Sir David, 1726–1792.
Annals of Scotland. From the accession of Malcolm III, surnamed Canmore, to the accession of Robert I. By Sir David Dalrymple. Edinburgh, printed by Balfour & Smellie. For J. Murray, London, 1776.
[8],401,[1]p., 4to. With an errata leaf. Price: 15*s*. 1000 copies printed (Murray took 750). Entered in the Stationers' Company Register, 10 Jan. 1776, 'The Author. The Whole'. A second volume covering the accession of Robert I, to the accession of the House of Stuart, was published by Murray in 1779. Stock: 74 (W).
ESTC t082751: L, qE/00729.
History. Murray alone.

122. Duncan, Andrew, 1744–1828, editor.
Medical and philosophical commentaries. By a Society of Physicians in Edinburgh. Volume fourth. . . . London, printed for J. Murray, W. Creech, and W. Drummond, Edinburgh; and T. Ewing, Dublin, 1776–77.
x,11–484p., 8vo. Price: 1*s*.6*d*. each number, or 6*s*. per vol.
Issued in four parts, with separate title pages. Pts. 2–4 dated 1777. Imprint of Pt. 2: London, J. Murray, W. Creech, C. Elliot, and Drummond, Edinburgh; and T. Ewing, Dublin. Pt. 4: London, J. Murray; W. Creech, C. Elliot and M. Drummond, Edinburgh. 1500 copies printed by Balfour and Smellie at Edinburgh on paper Murray shipped from London. Each part cost on average £9.12*s*. Pt. 2 entered in the Stationers' Company Register, 18 Mar. 1777. Pt. 3 entered 4 June 1777. Pt. 4 entered 29 Aug. 1777: 'J. Murray. The Whole'.

Pt. 1: second edition, London, J. Murray, 1790.
Pt. 2: second edition, J. Murray, 1791.
Sets consulted at Eu, L, Roy. Col. of Phys. Edin.
Medicine. Murray–with Agency.

123. The Edinburgh Magazine and Review.
Volume V. Edinburgh, Printed for W. Creech, successor to Mr Kincaid, C. Elliot, and W. Smellie; sold by J. Murray, London; and by T. Ewing, Dublin, 1776.
392p., 8vo. 1*s*. per monthly part.
Six parts (Mar.-Sept.). Edited by Gilbert Stuart and Wm Smellie, who printed it.
Primary location: E, R.B. 1735.
Miscellaneous. Agency–Edinburgh.

124. Euclid.
The Elements of Euclid, in which the propositions are demonstrated in a new and shorter manner than in former translations, . . . To which are annexed . . . tables . . . By George Douglas, . . . London, printed for J. Murray; and C. Elliot, Edinburgh, 1776.
xii,172,92p., plates, ill., 8vo. Price: 5*s*.6*d*.
Entered in the Stationers' Company Register, 14 Oct. 1776, 'George Douglas. The Whole'.
ESTC n031562: MiU, Buhr QA31.E88s732d73.
Science. Edinburgh co-publishing.

125. [Gordon, Thomas, d. 1750]
An inquiry into the powers of ecclesiastics, on the principles of scripture and reason. London, printed for J. Murray, 1776.
270p., 8vo. Price: 4*s*. boards.
300 copies printed. Printing and paper cost £28.1*s*.; 100 copies sent to Elliot at Edinburgh (AL, p. 311). Stock: 16 (H); 95 (W).
ESTC ID: t102377: L, 4105.cc.6
Religion. Murray alone.

126. Gray, Thomas, 1716–1771.
Poems by Mr. Gray. A new edition. London, printed for J. Murray, and C. Elliot, Edinburgh, 1776.
[2],146p., 2 plates, 8vo. Price: 3*s*.
1000 copies printed at Edinburgh by Murray & Cochrane for £8.8*s*.6*d*. on 20 reams thick post at 21*s*.6*d*./ream (£21.10*s*. total). AL records that Cook engraved two plates for 7 gns after designs by Hamilton (who was paid 5*s*.); however, the plate of 'The Bard' at p. 68 gives Page

as the engraver. AL also records that Johnson received 2 gns. for engraving the title page vignette; however the engraving itself gives Isaac Taylor as the engraver. Gilbert Stuart wrote the 'Life' for 3 gns. (AL, p. 41; see Plates 16 and 17).
ESTC t125811: L, 11633.e.49.
Poetry. Edinburgh co-publishing.

127. Innes, John, 1739–1777.
Eight anatomical tables of the human body; containing the principal parts of the skeletons and muscles represented in the large tables of Albinus; to which are added concise explanations. By John Innes. Edinburgh, printed by Balfour and Smellie; for J. Murray, London; Balfour, Drummond, Elliot and Schaw, 1776.
52p., 8 plates, 4to. Price: 6s.6d.
Another issue published the same year: Edinburgh, C. Elliot, and entered in the Stationers' Company Register, 20 Feb. 1776, 'Elliot. The Whole'.
ESTC t002070: L, T.310(2).
Medicine. Edinburgh co-publishing.

128. Innes, John, 1739–1777.
A short description of the human muscles, chiefly as they appear on dissection. . . . By John Innes. Edinburgh, printed by Balfour and Smellie: for J. Murray, London; Balfour, Drummond, Donaldson, Elliot and Schaw, Edinburgh, 1776.
vii,[1],223,[3]p., 8vo. Price: 3s. in boards.
Entered in the Stationers' Company Register, 10 Jan. 1776, 'J. Murray. The Whole'.
ESTC t048146: L, 1175.c.11(2).
Medicine. Edinburgh co-publishing.

129. Kearney, Michael, 1733–1814.
Lectures concerning history read during the year 1775, in Trinity College, Dublin, by Michael Kearney, . . . London, printed for J. Murray, 1776.
65,[1]p., 4to. With a half-title. Price: 2s.6d.
Stock: 200 (W).
ESTC t122143: L, 304.k.17.
History. Murray alone.

130. Languet, Hurbert
Huberti Langueti, Galli, epistolae ad Philippum Sydneium, equitem anglum. Accurante D. Dalrymple, de Hailes, Esq. Edinburgi ex officina A. Murray et J. Cochran. Veneunt Londini apud J. Murray, 1776.
ix,[1],329,[1]p., 8vo. Price: 6s. in boards.
ESTC t146492: L, 91.c.12.
Edited by Sir David Dalrymple. 250 copies printed. Stock: 7 (H); 166 (W).
History. Agency–Edinburgh.

131. Laurie, John, d. 1791.
Tables of simple and compound interest: calculated to ascertain the amount and present worth of principal sums and annuities; . . . To which are subjoined, a few remarks, in which Dr. Price's observations on reversionary payments, &c. &c. . . . By John Laurie, . . . Edinburgh, printed for the author; and sold by W. Creech, and W. Schaw. And by J. Murray, London, 1776.
viii,235,[1]p., 8vo.
ESTC t147479: L, 1027.l.3.
Economics. Agency–Edinburgh.

132. Le Beau, Charles, 1701–1778.
The history of Constantine the Great. Translated from the French of M. Le Beau. The second edition. London, printed for J. Murray; and J. Bew, 1776.
[3],vi–xxxi,[1],390p., 8vo. Price: 6s.
A translation of the first five books of Le Beau's *Histoire du Bas-empire*.
ESTC t224166. L, RB.23.a.7896.
History. London co-publishing.

133. The nightingale: a collection of ancient and modern songs, Scots and English; none of which are in Ramsay: and a variety of favourite songs and catches, . . . With toasts and sentiments. To which is added, The Edinburgh buck: an epilogue, written by Mr. R. Fergusson. Edinburgh, printed for J. Murray, 1776.
216p., 12mo.
ESTC t178319: O, Harding C 2240.
Poetry. Murray alone.

134. Perry, William, master of the Academy at Edinburgh.
The only sure guide to the English tongue; or, new pronouncing spelling-book. Upon the same plan as The Royal standard dictionary. designed for the use of schools, and private families. To which is added, a comprehensive grammar of the English language. By W. Perry, . . . Edinburgh, printed by Gavin Alston for the

author; and sold by J. Wilkie, T. Evans, and J. Murray, London; A. Donaldson, J. Bell, W. Creech, J. Dickson, C. Elliot, and R. Jamieson, Edinburgh; W. Charnley, Newcastle; C. Etherington, York; Cresswell, Nottingham; Norton, Bristol; Frederick, Bath; and by the author at his academy, 1776.

[12],144p., 12mo. Price: 1s. bound.

Reference: Alston iv. 734. Page [2] 'Entered in Stationers Hall according to Act of Parliament'.

ESTC t087433: L, 1212.h.6(1).

Language. Agency–Edinburgh.

135. Reports of cases concerning the revenue, argued and determined in the Court of Exchequer, from Easter term 1743, to Hilary term 1767. With an appendix, ... By Sir Thomas Parker, ... With two tables; ... London, printed by W. Strahan and M. Woodfall; and sold by W. Flexney, and J. Murray, 1776.

v,[3],283,[13]p., 2o. With a final leaf of errata. Price: 18s.

1000 copies printed. The original contract (dated 26 Feb. 1776) between Parker and Murray and Wm Flexney is in the Murray Archive (in a folder of sale catalogues). Parker paid for the paper and printing and received 10s. on each book sold, the account being settled every month.

ESTC t095680: L, 6128.ff.2.

Economics. Agency–London.

136. Richardson, John, 1741–1811?

A grammar of the Arabick language. In which the rules are illustrated by authorities from the best writers; principally adapted for the service of the Honourable East India Company. By John Richardson, ... London, printed by William Richardson, for J. Murray; and D. Prince, Oxford, 1776.

xii,211,[1]p., 4to. Price: 11s. (1786 advertised at 13s. bound).

Published 18 Jan. 1776.

ESTC t090668: L, 825.h.39.

Language. Provincial co-publishing.

137. [Stock, Joseph, 1740–1813. Bishop of Waterford.]

An account of the life of George Berkeley, D.D. late Bishop of Cloyne in Ireland. With notes, containing strictures upon his works. London, printed for J. Murray, 1776.

[2],iv,85,[1]p., 8vo. Price: 2s.

Wm Richardson printed 250 copies in Aug. 1776—sig. A-E, 5 half sheets at 6s.6d. per ½ sheet; Notes-Postscript in Pica, J to I., and Preface ¼ sheet. 6½ sheets at 8s. a ½ sheet—total: £4.8s.6d. (AL, p. 248 and loose sheet). Murray published a much enlarged second edn in 1784 (item 449).

ESTC t066487: L, 1415.d.9.

Biography. Murray alone.

138. Swieten, Gerard, Freiherr van, 1700–1772.

Commentaries upon Boerhaave's aphorisms concerning the knowledge and cure of diseases. By Baron Van Swieten, ... Translated from the Latin. ... Edinburgh, printed for Charles Elliot. Sold by J. Murray, London, 1776.

18v., 12mo. Price: 3s.6d. per vol. ; 3 gns bound. According to a newspaper advertisement in the Archive, published 16 Nov. 1776 and 'printed on a new letter case on purpose by Dr. Wilson, Glasgow ... '. First published in 18 vols 1744–73 by Horsfield and Longman. Stock: 4 sets (W).

ESTC n028227: NBuU-H, WZ260.S976c 1776.

Medicine. Agency–Edinburgh.

139. Thomson, John, 1733?–1807.

Tables of interest, at three per cent. From 1 to 365 days, in a regular progression of single days: ... By John Thomson, ... Edinburgh, printed for T. Cadell, and J. Murray, London, and William Creech, Edinburgh, 1776.

[2],129,[1]p., 12mo.

Also issued as part of Thomson's *Tables of interest, at* 3, 4, 4½, and 5 per cent. ... 1776 (*ESTC* n055006). Stock: 21 (W).

ESTC t172992: E, NG.1201.c.2(1).

Economics. Edinburgh co-publishing.

140. Thistlethwaite, James, b. 1751.

Edwald and Ellen, an heroic ballad. In two cantos. By Mr. Thistlethwaite. London, printed for J. Murray, 1776.

[4],32, 4to. Price: 1s.6d.

Paper cost £3.7s.6d. for 4½ reams at 15s./ream (AL, p. 318).

ESTC n009080: TxU, PR3729.T7E393.

Poetry. Murray alone.

141. Tucker, Nathaniel, 1750–1807.

The anchoret: a poem. By the author of the

Bermudian. London, printed for and sold by J. Murray, and W. Creech, Edinburgh, 1776.
32p., 4to.
ESTC t009196: L, 11602.gg.25(9).
Poetry. Edinburgh co-publishing.

142. Voltaire, Francois Marie Arouet de, 1694–1778.
Young James or the sage and the atheist. An English story. From the French of M. de Voltaire. London, printed for J. Murray, 1776.
[2],ii,[2],130p., 8vo. Price: 2s.6d.
A translation of *Histoire de Jenni*. Stock: 224 (W).
ESTC t137638: L, 012548.eeee.44.
Fiction. Murray alone.

143. The second edition.
[4],ii,130p., 8vo. Price: 2s.6d.
ESTC t179133: O, Vet.A5e.3196.
Fiction. Murray alone.

1777

144. [Arnot, Hugo, 1749–1786.]
An essay on nothing. A discourse delivered in a society. The third edition. London, printed for J. Murray; and C. Elliot, Edinburgh, 1777.
[2],104p., 8vo. Price: 1s.6d.
ESTC t059697: L, 12314.bb.28.
Philosophy. Edinburgh co-publishing.

145. Black, Joseph, 1728–1799.
Experiments upon magnesia alba, quick-lime, and other alcaline substances; By Joseph Black, M.D. . . . To which is annexed, An essay on the cold produced by evaporating fluids, . . . By William Cullen, M.D. . . . Edinburgh, printed for William Creech; and for J. Murray, and Wallis and Stonehouse, London, 1777.
[2],133,[1]p., ill., 8vo. Price 2s.
A reissue of an edition in the same year with Creech alone in the imprint.
ESTC t007640: L, T.433(1).
Science. Edinburgh co-publishing.

146. Carlyle, Alexander, 1722–1805.
The justice and necessity of the war with our American colonies examined. A sermon, preached at Inveresk, December 12. 1776, . . . By Alexander Carlyle, . . . Edinburgh, printed for J. Murray, London, and J. Dickson, Edinburgh, 1777.
[4],50p., 8vo. Price: 1s.

Reference: Adams 77–24.
ESTC t103681: L, 111.f.12.
Religion. Edinburgh co-publishing.

147. Cartwright, Edmund, 1743–1823.
Armine and Elvira, a legendary tale. In two parts. By Mr. Cartwright. The sixth edition. London, printed for J. Murray, 1777.
40p., 4to. with a half-title. Price: 2s.
Printed by Wm Richardson (AL, p. 248; see Plate 10).
ESTC t133058: L, 1480.bb.22.
Poetry. Murray alone.

148. Chambers, Ephraim, c. 1680–1740.
London, Jan. 1, 1777. Proposals for publishing in weekly numbers, Mr. Chambers's Cyclopaedia; or, universal dictionary of arts and sciences: with the supplement and modern improvements, incorporated in one alphabet. In four volumes. Illustrated with a great number of copper-plates. London, printed for W. Strahan, J. F. and C. Rivington, A. Hamilton, J. Hinton, T. Payne, W. Owen, B. White. D. Collins, T. Caslon, T. Longman, B. Law, T. Becket, C. Rivington, E. and C. Dilly, J. Baldwin, J. Wilkie, W. Nicoll, H. S. Woodfall, J. Robson and Co., J. Knox, W. Domville, T. Cadell, G. Robinson, R. Baldwin, W. Otridge, W. Davis, N. Conant, W. Stuart, J. Murray, J. Bell, W. Fox, S. Hayes, J. Donaldson, E. Johnson, and J. Richardson, 1777.
4p., 8vo.
Chambers's *Cyclopaedia* was published in 89 parts at 6d. per number and issued afterwards in five volumes 1778–1788 (see item 176). A variant issue of the Proposals is dated Dec. 15, 1778 (in the Gough Coll., Bodleian); the imprint begins 'printed for T. Longman.'
ESTC t120909: L, 1609/1132.
Miscellaneous. London syndicate.

149. Clarke, Henry, 1743–1818.
The rationale of circulating numbers, with the investigations of all the rules and peculiar processes used in that part of decimal arithmetic. To which are added, several curious mathematical questions; . . . By H. Clarke. London, printed for the author; and sold by Mr. Murray, 1777.
xiv,[3],16–215,[5]p., plates, 8vo. Price: 5s.
The last five pages contain an advertisement for

the Commercial and Mathematical School, in Salford, Manchester, and 'Emendations'.
ESTC t101233: L, 60.b.26.
Science. Agency–Murray alone.

150. Cullen, William, 1710–1790.
First lines of the practice of physic, for the use of students in the University of Edinburgh. By William Cullen, M.D. Vol. I. Edinburgh, printed for J. Murray, London; and William Creech, Edinburgh, 1777.
viii,417,[1]p., 8vo. Price: 6s.
1000 copies were printed by Balfour & Smellie, costing £24.2s.3d. (23 3/4 sheets at 18s./sheet). Murray paid Cullen £100 for the copyright of the first edn. (AL, loose sheet at p. 204, p. 230).
ESTC n032643: MdBJ–W, RBR C967f 1784.
Medicine. Edinburgh co-publishing.

151. Du Coudray, M. le chevalier, b. 1744.
Anecdotes of the Emperor Joseph II. during his residence in France, . . . Translated from the French of the Chevalier Coudray. London, printed for J. Murray, 1777.
xvi,79,[1]p., 8vo. Price: 1s.6d.
A translation of *Anecdotes intéressantes et historiques de l'illustre voyageur.* Printed by Wm Richardson (AL, p. 248). Entered in the Stationers' Company Register, 18 Sept. 1777, 'J. Murray. The Whole'.
ESTC n030238: MoU, Howey.
Biography. Murray alone.

152. Duncan, Andrew, 1744–1828, editor.
Medical and philosophical commentaries. By a Society of Physicians in Edinburgh. Volume fifth. London, printed for J. Murray, W. Creech, C. Elliot and M. Drummond, Edinburgh, 1777–78.
521p., 8vo. fold. table. Price: 1s.6d. each number, or 6s. per vol.
Issued in four parts, with separate title pages. Pts. 2–4, 1778. Pts. 3–4: London, J. Murray; J. Bell, W. Creech, C. Elliot, and M. Drummond. 1500 copies printed by Balfour and Smellie at Edinburgh on paper shipped from London by Murray. Each part cost on average £9.12s. Pt. 1 entered in the Stationers' Company Register, 18 Dec. 1777, 'J. Murray. The Whole'. 'First Five Vols. entered 17 Dec. 1778, 'J. Murray. By Purchase. The Whole'.
Primary location: Roy. Col. Phys. Edin.
Medicine. Murray–with Agency.

153. Fordyce, Sir, William, 1724–1792.
A new inquiry into the causes, symptoms, and cure, of putrid and inflammatory fevers; with an appendix on the hectic fever, and on the ulcerated and malignant sore throat. By William Fordyce, . . . The third edition. London, printed for T. Cadell; J. Murray; and W. Davenhill, 1777.
xvi,228p., 8vo. Price: 3s.
ESTC n019132: DNLM, W6P3 v.1910.
Medicine. London co-publishing.

154. The fourth edition.
ESTC t045782: L, 7320.c.24(2).
Medicine. London co-publishing.

155. Fordyce, Sir William, 1724–1792.
A review of the venereal disease, and its remedies. By William Fordyce, . . . The fourth edition, with considerable additions, and an appendix. London, printed by T. Spilsbury, for T. Cadell; and sold by J. Murray; and W. Davenhill, 1777.
[8],151,[1]p., 8vo. Price: 4s.
ESTC t123298: L, 1560/779.
Medicine. Agency–London.

156. Gray, Andrew, Minister of Abernethy, d. 1779.
A delineation of the parables of our blessed Saviour: to which is prefixed, a dissertation on parables and allegorical writings in general. By Andrew Gray, . . . London, printed for J. Murray; and J. Dickson, Edinburgh, 1777.
[viii],505,[1]p., 8vo. With an errata. Price: 6s. bound.
Murray had a 1/3 share with Dickson and John Balfour. Printed by Balfour and Smellie at Edinburgh at a cost of £30.19s. (AL, p. 128, loose sheet at p. 204)). Stock: 37 (H).
ESTC t137160: L, 220.g.8.
Another issue: Edinburgh, printed for J. Murray, London, and J. Dickson, Edinburgh, 1777.
ESTC t144204: Lu, Porteus.
Religion. Edinburgh co-publishing.

157. Hunter, William, 1718–1783.
Medical commentaries. Part I. Containing a plain and direct answer to Professor Monro jun. Interspersed with remarks on the structure, functions, and diseases of several parts of the human body. By William Hunter M.D. The second edition. London, printed for S. Baker

and G. Leigh; T. Cadell; D. Wilson and G. Nicoll; and J. Murray, 1777.
vii,[1],103[i.e.113],[1],33,[1]p., plates, 4to. Price: 6s. inboards.
Stock: 9 (H).
ESTC t062862: L, 44.h.8.
Medicine. London co-publishing.

158. [Johnson, Samuel, 1709–1784.]
March 1777. Proposals for printing by subscription, inscribed, by permission, to the Right Honourable the Earl of Eglinton: An analysis of the Scotch Celtic language. By William Shaw, native of one of the Hebrides. The book will be elegantly printed in one volume in quarto. Price half guinea, to be paid at the time of subscribing. The books will be delivered in November 1777, by J. Murray, Fleet-Street, J. Donaldson, Arundel Street, Strand, and Richardson and Urquhart, No. 91 Royal Exchange, London; C. Elliot, Edinburgh, and Dunlop and Wilson, Glasgow, where subscriptions are also received. The 'Proposals' for Shaw's *Analysis* are quoted in Boswell's *Life of Johnson* (Hill-Powell edn.), iii. 107. A copy of the 'Proposals' (1 of 3 known) with Boswell's annotations is at Yale University (Gen. MSS 89). The work itself was published in 1778 as *An analysis of the Galic language*, but Murray's name did not appear in the imprint (*ESTC* t084356).
Language. London co-publishing.

159. M'Mahon, Thomas O'Brien.
The candor and good-nature of Englishmen exemplified, in their deliberate, cautious, and charitable way of characterizing the customs, manners, constitution, and religion of neighbouring nations, ... To which are prefixed, proposals for printing by subscription, Eusebius, or, essays on the principal virtues, vices, and passions. ... By Thomas O Brien Mac Mahon, ... London, sold by Mess. Bew; Murray; Corrall; Riley; Lewis, 1777.
xii,292p., 8vo.
ESTC n003090: C-S, 204.M.
Miscellaneous. London co-publishing.

160. Murray, John, 1737–1793.
A letter to W. Mason, A.M. precentor of York, concerning his edition of Mr. Gray's poems. And the practices of booksellers. By a bookseller. London, printed for J. Murray, 1777.

64p., 8vo. With a half-title. Price: 1s.
Entered in the Stationers' Company Register, 29 May 1777, 'J. Murray. The Whole'. See the Bibliography of Pamphlets Written by Murray for details and Plate 44.
ESTC t004056: L, T.1164(11).
Law. Murray alone.

161. Ogilvie, John, 1732–1813.
Rona, a poem, in seven books, illustrated with a correct map of the Hebrides, and elegant engravings. By John Ogilvie, D.D. London, printed for J. Murray, 1777.
[2],xv,[1],219,[3]p., 7 plates, map, 4to. Each book has a frontispiece engraving and separate half-title. Price: 12s.6d. in boards.
500 copies printed. Entered in the Stationers' Company Register, 21 Dec. 1776, 'John Murray. The Whole', but BB, p. 5 records Murray with a half share. Stock: 19 (W).
ESTC t002707: L, 643.k.6(8).
Poetry. Murray alone.

162. Parkinson, Sydney, 1745?-1771.
A journal of a voyage to the South seas, in His Majesty's ship, the Endeavour. Faithfully transcribed from the papers of the late Sydney Parkinson, draughtsman to Joseph Banks, Esq. on his late expedition, ... round the world. Embellished with views and designs, ... London, printed for Stanfield Parkinson, the editor: and sold by Messrs. Richardson and Urquhart; Evans; Hooper; Murray; Leacroft; and Riley, 1773 [1777?].
xxiii,[1],22,212,[2]p., 27 plates, 4to. With a final errata leaf. Price: 1 gn. boards.
A reissue of the 1773 edition (see above, item 71) with the addition of 'Explanatory remarks on the preface to Sydney Parkinson's journal ... By John Fothergill'. The unsold copies of the 1773 edition were purchased by Fothergill in order to insert his explanation of the dispute between Stanfield Parkinson and publishers of the official account of the voyage of the Endeavour (See M. Holmes, *Captain James Cook. A bibliographical excursion*, pp. 53–5).
ESTC t152098: L, 566.k.13.
Travel–Topography. Agency–London.

163. Perry, Sampson, 1747–1823.
A disquisition of the stone and gravel, and other diseases of the kidneys, bladder, &c. By

S. Perry, . . . The fifth edition. London, printed for T. Becket; J. Murray; T. Evans; J. Southern; and Richardson and Urquhart, 1777.
[4],vi,ix–xv,[1],104,[2]p., 8vo. With a half-title and a final advertisement leaf. Price: 3s.
ESTC n006491: DNLM, 18th c.coll.
A variant issue (*ESTC* n065275) excludes J. Southern from the imprint.
Medicine. London co-publishing.

164. [Pratt, Samuel Jackson, 1749–1814.]
The sublime and beautiful of scripture: being essays on select passages of sacred composition. By Courtney Melmoth. In two volumes. London, printed for J. Murray, 1777.
Vol. 1: x,[6],208p.; vol. 2: [vii].173p., 8vo. With half-titles. Price: 3s. bound.
1000 copies printed by Wm Goldney. Expenses: £41: printing 27 sheets at 27s./sheet—£14.17s.8d.; 22 reams of paper supplied by Lepard at £15.6s./ream—£17.1s.; advertising, etc. £9.2s. Murray sold a half share to George Robinson for £20 and sold his 500 copies at 1s.6d.—£37.10s. Profit—£17 (BB, p. 29; Pratt, 1782). Entered in the Stationers' Company Register, 15 Feb. 1777, 'J. Murray. The Whole'.
ESTC t124076: L, 844.i.5.
Religion. London co-publishing.

165. Richardson, John, 1741–1811?.
A dictionary, Persian, Arabic, and English. By John Richardson, Esq. F.S.A. . . . To which is prefixed a dissertation on the languages, literature, and manners of eastern nations. Oxford, printed at the Clarendon Press. Sold by J. Murray, London; and by D. Prince, Oxford, 1777–80.
Vol. 1: xlviii 2144p.; vol. 2: xix,2286p., Fo. Price: 10 gns bound.
Text printed in double columns and numbered by columns. The title page to vol. 2 reads: 'A dictionary English, Persian and Arabic'. The 'Dissertation' was also issued separately. With a list of subscribers in vol. 2. Murray owned half the copyright, despite the wording of the imprint. Vol. 1 published 9 Dec. 1777 at 5 gns. Stock: 177 (W).
ESTC t090671: L, 67.i.4–5.
Language. Provincial co-publishing.

166. Richardson, John, 1741–1811?.
A dissertation on the languages, literature and

manners of eastern nations. Originally prefixed to a dictionary Persian, Arabic, and English. By John Richardson, Esq. . . . Oxford, printed at the Clarendon Press. Sold by J. Murray, London; and by D. Prince, Oxford, 1777.
[2],195,[49]p., 8vo. Price: 7s. bound.
Entered in the Stationers' Company Register, 29 Nov. 1777, 'J. Murray. The Whole' (see Richardson 1778, item 198).
ESTC t090662: L, 621.l.10.
Language. Provincial co-publishing.

*167. Saunders, William, 1743–1817.
Observations and experiments on the power of the mephytic acid in dissolving stones of the bladder. In a letter to Dr. Percival. By William Saunders, . . . London, printed in the year, 1777.
32p., 8vo. Price: 1s.
Monthly Review 59 (Aug. 1778), 154: 'Murray. 1777'. First published by Dr Percival in vol. 3 of *Philosophical, medical, and experimental essays*.
ESTC t138535: L, 1609/5459.
Medicine. Murray alone.

168. Thistlethwaite, James, b. 1751.
The child of misfortune; or, the history of Mrs. Gilbert. By Mr. Thistlethwaite. In two volumes. . . . London, printed for John Murray, 1777.
Vol. 1: 307p.; vol. 2: 287p., 12mo. Price: 6s.
Published Jan. 1776 in partnership with Wm Richardson, who printed 800 copies of the work. Production costs were £33.17s.3d. (AL, p. 248).
ESTC n027800: PU, Singer-Mendenhall PR3729.T7 C45 1777.
Fiction. London co-publishing.

169. [Voltaire, Francois Marie Arouet de, 1694–1778].
Historical memoirs of the author of The Henriade. With some original pieces. To which are added, genuine letters of Mr. de Voltaire. Taken from his own minutes. Translated from the French. London, printed for T. Durham; G. Kearsly, and J. Murray, 1777.
[2],ii,258,[2]p., 8vo. With a final advertisement leaf. Price: 3s.6d.
A translation of *Commentaire historique sur les oeuvres de l'auteur de la Henriade*, published in 1776 and variously attributed to Jean-Louis Wagnière, Durey de Morsan and Christin.

Theodore Besterman, however, believes it to be written or dictated by Voltaire himself. Additional notes and a letter by Voltaire have been added to this edition by the translator. On 13 March 1777 Murray paid £12.5*d*., his 1/3 share for the translation (BB, p. 5). Entered in the Stationers' Company Register, 31 Dec. 1776, T. Durham, Murray, and Kearsly 1/3 share each. *ESTC* t137668: L, 630.g.19.
Biography. London co-publishing.

1778

170. Adye, Stephen Payne, d. 1794.
A treatise on courts martial. . . . To which is added, I. An essay on military punishments and rewards. II. Considerations on the act for punishing mutiny and desertion, and the rules and articles for the government of His Majesty's land forces. By Stephen Payne Adye. . . . The second edition. London, printed for J. Murray, 1778.
160,53,[3]p., 8vo. With a final advertisement leaf.
ESTC t083271: L, 517.c.9.
Military. Murray alone.

171. Alves, Robert, 1745–1794.
Odes on several subjects. By Robert Alves, A.M. Edinburgh, printed for Creech; Murray, London, 1778.
[2],37,[1]p., 8vo. Price: 1*s*.
Pagination of NN copy: viii,10–37p
ESTC t227853 L, C.142.a.7
Poetry. Edinburgh co-publishing.

172. Boutcher, William.
A treatise on forest-trees: containing not only the best methods of their culture . . . but a variety of new and useful discoveries, . . . To which are added directions for the disposition, . . . of hedges . . . By William Boutcher, . . . The second edition. Edinburgh, printed for the author; and sold by J. Murray, London, 1778.
4,xlviii,259,[5]p., 4to. Price: 15*s* in boards.
The 1775 edition with a new title page. Stock: 78 (W).
ESTC t113532: L, 449.i.10.
Agriculture. Agency–Murray alone.

173. Breaks, Thomas.
A complete system of land-surveying, both in theory and practice, containing the best, the most accurate, and commodious methods of surveying and planning of ground by all the instruments now in use; . . . To which is added, the new art of surveying by the plain table. . . . To this work is annexed a true and correct table of logarithms of all numbers, . . . By Thomas Breaks. The second edition. London, printed for J. Murray, 1778.
[2],ii,593,[1]p., plates, 8vo.
A reissue of the 1771 Newcastle edition (see above, item 31), with a cancel title page. 'A table of the logarithms' has a separate divisional title page.
ESTC t113761: L, 530.f.13.
Science. Murray alone.

174. Brookes, Richard, fl. 1721–1763.
The general gazetteer: or, compendious geographical dictionary. Containing a description of all the empires, kingdoms, . . . and promontories in the known world; together with the government, policy, customs, manners, and religion of the inhabitants; . . . Embellished with nine maps. By R. Brookes, M.D. The fourth edition, improved, with additions and corrections, by Alex. Bisset, A.M. London, printed for J. F. and C. Rivington, T. Carnan, F. Newbery, and J. Johnson; S. Crowder, G. Robinson, R. Baldwin, W. Stuart, and Fielding and Walker; B. Law; T. Lowndes, and J. Murray; and T. Becket, 1778.
xvi,[678]p., plates, maps, 8vo. Price: 7*s*.
3000 copies printed. Murray bought a 103/3000 share on 8 Apr. 1777 at the Queen's Arms and paid 5 gns to Edward Johnston. On 10 Dec. he paid out £14.3*s*.3*d*. for paper and printing. The returns on his share (103 copies at 4*s*. each, wholesale) were £20.12*s*. (BB, p. 1). Entered in the Stationers' Company Register, 10 Nov. 1778, as listed in the imprint; shares not noted.
ESTC n030924: CoU, G102.B87 1778.
Travel–topography. London syndicate.

175. [Carlyle, Alexander, 1722–1805.]
A letter to His Grace the Duke of Buccleugh, on the national defence: with some remarks on Dr. Smith's chapter on that subject, in his book entitled, 'An enquiry in to the nature and causes of the wealth of nations'. London, printed for J. Murray, 1778.
[2],72p., 8vo.

200 copies printed (?). See To Carlyle, 1 May 1778.
ESTC t107064: L, 113.n.41.
Politics. Murray alone.

176. Chambers, Ephraim, *c.* 1680–1740.
Cyclopaedia: or, an universal dictionary of arts and sciences. . . . By E. Chambers, F.R.S. With the supplement, and modern improvements, incorporated in one alphabet. By Abraham Rees, D.D. In four volumes . . . London, printed for W. Strahan, J. F. and C. Rivington, A. Hamilton, J. Hinton, T. Payne, W. Owen, D. White. D. Collins, T. Caslon, T. Longman, B. Law, T. Durham, T. Backet, C. Rivington, E. and C. Dilly, H. Baldwin, J. Wilkie, W. Nicoll, H. S. Woodfall, J. Robson and Co., J. Knox, W. Domville, T. Cadell, G. Robinson, R. Baldwin, W. Otridge, W. Davis, N. Conant, W. Stuart, J. Murray, J. Bell, W. Fox, S. Hayes, J. Donaldson, E. Johnson, and J. Richardson, 1778–1788.
5 vols, unpaginated, plates, Fo.
Issued in 89 parts weekly at 6*d.* each. Vol. 2, 1779; vol. 3, 1781, and vol. 4, 1783, all listing only 26 other booksellers in London. Vol. 5, 'containing the addenda, index, arrangement of the plates, and the plates', is dated 1788. Murray's investment was £204; nett profit, £1199.5. He bought a 1/64 share at the Globe Tavern (John Crowder's sale) on 10 Sept. 1777 for £16, which he paid to George Robinson on 16 Jan. 1778; he later paid Robinson £29 more (12 'calls' at £2 each as the parts were published, plus a further £5). On 18 Oct. 1778 he paid £30 for an additional 3/128 share bought at Wm Stuart's bankruptcy sale; he also paid a £43.10*s.* 'advance' on the same. On 27 April 1779 he sold a 1/128 share to Hamilton for £10 and also was paid an 'advance' on that share of £14.10. The first 'dividend' (paid by Thomas Longman on 7 Oct. 1779) was £31.5*s.*; the second on 24 April 1780 was also £31.5*s.* On 12 Sept. 1780 Murray paid £33 for a further 1/128 share bought at an estate sale of the late Wm Davis on 25 July 1779. He received a dividend from Longman for £39.1*s.*3*d.* on 16 Feb. 1781. On 8 Nov. 1781 he paid a Capt. Richardson £52.10*s.* for a 1/32 share. Between 22 Dec. 1782 and 22 Dec. 1788 Murray received twelve dividends of £70.6*s.*3*d.* each on his 9/128 share. On 1 Jan. 1790 he sold a 2/128 share to Wm Goldsmith for £160. Between that date

and 11 Nov. 1793 he received five dividends of £54.13*s.*9*d.* each. After Murray's death a further dividend of £54.13*s.*9*d.* was received (11 Feb. 1794). His shares were sold at different times for a total of £149.11*s.* (BB, p. 8; for other editions see Chambers 1784, 1786, 1788, 1795).
ESTC t136235: L, 1221*s.*h.2.
Miscellaneous. London syndicate.

177. Clark, John, 1744–1805.
Observations on the diseases in long voyages to hot countries, and particularly on those which prevail in the East Indies. By John Clark, . . . A new edition. . . . London, printed for J. Murray, 1778.
xvi,366,[2]p., 8vo. With a final errata leaf. Price: 6*s.*
ESTC n041538: CU-BIOL, k-RC961.C6.
Medicine. Murray alone.

178. Cullen, William, 1710–1790.
First lines of the practice of physic, for the use of students in the University of Edinburgh. By William Cullen, M.D. & P. Second edition, corrected. Vol. I. Edinburgh, printed for William Creech. And sold in London by T. Cadell, and J. Murray, 1778.
viii,417,[1]p., 8vo. Price: 6*s.*
ESTC t084326: L, 1500/279.
Medicine. Edinburgh co-publishing.

179. Du Coudray, M. le chevalier, b. 1744.
Anecdotes of the Emperor Joseph II. during his residence in France, . . . Translated from the French of the chevalier Coudray. Second edition. London, printed for J. Murray, 1778.
xvi,79,[1]p., 8vo. With a half-title and publisher's advertisement. Price: 1*s.*6*d.*
A translation of *Anecdotes intéressantes et historiques de l'illustre voyageur*. Stock: 19 (H).
ESTC t114384: L, 615.a.31(3).
Biography. Murray alone.

180. Duncan, Andrew, 1744–1828.
Medical cases, selected from the records of the Public Dispensary at Edinburgh; with remarks and observations; being the substance of case-lectures, delivered during the years 1776–7, by Andrew Duncan, M.D. . . . Edinburgh, printed for Charles Elliot; and J. Murray, London, 1778.
xv,[1],370p., plate, port., 8vo. Price: 5*s.*

Entered in the Stationers' Company Register, 29 June 1778, 'Charles Elliot. The Whole'.
ESTC t059539: L, 1170.k.14(1).
Medicine. Edinburgh co-publishing.

181. Erskine, David Stewart, the Earl of Buchan, 1742–1829.
An account of the life, writings, and inventions of John Napier, of Merchiston; by David Stewart, Earl of Buchan, and Walter Minto, L.L.D. Illustrated with copper-plates. Perth, printed by R. Morison, junr. for R. Morison and Son; and sold by J. Murray, London; and W. Creech, Edinburgh, 1778.
134,3,[1]p., plates, port., 4to. With a two-leaf bibliography.
ESTC t141215: L, 1651/73.
Biography. Agency–Provincial.

182. Every merchant not his own ship-builder. Addressed to the proprietors of India stock. London, printed for J. Murray, 1778.
[4],75,[1]p., 8vo. With a half-title and advertisement at end.
A reply to *Considerations on the important benefits to be derived from the East-India Company's building and navigating their own ships.*
ESTC t084515: L, C.T.75(2).
Economics. Murray alone.

183. Ferguson, James, 1710–1776.
Astronomy explained upon Sir Isaac Newton's principles, and made easy to those who have not studied mathematics. To which are added, a plain method of finding the distances of all the planets from the sun, . . . By James Ferguson, . . . The sixth edition, corrected. London, printed for W. Strahan, J. Rivington and Sons, J. Hinton, T. Longman, T. Lowndes, S. Crowder, B. Law, G. Robinson, T. Becket, J. Murray, and T. Cadell, 1778.
[8],501,[15]p., plates, 8vo. Price: 9s.
1500 copies printed. Murray bought a 1/24 share on 8 Apr. 1777 at the Queen's Arms for £8.15s. On 3 July 1788 he paid Thomas Cadell (who organised the edition) £8.18s.6d. for paper and printing. The returns on his share (63 copies at 5s. each, wholesale) were 15 gns (BB, p. 2).
ESTC t018602: L, 52.f.15.
Science. London syndicate.

184. Gay, John, 1685–1732.
Fables by the late Mr. Gay. In one volume complete. London, printed for J. Buckland, W. Strahan, J. F. and C. Rivington, G. Keith, B. White, R. Horsfield, T. Lowndes, T. Caslon, S. Crowder, T. Longman, B. Law, T. Carnan, J. Wilkie, G. Robinson, T. Cadell, S. Bladon, H. L. Gardiner, F. Newbery, J. Wallis, W. Goldsmith, J. Murray, W. Stuart, and Fielding and Walker, 1778.
240p., plates, 12mo. Price: 3s.6d.
2200 copies printed. Murray bought a 1/20 share at the Globe Tavern (John Crowder's sale) on 10 Sept. 1777 for £10.5s. which he paid to George Robinson on 16 Jan. 1778. On 28 Sept. 1778 he paid Thomas Longman £3.3s.3d. for paper and printing. The returns on his share (110 books), paid on 28 Sept. 1778, were £6.1s. (BB, p. 9). At the same sale Murray purchased a 1/24 share of Gay's *Poems*, though, according to entry (BB, p. 9), an edition never appeared. The share was sold 23 Dec. 1794 to Stockdale for 3 gns.
ESTC t013857: L, 1164.c.58.
Poetry. London syndicate.

185. Gray, Thomas, 1716–1771.
Poems by Mr. Gray. A new edition. London, printed for J. Murray, 1778.
[6],[xxxix],[4],44–158p., plates, 8vo. Price: 3s.
See Gray 1776, item 126. Murray added a preface describing his dispute with Wm Mason over the copyright of three of Gray's poems. He also appended Gray's will to the 'Life' by Gilbert Stuart, added a poem attributed to J. Taite and issued an additional plate, 'The Fatal Sisters'.
ESTC n011839: MH–H, *EC75.G7948.B778p.
Poetry. Murray alone.

*186. [Hawkesworth, John, 1715?-1773].
The adventurer. . . . A new edition. Illustrated with frontispieces. London, printed for W. Strahan, J. Rivington and sons, J. Dodsley, T. Longman, B. Law, T. Caslon, T. Lowndes, J. Wilkie, T. Cadell, T. Davies, T. Becket, W. Flexney, F. Newbery, W. Goldsmith, W. Nicoll, W. Stewart, J. Conant, W. Fox, and E. Johnston, 1778.
Vol. 1: [4],308p.; vol. 2: [6],292p.; vol. 3: [6],298,[2]p.; vol. 4: [4],297,[2]p., plates, 12mo. With advertisements in vols. 3 and 4.

Essays by Hawkesworth, Joseph Warton, Samuel Johnson and others. The plates dated 1775 and published by T. Cadell. 2000 copies printed. Murray bought a 1/32 share on 8 April 1777 at the Queens Arms for which he paid 12 gns to Edward Johnston. The expenses for paper and printing, paid on 22 Dec. 1777 were £10.3s.1d. On the same day the returns on his share (62 books at 6s. each, wholesale) were £18.12s. (BB, p. 1). It is not clear why his name did not appear in the imprint.
ESTC t097975: L, 245.h.4–7.
Miscellaneous. London syndicate.

187. Hederich, Benjamin, 1675–1748.
Graecum lexicon manuale, primum a Beniamine Hederico institutum, post repetitas Sam. Patricii curas, auctum . . . cura Io. Augusti Ernesti, nunc iterum recensitum, . . . a T. Morell, . . . Londini, excudit H.S. Woodfall, impensis, C. Bathurst, J. F. & C. Rivington, J. Pote, J. Hinton, E. Johnson, W. Owen, T. Calson, S. Crowder, T. Longman, B. Law, E. and C. Dilly, T. Becket, T. Cadell, W. Ginger. G. Robinson, J. Johnson, H. Baldwin, T. Evans, W. Otridge, T. Beecroft, S. Hayes, W. Stuart, J. Murray, and C. Corbett, 1778.
viii,[828]p. (p. vii misnum. vi), 4to. Price: 1 gn. bound.
3000 copies printed. Murray bought a 1/64 share at the Queen's Arms sale on 25 Jan. 1776 for £8.17s.6d, which he paid to Thomas Becket. Production costs for the edition were £11.14s.9d. The returns on his share (47 copies at 14s. each, wholesale) were £32.18s. (BB, p. 3).
ESTC t140707: L, 66.e.16.
Language. London syndicate.

188. Horace.
A poetical translation of the works of Horace, with the original text, and critical notes collected from his best Latin and French commentators. By Philip Francis, D.D. In four volumes. . . . The eighth edition. London, printed for W. Strahan; J. Rivington and Sons; T. Caslon; B. Law; T. Cadell, G. Robinson; W. Stewart; T. Becket; J. Murray; W. Domville; J. Bell; and T. Evans. London, 1778.
Vol. 1: xxii,247,[5]p.; vol. 2: [2],309,[1]p.; vol. 3: [2],275,[1]p.; vol. 4: [1],267,[1]p., plate, 12mo.
Vols 2–4 have different title pages; vol. 2: 'The odes and carmen seculare of Horace'; vol. 3:

'The satires of Horace'; vol. 4: 'The epistles and art of poetry of Horace'. Parallel Latin and English texts. Murray purchased a 1/16 share on 10 Sept. 1777 at the Globe Tavern from S. Crowder, for which he paid George Robinson £5.10s. (BB, p. 8).
ESTC t042733: L, 1568/1327.
Poetry. London syndicate.

189. Hough, John, fl. 1778.
Second thought is best. An opera of two acts, performed at the Theatre Royal in Drury-Lane. Addressed to R. B. Sheridan, Esq; by J. Hough, of the Inner-Temple . . . [London], Published by Mr. Murray, bookseller, and of Mr. Greenlaw, 1788 [1778].
43,[1]p., 8vo. Price: 1s.
The play was performed on 30 Mar. 1778.
ESTC t115091: L, 11777.c.46.
Drama. London co-publishing.

190. Innes, John, 1739–1777.
A short description of the human muscles, chiefly as they appear on dissection. Together with their several uses, and the synonyma of the best authors. By John Innes. The second edition, greatly improved by Alex. Monro, M.D. Edinburgh, printed for Charles Elliot, and John Murray, London, 1778.
251,[1]p., 8vo. Price: 1s.6d.
ESTC t114728: L, 781.a.26.
Medicine. Edinburgh co-publishing.

191. Johnson, Samuel, 1709–1784.
A dictionary of the English language: in which the words are deduced from their originals, explained in their different meanings, . . . Abstracted from the folio edition, by the author Samuel Johnson, A.M. To which is prefixed, A grammar of the English language. In two volumes. . . . The sixth edition, corrected by the author. London, printed for W. Strahan, J. F. and C. Rivington, J. Hinton, L. Davies, W. Owen, T. Lowndes, T. Calson, S. Crowder, T. Longman, B. Law, T. Becket, E. and C. Dilly, J. Dodsley, W. Nicoll, G. Robinson, T. Cadell, J. Knox, J. Robson, W. Goldsmith, J. Ridley, T. Evans, J. Bew, J. Murray, W. Stuart, and Fielding & Walker, 1778.
2 vols, unpaginated, 8vo. Price: 10s.
5000 copies printed. Murray bought a 1/80 share at the Globe Tavern (John Crowder's

sale) on 10 Sept. 1777 for £17 which he paid to
George Robinson on 16 Jan. 1778. On 17
March 1778 he bought an additional 1/80 share
at the Globe for £16. He paid Thomas Longman £22.12s.11d. for paper and printing. The
returns on his share (126 books at 5s.6d. each,
wholesale) were £34 (BB, p. 10). Entered in the
Stationers' Company Register, 23 May 1778,
noting all those in the imprint but not their
shares.
ESTC t083960: L, 626.h.18.
Language. London syndicate.

192. Lind, James, 1716–1794.
An essay on the most effectual means of pre-
serving the health of seamen in the Royal Navy.
. . . By James Lind, . . . A new edition, much
enlarged and improved. London, printed for J.
Murray, 1778.
xx,363,[1]p., 8vo. Price: 6s.
ESTC n002011: MBCo, 1 Mk 371.
Medicine. Murray alone.

193. Lysias.
The orations of Lysias and Isocrates, translated
from the Greek: with some account of their
lives; and a discourse on the history, manners,
and character of the Greeks, . . . By John
Gillies, . . . London, printed for J. Murray;
and J. Bell, Edinburgh, 1778.
[36],cxxxv,[1],498,[2]p., plate, port., 4to. Price:
£1.1s. bound.
Entered in the Stationers' Company Register,
11 Mar. 1778, 'J. Murray. The Whole'. Stock: 71
(W).
ESTC t106138: L, 11391.k.5.
History. Edinburgh co-publishing.

194. Monro, Donald, editor, 1727–1802
Letters and essays on the small-pox and inoculation, the measles, the dry belly-ache, the
yellow, and remitting, and intermitting fevers
of the West Indies. To which are added,
thoughts on the hydrocephalus internus, and
observations on hydatides in the heads of
cattle. By different practitioners. London,
printed for J. Murray, and C. Elliot, Edinburgh,
1778.
xl,320p., 8vo. With a half-title. Price: 5s.
Monro's 35–page preface is followed by 'Letters
and Essays' by John Quier, Thomas Fraser,
John Hume, George Monro, Ambrose Dawson

and Dr Dodswell. Entered in the Stationers'
Company Register, 29 Nov. 1777, 'J. Murray.
The Whole'. Stock: 378 (W).
ESTC t060415: L, 1170.k.14(2).
Medicine. Edinburgh co-publishing.

195. O'Halloran, Sylvester, 1728–1807.
A general history of Ireland, from the earliest
accounts to the close of the twelfth century,
. . . By Mr. O'Halloran, . . . London, printed
for the author, by A. Hamilton: and sold by G.
Robinson; J. Murray; J. Robson; and by Mess.
Faulkner, Hoey, and Wilson, in Dublin, 1778.
Vol. 1: lvi,307,[11]p.; vol. 2: 416,[11]p., 4to. With
half-title in vol. 2. Price: 12s.6d. bound.
750 copies printed. Stock: 94 (W). A proposal
for this work to be published by James Williams
at Dublin was issued on 1 Aug. 1777 (O, Gough
Coll. Fiche 3 /G9), but this edition apparently
never appeared.
ESTC t056380: L, 186.c.12.
History. Agency–Provincial.

196. Plan of re-union between Great Britain
and her colonies. London, printed for J. Murray,
1778.
[2],xv,[1],211,[1]p., 8vo. Price: 3s.6d.
260 copies printed. In Murray's account ledger
under a 'Dr Ramsay, No. 1 Pallmall', but attributed (by Sabin) to Sir William Pulteney.
ESTC t042426: L, 102.g.44.
Politics. Murray alone.

*197. Richardson, George, c. 1736–1817.
Iconology; or, a collection of emblematical figures, moral and instructive; . . . By George
Richardson, . . . In two volumes. . . . London,
printed for the author, 1778–79.
Vol. 1: [10],vii[3],113p.; vol. 2: 115–161,[3]p.;
109 plates, 2o. With a two-page list of subscribers. Errata in vol. 1. Continuous pagination;
four parts bound in two volumes.
A loose translation and adaptation of Cesare
Ripa's *Iconologia*. The separate volume title pages
bear the date 1779 and 'printed by G. Scott' in
the imprint.
A newspaper advertisment in Murray's clipping
album hand-dated Jan. 1779: 'Sold by the
author, No. 105 Great Titchfield-street,
Cavendish-square; by Mr Taylor, in Holborn;
Mr. Nicol, and Mr. Elmsley, in the Strand; Mr.
Robson, in New Bond-street; Messrs Sayer and

Bennett, and Mr. Murray, in Fleet-street; Mr. Boydell, in Cheapside; and by the other booksellers in town and country. 6 guineas in 'coloured grounds'.
ESTC t101707: L, 92.1.4.
Arts. Agency–London.

198. Richardson, John, 1741–1811?.
A dissertation on the languages, literature, and manners of eastern nations. Originally prefixed to a dictionary, Persian, Arabic, and English. The second edition. To which is added, Part II. Containing additional observations. . . . By John Richardson, Esq. . . . Oxford, printed at the Clarendon Press. Sold by J. Murray, London; and by D. Prince, Oxford, 1778.
[12],288,[2],289–490p., 8vo. With a half-title and an errata slip. Price: 7s.
ESTC t090670: L, 280.g.5.
Murray paid the author 12 gns for this edition. He purchased 32 reams of paper for £26.8s. The copy was sold in May 1796 to Sewell for £10.s.6d. (See Richardson 1776, item 166; BB, p. 15).
Language. Provincial co-publishing.

199. Saunders, Robert.
Observations on the sore throat and fever, that raged in the north of Scotland, in the year 1777, in a letter to Dr. William Grant, by Robert Saunders, physician at Bamff. London, printed for J. Murray, 1778.
[4],50p., 8vo. Price: 1s.
ESTC n010336: MH-H, Tr 2057*.
Medicine. Murray alone.

200. Shakespeare, William, 1564–1616.
Shakespeare's history of the times: or the original portraits of that author. Adapted to modern characters, with notes and observations. London, printed for D. Browne; and J. Murray. And sold by all booksellers in town and country, 1778.
[4],iv,76[i.e.88]p., 12mo. With a half-title.
ESTC t064121: L, 1162.f.23(2).
Another issue: London, printed for D. Browne; and sold by J. Murray. And sold by all booksellers in town and country, 1778.
ESTC n044286: MH, 13483.68.
Politics. London co-publishing.

201. Shakespeare, William, 1564–1616.
The plays of William Shakspeare. In ten volumes. With the corrections and illustrations of various commentators; to which are added notes by Samuel Johnson and George Steevens. The second edition, revised and augmented. London, printed for C. Bathurst, W. Strahan, J. F. and C. Rivington, J. Hinton, L. Davis, W. Owen, T. Caslon, E. Johnson, S. Crowder, B. White, T. Longman, B. Law, E. and C. Dilly, C. Corbett, T. Cadell, H. L. Gardner, J. Nichols, J. Bew, J. Beecroft, W. Stuart, T. Lowndes, J. Robson, T. Payne, T. Becket, F. Newbery, G. Robinson, R. Baldwin, J. Williams, J. Ridley, T. Evans, W. Davies, W. Fox, and J. Murray, 1778.
Vol. 1: [iv],346,[6],372p.; vol. 2: 527p.; vol. 3: [ii],536p.; vol. 4: [ii],611p.; vol. 5: [ii],812,[3]p.; vol. 6: [2],v,[7]–566p.; vol. 7: [ii],500p.; vol. 8: [ii],562p.; vol. 9: [ii],[7],8–573p.; vol. 10: [ii],629,[4]p.; plates, port., music, 8vo. With half-titles in each vol. Price: £3.10s. bound.
1200 copies printed. Murray bought a 1/120 share at the Globe Tavern (D. Cornish's sale) on 17 Mar. 1778 for £9.15s. which he paid to George Robinson. On 19 Jan. 1779 he paid an advance on the share to Rivington of £14.15s.7½d. The returns on his share (10 sets at 40s. each, wholesale), paid on the same date, were £20. (BB, p. 12 and Plate 41). Entered in the Stationers' Company Register, 20 Jan. 1779. Murray's name does not appear in the 2-vol. *Supplement*, published in 1780 and edited by Edmond Malone.
ESTC t149955: L, 642.f.1–10.
Drama. London syndicate.

202. A sketch of the history of two acts of the Irish parliament, of the 2d and 8th of Queen Anne, to prevent the further growth of popery: . . . London, printed for J. Murray, 1778.
[2],80,[2]p., 8vo.
Stock: 88 (H).
ESTC t048418: L, T.771(3).
Religion. Murray alone.

203. Smellie, William, 1697–1763.
Thesaurus medicus: sive, disputationum, in academia Edinensi, ad rem medicam pertinentium, a collegio instituto ad hoc usque tempus, delectus, a Gulielmo Smellio, . . . habitus. . . . Edinburgi, typis academicis, prostant venales apud C. Elliot, J. Bell, et G. Creech; et Londini apud J. Murray, 1778–79.

Vol. 1: xii,483p.; vol. 2: x,523p., plates, 8vo. Price: 12s.
Vol. 2 imprint excludes J. Bell. Vols 3–4 were published in 1785 and bear the imprint: Edinburgi & Londini, apud C. Elliot 38; G. Robinson; Dublin, apud G. Gilbert; Parisiis, apud P. T. Barrois; Vienna & Lipsia, apud Rudolphum Graeffer, 1785.
ESTC t152289: GOT, 80Med.misc.454/7.
Medicine. Edinburgh co-publishing.

204. Stuart, Gilbert, 1743–1786.
A view of society in Europe, in its progress from rudeness to refinement: or, inquiries concerning the history of law, government, and manners. By Gilbert Stuart, LL.D. Edinburgh, printed for John Bell; and J. Murray, London, 1778.
xx,433,[3]p., 4to. With a half title and errata leaf. Price: 18s. in boards.
Entered in the Stationers' Company Register, 11 Mar. 1778, 'The Author. The Whole'.
ESTC t096549: L, 30.e.14.
History. Edinburgh co-publishing.

205. Taylor, George, geographer, fl. 1778.
Taylor and Skinner's maps of the roads of Ireland, surveyed 1777. [London], Published for the authors as the Act directs 14th. Novr. 1778. Sold by G. Nicol; J. Murray, London. and by W. Wilson, Dublin. Engraved by G. Terry, London, [1778].
xvi,288,16p., ill.,maps, 8vo. With a list of subscribers.
The title page, dedication and 288pp. of maps are engraved. Entered in the Stationers' Company Register, 12 Dec. 1778, 'Taylor & Skinner. The Whole'.
ESTC t145915: L, G.19825.
Travel-topography. Agency–provincial.

206. Thomson, James, 1700–1748.
The seasons, by James Thomson. A new edition. Adorned with a set of engravings from original designs. To which is prefixed an essay on the plan and character of the poem, by J. Aikin. London, printed for J. Murray, 1778.
xviii,xxi–xlv,[1],256p., plates, 8vo. Pp. xix and xx omitted in the pagination. Price: 5s. bound.
3000 copies printed by Wm Eyres at Warrington. Expenses total £243.7s.8d.: £140.5s.8d. for paper and printing; £56.16s. for engravings (£37.16s. to

Caldwal for engraving 8 plates; Hamilton 4 gns for 4 designs; £1.6s. to Page for 'writing to the plates'; £8 to Hicks for printing 8 plates, 1000 of each; 15s. additional copper plate paper); £20 for additional working of the plates; £10 to Aikin for essay; £1.6s. carriage from Warrington; £15 advertising. Profit on sale: £450 (probably an estimate). Nett profit: £206.12s.4d. (BB, p. 12). Aikin's 'Essay' entered in the Stationers' Company Register 23 June 1778, 'J. Murray by purchase. The Whole'.
ESTC t152194: GOT, 80P.Angl.6524.
Poetry. Murray alone.

207. Ward, William, 1708 or 9–1772.
An essay on grammar, as it may be applied to the English language. In two treatises. . . . A new edition. By William Ward, . . . London, printed for J. Murray, 1778.
xiv,[22],554,[2]p., 4to. With a final advertisement leaf.
Reference: Alston i. 265.
ESTC t165524: E, Milc.3.22.
Language. Murray alone.

208. Young, William, d. 1757.
A new Latin-English dictionary: containing all the words proper for reading the classic writers; with the authorities subjoined to each word and phrase. To which is prefixed, A new English-Latin dictionary, carefully compiled from the best authors in our language. . . . The fifth edition, corrected and improved. . . . By the Rev. Mr. William Young, editor of Ainsworth's dictionary. London, printed for B. White and Son, J. Pote, J. Buckland, C. Bathurst, W. Strahan, J. F. and C. Rivington, T. Caslon, T. Longman, B. Law, W. Ginger, T. Becket, H. Baldwin, J. Wilkie, J. Knox, G. Robinson, R. Baldwin, N. Conant, W. Stuart, J. Murray, T. Evans, J. Bew, H. Gardner, Fielding and Walker, and the executors of G. Knapp, 1778.
[1040]p., 8vo. With an initial imprimatur leaf.
8000 copies printed. Murray bought a 1/64 share at the Globe Tavern from S. Crowder on 10 Sept. 1777 for 10 gns which he paid to George Robinson on 16 Jan. 1778. On 19 Mar. he paid out £19.3s.9d. for paper and printing. The returns on his share (125 books at 4s. each, wholesale) were £25 (BB, p. 10).
ESTC t160495: GOT, 8 Ling.IV,4272.
Language. London syndicate.

1779

**209. Address to both houses of parliament. London, Murray, 1779.
No copy located. *Monthly Review* 61 (Dec. 1779), 468–70. Price: 1*s*.
Politics. Murray alone.

210. Aitken, John, d. 1790.
Systematic elements of the theory and practice of surgery: by John Aitken, . . . Edinburgh, printed for W. Gordon and W. Creech, and for J. Murray, London, 1779.
vii,[1],574p. (pp. 453, 495, 516 and 564 misnum. 435, 4, 416 and 558 respectively) 8vo. Price: 6*s*. in boards.
Entered in the Stationers' Company Register, 6 Jan. 1780, 'The Author. the Whole'.
ESTC t026148: L, 782.h.2.
Medicine. Edinburgh co-publishing.

211. Arnot, Hugo, 1749–1786.
The history of Edinburgh. By Hugo Arnot, . . . Printed for W. Creech; Edinburgh: and J. Murray, London, 1779.
xii,656,667–677,[1]p. (p. 423 misnum. 323), plates, map, 4to. Price: £1.5*s*.
1000 copies printed. Entered in the Stationers' Company Register, 30 July 1779, 'The Author. The Whole'.
ESTC t142880: L, 010370.dd.8.
History. Edinburgh co-publishing.

212. Buc'hoz, Pierre-Joseph, 1731–1807.
The toilet of Flora; or, a collection of the most simple and approved methods of preparing baths, essences, pomatums, . . . With receipts for cosmetics of every kind, . . . A new edition, improved. London, printed for J. Murray; and W. Nicoll, 1779.
[24],252p., plate, 12mo. Price: 3*s*. bound.
A translation, with alterations, of *La toilette de Flore*. See Buc'hoz 1784, item 400.
ESTC t145047: L, Cup.407.h.39.
Medicine. London co-publishing.

213. [Cartwright, Edmund, 1743–1823.]
The prince of peace; and other poems. London, printed for J. Murray, 1779.
[2],44,[i.e.48];[2]p. (pp.40–43 are repeated but text and register are continuous), 4to. With a half-title. Price: 2*s*.6*d*.
ESTC t127700: L, 162.l.60.

Entered in the Stationers' Company Register, 22 Mar. 1779. 'The Author. The Whole' (see Plate 39).
Another issue: large paper.
ESTC t044320: L, 11630.d.7(2).
Another issue: London, printed for J. Murray, and W. Creech, Edinburgh, 1779.
ESTC n039500: KU-S, Poems 383.
Poetry. Edinburgh co-publishing.

214. Clark, John, 1744–1805.
Observations on the diseases in long voyages to hot countries, and particularly on those which prevail in the East Indies. By John Clark, . . . A new edition. . . . London, printed for J. Murray, 1779.
xvi,366,[2]p., 8vo. With a half-title and a final leaf of errata. Price: 6*s*.
ESTC t117391: L, 1170.g.4.
Medicine. Murray alone.

215. Collins, Arthur, 1682?-1760.
The peerage of England; containing a genealogical and historical account of all the peers of that Kingdom, now existing either by tenure, summons, or creation: their descents and collateral lines: their births, marriages, and issue: famous actions both in war and peace . . . deaths, places of burial, monuments, epitaphs . . . Also their paternal coats of arms, crests, supporters and mottoes, curiously engraved on copper-plates . . . By Arthur Collins, Esq; In eight volumes. The fifth edition, carefully corrected, and continued to the present time [by Barak Longmate]. London, printed for W. Strahan, J. F. and C. Rivington, J. Hinton, T. Payne, W. Owen, S. Crowder, T. Caslon, T. Longman, C. Rivington, C. Dilly, J. Robson, T. Lowndes, G. Robinson, T. Cadell, H. L. Gardner, W. Davis, J. Nichols, T. Evans, J. Bew, R. Baldwin, J. Almon, J. Murray, W. Fox, J. White, Fielding and Walker, T. Beecroft, J. Donaldson, M. Folingsby, 1779.
Vol. 1: vi,[1],456,[24]p.; vol. 2: [1],528,[24]p.; vol. 3: [1],427,[25]p.; vol. 4: [1],431,[24]p.; vol. 5: [1],495,[30]p.; vol. 6: [1],423,[24]p.; vol. 7: [1],459,[24]p.; vol. 8: [1],452,[30]p., plates, 8vo. Price: £2.12*s*.6*d*. bound (£2.4*s*. in boards).
1250 copies printed. Murray purchased a 1/144 share on 8 Apr. 1777 at the Queen's Arms from Edward Johnston for £2.12*s*.6*d*. and a 1/72 share at Stuart's sale on 18 Oct. 1779 for 2

gns. Production costs for the edition were £24.14s. The returns on his share (26 copies at £1.10s. each, wholesale) were £39—a nett profit of £8.12s.6d. (BB, p. 1). A supplemental vol. followed in 1784. Stock: 2 (H). Shares sold 23 Dec. 1794 to Stockdale for £1.11s.6d. (BB, p. 1).
ESTC t139246: L, 9918.a.17.
Miscellaneous. London syndicate.

216. Crawford, Adair, 1748–1795.
Experiments and observations on animal heat, and the inflammation of combustible bodies. Being an attempt to resolve these phaenomena into a general law of nature. By Adair Crawford, A.M. London, printed for J. Murray; and J. Sewell, 1779.
[8],120p., 8vo. Price: 2s.6d.
Entered in the Stationers' Company Register, 12 Apr. 1788 [sic], 'Author. Whole'. Stock: 3 (H).
ESTC t033830: L, B.499(7).
Science. London co-publishing.

217. Cullen, William, 1710–1790.
First lines of the practice of physic, for the use of students in the University of Edinburgh. By William Cullen, M.D. & P. Vol. II. London, printed for J. Murray, 1779.
viii,408p., 8vo. Price: 6s.
ESTC t143257: L, 1500/279.
Medicine. Murray alone.

218. Dalrymple, Sir David, 1726–1792.
Annals of Scotland. from the accession of Robert I. surnamed Bruce, to the accession of the house of Stewart. By Sir David Dalrymple. Edinburgh, printed by Balfour & Smellie. For J. Murray, London, 1779.
[4],397,[3]p., 4to. With a half-title and a final advertisement leaf. Price: £1.7s.6d. (including the 1776 first vol.)
Entered in the Stationers' Company Register, 22 March 1779, 'The Author. The Whole'. Stock: 1 (H); 197 sets (W).
ESTC t141222: L, 600.i.11.
History. Murray alone.

219. Duncan, Andrew, 1744–1828, editor.
Medical and philosophical commentaries. By a Society of Physicians in Edinburgh. Volume sixth. London, printed for J. Murray, M.

Drummond, J. Bell, W. Creech, and C. Elliot, Edinburgh, 1779.
471,[12]p., 8vo. Price: 1s.6d. each part, or 6s. per vol.
Issued in four parts with separate title pages. Pt. 1 entered in the Stationers' Company Register, 2 Mar. 1779, 'J. Murray. The Whole'. Pt. 4, 3 Dec. 1779, 'John Murray by Purchase. the Whole'.
Primary Location: Roy. Col. of Phys. Edin.
Medicine. Murray–with Agency.

220. [Fitzgerald, Gerald, 1739 or 40–1819.]
The injured islanders; or, the influence of art upon the happiness of nature. London, printed for J. Murray; and W. Creech, Edinburgh, 1779.
8,25,[3]p., 4to. Price: 2s.
500 copies printed. Entered in the Stationers' Company Register, 11 Mar. 1779, 'J. Murray. By gift of The Author'. There was also a Dublin issue published by T. T. Faulkner for which Murray printed 25 title pages. (See To Faulkner, 12 Mar. 1779.)
ESTC t037228: L, 643.k.24.
Another issue: London, printed for J. Murray, 1779 (see title page, Plate 40).
ESTC t000419: L, 11630.d.7(3).
Poetry. Edinburgh co-publishing.

221. Foreign medical review: containing an account with extracts of all the new books published on natural history, botany, materia medica, chemistry, anatomy, surgery, midwifery and the practice of physic, in every part of the continent of Europe. Together with intelligence of new and interesting discoveries. . . . London, J. Murray, 1779–80.
Part 1: vi,[2],156p.; Part 4: [1],[1],167,[xii]p., 8vo Price: 2s.6d. each part or 10s. for the volume in boards.
Parts 2 and 3 (1780) were not published by Murray. The work was edited by François Xaviar Swediaur. See Plate 43. Pt. 1 entered in the Stationers' Company Register, 13 July 1779, 'J. Murray. The Whole.' Stock: 80 (H); 612 of No. 1; 200 No. 4 (W).
ESTC n061275: Ds, Widdess, room13A1 (Pt. 1 only); my own copy for other parts.
Medicine. Murray alone.

222. Frederick, II, King of Prussia, 1712–1786.
The panegyric of Voltaire, written by the King

of Prussia, and read at an extraordinary meeting of the Academy of Sciences and Belles Letters of Berlin, 26th November, 1778. London, printed for J. Murray, 1779.
[4],viii,[1],6–56p., 8vo. Price: 1s.6d.
A translation of *Eloge de Voltaire*. Entered in the Stationers' Company Register, 23 Jan. 1779, 'J. Murray, The Whole'. Another translation by the Rev. H.C. Newman was entered 6 Mar. 1787 in the translator's name.
ESTC t170324: Gu, Bh9–f.23.
Another issue: London, printed for J. Murray. And sold by J. Robson; M. Ridley; J. Walter: J. Sewel; and W. Creech, Edinburgh, 1779.
[4],viii,[1],6–56p., 8vo.
ESTC t091415: L, 1201.g.24(2).
Biography. Murray–with Agency.

223. Goldsmith, Oliver, 1728–1774.
The history of England, from the earliest times to the death of George II. By Dr. Goldsmith. The third edition, corrected. . . . London, printed for T. Becket, T. Cadell, and T. Evans; G. Robinson, and R. Baldwin; F. Newbery; and J. Murray, 1779.
Vol. 1: [3],viii,384,[23]p.; vol. 2: [iv],420,[28]p.; vol. 3: [iv],454,[22]p.; vol. 4: [iv],412,[24]p., ill.,-port., 8vo. With half-titles. Price: £1.4s.
1000 copies printed. In 1778 Murray paid George Robinson £3.13s.6d. for a 1/24 share bought at the Globe Tavern. In Apr. 1779 he paid Robinson £14.3s.6d. for paper and printing. The returns on his share (42 copies at 12s. each, wholesale) were £25.4s. (BB, p. 13). The imprint to vol. 3 has 'Cadel' instead of 'Cadell'.
ESTC n008382: MSaE, 942.662 1779.
History. London syndicate.

224. Grant, Donald.
Two dissertations on popish persecution and breach of faith. In answer to a book, entitled, 'A free examination of the common methods employed to prevent the growth of popery'. . . . To the whole is now added, A contrast between the popish oath of allegiance and the principles of popery. . . . By D. Grant, D.D. London, printed for J. Murray, J. Bell, J. Dickson, and C. Elliot, Edinburgh, 1779.
xiv,206,[2]p., 8vo. With a final errata leaf.
Murray took unsold copies from the 1771 edition and affixed a new title page. Grant added a

prefatory 'Contrast between the popish oath of allegiance and the principles of popery'.
ESTC t174984: E, L.16.d.
Religion. Edinburgh co-publishing.

225. Second edition.
xiv,[2],206,[2]p., 8vo.
ESTC t175214: E, L.16.d.
Religion. Edinburgh co-publishing.

226. Henry Home, Lord Kames, 1696–1782.
Essays on the principles of morality and natural religion: corrected and improved, in a third edition. Several essays added concerning the proof of a deity. Edinburgh, printed for John Bell; and John Murray, London, 1779.
x,[2],380p., 8vo. Price: 5s. bound.
ESTC n008388: MnU, 170 K12a.
Religion. Edinburgh co-publishing.

227. Innes, John, 1739–1777.
Eight anatomical tables of the human body; containing the principal parts of the skeleton and muscles represented in the large tables of Albinus. To which are added concise explanations. By John Innes, . . . The second edition. Edinburgh, printed for C. Elliot; and J. Murray, London, 1779.
iv,[1],4–52p., plates, 4to. Price: £1.11s.6d.
Plates engraved by Andrew Bell. Published Nov. 1779.
ESTC t151637: GOT, 80Zool.XI,2910.
Medicine. Edinburgh co-publishing.

228. Johnson, Samuel, 1709–1784.
Prefaces, biographical and critical, to the works of the English poets. By Samuel Johnson. . . . London, printed by J. Nichols; for C. Bathurst, J. Buckland, W. Strahan, J. Rivington and sons, T. Davies, T. Payne. L. Davis, W. Owen, B. White, S. Crowder, T. Caslon, T. Longman, B. Law, E. and C. Dilly, H. Baldwin, T. Becket, W. Davis, J. Dodsley, J. Wilkie, J. Robson, J. Johnson, T. Lowndes, G. Robinson, T. Cadell, J. Nichols, E. Newbery, T. Evans, J. Ridley, R. Baldwin, G. Nicol, Leigh and Sotheby, J. Bew, N. Conant, J. Murray, W. Fox, J. Bowen, 1779–81.
Vol. 1: xi,[166],128p.; vol. 2: [224],[40]p.; vol. 3: [350]p.; vol. 4: [32],[16],[28],20,12, 12,4,[10],12, 6,[6],[14],[12],42,64,4,[14]p.; vol. 5: 162,[54],20p.; vol. 6: 56,30,[44],38,[20],[64]p.; vol. 7: [374]p.; vol. 8: 112,30,12,[8],[12],[24],24p.; vol. 9: [148],

[8],40,[12],14p.; vol. 10: [114],8,16,20,18,22,[16], 56p., plate, port., 8vo. Price: £1.

Each life has a separate pagination. Vols. 1–4 are dated 1779, vols. 5–10: 1781; vols. 5–10 exclude E. and C. Baldwin, T. Becket, and W. Davis. One BL copy contains 'Directions to the binder' (vol. 1, pp. ix–x) for the first four volumes, showing that the lives were originally issued in parts. For details of expenses and profits, see 'Works of the English poets' 1779, item 250). Vols 1–4 entered in the Stationers' Company Register, 17 Mar. 1779, under 'Prefaces, Biographical & Critical to The Works of the English Poets. Samuel Johnson. The Whole'. Vols 5–10 entered, 8 May 1781, 'The author, the whole.

ESTC t044190: L, 1162.e.6–15
Biography. London syndicate.

229. A letter to J. C. Lettsom, M.D. F.R.S. S.A.S. &c. occasioned by Baron Dimsdale's Remarks on Dr. Lettsom's letter to Sir Robert Barker, and G. Stacpoole, Esq. upon general inoculation. By an uninterested spectator . . . London, printed for J. Murray, 1779.
39,[1]p., 8vo. Price: 1s.
Sometimes attributed to James Sims.
ESTC t068906: L, 7561.c.69(1).
Medicine. Murray alone.

230. Lind, James, 1716–1794.
An essay on the most effectual means of preserving the health of seamen in the Royal Navy. . . . By James Lind, . . . A new edition, much enlarged and improved. London, printed for J. Murray, 1779.
xx,363,[1]p., 8vo. Price: 6s.
ESTC n002012: DNLM, WZ260.L742e 1779.
Medicine. Murray alone.

231. Lorgna, Antonio Mario, 1730–1796.
A dissertation on the summation of infinite converging series with algebraic divisors. . . . Translated from the Latin of A.M. Lorgna, . . . To which is added, an appendix; . . . By H. Clarke. London, printed for the author; and sold by Mr. Murray, 1779.
xx,70,63–221,[1]p., plates, 4to. With a list of subscribers. Pp. 129–221 contain the 'Appendix'. Text and register continuous. Price: 10s.6d. in boards.
A *Supplement to Professor Lorgna's summation of*

series by Henry Clarke was published in 1782 (see item 304).
ESTC t105268: L, 50.k.15.
Science. Agency–Murray alone.

232. Lucas, Henry, fl. 1776–1795.
Poems to her Majesty: to which is added a new tragedy, entitled, The Earl of Somerset; literally founded on history: with a prefatory address, &c. By Henry Lucas, student of the Middle Temple, author of the Tears of Alnwick, Visit from the shades, &c. London, printed for the author, by William Davis. Sold also by J. Dodsley; J. Ridley; J. Murray; and by the author, 1779.
[4],iv,vii,[1],24,xlv,[1],146p., plates, 4to. Price: 10s.6d.
Edited and partly written by Samuel Johnson (see *Publications of the Bibliographical Society of America*, 41 (1947), 231–8).
ESTC t042678: L, 11630.e.8(2).
Poetry. Agency–London.

233. Malcolm, Alexander, 1685–1763.
Malcolm's Treatise of music, speculative, practical, and historical. Corrected and abridged by an eminent musician. Second edition. London, printed for J. Murray; and Luke White, Dublin, 1779.
[2],104p., music, 8vo.
Murray bought copies of the first edition of this abridgement from J. French along with copies of Rameau's *Treatise* (1779) and Rousseau's *Dictionary* (1779), and printed title pages for himself and Luke White. The three sold as a set wholesale for 3s.6d. (To White, 3 Nov. 1778). Stock: 128 (H).
ESTC n022576: CU-SB, MT6.M33 1779.
Miscellaneous. Provincial co-publishing.

234. March, R.
A treatise on silk, wool, worsted, cotton, and thread, describing their nature, properties and qualities, with instructions to clean the manufactures in the hosiery branch, . . . to which are added, descriptive remarks on frame-work knitting, . . . By R. March, . . . London, printed for the author, 1779; and sold by J. Murray; J. Almon; Mess. Richardson and Urquhart; and P. Brett, 1779.
44p., 8vo.
Entered in the Stationers' Company Register, 10 Aug. 1779, 'R. March. The Whole'.

ESTC t122196: L, 1029.a.28.
Science. Agency–London.

235. The medical register for the year 1779.
London, printed for J. Murray, 1779.
[12],44p. (p. 244 misnum. 44), 8vo. Price: 4s.6d.
Edited by Samuel Froart Simmons. 1000 copies
printed. Murray's expenses totalled £82.13s.
(£21 to Simmons for editing; £20.16s. for 32
reams of paper; £32 for printing 16 sheets;
£3.12s. for sewing 450 copies; 5 gns. advertising). He sold 450 copies at 3s.6d. (wholesale), or
£78.15s. (BB, p. 18). Entered in the Stationers'
Company Register, 1 May 1779, 'J. Murray. The
Whole'. Simmons assumed control the following year and entered the 1780 edition under his
own name in the Register, 24 July 1780.
ESTC n003634: MBCo, R713.29.M46.
Medicine. Murray alone.

236. Middleton, Joseph.
A complete book of interest, containing the
fullest tables of simple interest that have yet
appeared; ... By Joseph Middleton, ...
London, printed for J. Murray, Richardson
and Urquhart, and J. Robinson, 1779.
iv,284p., 8vo.
ESTC N068396: PPAmP, 658.M58c.
Economics. London co-publishing.

237. Millar, John, 1735–1801.
The origin of the distinction of ranks; or, an
inquiry into the circumstances which give rise
to influence and authority, in the different
members of society. By John Millar, ... The
third edition, corrected and enlarged. London,
sold by J. Murray, 1779.
viii,362p., 8vo. Price: 6s.
500 copies printed by Andrew Foulis at
Glasgow for £19.1s.8d. (To Millar, 14 Mar.
1780). Entered in the Stationers' Company
Register, 7 July 1780, 'Murray. Whole'.
ESTC t113007: L, 521.g.8.
History. Murray alone.

238. Murray, John, 1737–1793.
A catalogue of several thousand volumes; lately
purchased. The whole making a large assortment of valuable books, in most languages, arts,
and sciences, in very good condition; some of
them in elegant bindings ... which will be sold
cheap, at the prices marked in the catalogue 10

November 1779, by John Murray, facing St. Dunstan's Church, No. 32, Fleet-Street, London;
where the utmost value is given for any library
or parcel of books. Catalogues to be had at the
place of sale; of Mr. Elmsley; Mess. Richardson
and Urquhart; Mess. Fletcher and D. Prince,
Oxford; Mess. T. and J. Merril, at Cambridge;
C. Elliot and W. Creech, Edinburgh; and Luke
White and L. Flin, Dublin.
[4],132p., 8vo. Price: 6d.
ESTC t209350: Australia, NU, None Macd.
Miscellaneous. Murray–with Agency.

239. Palliser, Sir Hugh, 1723–1796.
The trial of Sir Hugh Palliser, vice-admiral of
the blue squadron, at a court-martial, held on
board His Majesty's ship the Sandwich, in
Portsmouth Harbour, on Monday, April 19th,
1779. ... for disobedience of orders, and
neglect of duty. To which is prefixed a glossary
of the technical terms and sea phrases used in
the course of the trial. London, for J. Murray;
and C. Etherington, 1779.
viii,232p., 8vo. Price: 3s.6d.
Stock: 20 (H).
ESTC n013821: MH-L, Trial.
Military. London co-publishing.

240. The third edition.
ESTC n013822: MH-L, Trial.
Military. London co-publishing.

241. Perry, Sampson, 1747–1823.
A disquisition of the stone and gravel; together
with strictures on the gout, when combined
with those disorders. By S. Perry, ... The sixth
edition, improved and enlarged. London,
printed for T. Becket; J. Murray; J. Bew; J.
Southern; and Richardson and Urquhart, 1779.
xvii,[1],220p., 8vo. Price: 3s.
ESTC t123217: L, 1507/1573.
Medicine. London co-publishing.

242. Rameau, Jean Philippe, 1683–1764.
A treatise of music, containing the principles of
composition. Wherein the several parts thereof
are fully explained, and made useful both to the
professors and students of that science. By Mr.
Rameau, ... Translated into English from the
original in the French language. Second edition.

London, printed for J. Murray; and Luke White, Dublin, 1779.

[7],4–180p., music,engr.music, 8vo.

A translation of *Traité de l'harmonie*. A reissue of the undated J. French edition, with a cancel title page. See Malcolm 1779, item 233 Stock: 167 (H).

ESTC t167735: L, R.M.5.i.5.

Miscellaneous. Provincial co-publishing.

243. Robertson, Robert, 1742–1829.

A physical journal kept on board His Majesty's Ship Rainbow, during three voyages to the coast of Africa, and West Indies, . . . to which is prefixed, a particular account of the remitting fever, which happened on board His Majesty's Sloop Weasel, . . . By Robert Robertson, . . . London, printed for J. Murray, 1779.

[2],xvi,196p., ill.,tables, 4to.

Stock: 262 (W).

ESTC t153715: GOT, 4oMed.pract.3678/85.

Travel-topography. Murray alone.

244. Rousseau, Jean-Jacques, 1712–1778.

A complete dictionary of music. Consisting of a copious explanation of all words necessary to a true knowledge and understanding of music. Translated from the original French of J. J. Rousseau. By William Waring. Second edition. London, printed for J. Murray; and Luke White, Dublin, 1779.

[4],468p., 2 plates, music, 8vo. The plates are numbered 469–470 to follow pagination.

A translation of *Dictionnaire de musique*. A reissue of the undated J. French edition, with a cancel title page. See Malcolm 1779, item 233 Stock: 15 (H).

ESTC n005070: OAU, SpC ML108.R82 1779.

Miscellaneous. Provincial co-publishing.

245. Stuart, Gilbert, 1743–1786.

Observations concerning the public law, and the constitutional history of Scotland: with occasional remarks concerning English antiquity. By Gilbert Stuart, LL.D. Edinburgh, printed for William Creech; and J. Murray, London, 1779.

xxii,[2],395,[1]p., 8vo.

Entered in the Stationers' Company Register, 22 Mar. 1779, 'The Author. The Whole' (misentered as 'Robert Gilbert, LLD.').

ESTC t096547: L, 228.g.18.

Law. Edinburgh co-publishing.

246. Thomson, James, 1700–1748.

The seasons, by James Thomson. A new edition. Adorned with a set of engravings from original designs. To which is prefixed An essay on the plan and character of the poem, by J. Aikin. London, printed for J. Murray, 1779.

xlv,[1],256p. (pp.xix–xx have been omitted in pagination, but the text and register are continuous), plates, 8vo. Price: 4s. in boards.

The 1778 edition (see above, item 206) with a new title page.

ESTC t044691: L, 1608/4271.

Poetry. Murray alone.

247. [Universal history]

London, Feb. 15, 1779. Proposals for publishing in monthly volumes, a new edition of the Universal history, ancient and modern compiled from original authors: with the histories of England, Scotland, and Ireland; and other considerable improvements; which will render this work a complete body of history, from the earliest time to the present. London, printed for G. Robinson; C. Bathurst, J. F. and C. Rivington, A. Hamilton, T. Payne, T. Longman, S. Crowder, B. Law, T. Becket, J. Robson, T. Cadell, J. and T. Bowles, S. Bladon, J. Murray, and W. Fox.

4p. 8vo.

The 'Conditions' include an anticipated 50 volumes, priced at 5s. each, the first published 1 Apr. 1779, 'and a Volume every succeeding month'.

Primary location, O, Gough Coll. Fiche 11/A2.

History. London syndicate.

248. An universal history, from the earliest accounts to the present time. Compiled from original authors. Illustrated with charts, maps, notes, &c. and a general index to the whole. . . . London, printed for C. Bathurst, J. F. and C. Rivington, A. Hamilton, T. Payne, T. Longman, S. Crowder, B. Law, T. Becket, J. Robson, F. Newbery, G. Robinson, T. Cadell, J. and T. Bowles, S. Bladon, J. Murray, and W. Fox, 1779–81.

18 vols., plates, maps, 8vo.

Vols. 10–17 are dated 1780; vol. 18, 1781. First published in 1736–44 as *An universal history, from the earliest account of time. The modern part of an universal history* was published commencing in

1780 (see item 260). A 2–vol. *Supplement* was published by Edward Dilly in 1790.
600 copies printed. Murray bought a 1/24 share for £7.10s. in 1779. He paid £51.5s. for paper and printing. The returns on his share (23 copies) were £62.2s. Share sold 23 Dec. 1794 to Stockdale for £10.6d. (BB, p. 16).
ESTC n036682: CCFB, 909.U58.
History. London syndicate.

249. Wastell, Henry.
Observations on the efficacy of a new mercurial preparation, for the cure of the venereal disease, in its most malignant state; . . . By Henry Wastell, surgeon, . . . London, printed for J. Murray, 1779.
viii,[2],104p., 8vo. Price: 2s.
ESTC n010734: DNLM.
Another issue: [2],ii,[1],vi–viii,[2],109,[1]p., 8vo.
ESTC t008448: L, T.281(2).
Medicine. Murray alone.

250. The works of the English poets. With prefaces, biographical and critical, by Samuel Johnson. . . . London, printed by H. Hughs; for C. Bathurst, J. Buckland, W. Strahan, J. Rivington and Sons, T. Davies, T. Payne, L. Davis, W. Owen, B. White, S. Crowder, T. Caslon, T. Longman, B. Law, E. and C. Dilly, J. Dodsley, H. Baldwin, J. Wilkie, J. Robson, J. Johnson, T. Lowndes, T. Becket, G. Robinson, T. Cadell, W. Davis, J. Nichols, F. Newbery, T. Evans, J. Ridley, R. Baldsin, G. Nicol, Leigh and Sotheby, J. Bew, N. Conant, J. Murray, W. Fox, J. Bowen, 1779–80.
60 vols., plates, ports., 8vo. Price: 2s.6d. per vol.; 10 gns. the set (£8.7s. in boards).
The first 58 vols. are dated 1779, and the last two, entitled: 'Index to the English poets.', dated 1780. The first eight vols. were printed by H. Hughs, and thenceforth, in various order and number of vols. done, by E. Cox, R. Hett, J. D. Cornish, J. Rivington, J. Nichols, H. Goldney, H. Baldwin and G. Bigg.
Murray originally acquired a 2/100ths share at the Chapter Coffee House. On 18 Apr. 1778 he paid Thomas Curtis £15 for paper. He purchased a further 1/100 share from George Robinson on 29 Oct. 1778 for £31, and on that date paid Thomas Cadell £25.10s. for expenses. The returns on his share (30 sets of 60 vols., at £1s.6d. for each vol., wholesale)

were £135—a nett profit of £63.10s. (see BB, p. 11, Plate 18, and *Works*, 1790).
ESTC t092171: L, 11601.c.2–21;11601.cc.1–16.
Poetry. London syndicate.

1780

251. An abstract of the trial of George Stratton, Henry Brooke, Charles Floyer, and George Mackay, Esquires, for deposing the Rt. Hon. Lord Pigot, late governor of Fort St. George, in the East Indies. London, printed for J. Murray; and W. Davis, 1780.
[4],84p., 8vo. With a half-title. Price: 1s.6d.
Stock: 72 (W).
ESTC t011473: L, T.686(8).
Law. London co-publishing.

252. Bruce, Peter Henry, 1692–1757.
London, Jan. 8, 1780. Proposals for printing by subscription, in one volume, quarto, Memoirs of Peter Henry Bruce, Esq. a military officer, and engineer in the services of Prussia, Russia, and Great-Britain. Containing, an account of his travels in Germany, Russia, Tartary, Turkey, the West Indies, &c . . .. To which is added an account of the British West Indies settlements . . . Subscriptions for this work are received by T. Payne and Son, B. White, J. Robson, T. Cadell, G. Nicol. J. Walter, J. Sewell, J. Murray, Mess. Fletcher, Oxon., Mess Merril, Cambridge, J. Balfour, Edinburgh, L. White, Dublin.
3p. 8vo.
The work was published in 1782, but Murray is not individually named in the imprint (see item 300).
Primary location, O, Gough Coll, Fiche 11/C7.
Travel-Topography. London syndicate.

253. Cullen, William, 1710–1790.
Synopsis nosologia methodica, exhibens clariss. virorum Sauvagesii, Linnai, Vogelii, et Sagari, systemata nosologica. Edidit suumque proprium systema nosologicum adjecit Gulielmus Cullen, . . . Editio tertia, emendata et plurimum aucta, duobus tomis. . . . Edinburgi, prostant venales, apud Gulielmum Creech; et Londini, apud Thomam Cadell, et Joannem Murray, 1780.
Vol. 1: iv,349p.; vol. 2: [1],xxix,41–417p., 8vo.
Price: 10s.
ESTC t134581: L, 1509/1620.
Medicine. Edinburgh co-publishing.

254. Dease, William, 1752?–1798.
An introduction to the theory and practice of surgery. By William Dease, . . . Vol. I. London, printed for J. Murray, 1780.
lv,[1],159,[1]p., 8vo. With a half-title, and an errata slip pasted to the verso of p. [viii]. Price: 3s. No more published. Entered in the Stationers' Company Register, 30 Nov. 1779, 'J. Murray the whole'. Stock: 97 (H); 199 (W).
ESTC t116752: L, 549.g.19.
Medicine. Murray alone.

255. Elliot, Sir John, 1736–1786.
Philosophical observations on the senses of vision and hearing; to which are added, a treatise on harmonic sounds, and an essay on combustion and animal heat. By J. Elliott, . . . London, printed for J. Murray, 1780.
viii,222,[4]p., 8vo. With two final advertisement leaves. Price: 3s.6d.
Entered in the Stationers' Company Register, 30 Nov. 1779, 'J. Murray. The Whole'. Stock: 20 (H).
ESTC t078105: L, 538.f.13(2).
Medicine. Murray alone.

256. Haller, Albrecht von, 1708–1777.
Letters from Baron Haller to his daughter, on the truths of the Christian religion. Translated from the German. London, printed for J. Murray; and William Creech, at Edinburgh, 1780.
xxxii,279,[1]p., 8vo. With a half-title. Price: 4s.
A translation of *Briefe über die wichtigsten Wahrheiten der Offenbarung*. Entered in the Stationers' Company Register, 7 July 1780, 'John Murray, the whole'.
ESTC t101699: L, 1019.d.27.
Religion. Edinburgh co-publishing.

257. Home, Francis, 1719–1813.
Clinical experiments, histories, and dissections. By Francis Home, M.D. Edinburgh, printed for William Creech, and J. Murray. London, 1780.
xvi,458,[2]p., 8vo. With a final errata leaf. Price: 7s.
ESTC t112609: L, 7444.de.16.
Medicine. Edinburgh co-publishing.

258. Manning, Henry, M.D.
Modern improvements in the practice of physic. By Henry Manning, . . . London, printed for G. Robinson; and J. Murray, 1780.

[10],240p. (pp. 434, 436, 438, 440 misnum. 234, 236, 238, 240 respectively), 8vo. With a half-title. Price: 5s.
Stock: 138 (W).
ESTC n005001: MBCo, 6.G.145.
Medicine. London co-publishing.

259. Manning Henry, M.D.
Modern improvements in the practice of surgery. By Henry Manning, . . . London, printed for G. Robinson; and J. Murray, 1780.
[4],423,[1]p., 8vo. Price: 5s.
Stock: 42 (H); 121 (W).
ESTC n004998: DNLM, 18th c. coll.
Medicine. Murray alone.

260. The modern part of an universal history, from the earliest accounts to the present time. Compiled from original authors. By the authors of the ancient part. . . . London, printed for C. Bathurst, J. F. C. Rivington, A. Hamilton, T. Payne, T. Longman, S. Crowder, B. Law, T. Becket, J. Robson, F. Newbery, G. Robinson, T. Cadell, J. and T. Bowles, S. Bladon, J. Murray, and W. Fox, 1780–84.
42 vols, plate, map. 8vo. Price: £15.
Vols. 1–4 dated 1780; vols. 5–15, 1781; vols. 16–28, 1782; vols. 29–37, 1783; vol. 38, 1784; vols. 39–41, 1783; vol. 42, 1784. The imprints of vols 4–42 exclude T. Becket and add (after Murray) J. Nichols and J. Bowen. 600 copies printed. See *Universal* 1779, item 248. Murray paid £52.8s.6d. for paper and printing. The returns on his share (22 copies) were £147.12s. (BB, p. 16). Stock: 4 sets in 60 vols. (both the ancient and modern parts) (W).
ESTC t041325: L, G.4596
History. London syndicate.

261. Monro, Donald, 1727–1802.
Observations on the means of preserving the health of soldiers; and of conducting military hospitals. And on the diseases incident to soldiers in the time of service, and on the same diseases as they have appeared in London. In two volumes. By Donald Monro, M.D. . . . The second edition. London, printed for J. Murray; and G. Robinson, 1780.
Vol. 1: xi,[7],374p.; vol. 2: vii,304,[2]p., 8vo. With 2pp. of advertisements in vol. 2. Price: 10s. in boards.
A greatly enlarged edition of his *Essay on the*

means of preserving the health of soldiers. Stock: 117 (W).
ESTC no10023: DNLM, 18th c.coll.
Medicine. London co-publishing.

262. Perry, William, lecturer in the Academy at Edinburgh.
The man of business; and gentleman's assistant: containing a complete system of practical arithmetic, ... book-keeping by single and double entry; ... By William Perry; ... The fourth edition with improvements. Edinburgh, printed for W. Anderson, Stirling; sold by him and C. Elliot, Edinburgh; W. Charnley, Newcastle and J. Murray, London, 1780.
212,[107],344–451,[1]p., 8vo. Price: 5s.6d.
ESTC no34751: FMU, HF5631.P45 1780.
Economics. Provincial co-publishing.

263. Richardson, William, 1743–1814.
A philosophical analysis and illustration of some of Shakespeare's remarkable characters. By W. Richardson, ... A new edition, corrected. London, printed for J. Murray, 1780.
207,[1]p., 8vo.
ESTC t136699: L, 11713.a.3.
Literary criticism. Murray alone.

264. Shaw, William, 1749–1831.
A Galic and English dictionary. Containing all the words in the Scotch and Irish dialects of the Celtic, that could be collected from the voice, and old books and MSS. By the Rev. William Shaw, A.M. ... London, printed for the author, by W. and A. Strahan; and sold by J. Murray; P. Elmsly; C. Elliot, J. Balfour, and R. Jamieson, Edinburgh; D. Prince, Oxford; Messrs. Merril, Cambridge; Wilson, Dublin; and Pissot, Paris, 1780.
Vol. 1: [380]p.; vol. 2: [308]p., 4to. With a four-page list of subscribers in vol. 1. Price: 2 gns. in boards.
500 copies printed by Wm Strahan, half on fine plain paper and half on ordinary Demy (BL Add. MS 48809, f. 7). 206 subscribers took 219 copies. Murray is not mentioned in the Prospectus (copy at O, J. Pros.249). Vol. 2 is entitled: *An English and Galic dictionary*.
ESTC t147710: L, 1502/410.
Language. Agency–London.

265. Simmons, Samuel Foart, 1750–1813.

The anatomy of the human body. By Samuel Foart Simmons, M.D. ... Vol. I. London, printed for J. Murray; and W. Creech, Edinburgh, 1780.
xix,[1],462p., 8vo. Price: 6s. in boards.
No more published. Murray paid Simmons £52.10s. for the copyright (BB, p. 22). Entered in the Stationers' Company Register, 30 Nov. 1779, 'J. Murray, the whole'. Stock: 166 (W).
ESTC t059542: L, 780.g.5.
Medicine. Edinburgh co-publishing.

266. Simmons, Samuel Foart, 1750–1813.
Observations on the cure of the gonorrhoea. By Samuel Foart Simmons, M.D. ... London, sold by J. Murray; Fielding and Walker; and J. Fisk, 1780.
viii,66,[2]p., 8vo. With a half-title and a final leaf of advertisements. Price: 1s.6d.
ESTC t055028: L, 783.k.5(1).
Medicine. London co-publishing.

267. Simmons, Samuel Foart, 1750–1813.
Practical observations on the treatment of consumptions. By Samuel Foart Simmons, M.D. ... London, Sold by J. Murray; Mess. Fielding and Walker; and J. Fisk, 1780.
87,[1]p., 8vo. With a half-title. Price: 2s.
ESTC t055655: L, T.316(3).
Medicine. London co-publishing.

268. [Smollett, Tobias George, 1721–1771.]
The adventures of Roderick Random. In two volumes. ... The tenth edition, illustrated with frontispieces. London, printed for W. Strahan, J. Rivington & Sons, T. Caslon, B. Law, C. Dilly, G. Robinson, T. Cadell, T. Lowndes, R. Baldwin, J. Murray, and J. Bowen, 1780.
Vol. 1: xvi,280p.; vol. 2: xii,316p., 2 plates, 12mo.
1500 copies printed. Murray bought a 1/32 share for £1.11s.6d. on 21 Jan. 1779 at the sale of Thomas Becket at the Queen's Arms. In July 1780 he paid Thomas Cadell £3.10s.6d. for paper and printing. The returns on his share (47 copies at 3s. each, wholesale) were £7.1s. (BB, p. 17).
ESTC t055375: L, 1486.aaa.14.
Fiction. London syndicate.

269. [Sterne, Laurence, 1713–1768.]
A sentimental journey through France and Italy.

By Mr. Yorick. . . . A new edition. London, printed for W. Strahan; T. Cadell; G. Robinson; J. Murray and T. Evans, 1780.
Vol. 1: 203p.; vol. 2: 208p., plates, ill., 8vo. Price: 5s.
1500 copies printed. Murray bought a quarter share for £51 on 21 Jan. 1779 at the sale of Thomas Becket at the Queen's Arms. He sold a 1/16 share to Thomas Evans on 28 Feb. 1780 for £13. On 11 July 1780 he paid Thomas Cadell £37.10s. for paper and printing. The returns on his share (375 sets at 2s. each, wholesale) were £37.10s. (BB, p. 18; see next).
ESTC t014707: L, 012641.de.8.
Fiction. London syndicate.

270. Another edition with the same imprint, in one volume.
[4],340,[4]p., ill., 12mo. With a half-title and two final advertisement leaves. Price: 3s.
1500 copies printed. On the same investment as above the returns on Murray's share in the one-vol. edition (375 copies at 1s.6d. each, wholesale) were £23.8s.9d. (BB, p. 18).
ESTC t014692: L, 1607/3568.
Fiction. London syndicate.

271. Sterne, Laurence, 1713–1768.
The works of Laurence Sterne. In ten volumes complete. Containing, I. the life and opinions of Tristram Shandy, Gent. II. A sentimental journey through France and Italy. III. Sermons. IV Letters. with a life of the author written by himself. London, printed for W. Strahan, J. Rivington and sons, J. Dodsley, G. Kearsley, T. Lowndes, G. Robinson, T. Cadell, J. Murray, T. Becket, R. Baldwin, and T. Evans, 1780.
Vol. 1: xx,[4],296p.; vol. 2: [4],307p.; vol. 3: [6],288p.; vol. 4: [8],264]p.; vol. 5: [3],242p.; vol. 6: [7],284p.; vol. 7: [12],276p.; vol. 8: [8],280p.; vol. 9: xx,208p.; vol. 10: vii,198p. 8vo. port. plates. Price: £2.
1000 copies printed. The details of Murray's original share purchases appear to be incomplete. On 21 Jan. 1779 he bought a 1/8 share of 'Vols 4, 5, 6' for £30 at the sale of Thomas Becket at the Queen's Arms, 1/16 of which he sold on 26 Jan. 1779 to Lowndes for 15 gns (BB, p. 15). On 3 May 1780 Murray paid £37.11d. for his 63/1000 share of paper and printing. The returns on his share (63 sets at

20s. each, wholesale) were £63 (BB, p. 23 and Plates 27 and 28). According to an undated newspaper advertisement the 'head of the author [is] by Sherwin, and other Plates from Designs of Hogarth, Rooker, and Edwards.'
Fiction. London syndicate.

272. Stuart, Gilbert, 1743–1786.
The history of the establishment of the reformation of religion in Scotland. By Gilbert Stuart, LL.D. London, printed for J. Murray; and J. Bell, at Edinburgh, 1780.
iv,[4],265,[3]p., port., 4to. With a final leaf of advertisements. Price: 10s.6d.
750 copies printed by Alexander Hamilton. Entered in the Stationers' Company Register, 7 Mar. 1780, 'The Author. the Whole'. Stock: 326 (W).
ESTC t096527: L, 203.e.14.
History. Edinburgh co-publishing.

273. Thoughts on a fund for the improvement of credit in Great Britain; and the establishement of a national bank in Ireland. London, printed for J. Murray, 1780.
[4],33p., 8vo. With a half-title. Price: 1s.
Published 21 Feb. 1780.
ESTC t085850: L, 104.c.41.
Economics. Murray alone.

274. [Wakefield, Gilbert, 1756–1801.]
Poems: consisting of original pieces; and translations, from the ancient, and modern classics. London, printed for J. Murray, 1780.
[8],96p., 8vo. With half-title.
ESTC t042609: L, 3755.d.10(3).
Poetry. Murray alone.

1781

275. Andree, John, c. 1740–ca. 1820.
Account of an elastic trochar, constructed on a new principle, for tapping the hydrocele, or watery rupture: . . . With a few words in favor of a larger trochar, on a similar construction, for tapping the abdomen. By John Andree, . . . London, printed for L. Davis; T. Caslon; G. Kearsley, and J. Murray; J. Ridley; R. Faulder; J. Sewell, W. Davis; and W. Clarke, 1781.
5,[2],10–41,[1]p., plate, 8vo. Price: 1s.
ESTC t006651: L, T.277(3).
Medicine. London co-publishing.

276. Andree, John, *c.* 1740–*c.* 1820.
An essay on the theory and cure of the venereal gonorrhoea, and its consequent diseases. By John Andree, ... The second edition, improved and enlarged. London, printed for L. Davis; T. Caslon; G. Kearsley; J. Murray; J. Ridley; R. Faulder; J. Sewell; W. Davis; and W. Clarke, 1781.
[2],85,[1]p., 8vo. With a half-title. Price: 1*s*.6*d.*
Entered in the Stationers' Company Register, 21 May 1781, 'The Author, the whole'.
ESTC to55029: L, 783.k.5(2).
Medicine. London co-publishing.

*277. Crébillon, Claude Propser Jolyot de, 1707–1777.
The Sopha: a moral tale. Translated from the French of Monsieur Crebillon. ... A new edition. London, printed for T. Cooper, 1781.
Vol. 1: [4],255,[1]p; vol. 2: [4],250p. 12mo. Price: 6*s.*
Listed in 'Books printed for J. Murray' in an advertisement to William Thomson, *The man in the moon,* 1783. A second edition appeared in 1787. First published in English in 1742. Stock: 25, 116 (W).
ESTC ID T115299: L, 1153.e.22.
Fiction. Murray alone?

278. Cullen, William, 1710–1790.
First lines of the practice of physic, for the use of students in the University of Edinburgh. By William Cullen, ... Third edition, corrected. Edinburgh, printed for William Creech; and sold in London by John Murray, 1781.
Vol. 1: viii,424p.; vol. 2: viii,406p., 8vo. Price: 12*s.*
The fourth edition of vol. 1, in which Murray did not have a share, was entered in the Stationers' Company Register, 6 Feb. 1784, 'Charles Elliot, the whole'; and vols. 2–4 10 June 1784 for Elliot.
ESTC t151831: GOT, 8oMed.pract.124/81.
Medicine. Agency–Edinburgh.

*279. Dancer, Thomas.
A brief history of the late expedition against Fort San Juan, so far as it relates to the diseases of the troops: together with some observations on climate, infection and contagion; and several of the endemial complaints of the West-Indies. By Thomas Dancer, M.D. physician to the

troops on that service. Kingston [Jamaica], printed by D. Douglass &; W. Aikman; and sold by them at the Royal Gazette Printing-Office, and at Wm. Aikman's shop in Kingston; by Alexander Aikman, in Spanish-Town; and by James Fannin, printer in Montego-Bay, 1781.
63,[1]p., 4to. Price: 2*s*.6*d.*
English Review 1 (May 1783), 378: 'sold by Murray in London'. Murray is also listed in the *Monthly Review* 68 (Apr. 1783), 361; *Critical Review* 54 (July 1782), 74.
ESTC t029630: L,T.35(18).
Medicine. Agency–provincial.

280. De Lolme, Jean Louis, 1740–1806.
The constitution of England, or an account of the English government; ... By J. L. de Lolme, ... The third edition. London, printed for G. Robinson; and J. Murray, 1781.
xvi,[4],479,[25]p., 8vo. With index and a final errata leaf. Price: 7*s.*
A translation of *Constitution de l'Angleterre* by Gilbert Stuart and first published by George Kearsley in 1775. Entered in the Stationers' Company Register, 22 Apr. 1775, 'The Author. The Whole'. This edition contains considerable additions.
1500 copies printed. Murray paid George Robinson £26.5*s.* for a ¼ share in Nov. 1780. He paid £34.7*s.*6*d.* for paper (£17 to Thomas Curtis) and printing (£17.7*s.*6*d.* to Arch. Hamilton). The returns on his share (375 copies at 4*s.*4*d,* each, wholesale) were £81.5*s.* (BB, p. 24).
ESTC t109392: L, 522.h.18.
History. London co-publishing.

281. Dodd, James Solas, 1721–1805.
The ancient and modern history of Gibraltar, and the sieges and attacks it hath sustained: with an accurate journal of the siege of that fortress by the Spaniards, from February 13, to June 23, 1727. Translated from the original Spanish, published by authority at Madrid. By J.S. Dodd, ... London, printed for John Murray, 1781.
[4],203,[1]p., 12mo. Price: 2*s*.6*d.*
ESTC t095130: L, 9180.bbb.16.
History. Murray alone.

282. Hamilton, Alexander, 1739–1802.
A treatise of midwifery, comprehending the management of female complaints, and the

treatment of children in early infancy. . . . By Alexander Hamilton, . . . London, printed for J. Murray; J. Dickson, W. Creech, and C. Elliot, Edinburgh, 1781.
xxiv,464p., 8vo. Price: 6s. in boards.
Entered in the Stationers' Company Register, 2 Jan. 1780, 'The Author, the whole'.
ESTC to51628: L, 1177.h.14.
Medicine. Edinburgh co-publishing.

283. Hints, on diseases that are not cured: address'd to the faculty only. London, printed for J. Murray, 1781.
[2],46p., Fo. Price: 1 gn.
ESTC to68079: L, 789.k.15.
Medicine. Murray alone.

284. Henry Home, Lord Kames, 1696–1782.
Loose hints upon education, chiefly concerning the culture of the heart. Edinburgh, printed for John Bell; and John Murray, London, 1781.
xi,381,[3]p., 8vo. Dedication signed: Henry Home. With a final advertisement leaf. Price: 5s.
Entered in the Stationers' Company Register, 30 Apr. 1781, 'J. Bell of Edinb: the whole by purchase from the author Henry Home'.
ESTC to58640: L, 1387.d.3.
Education. Edinburgh co-publishing.

285. Jackson, Seguin Henry, 1752–1816.
A treatise on sympathy, in two parts. . . . By Seguin Henry Jackson, . . . London, printed for the author; and sold by J. Murray, 1781.
xv,[1],274p. (p.xv misnum. ii), 8vo. Price: 4s. in boards.
ESTC t114944: L, 782.i.26.
Philosophy. Agency–Murray alone.

286. Johnson, Samuel, 1709–1784.
The lives of the most eminent English poets; with critical observations on their works. By Samuel Johnson. In four volumes. . . . London, printed for C. Bathurst, J. Buckland, W. Strahan, J. Rivington and Sons, T. Davies, T. Payne. L. Davis, W. Owen, B. White, S. Crowder, T. Caslon, T. Longman, B. Law, C. Dilly, J. Dodsley, J. Wilkie, J. Robson, J. Johnson, T. Lowndes, G. Robinson, T. Cadell, J. Nichols, E. Newbery, T. Evans, P. Elmsly, J. Ridley, R. Baldwin, G. Nicol, Leigh and Sotheby, J. Bew, N. Conant, W. Nicholl, J. Murray, S. Hayes, W. Fox, and J. Bowen, 1781.

Vol. 1: [1],vii,480p.; vol. 2: iii,471p.; vol. 3: iii,462p.; vol. 4: iii,505p., plate, port., 8vo. The final leaf of vol. 4 contains advertisements for books published by J. Nichols. Price: 1 gn.
ESTC t146734: L, 673.f.20–23.
3000 copies printed. Information in BB (p. 11) under 'Johnson's English Poets' surprisingly does not record this first octavo edition in which Murray certainly had an interest (See Johnson 1779, item 228; To Charles Elliot, 5 June 1781).
Biography. London syndicate.

287. The London medical journal. By a society of physicians. Vol. I. London, printed for the authors by W. Richardson; and sold by J. Murray, 1781.
iv,444,[8]p., 8vo.
Issued monthly. Edited by Samuel Foart Simmons. Superseded by *Medical facts and observations*. Stock: 250 Apr., 194 May, 246 June (W).
ESTC n062453: WU-M, Q 7L82.1
Medicine. London co-publishing.

288. The London mercury; containing the history, politics and literature of England, for the year 1780. London, printed for J. Murray, 1781.
[8],viii,392,151p., 8vo. Price: 5s. in boards.
Edited by William Thomson. Stock: 10 (H).
Primary location: CtY, Z17.303F.
Miscellaneous. Murray alone.

289. Lumley, Thomas.
A letter to Charles Turner, Esq; member of Parliament for the city of York, from the Rev. Thomas Lumley, L.L.B. London, printed for the author, and sold by J. Murray; W. Flexney; and by the booksellers in York, 1781.
[4],27,[1]p., 8vo.
ESTC n033595: Ct, X.29.11(4).
Politics. Agency–London.

290. Marmontel, Jean-François, 1723–1799.
Moral tales by M. Marmontel. . . . The third edition. Illustrated with sixteen elegant engravings. London, printed for T. Cadell, J. Murray, T. Becket, and H. Baldwin, 1781.
Vol. 1: [4],iv,260p.; vol. 2: [iv],288p.; vol. 3: [iv],251p., plates, 12mo. Price: 10s. 6d. bound.
A translation of *Contes moraux* by C. Denis and R. Lloyd. 1500 copies printed. Murray paid 2 gns for a ¼ share at Thomas Becket's sale on 21

Jan. 1779 at the Queen's Arms. He paid £56.5s. for paper (£37.15s.) and printing (£18.10). The returns on his share (375 copies at 5s.3d., each, wholesale) were £98.8s.9d. The share was sold on 23 Dec. 1794 to Vernor & Ogilvy for £2.5s. (BB, p. 20). Stock: 2 vol. 2; 3 vol. 3 (H). *ESTC* no35229: ViW, PQ2005.C5E5 1781. Religion. London co-publishing.

291. Millar, John, 1735–1801.
The origin of the distinction of ranks; or, an inquiry into the circumstances which give rise to influence and authority in the different members of society. By John Millar, Esq. . . . The third edition, corrected and enlarged. London, printed for J. Murray, 1781.
viii,362,[2]p., 8vo. With a half-title. Price: 6s. bound.
The 1779 edition (printed by Andrew Foulis) with a new title page. Entered in the Stationers' Company Register, 7 July 1780, 'Murray.' Stock: 1 (W).
ESTC t127481: L, 1509/793.
History. Murray alone.

292. Principles of law and government with An inquiry into the justice and policy of the present war, and most effectual means of obtaining an honourable, permanent, and advantageous peace. London, sold by J. Murray, 1781.
[2],iv,[2],202,[2];127;[1]p., 4to. With a half-title and an errata slip. Price: 7s.6d.
Sometimes attributed to David Williams, founder of the Literary Fund. In two parts, separately paginated. MH-L report errata leaf opposite p. iv making the pagination: iv,[4] &c. Entered in the Stationers' Company Register, 1 July 1781, 'The Author——Gordon, the whole'. Stock: 415 (W). Reference: Adams 81–58.
ESTC to57635: L, 521.k.22.
Politics. Murray alone.

293. Rutherford, William, 1745–1820.
The character, temper, qualifications, and duty, of a faithful minister. A sermon, preached the 22d of December, 1780, at the ordination of the Rev. Mr. Thomas Rutledge, . . . by the Rev. William Rutherford, . . . London, printed for J. Murray, 1781.
[4],39,[1]p., 8vo. Price: 1s.
ESTC t165367: E, L.114.g.1(8).
Religion. Murray alone.

294. Shaw, William, 1749–1831.
An enquiry into the authenticity of the poems ascribed to Ossian. By W. Shaw, . . . London, printed for J. Murray, 1781.
[4],87,[1]p., 8vo. With a half-title. Price: 1s.6d.
Revised by Samuel Johnson. (To Shaw, 26 Jan. 1782, which includes a transcribed note from Johnson on the subject). See Shaw 1782.
ESTC t143497: O, G.Pamph.374(2).
Literary criticism. Murray alone.

295. Thomson, Alexander, M.D.
An enquiry into the nature, causes, and method of cure, of nervous disorders. In a letter to a friend. By Alex. Thomson, M.D. London, printed for J. Murray, 1781.
[4],35,[1]p., 8vo. With a half-title. Price: 1s.
ESTC no09211: DNLM, 18th c.coll.
Medicine. Murray alone.

296. Wallis, George, 1740–1802.
An essay on the evil consequences attending injudicious bleeding in pregnancy. With an address in replication to the monthly reviewers. By George Wallis . . . The second edition. London, printed for J. Murray, 1781.
[4],19,[1];75,[1]p., 8vo. With a half-title.
ESTC t146912: L, 1178.i.6.
Medicine. Murray alone.

297. Walwyn, B., b. 1750.
The farce of Chit chat, or penance for polygamy. An interlude. Now performed at the Theatre Royal in Covent Garden. Written by B. Walwyn. London; sold by J. Murray, 1781.
[2],ii,[1],6–20p., 8vo. Price: 6d.
ESTC t223815: L, RB.23.b.1144.
Drama. Murray alone.

1782

298. Andree, John, c. 1740–c. 1820.
Account of an elastic trochar, constructed on a new principle, for tapping the hydrocele and abdomen. . . . The second edition, enlarged and improved. By John Andree, . . . London, printed for L. Davis; T. Caslon; J. Murray; R. Faulder; J. Sewell; W. Clark; P. Brett, and G. Bremner, 1782.
38,[2]p., plate, 8vo. With a half-title and a final advertisement leaf. Price: 1s.
ESTC t141547: L, 1568/388.
Medicine. London co-publishing.

299. Brookes, Richard, fl. 1721–1763.
The general gazetteer: or, compendious geographical dictionary. Containing a description of all the empires, . . . chief towns, . . . harbours, . . . and promontories in the known worlds; together with the governemnt, policy, . . . of the inhabitants; . . . Embellished with nine maps. By R. Brookes, M.D. The fifth edition, improved, with additions and corrections. London, printed for J. F. and C. Rivington, T. Carnan, and J. Johnson; S. Crowder, G. Robinson, R. Baldwin, B. Law, T. Lowndes, J. Murray and C. Dilly, 1782.
xvi,[682]p., plates, maps, 8vo. With a final errata leaf. Price: 7s.
3000 copies printed. Murray bought a 103/3000 share on 8 Apr. 1777 at the Queen's Arms and paid 5 gns to Edward Johnston. On 16 July 1782 he paid out £14.11s.10d. for paper and printing. The returns on his share (103 copies at 4s.4d. each, wholesale) were £22.6s.4d. (BB, p. 1; Brookes, 1778). Entered in the Stationers' Company Register, 18 July 1782, listed as in the imprint without the division of shares.
ESTC t113138: L, 793.h.7.
Travel–topography. London syndicate.

*300. Bruce, Peter Henry, 1692–1757.
Memoirs of Peter Henry Bruce, Esq. A military officer, in the services of Prussia, Russia, and Great Britain. Containing an account of his travels . . . London, printed for the author's widow; and sold by T. Payne, and Son; and all other booksellers, 1782.
[12],446p., 4to.
Murray is listed as an agent in the subscription proposal (see Bruce 1780, item 252).
ESTC t130369: L, 215.a.3.
Military. Agency–London.

301. Butter, William, 1726–1805.
A treatise on the infantile remittent fever. By William Butter, . . . London, printed for J. Robson; J. Murray; and J. Johnson, 1782.
50,[2]p., 8vo. With a half-title and a final advertisement leaf. Price: 1s.
ESTC t026549: L, 1177.d.12(2).
Medicine. London co-publishing.

302. Cervantes Saavedra, Miguel de, 1547–1616.

The history and adventures of the renowned Don Quixote. Translated from the Spanish of Miguel de Cervantes Saavedra. . . . By T. Smollett, M.D. Illustrated with twenty-eight new copper-plates, designed by Hayman, and elegantly engraved. The fifth edition, corrected. In four volumes. . . . London, printed for W. Strahan, J. F. and C. Rivington, T. Longman, T. Caslon, B. Law, T. Lowndes, W. Nicoll, Richardson and Urquhart, G. Robinson, T. Cadell, R. Baldwin, W. Goldsmith, J. Knox, J. Murray, E. Newbery, J. Debret, and J. Fox, 1782.
Vol. 1: [4],xl,293p.; vol. 2: [1],314p.; vol. 3: [1],xi,331p.; vol. 4: [1],322p., plates, 12mo. Price: 12s.
2040 copies printed. In Dec. 1782 issued a 3–month note to Cadell for £6.2s.6d. for expenses. The returns on his share (34 copies at 6s. each, wholesale) were £10.4s. (BB, p. 28).
ESTC t059488: L, 12491.b.14.
Fiction. London syndicate.

303. Chambaud, Lewis, d. 1776.
Chambaud improved; or, French and English exercises, . . . By James Nicolson, . . . London, printed for the author; and sold by J. Murray, 1782.
[8],219,[1]p., 12mo.
Originally published in 1750 as *Exercises to the rules of construction of French-speech.* Reference: Alston xii. 319. Entered in the Stationers' Company Register, 12 Dec. 1781, 'The Author, the whole'. In March 1784 Murray paid Nicolson £10 for the copyright (BB. p. 36) and published a second edition in 1789.
ESTC t054013: L, 1212.g.2(1).
Language. Agency–Murray alone.

304. Clarke, Henry, 1743–1818.
Supplement to Professor Lorgna's summation of series. To which are added, remarks on Mr. Landen's observations on the same subject. By the translator of the above work, Henry Clarke. London, printed for the author; and sold by J. Murray, 1782.
iv,56,[2]p., 4to. With a final advertisement leaf. Price: 2s.6d.
A supplement to *A dissertation on the summation of infinite converging series,* which Murray published in 1779 (item 231).
ESTC t105269: L, 50.k.15.
Science. Agency–Murray alone.

305. Combe, Charles, 1743–1817.
Nummorum veterum populorum et urbium, qui in museo Gulielmi Hunter asservantur, descriptio figuris illustrata. Opera et studio Caroli Combe, . . . Londini, ex officina J. Nichols: veneunt apud T. Cadell; P. Elmsly; G. Nicol; et J. Murray, 1782.
xi,[1],354,[2]p., 68 plates, 4to. With a final errata leaf.
ESTC t098595: L, 138.e.7.
Miscellaneous. London co-publishing.

306. Gast, John, 1716–1788.
The history of Greece, from the accession of Alexander of Macedon, till its final subjection to the Roman power; in eight books. By John Gast, D.D. Archdeacon of Glandelagh. London, printed for J. Murray; and sold by R. Moncrief, T. T. Faulkner, L. White and the rest of the booksellers at Dublin, 1782.
[4],vii–xxiv,711,[1]p., 4to. With a half-title and errata list. Price: 1 gn. in boards.
500 copies printed; expenses were £96.12s. for paper (92 reams of very fine Demy), printing and corrections £97.19s., advertising 14 guineas, 'publishing, warehouse and interest of money 10 guineas' (BB, p. 29 and correspondence with Gast; see Plate 24). Entered in the Stationers' Company Register, 29 Apr. 1782, 'J. Murray by purchase, the whole'. Stock: 56 (H).
ESTC t194372: DUc, N.III.62.
Another issue: London, printed for J. Murray, 1782.
ESTC t145508: L, 200.e.13.
History. Murray–with agency.

307. Heysham, John, 1753–1834.
An account of the jail fever, or typhus carcerum: as it appeared at Carlisle in the year 1781. By John Heysham . . . London, printed for T. Cadell, J. Murray, R. Faulder, and J. Milliken, Carlisle, 1782.
iv,59,[1]p., 8vo.
ESTC t108733: L, 7561.d.18.
Medicine. Provincial co-publishing.

308. Home, Francis, 1719–1813.
Clinical experiments, histories, and dissections. By Francis Home, M.D. . . . Second edition, corrected. London, printed for J. Murray, and William Creech, Edinburgh, 1782.
xii,499,[1]p. (pp. 167–176 are repeated in the

pagination, and numbers 177–186 are omitted), 8vo. Price: 7s.
Murray paid Home 50 gns for the work (To Home, 5 Nov. 1781).
ESTC n003186: MBCo, R854.G7H75 1782.
Medicine. Edinburgh co-publishing.

309. Home, Henry, Lord Kames, 1696–1782.
Loose hints upon education, chiefly concerning the culture of the heart. Second edition, enlarged. Edinburgh, printed for John Bell; Geo. Robinson, and John Murray, London, 1782.
xi,[1],419,[1]p., 8vo. Price: 5s.
ESTC t055415: L, 1030.g.6.
Education. Edinburgh co-publishing.

310. Jacob, Giles, 1686–1744.
A new law-dictionary: containing the interpretation and definition of words and terms used in the law; as also the law and practice, under the proper heads and titles. . . . Originally compiled by Giles Jacob. And now corrected and greatly enlarged by J. Morgan, . . . The tenth edition. London, printed by W. Strahan and W. Woodfall: for W. Strahan, J. Rivington and Sons, T. Payne, P. Iriel, W. Owen, T. Longman, S. Crowder, T. Caslon, D. Law, J. Robson, C. Dilly, G. Robinson, W. Domville, R. Cadell, T. Lowndes, W. Cater, J. Johnson, W. Flexney, W. Otridge, Richardson and Urquhart, J. Sewell, R. Baldwin, W. Nicoll, F. Newbery, E. Brooke, J. Murray, T. Evans, J. Fielding, J. Wade, W. Fox, and T. Whieldon, 1782.
[4],iii,[991]p., 20. Price: 2 gns.
2000 copies printed. Murray bought a 1/80 share at the Queens Arms on 25 Jan. 1777, paying Thomas Becket £13.7s.6d. cash for his share. In Nov. 1782 he paid £16.5s. for paper and printing. The returns on his share (25 copies at £1.8s. each, wholesale) were £35. Sold a 1/80 share 23 Dec. 1794 to Butterworth for £10.5s. Butterworth then paid an additional £6.17s.6d. (BB, p. 3).
ESTC t137458: L, 18.f.1.
Law. London syndicate.

311. [Le Sage, Alain René, 1668–1747.]
The adventures of Gil Blas of Santillane. A new translation, by the author of Roderick Random [Tobias Smollett]. Adorned with thirty-three cuts, neatly engraved. In four volumes. The

fifth edition. ... London, printed for W. Strahan, J. Rivington and Sons, J. Johnson, T. Longman, T. Caslon, J. Wilkie, B. Law, G. Robinson, T. Cadell, J. Knox, W. Nicoll, T. Lowndes, Richardson and Urquhart, J. Murray, T. Evans, J. Sewell, and R. Baldwin, 1782.

Vol. 1: xii,312p.; vol. 2: [4],263,[1]p.; vol. 3: vii,[1],292p.; vol. 4: iv,276p., 33 plates, 12mo. Price: 12s. bound.

Murray paid £1.17s. for a 1/32 share at Thomas Becket's sale on 21 Jan. 1779 at the Queen's Arms (BB, p. 25). No other records for this edition. See Le Sage 1792, item 890 Stock: 34 and 620 (W).

ESTC t130470: L, 12518.s.8.

Fiction. London syndicate.

312. Lieberkühn, Johann Nathanael, 1711–1756.

Joannis Nathanael Lieberkühn, ... dissertationes quatuor. ... Collecta & edita cura et studio Joannis Sheldon, ... Londini, prostant apud T. Cadell, & P. Elmsley; J. Murray; J. Johnson; E. & C. Dilly; J. Hayes; & W. Babbs, 1782.

[4],x,15,[1],[2],32,31–36,[17]–25,[1]p., plates, 4to. With an initial leaf of advertisements.

The French dissertations are part of an edition of the *Mémoires de l'Académie Royale des Sciences et Belles-Lettres de Berlin*, 1748.

ESTC t029102: L, T.40(2).

Medicine. London co-publishing.

313. Lucas, Henry, fl. 1776–1795.

The cypress-wreath; or meed of honor; an elegio-heroic poem, to the memory of the Right Honorable Captain Lord Robert Manners, ... By Henry Lucas, ... London, printed for the author; and sold by J. Stockdale; G. Kearsly; and J. Murray, 1782.

vi,[7]–19,[1]p., 4to. With a half-title. Price: 1s.

ESTC t034550: L, 11630.e.2(10).

Poetry. Agency–London.

314. [Macintosh, William]

Travels in Europe, Asia, and Africa; describing characters, customs, manners, laws, and productions of nature and art: containing various remarks on the political and commercial interests of Great Britain: and delineating, in particular, a new system ... in the East Indies: begun in ... 1777, and finished in 1781. In two volumes. ... London, printed for J. Murray, 1782.

Vol. 1: xxiii,[1],482p; vol. 2: xi,[1],503,[1]p., 8vo. With 2pp. of errata.

In the *Defence of Innes Munro*, 1790, Murray explained that 'a Gentleman from India, [Macintosh] being unpractised in literary composition, put sundry papers, which he wished to be published into the hands of Dr. [William] Thomson, who did his best to give them circulation by ... clothing them in tolerable language' (p. 17). Some of the letters included are 'addressed to J——M——Esq. London', presumably to Murray himself. Entered in the Stationers' Company Register, 29 Apr.l 1782, 'J. Murray by purchase, the whole'. An attack on this work was written by Capt. Joseph Price, *Some observations and remarks on a late publication, intitled, Travels in Europe, Asia, and Africa, in which the real author of this new and curious Asiatic Atalantis, his character and his abilities are fully made known to the publick*, 1782 (ESTC t122251).

ESTC t097734: L, 1045.h.6–7.

Travel–topography. Murray alone.

315. Pratt, Samuel Jackson, 1749–1814.

The sublime and beautiful of Scripture: being essays on select passages of sacred composition. By Mr. Pratt, ... A new edition. London, printed for J. Murray, and G. Robinson, 1782.

x,[4],xi–xii,[8],240p., 12mo. With a half-title and advertisements. Price: 3s. bound.

See Pratt 1777, item 164 Stock: 181 (W).

ESTC n037415: MBAt 32.P889.2.

Religion. London co-publishing.

316. Renny, George, c. 1760–1847.

A treatise on the venereal disease. By G. Renny, surgeon to the Athol Highlanders. London, printed for J. Murray, 1782.

xv,[1],171,[1]p., 8vo. With a half-title. Price: 3s. Stock: 80 (H).

ESTC t174442: E, NG.563.d.17.

Medicine. Murray alone.

317. Saunders, William, 1743–1817.

Observations on the superior efficacy of the red Peruvian bark, in the cure of agues and other fevers. Interspersed with occasional remarks on the treatment of other diseases by the same remedy. ... By William Saunders, M.D. ... Second edition, with considerable

additions. London, printed for J. Johnson, and J. Murray, 1782.
xii,iii,[1],76p., 8vo. Price: 2s. 6d.
ESTC no10078: MH-H, Tr 2048*
Medicine. London co-publishing.

318. The second edition with considerable additions. London, printed for J. Johnson, J. Murray; J. Sewell; and Hawkins, Southwark, 1782.
viii,158[i.e.176]p., 8vo.
ESTC to33057: L, B.72(1).
Medicine. London co-publishing.

319. Schotte, Johann Peter, 1744–1785.
A treatise on the synochus atrabiliosa, a contagious fever, which raged at Senegal in the year 1778, . . . By J. P. Schotte, M.D. London, printed for the author, by M. Scott, and sold by J. Murray, 1782.
169p. (pp. 169–170 misnum. 168–169), 8vo.
Price: 2s.6d.
Stock: 120 (H).
ESTC to18374: L, T.213(3).
Medicine. Agency–Murray alone.

320. Scott, Helenus, 1760–1821.
The adventures of a rupee. Wherein are interspersed various anecdotes Asiatic and European. London, printed for J. Murray, 1782.
[4],ix,[1],viii,264p., (p. 245 misnum. 249), 12mo. With a half-title. Price: 3s.6d.
The author identified in the 'Memoir of the author' as Helenus Scott, whom Murray paid 5 gns for the copyright (BB, p. 66). Entered in the Stationers' Company Register, 30 Nov. 1781, 'John Murray By purchase, the whole'.
ESTC to71896: L, N.1880.
Fiction. Murray alone.

321. A new edition. To which are prefixed, Memoirs of the life of the author. And to which there are annexed, his remarks concerning the inhabitants of Africa. London, printed for J. Murray, 1782.
[4],xx,257,[1]p., 12mo. With a half-title. Price: 3s.6d.
ESTC no03860: TxSaC, 823.79.S426.
Fiction. Murray alone.

322. A second letter to the Right Honourable Charles Jenkinson. London, printed for J. Murray, 1782.

[4],58p. 8vo. With a half-title. Price: 1s.
Signed: A citizen of the world, Brussels. Defending Charles Jenkinson and in answer to John Almon's anonymous *Letter to the Right Honourable Charles Jenkinson*, London, printed for J. Debrett, 1781 (*ESTC* to38384).
ESTC no62292: ICN, Case J54555.796.
Politics. Murray alone.

323. Shaw, William, 1749–1831.
An enquiry into the authenticity of the poems ascribed to Ossian. With a reply to Mr. Clark's Answer. The second edition corrected by W. Shaw, . . . London, printed for J. Murray, 1782.
[4],88p., 8vo. With a half-title. Price: 1s.6d.
Revised by Samuel Johnson. Stock: 274 (W), possibly copies of the 1781 edn.
ESTC t118399: L, 687.g.32(1).
Literary criticism. Murray alone.

324. [Sterne, Laurence, 1713–1768.]
Sentimental journey through France and Italy. By Mr Yorick. Complete in one volume. A new edition. London, printed for D. Payne, R. Gray, and G. [*sic*] Murray, 1782.
([2],267,[1]p.), ill., 12mo.
Also includes 'Yorick's sentimental journey continued. By Eugenius.' i.e. John Hall Stevenson. Presumably 'G. Murray' is a typographical error, although this edition is not listed in BB, p. 18 (see Sterne 1780, item 269).
ESTC to14700: L, 12643.p.71.
Fiction. London syndicate.

325. [Sterne, Laurence, 1713–1768.]
The life and opinions of Tristram Shandy, gentleman. . . . A new edition. London, printed for W. Strahan, J. Dodsley, G. Robinson, T. Cadell, T. Lowndes, and J. Murray, 1782.
Vol. 1: [4],229p.; vol. 2: 238,[1]p; vol. 3: [4],248p.; vol. 4: [8],224p.; vol. 5: [1],222p.; vol. 6: [1],205p., 6 plates, 8vo. Vol. 2 with advertisement; vol. 3 with half-title.
Murray bought a 1/8 share of 'Vols 4, 5, 6' for £30 on 21 Jan. 1779 at the sale of Thomas Becket at the Queen's Arms. On 26 Jan. 1779 he sold Lowndes a 1/16 share for £15.15s. On 6 Dec. 1782 Murray paid Thomas Cadell £10.3s. for paper and printing. The returns on his share (47 books at 7s.6d. each, wholesale) were £15.15s. — a loss of £8.13s. (BB, p. 15). Published 28 Dec. 1782.

ESTC n020570: CSmH, 247595.
Fiction. London syndicate.

326. Stuart, Gilbert, 1743–1786.
The history of Scotland, from the establishment of the Reformation, till the death of Queen Mary. By Gilbert Stuart . . . in two volumes . . . London, printed for J. Murray, 1782.
Vol. 1: [xii], 445,[2]p.; vol. 2: x,409,[1]p., 4to. With Murray's advertisements in both vols. Price: £1.5s.
Entered in the Stationers' Company Register, 29 Apr. 1782, 'John Murray, by purchase, the whole'.
ESTC t096525: L, 187.c.4.
Another issue: London, printed for J. Murray; and John Bell at Edinburgh, 1782.
ESTC n001050: CaOTU, E-10 2077.
History. Edinburgh co-publishing.

327. Stuart, Gilbert, 1743–1786.
A view of society in Europe, in its progress from rudeness to refinement: or, inquiries concerning the history of law, government, and manners. By Gilbert Stuart, . . . The second edition. London, printed for J. Murray, 1782.
xx,433,[3]p., 4to. With a half-title and errata leaf. Price: £1.
The 1778 edition with a cancel title page.
ESTC t141294: L, 521.l.19.
History. Murray alone.

328. Thomson, Alexander, M.D.
An enquiry into the nature, causes, and method of cure, of nervous disorders. In a letter to a friend. By Alex. Thomson, M.D. The second edition, with additions. London, printed for J. Murray, 1782.
[4],43,[1]p., 8vo. With a half-title. Price: 1s.
ESTC t164785: C, Hunter.b.78.8.
Medicine. Murray alone.

329. The third edition, with additions.
ESTC n006476: North America, MBU-M.
Medicine. Murray alone.

330. Virgil.
The works of Virgil: translated into English verse by Mr. Dryden . . . London, printed for C. Bathurst, J. Rivington and Sons, T. Caslon, J. Robson, B. Law, G. Robinson, T. Cadell, J.

Johnson, J. Murray, R. Baldwin, J. Debrett, W. Flexney. T. Evans, and J. Macqueen, 1782.
Vol. 1: 324p.; vol. 2: 318p.; vol. 3: 256, plates, 12mo.
1500 copies printed. Murray bought a 1/12 share for £6 at D. Cornish's sale on 17 Mar. 1782 at the Globe Tavern. In Dec. he paid £21.17s.1d. to Thomas Cadell for paper and printing. The returns of his share (125 copies at 6s. each, wholesale) were £37.10s. (BB, p. 13). The title pages of vols 2–4 vary and do not include Murray.
ESTC t177561: COCu, PR 3420.V5.
Poetry. London syndicate.

1783

331. Ariosto, Lodovico, 1474–1533.
Orlando furioso: translated from the Italian of Lodovico Ariosto; with notes: by John Hoole. In five volumes. . . . London, printed for the author: sold by C. Bathurst; T. Payne and Son; J. Dodsley; J. Robson; T. Cadell; G. Nicol; J. Murray; J. Walter; T. and W. Lowndes; J. Sewell; J. Stockdale; and J. Phillips, 1783.
Vol. 1: [8],cxxxi,334,p.; vol. 2: [1],407p.; vol. 3: [1],427p.; vol. 4: [4],438p.; vol. 5: [1],322,vi,[54], [2]p., plates, port., 8vo. With an Advertisement to the reader in vol. 1 and a list of subscribers and errata in vol. 5. Price: £1.11s.6d.
ESTC t133397: L, 1070.m.49.
Poetry. London syndicate.

332. Benjamin Ben Jonah, of Tudela.
Travels of Rabbi Benjamin, son of Jonah, of Tudela: through Europe, Asia, and Africa; from the ancient Kingdom of Navarre, to the frontiers of China. Faithfully translated from the original Hebrew; . . . By the Rev. B. Gerrans, . . . London, printed for the translator; sold by Messrs. Robson, J. Murray, T. Davis, W. Law, 1783.
xiii,[1],171,[1]p., 12mo.
Entered in the Stationers' Company Register, 15 Nov. 1783, 'The Translator, the whole'.
ESTC t051601: L, 303.c.3.
Travel–topography. Agency–London.

333. Bergman, Torbern, 1735–1784.
An essay on the usefulness of chemistry, and its application to the various occasions of life. Translated from the original of Sir Torbern

Bergman, . . . London, printed for J. Murray, 1783.
[4],163,[1]p., 8vo. Price: 3s.
A translation of *Anledning till föreslösningar öfver chemiens beskaffenhet och nytta* by François Xaviar Swediaur, to whom Murray paid 5 gns for the translation (BB, p. 66).
ESTC t011077: L, T.243(4).
Science. Murray alone.

334. Bergman, Torbern, 1735–1784.
Torberni Bergman, . . . sciagraphia regni mineralis, secundum principia proxima digesti. Londini, apud Johannem Murray, 1783.
165,[1]p., 8vo. Price: 2s.6d.
ESTC t201542: O, 18842e.66.
Science. Murray alone.

335. Bettesworth, John.
The seaman's sure guide, or, navigator's pocket remembrancer: wherein are given such plain instructions in every useful branch of navigation, as will in a short time form the complete mariner. Among the variety of essential articles contained . . . are, . . . A complete log of a ship's voyage, . . . By J. Bettesworth, . . . London, printed for the author, and S. Hooper; J. Murray; and D. Steel, 1783.
iv,160,[2]p., ill., 12mo. With a final advertisement leaf.
'A log of a ship's voyage, . . . in his Majesty's ship the Cumberland: kept by John Diligent' has a separate title page.
900 copies printed. Murray owned a half share. He paid Hooper £32 'for paper & print of 450 Seamans guide & 700 arithmetic' (see next). (BB, p. 36). Stock: 154 (W).
ESTC t114215: L, 533.f.23.
Travel–topography. London co-publishing.

*336. Bettesworth, John.
Arithmetic made easy, in the first four fundamental rules, with an appendix of reduction and the single rule of three. Also a collection of all the userful tables. . . . By J. Bettesworth, . . . London, printed for the author, by W. Mackintosh; and sold by A. Hogg and J. Macgowan, and H. Turpin, [1783].
67,[1]p., 12mo.
See previous item. Entered in Stationers' Company Register, 13 Oct. 1783, 'J. Murray, by purchase. The whole'. *ESTC* (t014604) lists another

issue with a different title page, pagination corrections and signature C partially reset.
ESTC t014605: L, 531.d.33(1).
Education. ?Agency–London

337. Boyer, Abel, 1667–1729.
Le dictionnaire royal françois-anglois et anglois-françois; tiré des meilleurs auteurs, . . . par Mr. A. Boyer. Nouvelle edition, rendue grammaticale . . . et soigneusement revue, corrigée, & augmentée . . . Par J. C. Prieur. . . . Londres, chez C. Bathurst, P. Vaillant, W. Strahan, J. F. and C. Rivington, J. Buckland, T. Payne and son, W. Owen, T. Caslon, T. Longman, G. Keith, J. Robson, T. Lowndes, E. Dilly, Richardson and Co., E. Johnson, G. Robinson, T. Cadell, J. Sewell, W. Ginger, P. Elmsley, W. Flexney, R. Baldwin, J. Nicholls, W. Domville, W. Nicoll, J. Murray, W. Goldsmith, H. Gardner, J. Bew, T. Beecroft, J. Russell, J. Bowen, J. Fielding, E. Newbery, and G. Wilkie, 1783.
2 vols., unpaginated, plate, table, port., 4to.
Title page to vol. 2 is 'The royal dictionary, French and English, and English and French; extracted from the writings of the best authors . . . '. Reference: Alston xii. 667.
ESTC t131046: L, 676.g.19.
Language. London syndicate.

338. Butter, William, 1726–1805.
An improved method of opening the temporal artery. Also, a new proposal for extracting the cataract. With descriptions and delineations of the instruments contrived for both operations. By the author, when a student at Edinburgh. . . . London, printed for J. Robson; J. Johnson; and J. Murray, 1783.
viii,213,[3]p., plate, 8vo. With a final advertisement leaf. Price: 4s.
The preface signed: Wm. Butter. Entered in the Stationers' Company Register, 16 Sept. 1783, 'The author, Wm Butter, the whole'.
ESTC t026550: L, 1186.i.3.
Medicine. London co-publishing.

339. [Cartwright, Edmund, 1743–1823.]
Sonnets to eminent men and an ode to the Earl of Effingham. London, printed for J. Murray, and T. Becket, 1783.
[2],15,[3]p., 4to. With a half-title and advertisements. Price: 1s.
ESTC t193937: L, qE-676.

Another issue: 'eminent men' is in roman rather than italic.
Stock: 253 (W).
ESTC t117733: L, 1601/311
Poetry. London co-publishing.

340. [Clarke, Henry, 1743–1818.]
Additional remarks on converging series, occasioned by the appendix to Mr. Landen's Observations on the same subject. London, printed for the author; and sold by J. Murray, 1783.
29,[3]p., 4to. With a final advertisement leaf. Price: 1s.6d.
ESTC t187474: Dt, L.dd.41 no.4.
Science. Agency–London.

341. The coalitionist. A satire. London, printed for the author: and sold by J. Murray; J. Johnson; J. Sewel; R. Blamire; and R. Faulder, [1783].
iv,28p., 4to. Price: 2s.
ESTC t114541: L, 1490.de.15.
Politics. Agency–London.

342. Crabbe, George, 1754–1832.
The skull; a poem. Inscribed to the prettiest woman in England. The second edition. London, printed by Millan and Rae; and sold by J. Murray; J. Debrett; J. Bowen; Mess. Richardson and Urquhart; T. Egerton; and J. Southerne, 1783.
[2],iv,[2],18,[2]p., 4to. With an additional title page, engraved, and a final advertisement leaf. Price: 2s.
ESTC no33459: MH, 18417.33.
Poetry. London co-publishing.

343. The English review; or, an abstract of English and foreign literature. ... London, printed for J. Murray, 1783.
Vol. 1: [viii],528,[8]p., 8vo; vol. 2: [1],[vi],480,[8]p., 8vo.
Published from Jan. in monthly parts (priced at 1s.); title page, contents, and index issued every six months. Apr. issue entered in the Stationers' Company Register, 22 May 1783, 'John Murray, the whole'; May issue, 2 June; June issue, 14 July; July issue, 5 Aug.; Aug. issue, 1 Sept.; Sept. issue, 1 Oct.; Oct. issue, 5 Nov.; Nov. issue, 1 Dec.
Primary location: NN, *DA.
Miscellaneous. Murray–with agency.

***344. Evans, Thomas, solicitor.
Réfutation des Mémoires de la Bastille, sur les principes généraux des loix, de la probalité et de la vérité; dans une suite de lettres à Monsieur Linguet, ... Par Thomas Evans, ... Londres, de l'imprimerie de Edw. Cox. Se vend chez J. Murray, 1783.
[4],68p., 8vo.
The imprint may be false, being a repetition of that of the English edition (next); possibly printed in the Netherlands.
ESTC t115266: L, R.64(3).
Politics. Agency–Murray alone.

345. Evans, Thomas, solicitor.
A refutation of the Memoirs of the Bastille, on the general principles of law, probability and truth; in a series of letters to Mr. Linguet, late advocate in the Parliament of Paris. By Thomas Evans, solicitor in Chancery, and one of the attorneys of the Court of King's-Bench, in England. ... London, printed for the author, by Edw. Cox, printer to the Honorable United East-India Company; and sold by J. Murray, 1783.
84p., 8vo. Price: 1s.6d.
ESTC to46648: L, T.244(13).
Politics. Agency–Murray alone.

346. Fielding, Henry, 1707–1754.
The works of Henry Fielding, Esq; with the life of the author. In twelve volumes. A new edition. To which is now first added, The fathers; or, the good-natured man. London, printed for W. Strahan, J. Rivington and Sons, S. Crowder, T. Longman, J. Robson, C. Dilly, G. Kearlsey, G. Robinson, T. Cadell, T. Lowndes, R. Baldwin, W. Cater, G. Nicoll, S. Bladon, J. Murray, W. Flexney, T. Evans, W. Otridge, J. Sewell, W. Love, J. Bowen, and W. Fox, 1783.
12 vols., plates, port., 12mo. Price: £1.16s.
Vols. 2–12 list an additional bookseller in the imprint, J. Nichols. 'An essay on the life and genius of Henry Fielding, Esq;' is by Arthur Murphy. In some copies, there is an additional title page to vol. 1 with the name 'G. Nicholl' in imprint.
Murray paid £4.12s. for a 1/12 share at the late Wm Caslon's sale on 5 June 1783 at the Globe Tavern. In Nov. he paid Thomas Cadell £29.19s.8d. for paper and printing. The returns

on his share (52 copies at 19s.3d. each, whole-sale) were £50.1s. (BB, p. 31). Stock: 12 (W). *ESTC* t089844: L, 633.d.14–25.
Fiction. London syndicate.

347. Gay, John, 1685–1732.
Fables by the late Mr. Gay. In one volume complete. London, printed for J. Buckland, W. Strahan, J. F. and C. Rivington, G. Keith, B. White, R. Horsfield, T. Lowndes, T. Caslon, S. Crowder, T. Longman, B. Law, T. Carnan, J. Wilkie, G. Robinson, T. Cadell. S. Bladon, R. Baldwin, J. Sewell, J. Johnson, H. L. Gardener, E. Newbery, W. Goldsmith, J. Murray, J. Walker, S. Hooper, and J. Bowen, 1783.
240p., plates, 12mo. Price: 3s. bound.
?5000 copies printed (some without plates). Murray bought a 1/20 share at the Globe Tavern (John Crowder's sale) on 10 Sept. 1777 for £10.5s. which he paid to George Robinson on 16 Jan. 1778. On 15 Nov. 1782 he paid Thomas Longman £5.19s.9d. for paper and printing. The returns on his share (250 books 'without plates'), paid on 15 Nov. 1782, were £12.10s. On 10 Apr. 1783 at the Globe Tavern Murray paid George Robinson £3.7s. for a 1/40 share (giving him 3/40ths in all). On 21 Aug. 1783 he paid Longman £7.17s.7d. The returns on his share (244 sets of 'cuts;' at 8d. each) were £8.2s.6d. On 23 Aug. 1783 he paid Longman an additional £1.6s.4d. and on the same day received £2.15s (55 books at 1s. each, whole-sale) (see Gay 1778, item 184; BB, p. 9).
ESTC t013861: L, 1161.d.40.
Poetry. London syndicate.

348. Grose, Francis, 1731?-1791.
London, August, 1783. Proposals for publishing an elegant edition, in eight volumes imperial octavo, of the Antiquities of England and Wales: being a collection of views of the most remarkable ruins and antient buildings accurately drawn on the spot. To each view is added an historical account of its situation, when and by whom built, with every interesting circumstance relating thereto. Collected from the best authorities. By Francis Grose, Esq; F.A.S. Printed for S. Hooper, and sold by J. Murray, and by all booksellers in Great Britain and Ireland.
Listed under 'Conditions' III. 'The first number will be published on Saturday, the 9th instat,

and to be continued every fortnight, till the whole is finished. Price: 1s.6d. each number.' This new edition, with the imprint 'printed for Hooper & Wigstead, was published 1783–97 (*ESTC* n036392). See *ESTC* t211089 for the announcement of the printing of the first number.
Primary location: O, Gough Coll. Fiche 2/A5.
Travel–topography. Agency–London.

349. [Hayes, Thomas, fl. 1783–1786.]
A serious and friendly address to the public, on the dangerous consequences of neglecting common coughs and colds so frequent in this climate; containing, a simple, efficacious, and domestic method of cure . . . By a gentleman of the faculty. London, printed for J. Murray, and Messrs. Shepherdson and Reynolds, 1783.
[2],ix,[1],42p., 8vo. Price: 1s.6d.
ESTC t047497: L, 1172.g.10(a).
Medicine. London co-publishing.

350. Hoffmann, Friedrich, 1660–1742.
A system of the practice of medicine; from the Latin of Dr. Hoffman. In two volumes. By the late William Lewis, . . . Revised and completed by Andrew Duncan, M.D. . . . London, printed for J. Murray; and J. Johnson, 1783.
Vol. 1: viii,591p.; vol. 2: vii,584p., 8vo. With half-titles. Price: 14s. bound.
A translation of *Medicina rationalis systematica*. Paper cost £97.10s. (130 reams at 15s./ream). Neill & Co. of Edinburgh printed the edition for £70.8s. from which Murray deducted £9.15s. for a 13–ream overcharge (BB, p. 30).
ESTC t063466: L, 1509/1552.
Medicine. London co-publishing.

351. Home, Francis, 1719–1813.
Clinical experiments, histories, and dissections. By Francis Home, M.D. . . . Third edition, corrected. London, printed for J. Murray, and William Creech, Edinburgh, 1783.
xii,499,[1]p. (pp. 167–176 are repeated in the pagination; 177–186 are omitted), 8vo. Price: 7s. Stock: 375 (H).
ESTC n003184: MBCo, R854.G7H75 1783.
Medicine. Edinburgh co-publishing.

352. Home, Robert, b. c. 1720.
The efficacy and innocency of solvents candidly examined; with experiments and cases. By

Robert Home, . . . London, printed for J. Murray, 1783.
78,[2]p., 8vo. With a half-title and a final advertisement leaf. Price: 1s.6d. stitched.
Published 10 Feb. 1783.
ESTC t128050: L, 1608/1434.
Medicine. Murray alone.

353. Homer.
The Iliad and Odyssey of Homer: translated by Pope. A new edition. In four volumes. . . . London, printed for C. Bathurst, J. Buckland, W. Strahan, J. Rivington and Sons, T. Davies, T. Payne. L. Davis, W. Owen, B. White, S. Crowder, T. Caslon, T. Longman, B. Law, C. Dilly, J. Dodsley, J. Wilkie, J. Robson, J. Johnson, T. Lowndes, G. Robinson, T. Cadell, J. Nichols, E. Newbery, T. Evans, P. Elmsly, R. Baldwin, G. Nicol, Leigh and Sotheby, J. Bew, N. Conant, W. Nicoll, J. Murray, S. Hayes, W. Fox, and J. Bowen, 1783.
Vol. 1: [2],376p.; vol. 2: [2],365,[1]; vol. 3: [2],325,[3]; vol. 4: [2],289,[1]p., 8vo.
Murray bought a 1/64 share for £1.11s.6d. on 21 Jan. 1779 at Thomas Becket's sale at the Queen's Arms (BB, p. 17). His profit, if any, is not recorded. The share was sold on 23 Dec. 1794 to Kearsley & Clark for 4 gns. (BB, p. 17). Stock: 6 and (H); 28 (W).
ESTC t127167: L, 1607/4322.
Poetry. London syndicate.

354. Hunter, Henry, 1741–1802.
The brevity, uncertainty, and importance of human life. A sermon preached at the protestant dissenting meeting house in Hammersmith, the twenty-second of June, 1783: on occasion of the sudden death of the late Rev. George Turnbull, Pastor of the Church of Christ there. By Henry Hunter, . . . London, printed for J. Murray, 1783.
36p., 8vo. With a half-title. Price: 6d.
ESTC t098650: L, 4481.aa.45.
Religion. Murray alone.

355. Hunter, Henry, 1741–1802.
Sacred biography: or, the history of the patriarchs from Adam to Abraham inclusively: being a course of lectures delivered at the Scots church, London Wall, by Henry Hunter, D.D. London, printed for the author, and sold by J. Murray, 1783.

xxxii,423,[1]p., 8vo. With a list of subscribers. Price: 7s.
The entire 6–vol. work was published in various editions between 1783 and 1792 (see item 422).
ESTC t098655: L, 4461.c.20.
Religion. Agency–Murray alone.

356. Inglefield, John Nicholson, 1748–1828.
Capt. Inglefield's narrative, concerning the loss of His Majesty's ship the Centaur, of seventy-four guns: and the miraculous preservation of the pinnace, with the Captain, Master and ten of the crew, in a traverse of near 300 leagues on the great Western Ocean; with the names of the people saved. Published by authority. London, printed for J. Murray; and A. Donaldson, 1783.
36,[4]p., 8vo. With a half-title; a leaf containing the names of those saved in the pinnace; and a final leaf of advertisements and errata. Price: 1s.
Entered in the Stationers' Company Register, 22 Jan. 1783, 'Captn. Inglefield. the whole'.
ESTC t113889: L, 533.d.12.
Military. London co-publishing.

357. A new edition, corrected.
36,[2]p., 8vo. In this edition, catchword on p. 21: period. With a half-title and a final leaf containing 'Names of the officers . . . ' and an advertisement. Price: 1s.
ESTC t019909: L, T.1095(11).
Military. London co-publishing.

358. Innes, George, d. 1781.
Fourteen discourses on practical subjects. By the late Reverend George Innes, . . . London, printed for J. Murray, 1783.
vi,269,[1]p., 12mo. Price: 3s.6d.
Stock: 12 (W).
ESTC t116277: L, 1024.b.7.
Religion. Murray alone.

359. Innes, John, 1739–1777.
Eight anatomical tables of the human body; containing the principal parts of the skeleton and muscles represented in the large tables of Albinus. To which are added concise explanations. By John Innes, late dissector to Dr Monro. The third edition. Edinburgh, printed for C. Elliot; and J. Murray, London, 1783.
iv,[1],4–52p., 8 plates, 4to.
ESTC t112465: L, 7421.aaa.15.
Medicine. Edinburgh co-publishing.

360. Johnson, Samuel, 1709–1784.

A dictionary of the English language: in which the words are deduced from their originals, explained in their different meanings, . . . Abstracted from the folio edition, by the author Samuel Johnson, A.M. To which is prefixed, A grammar of the English language. In two volumes. . . . The seventh edition, corrected by the author. London, printed for W. Strahan, J. F. and C. Rivington, L. Davis, W. Owen, T. Lowndes, T. Caslon, S. Crowder, T. Longman, B. Law, J. Dodsley, C. Dilly, G. Robinson, T. Cadell, J. Robson, W. Goldsmith, T. Evans, J. Bew, J. Murray, R. Baldwin, S. Hayes, and J. Bowen, 1783.

2 vols., unpaginated, plate, port., 8vo. Price: 10s. 5000 copies printed. Murray bought a 1/80 share at the Globe Tavern (John Crowder's sale) on 10 Sept. 1777 for £17 which he paid to George Robinson on 16 Jan. 1778; on 17 March 1778 he bought an additional 1/80 share at the Globe for £16; on 12 Sept. 1780 a 1/160 share for £6.10s. from the estate of the late Wm Davis, and on 10 May 1783 a 1/40 share (John Ridley's) for £24 which he paid to Thomas Evans. On 6 March 1783 he paid £26.11s.1d. for paper and printing, and on 23 Aug. 1783 he paid Longman a further £21.1s.10d. The returns on his share (282 books at 5s.10d. each, wholesale) were £82.5s. (See Johnson 1778, item 191; BB, p. 10).

ESTC n028411: NNC-T, V819.3.J631.

Language. London syndicate.

361. Johnson, Samuel, 1709–1784.

The lives of the most eminent English poets; with critical observations on their works. By Samuel Johnson. In four volumes. A new edition, corrected. London, printed for C. Bathurst, J. Buckland, W. Strahan, J. Rivington and Sons, T. Davies, T. Payne, L. Davis, W. Owen, B. White, S. Crowder, T. Caslon, T. Longman, B. Law, C, Dilly, J. Dodsley, J. Wilkie, J. Robson, J. Johnson, T. Lowndes, G. Robinson, T. Cadell, J. Nichols, E. Newbery, T. Evans, P. Elmsly, R. Baldwin, G. Nicol, Leigh and Sotheby, J. Bew, N. Conant, W. Nicoll, J. Murray, S. Hayes, W. Fox, and J. Bowen, 1783.

Vol. 1: [viii],454p.; vol. 2: [iv],440p.; vol. 3: [iv],432p.; vol. 4: [iv],[486]p., plate, port., 8vo. Price: 1 gn.

On 27 Jan. 1783 Murray issued notes to Cadell

totalling £24.9s.8d. for paper and printing. The returns of his share (60 copies at 14s. each, wholesale) were £42 (BB. p. 11).

ESTC t004514: L, 1066.g.20–23.

Biography. London syndicate.

362. Jones, Sir William, 1746–1794.

A grammar of the Persian language. By William Jones, . . . The third edition, with an index. London, printed by W. Richardson, for J. Murray, 1783.

[2],xix,[1],148,[42]p., plate, 4to. With advertisement leaves and an index. Price: 13s. bound (1786 advert.).

Stock: 240 (W).

ESTC t111360: L, 1483.c.25.

Language. Murray alone.

363. Kemeys, John Gardner.

Free and candid reflections occasioned by the late additional duties on sugars and on rum; submitted to the consideration of the British ministry, the members of both Houses of Parliament, and the proprietors of sugar estates in the West-India colonies. By John Gardner Kemeys, . . . London, printed for the author, and sold by T. Becket; T. Davies; S. Hooper, J. Johnson; G. Kearsley, and J. Murray; and J. Sewell, 1783.

13,[1],152p. (p. 116 misnum. 11), 8vo.

ESTC t122607: L, 104.i.28.

Economics. Agency–London.

364. [Kier, Adam.]

Hints for promoting a plan concerning the important subject of more effectually supplying the public with seamen and soldiers. Upon a comprehensive, equal, regular, and virtuous system. [London], Printed for J. Murray, 1783.

48p., 8vo. With a half-title. Price: 1s.

Signed A. K. 250 copies printed; only 11 sold (To Kier, 18 May 1789).

ESTC n049863: ICN, U645.405.

Military. Murray alone.

365. Lassone, M. de.

An opinion given (by order of government) upon a memoir concerning the method practised by the late M. Doulcet, (professor of physic at Paris, and one of the physicians of the Hotel Dieu,) in the cure of a disease, incident to lying-in-women, called the puerperal fever. Read at a meeting of the Royal Society of Medicine, held at the Louvre, the 6th of Sept. 1782. Translated by N. Maillard, M.D. London. Printed at Paris by Ph. D. Pierres, Printer in Ordinary to the King and Royal Society of Medicine, 1782. London, sold by A.[*sic*] Murray; and H. Payne, 1783.

42p., 8vo. With a half-title. Price: 1*s*.6*d*.

Signed at end: De Lassone. A translation of *Rapport fait par ordre du gouvernement sur un mémoire contenant la méthode employée par M. Doulcet . . . dans le traitement de fièvre puerpérale.*

ESTC n024520: C-S, P.E. 353 no.8.

Medicine. London co-publishing.

366. A letter from a clergyman to the Bishop of Landaff, on the subject of His Lordship's letter to the late Archbishop of Canterbury. London, printed for J. Murray, 1783.

18,[2]p., 4to. With a half-title and a final leaf of advertisements. Price: 1*s*.

See next and *A plain reply* below.

ESTC t037779: L, 4105.e.5.

Religion. Murray alone.

367. A letter to the Right Reverend Richard Lord Bishop of Landaff, on the projected reformation of the church: particularly respecting the inferior clergy. London, printed for J. Murray, 1783.

iv,47,[1]p., 4to. Price: 1*s*.6*d*.

Signed at end 'T. B. A Church of England-man'. On the reform of ecclesiastical revenues. See previous and *A plain reply* below. Stock: 350 (W).

ESTC t038432: L, 4105.e.30.

Religion. Murray alone.

368. The London kalendar, or, court and city register for England, Scotland, Ireland, and America, for the year 1783; . . . London, printed for J. Stockdale (from Mr. Almon's); T. Carnan; J. Fielding; J. Sewell; J. Murray; R. Faulder; D. Steel; J. Wallis; and A. Donaldson, [1783].

[4],284p., 12mo. Price: 1*s*.6*d*.

Another issue: headed 'A new edition corrected to the present time'.

ESTC t205634: L, P. P. 2506.k.

Miscellaneous. London co-publishing.

369. Macpherson, R.

A dissertation on the preservative from drowning; and swimmer's assistant. A new invention, . . . Together with an useful account of losses of lives by water. By R. Macpherson, Gent. London, printed for J. Murray, 1783.

viii,131,[1]p., plate, 8vo. With a half-title. Price: 2*s*.6*d*.

Entered in the Stationers' Company Register, 20th Sept. 1783, 'The author . . . one half. J. Murray . . . one half'.

ESTC t033011: L, 1040.f.12(3).

Medicine. Murray alone.

**370. Murray, John, 1737–1793.

No. 3. Murray's catalogue of books in medicine, surgery, anatomy, natural history, &c. For the use of the faculty, and practitioners in general. And which are to be sold (for ready money) at the prices marked against the several articles. London, printed for J. Murray, 1783.

No copy is extant; Murray mentioned the *Catalogue* in a letter to Patrick Hair, 9 July 1783 (see Murray 1784, item 437, for No. 4).

Miscellaneous. Murray alone.

371. Observations on a pamphlet entitled A defence of the Rockingham party, with the Right Honourable Frederic Lord North. These observations contain also a defence of Lord Shelburne from the charges brought against him, not only by the author of the defence, but also by the various anonymous writers, who have engaged on the same side of the question. London, printed for J. Murray; J. Faulder; J. Sewell; W. Flexney; R. Blamire; T. Babbs; J. Johnson, [1783].

[4],73,[1]p., 8vo. With a half-title. Price: 1*s*.

A defence of the Rockingham party, by Wm Godwin, was published in 1783 (*ESTC* n008450). Reference: Adams 83–66.

ESTC n041907: CSmH, 302628.

Politics. London co-publishing.

372. Parmentier, Antoine Augustin, 1737–1813. Observations on such nutritive vegetables as may be substituted in the place of ordinary food, in times of scarcity. Extracted from the French of M. Parmentier. London, printed for J. Murray, 1783.

viii,80p., plate, 8vo. With a half-title. Price: 1*s*.6*d*.

A translation of *Recherches sur les végétaux nourissants*.

ESTC t041760: L, 546.e.23(8).
Science. Murray alone.

373. Patrick, Simon, 1626–1707.
Consolatory discourses, comprehending, I. The heart's ease; . . . IV. A consolatory discourse in times of trouble and danger. By Symon Patrick, . . . The tenth edition. To which is added, a suitable collection of devotions, adapted to each of the discourses, from the best writers . . . Edinburgh, printed for W. Gordon; and sold by T. Longman, C. Dilly, J. Murray, and Richardson and Urquhart, London, 1783.
xxiii,[1],345,[3]p., 12mo.
Originally published in 1760 as *The heart's ease*.
ESTC t104260: L, 4408.dd.17.
Religion. Agency–Edinburgh.

374. Perfect, William, 1737–1809, M.D. of West Malling in Kent.
An address to the public, on the subject of insanity. London, Dodsley, Murray, &c, 1783.
[1],8 p., 4to. With a plate. Price: 1s.
English Review 2 (Nov. 1783), 382. Copy at Univ. London, but not seen.
Medicine. London co-publishing.

375. A plain reply to the strictures of Mr. Cumberland and the Country Curate, on the Bishop of Landaff's proposals; in a letter to Richard Cumberland, Esq. To which are added, observations on the right of patronage; and on the good policy and moral tendency of resignation bonds. By the author of A letter to the Bishop of Landaff on the projected reformation of the church. London, printed for J. Murray, 1783.
[3],6–60p., 4to.
See *A letter* (both) above. Richard Cumberland had written *A letter to Richard Lord Bishop Landaff, on the subject of his Lordship's letter to the late Archbishop of Canterbury*, published by Charles Dilly, 1783.
ESTC t148430: Lu, Porteus.
Religion. Murray alone.

376. Playfair, James, 1755–1794.
A method of constructing vapor baths, so as to render them of small expence, and of commodious use, in private families. With a design and description of a convenient hot water bath. By James Playfair, architect. London, printed by Millan and Rae; for J. Murray, 1783.

[2],19,[5]p., plates, 8vo. Price: 1s.
ESTC t039308: L, 1171.h.23(4).
Medicine. Murray alone.

377. Pratt, Samuel Jackson, 1749–1814.
The sublime and beautiful of scripture: being essays on select passages of sacred composition. By Mr. Pratt, . . . A new edition. London, printed for J. Murray, and G. Robinson, 1783.
xii,[8],240,[4]p. (p. 96 misnum. 97), 12mo. With a half-title and two final advertisement leaves. Price: 3s. bound.
ESTC t085830: L, 3125.df.4.
Religion. London co-publishing.

378. Robertson, James, 1714–1795.
Editio secunda grammatica Hebraa, priore in quibusdam partibus brevior, in aliis vero emendatior & auctior; prasertim in syntaxi, in qua singula partes orationis, tam nominum, quam verborum et temporum, exemplis idoneis ex sacro codice depromptis, illustrantur; . . . Auctore Jacobo Robertson, . . . [Edinburgh], Impensis auctoris, in adibus Mundell et Wilson, Edinburgi, excudebat Robertus Wilson junior, 1783. Prostant venales apud J. Balfour et Fil. A. Donaldson, W. Gordon, J. Bell, W. Creech, C. Elliot, J. Dickson, et W. Gray, Edinburgi; Dunlop et Wilson, Glasgua; Angus et fil. Aberdonia; Morison et fil. Perthi; E. et C. Dilly, T. Cadell, et J. Murray, Londini; bibliopolas, [1783].
xviii,346,89,[1]p., 8vo.
ESTC t100150: L, 12901.i.16.
Language. Agency–Edinburgh.

379. Robertson, Robert, 1742–1829.
Observations on the jail, hospital, or ship fever. By Robert Robertson, . . . London, printed for J. Murray, 1783.
x,[4],318p., 8vo. With a half-title. Price: 5s.
ESTC n041514: PPL, In Robe 1302.O.
Medicine. Murray alone.

380. [Robinson, Mary Darby]
The vis-à-vis of Berkley-Square: or, a wheel off Mrs. W*t**n's carriage. Inscribed to Florizel. London, sold by Murray; Bowen; and Southerne, [1783].
30p., 4to. With a half-title. Price: 1s.6d.
Dedication dated June 14, 1783. A verse satire on Mary Robinson's association with the Prince of Wales.

ESTC t060930: L, 1489.f.33.
Politics. London co-publishing.

381. Saunders, William, 1743–1817.
Observations on the superior efficacy of the red Peruvian bark, in the cure of agues and other fevers. Interspersed with occasional remarks on the treatment of other diseases by the same remedy. And an appendix containing a more particular account of its natural history. By William Saunders, . . . London, printed for J. Johnson, J. Murray, J. Sewell, and Hawkins, 1783.
xii,188p., 8vo. Price: 2s.6d.
Stock: 75 (W).
ESTC t198248: MRu, H 10 S3.
Medicine. London co-publishing.

382. Third edition, with considerable additions, London, printed for J. Johnson, J. Murray; J. Sewell; and Hawkins, 1783.
xii,188p., 8vo.
ESTC t138536: L, 1609/1587.
Medicine. London co-publishing.

383. Fourth edition, considerably enlarged. London, printed for J. Johnson, and J. Murray, 1783.
xii,181,[3]p., 8vo.
ESTC t033060: L, T.92(2).
Medicine. London co-publishing.

384. Scott, Helenus, 1760–1821.
The adventures of a rupee. Wherein are interspersed various anecdotes Asiatic and European. A new edition. To which are prefixed, Memoirs of the life of the author. And to which there are annexed, his remarks concerning the inhabitants of Africa. London, printed for J. Murray, 1783.
[4],xx,257,[1]p. (p. 93 misnum. 39), 12mo. With a half-title. Price: 3s.6d. bound.
Stock: 90 (H). See Scott 1782, item 320
ESTC t077688: L, 12613.d.4.
Fiction. Murray alone.

**385. A speech intended to have been spoken to the electors of Westminster, assembled at the Shakespeare Tavern, on Thursday, the third of April, 1783. London, Murray.
8vo. Price: 1s.
No copy located. *Monthly Review* 69 (Aug. 1783),

165: 'The design of this well-written pamphlet is to vindicate Mr Fox's connection with Lord North. The writer's arguments, if not convincing, at least are ingenious.' *Critical Review* 56 (Sept. 1783) wrongly gives 'April 13, 1783' in title.
Politics. Murray alone.

386. Sterne, Laurence, 1713–1768.
The works of Laurence Sterne. In ten volumes complete. Containing, I. the life and opinions of Tristram Shandy, Gent. II. A sentimental journey through France and Italy. III. Sermons. IV Letters. with a life of the author written by himself. London, printed for W. Strahan, J. Rivington, J. Dodsley, G. Kearsley, T. Lowndes, G. Robinson, B. Law, T. Cadell, J. Murray, T. Becket, R. Baldwin, and T. Evans, 1783.
Vol. 1: xx,[4],296p.; vol. 2: [4],307p.; vol. 3: [viii],276p.; vol. 4: [viii],280p.; vol. 5: [iii],242p.; vol. 6: [xii],284p.; vol. 7: [vi],288p.; vol. 8: [vi],284p.; vol. 9: xx,208p.; vol. 10: vii,198p.. 8vo. port. plates.
1000 copies printed. On 3 May 1780 Murray paid £37.11d. for his 63/1000 share of paper and printing. The returns on his share (63 sets at 20s. each, wholesale) were £63 (BB, p. 23).
ESTC t014701: L, 12270.aaa.11
Fiction. London syndicate.

387. Stuart, Gilbert, 1743–1786.
The history of Scotland, from the establishment of the Reformation, till the death of Queen Mary. To which are appended the observations concerning the public law and the constitution of Scotland . . . By Gilbert Stuart, . . . The second edition. London, printed for J. Murray, and G. Robinson, 1783–84.
Vol. 1: xxiv, 475,[1]p; vol. 2: [1],312,iv,5–160,[xxxii]p, port., 8vo.
Another issue: vol. 1 dated 1784; the portrait of Mary Queen of Scots faces right.
ESTC t096526: L, G.5100.5101.
History. London co-publishing.

388. Stuart, Gilbert, 1743–1786.
A view of society in Europe, in its progress from rudeness to refinement: or, inquiries concerning the history of law, government and manners. By Gilbert Stuart, . . . The second edition. London, printed for J. Murray, 1783.

xx,433,[3]p., 4to. With a half-title and an errata leaf. Price: 15s. in boards.

The 1782 edition with a new title page. Stock: 28 (H).

ESTC t096541: L, 9072.h.8.

History. Murray alone.

389. [Thomson, William, 1746–1817.]

The man in the moon; or, travels into the lunar regions, by the man of the people. . . . London, printed for J. Murray, 1783.

Vol. 1: 178,[6]p.; vol. 2: 214,[2]p., 8vo. With three leaves of advertisements at the end of the first volume and one at the end of the second. Price: 5s. (6s. in 1786 advert.).

Entered in the Stationers' Company Register, 30 Apr. 1782, 'J. Murray, the whole'. Stock: 46 (H).

ESTC t070735: L, N.1809,10.

Fiction. Murray alone.

390. Timour, 1336–1405.

Institutes political and military, written originally in the Mogul language, by the great Timour, improperly called Tamerlane: first translated into Persian by Abu Taulib Alhusseini; and thence into English, with marginal notes, by Major Davy, . . . and the whole work published with a preface, indexes, geographical notes, 38;c. 38;c. by Joseph White, B.D. . . . Oxford, at the Clarendon-Press, Sold by J. Murray, London; and by D. Prince and J. Cooke, Oxford, [1783].

li,[1],408,lxp., plates, 4to. Price: £1.1s.6d. (£1.11s.6d. in boards in 1786).

Parallel Persian and English texts. A prospectus for the work was circulated in 1780 (*ESTC* t152248) in which Murray's name was not included.

ESTC n008378: KMK, DS23.T58.

History. Provincial co-publishing.

391. Wilson, Andrew, M.D., of Newcastle-upon-Tyne.

Aphorisms, composed for a text to pratical [sic] lectures on the constitution and diseases of children. By Dr. Wilson, . . . London, sold by J. Murray, and J. Strahan, 1783.

x,75,[1]p., 12mo. Price: 1s.

A newspaper advertisement in the Archive dated 10 Feb. 1783 states that 'the Doctor begins his Course of Lectures upon the Aphorisms on

Wednesday, the 12th of February, at Six in the Evening, at his own house, Beauford Buildings, Strand.'

ESTC n016635: PPPH, R111.B57.

Medicine. London co-publishing.

1784

392. Abercrombie, John, 1726–1806.

Every man his own gardener. Being a new, and much more complete gardener's kalendar than any one hitherto published. . . . By Thomas Mawe, . . . John Abercrombie, . . . and other gardeners. The tenth edition, corrected, greatly enlarged, and wholly new-improved. London, printed for J. F. and C. Rivington, T. Longman, B. Law, T. and W. Lowndes, J. Johnson, G. Robinson, T. Cadell, W. Goldsmith, R. Baldwin, J. Murray, and E. Newbery, 1784.

[4],216,193–312,341–388,385–570,[18]p. (pp. 193–216, 385–388 repeated, and pp. 313–340 omitted in pagination), plate, 12mo. Price: 5s.

4000 copies printed. Murray paid Thomas Cadell 12 gns for a 1/32 share bought at Thomas Evans' sale on 3 July 1784. In Aug. he paid George Robinson £8.6s.8d. for paper and printing. The returns on his share (125 copies at 2s.10d. each, wholesale) were £17.14s.2d. (BB, p. 37). First published in 1767.

ESTC t129117: L, 1508/421.

Agriculture. London syndicate.

393. An account of the Scots Society in Norwich, from its rise in 1775, until it received the additional name of the Society of Universal Good-Will, in 1784. &c. The second edition. To which are added, the Articles, president's addresses, &c. &c. Norwich, printed and sold by W. Chase and Co. Sold also by J. Murray, London, 1784.

[2],3,[2],4–97,[1]p., 8vo. Price: 2s.6d.

ESTC t111434: L, 08282.h.37(1)

Religion. Agency–Provincial.

394. Benjamin Ben Jonah, of Tudela.

Travels of Rabbi Benjamin, son of Jonah, of Tudela: through Europe, Asia, and Africa; from the ancient Kingdom of Navarre, to the frontiers of China. Faithfully translated from the original Hebrew; . . . By the Rev. B. Gerrans, . . . London, printed for the translator; sold by Messrs Robson, J. Murray, T. Davis, W. Law, 1784.

xiii,[1],171,[1]p., 12mo.
A reissue of the 1783 edition with a new title
page.
ESTC to51602: L, G.15702.
Travel–topography. Agency–London.

395. Bergman, Torbern, 1735–1784.
An essay on the usefulness of chemistry, and its
application to the various occasions of life.
Translated from the original of Sir Torbern
Bergman, . . . London, printed for J. Murray,
1784.
[4],163,[1]p., 8vo. Price: 3s.
A re-issue of the 1783 translation (item 333)
with a new title page.
ESTC no01716: DNLM, WZ260.B512aE 1783.
Science. Murray alone.

396. Bergman, Torbern, 1735–1784.
Physical and chemical essays; translated from
the original Latin of Sir Torbern Bergman, . . .
By Edmund Cullen, M.D. . . . to which are
added notes and illustrations, by the translator.
London, printed for J. Murray; Balfour and Co.
W. Gordon, and J. Dickson, at Edinburgh; and
L. White, at Dublin, 1784.
Vol. 1: xl,464p.; vol. 2: xv,518p., 4 plates, 2
tables, 8vo. Price: 13s. in boards.
A translation of Opuscula physica et chemica.
Entered in the Stationers' Company Register,
19 Aug. 1784, 'J. Murray, by Purchase, the whole'.
ESTC no12248: MBCo, 1.Mk.69.
Science. Provincial co-publishing.

397. Blair, Hugh, 1718–1800.
Essays on rhetoric: abridged chiefly from Dr.
Blair's lectures on that science. London, printed
for J. Murray, 1784.
[8],384p., 12mo. With a half-title. Price: 4s.
Gilbert Stuart, who reviewed the 1783 edition
of Blair's Lectures in the English Review, may have
been the editor of this popular abridgement.
Five of Blair's original lectures (there were 47
in all) were omitted.
ESTC no09467: DeU.
Another issue in 8vo.
[12],384p., 8vo. With a half-title. Price: 4s.
Literary criticism. Murray alone.

398. Another edition
[16],533,[3]. 8vo. With a half-title and two preliminary and one final advertisement leaves.

ESTC no47431: North America, CSt,
PE1402.B7.
Literary criticism. Murray alone.

399. Brand, Thomas, surgeon.
Original letters that passed between Mess.
Brand and Ford, surgeons, on account of Mr.
Ford's conduct relative to Mr. Patterson, and
afterwards to one Sheldrake, a truss-maker,
who was convicted, . . . of being the author of
a false, scandalous, and malicious libel against
Mr. Brand. London, printed for J. Murray, 1784.
iv,48p., 8vo.
ESTC no10657: MBCo, 23.S.59 no.2.
Law. Murray alone.

400. Buc'hoz, Pierre-Joseph, 1731–1807.
The toilet of Flora; or, a collection of the most
simple and approved methods of preparing
baths, essences, pomatums, . . . with receipts
for cosmetics of every kind, . . . A new edition,
improved. London, printed for J. Murray; and
W. Nicoll, 1784.
[24],252p., plate, 12mo. With a half-title. Price:
3s.
A translation, with alterations, of La toilette de
Flore. Stock: 299 (H); 496, 294 (W), possibly
some from the 1779 edn (item 212).
ESTC to27163: L, 7956.aa.4.
Medicine. London co-publishing.

**401. Campbell, Coll.
An appeal to the public; by a neglected naval
officer, London, Murray, 1784.
8vo. Price: 1s.
No copy located. English Review 4 (Oct. 1784),
142; Critical Review 58 (Aug. 1784), 320. Murray
published a new edition in 1785 (item 460).
Military. Murray alone.

402. Chamberlaine, William, b. 1749.
A practical treatise on the efficacy of stizolobium, or, cowhage, internally administered, in
diseases occasioned by worms. To which are
added, observations on other anthelmintic
medicines of the West-Indies. By William
Chamberlaine, surgeon. London, printed for J.
Murray, 1784.
viii,77,[3]p., 8vo. With a half-title and final
advertisement leaf. Price: 1s.
ESTC t174240: C, VII–27–21/5.
Medicine. Murray alone.

403. The second edition.
ESTC t028456: L, T.215(2).
Medicine. Murray alone.

404. Chambers, Ephraim, *c.* 1680–1740.
Cyclopaedia: or, an universal dictionary of arts and sciences. . . . By E. Chambers, F.R.S. With the supplement, and modern improvements, incorporated in one alphabet. By Abraham Rees, D.D. In four volumes. . . . London, printed for W. Strahan, J. F. and C. Rivington, A. Hamilton, T. Payne, W. Owen, B. White, T. Longman, B. Law, C. Rivington, C. Dilly, H. Baldwin, J. Wilkie, H. S. Woodfall, J. Robson, J. Knox, W. Domville, T. Cadell, G. Robinson, A. Hamilton, Jun., R. Baldwin, W. Otridge, N. Conant, J. Murray, W. Fox, S. Hayes, J. Bowen, E. Johnson, S. A. Cumberledge, and D. Ogilvy, 1784–88.
5 vols, unpaginated, plates, 20.
Originally issued in 89 parts weekly at 6*d.* each (see Chambers 1778, item 176, for publishing information, BB, p. 8).
ESTC t135912: L, L.21.bb.5.
Miscellaneous. London syndicate.

405. Clark, Hugh.
A concise history of knighthood. Containing the religious and military orders which have been instituted in Europe. . . . In two volumes. . . . By Hugh Clark, . . . London, printed for W. Strahan, J. F. and C. Rivington, T. Payne, W. Owen, S. Crowder, T. Longman, C. Rivington, C. Dilly, J. Robson,. T. Lowndes, G. Robinson, T. Cadell, H. L. Gardner, J. Nichols, J. Bew, R. Baldwin, J. Murray, J. Debrett, W. Fox, J. White, J. Walker, T. Beecroft, M. Folingsby, 1784.
Vol. 1: x,285p.; vol. 2: 268,[1]p., 82 plates, 8vo. With an advertisement in vol. 2.
1000 copies printed. On 19 May 1784 Murray paid Thomas Longman 9 gns for paper and printing. The returns on his share (42 copies at 7*s.*4*d.* each, wholesale) were £15.8*s.* (BB, p. 37).
ESTC t144488: L, 200.c.22.
History. London syndicate.

406. Cooke, James, inventor.
Drill husbandry perfected. With other interesting circumstances in agriculture, respecting the most effectual methods of producing the greatest crops of corn, . . . with an elegant copper-plate of a new invented patent machine, . . . By the Rev. James Cooke, . . . Manchester, printed by J. Imison: and, sold by Mr. Murray, London, [1784?].
iii[i.e.iv],3–42p., plate, 8vo. Price: 1*s.*
ESTC n007495: PU, V630.8.Ag84.v.10.
Agriculture. Murray alone.

407. Cornwell, Bryan.
The domestic physician; or, guardian of health. Pointing out, in the most familiar manner, the symptoms of every disorder incident to mankind; together with their gradual progress, and the method of cure. . . . To which is added, an appendix, forming a complete dispensatory. By B. Cornwell, M.L. London, printed for the author, and sold at his house; J. Murray; J. Bew; and L. Davis, 1784.
xvi,650,[22]p., 8vo. Price: 7*s.*6*d.* bound.
ESTC n017822: CaOHM, B12087.
Medicine. Agency–London.

408. Defoe, Daniel, 1661?-1731.
The life and strange surprising adventures of Robinson Crusoe; of York, mariner: who lived eight and twenty years all alone in an uninhabited island on the coast of America, near the mouth of the great river Oroonoque; . . . Written by himself. The sixteenth edition, adorned with cuts. In two volumes. . . . London, printed for J. Buckland, W. Strahan, J. F. and C. Rivington, T. Longman, B. Law, J. Wilkie, T. and W. Lowndes, S. Bladon, J. Murray, R. Baldwin, and Scatcherd and Whitaker, 1784.
Vol. 1: 288p.; vol. 2: 275p., 5 plates, map, 12mo. Title page to vol. 2: 'The farther adventures of Robinson Crusoe'. J. Wallis is added to the list of publishers, after R. Baldwin. Vol. 2 does not bear an edition statement. Murray bought a 1/16 share of £4.10*s* at the sale of Catherine Caslon (widow of Thomas, who had died in March 1783) on 5 June 1783 at the Globe Tavern. He paid £8.17*s.*1*d.* for paper and printing (BB, p. 33 and loose sheet in BB; see Plate 26). Stock: 2 (W)
ESTC t072287: L, 1508/1530.
Fiction. London syndicate.

409. De Lolme, Jean Louis, 1740–1806.
The constitution of England, or an account of the English government; . . . By J. L. de Lolme,

. . . The fourth edition, corrected and enlarged. London, printed for G. Robinson; and J. Murray, 1784.
[8],xvi,540,[20]p.,plate, port., 8vo. Price: 7s.
1500 copies printed. The returns of Murray's share (375 copies at 4s.8d. each, wholesale) were £87.10s. This edition is about 60 pages longer than the previous one. (See De Lolme 1781, item 280; BB, p. 24).
ESTC t109210: L, 288.c.11.
History. London co-publishing.

410. Dewell, T.
The philosophy of physic, or, phlogistic system; . . . hence a concise plan of medical practice is proposed on fixed principles, . . . By T. Dewell, . . . Marlborough, printed by E. Harold; for J. Murray, J. Bew, London; and W. Taylor, Bath, [1784].
[6],xiv,47,[1]p., 8vo. With a half-title. Price: 1s.6d.
ESTC n019955: DNLM, 18th c.coll..
Medicine. Provincial co-publishing.

411. The English review; or, an abstract of English and foreign literature. . . . London, printed for J. Murray, 1784.
Vol. 3: [1],[vii],480,[8]p., 8vo; vol. 4: [1],[viii], 480,[8]p., 8vo.
Published in monthly parts (priced 1s.); title page, contents, and index issued every six months with each vol.
Primary location: NN, *DA.
Miscellaneous. Murray–with agency.

412. An essay to prove the insufficiency of a subaltern officer's pay in the army, compared with the necessary expences attending his station. To which is added, a plan for the more effectually recruiting the army, both in times of peace and war, by a subaltern. London, printed for S. Crowder; J. Murray, T. Stockdale; J. and J. Merrils, Cambridge; and S. Simmons, Lincoln, 1784
vii,[1],158p., 8vo.
ESTC t033437: L, T.380(10).
Military. London co-publishing.

***413. Evans, Thomas, solicitor.
Réfutation des Mémoires de la Bastille, sur les principes généraux des loix, de la probalité et de la vérité; dans une suite de lettres à M. Linguet, . . . Par T. Evans, . . . Seconde édition, revue & exactement corrigé. Londres, de l'imprimerie d'Edward Cox; et se trouve chez J. Murray, 1784.
50p., 12mo.
The imprint may be false, being a repetition of that of the 1783 English edition (item 345); possibly printed in the Netherlands.
ESTC n055505: KyU, 944.04 Ev16[2].
Politics. Murray alone.

414. Fielding, Henry, 1707–1754.
The works of Henry Fielding, Esq; with the life of the author. A new edition, in ten volumes. To which is now added, The fathers; or, the good-natured man. . . . London, printed for W. Strahan, J. Rivington and Sons, T. Payne, S. Crowder, T. Longman, J. Robson, J. Johnson, T. Cadell, T. Lowndes, R. Baldwin, W. Cater, G. Nicol, S Bladon, J. Murray, W. Otridge, J. Sewell, W. Lane, J. Bowen, and W. Fox, 1784.
Vol. 1: [iii],512p.; vol. 2: [iii],480p.; vol. 3: [iii],528p.; vol. 4: [4],vi,[7]-463p.; vol. 5: [ii],426p.; vol. 6: xxvi,534p.; vol. 7: xiv,537p.; vol. 8: [ii],480p.; vol. 9: vii,431p.; vol. 10: [iii],455p., plates, port., 8vo. Price: £3 bound.
'An essay on the life and genius of Henry Fielding, Esq.' is signed 'Arthur Murphy'. Murray paid £4.12s. for a 1/12 share at the late Wm Caslon's sale on 5 June 1783 at the Globe Tavern. In Nov. 1784 he paid Thomas Cadell £38.2s.10d. for paper and printing. The returns on his share (26 copies at 36s.6d. each, wholesale) were £47.13s.4d. Shares sold May 1796: 1/24 to Murray 38; Co. for 10s.6d.; 1/24 to Rivington for £15s. (See Fielding 1783, item 346; BB, p. 31). According to a newspaper advertisement of 1785, the plates were 'designed by Rooker and engraved by Collyer. Stock: 2 (W).
ESTC t089845: L, 635.f.1–10.
Fiction. London syndicate.

415. Gardiner, John.
Observations on the animal oeconomy, and on the causes and cure of diseases. By John Gardiner, . . . Edinburgh, printed for William Creech; and sold in London by T. Longman, J. Johnson, and J. Murray, 1784.
xxx,[2],458p., 8vo. Price: 6s. bound.
Murray took 100 copies from Creech in Nov.

1784 and by Sept. 1786 had sold 55 (To Gardiner, 9 Sept. 1786).
ESTC t121886: L, 1609/4884.
Medicine. Edinburgh co-publishing.

416. [Godwin, William, 1756–1836.]
The herald of literature; or, a review of the most considerable publications that will be made in the course of the ensuing winter: with extracts. London, printed for J. Murray, 1784.
[4],113,[3]p., 8vo. With a half-title and a final advertisement leaf. Price: 2*s*.
Murray explained the parodic nature of this publication to Richard Moncrieffe (26 April 1784); 'There is no novel *Louisa* by Miss Burney. There is a fictitious review of this and other books that never existed in the Herald of Literature.'
ESTC t106123: L, T.857(5).
Literary criticism. Murray alone.

417. [Godwin, William, 1756–1836.]
Instructions to a statesman. Humbly inscribed to the Right Honourable George Earl Temple. London, printed for J. Murray; J. Debrett; and J. Sewell, 1784.
xx,71,[1]p., 8vo. Price: 2*s*.
ESTC n028751: CSmH, 319612.
Politics. London co-publishing.

418. Goldsmith, Oliver, 1728–1774.
The history of England, from the earliest times to the death of George II. By Dr. Goldsmith. The fourth edition, corrected. . . . London, printed for J. F. and C. Rivington, B. Law, Richardson and Urquhart, G. Robinson, T. Cadell, J. Murray, T. Evans, J. Sewell, R. Baldwin, S. Hayes, and E. Newbery, 1784.
Vol. 1: v,[1],384,[20]p.; vol. 2: [1],420,[28]p., ill.,-ports., 8vo. Price: £1.4*s*.
1000 copies printed. In 1778 Murray paid George Robinson £3.13*s*.6*d*. for a 1/24 share bought at the Globe Tavern. In Apr. 1784 he paid £15.6*s*.6*d*., for paper and printing. The returns on his share (42 copies at 14*s*. each, wholesale) were £29.8*s*. (See Goldsmith 1779, item 223; BB, p. 13).
ESTC t146091: L, 1609/4121.
History. London syndicate.

419. [Gordon, Thomas.]
General remarks on the British fisheries. By a North Briton. London, printed for J. Murray; G. and T. Wilkie; and F. Jones. Sold also at New Lloyd's Coffee-house, Royal Exchange; and at the British Coffee-house, Charing-Cross, 1784.
[4],60p., 8vo. With a half-title. Price: 1*s*.6*d*.
Published in Dec. 1784. A larger work by Gordon (see item 475) was not published.
ESTC t082786: L, E.1248(8).
Economics. London co-publishing.

420. [Hill, John, 1714?–1775.]
The virtues of honey, in preventing many of the worst disorders; and in the certain cure of several others; . . . London, printed for J. Murray, 1784.
[2],74p., 12mo. With a half-title.
ESTC t050940: L, 7461.a.76.
Medicine. Murray alone.

421. Hodson, Thomas.
Cursory observations on a treatise intitled, 'Medical advice to the consumptive and asthmatic people of England, by Philip Stern, M.D.' London, printed for J. Murray, 1784.
vii,[1],31,[1]p., 8vo. With a half-title. Price: 1*s*.
ESTC n067646. CtY, Med.
Medicine. Murray alone.

422. Hunter, Henry, 1741–1802.
Sacred biography: or, the history of the patriarchs from Isaac to the birth of Moses inclusively: being a course of lectures delivered at the Scots church, London Wall, by Henry Hunter, D.D. . . . London, printed for the author, and sold by J. Murray; and James Dickson, Edinburgh, 1784–91.
vol. 1: [4],viii,429p.; vol. 2: xv,461p.; vol. 3: xvi,493p.; vol. 4: xiii,464p.; vol. 5: xiii,439p., 8vo, port. Price for 5 vol. set: £1.10*s*.
The title pages of vols. 3–5 read 'Sacred biography; or the history of the patriarchs. Being a course of lectures, delivered at the Scots church, London-Wall. By Henry Hunter, D.D. . . . ', with some variation in punctuation from volume to volume. The title pages to vols. 3 and 4 are dated 1786 and 1788. Vol. 3 bears the imprint: printed for the author, by Robert Hawes: and sold by J. Murray; and James Dickson, Edinburgh; that to vol. 4: printed for the author, by Ritchie and Sammells, and sold by John Murray; and James

Dickson, Edinburgh; and that to vol. 5: printed for the author, by Ritchie & Sammells, and sold by J. Murray; and James Dickson, Edinburgh. A sixth vol. 'Being a sequel to the history of the patriarchs' appeared in 1792.
ESTC n062270 (CaQMMD, RB CBE.H94) is 'a new edition' of vol. 1, 1784 with the pagination: xxxii,431p.
ESTC n036204: CaOHM, B5306-9.
Religion. Agency–London.

423. Innes, John, 1739–1777.
A short description of the human muscles, chiefly as they appear on dissection. Together with their several uses, and the synonyma of the best authors. By John Innes. A new edition, greatly improved by Alex. Monro, M.D. Edinburgh, printed for Charles Elliot; and G. Robinson and J. Murray, London, 1784.
240p., 12mo.
ESTC n022648: MBCo, QM151.16 1784.
Medicine. Edinburgh co-publishing.

424. Johnson, Samuel, 1709–1784.
A dictionary of the English language: in which the words are deduced from their originals, and illustrated in their different significations by examples from the best writers. . . . By Samuel Johnson. . . . The fifth edition. London, printed by W. & A. Strahan; for W. Strahan, J. F. & C. Rivington, L. Davis, T. Payne & Son, W. Owen, T. Longman, B. Law, J. Dodsley, C. Dilly, T. & W. Lowndes, G. Robinson, T. Cadell, T. Evans, Jo. Johnson, J. Robson, Richardson & Urquhart, J. Nichols, R. Baldwin, W. Goldsmith, J. Murray, W. Stuart, W. Fox, S. Hayes, J. Bowen, S. A. Cumberlege, and M. Newbery, 1784.
2 vols, unpaginated, Fo. Price: £4.10s. bound
There is no costing information about this folio edition, but see Johnson 1778, item 191; BB, p. 10. Published in Feb. 1785.
ESTC t116656: L, L.R.300.bbb.11.
Language. London syndicate.

425. [Johnson, Samuel, 1709–1784.]
The Rambler. In four volumes. The tenth edition. London, printed for W. Strahan, J. Rivington and Sons, B. Collins, T. Longman, B. Law, C. Dilly, T. Carnan, J. Robson, G. Robinson, T. Lowndes, T. Cadell, W. Cater, H. Baldwin, T. Newbery, J. Knox, J. Bew, J.

Nichols, W. Goldsmith, J. Murray, T. Evans, W. Fox, and J. Macqueen, 1784.
Vol. 1: [4],322,[1]p.; vol. 2: [iv],304p.; vol. 3: [iv],319p.; vol. 4: [iv],264,[32]p., port. in vol. 1; frontispiece plates to vols. 2–4, 12mo. Price: 12s. bound.
2000 copies printed. On 14 Aug. 1781 at John Hinton's sale Murray paid 4 gns for a 1/32 share. On 24 Dec. 1783 he paid £10.11s.4d. expenses. The returns on his share (63 copies at 6s. each, wholesale) were 18 gns. (BB, p. 28).
ESTC t098572: L, P.P.5251.a.
Education. London syndicate.

426. Juvenal.
The tenth satire of Juvenal. Translated by Thomas Morris, Esq; late Captain in his Majesty's XVIIth Regiment of Foot. Published as a specimen of his translation of that author. London, printed for J. Murray; J. Walter; and T. Hookam and R. Faulder, 1784.
[4],35,[1]p., 4to.
ESTC n054299: Ct, H.10.141[2].
Poetry. London syndicate.

427. The London kalendar, or, court and city register for England, Scotland, Ireland, and America, for the year 1784; . . . London, printed for J. Stockdale (from Mr. Almon's); T. Carnan; A. Donaldson; J. Fielding; J. Sewell; D. Steel; R. Faulder; and J. Murray, [1784].
[4],296p., 12mo. Price: 1s. 6d. sewed.
ESTC t205634: D, 9142.L4.
Another issue: headed 'corrected to the 1st of Dec. 1783'; without J. Fielding in the imprint. Same pagination.
ESTC t205634: D, 9142.L4.
Miscellaneous. London syndicate.

428. Longmate, Barak.
A supplement to the fifth edition of Collins's peerage of England; containing a general account of the marriages, births, promotions, deaths, &c. which have occurred in each family, from the publication, in the year 1779, to the present time. Also, genealogical and historical accounts of those families which have been advanced to the English peerage, whether by descent or creation, since that period. With their paternal coats of arms, crests, supportes, and mottoes, engraved on thirty-four copper plates . . . By B. Longmate, editor of the fifth

edition of Collins's peerage. London, printed for W. Strahan, J. F. and C. Rivington, T. Payne and Son, W. Owen, S. Crowder, T. Longman, C. Rivington, C. Dilly, J. Robson, T. and W. Lowndes, G. Robinson, T. Cadell, H. L. Gardner, J. Nichols, J. Bew, R. Baldwin, J. Murray, J. Debrett, W. Fox, J. White, J. Walker, T. Beecroft, and M. Folingsby, 1784.
xv,[1],300,[16],301–435,[9]p., plates, 8vo.
See Collins 1779, item 215. Murray bought a 1/48 share at Caslon's sale on 5 June 1783 for 19s. in addition to the 3/144 share he already owned. There is no record of his profit (if any) on this supplemental volume.
ESTC t120340: L, 9918.a.18.
Another issue: with a cancel title page; the imprint ends with 'W. Bent and M. Follingsby'.
ESTC t120339: L, 139.b.18.
Miscellaneous. London syndicate.

429. Lunardi's grand aerostatic voyage through the air, containing a complete and circumstantial account of the grand aerial flight made by that enterprising foreigner, in his air balloon, on September 15, 1784, . . . London, printed for J. Bew; J. Murray; Richardson and Urquhart; and R. Ryan; and sold by all the town and country booksellers, 1784.
[4],15,[1]p., plate, port., 4to. With a half-title.
Entered in the Stationers' Company Register, 23 Dec. 1784, 'The Author, the whole'.
ESTC t038779: L, 537.k.7(1).
Science. London co-publishing.

430. [Maurice, Thomas, A.B. of University College Oxford, 1754–1824].
Ode sacred to the genius of Handel. By a gentleman of Oxford. London, printed for the author, and sold by J. Murray; and J. Dodsley, [1784?].
7,[1]p., 4to.
ESTC t065501: L, 1486.l.9.
Poetry. Agency–London.

*431. Maurice, Thomas, A.B. of University College Oxford, 1754–1824.
Westminster-Abbey: an elegiac poem. By the Revd. Thomas Maurice, . . . London, printed for the author, and sold by J. Dodsley, and G. Kearsley; and by Messrs. Fletcher and Prince, in Oxford, and J. Merrill, Cambridge, 1784.
x,22p., 4to. Price: 3s.

Monthly Review 72 (June 1785) 463–65: 'Murray'
ESTC t052343: L, 11630.e.25.
Poetry. Agency–London.

432. McArthur, John, 1755–1840.
The army and navy gentleman's companion; or a new and complete treatise on the theory and practice of fencing. Displaying the intricacies of small-sword play; . . . Illustrated by mathematical figures, and adorned with elegant engravings . . . A new edition revised with a glossary and improvements, by J. Mc.Arthur . . . London, printed for J. Murray, 1784.
[6],xxii,162p., 19 plates, 4to. Engraved title page. With a list of subscribers. Price: 15s. in boards.
ESTC t118279: L, 1601/65.
Military. Murray alone.

433. Mitford, William, 1744–1827.
The history of Greece. By William Mitford, Esq. The first volume. London, printed by T. Wright, for J. Murray; and J. Robson, 1784.
[12],450p., plate, map, 4to. With a half-title. Price: 16s. in boards.
Published 22 July 1784. The second and subsequent volumes appeared after the second edition of vol. 1 of 1789, neither published by Murray. Stock: 2 sets; 1 vol. 1 (H).
ESTC t119958: L, 585.h.32(vol. 1).
History. London co-publishing.

434. [Moir, John.]
Female tuition; or, an address to mothers, on the education of daughters. London, printed for J. Murray, 1784.
vi,[2],306,[2]p., 8vo. With a half-title and a final leaf of advertisements. Price: 3s.
Entered in the Stationers' Company Register, 19 Aug. 1784, 'The author J. Moir, one half; J. Murray, one half'.
ESTC t078347: L, 1031.e.10.
Education. Murray alone.

435. Montagu, Lady, Mary Wortley, 1689–1762.
Letters of the Right Honourable Lady M——y W——y M——e: written during her travels in Europe, Asia, and Africa, to persons of distinction, men of letters, &c. in different parts of Europe. Which contain among other curious relations, accounts of the policy and manners of the Turks; drawn from sources that have

been inaccessible to other travellers. A new edition. To which are now first added, poems, by the same author. In two volumes. London, printed for T. Cadell, and T. Evans; J. Murray; and R. Baldwin, 1784.

Vol. 1: [iii]–ix,[2],220; vol. 2: [4],272p., 8vo.

With a 'Preface, by a lady' signed 'M. A.', i.e. Mary Astell. 1000 copies printed. Murray paid £1.11s.6d. for a 1/8 share at Thomas Becket's sale on 21 Jan. 1779 at the Queen's Arms. In Oct. 1783 he paid £10.8s.4d. for paper and printing. The returns on his share (125 copies at 3s. each, wholesale) were £18.15 (BB, p. 21). ESTC t066781: L, 1486.de.31.

Travel–topography. London co-publishing.

436. Murray, John, 1737–1793.

An author's conduct to the public, stated in the behaviour of Dr. William Cullen, His Majesty's physician at Edinburgh. London, printed for J. Murray, 1784.

[4],ii,41,[1]p., 8vo. Price: 1s.

See Bibliography of Pamphlets Written by Murray for details; Plate 45.

ESTC n015092: DNLM, WZ260.M983a 1784.

Miscellaneous. Murray alone.

437. Murray, John, 1737–1793.

No. 4. Murray's catalogue of books in medicine, surgery, anatomy, natural history, &c. For the use of the faculty, and practitioners in general. And which are to be sold (for ready money) at the prices marked against the several articles. London, printed for J. Murray, No. 32. Fleet-Street, where orders for books in this catalogue are received, 1784.

[2],54,[1]p. 8vo.

Murray's signed 'Advertisement' is dated February 1784. See Plate 32.

ESTC n63772: KU-S WZ260.J65n. 1784

Medicine. Murray alone.

438. A new and general biographical dictionary; containing an historical and critical account of the lives and writings of the most eminent persons in every nation; particularly the British and Irish; from the earliest accounts of time to the present period, wherein their remarkable actions and sufferings, their virtues, parts, and learning are accurately displayed. With a catalogue of their literary productions. A new edition, in twelve volumes, greatly enlarged and improved. . . . London, printed for W. Strahan, T. Payne and Son, J. Rivington and Sons, W. Owen, B. White, T. and W. Lowndes, B. Law, J. Robson, J. Johnson, G. Robinson, J. Nichols, J. Murray, W. Goldsmith, G. Nicol, P. Macqueen, T. Bowles, W. Chapman, and E. Newbery, 1784.

Vol. 1: xxx,421,[2]p.; vol. 2: [3],482,[3]p.; vol. 3: [3],480,[3]p.; vol. 4: [3],534,[3]p.; vol. 5: [3],5 47p.; vol. 6: [3],492,[3]p.; vol. 7: [3],531,[4]p.; vol. 8. [3],493p.; vol. 9: [3],548p.; vol. 10: [3], 540,[3]p.; vol. 11: [3],596p.; vol. 12: [3],758p., 8vo. With half-titles. Price: £3.12s. in boards.

2000 copies printed. Murray paid £2.7s. for a 31/2000 share at Thomas Becket's sale at the Queen's Arms on 21 Jan. 1779. In May 1784 he paid £41.6s.1d. to Nichols for paper and printing. The returns on his share (31 copies at £2.12s. each, wholesale) were £62.8s. Share sold 23 Dec. 1794 to Davies for £11 (BB, p. 19). ESTC t133607: L, 10604.m.17.

Biography. London syndicate.

439. O'Gallagher, Felix.

An essay on the investigation of the first principles of nature: together with the application thereof to solve the phenomena of the physical system. Part I. Containing a new philosophical theory; . . . By Felix O'Gallagher. London, printed for J. Murray, 1784.

xi,[1],388p., 8vo. Price: 5s. in boards.

250 copies printed (To O'Gallagher, 26 Apr. 1784). Entered in the Stationers' Company Register, 'The author, the whole'. Part II published in 1786 (item 538). Stock: 178 (W).

ESTC n031268: NCorniM *364.

Medicine. Murray alone.

440. Perfect, William, 1737–1809.

Cases in midwifery: with references and remarks. By William Perfect, . . . Second edition, corrected and improved. Rochester, printed for the author, by T. Fisher: and sold by J. Bew; and J. Murray, London, 1784.

Vol. 1: [xii],401p.; vol. 2: [xii],530p., 8vo. Price: 12s.

ESTC n014595: DNLM, 18th c.coll.

Medicine. Agency–provincial.

**441. A review of the proceedings against Lieutenant Charles Bourne, in the Court of King's Bench, upon a libel and assault, on the prosecution of Sir James Wallace, June 5 and

July 8, 1783 ... with explanatory notes and observations. London, Murray, 1784.
No copy located. *Monthly Review* 71 (Aug. 1784), 152–3. Price: 1s.6d. *ESTC* records three different editions in 1783: n013791, t113391, n024513.
Law. Murray alone.

442. Richardson, William, 1743–1814.
Essays on Shakespeare's dramatic characters of Richard the Third, King Lear, and Timon of Athens. To which are added, an essay on the faults of Shakespeare and additional observations on the character of Hamlet. By Mr. Richardson, ... London, printed for J. Murray, 1784.
[6],vi,[1],4–170,[4]p., 8vo. With a half-title, two final advertisement leaves, and an errata slip pasted in at p. 170. Price: 3s.
Entered in the Stationers' Company Register, 28 Nov. 1783, 'J. Murray, by purchase, the whole'.
ESTC t136684: L, 642.b.33.
Literary criticism. Murray alone.

443. Richardson, William, 1743–1814.
A philosophical analysis and illustration of some of Shakespeare's remarkable characters. By W. Richardson, ... The third edition, corrected. London, printed for J. Murray, 1784.
207,[1]p., 8vo. Price: 2s.6d. sewed.
A reissue of the 'New edition, corrected', London, 1780, with a cancel title page.
ESTC t136698: L, 11764.b.7.
Literary criticism. Murray alone.

444. Ruspini, Bartholomew, 1728–1813.
A treatise on the teeth: wherein an accurate idea of their structure is given, the cause of their decay pointed out, ... By Barth. Ruspini, ... A new edition: with an appendix of new cases. London, printed for the author, and may be had at his house in Pall-Mall; and of Mr. Johnson, St. Paul's Church-yard, and of Messrs. Kearsley and Murray, Fleet-Street, 1784.
[4],vii,[1],96p., 8vo.
ESTC n049621: DNLM, W6.P3 v.548.
Medicine. Agency–London.

445. Shakespeare, William, 1564–1616.
Othello, the Moor of Venice, a tragedy, written by William Shakespeare, marked with the varia-

tions in the manager's book, af [*sic*] the Theatre-Royal in Drury-Lane. London, printed for C. Bathurst, W. & A. Strahan, J. F. & C. Rivington, L. Davis, T. & W. Lowndes, W. Owen & Son, S. Crowder, B. White, T. Longman, B. Law, C. Dilly, T. Cadell, T. Payne & Son, J. Robson, G. Robinson, T. Davies, T. Bowles, R. Baldwin, H. L. Gardner, J. Nicholls, J. Bew, W. Cater, J. Murray, W. Stuart, S. Hayes, W. Bent, S. Bladon, W. Fox, & E. Newbery, 1784.
91,[1]p., plate, 12mo.
ESTC t062199: L, 11765.aaa.3.
Drama. London syndicate.

446. Sheldon, John, 1752–1808.
The history of the absorbent system, part the first. Containing the chylography, or description of the human lacteal vessels, ... Illustrated by figures, by John Sheldon, ... London, printed for the author, sold by T. Cadell, and P. Elmsly; J. Murray; J. Johnson; C. Dilly; C. Heydinger; and W. Babbs, 1784.
[4],ii,[6],vi,52,[14]p.,6 plates, 4to. With a half-title, a list of subscribers, and leaf of errata.
Each plate is accompanied by an explanatory leaf.
Another issue: London, printed for the author, and may be had at his house in Great Queen-street.
ESTC t091103: L, 435.h.4.
Medicine. Agency–London.

447. Spallanzani, Lazzaro, 1729–1799.
Dissertations relative to the natural history of animals and vegetables. Translated from the Italian of the Abbé Spallanzani, ... To which are added two letters from Mr. Bonnet to the author. And (to each volume of this translation) an appendix, ... London, printed for J. Murray, 1784.
Vol. 1: [xl],[7]-328,[14],[1]p.; vol. 2: iii,[5]–385, [17],[2]p., plates, 8vo. Price: 10s.6d. in boards.
A translation by Thomas Beddoes of *Opuscoli di fisica animale e vegetabile*; (To Beddoes, 14 July 1784).
ESTC t131278: L, 956.h.14,15.
Science. Murray alone.

448. Spence, David, 1747–1786.
A system of midwifery, theoretical and practical. Illustrated with copper-plates. By David Spence, M.D. ... Edinburgh, printed for William

Creech; and sold in London by T. Longman and J. Murray, 1784.
xii,407,[4],410–589,[1]p., 26 plates, 8vo. Part II has a separate title page inserted after p. 407. Price: 12*s.* bound.
ESTC t051040: L, 1177.h.16.
Medicine. Agency–Edinburgh.

449. [Stock, Joseph, 1740–1813.]
Memoirs of George Berkeley, D.D. late Bishop of Cloyne in Ireland. The second edition, with improvements. London, printed for J. Murray; and R. Faulder, 1784.
iv,186,[2]p., plate, 8vo. With a final advertisement leaf. Price: 3*s.6d.*
This edition is more than double the length of the 1776 edition and includes 140 pages of correspondence. The portrait of Berkeley, dated 1 Aug. 1781, was published by Murray and Wm Hallhead at Dublin for the Dublin edition of Berkeley's *Works*. Stock: 29 (W).
ESTC t147009: L, 1372.d.10.
Biography. London co-publishing.

450. [Taylor, Edward, 1741?–1797.]
Werter to Charlotte. A poem. London, printed for J. Murray, 1784.
23,[1]p., 4to. Price: 1*s.*
ESTC t102939: L, 11632.d.49(1).
Poetry. Murray alone.

451. Trye, Charles Brandon, 1757–1811.
Remarks on morbid retentions of urine. By Charles Brandon Trye, . . . Glocester, printed by R. Raikes. And sold by J. Murray, London; Evans and Hazell, and S. Harward, Glocester, 1784.
vii,[1],84p., plates, 8vo. Price: 2*s.6d.*
100 copies printed (To Trye, 20 Aug. 1784).
ESTC t007906: L, T.343(1).
Medicine. Provincial co-publishing.

452. Vanity of fame. A poem: illustrated by some characters of the present age. Written in imitation of Pope's didactic essays. Addressed to Sir Carnaby Haggerston, Bart. London, Printed for J. Murray, R. Faulder, and J. Walter, 1784.
49,[1]p., 4to. With advertisement and errata slip pasted onto p. 49. Price: 2*s.6d.*
Primary location: CtY, Beinecke 1975 2570.
Poetry. London co-publishing.

453. White, Thomas, b. 1753.
A treatise on struma or scrofula, commonly called the King's evil; . . . By Thomas White, . . . London, printed for J. Murray; and R. Turner, 1784.
xvi,110p., 8vo. With a half-title. Price: 2*s.*
ESTC t056779: L, T.214(5).
Medicine. London co-publishing.

1785

454. Adye, Stephen Payne, d. 1794.
A treatise on courts martial. To which is added, an essay on military punishments and rewards. The third edition, with additions and amendments, by Stephen Payne Adye, . . . London, printed for J. Murray, 1785.
viii,284,[4]p., 8vo. With two final advertisement leaves. Price: 3*s.6d.* in boards.
ESTC n013707: MH-L, S UK 989.ADY.
Military. Murray alone.

*455. Arnot, Hugo, 1749–1786.
A collection and abridgement of celebrated criminal trials in Scotland, from A.D. 1536, to 1784. With historical and critical remarks. By Hugo Arnot, . . . Edinburgh, printed for the author; by William Smellie, 1785.
xxiii,[1],400p., 4to. With a list of subscribers. Price: 18*s.* in boards.
Monthly Review 77 (Sept. 1787) 213–16: 'Edinburgh printed, sold by Murray in London'. Also listed in several advertisements at the end of Murray's publications.
ESTC t142881: L, G.5398.
Law. Agency–Edinburgh.

456. Bergman, Torbern, 1735–1784.
A dissertation on elective attractions. By Torbern Bergmann. . . . Translated from the Latin by the translator of Spallanzani's dissertations. London, printed for J. Murray; and Charles Elliot, Edinburgh, 1785.
xiv,[2],382,[2]p.,tables, plates, 8vo. With a final errata leaf.
Translated by Thomas Beddoes. First published in 1775 as *Disquisitio de attractionibus electivis* in vol. 2 of *Nova acta Regia societatis scientiarum upsaliensis*. Entered in the Stationers' Company Register, 1 Oct. 1785, 'John Murray. The Whole'. 1000 copies printed. Expenses from 6 Aug. 1785: £2.7*s.6d.* for copper-plate paper; printing and paper, £134.8*s.3d.* The returns on

1000 copies (at 4s.4d. each, wholesale) were £216.15s.4d., a nett profit of £79.17s. (BB, p. 40). Stock: W (7).
ESTC n008840: DNLM, WZ260.B512dE 1785.
Science. Murray alone (despite imprint).

457. Blair, Hugh, 1718–1800.
Essays on rhetoric: abridged chiefly from Dr. Blair's lectures on that science. The second edition, with additions and improvements. London, printed for J. Murray, 1785.
[16],533,[3]p., 12mo. With a half-title and a final advertisement leaf. Price: 4s.
ESTC t129564: L, 11806.a.30.
This edition was reprinted over 70 times in America between 1802 and 1871 (see Blair 1784, item 397).
Literary criticism. Murray alone.

458. Blane, Sir, Gilbert, 1749–1834.
Observations on the diseases incident to seamen. By Gilbert Blane, . . . London, printed by Joseph Cooper; and sold by John Murray, and by William Creech, in Edinburgh, 1785.
viii,xiv, 16–502,xv,[1]p.,tables, 8vo. Price: 6s. in boards.
ESTC t100609: L, 45.a.7.
Medicine. Edinburgh co-publishing.

459. Brand, Thomas, surgeon.
Chirurgical essays on the cure of ruptures, and the pernicious consequences of referring patients to truss-makers: with cases. By T. Brand, . . . The second edition. London, sold by J. Dodsley; J. Bew; J. Murray; and T. Lewis, 1785.
[22],119,[1]p., 8vo.
First published as *Chirurgical essays, on the causes and symptoms of ruptures*, and entered in the Stationers' Company Register, 1 Aug. 1782, 'The Author, the whole'.
ESTC n015069: MBCo, 23.S.59.
Medicine. London co-publishing.

460. Campbell, Coll.
A new edition of the appeal of a neglected naval officer; to which are now added, the reply of Sir Roger Curtis, intersected with remarks by Lieut. Campbell; and . . . letters on the blockade of Mahon, . . . Together with a letter to Lord Howe, . . . on his treatment of Mr. Campbell.

London, printed for J. Murray; and W. Richardson, [1785].
[2],128p., 8vo.
ESTC t108609: L, 8132.e.15.
Military. London co-publishing.

461. Campbell, John, 1708–1775.
Lives of the British admirals: containing a new and accurate naval history from the earliest periods. By Dr. J. Campbell. With a continuation down to the year 1779, . . . Written under the inspection of Doctor Berkenhout. The whole illustrated with correct maps; and frontispieces . . . In four volumes. . . . London, printed for J. Murray, 1785.
Vol. 1: [1],xv,vi,578p.; vol. 2: iv,558p.; vol. 3: [iii],520p.; vol. 4: xx,521p., plates, maps, 8vo. Price: £1.8s. bound.
A reprint of the 1779 edition. The frontispieces are dated 'Jany. 1st. 1779', and are published by A. Donaldson. Another issue published, London, printed for G. G. J. and J. Robinson, 1785. Stock: 14 (H); 44 (W).
ESTC t126073: L, 1509/149.
Biography. Murray alone.

462. Chamberlaine, William, b. 1749.
A practical treatise on the efficacy of stizolobium, or, cowhage, internally administered, in diseases occasioned by worms. To which are added, observations on other anthelmintic medicines of the West-Indies. By William Chamberlaine, surgeon. The third edition. London, printed for J. Murray, 1785.
viii,77,[3]p., 8vo. With a half-title and a final advertisement leaf.
ESTC n020682: KU-S, Brodie 31.4.
Medicine. Murray alone.

463. Coley, William.
An account of the late epidemic ague, particularly as it appeared in the neighbourhood of Bridgnorth in Shropshire, in the year 1784; with a successful method of treating it: to which are added, some observations on a dysentery, that prevailed at the same time. By William Coley, . . . London, printed for the author; and sold by J. Murray, and Messrs Robinsons, 1785.
xiii,[1],58p., 8vo. With a half-title. Price: 1s.
ESTC t183584: C, Syn.7.78.61/6.
Medicine. Agency–London.

464. Cullen, William, 1710–1790.
Synopsis nosologia methodica, exhibens clariss. virorum Sauvagesii, Linnai, Vogelii, Sagari, et Macbridii, systemata nosologica. Edidit suumque proprium systema nosologicum adjecit Gulielmus Cullen, . . . Editio quarta, emendata et plurimum aucta, duobus tomis. . . . Edinburgi, prostant venales apud Gulielmum Creech; et J. Murray, London, 1785.
Vol. 1: iv,368p.; vol. 2: [4],xl,417p., 8vo.
Entered in the Stationers' Company Register, 13 May 1785, 'Mr Wm Creech Edinb: the whole'.
ESTC no23219: DNLM, WZ260.C967s 1785.
Medicine. Edinburgh co-publishing.

465. De Lolme, Jean Louis, 1740–1806.
Constitution de l'Angleterre, ou état du gouvernement anglois, comparé avec la forme républicaine & avec les autres monarchies de l'Europe. Par M. de Lolme, . . . Quatrieme édition, entiérement revue & augmentée de la moitié, sur l'édition angloise, . . . Londres, chez G. Robinson. J. Murray, 1785.
Vol. 1: [4],xxvi,[2],230; vol. 2: 262,[2], 8vo.
500 copies printed. Murray paid George Robinson £60.19s.6d. for the whole share of this edition in Mar. 1784 and July 1785. He paid £54.3s.4d. for paper and printing. The returns on 500 copies at 4s.8d., each, wholesale, were £116.13s.4d. (BB, p. 24; see De Lolme 1781, item 280 and 1784, item 409).
ESTC no03558: MH-L, UK 961.LOL.AF.
History. London co-publishing.

466. Dewell, T.
The philosophy of physic, founded on one general and immutable law of nature, the necessarily relative agency of elementary fire. By T. Dewell, . . . The second edition, revised & corrected. Marlborough, printed by E. Harold; for J. Murray, J. Bew, London; W. Taylor, Bath; and J. Elliot, Edinburgh, 1785.
vii,[3],xliii,[1],84p., 8vo. With a half-title.
ESTC t136100: L, 1507/1794.
Medicine. Provincial co-publishing.

467. Dickson, Adam, 1721–1776, Minister at Dunse.
A treatise of agriculture. A new edition, by Adam Dickson, A.M. Edinburgh, printed for J. Dickson. London, for B. White and J. Murray, 1785.

Vol. 1: [8],lxv,487p.; vol. 2: [8],564p., plates, 8vo.
First published in 1762 'for the author' by Alex. Donaldson and J. Reid. Stock: 1 (H); 3 (W).
ESTC t176569: D, 6302.d3.1.
Agriculture. London co-publishing.

468. Duncan, Andrew, 1744–1828, editor.
Medical Commentaries, for the years 1783–84; exhibiting a concise view of the latest and most important discoveries in medicine and medical philosophy. Collected and published by Andrew Duncan, M.D.F.R. & A.S.Ed . . . Volume Ninth. London, printed for J. Murray, and C. Dilly; and for W. Gordon and C. Elliot, Edinburgh, 1785.
xvi,516p. 8vo. Price: 6s.
Stock: 79 (W).
Primary location: Roy. Col. Phys. Edin.
Medicine. Edinburgh co-publishing.

469. The English review; or, an abstract of English and foreign literature. . . . London, printed for J. Murray, 1785.
Vol. 5: [1],[vi],480,[8]p., 8vo; vol. 6: [1],[viii], 464,*425–*464–480,[8]p., 8vo.
Published in monthly parts (priced 1s.); title page, contents, and index issued every six months.
Primary location: NN, *DA.
Miscellaneous. Murray–with agency.

470. An epistle from John, Lord Ashburton, in the shades, to the Right Hon. William P–tt, in the sunshine. With notes political, critical, historical, and explanatory. London, sold by J. Murray; and T. Southerne, 1785.
[2],36p., 4to. With a half-title. Price: 2s.
ESTC no06828: MH-H, *EC75.A100 785e.
Politics. London co-publishing.

471. Ferguson, James, 1710–1776.
Astronomy explained upon Sir Isaac Newton's principles, and made easy to those who have not studied mathematics. To which are added, a plain method of finding the distances of all the planets from the sun, . . . By James Ferguson, . . . The seventh edition. London, printed for W. Strahan. J. Rivington and Sons, T. Longman, B. Law, G. Robinson, T. Cadell, J. Johnson, J. Bew, J. Murray, R. Baldwin, T. Evans, W. Lowndes, and C. Bent, 1785.

[8],501,[15]p., plates, 8vo. With an index. Price: 9s.

1500 copies printed. Murray bought a 1/24 share on 8 Apr. 1777 at the Queen's Arms for £8.15s. On 10 Dec. 1784 he paid Thomas Cadell (who organised the edition) £9.14s.3d. for paper and printing. The returns on his share (63 copies at 5s. each, wholesale) were 15 gns. (BB, p. 2; Ferguson 1778, item 183).
ESTC t018583: L, 8562.bbb.5.
Science. London syndicate.

472. Fordyce, Sir William, 1724–1792.
A review of the venereal disease, and its remedies: with an appendix. By Sir William Fordyce, M.D. The fifth edition. London, printed by T. Spilsbury, for T. Cadell; and sold by J. Murray; and W. Davenhill, 1785.
[8],151,[1]p., 8vo. With a half-title. Price: 3s.
ESTC t045783: L, 7320.c.24(3).
Medicine. Agency–London.

473. Garrick, David, 1717–1779.
The winter's tale, or Florizel and Perdita. A dramatic pastoral, altered from Shakspeare, by David Garrick, Esq. Marked with the variations in the manager's book, at the Theatre-Royal in Drury-Lane. London, printed for C. Bathurst, W. & A. Strahan, J. F. & C. Rivington, L. Davis, W. Owen & Son, S. Crowder, B. White & Son, T. Longman, B. Law, C. Dilly, T. Cadell, T. Payne & Son, J. Robson, G. G. J. and J. Robinson, T. Davies, T. Bowles, R. Baldwin, H. L. Nichols, J. Bew, W. Cater, J. Murray, W. Stuart, S. Hayes, W. Lowndes, G. & T. Wilkie, S. Bladon, W. Fox, and E. Newbery, 1785.
48p., plate, 12mo.
ESTC t062749: L, 11763.ppp.61.
Drama. London syndicate.

474. Gay, John, 1685–1732.
Fables by the late Mr. Gay. In one volume complete. London, printed for J. Buckland, A. Strahan, J. F. and C. Rivington, B. White, T. Longman, B. Law, T. Carnan, G. G. J. and J. Robinson, T. Cadell, S. Bladon, R. Baldwin, J. Sewell, J. Johnson, H. L. Gardner, W. Goldsmith, J. Murray, W. Lowndes, G. and T. Wilkie, W. Bent, and E. Newbery, 1785.
240p., plates, 12mo. Price: 3s. bound.
?5000 copies printed (some without plates). Murray bought a 1/20 share at the Globe

Tavern (John Crowder's sale) on 10 Sept. 1777 for £10.5s. which he paid to George Robinson on 16 Jan. 1778 and on 10 April 1783 at the Globe Tavern he paid Robinson £3.7s. for an additional 1/40 share (3/40ths in all). On 15 Sept. 1785 Murray paid Thomas Longman £7.12s.6d. for paper and printing. The returns on his share (305 books 'no cuts' at 1s. each, wholesale), paid on 15 Sept. 1785, were £15.5s. (see BB, p. 9; Gay 1778, item 184 and 1783, item 347).
ESTC t013864: L, 1164.c.57.
Poetry. London syndicate.

475. Gordon, Thomas.
Proposals for printing by subscription, in one volume quarto, price one guinea, (half to be paid at the time of subscribing, and the other half on delivery of the book in boards), The spirit of commerce. In three parts. Part I. An account of all the different real coins . . . .. Part II. Simulated accounts. . . . Part III. An account of the most considerable manufacturing towns in Europe . . . .. By Thomas Gordon, Esq. Lesmoir. Subscriptions are received by J. Murray; G. and T. Wilkie; at New Lloyd's Coffee-house; and at the British Coffee-house.
Information taken from a newspaper clipping in the Archive, hand-dated 1785. No copy of the separately printed proposal (if there was one) is located nor is the work itself.
Economics. London co-publishing.

476. [Harrington, Robert, 1751–1837.]
Thoughts on the properties and formation of the different kinds of air; with remarks . . . on the different theories upon air. London, printed for R. Faulder; J. Murray; and R. Cust, 1785.
vii,[3],330p., 8vo. Price: 5d. in boards.
ESTC t210218: Di, MR 30 I 28.
Science. London co-publishing.

477. Hayes, Thomas, fl. 1783–1786.
A serious address on the dangerous consequences of neglecting common coughs and colds; containing, a simple, efficacious, and domestic method of cure. . . . The second edition. To which is now added, successful directions to prevent and cure consumptions. By Thomas Hayes. . . . London, printed for J. Murray, and Messrs. Shepperson and Reynolds, 1785.

92p., 8vo. Price: 2s.
First published by Murray in 1783 as *A serious and friendly address.*
ESTC n022078: DNLM, WZ260.H418s 1785.
Medicine. London co-publishing.

478. Hunter, Henry, 1741–1802.
Sacred biography. Or the history of the patriarchs: being a course of lectures delivered at the Scots church, London Wall, by Henry Hunter, D.D. The third edition. Volume I. London, printed for the author, at the Logogrhphic-Press [i.e. Logographic Press], and sold by J. Murray; and James Dickson, Edinburgh, 1785. [4],viii,431,[1]p., port., 8vo. Price: 7s.
ESTC n036201: CaOHM, B5304.
Religion. Agency–London.

479. Imison, John, d. 1788.
The school of arts; or, an introduction to useful knowledge, being a compilation of real experiments and improvements, in several pleasing branches of science, . . . By John Imison. London, printed for the author, and sold by J. Murray, [1785].
[4],iii,[5],264;124p., plates, 8vo. Price: 8s in boards.
In two parts, the second, 'Curious and entertaining miscellaneous articles', with separate pagination and register. *English Review* 6 (Dec. 1785), 425.
ESTC t130627: L,1609/5462.
Science. Agency–Murray alone.

480. Johnson, Samuel, 1709–1784.
A dictionary of the English language: in which the words are deduced from their originals, and illustrated in their different significations by examples from the best writers. . . . By Samuel Johnson, . . . The sixth edition. London, printed for J. F. and C. Rivington, L. Davis, T. Payne and Son, T. Longman, B. Law, J. Dodsley, C. Dilly, W. Lowndes, G. G. J. and J. Robinson, T. Cadell, Jo. Johnson, J. Robson, W. Richardson, J. Nichols, R. Baldwin, W. Goldsmith, J. Murray, W. Stuart, P. Elmsley, W. Fox, S. Hayes, A. Strahan, W. Bent, T. and J. Egerton, and M. Newbery. 1785.
[1150]p., plate, port., 4to.
Published in 84 weekly numbers at 6d. each (or 2 gns. in sheets). Murray described this edition as 'Jarvis's Johnson' (To Creech, 24 Feb. 1787). Stock: 8 (W).

ESTC t116655: L, 1890.b.3(97).
Language. London syndicate.

481. The seventh edition.
ESTC t116652: L, 1483.dd.2.
Language. London syndicate.

482. The London calendar, or court and city register for England, Scotland, Ireland, and America, for the year 1785; . . . London, printed for John Stockdale; T. Carnan; J. Sewell, D. Steel; R. Faulder; J. Murray; and Scatcherd and Whitaker, [1785].
[4],296p., 12mo. Price: 1s.6d. sewed; 2s. in red morocco; 2s.9d. with an almanack.
ESTC t139275: L, C.108.c.57(2).
An undated newspaper advertisement in the Archive states that 'the Royal Kalendar, and the Court and City Register are the same book, printed verbatim, except about 36 pages, from page 21 to page 58'.
Miscellaneous. London syndicate.

483. Lovat, Simon Fraser, Lord, 1667?–1747.
Memoirs of the life of Simon Lord Lovat, written by himself in the French language, and now first translated from the original manuscript. London, printed for J. Murray, 1785.
xvi,468p., 8vo.
A translation by William Godwin of *Memoires de la vie du Lord Lovat.* Murray paid Alex. Fraser £40 for the Memoirs (To Fraser, 9 Nov. 1784). This edition was suppressed (To John Bell, 15 Mar. 1785). The sheets were reissued by George Nicol with a new title page in 1797. Stock: 'Memoirs of ***** of ******' 49 copies (H).
ESTC t173534: E, NF.1348.a.3
Biography. Murray alone.

484. Motherby, George, 1732–1793.
A new medical dictionary; or, general repository of physic. Containing an explanation of the terms, and a description of the various particulars. . . . By G. Motherby, M.D. The second edition, considerably enlarged and improved, and the whole carefully corrected. London, printed for J. Johnson; G. G. J. and J. Robinson; A. Hamilton, jun. and J. Murray, 1785.
vi,[714]p., 26 plates, Fo. Price: 2 gns. in boards. 1250 copies printed. Murray bought a 1/8 share in July 1778. In Feb. 1785 he paid Joseph Johnson £108.16s.6d. for his share of paper and printing.

The returns on his share (157 copies at 28s. each, wholesale) were £219.12s.6d. (BB, p. 7). Published 8 Feb. 1785.
ESTC t066033: L, 1486.gg.4.
Medicine. London co-publishing.

485. Murray, John, 1737–1793.
No. V. Murray's catalogue of books, in medicine, surgery, anatomy, natural history &c. for the use of the faculty, . . . London, printed for J. Murray, 1785.
[2],76p. 8vo.
ESTC t227242: L, RB.23.a.11377.
Medicine. Murray Alone.

486. The novelties of a year and a day, in a series of picturesque letters on the characters, manners, and customs of the Spanish, French, and English nations; . . . by Figaro. London, printed for the author; at the Logographic Press, and sold by J. Murray, [1785?].
[4],222,[2]p., 12o. With a final advertisement leaf. Price: 3s.
Last letter dated May 28th, 1785. *English Review* 7 (March 1786), 223.
ESTC t128782: L, 12352.ee.14.
Travel-Topography. Agency–Murray alone.

487. Observations on the jurisprudence of the Court of Session in Scotland; wherein some improprieties in the present mode of procedure are pointed out, and amendments submitted. London, printed for J. Murray; and C. Elliott, Edinburgh, 1785.
34p., 8vo. Price: 1s.
ESTC n010156: MH-L, UK 991.Sc.OBS.
Law. Edinburgh co-publishing.

488. Perry, Sampson, 1747–1823.
A disquisition of the stone and gravel; with strictures on the gout, when combined with those disorders. By S. Perry, surgeon. The seventh edition, improved and enlarged. London, printed by H. Reynell, for T. Becket; J. Bew; J. Murray; J. Southern; and Richardson, 1785.
xix,[1],248p., 8vo. With a half-title. Price: 3s.
ESTC t064159: L, 1189.d.23.
Another issue: London, printed by H. Reynell, for J. Murray; J. Bew; T. Becket; J. Southern; and Richardson, 1785.
ESTC n006494: MBCo 18.B.384.

Another issue: London, printed by H. Reynell, for J. Bew; J. Murray; T. Becket; J. Southern; and Richardson, 1785.
ESTC n006493: DNLM, 18th c. coll.
Medicine. London co-publishing.

489. The political magazine and parliamentary, naval, military, and literary journal, for the year, 1785. London, printed for J. Murray, and sold by every bookseller and news carrier in Great Britain.
Vol. 8: Jan.–June. [ii],480,[13]p., 8vo. With an index, plates and maps; vol. 9: July–Dec. [viii],476p., 8vo. With plates and maps.
Issued in monthly parts at 1s. each; 2000 copies printed (To John Trusler, 5 Oct. 1786).
Primary location: CtY, Franklin Coll.
Miscellaneous. Murray alone.

490. Practical benevolence, in a letter, addressed to the public. By a universal friend; to whom persons of all ranks and denominations may have recourse for advice, in the most critical situations, and most delicate circumstances of human life. London, printed for the author, and sold by J. Murray, 1785.
22p., 8vo. Price: 1s.
ESTC t099729: L,8404.aaa.12.
Religion. Agency–Murray alone.

491. Richardson, William, 1743–1814.
Essays on Shakespeare's dramatic characters of Macbeth, Hamlet, Jaques, and Imogen. To which are prefixed, an introduction. The fourth edition. By Mr. Richardson, . . . London, printed for J. Murray, 1785.
[4],203,[1]p., 8vo. Price: 5s.
ESTC t136701: BMp, S450.
Literary criticism. Murray alone.

492. Richardson, William, 1743–1814.
Essays on Shakespeare's dramatic characters of Richard the Third, King Lear, and Timon of Athens. To which are added, an essay on the faults of Shakespeare; . . . By Mr. Richardson, . . . London, printed for J. Murray, 1785.
viii,170p., 8vo. Price: 5s.
ESTC t167517: L, uk PR 2975.R3(1785).
Literary criticism. Murray alone.

493. The second edition.
viii,[1],4–170p., 8vo.

ESTC t119255: L, 1607/1747.
Literary criticism. Murray alone.

494. Salmon, Thomas, 1679–1767.
Salmon's geographical and astronomical grammar, including the ancient and present state of the world; . . . The thirteenth edition; with considerable corrections and additions, in which the history of the various countries in every quarter of the globe is continued to the year 1785, . . . London, printed for C. Bathurst, W. Strahan, J. F. and C. Rivington, S. Crowder, T. Longman, B. Law, J. and T. Pote, C. Dilly, G. G. J. and J. Robinson, T. Cadell, R. Baldwin, J. Nichols, J. Sewell, W. Goldsmith, W. Nicoll, J. Murray, J. Bew, W. Lowndes, Scatcherd and Whitaker, and W. Stuart, 1785.
vi,770p., plates, maps, 8vo.
5000 copies printed. Murray paid £5.6s. for a 1/32 share bought at Caslon's sale on 5 June 1783. He paid expenses of £32.18s.3d. on 8 July 1785. The returns on his share (188 copies at 4s.8d. each, wholesale) were £43.17s.4d. Stock: 2 (H); 77 (W).
ESTC t069013: L, 570.d.8.
Travel–topography. London syndicate.

495. Shakespeare, William, 1564–1616.
The plays of William Shakspeare. In ten volumes. With the corrections and illustrations of various commentators; to which are added notes by Samuel Johnson and George Steevens. The third edition, revised and augmented by the editor of Dodsley's collection of old plays [Isaac Reed]. London, printed for C. Bathurst, J. Rivington and Sons, T. Payne and Son, L. Davis, W. Owen, B. White and Son, T. Longman, B. Law, T. Bowles, J. Johnson, C. Dilly, J. Robson, G. G. J. and J. Robinson, T. Cadell, H. L. Gardner, J. Nichols, J. Bew, W. Stuart, R. Baldwin, J. Murray, A. Strahan, T. Vernor, J. Barker, W. Lowndes, S Hayes, G. and T. Wilkie, Scatcherd and Whitaker, T. and J. Egerton, W. Fox, and E. Newbery, 1785.
Vol. 1: [3],iv,362,414p.; vol. 2: [3],560p.; vol. 3: [3],560p.; vol. 4: [3],644p.; vol. 5: [3],651p.; vol. 6: [3],v,[7]–584p.; vol. 7: [3],512p.; vol. 8: [3],588p.; vol. 9: [3],618p.; vol. 10: [3],754p., plates, ports., 8vo. Price: £3.10s. in boards.
1200 copies printed. Murray bought a 1/120 share at the Globe Tavern (D. Cornish's sale) on 17 March 1778 for £9.15s. which he paid to

George Robinson. On 14 Aug. 1781 at John Hinton's sale he purchased a 1/60 share for £7.17s.6d. and on 10 May 1783 he acquired a further 1/60 share (John Ridley's) for £9, which he paid to Thomas Evans. On 8 Nov. 1785 he paid £78.12s.6d. for paper and printing in cash to Rivington. The returns on his share (51 sets at £2.3s.4d. each, wholesale), paid on 8 Dec. 1785, were £110.10s. (BB, p. 12, Plate 41; see Shakespeare 1778, item 201). Entered in the Stationers' Company Register, 7 Dec. 1785, 'John Francis & Charles Rivington & the rest of the Proprietors, Whole'.
ESTC t138853: L, 642.f.11–20.
Drama. London syndicate.

496. Shakespeare, William, 1564–1616.
Macbeth. A tragedy. Written by William Shakspeare, with the additions set to music by Mr. Locke and Dr. Arne. Marked with the variations in the manager's book, at the Theatre-Royal in Drury-Lane. London, printed for C. Bathurst, W. and A. Strahan, J. F. & C. Rivington, L. Davis, W. Lowndes, W. Owen & Son, B. White & Son, T. Longman, B. Law, C. Dilly, T. Cadell, T. Payne & Son, J. Robson, G. G. J. and J. Robinson, T. Davies, T. Bowles, R. Baldwin, H. L. Gardner, J. Nicholls, J. Bew, W. Cater, J. Murray, W. Stuart, S. Hayes, W. Bent, S. Bladon, W. Fox, & E. Newbery, 1785.
67,[5]p., plate, 12mo. With two final advertisement leaves.
ESTC n004559: CaOTU, B-10 6562.
Drama. London syndicate.

497. Shakespeare, William, 1564–1616.
The tempest, a comedy; written by William Shakspeare: the music by Purcel and Dr. Arne; with the additional airs and choruses, by the late Mr. Linley, jun. Marked with the variations in the manager's book, at the Theatre-Royal in Drury-Lane. London, printed for C. Bathurst, W. and A. Strahan, J. F. and C. Rivington, L. Davis, W. Owen & Son, B. White & Son, T. Longman, B. Law, C. Dilly, T. Payne & Son, J. Nicholls, T. Cadell, J. Robson, G. G. J. and J. Robinson, T. Bowles, R. Baldwin, H. L. Gardner, J. Bew, W. Cater, J. Murray, W. Stuart, S. Hayes, W. Lowndes, S. Bladon, G. & T. Wilkie, W. Fox, Scatcherd & Whitaker, and E. Newbery, 1785.
62,[2]p., plate, 12mo.

ESTC t177479: BMp, S 347.1785.
Drama. London syndicate.

498. Stevens, George Alexander, 1710–1784.
The dramatic history of Master Edward, Miss Ann, and others, the extraordinaries of these times. Collected from Zaphaniel's original papers. By George Alexander Stevens, author of the celebrated Lecture upon heads. To which are prefixed, memoirs of the life of the author. A new edition, illustrated with copper-plates. London, printed for J. Murray, 1785.
xi,[1],2,192p., plates, 12mo. Price: 4*s.* in boards.
Apparently a reissue of the Waller 1743 [1763] edition (*ESTC* t116476), with a cancel title page and the addition of 'An account of the life of the author'.
ESTC t110830: L, 10825.b.40.
Fiction. Murray alone.

**499. [Taylor, Edward, 1741–1797.]
Julia to St. Preux. a poem. By the author of Werter to Charlotte. London, Murray, 1785.
4to. Price: 1*s.*
No copy located. *English Review* 6 (Sept. 1785), 229–30 (Forster, 2330).
Poetry. Murray alone.

500. [Trusler, John, 1735–1820.]
Modern times, or, the adventures of Gabriel Outcast. Supposed to be written by himself. In imitation of Gil Blas. . . . The second edition, with additions. London, printed for the author; and sold by J. Murray, 1785.
Vol. 1: iv,212p.; vol. 2: iv,191p.; vol. 3: iv,207p. 12mo. With half-titles in vols 2–3. Price: 9*s.* sewed.
The first edition was 'printed for the author and sold by J. Walter' in 1785.
ESTC t100116: L, G.17721.
Fiction. Agency–Murray alone.

**501. Wells, the Rev. Charles, Rector of Leigh.
A brief account of the seminary of learning, established at Margate in Kent, for the reception of twelve young gentlemen. By a Clergyman.
12mo. Price: 6*d.*
No copy located. *English Review* 5 (May 1785), 391. 'Murray'. A newspaper clipping in the Archive hand-dated 1785 reads: 'Margate. Sea Bathing and Private Tuition. A beneficed Clergyman, who has a few Pupils, of a very genteel

and respectable description, under his care, purposes passing the Summer with them at Margate, in order to give them the benefit and advantages of sea air, and sea bathing, without suffering their studies to meet with any interruption. The advertiser has a large and commodious house in the most airy part of Church Field, and as it is calculated to accommodate more young gentlemen than are at present in his family. . . . For further particulars, application may be made to Mr. Murray, Bookseller, Fleet-street, or to Mr. Hall, Bookseller, at Margate.'
Education. Murray alone.

1786

502. The adventures of George Maitland, Esq. In three volumes. . . . London, printed for J. Murray, 1786.
Vol. 1: [iii],283p.; vol. 2: [iii],284p.; vol. 3: [iii],271,[1]p., 12mo. Price: 9*s.*
750 copies printed. Paper and printing (by Simmons & Kirby at Canterbury) cost £100 (BB, p. 38; To Simmons & Kirby, 22 Apr. 1785). Originally published in 1755 as the *Life and adventures of James Ramble*, by Edward Kimber. Entered in the Stationers' Company Register, 1 Oct. 1785, 'John Murray. The Whole'. Stock: 133 (H).
ESTC t074441: L,N.2202.
Fiction. Murray alone.

503. Adye, Stephen Payne, d. 1794.
A treatise on courts martial. To which is added, an essay on military punishments and rewards. The third edition, with additions and amendments, by Stephen Payne Adye, . . . London, printed for J. Murray, 1786.
viii,284,[4]p., 8vo. With two final advertisement leaves. Price: 3*s.*6*d.* in boards.
A reissue of Murray's 1784 edition with a cancel title page. Stock: 184 (H).
ESTC n047734: Osj.
Military. Murray alone.

504. Aitken, John, d. 1790.
Principles of anatomy and physiology by John Aitken, M.D. . . . London, printed for J. Murray, 1786.
Vol. 1: [ii],viii,187p.; vol. 2: [vi],162p., plates, 8vo. Price: 10*s.* in boards.
Vol. 1 includes 98 unnumbered pages with 31

plates; vol. 2 includes 62 unnumbered pages with 26 plates.
ESTC no11781: DNLM, WZ260.A298pa 1786.
Medicine. Murray alone.

505. Aitken, John, d. 1790.
Principles of midwifery, or puerperal medicine. By John Aitken, . . . The third edition, enlarged and illustrated with engravings. For the use of students. London, printed for J. Murray, [1786]. xiv,210,[72],8p., plates, ill. port., 8vo.
ESTC t121343: L, 1609/680.
Medicine. Murray alone.

506. Aitken, John, d. 1790.
A system of obstetrical tables, with explanations; representing the foundations of the theory and practice of midwifery. By John Aitken, . . . For the use of students. London, printed for J. Murray, 1786.
[76],8p., plates, ill., 8vo.
ESTC no23197: MBCo, 25.A.308.
Medicine. Murray alone.

507. Anderson, John, c. 1730–1804.
An essay on evacuations. London, printed for the author, and sold by J. Murray, Fleet-Street, and by J. Donaldson, Edinburgh, 1786.
viii,86p., 8vo.
ESTC t033310: L, T.380(7).
Medicine. Agency–London.

508. Bacon, Francis, Viscount St. Albans, 1561–1626.
The history of Henry VII. of England, written in the year 1616. By Francis Bacon, . . . Now first new written 1786. London, printed for the editor, at the Logographic Press, by the Literary Society: and sold by J. Murray, 1786.
iv,288,iii,[1]p., 8vo. Price: 5s. in boards.
ESTC t089370: L, 989.b.17.
History. Agency–London.

509. Beatson, Robert, 1742–1818.
A political index to the histories of Great Britain and Ireland; or, a complete register of the hereditary honours, public offices, and persons in office, from the earliest periods to the present time. By Robert Beatson, Esq;. Edinburgh, printed for the author. Sold by William Gordon and William Creech, Edinburgh; and by G.

Robinson, J. Murray and A. Strahan, London, 1786.
xi,[1],211,[1];372;117,[1]p., 8vo. Price: 2s.6d.
ESTC t143101: L, 808.k.3.
History. Agency–Edinburgh.

***510. Blackstone, Sir William, 1723–1780.
Commentaries on the laws of England. In four books. By Sir William Blackstone, . . . The tenth edition. London, printed for J. Murray, J. Jarvis, & J. Fielding, 1786.
Vol. 1: vi,[1],485p.; vol. 2: [missing]; vol. 3: [iv],455,xxviip.; vol. 4: [iv],443,viii,[50]p., plates, port., 12mo.
On 3 Nov. Murray told Thomas Cadell, who owned the copyright: 'I have never seen the book, and have no concern whatever in the adventure, and my name is printed whole against my consent or knowledge'. Possibly an Irish edition.
ESTC t183793: L, Vu Y 78.3.449–452.
Law. London co-publishing.

511. Boyer, Abel, 1667–1729.
Boyer's Royal dictionary abridged. In two parts, I. French and English II. English and French. . . . The sixteenth edition, carefully corrected and improved, . . . By J.C. Prieur. London, printed for Messrs. Bathurst, Pote, Rivingtons, Owen, Buckland, Longman, Law, Pritchard, Robson, Dilly, Johnson, Elmsley, Ginger, Robinson, Cadell, Nicol, Baldwin, Short, Domville, Sewel, Goldsmith, Bew, Murray, Hayes, Lowndes, Scatcherd and Whitaker, Egerton, and Bent, 1786.
[914]p., table, 8vo.
Reference: Alston xii. 688.
ESTC t132563: L, 1560/1938.
Language. London syndicate.

512. Brookes, Richard, fl. 1721–1763.
The general gazetteer: or, compendious geographical dictionary. Containing a description of all the empires, . . . chief towns, . . . harbours, . . . and promontories in the known world; together with the governemnt, policy, . . . of the inhabitants; . . . Embellished with nine maps. By R. Brookes, M. D. The sixth edition, improved, with additions and corrections. London, printed for J. F. C. Rivington, T. Carnan, and J. Johnson; G. G. J. & J. Robinson, R. Baldwin, J. Bent, B.

Law, T. Lowndes, J.Murray, C. Dilly, T. Vernor, S. Hayes, 1786.

xvi,[696]p., plates, maps, 8vo. With five pages of advertisements. Price: 7s.

3000 copies printed. Murray bought a 103/3000 share on 8 Apr. 1777 at the Queen's Arms and paid 5 gns. to Edward Johnston. On 26 Dec. he paid out £18.16s.9d. for paper and printing. The returns on his share (137 copies at 4s.4d. each, wholesale) were £29.13s.8d. (BB, p. 1; See Brookes 1778, item 174 and 1782, item 299). Entered in the Stationers' Company Register, 22 Dec. 1786, T. Carnan, Whole'.

ESTC t143954: L, 793.g.30.

Travel–topography. London syndicate.

513. Chambers, Ephraim, c. 1680–1740.

Cyclopaedia: or, an universal dictionary of arts and sciences. . . . By E. Chambers, F.R.S. With the supplement, and modern improvements, incorporated in one alphabet. By Abraham Rees, D.D. In four volumes. . . . London, printed for J. F. and C. Rivington, A. Hamilton, T. Payne and Son, W. Owen, B. White, T. Longman, B. Law, C. Rivington, C. Dilly, H. Baldwin, H. S. Woodfall, J. Robson, J. Knox, W. Domville, G. G. J. and J. Robinson, T. Cadell, A. Hamilton, Jun., R. Baldwin, W. Otridge, N. Conant, J. Murray, A. Strahan, W. Fox, S. Hayes, E. Johnson, J. Bent, D. Ogilvy, S. and T. Wilkie, and W. Collins, 1786–88.

5 vols., unpaginated, plates, Fo.

Originally issued in 89 parts weekly at 6d. per number. Vols. 1, 2, 3 and 5 are dated 1788, vol. 4 1786. Vol. 5 contains 'addenda, index, arrangement of the plates, and the plates' (see Chambers 1778, item 176, for publishing information, BB, p. 8).

ESTC t136237: L, 12214.bb.1.

Miscellaneous. London syndicate.

514. Clubbe, John, b. 1742.

An essay on the virulent gonorrhoea; in which the different opinions respecting the treatment of the disease are carefully examined; and a method of cure deduced from them, . . . By J.Clubbe, . . . London, printed for J. Murray, 1786.

[4],viii,77,[1]p., 8vo.

ESTC t033416: L,T.97(7).

Medicine. Murray alone.

515. Curry, John, d. 1780.

An historical and critical review of the civil wars in Ireland, from the reign of Queen Elizabeth, to the Settlement under King William. With the state of the Irish Catholics, . . . By John Curry, M.D. In two volumes. . . . London, printed for G. G. J. and J. Robinson, and J. Murray, 1786. Vol. 1: xxiii,400p.; vol. 2: vi,400.[12]p., 8vo. Price: 13s.

A Dublin issue printed for Luke White was also published in 1786 (ESTC: t110536). See Curry 1775, item 101. Stock: 12 (H).

ESTC t131404: L, 286.b.28–29.

History. London co-publishing.

*516. Duncan, Andrew, 1744–1828.

A short account of the late Dr John Parsons, . . . Dr Richard Huck Saunders, . . . Dr Charles Colignon, . . . and Sir Alexander Dick . . . From the Edinburgh medical commentaries, Vol. X. Page 322. et seq. Edinburgh, 1786.

24p, 8vo. Price: 1s.

English Review 8 (Oct. 1786), 312. 'Murray'.

ESTC n022437: DNLM, WZ260.S559 1786.

Biography. Murray alone.

*517. Duncan, Andrew, 1744–1828.

Heads of lectures on the materia medica. By Andrew Duncan, M.D. . . . . Edinburgh, 1786.

80p, 8vo. Pp.78–80 are advertisements. Price: 1s.6d.

English Review 9 (Feb. 1787), 146: 'Murray, London; Elliot, Edinburgh'.

ESTC n003577: DNLM, 18th c. coll.

Medicine. Edinburgh co-publishing.

518. Duncan, Andrew, 1744–1828, editor.

Medical Commentaries, for the year 1785; exhibiting a concise view of the latest and most important discoveries in medicine and medical philosophy. Collected and published by Andrew Duncan, M.D.F.R. & A.S.Ed . . . Volume Tenth. London, printed for J. Murray, and C. Elliot, Edinburgh, 1786.

xvi,469p. 8vo. Price of the complete 10–vol. set: £3 in boards, £3.10s. bound.

1250 copies printed. Stock: 331 (W).

Primary location: Roy. Col. of Phys. Edin.

Medicine. Edinburgh co-publishing.

519. The Edinburgh magazine, or literary

miscellany, . . . Edinburgh, Printed for J. Sibbald: and sold by J. Murray, London, 1786.
Vol. 3: [1],494pp. 8vo. plates; vol. 4: [1],492pp. 8vo. plates. First published in 1785 by James Sibbald. Published in monthly parts; title page, contents, and index issued every six months. Printed by Macfarquhar and Elliot, Edinburgh.
Primary location: E, NH 295.
Miscellaneous. Agency–Edinburgh.

520. The English review; or, an abstract of English and foreign literature. . . . London, printed for J. Murray, 1786.
Vol. 7: [1],[vii],480,[6]p., 8vo; vol. 8: [1],[vii], 440,[6]p., 8vo.
Published in monthly parts (priced at 1s.); title page, contents, and index issued every six months.
Primary location: NN, *DA.
Miscellaneous. Murray–with agency.

521. Fielding, Henry, 1707–1754.
The virgin unmasked: a musical entertainment, in one act. By Henry Fielding, Esq; with alterations. As performed at the Theatres-Royal in Drury-Lane, and Covent-Garden. London, printed for T. Payne and Son, J. Nichols, G. G .J. and J. Robinson, T. Cadell, J. Murray, G. Nicol, S. Bladon, W. Lowndes, W. Nicoll, W. Fox, and D. Ogilvy, 1786.
27,[5]p., 8vo. With two final advertisement leaves. Price: 1s.
First published in 1735 as *An old man taught wisdom*.
ESTC t089913: L, 643.h.20(9).
Drama. London syndicate.

522. Foot, Jesse, 1744–1826.
A critical enquiry into the ancient and modern manner of treating the diseases of the urethra. With an improved method of cure. By Jesse Foot, . . . The fourth edition, with additional cases. London, sold by Becket; Faulder; Murray, and Stockdale, 1786.
[2],vii,[1],76p., 8vo. With a half-title.
ESTC t033068: L, T.147(2).
Medicine. London co-publishing.

523. Garrick, David, 1717–1779.
The taming of the shrew; or Catherine and Petruchio. A comedy. Altered from Shakspeare, by David Garrick, Esq. Marked with the varia-

tions in the manager's book, at the Theatre-Royal in Covent-Garden. London, printed for C. Bathurst, J. F. & C. Rivington, L. Davis, W. Owen & Son, B. White & Son, T. Longman, B. Law, C. Dilly, T. Payne & Son, J. Nichols, T. Cadell, J. Robson, G. G. J. & J. Robinson, T. Bowles, R. Baldwin, H. L. Gardner, J. Bew, W. Cater, J. Murray, W. Stuart, S. Hayes, W. Lowndes, S. Bladon, G. & T. Wilkie, W. Fox, Scatcherd & Whitaker, E. Newbery, J. Barker, T. & J. Egerton, and D. Ogilvy, 1786.
34,[2]p., 12mo. With a final leaf of advertisements.
First published as *Catharine and Petruchio* in 1756.
ESTC t062750: L, 11763.aa.11.
Drama. London syndicate.

524. Goldsmith, Oliver, 1728–1774.
The poetical and dramatic works of Oliver Goldsmith, M. B. A new edition. With an account of the life and writings of the author. In two volumes. London, printed by H. Goldney, for Messieurs Rivington, T. Carnan, E. Newbery, and W. Nicoll; W. Lowndes and J. Murray; and J. Debrett, 1786.
Vol. 1: viii, lxiv,120p.; vol. 2: viii, 271p., plate, port., 8vo. With half-titles. Price: 6s. in boards. 1250 copies printed. Murray paid £9 for a 1/5 share bought at Thomas Evans' sale on 3 July 1784. In June 1786 he paid £24.4s.4d. for paper and printing. The returns of his share (250 copies at 3s.10d. each, wholesale) were £47.18s.4d. (BB, p. 38).
ESTC t146129: L, 81.a.33.
Poetry (and Drama). London syndicate.

525. Gray, Thomas, 1716–1771.
Poems. By Mr. Gray. A new edition. London, printed for J. Murray, 1786.
[1],xxxix,[41]–178p., 7 plates, 8vo. Price: 4s.3d. in boards.
1250 copies printed (250 large paper). Expenses: £93.1s.6d. Sales: £225 (1000 copies at 3s.; 250 large paper copies at 6s. each, wholesale). Profit: £131.1s. (AL, p. 41; Gray, 1776, 1778). In this edition Murray replaced the title page vignette, with a cypher of his initials. The untrimmed large paper copy in the Archive measures 23.6 × 15 cms.
ESTC t132351: L, 11643.b.36.
Poetry. Murray alone.

526. Hancock, Blyth, 1721 or 2–1795.
The astronomy of comets. In two parts. Part I. Containing a physical account of the solar system; . . . Part II. Containing the practical methods of calculation. . . . By Blyth Hancock, . . . Bury St. Edmund's, printed by P. Gedge, for J. Murray, London; and sold by all the booksellers, 1786.
xvi,90p., plate, 8vo. With a list of subscribers. Price: 2s.6d.
ESTC t110886: L, 1651/402.
Science. Murray alone.

527. Hastings, Warren, 1732–1818.
Memoirs relative to the state of India. By Warren Hastings, . . . A new edition, with additions. London, printed for J. Murray, 1786.
viii,218,[2]p., plate, port., 8vo. With an advertisement leaf. Price: 4s.
An unauthorised edition published by George Kearsley appeared before this edition in the same year with the title *Mr. Hastings' review of the state of Bengal*. Murray 'applied to Mr. Hastings, and obtained his consent' to publish this 'authentic' edition (Editor's preface). Murray himself was probably the editor. Appendix II (pp. 197–218) contains the National Affairs article from Murray's *English Review* for June 1786 on the 'Impeachment of Mr. Hastings'. Entered in the Stationers' Company Register, 10 Oct. 1786, 'John Murray, Whole'.
ESTC t039163: L, 583.g.3(1).
Another issue: viii,196,[2]p., plate, port., 8vo. Price: 4s. With an advertisement leaf.
In this issue the final twenty-two pages (Appendix II) are removed, and the catchword 'Appendix' at p. 196 is pasted over with a paper slip. P. 12 line 4 begins: 'perty . . . '; p. 92 line 19 reads: 'his pleasure.'; p. 131 line 2 begins: 'a single . . . '. See Hastings 1787, items 589–90, for new issues of this and the next.
Politics. Murray alone.

528. Another edition.
viii,196,[4]., plate, port., 8vo. With two advertisement leaves. Price: 4s.
This edition is completely reset, errors corrected (for example, p. 3, line 25, 'reservation' for 'reversion'), and there is no catchword at p. 196. P. 12 line 4 begins 'property . . . '; p. 92 line 19 reads: 'pleasure'.; p. 131 line 2 begins 'to a single . . . '. The advertisement is headed 'For

gentlemen going to India. Books printed for J. Murray.'
ESTC t200084: O, Vet.A5e,321.
Politics. Murray alone

529. Hayes, Thomas, fl. 1783–1786.
A serious address on the dangerous consequences of neglecting common coughs and colds; with successful directions how to prevent and cure consumptions. . . . To which are now added, Observations on the hooping cough and asthma. By Thomas Hayes. . . . The third edition. London, printed for J. Murray, and Messrs. Shepperson and Reynolds, 1786.
152p. (pp. 130–131 misnum. 140–141), 8vo. Price: 2s.6d.
First published by Murray in 1783 as *A serious and friendly address to the public, on the dangerous consequences of neglecting common coughs and colds*.
ESTC t018391: L, T.104(3).
Medicine. London co-publishing.

530. The fourth edition.
[2],150p., 8vo. With a half-title.
ESTC t018386: L, T.724(1).
Medicine. London co-publishing.

531. Hunter, Henry, 1741–1802.
Sacred biography: or the history of the patriarchs. Being a course of lectures delivered at the Scots church, London Wall, by Henry Hunter, D.D. The second edition. Volume II. London, printed for the author, by Ritchie & Sammells, and sold by J. Murray; and James Dickson, Edinburgh, 1786.
xv,[1],461,[1]p., 8vo. Price: 6s. in boards.
ESTC n036200: CaOHM, B5305.
Religion. Agency–London.

532. Johnson, Samuel, 1709–1784.
A dictionary of the English language: in which the words are deduced from their originals, explained in their different meanings, . . . Abstracted from the folio edition, by the author, Samuel Johnson, A.M. To which is prefixed, A grammar of the English language. In two volumes. . . . The eighth edition. London, printed for J. F. and C. Rivington, L. Davis, W. Owen, T. Longman, B. Law, J. Dodsley, C. Dilly, G. G. J. and J. Robinson, T. Cadell, J. Robson,

W. Goldsmith, J. Bew, J. Murray, R. Baldwin, S. Hayes, and G. and T. Wilkie, 1786.
2 vols., unpaginated, 8vo. Price: 10s.
5000 copies printed. Murray bought a 1/80 share at the Globe Tavern (John Crowder's sale) on 10 Sept. 1777 for £17 which he paid to George Robinson on 16 Jan. 1778; on 17 March 1778 he bought an additional 1/80 share at the Globe for £16; on 12 Sept. 1780 he bought a 1/160 share for £6.10 from the estate of the late Wm Davis; and on 10 May 1783 he bought a 1/40 share (John Ridley's) for £24 paid to Thomas Evans. On 13 Dec. 1785 he paid Thomas Longman £48.15s.8d. for paper and printing. The returns on his share (282 books at 5s. each, wholesale) were £70.2s. (See Johnson 1778, item 191 and 1783, item 360; BB, p. 10).
ESTC t083956: L, 12983.f.26.
Language. London syndicate.

*533. Kelso, Hamilton.
A treatise on elementary air. By Hamilton Kelso, M.D. Strabane, printed by J. Alexander, 1786.
16p., 8vo. Price: 1s.
Monthly Review 77 (Aug. 1787) 163–4: '12mo. Murray'. *Critical Review* 64 (Sept. 1787), 238: 'No Publisher—or Price'
ESTC t193109: D, Strabane 1786(1).
Science. Murray alone.

534. The London kalendar, or court and city register for England, Scotland, Ireland, and America, for the year 1786; . . . London, printed for John Stockdale; T. Carnan; J. Sewell, D. Steel; R. Faulder; J. Murray; and Scatcherd and Whitaker, [1786].
[4],296p., 12mo. Price: 2s.
ESTC t139276: L, P.P.2506.K.
Miscellaneous. London syndicate.

535. M'Farlan, John.
Tracts on subjects of national importance. I. On the advantages of manufactures, commerce, and great town, to the population or prosperity of a country. II. Difficulties stated to a proposed assessment of the land tax: . . . By the Rev. John M'Farlan, . . . London, printed for J. Murray; and James Dickson, Edinburgh, 1786.
[8],88p., 8vo. With a half-title. Price: 1s.6d.
ESTC t117751: L, 1600/821.

Economics. Edinburgh co-publishing.

536. [Moir, John.]
Female tuition; or, an address to mothers, on the education of daughters. The second edition. London, printed for J. Murray, 1786.
vi,[2],268,[4]p., 8vo. With a half-title and two final advertisement leaves. Price: 3s.
ESTC t078345: L, 08416.f.23.
Education. Murray alone.

537. Nolan, William.
An essay on humanity: or a view of abuses in hospitals. With a plan for correcting them. By William Nolan. London, printed for the author, and sold by J. Murray, 1786.
49,[1]p., 8vo. Price: 1s.
ESTC n001634: DNLM, 18th c. coll.
Medicine. Agency–Murray alone.

538. O'Gallagher, Felix.
A essay on the investigation of the first principles of nature: together with the application thereof to solve the phenomena of the physical system. Part II. . . . By Felix O'Gallagher. London, printed for the author, and sold by J. Murray, 1786.
399,[1]p., 8vo. Price: 5s.
Part I published in 1784.
ESTC n031266: NCorniM, *364.
Medicine. Agency–Murray alone.

539. Ogilvie, James, 1760–1820.
Sermons on various subjects. By James Ogilvie, . . . London, printed for J. Murray, 1786.
[36],39,[4],42–65,[4],68–113,[4],116–308p., 8vo. With a list of subscribers. Price: 6s. in boards. Eleven sermons, each with it own divisional title page, though those to sermons, 2, 3, 5 are not included in the register and pagination. Stock: 65 (H).
ESTC t116145: L, 1024.c.23.
Religion. Murray alone.

540. Perry, Sampson, 1747–1823.
A dissertation on the lues venerea, gonorrhoa, and tabes dorsalis, or gleet; in which, the theory of these diseases though new, is divested of all subtilty, and the practice laid down . . . pointing out in what esteem mercury ought to be held in the cure of these complaints. By S. Perry, Surgeon. London, printed by W. Justins, for J.

Murray; J. Bew; J. Richardson; and J. Southern, 1786.
107,[1]p., 8vo. With a half-title. Price: 2s.
ESTC n028561: NBuU-H, WZ260.P465d 1786.
Medicine. London co-publishing.

541. The political magazine and parliamentary, naval, military, and literary journal, for the year, 1786. London, printed for J. Murray, and sold by every bookseller and news carrier in Great Britain.
Vol. 10: Jan.–June. [ii],484,[13]p., 8vo; vol. 11: July–Dec. [i],480,[12]p., 8vo. With index, plates, and maps in both vols.
Issued in monthly parts at 1s. each; 2000 copies printed (To John Trusler, 5 Oct. 1786).
Primary location: CtY, Franklin Coll.
Miscellaneous. Murray alone.

*542. Raspe, Rudolf Erich, 1737–1794.
Account of the present state and arrangement of Mr. James Tassie's collection of pastes and impressions from ancient and modern gems; with a few remarks on the origin of engraving on hard stones, . . . By R. E. Raspe. London, 1786.
35,[1]p., 8vo.
Murray had published Tassie's *Catalogue* in 1775 and the *Catalogue raisonné* in 1791.
ESTC n016127: MH-H, *EC75.R1847.786a.
Arts. Agency–London.

543. Richardson, William, 1743–1814.
Essays on Shakespeare's dramatic characters of Richard the Third, King Lear, and Timon of Athens. To which are added, an essay on the faults of Shakespeare; and additional observations on the character of Hamlet. The second edition. By Mr. Richardson, . . . London, printed for J. Murray, 1786.
viii,[1],4–170p., 8vo. Price: 5s.
ESTC t136700: L, 840.b.28.
Literary criticism. Murray alone.

544. Richardson, William, 1743–1814.
Essays on Shakespeare's dramatic characters of Macbeth, Hamlet, Jaques, and Imogen. To which are prefixed, an introduction. The fourth edition. By Mr. Richardson, . . . London, printed for J. Murray, 1786.
[4],203,[1]p., 8vo. Price: 5s.
ESTC n008399: NjP, 3925.88.4.

Literary criticism. Murray alone.

545. Scheele, Karl Wilhelm, 1742–1786.
The chemical essays of Charles-William Scheele. Translated from the transactions of the Academy of Sciences at Stockholm. With additions. London, printed for J. Murray; W. Gordon and C. Elliot, Edinburgh, 1786.
xiii,[1],ii,406p., 8vo. Price: 6s. in boards.
Preface signed: Thomas Beddoes [the transla-tor]. 750 copies printed by Neill & Co. (To Neill & Co., 6 Feb. 1786). Entered in the Stationers' Company Register, 25 Mar. 1786, 'John Murray, the Whole'. Stock: 58 (W).
ESTC n014683: MBCo, 1.Mk.302.
Science. Edinburgh co-publishing.

546. Shakespeare, William, 1564–1616.
The plays of William Shakspeare. Accurately printed from the text of Mr. Malone's edition; with select explanatory notes. In seven volumes. . . . London, printed for J. Rivington and Sons, L. Davis, B. White and Son, T. Longman, B. Law, H. S. Woodfall, C. Dilly, J. Robson, J. Johnson, T. Vernor, G. G. J. and J. Robinson, T. Cadell, J. Murray, R. Baldwin, H. L. Gardner, J. Sewell, J. Nichols, J. Bew, T. Payne Jun., S. Hayes, R. Faulder, W. Lowndes, G. and T. Wilkie, Scratchard and Whitaker, T. and J. Egerton, C. Stalker, J. Barker, J. Edwards, Ogilvie and Speare, J. Cuthell, J. Lackington, and E. Newbery, 1786–90.
Vol. 1: [4],xxiv,74,[4],72,95,[1],100,59,[1]p.; vol. 2: [4],85,[1],98,78,84, 96,90p.; vol. 3: [4],99,[1], 90,105,[1],104,97,[1]p.; vol. 4: [4],91,[5],104,120, [2],6,118,96p.; vol. 5: [4],112,100,124,121,[1], 118p.; vol. 6 [43],192,118,80p.; vol. 7: [4],126, 138,109,[1],274p., 12mo.
Vol. 1, with cancel title page and half-title, is dated 1790 and vols 2–7 dated 1786, and whose imprints read: 'printed for C. Bathurst, T. Payne and Son, W. and A. Strahan, J. F. and C. Rivington, L. Davis, W. Owen, B. White, T. Longman, B. Law, C. Dilly, J. Robson, T. Cadell, G. G. J. and J. Robinson, H. L. Gard-ner, J. Nicholls, R. Baldwin, J. Bew, J. Murray, W. Lowndes, and the rest of the proprietors. Each play with separate pagination and divi-sional half-title; the register in each volume is continuous. See Shakespeare 1790, item 791, for publication details of this 'problem' edition.

ESTC t135348: L, 642.c.9–15.
Drama. London syndicate.

547. Shakespeare, William, 1564–1616.
As you like it. A comedy. Written by William
Shakspeare. Marked with the variations in the
manager's book, at the Theatre-Royal in
Covent-Garden. London, printed for C. Bath-
urst, J. F. & C. Rivington, L. Davis, W. Owen &
Son, B. White & Son, T. Longman, B. Law, C.
Dilly, T. Payne & Son, J. Nichols, T. Cadell, J.
Robson, G. G. J. and J. Robinson, A. Strahan, T.
Bowles, R. Baldwin, H. L. Gardner, J. Bew. W.
Cater, J. Murray, W. Stuart, S. Hayes, W.
Lowndes, S. Bladon, G & T. Wilkie, W. Fox,
Scatchard & Whitaker, E. Newbery, and J.
Barker, 1786.
75,[1]p., plate, 12mo.
ESTC t022531: L, 11763.aaa.21.
Drama. London syndicate.

548. Shakespeare, William, 1564–1616.
Coriolanus. A tragedy. Written by William
Shakspeare. Marked with the variations in the
manager's book, at the Theatre-Royal in Drury-
Lane. London, printed for C. Bathurst, J. F. &
C. Rivington, L. Davis, W. Owen & Son, B.
White & Son, T. Longman, B. Law, C. Dilly,
T. Payne & Son, J. Nicholls, T. Cadell, J.
Robson, G. G. J. and J. Robinson, A. Strahan,
T. Bowles, R. Baldwin, H. L. Gardner, J. Bew.
W. Cater, J. Murray, W. Stuart, S. Hayes, W.
Lowndes, S. Bladon, G. & T. Wilkie, W. Fox,
Scatcherd & Whitaker, E. Newbery, and J.
Barker, T. & J. Egerton, D. Ogilvy, and R.
Faulder, 1786.
102,[2]p., 12mo.
ESTC t034181: L, 11767.a.111(2).
Drama. London syndicate.

549. Shakespeare, William, 1564–1616.
Julius Caesar. A tragedy. Written by William
Shakspeare. Marked with the variations in the
manager's book, at the Theatre-Royal in Drury-
Lane. London, printed for C. Bathurst, J. F. &
C. Rivington, L. Davis, W. Owen & Son, B.
White & Son, T. Longman, B. Law, C. Dilly,
T. Payne & Son, J. Nicholls, T. Cadell, J.
Robson, G. G. J. and J. Robinson, A. Strahan,
T. Bowles, R. Baldwin, H. L. Gardner, J. Bew.
W. Cater, J. Murray, W. Stuart, S. Hayes, W.
Lowndes, S. Bladon, G. & T. Wilkie, W. Fox,

Scatcherd & Whitaker, E. Newbery, and J.
Barker, T. & J. Egerton, D. Ogilvy, and R.
Faulder, 1786.
72p., plate, 12mo.
ESTC n031699: NjP, 3925.999 v.2.
Drama. London syndicate.

550. Shakespeare, William, 1564–1616.
King Henry the Eighth, a tragedy: written by
William Shakspeare. Marked with the variations
in the manager's book at the Theatre-Royal in
Covent-Garden. London, printed for C. Bath-
urst, J. F. & C. Rivington, L. Davis, W. Owen &
Son, B. White & Son, T. Longman, B. Law, C.
Dilly, T. Payne & Son, J. Nicholls, T. Cadell, J.
Robson, G. G. J. and J. Robinson, A. Strahan, T.
Bowles, R. Baldwin, H. L. Gardner, J. Bew. W.
Cater, J. Murray, W. Stuart, S. Hayes, W.
Lowndes, S. Bladon, G. & T. Wilkie, W. Fox,
Scatcherd & Whitaker, J. Barker, and E.
Newbery, 1786.
86,[2]p., 12mo. With a final advertisement leaf.
ESTC n004668: PU, Furness C94.35 1786C.
Drama. London syndicate.

551. Shakespeare, William, 1564–1616.
Twelfth-night: or, what you will. Written by
William Shakspeare. Marked with the variations
in the manager's book, at the Theatre-Royal in
Drury-Lane. London, printed for C. Bathurst, J.
F. & C. Rivington, L. Davis, W. Owen & Son, B.
White & Son, T. Longman, B. Law, C. Dilly, T.
Payne & Son, J. Nicholls, T. Cadell, J. Robson,
G. G. J. and J. Robinson, T. Bowles, R. Baldwin,
H. L. Gardner, J. Bew, J. Murray, W. Stuart, S.
Hayes, W. Lowndes, S. Bladon, G. & T. Wilkie,
W. Fox, Scatcherd & Whitaker, E. Newbery, J.
Barker, T. & J. Egerton, D. Ogilvy, and R.
Faulder, 1786.
72p., plate, 12mo.
ESTC t174784: C, S724.d.78.1/1.
Drama. London syndicate.

552. Skeete, Thomas, 1757–1789.
Experiments and observations on quilled and
red Peruvian bark: among which are included,
some remarkable effects arising from the action
of common bark and magnesia upon each
other. . . . By Thomas Skeete, M.D. London,
printed for J. Murray; and sold by W. Creech
and C. Elliot, Edinburgh; and Luke White and
W. Gilbert, Dublin, 1786.

xxiv,355,[21]p., 8vo. With a half-title and adver-
tisements. Price: 5s. in boards.
Stock: 28 (H); 346 (W).
ESTC to58312: L, 7510.ee.12.
Medicine. Murray–with agency.

553. Smith, Joseph, d. *c.* 1798.
Observations on the use and abuse of the
Cheltenham waters, in which are included occa-
sional remarks on different saline compositions.
By J. Smith, . . . Cheltenham, printed and sold
by S. Harward; sold also at his shops in
Gloucester and Tewkesbury; by Murray, Elmsly,
and Cadell, London; and by the booksellers in
Oxford and Bath, 1786.
[2],67,[1]p., 8vo. Price: 1s.6d.
This is the earliest recorded Cheltenham
imprint (excluding periodicals).
ESTC to98929: L, 234.k.20.
Medicine. Agency–provincial.

554. Stevens, George Alexander, 1710–1784.
The dramatic history of Master Edward. Miss
Ann, and the others. The extraordinaries of
these times. Collected from Zaphaniel's original
papers. By George Alexander Stevens. . . . To
which are prefixed, memoirs of the life of the
author. A new edition illustrated with copper
plates. London, printed for J. Murray, 1786.
xi,[1],2,192. plates, 12mo. Price: 4s. in boards.
A reissue of Stevens 1785, item 498. Stock: 380
(W).
ESTC no08969: CaOTU, B-10 5720.
Fiction. Murray alone.

555. Trusler, John, 1735–1820.
The country lawyer: containing, not only large
abstracts of the several acts of Parliament, . . .
but all the doctrine and adjudged cases, . . . By
Dr. John Trusler. . . . London, sold by J.
Murray, 1786.
xiii,[1],204,[4]p., 12mo. With two final errata
leaves. Price: 3s.
ESTC t151087: GOT, 80J.stat.XIV,6442
Law. Agency–Murray alone.

556. [Trusler, John, 1735–1820.]
Modern times, or, the adventures of Gabriel
Outcast. Supposed to be written by himself.
In imitation of Gil Blas. . . . The third edition,
with alterations. London, printed for the
author; and sold by J. Murray, 1786.

Vol.1: iv,224p.; vol. 2: [ii],222p.; vol. 3:
[ii],214p.,12mo. Price: 9s. sewed.
Some copies (C, CtY) contain twelve plates, but
these plates were apparently intended for the
1789 fourth edition: 'printed for the author, and
sold at the Literary-Press'.
ESTC t153576: GOT, 80Fab.IX,1935.
Another issue: third edition with additions.
ESTC no59914: In U-Li, PR3736.T75Mb.
Fiction. Agency–Murray alone.

557. Turnbull, William, *c.* 1729–1796.
An inquiry into the origin and antiquity of the
lues venerea; with observations on its introduc-
tion and progress in the islands of the South
Seas. To which is added, a short view of the
various remedies . . . By William Turnbull, . . .
London, printed for J. Murray, 1786.
xii,115,[1]p., 8vo. Price: 2s.
ESTC no02223: CaOTU, J. A. Hannah Coll.
Medicine. Murray alone.

558. Urquhart, George, scientist.
Institutes of hydrostatics: illustrated with plates.
To which is added, a philosophical essay on air-
balloons; and an appendix, . . . London, printed
for the author by H. D. Steel; and sold by the
following booksellers: Mr. Murray: Mr. Richardson; Mess. Steel and Son, 1786.
vii,[1],254,[2]p.,fold. plates, 8vo. With a half-title
and a final errata leaf.
Entered in the Stationers' Company Register,
24 Apr. 1786, 'Geo. Urquhart. Whole'.
ESTC to37282: L, 537.d.24(3).
Science. Agency–London.

559. Wright, James, d. 1812, minister of the
gospel at Maybole.
A recommendation of brotherly love, upon the
principles of Christianity. To which is subjoined, An inquiry into the true design of the
institution of Masonry. In four books. By James
Wright, . . . Edinburgh, printed for J. Dickson,
and C. Elliot; and J. Murray, London, 1786.
vi,[1],10–331,[1]p., 8vo. Price: 4s. in boards.
Murray wrote to the Edinburgh booksellers
Wilson and Mundell, 'I did what I could to
promote the sale of the work, and wish I had
been able to make a more favourable return' (27
Apr. 1787).
ESTC t116113: L, 854.c.21.
Religion. Edinburgh co-publishing.

1787

560. Abercrombie, John, 1726–1806.
Every man his own gardener. Being a new, and much more complete gardener's kalendar, and general director, than any one hitherto published. ... By Thomas Mawe, ... John Abercrombie, ... and other gardeners. The eleventh edition, corrected, and greatly enlarged, ... London, printed for J. F. and C. Rivington, T. Longman, B. Law, J. Johnson, G. G. J. and J. Robinson, T. Cadell, W. Goldsmith, R. Baldwin, J. Murray, E. Newbery, and W. Lowndes, 1787.
[4],616,[20]p., plate, 12mo. Price: 5s.
4000 copies printed. Murray paid Thomas Cadell 12 gns. for a 1/32 share bought at Thomas Evans' sale on 3 July 1784. In Aug. Murray paid £11.9s.2d. for paper and printing. The returns on his share (125 copies at 2s.11d. each, wholesale) were £18.4s.7d. (Abercrombie 1784, item 392; BB, p. 37).
ESTC n009524: CaOLU, Main SpC SB466.G7M46.
Agriculture. London syndicate.

561. An account of the loss of His Majesty's ship Deal Castle. Commanded by Capt. James Hawkins, off the island of Porto Pico, during the hurricane in the West-Indies, in the Year 1780. London, printed for J. Murray, 1787.
[2],ii,48,2p., 8vo. With a final leaf of errata. Price: 1s.
Expenses totalled 11 gns: 5 gns for printing 3.5 sheets at 30s. and paper, 7 reams at 18s. (To Robert Young, 16 Dec. 1786). Young may be the author.
ESTC t102124: L, 103.f.61.
Military. Murray alone.

562. An account of the Scots Society in Norwich, from its rise in 1775, until it received the additional name of the Society of Universal Good-Will, in 1784. &c. The second edition. To which are added, the Articles, president's addresses, &c. &c. Norwich, printed and sold by W. Chase and Co. Sold also by J. Murray, London, 1787.
[4],46,[3],48–65,[1],6,65–97,[1]p., 8vo.
A reissue of the 1784 second edition with new preliminaries, and with pp. [47]-64 ('Articles and regulation for the Scots Society in Norwich') replaced by 'Articles and regulations for the

Society of Universal Goodwill', with separate title page and register, and numbered: [3], 48–65, [1], 6p. A variant has the interpolated section numbered: 21, 6p.
ESTC t018708: L, T.91(5).
Religion. Agency–provincial.

563. Aitken, John, d. 1790.
A system of anatomical tables, with explanations. By John Aitken, ... London, printed for J. Murray, 1786.
Pp.[144], plates, 8vo.
ESTC n024699: MnU-B, B611.fAi93.
Medicine. Murray alone.

564. Anderson, John, c. 1730–1804.
Medical remarks on natural, spontaneous and artificial evacuation. By John Anderson, M.D. London, printed for the author, and sold by J. Murray, and by J. Donaldson, Edinburgh, 1787.
vi,[2],122p., 8vo. Price: 2s.6d.
An enlarged edition of the *Essay on evacuations*, 1786.
ESTC t039099: L, T.157(1).
Medicine. Agency–London.

565. [Bennett, John, Curate of St. Mary's, Manchester.]
Strictures on female education; chiefly as it relates to the culture of the heart, in four essays. By a clergyman of the Church of England. London, printed for the author, and sold by T. Cadell; J. J. G. and J. Robinsons; Rivington; J. Murray; and Dodsley, [1787].
xiv,152p., 8vo. With a half-title. Price: 3s.
ESTC t129430: L, 1508/119.
Education. Agency–London.

566. Berquin, Arnaud, 1747–1791.
L'ami des enfans, par M. Berquin. Embelli d'un frontispice. ... A Londres, chez J. Stockdale; J. Rivington & Fils; B. Law; J. Johnson; C. Dilly; J. Murray; J. Sewell: & W. Creech, Edinburgh, 1787.
Vol. 1: iv,207p.; vol. 2: [2],206p.; vol. 3: [2],235,[1]p.; vol. 4: [4],212p., plates, 12mo. With advertisements in vols 3–4. Price: 8s.
1000 copies printed. On 8 May 1787 Murray paid John Stockdale £26.5s. for a 1/8 share of the copyright. He paid £20.8d. for expenses. The returns on his share (125 copies at 4s. each, wholesale) were £25 (BB, p. 45). Origin-

ally published in parts in 1783. See Stationers' Company Register, 20 May 1783, 6 Sept. 1783, 8 March 1783. Also entered in the Register, 8 March 1784, vols 1–6, 'The author, the whole'. *ESTC* n030038: MA, Uncat. (Berquin). Education. London co-publishing.

567. Berquin, Arnaud, 1747–1791.
Select stories for the instruction and entertainment of children, from the French of M. Berquin. . . . London, printed for J. Stockdale; J. Rivington and Sons; B. Law; J. Johnson; C. Dilly; J. Murray; J. Sewell; and W. Creech, Edinburgh, 1787.
xii,300p., plates, 12mo. Price: 3s.
Translated selections of *L'ami des enfans* by J. Cooper. 3000 copies printed. See above. Murray paid £42.3s.9d. for expenses. The returns on his share (375 copies) were £75 (BB, p. 45). Stock: 160 (W).
ESTC t090039: L, Ch.780/49.
Education. London co-publishing.

568. Blair, Hugh, 1718–1800.
Essays on rhetoric: abridged chiefly from Dr. Blair's Lectures on that science. The third edition, with additions and improvements. London, printed for J. Murray, 1787.
viii,[4],420p., 12mo. Price: 4s.
1500 copies printed by Simmons at Canterbury (To Simmons, 30 Apr. 1787). Stock: 63 (H); 602, 61 'fine' (W).
ESTC t129565: L, 11806.a.48.
Literary criticism. Murray alone.

569. Boyd, Robert, d. 1793.
The office, powers, and jurisdiction, of His Majesty's justices of the peace, and commissioners of supply. In four books. By Robert Boyd, . . . Edinburgh, printed for the author; and sold by E. Balfour, and J. Murray, London, 1787.
xxvi,1028,xxp., 4to. With a list of subscribers. Price: £1.11s.6d. in boards.
Murray took 75 or 100 copies (To Boyd, 27 Apr. 1787) and sold only six (To Wm Smellie, 4 Oct. 1787). Entered in the Stationers' Company Register, 'Author, Whole. Certificate given March 6. 1794'.
ESTC t113285: L, 516.l.15,16.
Law. Agency–Edinburgh.

570. Brand, Thomas, surgeon.
The case of a boy, who had been mistaken for a girl; with three anatomical views of the parts, before and after the operation and cure; by Thomas Brand, . . . London, printed for the author, and sold by G. Nicol; J. Murray; and J. Bew, 1787.
8p., plates, 4to. Price: 1s.6d.
ESTC t149076: GOT, 4oZool.XIII,3397.
Medicine. Agency–London.

571. Brand, Thomas, surgeon.
Strictures in vindication of some of the doctrines misrepresented by Mr. Foot in his two pamphlets entitled, Observations upon the new opinions & John Hunter, in his late treatise on the venereal disease; including Mr. Pott's plagiarisms and misinformation . . . London, printed for G. Nicol; J. Bew; T. Murray; and J. Debrett, 1787.
[4],56p., 4to.
See Trye 1787, item 621 and Peake 1788, item 676, for other works on this topic.
ESTC t055612: L, 07305.l.7(1).
Medicine. London co-publishing.

**572. A brief account of a seminary established at Hampstead for the reception of a limited number of young gentlemen of a respectable description. By a clergyman. London, Murray, 1787.
12mo. Price: 6d.
No copy located. *English Review* 10 (Dec. 1787), 475.
Education. Murray alone.

**573. Brown, John, 1735–1788.
Joannis Brunonis, M.D. De medicina pralectoris, societatis medicae praesidarii, antiquariorum apud Scotos ab epistolis latinis, Elementa medicina. Editio altera plurimum emendata, et integrum demum opus exhibens. [1787].
2 vols, 8vo. Price: 8s.
No copy located. *Critical Review* 63 (Apr. 1787), 241–8: 'Murray'.
First published in one vol. in 1780: Edinburgh, Charles Elliot (*ESTC* n003657). Stock: 19 (H).
Medicine. ?Agency–Edinburgh (see next).

*574. [Brown, John, 1735–1788.]
Observations on the principles of the old system

of physic, exhibiting a compend of the new doctrine. The whole containing a new account of the state of medicine from the present times, backward, to the restoration of the Grecian learning in the western parts of Europe. By a gentleman conversant in the subject. Edinburgh, from the Apollo Press, by Martin and M'Dowell; for the author. Anno, 1787.
[2],ccxliii,[1],141,[1]p., 8vo. Price: 6s.
Monthly Review 79 (July 1788), 25–7: 'Edinburgh, printed; and sold by Murray, in London.' *Critical Review* 64 (Aug. 1787), 89–93, does not list Murray.
ESTC t055485: L, 541.f.27.
Medicine. Agency–Edinburgh.

575. [Colman, George, 1732–1794.]
A very plain state of the case, or the Royalty Theatre versus the Theatres Royal. . . . London, printed for the author, and sold by J. Murray, 1787.
vii,[1],54,[2]p., 8vo. With a half-title and errata leaf. Price: 1s.6d.
  1000 copies printed (To John Palmer, 28 Jan. 1788). See Jackman 1787, item 600.
ESTC t005907: L, 641.d.31(19).
Drama. Agency–London.

576. Cornwell, Bryan.
The domestic physician, or guardian of health. Pointing out, in the most familiar manner, the symptoms of every disorder incident to mankind; together with their gradual progress and method of cure. . . . To which is added, an appendix, forming a complete dispensatory. A new edition. By B. Cornwell, . . . London, printed for the author; and sold by J. Murray; J. Bew; and L. Davis, 1787.
xvi,650,[22]p., 8vo. With an index. Price: 7s.6d. bound.
Murray was a partner (To Cornwell, 26 Dec. 1786).
ESTC n028633: PPL, In Corn 7930.O.
Medicine. London co-publishing.

577. Dalzel, Andrew, editor.
Analekta Hellénika héssona. Sive collectanea Graeca minora: cum notis philologicis, atque parvo lexico: . . . Edinburgi, excudebat Adamus Neill cum sociis. Veneunt autem ibi apud Joannem Bell et Jacobum Dickson. Londini: apud Joannem Murray, 1787.

xii,100;[96];87,[1]p., 8vo. Price: 5s.
Entered in the Stationers' Company Register, 28 June 1787, 'Author. Whole'.
ESTC t114705: L, 832.e.17.
Language. Edinburgh co-publishing.

578. Drysdale, William.
The Albanaut: a poem. Being a journal of His Majesty's ship Saint Alban's, of sixty-four guns, commanded by Charles Inglis, . . . By the Rev. William Drysdale, . . . London, printed for J. Murray, 1787.
[4],48pp., 8vo.
ESTC n029633: O, G.Pamph.1296(7).
Poetry. Murray alone.

579. The Edinburgh magazine, or literary miscellany, . . . Edinburgh, Printed for J. Sibbald: and sold by J. Murray, London, 1787.
Vol. 5: [1],494p., 8vo. plates; vol. 6: [1],494p., 8vo. plates.
Published in monthly parts; title page, contents, and index issued every six months. Printed by Macfarquhar and Elliot, Edinburgh.
Primary location: E, NH 295.
Miscellaneous. Agency–Edinburgh.

580. The English review; or, an abstract of English and foreign literature. . . . London, printed for J. Murray, 1787.
Vol. 9: [1],[vii],480,[6]p., 8vo; vol. 10: [1],[vii], 482,[6]p., 8vo.
Published in monthly parts (priced at 1s.); title page, contents, and index issued every six months.
Primary location: NN, *DA.
Miscellaneous. Murray–with agency.

581. Fletcher, Charles, M.D.
The cockpit: a poem. By Charles Fletcher, M.D. . . . London, printed by J. Stevenson. For J. Murray; W. Richardson; and T. and J. Egerton, 1787.
28p., ill., 4to. With a half-title. Price: 2s. sewed.
Entered in the Stationers' Company Register, 25 Oct. 1788, 'Author. Whole'.
ESTC t188432: O, 40 W 67(13) Jur.
Poetry. London co-publishing.

*582. Florian, 1755–1794.
The adventures of Numa Pompilius, second King of Rome. Translated from the French of

M. de Florian. In two volumes. . . . London, printed for C. Dilly; J. Stockdale; and W. Creech, Edinburgh, 1787.
Vol. 1: [4],iv,267,[1]p; vol. 2: [2],iii,[1],290,[2]p., 8vo. With Murray's advertisement. Price: 6s. in boards.
Entered in the Stationers' Company Register, 28 June 1787, 'J. Murray, C. Dilly, J. Stockdale, 38; Wm. Creech, by purchase. Whole'. Also recorded in BB, p. 66.
ESTC t113862: L, 634.b.34.
Fiction. Edinburgh co-publishing.

583. Fontana, Felice, 1730–1805.
Treatise on the venom of the viper; on the American poisons; and on the cherry laurel, and some other vegetable poisons. To which are annexed observations on the primitive structure of the animal body. . . . With ten descriptive plates. Translated from the original French of Felix Fontana, . . . By Joseph Skinner, . . . In two volumes. . . . London, printed for J. Murray, 1787.
Vol. 1: [1],xix,409,xivp.; vol. 2: [3],ii,[1],395,xi,x–xiip., 10 plates, 8vo. With half-titles. Price: 12s.
A translation of Traité sur le vénin de la vipère.
Stock: 162 of which 103 are folded; 248 vol. 1 (W).
ESTC t059341: L, 7509.c.2.
Science. Murray alone.

584. Fuller, Anne, d. 1790.
Alan Fitz-Osborne, an historical tale. In two volumes. . . . By Miss Fuller. Second edition. London, printed and sold by T. Wilkins. Sold also by Murray; Bew; Hookham; Jones; and Keating, 1787.
Vol. 1: x,[11]–288p.; vol. 2: [3]-364p., 12mo. Price: 5s.
Entered in the Stationers' Company Register, 3 Jan. 1787, 'Ann Fuller, Whole'.
ESTC t119103: L, 1607/1764.
Fiction. Agency–London.

585. Girdlestone, Thomas.
Essays on the hepatitis and spasmodic affections in India; founded on observations made whilst on service with his Majesty's troops in different parts of that country. By Thomas Girdleston, M.D. London, printed for J. Murray, 1787.
x,7–50,[1],[51]-65p., 8vo. With half-title.

Stock: 125 (W).
ESTC t064134: L, 7306.bb.16(1).
Medicine. Murray alone.

586. Goldsmith, Oliver, 1728–1774.
The history of England, from the earliest times to the death of George II. By Dr. Goldsmith. The fifth edition, corrected. . . . London, printed for L. Davis, J. F. and C. Rivington, T. Payne and Son, B. Law, G. G. J. and J. Robinson, T. Cadell, J. Murray, J. Sewell, W. Richardson, R. Baldwin, S. Hayes, and E. Newbery, 1787.
Vol. 1: viii,384,[20]p.; vol. 2: 420,[28]p.; vol. 3: 454,[22]p.; vol. 4: 412,[23]p., ill.,port., 8vo. Price: £1.4s.
The imprint to vol. 3 includes J. Nichols.
1000 copies printed. In 1778 Murray paid George Robinson £3.13s.6d. for a 1/24 share bought at the Globe Tavern. In April 1787 he paid £14.1s.3d. for paper and printing. The returns on his share (42 copies at 14s. each, wholesale) were £29.8s. (BB, p. 13; Goldsmith 1779, item 223, and 1784, item 418).
ESTC t146092: L, 9505.cc.1.
History. London syndicate.

587. Goldson, William.
An extraordinary case of lacerated vagina, at the full period of gestation. With observations, tending to show that many cases related as ruptures of the uterus, have been lacerations of the vagina. By William Goldson, . . . London, printed for J. Murray; and C. Elliot, Edinburgh, 1787.
77,[1]p., 8vo. Price: 1s.6d.
ESTC t088982: L, 1178.i.8.
Medicine. Edinburgh co-publishing.

588. Hamilton, Robert, 1749–1830.
The duties of a regimental surgeon considered: with observations on his general qualifications; and hints relative to a more respectable practice, and better regulation of that department. . . . By R. Hamilton, M.D. . . . In two volumes. . . . London, printed and sold by J. Johnson; J. Murray; T. Longman; and J. Shave, Ipswich, [1787].
Vol. 1: [4],iv,[xiv],369p.; vol. 2: [4],[x],357p., plate, 8vo.
ESTC n002268: DNLM, WZ260.H231du 1787.
Medicine. London co-publishing.

589. Hastings, Warren, 1732–1818.
Memoirs relative to the state of India. By
Warren Hastings, . . . A new edition, with addi-
tions. London, printed for J. Murray, 1787.
viii,196,[2]p., plate, port., 8vo. With two adver-
tisement leaves. Price: 4s.
A reissue of the 1786 edition (catchword on p.
196 pasted over) with a new title-page.
ESTC t062147: L, 8023.d.34.
Politics. Murray alone.

590. Another edition.
vii,196,[4]p., plate, port., 8vo. With one adver-
tisement leaf. Price: 4s.
A further reissue of the 1786 second edition (no
catchword on p. 196) with a new title-page.
Stock: 226 (H).
ESTC t163703: GOT, 80H.As.II,2108.
Politics. Murray alone.

591. Hawkins, Sir John, 1719–1789.
The life of Samuel Johnson, LL.D. By Sir John
Hawkins, Knt. London, printed for J. Buckland,
J. Rivington and Sons, T. Payne and Sons, L.
Davis, B. White and Son, T. Longman, B. Law,
J. Dodsley, H. Baldwin, J. Robson, J. Johnson,
C. Dilly, T. Vernor, W. Nicoll, G. G. J. and J.
Robinson, T. Cadell, T. Carnan, J. Nichols, J.
Bew, R. Baldwin, N. Conant, P. Elmsley, W.
Goldsmith, J. Knox, R. Faulder, Leigh and
Sotheby, G. Nicol, J. Murray, A. Strahan, W. Low-
ndes, T. Evans, W. Bent, S. Hayes, G. and T.
Wilkie, T. and J. Egerton, W. Fox, P. Macqueen,
D. Ogilvie, B. Collins, and E. Newbery, 1787.
[2],602,[16]p., 8vo. With a half-title. Price: 7s. in
boards.
See Johnson, *Works* 1787, item 602. The
engraved portrait sold only with the *Works*
(To James Fletcher, 9 Mar. 1787). Entered in
the Stationers' Company Register, 6 Mar. 1787
according to the imprint.
ESTC t110655: L, 10861.h.7.
Biography. London syndicate.

592. Second edition, revised and corrected.
[4],605,[15]p., 8vo. With a half-title. Price: 7s.
ESTC t113903: L,633.k.2.
Biography. London syndicate.

593. [Heriot, John, 1760–1833.]
The sorrows of the heart, a novel. In two

volumes. . . . London, printed for J. Murray,
1787.
Vol. 1: vi,209p.; vol. 2: iv,205,[3]p., 12to. With
publisher's advertisement. Price: 5s sewed.
Murray paid Heriot £10 for the copyright (BB,
p. 66). Entered in the Stationers' Company
Register, 30 Jan. 1787, 'J. Murray, Whole'. Stock:
42 (H).
ESTC t073503: L, N.2058.
Fiction. Murray alone.

594. Hunter, Henry, 1741–1802.
The tabernacle of God with men. A sermon,
preached at the opening of a meeting-house, in
Marsh-street, Walthamstow, on Wednesday, the
6th of June, 1787: and at the Scots church,
London-wall, previous to the dispensation of
the sacrament of the Lord's supper, June 24,
1787. By Henry Hunter, . . . London, printed
for the author, by Ritchie and Sammells; and
sold by John Murray, [1787].
vii,,37,[3]p., 8vo. With a half-title and three
pages of advertisements. Price: 1s.
ESTC t016200: L, 4473.g.8(1).
Religion. Agency–Murray alone.

595. Imison, John, d. 1788.
The school of arts; or, an introduction to useful
knowledge, being a compilation of real experiments and improvements, in several pleasing
branches of science, . . . The second edition,
with very considerable additions. By John
Imison. London, printed for the author, and
sold by J. Murray, [1787].
xv,[1],318,[6];[8],176p., 24 plates, 8vo. Price:
11s.6d.
In two parts, the second, 'Curious and useful
miscellaneous articles.', with separate half-title,
pagination, register, and part numbers. Each
section published in 20 parts. Entered in the
Stationers' Company Register, 16 Mar. 1787,
'Author. Whole'. Stock: 300 copies of numbers
1–9, 11–12, 17–18 (H).
ESTC t130626: L, 1609/4182.
Another issue: This second edition not issued
in numbered parts.
xv,[1],319,[5];[8],112,133–176p. (pp. 113–132 of
the second part have been omitted in pagination; but text and register are continuous),
plates, 8vo.
ESTC t055151: L, 1135.l.4.
Science. Agency–Murray alone.

596. Imison, John, d. 1788.
A treatise of the mechanical powers. I. of the lever, II. the wheel and axle, III. the pulley, IV. the screw, V. the wedge, and VI, the inclined plane. To which are added, several useful improvements in mill work, bevel geer, friction, the best shape for teeth in wheels, &c. By John Imison. London, printed for the author, and sold by J. Murray, [1787].
[4],41,[1]p., 2 plates, 8vo.
Stock: 500 '4 first ½ sheets' (H). In 1794 Hester Murray printed a new title page and published the second edition (item 994).
ESTC t055770: L, 8776.cc.15(2).
Science. Agency–Murray alone.

597. Inglefield, Ann.
The arguments of counsel in the Ecclesiastical Court, in the cause of Inglefield. With the speech of Doctor Calvert; on the twenty-second of July, 1786, at giving judgment. . . . London, printed for J. Murray, 1787.
[2],110p., 8vo.
ESTC t125878: L, 1509/412(1).
Law. Murray alone.

598. [Inglefield, John Nicholson, 1748–1828].
An answer to the pamphlet, entitled, 'Mrs. Inglefield's reply'. London, printed for J. Murray, 1787.
[2],13,[1]p., 8vo.
ESTC n029376: NIC, Rare K C92 no.3.
Law. Murray alone.

599. Inglefield, John Nicholson, 1748–1828.
Captain Inglefield's vindication of his conduct: or, a reply to a pamphlet, intitled, 'Mrs. Inglefield's justification'. London, printed for Captain Inglefield, the author: and sold by J. Murray, 1787.
[4],68p., 8vo. With a half-title. Price: 1s.6d.
ESTC t111008: L, 1414.i.29.
Law. Agency–Murray alone.

600. [Jackman, Isaac, fl. 1776–1795.]
Royal and Royalty Theatres. Letter to Phillips Glover, Esq. of Wispington, in Lincolnshire; in a dedication to the burletta of Hero and Leander, . . . at the Royalty Theatre, in Goodman's Fields. London, printed for John Murray, 1787.
vii,[1],84p., 8vo. Price: 2s.
2000 copies printed. On 21 Sept. 1787 Murray

paid Jackman £50 'for the Copy'. Entered in the Stationers' Company Register, 25 Sept. 1787, 'J. Murray, Whole'. See Colman above, item 575.
ESTC t045253: L, 643.e.15(7).
Drama. Murray alone.

601. James, I, King of Scotland, 1394–1437.
The works of James I, King of Scotland. Containing The King's quair, Christis kirk of the grene, and peblis to the play. Perth, printed by R. Morison, junior, for R. Morison and Son; and sold by J. Murray, London, 1787.
[8],iv,112,[5],116–121,[1]p., plates, ports, 12mo.
ESTC t104669: L, 1606/2017(1).
Poetry. Agency–Provincial.

602. Johnson, Samuel, 1709–1784.
The works of Samuel Johnson, LL.D. Together with his life, and notes on his Lives of the poets, by Sir John Hawkins, Knt. In eleven volumes. . . . London, printed for J. Buckland, J. Rivington and Sons, T. Payne and Sons, L. Davis, B. White and Son, T. Longman, B. Law, J. Dodsley, H. Baldwin, J. Robson, J. Johnson, C. Dilly, T. Vernor, W. Nicoll, G. G. J. and J. Robinson, T. Cadell, T. Carnan, J. Nichols, J. Bew, R. Baldwin, N. Conant, P. Elmsley, W. Goldsmith, J. Knox, R. Faulder, Leigh and Sotheby, G. Nicol, J. Murray, A. Strahan, W. Lowndes, T. Evans, W. Bent, S. Hayes, G. and T. Wilkie, T. and J. Egerton, W. Fox, P. M'Queen, S. Ogilvie, B. Collins, E. Newbery, and R. Jameson, 1787.
Vol. 1: x,602,[16]p.; vol. 2: [5],477p.; vol. 3: [3],418p.; vol. 4: iv,637p.; vol. 5: [7],446p.; vol. 6: [5],443p.; vol. 7: [5],397p.; vol. 8: [7],410p.; vol. 9: [4],446p.; vol. 10: [5],522p.; vol. 11: [6],430,[90]p., plates, port., 8vo. Price: £3.6s. in boards.
On 8 Aug. 1785 Murray advanced £37.11s.8d. for paper, and on 3 Mar. 1787 he issued a note for £15.8s.5d. at two months and a further note for the same amount at six months. Murray issued a final note on 31 May 1787 for £6.10d. at five months — a total outlay of £74.8s.11d. The returns on his share (44 sets at £2.18s.8d., each, wholesale) were £129.1s.4d. On 27 copies of Johnson's 'Life' by Hawkins the returns were £6.6s. — nett profit £60.18s.5d. (BB, p. 43). An additional two vols, numbered twelve and thirteen, were issued in the same year entitled 'The works of Samuel Johnson, LL.D. In thirteen

volumes'; and a fourteenth vol., was issued in 1788.

ESTC t083967: L, 93.e.1–11.

Another issue:

Vol. 1: [5],viii–x,[4],602,[16]p., 8vo.

A separate issue of vol. 1, with an added title page 'The life of Samuel Johnson LL.D. By Sir John Hawkins, Knt.,' London, 1787; apparently different from Hawkins's separately issued 'Life'. The imprint excludes R. Jameson.

ESTC t082917: L, 633.k.1.

Miscellaneous. London syndicate.

603. Kentish, Richard, 1730–1792.

An essay on sea-bathing, and the internal use of sea-water. By Richard Kentish, M.D. . . . London, printed for J. Murray; and sold by J. Johnson; P. Elmsly; and the booksellers of Brighthelmstone, Margate, Weymouth, and Southampton, 1787.

[4],vii,[1],71,[1]p.,table, 8vo. With a half-title. Price: 1*s*.6*d*.

Entered in the Stationers' Company Register, 'Author. Whole'.

ESTC t018373: L, T.724(2).

Medicine. Murray–with agency.

**604. Lavater, Johann Caspar, 1741–1801.

Proposals for printing by subscription, a translation of that ingenious and instructive work. Essays on Physiognomy, by John Gaspard Lavater. . . . Subscriptions are taken in by John Murray, Bookseller; by Henry Hunter, the translator; and by Thomas Holloway, the Engraver. Also sold by G. Nicol; J. Sewell; J. Walter; J. Stockdale; J. Debret; R. Faulder; J. and J. Fletcher, Oxford; J. and J. Merrill, Cambridge; and by W. Creech, Edinburgh, [1787].

4to, plate. Price: 2*s*.6*d*.

No copy located. However, an advertisement for the Proposals is bound into the Edinburgh University copy of Florian's *Adventures of Numa Pompilius*, 1787.

Religion. London co-publishing.

605. Leake, John, 1729–1792.

Introduction to the theory and practice of midwifery: . . . To which are added, a description of the author's new forceps, illustrated with elegant copper plates. Also a syllabus of obstetric lectures . . . delivered at his theatre, in Craven-Street, London. By John Leake, . . . London, printed for R. Baldwin; and A.[*sic*] Murray, 1787.

viii,126p., plate, 8vo. With two preliminary advertisement pages.

ESTC n002144: DNLM, 18th c. coll.

Medicine. London co-publishing.

606. Leake, John, 1729–1792.

Medical instructions towards the prevention and cure of chronic diseases peculiar to women: . . . To which are added, prescriptions, . . . By John Leake, . . . Sixth edition, with additions. London, printed for Baldwin; Murray; and Egerton, 1787.

Vol. 1: viii,9–454p.; vol. 2: 423,[18]p., plate, port., 8vo. Price: 11*s*.

Vol. 1 was first published in 1777 as *Medical instructions towards the prevention and cure of chronic or slow diseases peculiar to women*. Vol. 2: *Practical observations on the child-bed fever, and acute diseases most fatal to women during the state of pregnancy*, London, printed for R. Baldwin; and A. Murray, 1787.

ESTC n003714: DNLM, 18th c. coll..

Medicine. London co-publishing.

607. Leake, John, 1729–1792.

Syllabus or general heads of a course of lectures on the theory and practice of midwifery: including the nature and treatment of diseases incident to women and children. . . . By John Leake, . . . London, printed for J. Murray, and sold by the principal booksellers in England, 1787.

53,[1]p., 8vo. Price: 1*s*.

ESTC n024435: CaOTU, J. A. Hannah Coll. pam.

Medicine. Murray alone.

608. [Logan, John, 1748–1788.]

A dissertation on the governments, manners, and spirit of Asia. London, printed for J. Murray; J. Walter; J. Stockdale; R. Faulder; and W. Creech, Edinburgh, 1787.

27,[1]p., 4to. With a half-title. Price: 1*s*.6*d*.

Entered in the Stationers' Company Register, 8 June 1787, 'J. Murray. Whole'.

ESTC t034663: L, 583.h.11(4).

History. Edinburgh co-publishing.

609. The London calendar, or court and city register for England, Scotland, Ireland, and America, for the year 1787; . . . London,

printed for John Stockdale; T. Carnan; J. Sewell; D. Steel, and Son; R. Faulder; J. Murray; and Scatcherd and Whitaker. Sold also by T. Lewis; T. Booker; W. Babbs; T. Cornel; and W. Clarke, [1787].
[4],296p., 12mo.
ESTC t139276: L, P.P.2506.K.
Miscellaneous. London syndicate.

610. MacGilvray, John.
Poems. By John MacGilvray, A.M. Master of the Grammar School at Lestwithiel. London, printed for J. Bew; and J. Murray, 1787.
[1],109p., 4to. Price: 4s.
Entered in the Stationers' Company Register, 'J. Bew. Whole'.
ESTC t000678: L, 11630.e.8(3).
Poetry. London co-publishing.

611. Millar, John, 1735–1801.
An historical view of the English government, from the settlement of the Saxons in Britain to the accession of the house of Stewart. By John Millar, Professor of Law in the University of Glasgow. London, printed for A. Strahan, and T. Cadell ; and J. Murray, 1787.
vii,[9],565,[19]p., 4to. With a half-title, index, and errata. Price: 18s. in boards.
750 copies printed by Henry Hughs. Murray and Cadell each owned a quarter share; the author a half share. Expenses: Murray bought half the edition for £150; paper bought from Thomas Curtis at £79.6.; printing — £61.9s.; index — 6 gns.; advertising — £22.14s. 485 copies sold — £339.10s. nett profit — £19.10. To compensate for the smallness of Millar's share (£9.15s.), Murray gave Millar an additional £40 in 1789. Murray's loss: £30.10s. (BB, p. 45). Entered in the Stationers' Company Register, 30 Jan. 1787, 'A. Strahan 38; T. Cadell, Whole. Certificate given Dec. 20 1802' — an apparent contradiction.
ESTC t117422: L, 188.b.6.
History. London co-publishing.

612. Murray, John, 1737–1793.
No. VI. Murray's catalogue of books in medicine, surgery, anatomy, natural history, &c. For the use of the faculty and practioners in general; and which are to be sold at the prices marked against the several articles. London, J. Murray, 1787.
[4],70p., 8vo. Price: 3s.

The Advertisement on p. [2] is dated August 1786.
ESTC t227244: L, RB.23.a.11376
Medicine. Murray alone.

613. [Ogilvie, John, 1732–1813.]
The fane of the druids. A poem. London, printed for J. Murray, 1787.
viii,50p., 4to. With a half-title. Price: 2s.6d.
A stamp duty levied on the edition was 17s. (BB, p. 49). Stock: 203 (W).
ESTC t035356: L, 11630.e.15(4).
Poetry. Murray alone.

614. Perfect, William, 1737–1809.
Select cases in the different species of insanity, lunacy, or madness. By William Perfect, . . . Rochester, printed and sold by W. Gillman; sold also by J. Murray, and J. Bew, London, 1787.
viii,335,[1]p., 8vo. With a half-title. Price: 6s.
ESTC t126963: L, C.175.d.16.
Medicine. Agency–provincial.

**615. Pirie, Alexander, of Newburgh.
Critical and practical observations on scripture texts. Murray, London.
12mo. Price: 2s.
No copy located. *English Review,* 14 (Feb. 1787), 152.
Religion. Murray alone.

616. [Playfair, William, 1759–1823.]
Joseph and Benjamin, a conversation. Translated from a French manuscript. London, printed at the Logographic Press, for J. Murray, 1787.
[6],xv,[1],238[i.e.239],[1]p. (p.217 is misnum. 216 and the error is perpetuated), 12mo. With a half-title. Price: 3s.
Joseph is Joseph II; Benjamin is Benjamin Franklin. Stock: 32 (H). Reference: Sabin 36665.
ESTC t112793: L, 8007.bb.21.
Politics. Murray alone.

617. The political magazine and parliamentary, naval, military, and literary journal, for the year, 1787. London, printed for J. Murray, and sold by every bookseller and news carrier in Great Britain.
Vol. 12: Jan.–June. [vi],480,[12]p., 8vo. With an index, plates, and maps; vol. 13: July–Dec.

[iv],960 (481–960),[12]p., 8vo. With an index, plates, and maps.

Issued in monthly parts at 1s. each; 2000 copies printed (To John Trusler, 5 Oct. 1786). John Walter printed vol. 12 only (To Walter, 2 June 1787).

Primary location: CtY, Franklin Coll.

Miscellaneous. Murray alone.

618. Rutherford, William, 1745–1820.

Elements of Latin grammar, for the use of the academy at Uxbridge.

12mo. Price: 3s.

No copy located. *English Review,* 9 (May 1787), 388. 'Murray'.

Language. Murray alone.

619. Schrevel, Cornelis, 1608–1644.

Cornelii Schrevelii lexicon manuale Graco-Latinum & Latino-Gracum: studio atque opera Josephi Hill, Johannis Entick, necnon Gulielmi Bowyer, . . . ad calcem adjecta sunt sententia Graco-Latina, . . . Item tractatus duo: . . . Editio XIV, prioribus multo auctior et emendatior. Londini, ex officina M. Brown. Sumptibus J. F. & C. Rivington; T. Longman; B. Law; T. Pote; W. Ginger; S. Bladon; C. Dilly; J. Johnson; G. G. J. & J. Robinson; H. Gardner; R. Baldwin; J. Nichols; J. Murray; T. Evans; W. Goldsmith; J. Bew; P. Wynne; S. Hayes; J. Philips; D. Ogilvie; W. Lowndes; Scatcherd & Whtaker; W. Bent; G. & T. Wilkie; et C. Stalker, 1787.

viii,[680],176p., 8vo.

6000 copies printed. On 5 June 1783 Murray paid £4.10s for '100 books in 4000' at the sale of Catherine Caslon. He issued notes at two and six months on 1 Sept. 1787 totalling £21.11s.3d, for paper and printing. The returns on his 1/40 share (150 books at 4s.8d. each, wholesale) were £35 (BB, p. 34).

ESTC n003606: OClW, 483.S37n.

Language. London syndicate.

620. Shakespeare, William, 1564–1616.

Twelfth-night: or, what you will. Written by William Shakspeare. Marked with the variations in the manager's book, at the Theatre-Royal in Drury-Lane. London, printed for C. Bathurst, J. F. and C. Rivington, L. Davis, W. Owen & Son, B. White & Son, T. Longman, B. Law, C. Dilly, T. Payne & Son, J. Nichols. T. Cadell, J. Robson, G. G. J. and J. Robinson, T. Bowles, R. Baldwin,

H. L. Gardner, J. Bew, J. Murray, W. Stuart, S. Hayes, W. Lowndes, S. Beadon, G. & T. Wilkie, W. Fox, Scatcherd & Whitaker, Newberry, J. Barker, T. & J. Egerton, D. Ogilvy, and R. Faulder, 1787.

72p., 12mo.

ESTC t174786: BMp, S 352.1787.

Drama. London syndicate.

621. Trye, Charles Brandon, 1757–1811.

A review of Jesse Foote's Observations on the new opinions of John Hunter, in his late Treatise on the venereal disease. By Charles Brandon Trye, . . . [London], Printed for John Murray, London, 1787.

[4],vii,[1],68p., 8vo. Price: 1s.6d.

See Brand 1787, item 571, and Peake 1788, item 676, for other works on this topic.

ESTC t198385: C, VII-27–16/5.

Medicine. Murray alone.

622. Walsh, Philip Pitt, 1761?-1787.

Practical observations on the puerperal fever: wherein the nature of that disease is investigated, and a method of cure, which has hitherto proved successful, recommended. By Philip Pitt Walsh, . . . London, printed for C. Dilly; J. Murray; and B. Law, 1787.

viii,59,[1]p., 8vo.

ESTC t117764: L, 1177.d.13(2).

Medicine. London co-publishing.

623. Wells, Charles.

A sermon preached at the church of St. Peter, &c. London, Murray, 1787.

No copy located. *English Review* 9 (June 1787), 471. Wells delivered the sermon before the freemasons of the county of Kent. Murray took 50 copies from Thomas Smith, the printer at Canterbury (To Smith, 26–29 Sept. 1786).

Religion. Murray alone.

624. Whitaker, John, 1735–1808.

Mary Queen of Scots vindicated. By John Whitaker, . . . London, printed for J. Murray, 1787.

Vol. 1: [1],ix,11–534p.; vol. 2: [1],431p.; vol. 3: [1],408p., 8vo. Price: 18s.

Vols. 2–3 bear the imprint: printed for J. Murray; and W. Creech, Edinburgh.

750 copies printed by Henry Hughes (To Whitaker, 9 Aug. and 25 Sept. 1786). Entered

in the Stationers' Company Register, 28 June 1787, 'Author. Whole'.
ESTC t148526: L, 600.f.14–16.
History. Murray alone.

625. White, Thomas, b. 1753.
A treatise on the struma or scrofula, commonly called the King's evil; in which the common opinion of its being a hereditary disease is proved to be erroneous; more rational causes are assigned; and a successful method of treatment is recommended. By Thomas White, . . . The second edition. London, printed for J. Murray; J. Walter; and R. and T. Turner, 1787.
viii,100p., 8vo. Price: 2s.6d.
ESTC t071039: L, 1485.ff.1.
Medicine. London co-publishing.

626. Young, Robert, social reformer.
An examination of the third and fourth definitions of the first book of Sir Isaac Newton's Principia, and of the three axioms or laws of motion. By Robert Young. London, printed for the author; and sold by T. Becket; J. Johnson; and J. Murray, 1787.
xx,63,[1]p., 8vo.
ESTC t078094: L, 538.f.13(3).
Science. Agency–London.

627. Young, William, d. 1757.
A new Latin-English dictionary: containing all the words proper for reading the classic writers; with the authorities subjoined to each word and phrase. To which is prefixed, A new English-Latin dictionary, carefully compiled from the best authors in our language. . . . The seventh edition, corrected and improved. . . . By the Rev. Mr. William Young, . . . London, printed for B. White and Son, J. Buckland, J. F. and C. Rivington, T. Longman, B. Law, W. Ginger, H. Baldwin, T. Pote, J. Johnson, G. G. J. and J. Robinson, R. Baldwin, T. Cadell, J. Sewell, J. Murray, T. Evans, H. L. Gardner, J. Bew, S. Hayes, W. Bent, W. Lowndes, G. and T. Wilkie, Scatcherd and Whitaker, 1787.
[1032]p., 4to.
8000 copies printed. Murray bought a 1/64 share at the Globe Tavern from S. Crowder on 10 Sept. 1777 for 10 gns which he paid to George Robinson on 16 Jan. 1778. On 18 Aug. 1787 he paid out £19.18s.7d. for paper and printing. The returns on his share (125 books

at 4s.8d. each, wholesale) were £29.3s.4d. (BB, p. 10; See Young 1778, item 208).
ESTC t128558: L, 1651.
Language. London syndicate.

1788

628. Abercrombie, John, 1726–1806.
Every man his own gardener. Being a new, and much more complete gardener's kalendar, than any one hitherto published. . . . By Thomas Mawe, . . . John Abercrombie, . . . and other gardeners. The twelfth edition, corrected, and greatly enlarged,. London, printed for J. F. and C. Rivington, T. Longman, B. Law, J. Johnson, G. G. J. and J. Robinson, T. Cadell. W. Goldsmith, R. Baldwin, J. Murray, E. Newbery, and W. Lowndes, 1788.
[4],616,[20]p., plate, 12mo. Price: 5s.
5000 copies printed. Murray paid Thomas Cadell 12 gns for a 1/32 share bought at Thomas Evans's sale on 3 July 1784. In Feb. 1788 he paid £11.2s.9d. for paper and printing. The returns on his share (157 copies at 2s.11d. each, wholesale) were £22.17s.11d. (BB, p. 37; Abercrombie 1784, item 392, and 1787, item 560).
ESTC t033567: L, 1508/847(1).
Agriculture. London syndicate.

629. Addison, Joseph, 1672–1719.
The spectator. . . . London, printed for Messrs. Payne, Rivington, Davis, Longman, Dodsley, White, Law, Robson, Crowder, Johnson, Nichols, Dilly, Robinson, Cadell, Stuart, Bowles, Sewell, Murray, Flexney, Baldwin, Goldsmith, Lowndes, Knox, Otridge, Hayes, Piquinet, Macqueen, & Newbery, [1788].
Vol. 1: [1],[i],iv,322,[12]p.; vol. 2: [1],346,[12]p.; vol. 3: [1],ii,337,[ii]p.; vol. 4: [1],iv,320,[9]p.; vol. 5: [1],[ii],324,[10]p.; vol. 6: [1],ii,329,[19]p. vol. 7: ii,[3]–342,[13]p.; vol. 8: iv,[5]–300,[12]p., plates, 12mo.
Entered in the Stationers' Company Register, 24 Apr. 1788.
ESTC n024154: CSmH, 140959.
Miscellaneous. London syndicate.

630. Aikin, John, 1747–1822.
An essay on the plan and character of Thomson's Seasons, by J. Aikin. London, printed for J. Murray, 1788.
xlv,[1]p., 8vo. Price: 2s.

ESTC t064088: L, 1162.f.23(1).
Literary criticism. Murray alone.

631. Alderson, John, 1757–1829.
An essay on the nature and origin of the contagion of fevers. By John Alderson, . . . Hull, printed and sold by G. Prince; sold also by Creech, Edinburgh; Murray, London; Todd, York; Binns, Leeds; and Drury, Lincoln, 1788. [6],58p., 8vo. With a half-title.
Murray took 50 copies and advertised the work in London (To Alderson, 21 Apr. 1785).
ESTC t033391: L, T.182(5).
Medicine. Agency–Provincial.

632. Anderson, John, *c.* 1730–1804.
Medical remarks on natural, spontaneous and artificial evacuation. By John Anderson, . . . The second edition. London, printed for the author, and sold by J. Murray; and J. Johnson, 1788.
x,[2],171,[1]p., 12mo. With a half-title. Price: 3s.
ESTC t135973: L, 1189.e.15.
Medicine. Agency–London.

633. Andree, John, *c.* 1740–*c.* 1820.
Considerations on bilious diseases: and some particular affections of the liver, and the gall bladder. By John Andree, M.D. Hertford, printed for the author, and sold by J. Murray, and W. Lowndes, London; and T. Simson, Hertford, 1788.
[iv],58p. (p. iv misnum. vi; 58 misnum. 38). 8vo. Price: 1s.6d.
Murray and Lowndes took 50 copies each (To Andree, 21 May 1788).
ESTC n001929: DNLM, WZ260.A561c 1788.
Medicine. Agency–provincial.

634. Articles exhibited by the knights, citizens, and burgesses, in Parliament assembled, in the name of themselves and of all the commons of Great Britain, against Warren Hastings, Esq. late governor general of Bengal, in maintenance of their inpeachment against him for high crimes and misdemeanors. With the amendments. London, printed for John Murray; and John Stockdale, 1788.
216p., 8vo.
ESTC t187142: MRu, R45972.
Politics. London co-publishing.

635. Another edition.
112p., 8vo.
ESTC t126292: L, 6495.c.11(1).
Politics. London co-publishing.

636. Articles of charge of high crimes and misdemeanors, against Sir Elijah Impey, . . . Presented to the House of Commons, upon the 12th day of December 1787. London, printed for John Stockdale; John Murray; John Sewell; W. Creech, Edinburgh; and A. Gerna, Dublin, 1788.
143,[1]p., 8vo.
ESTC t094377: L, 8023.i.2(2).
Politics. Provincial co-publishing.

637. Bergman, Torbern, 1735–1784.
Physical and chemical essays: translated from the original Latin of Sir Torbern Bergman, . . . By Edmund Cullen, M.D. . . . To which are added notes and illustrations, by the translator. . . . London, printed for J. Murray; and William Creech, Edinburgh, 1788.
Vol. 1: xl,464p.; vol. 2: xv,518p., 4 plates, 2 tables, 8vo. Price: 13s. in boards.
The 1784 edition with cancel title pages. A third volume appeared in 1791 (Edinburgh, G. Mudie, J. & J. Fairbairn; and J. Evans, London), though judging from his stock, Murray probably had a financial stake in this volume. Stock: 7 (H); 228 vols. 1–2; 40 vol. 2; 67 vol. 3 (W).
ESTC n012249: MBCo, 1.Hbs.28.
Science. Edinburgh co-publishing.

638. Berquin, Arnaud, 1747–1791.
The children's friend. Translated from the French of M. Berquin; complete in four volumes. Ornamented with frontispieces. A new corrected edition; with additions. London, printed for J. Stockdale; J. Rivington and sons; B. Law; J. Johnson; C. Dilly; J. Murray; J. Sewell; and W. Creech, Edinburgh, 1788.
Vol. 1: xii,200p.; vol. 2: iv,198,[2]p.; vol. 3: iv,218p.; vol. 4: iv,244p., plates, 12mo. With a final leaf of advertisements in vol. 2.
Translated by J. Cooper. On 8 May 1787 Murray paid John Stockdale £26.5s. for 1/8 of the copyright (BB, p. 45). Stock: 153 (W).
ESTC t089228: L, 012806.f.21.
Education. Edinburgh co-publishing.

639. Blane, Sir, Gilbert, 1749–1834.

A lecture on muscular motion, read at the Royal Society, the 13th and 20th of November, 1788. By Gilbert Blane, M.D. F.R.S. London, printed by Joseph Cooper; and sold by J. Murray; J. Johnson; and J. Stockdale, [1788].
[2],57,[1]p., 4to. Price: 2s.6d.
ESTC t104111: L, 115.i.58.
Medicine. London co-publishing.

640. Brown, William Laurence, 1755–1830.
An essay on the folly of scepticism; the absurdity of dogmatizing on religious subjects; and the proper medium to be observed between these two extremes. ... By W. L. Brown, ... London, printed for J. Murray; and W. Creech, Edinburgh, 1788.
xxi,[3],192p., 8vo. With a half-title. Price: 2s.6d.
750 copies printed; 100 sent to Wm Creech (To Creech, 27 Dec. 1787). In 1794 only 145 copies had been sold (Hester Murray to Brown, 21 Feb. 1794). Stock: 516 (W).
ESTC t101613: L, 4016.a.10.
Religion. Edinburgh co-publishing.

641. Carter, Francis, editor.
An account of the various systems of medicine, from the days of Hipocrates, to the present time: collected from the best Latin, French and English authors, particularly from the works of John Brown, ... By Francis Carter, M.D. ... London, printed for the author, and co. and sold by Mr. Murray; Mr. Balfour, Edinburgh; Mr. White, Dublin; and most of the principal booksellers in Great Britain and Ireland, 1788.
Vol. 1: vi,200p.; vol. 2: 239,[2]p., 8vo. With an errata leaf. Price: 10s.6d.
ESTC n016586: DNLM, 18th c. coll.
Medicine. Agency–provincial.

642. Cases, medical, chirurgical, and anatomical, with observations. ... By Loftus Wood, M.D. London, printed for J. Murray, 1788.
xii,vii,[1],13–480p., 8vo.
Abridged translations (by Wood) of the *Académie Royale des sciences*.
ESTC t189367: MRu, J6 W52.
Medicine. Murray alone.

643. Cornwell, Bryan.
The domestic physician, or guardian of health. Pointing out, in the most familiar manner, the symptoms of every disorder incident to mankind; together with their gradual progress and method of cure. ... To which is added, an appendix, forming a complete dispensatory. A new edition. By B. Cornwell, ... London, printed for the author; and sold by J. Murray; J. Bew; and L. Davis,
1788.
xvi,650,[22]p., 8vo.
Stock: 136 (W).
ESTC n009859: DNLM, WZ260.C813d 1788.
Medicine. London co-publishing.

644. De Lolme, Jean Louis, 1740–1806.
The constitution of England, or an account of the English government; in which it is compared, both with the republican form of government, and the other monarchies in Europe. By J. L. de Lolme, ... A new edition, corrected. London, printed for G. G. J. & J. Robinson; and J. Murray, 1788.
[8],xvi,540,[20]p., plate, port., 8vo. Price: 7s.
500 copies printed. Murray paid £32.5s.10d. for paper and printing. The returns on 250 copies at 4s.8d., each, wholesale, were £58.16.8d. (BB, p. 24).
ESTC t105987: L, 1609/1750.
History. London co-publishing.

645. Dickson, Adam, 1721–1776.
Proposals for printing by subscription, an enquiry into the husbandry of the ancients. By the Reverend Adam Dickson, ... [London], subscriptions are taken, at London, by B. White and J. Murray; at York, by John Todd and Thomas Wilson; at Leeds, by J. Binns, [1788].
[4]p., 8vo.
The *Husbandry of the ancients* was published in 1788 by Creech, Edinburgh; Robinson and Cadell, London.
ESTC t042918: L, 1339.h.11(13).
Agriculture. Agency–provincial.

646. Douglas, Gawin, 1474?–1522.
Select works of Gawin Douglass, ... Containing Memoirs of the author, The palace of honour, Prologues to the Aneid, and a glossary of obsolete words; to which is added an old poem, author unknown. Perth, printed by R. Morison, junior, for R. Morison and Son; and sold by J. Murray, London, 1788.
[4],lxi,[1],156p., plate, port., 12mo.

ESTC t104661: L, 1606/2017(2).
Poetry. Agency–provincial.

647. Dunbar, William, 1460?–1520?.
Select poems of Wil. Dunbar. Part first. From
the M.S. of George Bannatyne, published 1568.
Perth, printed by R. Morison, junr. For R.
Morison & Son; and sold by J. Murray, London,
and C. Elliot, Edinburgh, 1788.
[2],100p., plate, 12mo.
ESTC t104668: L, 1606/2017(3).
Poetry. Agency–provincial.

648. The Edinburgh magazine, or literary mis-
cellany, . . . Edinburgh, Printed for J. Sibbald:
and sold by J. Murray, London, 1788.
Vol. 7: [1],472,90p., 8vo. plates; vol. 8:
[1],434,194,[2]p., 8vo. plates.
Published in monthly parts; title page, contents,
and index issued every six months. Printed by
Macfarquhar and Elliot, Edinburgh.
Primary location: E, NH 295.
Miscellaneous. Agency–Edinburgh.

649. The English review; or, an abstract of
English and foreign literature. . . . London,
printed for J. Murray, 1788.
Vol. 11: [1],[viii],480,[6]p., 8vo; vol. 12: [1],[viii],
480,[6]p., 8vo.
Published in monthly parts (priced at 1s.); title
page, contents, and index issued every six
months.
Primary location: NN, *DA.
Miscellaneous. Murray–with agency.

650. Falconar, Maria, b. 1770 or 1, and Harriet.
Poems on slavery: by Maria Falconar, aged 17,
and Harriet Falconar, aged 14. London, printed
for Messrs. Egertons; Mr. Murray; and Mr. J.
Johnson, 1788.
vii,[1],25,[1]p., 12mo. With a half-title. Price:
1s.6d.
Murray's address is given as Temple-Bar (not
far from 32 Fleet St).
ESTC t061945: L, 1164.e.23.
Poetry. London co-publishing.

651. Familiar letters from a gentleman to a few
select friends; with some original poems on
various subjects. London, printed for the
author by S. Gosnell, and sold by J. Murray;
Messrs. White and Son; and J. Debrett, 1788.

vii,[1],246p., plate, 8vo. Price: 4s.
ESTC n009648: DeU, SpC PR3291.A1F33.
Poetry. Agency–London.

652. Fergusson, Robert, 1750–1774.
Poems on various subjects by R. Fergusson. In
two parts. Perth, printed by R. Morison, Junr.
for R. Morison and Son, booksellers; and sold
by J. Murray, London, 1788–89.
Pt. 1: viii,104; pt. 2: iv,128. port, plates, 12mo.
The title page to pt. 2 adds G. Mudie,
Edinburgh, to the imprint.
ESTC t077054: L, 11631.a.19.
Poetry. Agency–provincial.

653. Fielding, Henry, 1707–1754.
The miser. A comedy of five acts. Written by
Henry Fielding, Esq. with the variations in the
manager's book at the Theatre Royal Covent
Garden. London, printed for T. Payne and
Sons, J. Nichols, G. G. J. and J. Robinson, T.
Cadell, J. Murray, G. Nicol,, S. Bladon, W.
Lowndes, W. Nicholl, W. Fox, and Ogilvie and
Speare, 1788.
67,[1]p., 12mo. Price: 1s.
Adapted by Fielding from Molière's *L'Avare*,
itself based on the *Aulularia* of Plautus.
ESTC n004488: KyU,*822.F46m 1788.
Drama. London syndicate.

*654. Florian, 1755–1794.
The adventures of Numa Pompilius, second
King of Rome. Translated from the French of
M. de Florian. In two volumes. . . . London,
printed for C. Dilly; J. Stockdale; and W.
Creech, Edinburgh, 1788.
Vol. 1: [4],iv,267,[1]p; vol. 2: [2],iii,[1],290p., 8vo.
A reissue of Florian, 1787, above.
ESTC n050007: L, 152.1.7.
Fiction. Edinburgh co-publishing.

655. Gay, John, 1685–1732.
Fables by the late Mr. Gay. In one volume
complete. London, printed for J. Buckland, J.
F. and C. Rivington, B. and B. White, T. Longman, B. Law, T. Carnan, G. G. J. and J. Robinson, T. Cadell, S. Blandon, R. Baldwin, J. Sewell,
J. Johnson, H. L. Gardner, J. Bew, W. Goldsmith, J. Murray, W. Lowndes, J. Scatherd and
J. Whitaker, G. and T. Wilkie, and E. Newbery,
1788.
[8],232p., plates, 12mo. Price: 2s.

?5693 copies printed. Murray bought a 1/20 share at the Globe Tavern (John Crowder's sale) on 10 Sept. 1777 for £10.5s. which he paid to George Robinson on 16 Jan. 1778 and on 10 April 1783 at the Globe Tavern he paid Robinson £3.7s. for an additional 1/40 share (3/40 in all). On 13 Aug. 1787 Murray paid Thomas Longman £3.11s.2d. for the cost of the plates. The returns on his share (122 set of cuts at 8d. each, wholesale), paid on 13 Aug. 1785, were £4.1s.3d. On 21 Oct. 1788 he paid Longman £12.14s.6d. paper and printing. The returns on his share (427 books at 1s. each, wholesale), paid on 23 Oct. 1788, were £21.7s. (see BB, p. 9; Gay 1778 item 184, 1783, item 347, and 1785, item 474).
ESTC to13866: L, 1161.f.38.
Poetry. London syndicate.

656. Graham, Robert, c. 1735–1797.
A letter to the Right Honourable William Pitt, Chancellor of the Exchequer, on the reform of the internal government of the royal boroughs of Scotland. By Robert Graham, . . . With an appendix. London, printed for J. Murray, 1788. 56p., 8vo. Price: 1s.6d.
ESTC to11234: L, E.2157(1).
Politics. Murray alone.

657. Harrington, Robert, 1751–1837.
A letter addressed to Dr. Priestley, Messrs. Cavendish, Lavoisier, and Kirwan; endeavouring to prove, that their newly adopted opinions of inflammable and dephlogisticated airs, forming water; and the acids being compounded of the different kinds of air, are fallacious. By Robert Harrington, M.D. London, printed for R. Faulder; J. Murray; and R. Cust, 1788. v,[3],136p., 8mo.
ESTC no02104: CaOTU, Science.
Science. London co-publishing.

658. Hastings, Warren, 1732–1818.
The answer of Warren Hastings Esquire, to the articles exhibited by the knights, citizens, and burgesses in Parliament assembled, . . . in maintenance of their impeachment against him for high crimes and misdemeanours supposed to have been by him committed. Delivered at the bar of the house of peers, on Wednesday, November 28th, 1787. London, printed for John Stockdale; John Murray; John Sewell; W. Creech, Edinburgh; and Anthony Gerna, Dublin, 1788.
[1],261,[1]p., 8vo.
ESTC to61286: L, 8022.dd.19.
Another issue: London, printed for John Murray; John Stockdale; John Sewell; W. Creech, Edinburgh; and Anthony Gerna, Dublin, 1788.
[2],261,[1]p., 8vo.
ESTC no05591: MCh B, SpC DS473.3.A3 no.2.
Politics. Provincial co-publishing.

659. [Hawkesworth, John, 1715?–1773].
The adventurer. . . . A new edition. Illustrated with frontispieces. London, printed by H. Goldney, for J. Rivington and sons, L. Davis, J. Dodsley, T. Longman, B. Law, J. Robson and Co., G. G. J. and J. Robinson, T. Cadell, J. Murray, R. Baldwin, W. Flexney, S. Hayes, W. Goldsmith, W. Nicoll, W. Fox, W. Lowndes, E. Newbery, and G. and T. Wilkie, 1788.
Vol. 1: [4],308p.; vol. 2: [6],292p.; vol. 3: [6],298,[2]p.; vol. 4: [4],297,[2]p., plates, 12mo. With advertisements in vols. 3–4.
Essays by Hawkesworth, Joseph Warton, Samuel Johnson and others. 1500 copies printed. Murray bought a 1/32 share on 8 Apr. 1777 at the Queens Arms for which he paid 12 gns to Edward Johnston. He bought another 1/32 share at Thomas Becket's sale on 21 Jan. 1779 at the Queen's Arms for £2.5s. The expenses for paper and printing, paid on 8 July 1788, came to £16.1s.10d. On the same day the returns on his share (95 books at 6s.6d. each, wholesale) were £30.3s.2d. (BB, p. 1; Hawkesworth 1778, item 186).

660. Hollingsworth, S.
A dissertation on the manners, governments, and spirit, of Africa. To which is added, observations on the present applications to Parliament for abolishing Negroe slavery in the British West Indies. By S. Hollingsworth, . . . Edinburgh, printed for William Creech; and J. Stockdale, and J. Murray, London, 1788.
[6],24;[2],43,[1]p., 4to. Price: 2s.6d.
'Observations on the slave trade' has a divisional title page as well as separate pagination and register.
ESTC no06457: MH-H, *EC75.H7258.788d.
Politics. Edinburgh co-publishing.

661. [Homer, Philip Bracebridge, 1765–1838.]

The garland; a collection of poems. Oxford, printed for C. S. Rann; and sold by Robson and Clarke, and by Murray, London; and likewise by the booksellers at Coventry, Birmingham, and Warwick, [1788].
[8],39,[1]p., 4to. With a half-title. Price: 2s.6d.
ESTC to40429: L, 11630.d.4(7).
Poetry. Agency–provincial.

662. Humpage, Benjamin.
An essay on the rupture called hydrocele: explaining the anatomy of the parts affected; with objections to the incision, . . . In which is communicated an improved method of radically curing that disorder, . . . By Benjamin Humpage, . . . London, printed by H. Reynell. And sold by J. Murray, and T. Hookham, 1788.
[2],ii,38p., 8vo. Price: 1s.
ESTC n000551: DNLM, 18th c. coll.
Medicine. London co-publishing.

663. Hunter, Henry, 1741–1802.
The universal and everlasting dominion of God, a perpetual source of joy and praise. A sermon, preached before the Scottish presbytery, in London, at the Scots Church, London-Wall, on Tuesday the 4th of November, 1788, in commemoration of the Glorious Revolution in 1688 . . .. By Henry Hunter, D.D. London, printed for the author, by Ritchie and Sammells; and sold by John Murray, 1788.
64p., 8vo. With a half-title.
ESTC to11498: L, T.1049(2).
Religion. Agency–Murray alone.

664. [Inglefield, John Nicholson, 1748–1828.]
A short account of the naval actions of the last war; in order to prove that the French nation never gave such slender proofs of maritime greatness as during that period; with observations on the discipline, and hints for the improvement, of the British navy. By an officer. London, printed for J. Murray, 1788.
viii,148p.,table, 8vo. With a half-title. Price: 2s.6d.
750 copies printed by Wayland. Inglefield had a half share. Expenses: paper — (15.5 reams at 18s. each) £13.19; printing 10¼ sheets 'English' with notes — £11.7s. plus £2.5s. for alterations; 4s.6d. a cancel leaf minus 10s. overcharge; advertising — £9.6d.; stitching in blue paper — £1.10s. Receipts: 750 books at £9.12s. per hundred —

£72 (BB, p. 49). Nett profit £32.4s. (divided equally). Entered in the Stationers' Company Register, 13 Sept. 1788, 'J. Murray. Whole'.
ESTC to11093: L, E.2064(1).
Military. Murray alone.

665. Jameson, Thomas, surgeon, Royal Navy.
A treatise on diluents, and an enquiry into the diseases of the fluids of the human body, to ascertain the operation of diluents upon them. . . . By Thomas Jameson, . . . London, printed for the author by J. Davis; and sold by J. Murray, and C. Elliot, Edinburgh, 1788.
134p., 8vo. With a half-title. Price: 2s.6d.
ESTC to08296: L, T.191(4).
Medicine. Agency–London.

666. A letter to Philip Francis, Esq. from the Right Hon. Edmund Burke, Chairman, . . . members of the committee for managing the impeachment of Mr. Hastings. With remarks. London, printed for John Murray; and John Stockdale, 1788.
[2],33,[1]p., 8vo. With a half-title.
ESTC to11505: L, RB.23.a.1088.
Politics. London co-publishing.

667. A letter to the author of Thoughts on the manners of the great. London, printed for J. Murray, 1788.
[4],142,[2]p., 8vo. With a half-title and final leaf of errata. Price: 2s.
A reply to Hannah More.
ESTC to28260: L, 225.a.21.
Miscellaneous. Murray alone.

668. Lind, James, 1716–1794.
An essay on diseases incidental to Europeans in hot climates. With the method of preventing their fatal consequences. By James Lind, . . . To which is added, an appendix concerning intermittent fevers. And, a simple and easy way to render sea water fresh, . . . The fourth edition. London, printed for J. Murray, 1788.
xvi,357,[9]p., 8vo. Price: 6s.
750 copies printed. Murray paid £2.6s. for a half share at Thomas Becket's sale on 21 Jan. 1779 at the Queen's Arms. (He presumably already owned the other half.) He paid out £59.18s. for paper, printing and advertising and sold the copies for £131.5s., or 3s.6d. each, wholesale (BB, p. 16).

ESTC n002084: CaBVaU, WZ260.L47 1788.
Medicine. Murray alone.

669. The London calendar, or court and city register for England, Scotland, Ireland, and America, for the year 1788; ... London, printed for John Stockdale; T. Carnan; J. Sewell; D. Steel, and Son; R. Faulder; J. Murray, T. Whieldon and T. Wright; T. Booker and T. Hookham; W. Babbs, and Shepperson and Reynolds, T. Cornell; J. Deighton, Ogilvy and Speare, and J. Cuthell; P. M. Queen, and J. Strahan; W. Clarke; T. Axtell, and W. Creech, Edinburgh, [1788].
[4],294p., 12mo.
ESTC t139277: L, P.P.2506.K.
Miscellaneous. London syndicate.

670. [Macdonald, Thomas.]
A review of the laws and regulations respecting the distillery of Scotland; with the circumstances which gave rise to them considered upon principle. London, printed for John Murray, 1788.
v,49p., 8vo. Price: 1s.6d.
ESTC t176222: O, G.Pamph.1949(12).
Law. Murray alone.

671 [M'Donald, Andrew, 1755?-1790].
Twenty-eight miscellaneous sermons. By a clergyman of the Church of England. London, printed for J. Murray, 1788.
[2],390p., 8vo. Price: 5s. in boards.
ESTC n054279: MBAt, 3YE.M143
Religion. Murray alone.

672. M'Donald, Andrew, 1755?-1790.
Vimonda: a tragedy, by A. M'Donald; performed at the Theatre-Royal, Hay-Market. London, printed for J. Murray; J. Walter; J. Stockdale; R. Faulder; and J. Sewell, 1788.
[4],82,[2]p., 8vo. Price: 1s.6d.
Murray paid the author £30 for the copyright (BB, p. 69). Entered in the Stationers' Company Register, 11 July 1788, 'John Murray. Whole'.
ESTC t050806: L, 643.e.18(9).
Drama. London co-publishing.

673. The second edition.
ESTC t194664: O, Mal.B 44(13).
Drama. London co-publishing.

674. Murray, John, 1737-1793.
A letter to W. Mason, A.M. precentor of York, from J. Murray, bookseller, in London. The second edition, corrected. London, printed for J. Murray, 1788.
32,[2]p., 12mo. Price: 6d.
The same text as Murray's 1777 edition, with a few passages toned down. See the Bibliography of Pamphlets Written by Murray for details.
ESTC n033836: Ct, X.34.21(2).
Law. Murray alone.

675. [Paterson, Samuel, 1728-1802.]
Speculations upon law and lawyers; applicable to the manifest hardships, uncertainty, and abusive practice of the common law. London, printed [by G. Auld for the author,] for Messrs. Robson and Clarke; Debrett; Beckett and Edwards; Egerton; Murray and Wheildon; Robinson; and Richardson, 1788.
[8],103,[1]p., 8vo.
ESTC t065087: L, 518.h.18(2).
Law. Agency–London.

676. Peake, John.
A candid review of Jessie Foot's observations on the new opinions of John Hunter, in his late treatise on the venereal disease, ending with the subject of gonorrhoea. By John Peake, surgeon. London, sold by J. Johnson; J. Murray; and T. and J. Egerton, 1788.
[2],v–vii,[1],77,[1]p., 8vo.
See Brand and Trye 1787 (items 571 and 621) for other works on this topic.
ESTC n003833: DNLM, W6.P3 v.2542.
Medicine. London co-publishing.

677. Perry, William, lecturer in the Academy at Edinburgh.
The royal standard English dictionary. In which the words are not only rationally divided into syllables, accurately accented, their part of speech properly distinguished, and their various significations arranged in one line; but likewise ... it exhibits their true pronunciation, ... To which is prefixed, a comprehensive grammar ... The fifth edition. In which is now added the Scripture proper names, ... By W. Perry, ... Edinburgh, printed for, and sold by J. Bell and J. Dickson; and J. Murray, London, 1788.
[4],559,[1],36p., oblong 12mo. Price: 3s. bound
The Appendix has a separate title page,

pagination and register. Reference: Alston v. 294. In Aug. 1785 Murray paid Neill, printer at Edinburgh, 4 gns. for one half of the copy of 'Perry's Dictionary & Works'. On 11 July 1788 he issued a note at three month to Cadell & Co. Stationers, for £84.10s. for 338 reams of paper and paid Neill & Co. £55.18s.6d. for printing. The returns on his share (ambiguously recorded on BB, p. 42, as 500 books at 1s.6d. each; 1200 books at 1s.6d. each; and 1362 books at 1s.6d. each) were £37.10s. £90, and £102.2s. respectively.

ESTC t209097: WAu, 18.16.12.17.
Language: Edinburgh co-publishing.

678. Pirie, Alexander, of Newburgh.
Appendix to a Dissertation on baptism. In a series of letters addressed to Mr. M'Lean, of Edinburgh. London, Murray, 1788.
12mo. Price: 2s.
No copy located. *English Review* 13 (Feb. 1789), 152.
Religion. Murray alone.

679. Pirie, Alexander, of Newburgh.
A dissertation on baptism; intended to illustrate the origin, history, design, mode, and subjects, of that sacred institution, &c. To which is added an inquiry into the lawfullness of eating blood. Perth, Morison; Murray, London, 1788.
12mo. Price: 1s.6d.
No copy located. *English Review* 13 (Feb. 1789), 152.
Religion. Agency–provincial.

680. The political magazine and parliamentary, naval, military, and literary journal, for the year, 1788. London, printed for J. Murray, and sold by every bookseller and news carrier in Great Britain.
Vol. 14: Jan.–June. [1],[iv],496,[10]p. 8vo. With an index, plates, and maps; vol. 15: July–Dec. [i],516,[14]p. 8vo. With an index, plates, and maps. Issued in monthly parts at 1s. each; 2000 copies printed (To John Trusler, 5 Oct. 1786).
Primary location: CtY, Franklin Coll.
Miscellaneous. Murray alone.

681. Ramsay, Allan, 1685–1758.
The gentle shepherd, a pastoral comedy; by Allan Ramsay. Glasgow, printed by A. Foulis, and sold by D. Allan, Edinburgh, also by J. Murray, and C. Elliot, London, 1788.

[4],x,[2],111,[3],17,[1]p. 4to. With a half-title, plates, engr. music, port.
The artist David Allan owned part of the work and in October 1792 Murray agreed to take sixty remaining copies at 9s. each (JM to David Allan, 22 Oct. 1791; Gaskell, *Foulis* 688).
ESTC t060190: L, 644.l.23.
Drama. Provincial co-publishing.

682. Reflections upon a late extraordinary promotion of sixteen admirals. London, Murray, 1788.
8vo. Price: 1s.
No copy located. *English Review* 11 (Mar. 1788), 232; and (May 1788), 391.
Military. Murray alone.

683. A review of the principal charges against Warren Hastings Esquire, late Governor General of Bengal. London, printed for John Stockdale; and John Murray, 1788.
111,[1]p., 8vo. Advertisements last 6 pp.
ESTC t143514: Lu, Porteus BP99.
Politics. London co-publishing.

684. Richardson, William, 1743–1814.
Essays on Shakespeare's dramatic character of Sir John Falstaff, and on his imitation of female characters. To which are added, some general observations on the study of Shakespeare. By Mr. Richardson, . . . London, printed for J. Murray, 1788.
[4],96p., 8vo. With a half-title. Price: 2s.
On 27 Sept. 1788 Murray paid Richardson £20 'for falstaff &c'; 3 gns. for a portrait of the author by John Donaldson; and £2 for a copy of 'Capeles Shakespeare' for Richardson. (BB, p. 7). Entered in the Stationers' Company Register, 30 Sept. 1788, 'John Murray. Whole'.
ESTC n008400: TxHR, WRC PR2989.R4.
Literary criticism. Murray alone.

685. [Robertson, George, d. 1791.]
A short account of a passage from China, late in the season, down the China Seas, through the Southern Natuna Islands, along the west coast of Borneo, through the Straits of Billitton or (Clements Straits) to the Straits of Sunda. . . . London, printed for J. Murray, 1788.
iv,24p., 4to.
ESTC t181538: E, E.120.a.18(2).
Travel–topography. Murray alone.

686. Rutherford, William, 1745–1820.

A view of antient history; including the progress of literature and the fine arts. By William Rutherford, ... London, printed for the author; and sold by J. Murray, 1788–91.

Vol. 1: x,450,[2]p., 8vo. With a plate, map, and advertsiement; Vol. 2: iv,528p. With a map. Price: 14s. in boards.

Vol. 1 entered in the Stationers' Company Register, 7 Mar. 1788, 'J. Murray. Whole'; vol. 2 entered 30 Dec. 1790 'J. Murray'.

ESTC t114185: L, 581.f.11,12.

History. Agency–Murray alone.

687. Seally, John, c. 1747–1795.

The lady's encyclopedia: or, a concise analysis of the belles lettres, the fine arts, and the sciences, in three volumes. Illustrated with fifty engraved heads, and thirty-four maps, &c. By the Rev. J. Seally, ... London, printed for J. Murray, and W. Creech, Edinburgh, 1788.

Vol. 1: [viii],371p.; vol. 2: xi,391p.; vol. 3: xi,[1],503p., plates, maps, ports., 12mo. Price: 12s. Reference: Alston iii. 387. Stock: 64 sets, 260 vol. 3 (W).

ESTC t124906: L, 1422.c.19.

Education. Edinburgh co-publishing.

688. Shaw, James.

A review of the affairs of the Austrian Netherlands, in the year 1787. London, printed for J. Murray, 1788.

[6],108p., 8vo. With a half-title. Price: 2s.

Entered in the Stationers' Company Register, 11 July 1788, 'John Murray. Whole'. Stock: 53 (H). Stock: 150 (W).

ESTC t062290: L, 590.c.22.

Politics. Murray alone.

689. Shaw, James.

Sketches of the history of the Austrian Netherlands: with remarks on the constitution, commerce, arts, and general state of these provinces. The second edition. London, printed for J. Murray, 1788.

[4],310p., 8vo. With a half-title.

Murray paid Shaw £31.10s, apparently for the copyright (BB, p. 43). The first edition had been published the year before by George Robinson. Copy located in a Christie's sale (London), 25 Apr. 1997, lot 87.

Politics. Murray alone.

690. Skeete, Thomas, 1757–1789.

Syllabus of a course of lectures upon the animal oeconomy. By Thomas Skeete, ... London, sold by C. Dilly; J. Johnson; and J. Murray, 1788. vi,50p., 8vo.

ESTC n023213: DNLM, 18th c.coll.

Science. London co-publishing.

691. Staehlin, Jakob von, 1709–1785.

Original anecdotes of Peter the Great, collected from the conversation of several persons of distinction at Petersburgh and Moscow. By Mr. Stahlin, ... London, printed for J. Murray; J. Sewell; and W. Creech, at Edinburgh, 1788.

[2],viii,[3]–448p., 8vo. Price: 6s.

A translation of *Originalanekdoten von Peter dem Grossen*, 1785. French and Russian versions had appeared in 1787. Entered in the Stationers' Company Register, 11 July 1788, 'John Murray. Whole'. Stock: 45 (H); 388 (W).

ESTC t107832: L, 1200.f.5.

Biography. Edinburgh co-publishing.

692. Sterne, Laurence, 1713–1768.

The works of Laurence Sterne. In ten volumes complete. Containing, I. the life and opinions of Tristram Shandy, Gent. II. A sentimental journey through France and Italy. III. Sermons. IV. Letters. with a life of the author written by himself. London, printed for J. Rivington and sons, J. Dodsley, G. Kearsley, J. Johnson, G. G. J. and J. Robinson, T. Cadell, J. Murray, T. Becket, R. Baldwin, A. Strahan, W. Lowndes, W. Bent, G. and T. Wilkie, and G. Ogilvie, 1788.

Vol. 1: xx,[4],296p.; vol. 2: [1],307p.; vol. 3: [11],288p.; vol. 4: [1],264p.; vol. 5: [3],242p.; vol. 6: [12],284p.; vol. 7: [8],276p.; vol. 8: [6],280p.; vol. 9: vii,208p.; vol. 10: vii,198p.; port. plates. 8vo. Price: £2.

1000 copies printed. On 8 July 1788 Murray paid £32.18s.8d. for his 63/1000 share of paper and printing. The returns on his share (63 sets at 20s. each, wholesale) were £63 (BB, p. 23 and Plate 27).

ESTC t014785: L, 1608/5467.

Fiction. London syndicate.

693. Tassie, James, 1735–1799.

Proposals for printing a descriptive catalogue of a collection of pastes and impressions of ancient and modern gems: formed and selling by James Tassie ... The work will contain

about 100 sheets letter-press: It is now printing with this type, and on this paper. A few
copies will be taken off on larger and finer
paper. The price on this paper, in boards, will
not be above one guinea and a half; a propor-
tionable price will be charged for the copies
on large paper ... The virtuosi, encouragers
and professors of the arts, who have hitherto
liberally encouraged the Proprietor's well
meant pursuits and perseverance, are humbly
requested to honour this undertaking with
their subscription, which will be taken in at
his house, No. 20, Leicester Fields; and at Mr.
Murray's No. 32, Fleet Street. No payment
expected till the delivery of the work. London
December 22, 1788.
The prospectus in French is bound into the
British Library copy (141.e.6–7): 'Avertisse-
ment d'un catalogue raisonné de la collection
de pates et impressions de pierres Gravées
antiques & modernes: qui a eté formée et se
vend par James Tassie'. Published in 1791,
item 850.
Primary location: L, 787.1.17.
Arts. Agency–London.

694. [Thomson, Alexander, 1763–1803.]
The choice. Edinburgh, printed for William
Creech; and sold by J. Murray,
London, 1788.
[2],38p., 4to. Price: 1s.6d.
ESTC t001020: L, 11630.f.12.
Poetry. Agency–Edinburgh.

695. Thomson, James, 1700–1748.
The works of James Thomson. With his last
corrections and improvements. In three
volumes complete. To which is prefixed the
life of the author, by Patrick Murdoch, ...
London, printed by A. Strahan; for J. Rivington
and Sons, T. Payne and Sons, S. Crowder, T.
Longman, B. Law, G. G. J. and J. Robinson, T.
Cadell, J. Nichols, R. Baldwin, W. Goldsmith,
W. Stuart, J. Murray, J. White, W. Lowndes, W.
Bent, S. Hayes, G. and T. Wilkie, D. Ogilvy, and
Scatcherd and Whitaker, 1788.
Vol. 1: xxxii,280p.; vol. 2: [iv],306,[307]p.; vol. 3:
[iv],308,[309],[1]p., plates, port., 8vo.
1500 copies printed. Murray paid £1.3s.6d. for a
1/48 share to George Robinson on 3 June 1779.
In Dec. 1787 he paid £3.9s.7d. for expenses of
the edition. The returns of his share (32 books
at 4s. each, wholesale) were £6.8s. (BB, p. 47).

ESTC t137447: L, 1608/4351.
Poetry. London syndicate.

696. Thomson, James, 1700–1748.
The works of James Thomson. In two volumes.
... London, printed for J. Rivington and Sons,
T. Payne and Sons, S. Crowder, T. Longman, G.
G. J. and J. Robinson, T. Cadell, J. Nichols, R.
Baldwin, W. Goldsmith, W. Stuart, J. Murray, J.
White, W. Lowndes, W. Bent, S. Hayes, G. and
T. Wilkie, D. Ogilvy, and Scatcherd and
Whitaker, 1788.
Vol. 1: xxiv,403p.; vol. 2: 435,[1]p., plates, port.,
12mo.
See above. In Dec. 1788 Murray paid Thomas
Cadell £8.7s.2d. The returns on his share were
£12.16s. In May 1796 1/48 share sold to Vernor
for 14s.6d.(BB, p. 47). Stock: 9 (H); 30 (W).
ESTC t038138: L, 11607.f.15.
Poetry. London syndicate.

697. [Thomson, William, 1746–1817.]
Memoirs of the late war in Asia. With a narrative of the imprisonment and sufferings of our
officers and soldiers: by an officer of Colonel
Baillie's detachment. ... London, printed for
the author; and sold by J. Murray, 1788.
Vol. 1.: vii,512p.; vol. 2: [1],304p., plates, map,
8vo. Price: 1s.6d.
Thomson based his account on the MS journals
of Capt. Thomas Boswer and a Capt. Lamont
(*Defence of Innes Munro*, p. 7). A second edition
was published in 1789 as *Memoirs of the war in
Asia, from* 1780 to 1784. Entered in the Stationers' Company Register, 7 Mar. 1788, 'J. Murray. The Whole'.
ESTC t092655: L, 802.k.7,8.
Military. Agency–Murray alone.

698. Timbury, Jane.
The male coquet. A novel. In two volumes. By
Jane Timbury, ... London, printed for J.
Murray, 1788.
Vol. 1: iv,166p.; vol. 2: iv,150,[2]p., 12mo. With
publisher's advertisements. Price: 4s.
ESTC n004439: CLU-S/CPR5671.T222m 1788.
Murray paid the author 5 gns. on 20 Mar. 1788
(BB, p. 43). Entered in the Stationers' Company
Register, 11 July, 1788, 'John Murray. Whole'.
Stock: 22 (H); 408 (W).
Fiction. Murray alone.

699. Trenck, Friedrich, Freiherr von der, 1726–1794.
The life of Frederick, Baron Trenck. Written by himself, and translated from the German. . . . London, printed for J. Murray, 1788.
Vol. 1: 231,[1]; vol. 2: [1],211,[3]p., plate, 12mo. With errata slip tipped in p. 1 vol. 1; advertisements in both vols. Price: 5s.
A translation by John Skinner (who was paid 20s. per sheet of original) of Merkwürdige Lebensgeschichte (To Skinner, 14 Feb. 1788). Thomas Holcroft's translation appeared a few months before. Stock: 1 (H).
ESTC t118779: L, 1607/443.
Biography. Murray alone.

*700. [Tytler, James, M.A., of Brechin, Forfarshire.]
A new and concise system of geography; containing a particular account of the empires, kingdoms, states, provinces, and islands in the known world. In which is included a comprehensive history of remarkable and interesting events. With an introduction, exhibiting the principles of astronomy, as they are connected with the knowledge of geography. By the author of the continuation of Salmon's geographical grammar [Tytler]. Embellished with a set of accurate maps engraved purposely for the work. Edinburgh, printed for Peter Hill, 1788.
[6],18,397,[3]p., plates, maps, 8vo. With a final errata leaf. Price: 5s.
English Review 12 (Aug. 1788), 93–94: 'Edinburgh, printed for Peter Hill; Murray, London.' Entered in the Stationers' Company Register, 11 Mar. 1788, 'A. Kincaid. Whole' (The son and namesake of the publisher Alexander Kincaid, he may also have been the author).
ESTC t068977: L, 570.d.12.
Travel–topography. Edinburgh co-publishing.

701. Voltaire, Francois Marie Arouet de, 1694–1778.
The white bull, an Oriental history. From an ancient Syrian manuscript. Communicated by Mr. Voltaire. Cum notis editoris et variorum: . . . The whole faithfully done into English. London, printed for J. Murray, 1788.
[4],ix–cxliv,[3],vi–viii,168,[4]p., 8vo. Two final errata leaves.
A translation of Le taureau blanc, attributed to

Jeremy Bentham. See Voltaire 1774, item 93.
Stock: 62 (H); 68 (W).
ESTC n025617: MH-H *FC7.V8893.Eg774ba.
Fiction. Murray alone.

702. Whitaker, John, 1735–1808.
Mary Queen of Scots vindicated. By John Whitaker, . . . In three volumes. . . . London, printed for J. Murray; and W. Creech, Edinburgh, 1788.
Vol. 1: [1],ix,11–534p.; vol. 2: [1],431; vol. 3: [1],408p., 8vo. Price: 18s. in boards.
A reissue of the 1787 edition with new title pages.
ESTC t148717: L, 287.f.8–10.
History. Edinburgh co-publishing.

703. [Wilson, Andrew, M.D., of Newcastle-upon-Tyne.]
Bath waters, a conjectural idea of their nature and qualities, in three letters, to——To which is added, putridity and infection unjustly imputed to fevers, a cruel public grievance, attempted to be redressed; with some account of the nature and management of plain fevers. By A. W. M.D. . . . Bath, printed and sold by S. Hazard; sold also by G. G. J. and J. Robinson, Murray, and Strahan, London, 1788.
[4],87,[3]p., 8vo. With a final advertisement leaf. Price: 2s.
ESTC n015476: MH-H, Tr2066*.
Medicine. Agency–provincial.

704. Young, Robert, social reformer.
An essay on the powers and mechanism of nature; intended, by a deeper analysis of physical principles, to extend, improve, and more firmly establish, the grand superstructure of the Newtonian system. By Robert Young. London, printed for the author, by Fry and Couchman; sold by T. Becket, J. Johnson, and J. Murray, 1788.
xxiii,[1],336p., plates, 8vo.
Stock: 18 (H).
ESTC t078101: L, 528.g.7.
Science. Agency–London.

1789

705. Addison, Joseph, 1672–1719.
The spectator. . . . London, printed by H. Hughs; for Messrs. Payne, Rivington, Davis, Longman, Dodsley, White, Law. Robson, Crowder, H.

Baldwin, Johnson, Nichols, Dilly, Robinson, Cadell, Stuart, Sewell, Murray, Flexney, R. Baldwin, Faulder, Goldsmith, Knox, Otridge, Hayes, Piguenit, McQueen, Newbery, Lowndes, Edwards, and Stalker, 1789.
Vol. 1: [1],iv,476,[12]p.; vol. 2: [1],iii,[1],506, [12]p.; vol. 3: [1],479,[13]p.; vol. 4: [1],443,[9]p.; vol. 5: [1],460,[12]p.; vol. 6: [1],459,[19]p.; vol. 7: [1],486,[11] .; vol. 8: [1],408,[10]p., ill., 8vo.
Vols 3 and 4 printed by T. Wright; vols 5 and 6 by T. Spilsbury; vols 7 and 8 by T. Bensley. Stock: 44 (W).
ESTC t097954: L, P.P.5250.eba.
Miscellaneous. London syndicate.

706. Bennett, John, Curate of St. Mary's, Manchester.
Letters to a young lady, on a variety of useful and interesting subjects, calculated to improve the heart, to form the manners, and enlighten the understanding: ... By the Rev. John Bennett, ... Warrington, printed by W. Eyres, for the author, and sold by G. G. J. and J. Robinsons; Messrs. Rivingtons, and J. Johnson; T. Cadell; J. Murray, London; and I. Clarke, Manchester, 1789.
Vol. 1: 1,xv,[3]—244p.; vol. 2: [4],271p., 12mo. With half-titles. Price: 5s.6d. sewed.
Entered in the Stationers' Company Register, 23 April 1789, 'Author. Whole'.
ESTC t099560: L, 1031.e.12.
Education. Agency–provincial.

707. Berkeley, George, 1733–1795.
The English revolution vindicated from the misrepresentation of the adherents of the House. of Stuart: in a discourse preached at Cookham, in the diocese of Sarum, on Sunday, October 25, 1789. . . . By George Berkeley, . . . London, printed for Elliot and Kay; and sold by T. Cadell, and J. Gardner; and J. Murray, London; Simmons, Canterbury; Prince, Oxford; T. & J. Merrill, Cambridge; Todd, York; Smart, Worcester; Raikes, Gloucester; Pote, Eton; and Cruttwell, Bath, [1789].
[4],31,[1]p., 4to. With a half-title. Price; 1s.6d.
The *London Chronicle* gives 3 Dec. 1789 as the date of publication.
ESTC t007150: L, 694.k.9(10).
History. Agency–London.

708. Blane, Sir, Gilbert, 1749–1834.

Observations on the diseases of seamen. By Gilbert Blane, . . . The second edition, with corrections and additions. London, printed by Joseph Cooper; and sold by John Murray; J. Johnson; and by William Creech, in Edinburgh, 1789.
viii,560,4,xv,[1]p.,tables, 8vo.
First issued as *Observations on the diseases incident to seamen.* This edition published 3 Dec. 1789 (*London Chronicle*, which notes that 'the additions to this edition, consisting chiefly of a Pharmacopoeia, may be had separately at Mr. Murray's').
ESTC n010703: DNLM, WZ260.B6420 1789 2cop.
Medicine. Edinburgh co-publishing.

*****709.** Brisson, Pierre-Raymond de. 1745–1820?
An account of the shipwreck and captivity of M. de Brisson: containing a description of the deserts of Africa, from Senegal to Morocco. Translated from the French. London printed for J. Johnson, 1789.
[2],xii,173,[3]p., 8vo.
A translation of *Histoire du naufrage et de la captivité de M. Brisson.* Murray and Joseph Johnson each had a half share. Murray's expenses for printing and paper in Sept. 1789 were £20.2s.6d. (BB, p. 60).
ESTC n030247: MSaE, 910.42.B85
Travel–topography. London co-publishing.

710. Burney, William.
Dumfries, a poem. By William Burney. Sold by J. Murray, and W. Richardson, London; W. Creech, Edinburgh; W. Boyd, and other booksellers,
Dumfries, 1789.
16p., 8vo. With a half-title.
ESTC t198236: O, Gough Col. Scotl.156(8).
Poetry. Provincial co-publishing.

711. Chambaud, Lewis, d. 1776.
Chambaud improved; or, French and English exercises, with their respective grammar-rules . . . By James Nicholson, . . . The second edition. London, printed for J. Murray, 1789.
iv,[4],219,[1]p., 8vo.
Originally published in 1750 as *Exercises to the rules of construction of French-speech.* Reference: Alston xii. 325. In Mar. 1784 Murray had paid

Nicolson £10 for the copyright, which was sold in May 1796 to Murray & Highley for 4 gns. (BB, p. 36). Stock: 233 (H); 22 (W).
ESTC t121194: L, 1608/4962.
Language. Murray alone.

712. Dalzel, Andrew, editor.
Analekta Hellénika. Sive collectanea Graeca: ad usum academica juventutis accommodata. Tom. I. complectens excerpta ex variis orationis solutae scriptoribus Cum notis philologicis; quas partim collegit, partim scripsit Andreas Dalzel, . . . Editio secunda emendatior. Edinburgi, excudebat Adamus Neill cum sociis. Veneunt autem ibi apud Joannem Bell et Jacobum Dickson. Londini: apud Joannem Murray, 1789.
xvi,348;184p., plate, map, 8vo. With a half-title. Price: 5s.
The 'Nota philologica' have separate title page, pagination and register. Entered in the Stationers' Company Register, 25 May 1789, 'Author, Whole'. Stock: 36 (H).
ESTC t150559: L, 997.i.4.
Language. Edinburgh co-publishing.

713. Davidson, David.
Thoughts on the seasons, &c. partly in the Scottish dialect, by David Davidson. London, printed for the author; and sold by J. Murray; and W. Creech, Edinburgh, 1789.
viii,189,[1]p., 8vo. With a half-title. Price: 5s.
ESTC t175906: C, 7720.c.179.
Poetry. Agency–London.

714. De Lolme, Jean Louis, 1740–1806.
The constitution of England; or, an account of the English government: . . . By J. L. de Lolme, . . . A new edition, corrected. London, printed for G. G. J. and J. Robinson; and J. Murray, 1789.
[8],xvi,540,[20]p., plate, port., 8vo. Price: 7s.
Possibly the 1788 edition (item 644) with a new title page as it is not listed under the account in BB, p. 24.
ESTC t110146: L, G.16288.
History. London co-publishing.

715. The Edinburgh magazine, or literary miscellany, . . . Edinburgh, Printed for J. Sibbald: and sold by J. Murray, London, 1789.

Vol. 9: [1],[2],434,100p., 8vo. plates; vol. 10: [1],[2],436,92,[2]p., 8vo. plates.
Published in monthly parts; title page, contents, and index issued every six months. Printed by Macfarquhar and Elliot, Edinburgh.
Primary location: E, NH 295.
Miscellaneous. Agency–Edinburgh.

716. The English review; or, an abstract of English and foreign literature. . . . London, printed for J. Murray, 1789.
Vol. 13: [1],[viii],480,[6]p., 8vo; vol. 14: [1],[viii], 480,[6]p., 8vo.
Published in monthly parts (priced at 1s.); title page, contents, and index issued every six months.
Primary location: NN, *DA.
Miscellaneous. Murray–with agency.

717. An epistle, in verse. Written from Somersetshire, in the year 1776, to ***** ******** ******, Esq. in Scotland. London, printed for J. Murray, by J. Cooper, with his new-invented ink, 1789.
[4],30,[2]p., 4to. With a half-title and a final advertisement leaf. Price: 1s.6d.
ESTC t000196: L, 643.k.18(15).
Poetry. Murray alone.

718. Equiano, Olaudah, b. 1745.
The interesting narrative of the life of Olaudah Equiano, or Gustavus Vassa, the African. Written by himself. . . . London, printed for and sold by the author; sold also by Mr. Johnson; Mr. Murray, Fleet-Street; Messrs. Robson and Clark; Mr. Davis; Messrs. Shepperson and Reynolds; Mr. Jackson; Mr. Lackington; Mr. Matthews; Mr Murray, Prince's-Street, Soho; Mess. Taylor and Co.; Mr. Button; Mr. Parsons; and may be had of all the Booksellers in town and country. Entered at Stationer's Hall, [1789].
Vol. 1: [xiv],272p.; vol. 2: [ii],255p., plates, port., 12mo. With a list of subscribers in vol. 1.
The only publication located listing both John Murrays active in London at the time. Entered in the Stationers' Company Register, 25 Mar. 1789, 'Author. Whole'.
ESTC t140573: L, 615.d.8.
Biography. Agency–London.

719. Henderson, William.
A few observations concerning those things

which are probable, or in some measure ascertained, relative to the history and cure of the plague. By William Henderson, . . . London, printed for J. Murray, 1789.
[2],iv,[2],79,[1]p., 8vo. Price: 1s.6d.
750? copies printed at a cost of £5.10s. (To Henderson, 7 July 1791). Henderson was a surgeon at St. Andrew Street, Glasgow. Stock: 342 (W).
ESTC t151822: GOT, 80Med.pract.2378/89.
Medicine. Murray alone.

720. Higgins, William, 1763–1825.
A comparative view of the phlogistic and antiphlogistic theories. With inductions. To which is annexed, an analysis of the human calculus, . . . By William Higgins, . . . London, printed for J. Murray, 1789.
[6],xiv,316,[2]p., 8vo. With a half-title and a final errata leaf. Price: 7s.
ESTC t149794: GOT, 80Chem.II,4614.
Medicine. Murray alone.

721. The historian's pocket dictionary; annexing dates to the memorable occurrences, from the earliest period of history to the present time: . . . Also the sovereigns of England and Scotland, distinguished painters, &c. and eminent men of all professions. London, printed for J. Murray, and G. and T. Wilkie, [1789].
viii,352p., 12mo. Price: 3s.
On 13 Nov. 1787 Murray paid 5 gns. for the whole assignment (BB, p. 48). Stock: 24 (H); 522 (W). The publication of this work involved Murray in a law suit with John Trusler in 1789.
ESTC no17781: CaOHM, A1510.
History. London co-publishing.

722. Homer, Philip Bracebridge, 1765–1838.
Anthologia: or, a collection of flowers. In blank verse. By the Rev. Philip Bracebridge Homer, . . . London, printed for the author; and sold by Robson and Clarke, and by Murray; and likewise by the booksellers at Coventry, Birmingham and Warwick, [1789].
[2],25,[1]p., 4to. Price: 1s.
ESTC t022160: L, 11630.e.12(1).
Poetry. Agency–London.

723. An inquiry into the origin, progress, & present state of slavery: with a plan for the gradual, reasonable, & secure emancipation of slaves. By a member of the Society of Universal Goodwill, in London and Norwich. [London], printed for John Murray, London, 1789.
43,[1]p., 8vo.
ESTC t006217: L, T.700(8).
Politics. Murray alone.

724. Jamieson, John, 1759–1838.
The sorrows of slavery, a poem. Containing a faithful statement of facts respecting the African slave trade. By the Rev. J. Jamieson, . . . London, printed for J. Murray, 1789.
80p., 8vo. Price: 1s.6d.
ESTC t124941: L, 11632.bb.24.
Poetry. Murray alone.

725. Jure divino: or, the true grounds and reasons for the support of the Christian ministry. Occasioned by the present contested election at the asylum. The second edition. London, printed for the author; and sold by J. Johnson; W. Richardson; J. Murray; and J. Mathews, 1789.
iv,45,[1]p., 4to.
ESTC n64276: Cpe, 5.4.34.
Religion. London co-publishing.

726. [Johnson, Samuel, 1709–1784.]
The Rambler. . . . The eleventh edition. London, printed for J. Rivington and Sons, T. Longman, B. Law, H. Baldwin, Robson and Clark, C. Dilly, G. G. J. and J. Robinson, T. Cadell, T. Carnan, J. Nichols, J. Bew, W. Goldsmith, J. Knox, J. Murray, W. Otridge, W. Lowndes, S. Hayes, G. and T. Wilkie, W. Fox, P. M'Queen, B. Collins, E. Newbery, and R. Jameson, 1789.
Vol. 1: [4],322,[2]p.; vol. 2: [4],304p.; vol. 3: [4],319,[1]p; vol. 4: [4],264,[28]p., port. in vol. 1; frontispiece plates to vols. 2–4, 12mo. With an advertisement in vol. 1. Price: 12s.
This edition is not noted in BB, p. 28 (see Johnson's *Rambler* 1784, item 425).
ESTC t098573: L, P.P.5251.aa.
Miscellaneous. London syndicate.

727. Lavater, Johann Caspar, 1741–1801.
Essays on physiognomy, designed to promote the knowledge and the love of mankind. By John Caspar Lavater, citizen of Zurich, and minister of the Gospel. Illustrated by more than eight hundred engravings accurately copied: and some duplicates added from origi-

nals. Executed by, or under the inspection of, Thomas Holloway. Translated from the French by Henry Hunter, . . . London, printed for John Murray; H. Hunter; and T. Holloway, 1789–98. Vol. 1: [xii],[x],iv,[x],281p.; vol. 2: xii,238p. (part 1); [vi],[239]–444p. (part 2); vol. 3: xii,252p. (part 1); [vi],253–437,[8]p. (part 2), plates, ill.,ports., 4to. With half-titles.

1000 copies printed by Thomas Bensley. Vol. 2 dated 1792; vol. 3, 1798, both in two parts. With a 10–page list of subscribers in vol. 1 (743 names for 748 copies). Joseph Johnson owned a ¼ share though not named in the imprint (see Ch. 5, p. 83).

Issued in forty-one parts between Jan. 1788 and Mar. 1799. Copies in parts with printed wrappers note the publication date, the number of engravings and the price to subscribers (12s. per part). On the back wrappers are printed notes 'To the Subscribers' with commentary, binding instructions, etc. The information below is taken from a set of original parts in the Arents Collection of the New York Public Library.

Vol. 1. London, printed for John Murray; H. Hunter; and T. Holloway, 1789.

Part 1. January 1788: London, printed for John Murray; Henry Hunter, D. D. translator; and Thomas Holloway, the engraver.

2. March 1788: London, printed for John Murray; Henry Hunter, D. D. translator; and Thomas Holloway, the engraver. Sold also by G. Nicol; J. Walter; and J. Sewell (see Plates 21 and 22a).

3. May 1788: London, printed for John Murray; Henry Hunter, D. D. the translator; and Thomas Holloway, the engraver. Sold also by G. Nicol; J. and J. Boydell; J. Walter; and J. Sewell.

4. June 1788: same imprint.

5. July 1788: same imprint.

6. October 1788: same imprint.

7. November 1788: same imprint.

8. February 1789: same imprint.

9. May 1789: same imprint.

10. October 1789: same imprint.

Vol. 2. London, printed for John Murray; H. Hunter; and T. Holloway, 1792.

11. December 1789: same imprint.

12. March 1790: same imprint.

13. May 1790: London, printed for John Murray; Henry Hunter, D. D. the translator; and Thomas Holloway, the engraver. Sold

also by G. Nicol; W. Clark; J. and J. Boydell; J. Walter; and J. Sewell.

14. June 1790: same imprint.

15. August 1790: same imprint.

16. October 1790: same imprint.

17. December 1790: same imprint.

18. March 1791: same imprint.

19. May 1791: same imprint.

20. December 1791: same imprint.

21. December 1791: same imprint.

22. January 1792: same imprint.

23. April 1792: same imprint.

24. July 1792: same imprint.

Vol. 3. London, printed for Murray & Highley; H. Hunter; and T. Holloway, 1798.

25. December 1792: same imprint.

26. Januray 1793: same imprint.

27. April 1793: same imprint.

28. July 1793: same imprint.

29. September 1793: same imprint.

30. November 1793: same imprint.

31. January 1794: London, printed for Hester Murray; Henry Hunter, D. D. the translator; and Thomas Holloway, the engraver. Sold also by G. Nicol; W. Clark; J. and J. Boydell; J. Walter; and J. Sewell.

32. May 1794: same imprint.

33. May 1794: same imprint.

34. August 1794: same imprint.

35. October 1794: same imprint.

36. January 1795: same imprint.

37. April 1795: same imprint.

38. August 1795: same imprint.

39. March 1796: same imprint.

40. May 1797: London, printed for Murray & Highely, Henry Hunter, D. D. the translator; and Thomas Holloway, the engraver. Sold also by G. Nicol; W. Clark; J. and J. Boydell; J. Walter; and J. Sewell.

41. March 1799: same imprint.

The only account of this work in the Archive is recorded for the thirty-ninth number: 1000 copies printed; 500 sold Mar.–Sept. 1796 at 10s. each, wholesale. Stitching 1000 copies (at 1 gn. per hundred), 10 gns. (DB3, p. 241); stamp duty for the number, 6s.; 5 reams of tissue (at 9s./ream), £2.5s. (DB3, p. 168).

Religion. London co-publishing.

728. Lewis, Jenkin.

Memoirs of Prince William Henry, Duke of Glocester, from his birth, July the 24th, 1689,

to October, 1697; from an original tract, written by Jenkin Lewis, . . . and continued to the . . . Duke's death, July 29, 1700, . . . by the editor. London, printed for the editor, and sold by Mess. Payne; J. Murray; Messrs. Robson and Clarke: Messrs. Prince and Cooke, and J. Fletcher, Oxford, 1789.
vii,[1],116p., plate, music, 8vo.
ESTC t009532: L, 613.k.10(2).
Biography. Agency–London.

*729. M'Nayr, James, 1757 or 8–1808.
A system of English conveyancing, adapted to Scotland. By James McNayr, writer. Glasgow, printed by David Niven, 1789.
vii,[1],320p., 4to. Price: 12s.6d.
Monthly Review, 2 (June 1790), 'Murray &c.'
ESTC no23209: MH-L, S.Uk 916.7sc.MAC.
Law. Agency–provincial.

730. Mortimer, Thomas, 1730–1810.
The student's pocket dictionary; or, compendium of universal history, chronology, and biography, from the earliest accounts to the present time; with authorities. In two parts. Part I. Containing a compendium of universal history. Part II. Containing a compendium of biography. By Thomas Mortimer, Esq. The second edition, with considerable emendations and additions. London, printed for J. Johnson; and J. Murray, 1789.
[396]p., 12mo. With a half title and a final advertisement leaf.
3000 copies printed. In June 1789 Murray paid £53.2s.6d., a ¼ share of the expenses to Joseph Johnson. The returns on his share (750 copies at 2s.4d. each, wholesale) were £87.10s. Share sold May 1796 to Ogilvie for 10s.6d. (BB, p. 52). Stock: 146 (W). The advertisement is Joseph Johnson's 'Catalogue of books composed for the use of young persons'.
ESTC t087412: L, 10603.aa.18.
Education. London co-publishing.

731. [Ogilvie, John, 1732–1813.]
The fane of the druids. A poem. Book the second; . . . By the author of the first book. London, printed for J. Murray, 1789.
[6],38,[2]p., 4to. With a half-title and a final advertisement leaf. Price: 2s.
See Ogilvie 1787 (item 613) for Bk 1. Stock: 257 Bk 2; 150 of both (W).

ESTC t035357: L, 11630.d.4(12).
Poetry. Murray alone.

732. [Oswald, John, d. 1793.]
Poems; to which is added, The humours of John Bull, an operatical farce, in two acts. By Silvester Otway. London, printed by Macrae, for J. Murray, 1789.
xii,[5],20–62,[3],58–69,[6],80–137p., plate, 8vo. With a list of subscribers. Despite the pagination, the text is continuous. Price: 3s.
ESTC t212732: E, Hall.149.1.
Poetry. Murray alone.

733. Perfect, William, 1737–1809.
Cases in midwifery: principally founded on the correspondence of . . . Dr. Colin Mackenzie, with references, quotations, and remarks, by William Perfect, . . . In two volumes. Third edition. . . . Rochester, printed by W. Gillman, at the Phoenix Printing Office. And sold by Bew; Murray; and Foster, London, 1789.
Vol. 1: 400p.; vol. 2: 530p., plate, 8vo. Price: 12s.
ESTC no16020: MnU-B, B618.2.P416 1789.
Medicine. Provincial co-publishing.

734. Perry, Sampson, 1747–1823.
Observations on the stone, gravel, and all other calculous obstructions of the urinary passages, . . . By S. Perry, surgeon. London, printed for J. Murray; J. Bew; J. Southern; and Richardson, 1789.
[4],68p., 8vo. Price: 1s.
ESTC t186026: MRu, J15.4 P25.
Medicine. London co-publishing.

735. Perry, Sampson, 1747–1823.
Further observations on the stone, gravel, and all other calculous obstructions of the urinary passages, with additional proofs of the efficacy of a new discovery in the cure of these diseases. By S. Perry, Surgeon. London, printed for J. Murray; J. Bew; T. Becket; J. Southern; and Richardson, 1789.
[4],68p., 8vo. Price: 1s.
ESTC no03288: DNLM, 18th c.coll.
Medicine. London co-publishing.

736. The political magazine and parliamentary, naval, military, and literary journal, for the year, 1788. London, printed for J. Murray, and sold by every bookseller and news carrier in Great Britain.

Vol. 16: Jan.–June. [xv],504,[14]p., 8vo. With an index, plates, and maps.

Issued in monthly parts at 1s. each; 2000 copies printed (To John Trusler, 5 Oct. 1786). In July the periodical was taken over by Robert Butters, printer at 79 Fleet Street.

Primary location: CtY, Franklin. Col.

Miscellaneous. Murray alone.

*737. Rannie, John.

Poems. By John Rannie. London, printed for, and sold by G. Sael, at his circulating library, 1789.

[4],75,[1]p., 4to. Price: 3s.

English Review 14 (Sept 1789), 226–27: 'Murray'.

ESTC t042595: L, 11630.e.12(2).

Poetry. ?Agency–London.

738. Report from the committee appointed to examine the physicians who have attended His Majesty, during his illness, touching the present state of His Majesty's health. Ordered to be printed 13th January 1789. London, printed for J. Murray, 1789.

132p., 8vo.

ESTC no12656: MBCo, 19.S.308.

Medicine. Murray alone.

739. Richardson, William, 1743–1814.

Essays on Shakespeare's dramatic character of Sir John Falstaff, and on his imitation of female characters. To which are added, some general observations on the study of Shakespeare. By Mr. Richardson, . . . London, printed for J. Murray, 1789.

[4],96p., 8vo. With a half-title. Price: 2s.

In May 1796 the copyright was sold to Murray & Co (i.e. & Highley) for £15 (BB, p. 7). Stock: 317 (W).

ESTC t028217: L, 642.d.33.

Literary criticism. Murray alone.

740. Robinson, Pollingrove.

Cometilla; or views of nature. By Pollingrove Robinson, Esq. Vol. I. Being an introduction to astronomy. London, printed for J. Murray, 1789.

xv,[1],262p., 8vo. Price: 3s.3d.

Pollingrove Robinson may be a pseudonym.

ESTC t140633: L, 49.a.24.

Science. Murray alone.

741. Rollin, Charles, 1661–1741.

The ancient history by Charles Rollin, . . . In eight volumes. Containing an account of the Egyptians, Carthaginians, Assyrians, Babylonians, Medes and Persians, Macedonians, and Grecians. The eighth edition. Illustrated with a new and complete set of maps of ancient geography, neat engravings of Egyptian antiquities, &c. adapted to the work. Edinburgh, at the Apollo Press, by Martin and McDowall. Printed for A. Guthrie; and J. Murray, London. 1789–90.

Vol. 1: 15,424p.; vol. 2: 7,422p.; vol. 3: 7,444p.; vol. 4: 7, 485p.; vol. 5: 5,431p.; vol. 6: 5,514p.; vol. 7: 6,426p.; vol. 8: 4,402p. With plates, maps, 8vo.

A translation of *Histoire ancienne des Égyptiens*. Vols. 1–2 dated 1789; Vols. 3–8 dated 1790, with imprint: Edinburgh, printed by Mundell and Son; for A. Guthrie, and J. Murray, London. Stock: 2 (W).

ESTC t042518: E, NF.842.c.15.

History. Edinburgh co-publishing.

742. The second report and address of the Philanthropic Society; instituted September 1788, for the prevention of crimes. Containing remarks upon education, . . . London, sold by T. Becket; Messrs Robinsons; J. Johnson; J. Murray; T. Hookam; Messrs. White and Son; and Debrett, 1789.

xii,59,[1]p., 8vo. Price: 1s.

ESTC t047362: L, T.261(5).

Law. London co-publishing.

743. Spallanzani, Lazzaro, 1729–1799.

Dissertations relative to the natural history of animals and vegetables. Translated from the Italian of the Abbé Spallanzani, . . . In two volumes. A new edition corrected and enlarged. London, printed for J. Murray, 1789.

Vol. 1: ii, 391,[14]p.; vol. 2: iii,486,[20]p., 3 plates, 8vo. Price: 10s.6d.

Advertisement signed: Thomas Beddoes. A translation of *Opuscoli di fisica animale e vegetabile*. Printed by Simmons at Canterbury on 90 reams fine Demy (To Simmons, 15 Feb. 1788). Stock: 6 (H); 258 (W).

ESTC t131279: L, 973.g.2,3.

Science. Murray alone.

744. [Swinton, John, Lord Swinton.]

A proposal for uniformity of weights and measures in Scotland, by execution of the laws now in force. With tables of the English and Scotch standards, . . . The second edition. Edinburgh, printed for Peter Hill; and John Murray, London, 1789.
vii,[1],144, [1]p., 8vo. With a half-title. Price: 3s.6d.
ESTC no39788: KU-S, C7235.
Economics. Edinburgh co-publishing.

745. Thomas, Andrew, Clerk to Robert Herries and Co.
Tables of exchange to and from France from 25d to 28 15/16, the French crown. London, Murray, 1789.
royal 8vo. Price: 7s.6d.
No copy located. *English Review* 15 (Feb. 1790), 150–51. Stock: 142 (W)
Economics. Murray alone.

746. [Thomson, William, 1746–1817.]
Mammuth; or, human nature displayed on a grand scale: in a tour with the tinkers, into the inland parts of Africa. By the man in the moon. In two volumes. . . . London, printed for J. Murray, 1789.
iv,285; iv,320,[2]p., 12mo. With a final page of errata. Price: 6s.
ESTC no04435: MnU, 824.T387.OM.
Fiction. Murray alone.

747. Whitaker, John, 1735–1808.
Additions and corrections made in the second edition of Mary Queen of Scots vindicated. By John Whitaker, . . . London, printed for J. Murray; and W. Creech, Edinburgh, 1789.
xiii,[3],453,[1]p., 8vo. Price: 7s. in boards.
500 copies printed (To Whitaker, 12 Apr. 1790).
Stock: 45 (H); 332 (W).
ESTC t127853: L, 1609/660.
History. Edinburgh co-publishing.

1790

748. Ainsworth, Robert, 1660–1743.
An abridgement of the last quarto edition of Ainsworth's dictionary, English and Latin. . . . By Thomas Morell, . . . The third edition. London, printed by Charles Rivington, for J. Rivington and Sons, L. Davis, T. Payne and Son, T. Longman, B. Law, C. Dilly, G. G. J. and J. Robinson, T. Pote, T. Cadell, J. Johnson, J. Robson, W. Ginger, R. Baldwin, J. Sewell, J.

Nichol. J. Bew, S. Hayes, W. Goldsmith, P. Elmsley, J. Murray, W. Lowndes, W. Bent, G. and T. Wilkie, W. Otridge, Scatcherd and Whitaker, C. D. Piguenitt, C. Stalker, 1790.
[1150]p., 8vo.
8000 copies printed. Murray paid £4.7s.6d. for a 1/45 share at the late Wm Strahan's sale on 24 Mar. 1786. In Mar. 1790 he paid £17.16s. and in Oct. £18.10s.10d. for expenses of the edition. The returns on his share (178 copies at 5s. 8d. each, wholesale) were £54.18s.8d. Shares sold 23 Dec. 1794: 1/45 to Lowndes for £21.10s.; 1/80 to Davies for £12.17s. (BB, p. 44).
ESTC no42983: PPL, O Latin Ain 74916.O.
Language. London syndicate.

749. Aitken, John, d. 1790.
Essays on fractures and luxations. By John Aitken, M.D. . . . Illustrated with eleven plates. London, printed for T. Cadell, and J. Murray, 1790.
xi,[1],173,[3]p., plates, 8vo. Price: 4s.
ESTC no01886: DNLM, WZ260.A298er 17 90.
Medicine. London co-publishing.

750. Andree, John, c. 1740–c. 1820.
Considerations on bilious diseases: and some particular affections of the liver, and the gall bladder. The second edition, enlarged and improved By John Andree, M.D. London, printed for J. Murray; J. Johnson; W. Clarke; P. Hill, and Watson, Elder and Co. Edinburgh; A. Clarke and T. Simson, Hertford, 1790.
vii,[1],61,[3]p., 8vo. With a half-title. Price: 1s.6d.
ESTC to55931: L, 7306.df.21(2)
Medicine. Provincial co-publishing.

751. Baudelocque, Jean Louis, 1745–1810.
A system of midwifery: translated from the French of Baudelocque, by John Heath, . . . London, printed for the author, and sold by J. Parkinson; and J. Murray, 1790.
Vol. 1: xx,xlvii,453p.; vol. 2: xiii,473,[1]p.; vol. 3: [x],504p., plates (some fold.), 8vo. With half-titles. Price: £1.1s.
A translation of *Art des accouchemens*.
ESTC to91307: L, 1176.g.3–5.
Medicine. Agency–London.

752. Beddoes, Thomas, 1760–1808.
A guide for self preservation, and parental affection; or plain directions for enabling people to

keep themselves and their children free from several common disorders. By Thomas Beddoes, M.D. Bristol, printed by Bulgin and Rosser, for J. Murray; and J. Johnson, London, [1790?].

24p., 12mo.

Last date in text is 1788 (p.21); 3rd edn. dated [1794].

ESTC n017914: MH-H, Tr 2362*.

Medicine. London co-publishing.

753. Carmichael, James, of Edinburgh.

Various tracts concerning the peerage of Scotland, collected from the public records, original instruments, and authentic manuscripts; to which is annexed an appendix, containing many original papers . . . Edinburgh, printed for the editor, sold by Watson, Elder, and Company; and J. Murray, London, 1790.

[4],vi,[2],164p., 4to. Price: 7s.6d.

Entered in the Stationers' Company Register, 29 Jan. 1791, 'J. Carmichael. Whole'.

ESTC t062662: L, 600.i.16(4).

Miscellaneous. Agency–Edinburgh.

754. [Dalrymple, Sir David, 1726–1792.]

The little freeholder, a dramatic entertainment, in two acts. London, printed for J. Murray; and A. Guthrie, Edinburgh. Anno, 1790.

[4],63,[1]p., 8vo. Price: 1s.6d.

Variant copies have a dagger added to the signature on A1. Entered in the Stationers' Company Register, 30 Oct. 1790, 'A. Guthrie'.

ESTC t055515: L, 643.e.19(4).

Drama. Edinburgh co-publishing.

755. De Lolme, Jean Louis, 1740–1806.

The constitution of England; or, an account of the English government: in which it is compared, both with the republican form of government, and the other monarchies in Europe. By J. L. de Lolme, . . . A new edition, corrected. London, printed for G. G. J. and J. Robinson; and J. Murray, 1790.

[8],xv,[1],540,[20]p., plate, port., 8vo. Price: 7s. 500 copies printed, some large paper. Murray paid Robinson £43.1s. for paper and printing. The returns on his share (250 copies at 4s.8d., each, wholesale) were £58.16.8d. For 63 large paper copies at 7s.6d. each, wholesale, the returns were £23.12s.6d. (BB, p. 24).

ESTC n003555: MH-L, UK 961.DEL.

History. London co-publishing.

756. Donaldson, John, fl. 1790–1795.

Miscellaneous proposals for increasing our national wealth twelve millions a year; and also for augmenting the revenue without a new tax, or the further extension of the excise laws. By John Donaldson, Esquire. London, printed for the author; and sold by J. Murray, 1790.

[6],viii,58p., 8vo. Price: 1s.6d.

Entered in the Stationers' Company Register, 14 July 1790, 'Author. Whole'.

ESTC t039432: L, E.2064(7).

Politics. Agency–Murray alone.

757. The Edinburgh magazine, or literary miscellany, . . . Edinburgh, Printed for J. Sibbald: and sold by J. Murray, London, 1790.

Vol. 11: 440,96,[2]p., 8vo. plates; vol. 12: [1],436,92,[2]p., 8vo. plates.

Published in monthly parts, title page, contents, and index issued every six months. Printed by Macfarquhar and Elliot, Edinburgh.

Primary location: E, NH 295.

Miscellaneous. Agency–Edinburgh.

758. The English review; or, an abstract of English and foreign literature. . . . London, printed for J. Murray, 1790.

Vol. 15: [1],[viii],480,[6]p., 8vo; vol. 16: [1],[viii], 480,[6]p., 8vo.

Published in monthly parts (priced at 1s.); title page, contents, and index issued every six months.

Primary location: NN, *DA.

Miscellaneous. Murray–with agency.

759. [Ettrick, William, 1756 or 7–1847.]

The blunders of loyalty, and other miscellaneous poems; being a selection of certain ancient poems, . . . Together with the original notes and illustrations, &c. The poems modernized by Ferdinando Fungus, gent. London, printed for J. Murray, 1790.

44p., 4to. Price: 2s.6d.

See 'Fungus' below.

ESTC t125900: L, 11660.c.15.

Poetry. Murray alone.

760. Ferguson, James, 1710–1776.

Astronomy explained upon Sir Isaac Newton's principles, and made easy to those who have not studied mathematics. To which are added, a plain method of finding the distances of all the planets from the sun, . . . By James Ferguson, . . . The eighth edition. London, printed for J. F. and C. Rivington, T. Longman, B. Law, J. Johnson, G. G. J. and J. Robinson, T. Cadell. J. Bew, J. Murray, R. Baldwin, W. Lowndes, W. Bent, and J. Evans, 1790.

[8],503,[17]p., plates, 8vo. With an index. Price: 9s.

2000 copies printed. Murray bought a 1/24 share on 8 Apr. 1777 at the Queen's Arms for £8.15s. On 3 Feb. Murray paid Thomas Cadell (who organised the edition) £11.17s.6d. for paper and printing. The returns on his share (84 copies at 5s.5d. each, wholesale) were £32.2s. Shares sold 23 Dec. 1794: 1/48 to Scatcherd for £3.5s.; 1/48 to Vernor for £3.5s. (BB, p. 2; see Ferguson 1778, item 183, and 1785, item 471).
ESTC to18588: L, 531.i.7.
Science. London syndicate.

*761. Fungus, Ferdinando.
New facts, or the White-washer, or the second part of Gabriel Outcast. Being an ancient poem, revis'd and now first published by Ferdinando Fungus, gent. [London], Printed in 1790.
[2],xvi,3–24p., 8vo. Price: 1s.6d.
Ferdinando Fungus is sometimes identified as William Ettrick, Gabriel Outcast as Robert Burd Gabriel. Monthly Review 1 (Mar. 1790), 339: 'Murray.'
ESTC to39840: L, 11641.bb.29.
Poetry. Murray alone.

762. Goldsmith, Oliver, 1728–1774.
The history of England, from the earliest times to the death of George II. By Dr. Goldsmith. The sixth edition, corrected. . . . London, printed for L. Davis, J. F. and C. Rivington, T. Payne and Son, B. Law, G. G. J. and J. Robinson, W. Richardson, T. Cadell, J. Murray, J. Sewell, R. Baldwin, S. Hayes, and E. Newbery, 1790.
Vol. 1: [2],viii,411,[33]p.; vol. 2: [2],434,[32]p.; vol. 3: [2],413,[27]p., plate, port., 8vo. Price: £1.1s.
1500 copies printed. In 1778 Murray paid George Robinson £3.13s.6d. for a 1/24 share bought at the Globe Tavern. In March 1790 he paid £17.3s. for paper and printing. The returns on his share (63 copies at 13s. each, wholesale)

were £40.19s. (BB, p. 13; Goldsmith, 1779, 1784, 1787). Shares sold Dec. 1794 to Richardson for £5.15s. (BB, p. 13).
ESTC no17554: ICU, DA32.G6.
History. London syndicate.

*763. [Grant, James, 1743–1835].
A letter, addressed to the heritors or landed proprietors of Scotland, holding their lands of subject superiors, or mediately of the Crown. Edinburgh, printed for Peter Hill, 1790.
[2],37,[1]p., 8vo. Price: 1s.6d.
Signed at end: Scoto-Britannus, i.e. James Grant.
English Review 17 (June 1791), 270–74, 'John Murray, London'.
ESTC t147359: L, Cup.407.ff.1
Law. Edinburgh co-publishing.

764. Gray, Thomas, 1716–1771.
Poems. By Mr. Gray. A new edition. London, printed for J. Murray, 1790.
[2],178p., 7 plates, 8vo.
Stock: 682 (240 without plates) (H).
ESTC t124973: L, 11631.bbb.17.
Poetry. Murray alone.

765. Hamilton, James Edward.
A letter to the people of England, upon the present crisis; by James Edward Hamilton, Esq;. London, printed for the author, and sold by J. Debrett, Richardson, Dilly, Johnson, Murray, [1790].
[2],15,[1]p., 8vo.
Entered in the Stationers' Company Register, 26 May 1790, 'Author. Whole'.
ESTC to11096: L, E.2064(8).
Politics. Agency–London.

766. Happiness, a poem. London, printed, and sold by J. Ridgeway, and J. Murray, 1790.
19,[1]p., ill., 4to. Price: 1s.6d.
ESTC t192540: O, G.Pamph.1704(13).
Poetry. London co-publishing.

767. Hederich, Benjamin, 1675–1748.
Graecum lexicon manuale, primum a Benjamine Hederico institutum: dein post repetitas Sam. Patricii curas, auctum myriade amplius verborum: postremo innumeris vitiis repurgatum, plurimisque novis significatibus verborum locupletatum cura Io. Augusti Ernesti: et nunc

iterum recensitum, et quam plurimam in utra-
que parte auctum a T. Morell, . . . Editio nova,
prioribus longè emendatior. Londini, excudit
H.S. Woodfall, impensis, J.F. & C. Rivington,
T. Longman, B. Law, T. Pote, J. Johnson, C.
Dilly, G. G. J. and J. Robinson, T. Cadell, W.
Ginger, J. Bew, R. Baldwin, J. Murray, W.
Lowndes, S. Hayes, P. Elmsley, W. Otridge, G.
and T. Wilkie, J. Evans, & W. Lepard, 1790.
viii,[828]p., 4to. Price: 1 gn. bound.
3000 copies printed. Murray bought a 1/64
share at the Queen's Arms sale on 25 Jan.
1776 for £8.17s.6d, which he paid to Thomas
Becket. Production costs for the edition were
£11.8s. The returns on his share (47 copies at
14s. each, wholesale) were £37.11s. Share sold
May 1796: 1/64 to Richardson for £3.10s. (BB,
p. 3; Hederich 1778, item 187). Stock: 2 (H); 4
(W).
ESTC t142062: L, 1562/255.
Language. London syndicate.

*768. Henry, the Minstrel, fl. 1470–1492.
The metrical history of Sir William Wallace,
Knight of Ellerslie, by Henry, commonly called
Blind Harry: carefully transcribed from the M.S.
copy of that work, in the Advocates' Library,
under the eye of the Earl of Buchan. . . . In
three volumes. . . . Perth, printed by R.
Morison junior, for R. Morison and Son, 1790.
Vol. 1: [viii],146p.; vol. 2: 171,[12]p.; vol. 3:
90,61,[6]p., plates, port., 12mo. With a list of
subscribers in vol. 3. Price: 6s.
English Review 17 (Feb. 1791), 100–103, 'J.
Murray London'. A copy in its original printed
wrappers gives the additional imprint: 'and sold
by John Murray, London; George Mudie &
Peter Hill, Edinburgh; William Coke, Leith;
James Duncan Senior, Glasgow; Angus &
Son, Aberdeen; and the other Booksellers in
the Kingdom'. Based on the Latin prose history
of Wallace by John Blair.
ESTC t071686: L, 1479.a.2.
Poetry. Provincial co-publishing.

769. Homer.
Homeri Ilias, Graece et Latine. Annotationes in
usum serenissimi principis Gulielmi Augusti,
ducis de Cumberland, &s. regio jussu scripsit
atque edidit Samuel Clarke, S.T.P. . . . Editio
undecima. Londini, impensis J. F. C. Rivington,
B. & B. White, T. Longman, B. Law, G. G. J. & J.

Robinson, J. Johnson, R. Baldwin, T. Pote, J.
Nichols, G. Richardson, J. Bew, J. Murray, S.
Hayes, Scatcherd & Whitaker, G. & T. Wilkie,
E. Newbery, & J. Evans 1790.
Vol. 1: [1],vii,510p.; vol. 2: [1],iii,510,[16]p., plate,
map. 8vo.
Murray bought a 1/48 share at Caslon's sale on
5 June 1783 for 3 gns. On 14 Dec. 1789 he paid
Wright & Gill 4 gns. and on 19 May 1790 he
made out a six-month note to Rivington for
£6.2s.6d. The returns on his share (42 copies at
7s.6d. each, wholesale) were £15.8s. Share sold
Dec. 1794 to Lowndes for 5 gns. (BB, p. 32).
ESTC ID. N008366: ViLxW, Rare PA4019.A2
1790.
Poetry. London syndicate.

770. [Inglefield, John Nicholson, 1748–1828.]
A short account of the naval actions of the last
war; in order to prove that the French nation
never gave such slender proofs of maritime
greatness as during that period; with observations on the discipline, . . . of the British navy.
The second edition. By an officer. London,
printed for J. Murray, 1790.
viii,147,[1]p., plates, maps, 8vo. With a half-title.
See Inglefield 1788, item 664. Stock: 376 (W).
ESTC t072998: L, 1397.d.21.
Military. Murray alone.

771. [Innes, William, *c.* 1720–1795].
The slave-trade indispensable: in answer to the
speech of William Wilberforce, Esq. on the 13th
of May, 1789. By a West-India-merchant.
London, sold by W. Richardson; J. Murray;
and J. Debrett, 1790.
[2],77,[3]p., 8vo.
ESTC n021364: MnU, Y326.1.In6.
Politics. London co-publishing.

772. Johnson, Samuel, 1709–1784.
A dictionary of the English language: in which
the words are deduced from their originals,
explained in their different meanings, . . .
Abstracted from the folio edition, by the
author, Samuel Johnson, A.M. To which is prefixed, A grammar of the English language. The
ninth edition. London, printed for J. F. and C.
Rivington, L. Davis, T. Longman, B. Law, J.
Dodsley, C. Dilly, G. G. J. and J. Robinson, T.
Cadell, J. Robson, W. Goldsmith, J. Bew, J.

Murray, R. Baldwin, S. Hayes, G. and T. Wilkie, and C. Stalker, 1790.
2 vols. [1032]p., 8vo. Price: 12s.
5000 copies printed. Murray bought a 1/80 share at the Globe Tavern (John Crowder's sale) on 10 Sept. 1777 for £17 which he paid to George Robinson on 16 Jan. 1778; on 17 Mar. 1778 he bought an additional 1/80 share at the Globe for £16; on 12 Sept. 1780 he bought a 1/160 share for £6.10 from the estate of the late Wm Davis; and on 10 May 1783 he bought a 1/40 share (John Ridley's) for £24 paid to Thomas Evans. On 19 Jan. 1790 he paid Thomas Longman £54.4s.10d. for paper and printing. The returns on his share (378 books at 5s. each, wholesale) were £99.10s. (See Johnson 1778, item 191, 1783, item 360, 1785, item 480, and 1786, ite, 532; BB, p. 10).
ESTC t083958: L, 1560/1920.
Language. London syndicate.

773. Johnson, Samuel, 1709–1784.
The lives of the most eminent English poets, with critical observations on their works. By Samuel Johnson. A new edition, corrected. In four volumes. ... London, printed for J. Rivington & Sons, L. Davis, B. White & Son, T. Longman, B. Law, J. Dodsley, H. Baldwin, J. Robson, C. Dilly, T. Cadell, J. Nichols, J. Johnson, G. G. J. and J. Robinson, R. Baldwin, H. L. Gardner, P. Elmsley, G. Nicol, Leigh & Sotheby, J. Bew, J. Murray, J. Sewell, W. Goldsmith, T. Payne, W. Richardson, T. Vernor, W. Lowndes, W. Bent, W. Otridge, T. & J. Egerton, S. Hayes, R. Faulder, J. Edwards, G. & T. Wilkie, W. Nicol, Ogilvy & Speare, Scatcherd & Whitaker, J. Evans, W. Fox, C. Stalker, and E. Newbery, 1790–91.
Vol. 1: iii,464p.; vol. 2: iii.452p.; vol. 3: [iii],436p.; vol. 4: [iii],491p., plate, port., 8vo. Price: £1.4s.
Vols. 1–2 dated 1790; vols. 3–4, 1791. On 10 Mar. 1791 Murray issued a note for £14.6s.8d. and received his share of the profits, £29.6s.8d. (40 sets at 14s.8d. each, wholesale). Some sets from this edition were used for the 1792 edition of Johnson's 'Works' (See Johnson 1779, item 250; BB, p. 43).
ESTC t116667: L, 1066.g.24–27.
Biography. London syndicate.

*774. [Kincaid, Alexander, editor]
A new geographical, historical, and commercial grammar; and present state of the several empires and kingdoms of the world. The whole executed on a plan similar to that of Will. Guthrie, Esq. By a society in Edinburgh. ... Edinburgh, printed for Alexander Kincaid, 1790.
Vol. 1: 576p.; vol. 2: viii,598,[2]p., plates, maps. 8vo. With an errata slip and directions. Price: 10s.6d.
Published in 18 parts. *Critical Review* 2 (May 1791), 73–80: 'Murray.' Also 'Murray' in *Monthly Review* 3 (May 1791) 73–4. Entered in the Stationers' Company Register, 23 Aug. 1790, 'No 8 to 16 of a New Geographical ... ' Stock: 26 (H).
ESTC t095404: L, 570.d.13.14.
Travel–topography. Agency–Edinburgh.

775. La Fite, Madame de, (Marie-élisabeth), 1750?–1794.
Reponses à démêler: ou, essai d'une maniere d'exercer l'attention. On y a joint divers morceaux, qui ont pour but d'instruire ou d'amuser les jeunes personnes. Par Madame de La Fite. Londres, chez J. Murray, 1790.
iv,271,[1]p., 12mo.
Entered in the Stationers' Company Register, 31 Dec. 1790, 'J. Murray. Whole' (see La Fite 1791, item 834). Stock: 85 (H); 508 (W).
ESTC t155260: L, 1031.c.3(1).
Education. Murray alone.

776. Le Couteur, John, 1761–1835.
Letters chiefly from India; containing an account of the military transactions on the coast of Malabar, during the late war: ... By John Le Couteur, ... Translated from the French. London, printed for J. Murray, 1790.
vii,[1],xiii,[1],407,[1]p., 8vo. Price: 6s. in boards.
Stock: 5 (H); 526 (W).
ESTC t092283: L, 802.h.14.
Military. Murray alone.

777. The London calendar, or court and city register, for England, Scotland Ireland, and America, for the year, 1790; ... A new edition, corrected to the 20th of February. London, printed for John Stockdale; and sold also by D. Steele, J. Murray, and T. Whieldon; R. Faulder, T. Booker, and T. Hookham; T. Cornell; Shepperson and Reynolds, and Smith and Gardner; J. Woodmason; J. Deighton, J. Strahan; W. Clarke; and C. Forster, [1790]. iv,21,[4],23–281p., 12mo. Price: 2s. bound. *ESTC* t139278: L, P.P.2506.K. Miscellaneous. London syndicate.

778. Macdonald, Andrew. 1755–1790. Twenty-eight miscellaneous sermons. By A. Macdonald, . . . The second edition. London, printed for J. Murray, 1790. viii,390p., 8vo. Stock: 825 (H); 44 (W). *ESTC* t226272: L, RB.23.a.10348. Religion. Murray alone.

779. [Mackenzie, Alexander, of Edinburgh.] A view of the political state of Scotland at the late general election. . . . Exhibiting the manner in which every peer, freeholder, and borough in Scotland voted at the late general election; with other interesting political information. Edinburgh, printed by Mundell and Son; for J. Ainslie; and P. Hill: and T. Cadell, Elliot & Kay, and J. Murray, London. Anno, 1790. viii,[2],55,[1],262p.,tables, 8vo. With a half-title. Price: 7s.6d. Entered in the Stationers' Company Register, 1 Dec. 1790, 'A. McKenzie & J. Ainslie'. *ESTC* t083148: L, 601.e.24. Politics. Edinburgh co-publishing.

780. Mayow, John, 1640–1679. Chemical experiments and opinions. Extracted from a work published in the last century. Oxford, at the Clarendon Press. Sold by D. Prince and J. Cooke, and J. Fletcher, Oxford. And J. Murray, London, 1790. [2],xli,[1],18,[2],63,[1]p., plates, 8vo. Extracts from *Tractatus quinque medico-physici . . . Studio Johannis Mayow,* Oxford, 1674, translated and edited by Thomas Beddoes, who signed the preface. *ESTC* t099158: L, 45.f.26. Science. Provincial co-publishing.

781. Milton, John, 1608–1674. Paradise lost. A poem, in twelve books. The author John Milton. The ninth edition, with notes of various authors, by Thomas Newton, . . . In two volumes. . . . London, printed for J. F. C. Rivington, L. Davis, B. White and Son, T. Longman, B. Law, J. Dodsley, C. Dilly, G. G. J.

and J. Robinson, J. Johnson, T. Cadell, J. Robson, J. Sewell, J. Knox, W. Otridge, J. Bew, J. Murray, R. Baldwin, E. Newbery, Scatcherd and Whitaker, W. Lowndes, G. and T. Wilkie, R. Ryan, B. C. Collins, 1790. Vol. 1: [24],lxxxvi,[26],510p.; vol. 2: 463,[184] p.,120 plates, port., 8vo. With an advertisement in vol. 2. 4000 copies printed. Murray bought a 1/80 share for £8.10s. on 17 March 1778 at the D. Cornish sale at the Globe Tavern. On 20 Feb. 1790 he paid Curtis £5.4s.6d. by a note at three months for paper and printing, and on 26 June he paid Dilly £1.1s.10d. for paper and printing. The returns on his share (19 copies at 18s. each, wholesale), paid on 20 Feb. were £7.12s. The returns on his share of the edition below (31 copies at 2s.3d. each, wholesale) were £3.7s.2d. 1/80 share sold May 1796 to Vernor for £3 (BB, p. 14). Stock: 7 (W). *ESTC* t133893: L, 11626.ee.10,11. Poetry. London syndicate.

782. Another edition. Printed from the text of Tonson's correction edition of M.DCC.XI. London, printed for J. F. and C. Rivington, L. Davis, B. White and Son, T. Longman, B. Law, J. Dodsley, J. Johnson, J. Robson, C. Dilly, G. G. J. and J. Robinson, T. Cadell, J. Nichols, R. Baldwin, J. Sewell, J. Knox, J. Murray, W. Lowndes, J. Bew, W. Goldsmith, W. Otridge, G. and T. Wilkie, R. Ryan, and E. Newbery, 1790. [3],vi–xxxv,[1],345,[1]p., plate, port., 12mo. Includes the life of Milton by Elijah Fenton. *ESTC* t133894: L, 11634.de.4. Poetry. London syndicate.

783. Montagu, Lady, Mary Wortley, 1689–1762. Letters of the Right Honourable Lady M—y W—y M—e: written during her travels in Europe, Asia, and Africa, to persons of distinction, men of letters, &c. in different parts of Europe. Which contain among other curious relations, accounts of the policy and manners of the Turks; . . . drawn from sources that have been inaccessible to other travellers. A new edition. To which are added, poems, by the same author. In two volumes. . . . London, printed for T. Cadell; J. Murray; and R. Baldwin, 1789 [1790].

Vol. 1: ix,[2],220p.; vol. 2: 272p., plate, port., 8vo.
The preface is signed: M.A., i.e. Mary Astell. The portrait is dated Jan. 14, 1790. 1000 copies printed. Murray paid £1.11s.6d. for a 1/8 share at Thomas Becket's sale on 21 Jan. 1779 at the Queen's Arms. In Feb. 1790 Murray paid £12.10s to Thomas Cadell for paper and printing. The returns on his share (125 copies at 3s. each, wholesale) were £18.15 (BB, p. 21; Montagu 1784, item 435). Stock: 12 (W).
ESTC t129187: L, 1607/4745.
Travel–topography. London co-publishing.

784. Morison, John, of Edinburgh.
Tables of interest, at 3, 4, 4½, and 5 per cent. From L.1 to L.10,000, in a regular succession of days, from 1 to 365, . . . Also, tables of exchange or commission, . . . By John Morison, . . . Edinburgh, printed for William Creech: and sold in London by J. Murray, and T. Kay, 1790.
[4],613,[1]p., 8vo.
ESTC t173094: E, ICAS.606.
Economics. Agency–Edinburgh.

785. The perfidious guardian; or, vicissitudes of fortune, exemplified in the history of Lucretia Lawson. In two volumes. . . . London, printed and sold by T. Wilkins. Sold also by J. Bew; T. Hookham; J. Murray; and W. Richardson, 1790.
Vol. 1: xi,206p.; vol. 2: 237p., 12mo. Price: 6s.
ESTC t127127: L, C.175.m.37.
Fiction. Agency–London.

786. Pott, Percivall, 1714–1788.
The chirurgical works of Percivall Pott, F.R.S. Surgeon to St. Bartholomew's Hospital. A new edition, with his last corrections. To which are added a short account of the life of the author, . . . and occasional notes and observations. By James Earle, Esq. . . . In three volumes. . . . London, printed for J. Johnson, G.G.J. and J. Robinson, T. Cadell, J. Murray, W. Fox, J. Bew, S Hayes, and W. Lowndes, London, 1790.
Vol. 1: viii,xlv,477,[3]p.; vol. 2: iv,487p.; vol. 3: vi,507,[32]p., port., 19 plates, 8vo. With Joseph Johnson's advertisements in vol. 1. Price: £1.4s.
?960 copies printed. Murray paid £9.2s.6d. for a 1/16 share at Thomas Evans's sale on 3 July 1784. In May 1990 he paid to Joseph Johnson £27.2s.6d. for paper and printing. The returns

on his share (60 copies at 14s. each, wholesale) were £42 (BB, p. 39). Entered in the Stationers' Company Register, 4 May 1790, 'J. Johnson & the rest of the Proprietors. Whole'.
ESTC t030599: L, 782.1.7–9.
Medicine. London syndicate.

787. Quin, Charles William, b. 1755.
A treatise on the dropsy of the brain, illustrated by a variety of cases. To which are added, observations on the use and effects of the digitalis purpurea in dropsies. By Charles William Quin, M.D. . . . . London, printed for J. Murray, and W. Jones, successor to L. White, Dublin, 1790.
227,[1]p., 8vo. With a half-title. Price: 3s.6d.
ESTC t008048: L, T.139(1).
Medicine. Provincial co-publishing.

788. Ray, John Mead.
A comprehensive view of various systems, philosophical, political & theological, from the creation to the present time, among patriarchs, pagans, mahomedans, Jews, & Christians. In which is shewn, I. Wherein the various parties agree. . . . III. What is right and wrong, . . . A new edition, with additions and improvements, from some years further observationsand investigations, and the remarks of the most learned and judicious of all professions. By J. M. Ray, L.L.O.O. P S.T.D. First printed in the year M.DCC.LXXXV. London, Sold by J. Murray, [1790?].
[2],320p., 8vo.
Dated on the evidence of a letter printed on the verso of the title leaf.
ESTC n052298: PPL, Ia.Ray.Log.2429.O.
Religion. Murray alone.

789. Ross, David, 1728–1790.
Proposals for publishing by subscription, in one volume, quarto, price one guinea, the history of the rise and progress of the English stage, from the first institution of a theatre in London, to the year 1790; with remarks and anecdotes of the principal actors; who were contemporaries with the author David Ross, late patentee of the Theatre-Royal, Edinburgh; . . . with many curious anecdotes never before published. A few copies will be printed on fine royal paper, price two guineas. Subscriptions taken in by John

Murray, Bookseller, Fleet-street, London. The names of the subscribers will be printed.
[1], Fo.
On 29 May 1790 James Boswell recorded in his journal that he spoke with Ross 'of a History of the English Stage which Ross was to publish by subscription'. Ross died on 14 Sept. 1790, and the work did not appear.
Primary location: CtY, Gen. MSS 89.
Drama. Murray alone.

790. Ruspini, Bartholomew, 1728–1813.
A treatise on the teeth: wherein an accurate idea of their structure is given, the cause of their decay pointed out, and their various diseases enumerated. To which is added, the most effectual method of treating the disorders of the teeth and gums, . . . By the Chevalier Ruspini, . . . A new edition: with an appendix of new cases. London, printed for the author, and may be had at his house in Pall-Mall; and of Mr. Johnson; and of Messrs. Kearsley and Murray, 1790.
90p., 8vo.
ESTC t089332: L, 1651/790.
Medicine. Agency–London.

791. Shakespeare, William, 1564–1616.
The plays and poems of William Shakspeare, in ten volumes; collated verbatim with the most authentick copies, and revised: with the corrections and illustrations of various commentators; to which are added, an essay on the chronological order of his plays; an essay relative to Shakspeare and Jonson; a dissertation . . . an historical account . . . by Edmond Malone. London, printed by H. Baldwin, for J. Rivington and Sons, L. Davis, B. White and Son, T. Longman, B. Law, H. S. Woodfall, C. Dilly, J. Robson, J. Johnson, T. Vernor, G. G. J. and J. Robinson, T. Cadell, J. Murray, R. Baldwin, H. L. Gardner, J. Sewell, J. Nichols, J. Bew, T. Payne, Jun., S. Hayes, R. Faulder, W. Lowndes, G. and T. Wilkie, Scatcherd and Whitaker, T. and J. Egerton, C. Stalker, J. Barker, J. Edwards, Ogilvie and Speare, J. Cuthell, J. Lackington, and E. Newbery, 1790.
11 vols, plates, ports., 8vo. £3.17s. in boards.
Vol. 1 is in two parts, each with separate title page, pagination and register. Murray described two issues, 'one in 11 thick vols. cr[own]; another in 7 vols. 12mo . . . sold for a Guinea

bound' (To James Sibbald, 4 Dec. 1790). 1000 copies printed (To Bell & Bradfute, 27 Nov. 1790).
1200 copies printed. Murray bought a 1/120 share at the Globe Tavern (D. Cornish's sale) on 17 Mar. 1778 for £9.15s. which he paid to George Robinson. On 14 Aug. 1781 at John Hinton's sale he purchased a 1/60 share for £7.17s.6d. and on 10 May 1783 he acquired a further 1/60 share (John Ridley's) for £9, which he paid to Thomas Evans. He paid £48.11s.6d. for paper on 19 Aug. 1788; for printing (to Henry Baldwin) £48.7s.6d. on 8 May 1790; and he issued a note for £20 on 13 Dec. 1790. Total expenses, £116.19s. The returns on his share (39 sets at £2.15s. each, wholesale) were £107.5s.; and on the 7 vol. edition (61 sets at 16s.4d. each, wholesale), £49.16s.4d. — both paid on 13 Dec. 1790. Total profit, £157.1s.4d. (BB, p. 12; see Shakespeare Plays 1778, item 201, and 1785, item 495). Apparently 1200 sets of each edition were printed, although Murray's share in each varied. Entered in the Stationers' Company Register, 24 Nov. 1790; names as in imprint. Stock: 11 sets of the 7-vol. edn. (W).
ESTC t138858: L, 11763.r.37.
Drama. London syndicate.

792. A short journey in the West Indies, in which are interspersed, curious anecdotes and characters. In two volumes. . . . London, printed for the author, and sold by J. Murray, and J. Forbes, 1790.
Vol. 1: 155p.; vol. 2: 161p., 8vo. Price: 5s. sewed.
ESTC t110820: L, 10480.aa.12.
Travel–topography. Agency–London.

793. Sonnets to Eliza, by her friend. London, printed for J. Murray, 1790.
iv,63,[1]p., 4to. Price: 2s.
Stock: 477 (W).
ESTC t207964: AWn, PR 5292 A1 e08(4to).
Poetry. Murray alone.

794. [Sterne, Laurence, 1713–1768.]
A sentimental journey through France and Italy. By Mr. Yorick. A new edition. London, printed by A. Strahan, for J. Johnson, G. G. J. & J. Robinson, T. Cadell, J. Murray, W. Lowndes, G. & T. Wilkie, Ogilvy & Speare, and W. Bent, 1790.
[4],251,[1]p., plates, ill., 8vo.

ESTC to14696: L, 1050.e.14.
1500 copies printed. Murray bought a quarter share for £51 on 21 Jan. 1779 at the sale of Thomas Becket at the Queen's Arms. He sold a 1/16 share to Thomas Evans on 28 Feb. 1780 for £13. In 1790 he paid Thomas Cadell £17.19s.4d. for paper and printing. The returns on his share (376 copies (half on fine paper at 2s. each, wholesale and half on coarse paper at 1s.1d.) were £28.14s.6d. (£18.10s. fine and £10.4s.6d. coarse). See BB, p. 18. Stock: 6 (H); 16 (W).
Fiction. London syndicate.

795. Sydney and Eugenia. A novel. By a lady. London, printed and sold by T. Wilkins, sold also by J. Bew; J. Murray; W. Richardson; and T. Hookham, 1790.
Vol. 1: [2],304p.; vol. 2: [4],322p., 12mo. Price: 6s.
ESTC t198975: MRu, R 54260.
Fiction. Agency–London.

796. Thomson, Frederick.
An essay on the scurvy: shewing effectual and practicable means for its prevention at sea. With some observations on fevers, and proposals for the more effectual preservation of the health of seamen. By Frederick Thomson, . . . London, printed for the author; and sold by G. G. J. and J. Robinson; C. Dilly; J. Murray; and T. and J. Egerton, 1790.
vii,[6],xii–xxiv,206p., 8vo. With a half-title. Price 4s. in boards.
ESTC to99794: L, 42.d.1.
Medicine. Agency–London.

797. Toleration and charity peculiar to the Christian religion. Written originally in French, (but never published), by A. B. Bishop of—, in Languedoc, to his friend, a bishop in Normandy. Translated by a friend to the author, and dedicated to the Rt. Hon. Charles James Fox. London, printed for J. Murray, 1790.
32p., 8vo. Price: 1s.6d.
ESTC t177104: O, 80 X 288(7)BS.
Religion. Murray alone.

798. [Trist, Jeremiah.]
Historical memoirs of religious dissension; addressed to the seventeenth parliament of

Great Britain. London, printed for J. Murray, 1790.
xvi,99,[1]p., 8vo. With a half-title. Price: 2s.
500 copies printed. Rev. Trist, at Veryan near Tregony, was a regular correspondent of Murray's (To Trist, 4 Aug. 1791).
ESTC to59441: L, 4135.bb.37.
Religion. Murray alone.

799. Walker, Robert, M.D.
An inquiry, into the small-pox, medical and political: wherein a successful method of treating that disease is proposed, the cause of pits explained, and the method of their prevention pointed out; with an appendix, representing the present state of small-pox. By Robert Walker, M.D. . . . London, printed for J. Murray, and W. Creech, C. Elliot, P. Hill, J. Elder, and G. Mudie, Edinburgh, 1790.
xvi,499,[1]p., 8vo. Price: 6s. in boards.
600 copies printed by Neill & Co. (To Walker; to Neill & Co, 17 Nov. 1789). Stock: 303 (W).
ESTC to60418: L, 41.e.13.
Medicine. Edinburgh co-publishing.

800. Whitaker, John, 1735–1808.
Mary Queen of Scots vindicated. By John Whitaker, . . . In three volumes. The second edition, enlarged and corrected. . . . London, printed for J. Murray, 1790.
Vol. 1: [1],xix,21–574,[12]p.; vol. 2: [1],522,xp.; vol. 3: [1],625,[15]p., 8vo. Price: 18s.
Stock: 3 (H); 554 (W).
ESTC to82377: L, 600.f.17–19.
History. Murray alone.

801. The works of the English poets. With prefaces, biographical and critical, by Samuel Johnson. . . . London, printed by John Nichols; for J. Buckland, J. Rivington and Sons, T. Payne and Sons, L. Davis, B. White and Son, T. Longman, B. Law, J. Dodsley, H. Baldwin, J. Robson, C. Dilly, T. Cadell, J. Nichols, J. Johnson, G. G. J. and J. Robinson, R. Baldwin, H. L. Gardner, P. Elmsley, T. Evans, G. Nicol, Leigh & Sotheby, J. Bew, N. Conant, J. Murray, J. Sewell, W. Goldsmith, W. Richardson, T. Vernor, W. Lowndes, W. Bent, W. Otridge, T. & J. Egerton, S. Hayes, R. Faulder, J. Edwards, G. & T. Wilkie, W. Nicol, Ogilvy & Speare, Scatcherd & Whitaker, J. Evans, W. Fox, C. Stalker, and E. Newbery, 1790.

75 vols, 8vo. Price: £11.5s. in boards.
Vols. 1–6 contain the lives of the poets; vols. 74–75, general index. Half-title to vol. 1: 'The works of the English poets. . . . In seventy-five volumes'.

Murray originally acquired a 2/100 share at the Chapter Coffee House. On 29 Oct. 1778 he paid George Robinson £31 for a further 1/100 share; on 18 June 1783 he paid Stanley Crowder £18 for a 1/25 share; and on 5 June 1783 he bought a 1/50 share at the Caslon sale for £9.17s.6d. On 1 Nov. 1788 Murray issued notes at three and four months to the stationers Thomas Wright and Wm Gill for paper amounting to £160 and paid a further £16 in 'cash for incidents'. Murray sold shares in Nov. 1789: 1/100 to Wm Goldsmith for £6; 3/100 to Wm Richardson for £19.10s. Both men paid Murray £22 per share for the advance he had paid on the paper. On 22 March 1790 Murray issued four notes (at two, three, four and five months) for printing expenses totalling £198.17s.6d. The returns on his share (60 sets of 75 volumes at £7 each set, wholesale) were £420. In addition he received £9, the value of ten copies of a 9 vol. set (18s. each, wholesale). Murray's nett profit on the edition was £133.16s. His shares (4/100ths) were sold individually on 23 Dec. 1794: three at £2.5s.6d. each and one at £1.5s. — £8.1s.6d. in total (BB, p. 11; Plates 18–19; *The Works* 1779, item 250). Shares sold Dec. 1794: 1/100 to J. Walker for £1.5s.; 1/100 to Stockdale for £2.5s.6d.; 1/100 to Scatcherd for £2.5s.6d.; 1/100 to Otridge for £2.5s.6d. Stock: 11 sets (W).
ESTC t152606: L, 237.d.1–39 and 238.d.1–36
Poetry. London syndicate.

802. Young, Robert, social reformer.
Essays and reflections on various subjects of politics and science. By Robert Young. London, sold by T. Becket; Messrs. Robinson; J. Johnson; J. Murray; Debrett Messrs. White and Son; and T. Hookham, 1790.
Pp.viii,1–136, 8vo.
Published in parts.
ESTC t121809: L, 1609/2473.
Politics. London co-publishing.

1791

803. Abercrombie, John, 1726–1806.
Every man his own gardener. Being a new and much more complete gardener's kalendar, . . . than any one hitherto published. . . . By Thomas Mawe, . . . John Abercrombie, . . . and other gardeners. The thirteenth edition, corrected, and greatly enlarged, . . . London, printed for J. F. and C. Rivington, T. Longman, B. Law, J. Johnson, G. G. J. and J. Robinson, T. Cadell, W. Goldsmith, R. Baldwin, J. Murray, E. Newbery, and W. Lowndes, 1791.
[4],616,[20]p., 12mo. Price: 5s.
5000 copies printed. Murray paid Thomas Cadell 12 gns. for a 1/32 share bought at Thomas Evans's sale on 3 July 1784. In March 1788 Murray paid £11.2s.9d. for paper and printing. The returns on his share (157 copies at 2s.11d. each, wholesale) were £22.17s.11d. Shares sold May 1796: 1/64 to Rivington for £10.15s; 1/64 to Kay for 11 gns (BB, p. 37; see Abercrombie 1784, item 392, 1787, item 560, and 1788, item 628). Stock: 27 (W).
ESTC to33568: L, 1508/848
Agriculture. London syndicate.

804. Anderson, Walter, 1723–1800.
The philosophy of ancient Greece investigated, in its origin and progress, to the aeras of its greatest celebrity, in the Ionian, Italic, and Athenian schools: . . . By Walter Anderson, . . . Edinburgh, printed by Smellie. Sold in London, by C. Dilly; G. G. J. and J. Robinsons; J. Johnson; J. Murray; T. Payne; G. Nicol; J. Debrett; and J. Clarke, 1791.
[2],xiv,588p., 4to. With a half-title and errata. Price: £1.5s
A variant has the final page misnum. 88.
ESTC to87876: L, 29.e.16.
Philosophy. London co-publishing.

805. Bell, Benjamin, 1749–1806.
A system of surgery. By Benjamin Bell, . . . Illustrated with copperplates. . . . The fifth edition. Edinburgh, printed for Bell & Bradfute; and G. G. J. and J. Robinson, and J. Murray, London, 1791.
Vol. 1: 568p.; vol. 2: iv,[9]–488p.; Vol. 3: viii,540p.; vol. 4: 422,[2]p.; vol. 5: 564p.; vol. 6: 529,[1]p., plates, port., 8vo. Price: £2.9s. (with next)
1500 copies printed at Edinburgh by Neill & Co.. In Sept. 1790 Murray paid £258 for a ¼ share at Charles Elliot's estate sale at Edinburgh, and he received copies in varying

numbers of vols. 2–6. He paid £227 for his share of Demy paper (£117.7s.2d.), printing (£57.9s.6d.), printing plates (£15.8s.), Demy paper for plates (£11.16s.6d.), payment to the author (£25), engraved head of Bell (£3.3s.), payment to Lizars (£15.8s) and other expenses (£9.7s.3d.). The returns on share (375 copies at 24s. each, wholesale) were £400. Murray sold this work together with the following item. Shares sold May 1796: 1/8 to Murray for £126; 1/16 to Kay for £65; 1/16 to Cawthorn for £65 (BB, p. 59). Vol. 1 originally entered in the Stationers' Company Register, 10 Jan. 1783, 'C. Elliot, the whole'; vol. 5 entered 17 Mar. 1787, 'C. Elliot. Whole'; vol. 6, 6 May 1788, 'Chas. Elliot. Whole'. Stock: 10 vol. 2; 10 vol. 4; 13 vol. 5 (H); 90 vol. 6, 29 without 'cuts' (W). *ESTC* t121335: L, 1609/566.
Medicine. Edinburgh co-publishing.

806. Bell, Benjamin, 1749–1806.
A treatise on the theory and management of ulcers: with a dissertation on white swellings of the joints. To which is prefixed, an essay on the chirurgical treatment of inflammation and its consequences. By Benjamin Bell, ... A new edition. Edinburgh, printed for Bell & Bradfute; and for G. G. J. & J. Robinson, and J. Murray, London, 1791.
486,[2]p., plate, 8vo. With a final advertisement leaf. Price: 6s.
1500 copies printed. In Sept. 1790 Murray paid £43 for a ¼ share at Charles Elliot's estate sale at Edinburgh. The returns on his share (375 copies at 4s. each, wholesale) were £75 (BB, pp. 52, 60). Bell & Bradfute ledger 6, item 285, records the purchase of 56 reams of paper from Charles Cowan between 23 Apr. and 25 July, for £39 supplied to the printer David Willison (Edinburgh City Archive). Originally entered in the Stationers' Company Register, 30 Apr. 1778, 'The Author. The Whole'. Stock: 15 (H); 83 (W).
ESTC t099024: L, 1188.c.37(1).
Medicine. Edinburgh co-publishing.

807. Bell, John, 1763–1820.
An inquiry into the causes which produce, and the means of preventing diseases among British officers, soldiers, and others in the West Indies. Containing observations on the ... action of spirituous liquors on the human body; on the use of malt liquor, and on salted provisions; ... By John Bell, ... London, printed for J. Murray, 1791.
xv,[1],180p., 8vo. Price: 3s.3d.
ESTC n002391: DNLM, W6.P3 v.1158 no.2.
Medicine. Murray alone.

808. Boyer, Abel, 1667–1729.
Boyer's Royal dictionary abridged. In two parts, I. French and English II. English and French. ... The seventeenth edition, carefully corrected ... By J. C. Prieur. London, printed for Messrs. Rivingtons, Pote, Longman, Law, Pritchard, Robson, Dilly, Johnson, Elmsley, Ginger, Robinson, Cadell, Richardson, Baldwin, Stuart, Domville, Sewell, Goldsmith, Murray, Hayes, Lowndes, Scatcherd and Whitaker, Egertons, W. Bent, G. and T. Wilkie, and P. Wynne, 1791.
[402]p.; [512]p.,table, 8vo.
In two parts each with separate register; unpaginated throughout. Reference: Alston xii. 690. Stock: 29 (W).
ESTC t145178: L, 1560/1919.
Language. London syndicate.

809. Brookes, Richard, fl. 1721–1763.
The general gazetteer: or, compendious geographical dictionary. Containing a description of all the empires, ... chief towns, ... harbours, ... and promontories in the known works; together with the governemnt, policy, ... of the inhabitants; ... Embellished with nine maps. By R. Brookes, M. D. The seventh edition, improved, with additions and corrections. London, printed for J. F. C. Rivington, F. Power and Co. and J. Johnson; G. G. J. J. Robinson, R. Baldwin, J. Bent; B. Law. T. Lowndes; J. Murray; C. Dilly; T. Vernor; and S. Hayes, 1791.
xvi,[696]p., plates, maps, 8vo. With five pages of advertisements. Price: 7s.
3000 copies printed. Murray bought a 103/3000 share on 8 Apr. 1777 at the Queen's Arms and paid 5 gns. to Edward Johnston. On 12 May he paid £23.10s.3d. for paper and printing. The returns on his share (177 copies at 4s.4d. each, wholesale) were £37.1s. (BB, p. 1; see Brookes 1778, item 174, 1782, item 299, and 1786, item 512).
ESTC t151867: GOT, 8 Geogr. B87.
Travel–topography. London syndicate.

810. Carr, George, 1705–1776.

Sermons. By the late Rev. George Carr, . . . In two volumes. . . . The seventh edition. To which are prefixed, an elegant engraving, and some account of the author. Edinburgh, printed for Bell & Bradfute; and G. G. J. & J. Robinson, and J. Murray, London, 1791.

Vol. 1: x,[11]–414, [2]p.; vol. 2: iv,396p., 8vo. With advertisements in vol. 1. Price: 10s. boards.

1500 copies printed. Murray owned a ¼ share, purchased at the estate sale of Charles Elliot. Expenses: £44.3s.6d. (¼ of 160 reams Demy at 14s./ream, £29.9s.9d.; printing — £14.13s.9d. The returns on his share (375 copies at 7s.4d. each, wholesale) were £137.10s. Share sold May 1796 to Piguenit for £3.15s. (BB, p. 56). Bell & Bradfute ledger 6, item 158, records the purchase of 160 reams of Demy paper from Charles Cowan between 25 Oct. and 30 Nov. for £112. item 348 records that David Willison printed the work for £58.15s. (23s. per sheet, with a small additional charge for pica and small pica). A further notes states that the book 'required 167½ reams paper — besides 1 ream coarse for proof, tympan, & slip sheets' (Edinburgh City Archive). The advertisement lists 'Books printed for the publishers named in the imprint. Stock: 250 (W).

ESTC t121691: L, 1609/3772.

Religion. Edinburgh co-publishing.

811. Carter, George, 1737–1794.

A narrative of the loss of the Grosvenor East Indiaman, which was unfortunately wrecked upon the coast of Caffraria, . . . on the 4th of August, 1782, compiled from the examination of John Hynes, one of the unfortunate survivors. By Mr. George Carter, . . . with copper plates descriptive of the catastrophe, engraved from Mr. Carter's designs. London, printed at the Minerva Press, for J. Murray, and William Lane, 1791.

[4],174p., plates, 8vo. With a half-title. Price: 3s. 1250 copies printed by Lane, who had a half share. Expenses — £52.7s.3d. Returns — £56.14s. Murray sold 603 copies for £46.10s.; Lane sold 147 for £10.4s. Profit — £4.6s.9d. (BB, p. 50).

ESTC t136158: L, G.15731.

Travel–topography. London co-publishing.

812. Cullen, William, 1710–1790.

First lines of the practice of physic. By William Cullen, M.D. . . . In four volumes. With prac-

tical and explanatory notes, by John Rotheram, . . . Edinburgh, printed for Bell & Bradfute, and William Creech, Edinburgh; G. G. J. & J. Robinsons, and J. Murray, London, 1791.

Vol. 1: xii,448p.; vol. 2: viii,9–480p.; vol. 3: x,11–444p.; vol. 4: [1],viii,492p., 8vo. With half-titles. 1500 copies printed. Murray paid £54.10d. for a 1/6 share. Expenses: £84.9s.8d. The returns on his share (250 copies at 16s. each, wholesale) were £200. Bell & Bradfute ledger 6, item 251, for 25 Nov. 1791 records Smellie as the printer of vols. 1 and 3 and Patterson of vols. 2 and 4 on paper supplied by Strachan & Cameron at 16s. per ream — in all 394 reams costing £315.12s. (Edinburgh City Archive). Shares sold May 1796: 1/12 to Murray for £49; 1/12 to Longman for £51 (BB, p. 54). Stock: 41 and 33 (W).

ESTC n006779: DNLM, WZ260.C967f 1791.

Medicine. Edinburgh co-publishing.

813. [Andrew Dalzel, editor.]

Analekta Hellénika héssona. Sive collectanea Graeca minora: cum notis philologicis, atque parvo lexico: . . . Editio secunda emendatior. Edinburgi, excudebat Adamus Neill cum sociis. Veneunt ibidem, apud Bell and Bradfute, et Jacobum Dickson. Londini: apud Joannem Murray, 1791.

xii,100;87,[1];[96]p., 8vo.

The 'Nota' have separate pagination and the 'Parvum lexicon' is unpaginated. Stock: 2 (H).

ESTC t146290: L, 998.i.1.

Language. Edinburgh co-publishing.

814. [Defoe, Daniel, 1661?–1731.]

The life and strange surprising adventures of Robinson Crusoe, of York, mariner: who lived eight and twenty years all alone in an uninhabited island on the coast of America, near the mouth of the great river Oroonoque; . . . Written by himself. The seventeenth edition, adorned with cuts. In two volumes. . . . London, printed for J. F. and C. Rivington; T. Longman; B. Law; S. Bladon; J. Murray; W. Goldsmith; R. Baldwin; R. Faulder; J. Bew; Scatcherd and Whitaker; W. Lowndes, and G. and T. Wilkie, 1791.

Vol. 1: iv,[5]–288p.; vol. 2: iv,[5]–275p., plates, map, 12mo.

Title page to vol. 2: 'The farther adventures of Robinson Crusoe'. Murray bought a 1/16 share

for £4.10s at the sale of Catherine Caslon on 5
June 1783 at the Globe Tavern and a further
1/64th share at James Buckland's sale on 10
June 1790 for £1.11s.6d (BB, p. 33 and loose
sheet in BB; Defoe, 1784; see Plate 26). Stock:
4 (W).Stock: 20 (H); 124 (W).
ESTC t072292: L, 12611.h.3.
Fiction. London syndicate.

815. [Disraeli, Isaac, 1766–1848.]
Curiosities of literature. Consisting of anecdotes, characters, sketches, and observations,
literary, critical, and historical. London, printed
for J. Murray, 1791.
xi,[5],531,[13]p., 8vo. With a half-title and final
index. Price: 6s. in boards.
Entered in the Stationers' Company Register, 13
Feb. 1792, 'John Murray. Whole'.
ESTC t115852: L, 1087.e.6.
Literary criticism. Murray alone.

816. The Edinburgh magazine, or literary miscellany, . . . Edinburgh, Printed for J. Sibbald.
sold by Lawrie, Symington, and Co. Edinburgh;
and J. Murray, London, 1791.
Vol. 13: 526p., 8vo. plates; vol. 14: 528p., 8vo.
plates.
Published in monthly parts; the title page, contents, and index issued every six months.
Printed by Macfarquhar and Elliot, Edinburgh.
Primary location: E, NH 295.
Miscellaneous. Agency–Edinburgh.

817. The English review; or, an abstract of
English and foreign literature. . . . London,
printed for J. Murray, 1791.
Vol. 17: [1],[viii],480,[6]p., 8vo; vol. 18: [1],
[viii],480,[6]p., 8vo.
Published in monthly parts (priced at 1s.); title
page, contents, and index issued every six
months.
Primary location: NN, *DA.
Miscellaneous. Murray–with Agency.

818. Epistles, elegant, familiar, & instructive,
selected from the best writers, ancient as well
as modern; intended for the improvement of
young persons, and for general entertainment:
being a proper supplement to extracts in prose,
& in poetry. London, printed for Messrs.
Rivingtons, Longman, Law, Dodsley, Whites,
Johnson, Robinsons, Cadell, Murray, Richardson,

Baldwin, Bew, Goldsmith, Faulder, Hayes,
Ogilvy & Co. Scatcherd & Co. Vernor, Wynne,
Wilkie, Lowndes, Evans, & Kearsley, 1791.
[1],iv,[11],776p. 8vo. With an engraved title
page. Price: 9s. bound.
5000 copies printed. For his 6/100 share of the
expenses for this work, the *Extracts . . . in poetry*,
and the *Extracts in prose* (below) Murray paid
out £212.10s. (in four notes). On 7 Oct. 1791 he
received £285 (300 books at 19s. each, wholesale), a profit of £72.10s. (BB, p. 39).
Education. London syndicate.

819. Ewing, Alexander, d. 1804.
A synopsis of practical mathematics. Contain-
ing plain trigonometry, mensuration of heights,
. . . With tables of the logarithms of numbers,
and of sines and tangents. . . . By Alexander
Ewing, . . . Third edition. Edinburgh, printed
for J. & J. Fairbairn, and A. Guthrie; and sold by
T. Cadell, J. Murray, and J. Cuthell, London,
1791.
iv,272,[156]p., plates, 8vo.
ESTC t199044: E, NG.1202.d.9.
Science. Agency–Edinburgh.

820. Extracts, elegant, instructive, and enter-
taining, in poetry from the most approved
authors: disposed under proper heads: intended
to assist in introducing young persons to an
acquaintance with useful and ornamental
knowledge. London, printed for Messrs.
Rivingtons, Longman, Law, Dodsley, Whites,
Johnson,   Robinson,   Cadell,   Murray,
Richardson, Baldwin, Bew, Goldsmith, Faulder,
Hayes, Ogilvy & Co., Bent, Scatchert & Co.,
Vernor, Wynne, Wilkie, Lowndes, Evans, &
Kearsley, 1791.
Vol. 1: [viii],472p.; vol. 2: 472p., 8vo. Price:
10s.6d. bound.
Compiled by Vicesimus Knox. The title pages
are engraved, that to vol. 2 reading 'Extracts,
elegant, instructive, & entertaining, in verse;
books third, fourth, & fifth'.
5000 copies printed. See *Epistles* 1791, item 818;
BB. p. 39.
ESTC t129577: L, 1465.k.26.
Education. London syndicate.

821. Extracts, elegant, instructive, and entertaining, in prose; selected from the best modern
authors, and disposed under proper heads:

intended to assist in introducing young persons to an acquaintance with useful and ornamental knowledge. London, printed for Messrs. Rivingtons, Longman, Law, Dodsley, Whites, Johnson, Robinson, Cadell, Murray, Richardson, Baldwin, Bew, Goldsmith, Faulder, Hayes, Ogilvy & Co., Bent, Scatchert & Co., Vernor, Wynne, Wilkie, Lowndes, Evans, & Kearsley, 1791.

Vol. 1: [viii],472p.; vol. 2: 524p., 8vo. Price: 10s.6d. bound.

Compiled by Vicesimus Knox. The title pages are engraved, that to vol. 2 reading *Extracts, elegant, instructive, & entertaining, in prose, &c. Books third, fourth, & fifth.*

5000 copies printed. See *Epistles* 1791 item 818; BB, p. 39.

ESTC t142184: L, 12298.h.7.

Education. London syndicate.

822. Fielding, Henry, 1707–1754.

The virgin unmasked: a musical entertainment in one act; written by Henry Fielding, Esq. With the variations in the managers books at the Theatre Royal Drury Lane and Covent Garden. London, printed for T. Payne and Son, J. Nichols, G. G. J. and J. Robinson, T. Cadell, J. Murray, G. Nicol. S. Bladon, W. Lowndes, W. Nicoll, W. Fox, and Ogilvy and Speare, 1791.

24p., plate, 12mo. Price: 1s.

First published in 1735 as *An old man taught wisdom.*

ESTC t050923: L, 11777.b.8(3).

Drama. London syndicate.

823. Fraser, Simon.

Reports of the proceedings before select committees of the House of Commons, in the following cases of controverted elections; . . . heard and determined during the first session of the seventeenth Parliament . . . By Simon Fraser, . . . London, printed for J. Murray; and Whieldon and Butterworth, 1791–93.

Vol. 1: xiii,416,xxxiip.; vol. 2: [1],iv,xiv,456p., plates., maps, 8vo. Price: 6s.6d. in boards.

The separate title page to vol. 2 reads 'Reports of the proceedings . . . during the second session of the seventeenth Parliament . . . Vol. II.' and bears the imprint: printed for J. Murray, C. Dilly, E. and R. Brooke, Whieldon and Butterworth, J. Debrett, and T. and J. Egerton. 1793.

ESTC t130233: L, 228.e.21,22.

Politics. London co-publishing.

824. Gertrude; or, the orphan of Llanfruist. A novel. In two volumes. . . . London, printed and sold by T. Wilkins; sold also by Messrs. Robinsons, and H. D. Symonds, T. Hookham; J. Murray, and W. Richardson, 1791.

Vol. 1: [3],[xii],207,[1]p.; vol. 2: [4],269,[3]p., 12mo. With publisher's advertisement. Price: 6s.

ESTC n016948: CtY, Im.G328.791.

Fiction. London co-publishing.

825. Goldsmith, Oliver, 1728–1774.

The poetical and dramatic works of Oliver Goldsmith, M.B. A new edition. With an account of the life and writings of the author. In two volumes. London, printed by H. Goldney, for Messieurs Rivington, F. Power and Co. and E. Newbery; T. Cadell; W. Lowndes, and J. Murray; and J. Debrett, 1791.

Vol. 1: lxiv,120p.; vol. 2: viii,271p., plate, port., 8vo.

?1200 copies printed. Murray paid £9 for a 1/5 share bought at Thomas Evans' sale on 3 July 1784. In 1791 he paid £25.16s.2d. for paper and printing. The returns on his share (234 copies at 3s.10d. each, wholesale) were £44.17s. (see Goldsmith 1786, item 524; BB, p. 38). Stock: 88 (H).

ESTC t146130: L, 1608/4215.

Poetry (drama). London syndicate.

826. Higgins, William, 1763–1825.

A comparative view of the phlogistic and antiphlogistic theories. With inductions. To which is annexed, an analysis of the human calculus, with observations on its origin, &c. By William Higgins, . . . The second edition. London, printed for J. Murray, 1791.

[6],xiv,[2],316p., 8vo.

Stock: 40 (H) possibly including the 1789 edn.

ESTC t071356: L, 1489.tt.30.

Medicine. Murray alone.

827. The history of Jane Grey, . . . with a defence of her claim to the crown. London, printed and sold by T. Wilkins; sold also by H. D. Symonds; T. Hookham; J. Murray; and W. Richardson, 1791.

xii,168p., plate, port., 12mo.

Edited by Thomas Wilkins.

ESTC t117589: L, 1202.f.31.
History. London co-publishing.

828. Horace.
A poetical translation of the works of Horace,
with the original text, and critical notes collected from his best Latin and French commentators. By Philip Francis, D.D. In four volumes.
. . . The ninth edition. London, printed for T.
Payne and Son; J. Rivington and Sons; B. Law; J.
Johnson; G. G. J. and J. Robinson; T. Cadell; J.
Sewell; J. Murray; W. Richardson; S. Hayes; W.
Lowndes; and D. Ogilvy and Co., 1791.
Vol. 1: xx,247p.; vol. 2: [1],309,[2]p.; vol. 3: [1],
275p.; vol. 4: [1]267p., 12mo. With half-titles
and a list of 'Books printed for the Proprietors'
in vol. 2.
1500 copies printed. Murray paid £15.5s.6d. for
his 1/16 share. The returns on his share (94
copies at 6s.5d. each, wholesale) were
£29.13s.2d. Shares sold 23 Dec. 1794: 1/16 to
Kearsley for 10s.6d. (BB, p. 8). Stock: 20 (W).
ESTC t042734: L,E/03837.
Poetry. London syndicate.

829. Innes, John, 1739–1777.
A short description of the human muscles,
chiefly as they appear on dissection; together
with their several uses, . . . By John Innes. A
new edition. Greatly improved by Alex. Monro,
M.D. London, printed by E. Hodson, for J.
Murray; and J. Cuthell, 1791.
240p., 12mo.
Stock: 221 (W).
ESTC t111987: L, 7421.aaa.2.
Medicine. London co-publishing.

830. Jackson, Robert, 1750–1827.
A treatise on the fevers of Jamaica, with some
observations on the intermitting fever of America, and an appendix, containing some hints on
the means of preserving the health of soldiers
in hot climates. By Robert Jackson, M.D.
London, printed for J. Murray, 1791.
viii,424,115,[1]p., 8vo. Price: 6s.6d. in boards.
750 copies printed at Canterbury by Simmons &
Kirby at 18s. per sheet (to Hall & Elliot, 24 May
1791). Entered in the Stationers' Company Register, 21 Apr. 1791, 'J. Murray. Whole'. Stock:
340 (W).
ESTC t135519: L, 1168.h.9.
Medicine. Murray alone.

831. Keith, George Skene, 1752–1823.
Tracts on weights, measures, and coins. Viz. I.
Synopsis of a system of equalization of weights
and measures of Great Britain. . . . VI. Remarks
on Dr Rotheram's observations on the proposed plan for equalizing all our weights and
measures. By George Skene Keith, . . .
London, printed for J. Murray; and Cornelius
Elliot, Edinburgh, 1791.
20p., 4to. Printed in double columns. Price:
1s.6d.
ESTC n034491: CaOTU, Science Pam.
Economics. Edinburgh co-publishing.

832. Kentish, Richard, 1730–1792.
Advice to gouty persons, by Dr. Kentish. . . .
London, printed for J. Murray; and sold by J.
Johnson; T. Cadell, and P. Elmsly; T. Hookham;
and other booksellers in town and country,
1789 [1791].
[2],v[i.e.vii],[1],100p. (pp.ii and vii misnum. i and
v respectively), 8vo. Price: 1s.6d.
The dedication is dated July 1st, 1791.
ESTC n016245: DNLM, WZ260.K373a 1789.
Medicine. Murray–with agency.

833. Second edition:
ESTC t020979: L, 7620.b.44.
Medicine. Murray–with agency.

834. La Fite, Madame de, (Marie-élisabeth),
1750?-1794.
Questions to be resolved: or, a new method of
exercising the attention of young people. Interspersed with various pieces, calculated for
instruction and amusement. Translated from
the French of Madame de La Fite. London,
printed for J. Murray, 1791.
iv,273,[3]p., 12mo. Price: 5s. sewed.
A translation of *Reponses à démêler* (see La Fite
1790, item 775). Entered in the Stationers'
Company Register, 31 Dec. 1790. 'J. Murray.
Whole'.
ESTC t160013: L, 1031.c.3(2).
Education. Murray alone.

*835. Lanségúe, M. de.
A short compendium of ancient and modern
historical geography. Translated from the
French, and dedicated, . . . to Miss Billings,
by Mr. de Lanségúe. London, printed at the

Logographic Press; and sold by T. Cadell; Baldwin; B. Law; and J. Walter, 1791.
viii,480p., 8to. With a half-title. Price: 6s.6d.
Critical Review 2 (Mov. 1791), 360: 'Murray'. No French original found.
ESTC t114314: L, 570.d.16.
Miscellaneous. London co-publishing.

836. A letter from a Scotch nun, to a bachelor, containing the reasons why so few are married; with wholesome advices to both sexes in all ranks, how to get married, and that soon. London, sold by C. Dilly, and J. Murray, W. Creech and J. Hill, Edinburgh; J. Gillies and R. Morison, Perth; J. Duncan, Glasgow, 1791.
32p., 12mo. With a half-title.
ESTC t181054: E, 1928.20.
Miscellaneous. Provincial co-publishing.

837. Luckombe, Philip, d. 1803.
The beauties of England: giving a descriptive view of the chief villages, market-towns, and cities; . . . in England and Wales; . . . By Philip Luckombe. . . . The fifth edition, enlarged. London, printed for W. Richardson, J. Murray, W. Goldsmith, and R. Baldwin, 1791.
Vol. 1: xxiii,234p.; vol. 2: 384p., plate, map, 12mo.
1000 copies printed. Murray paid £10 for a ¼ share in Sept. 1791 at the sale of the late Lockyer Davis. In June he paid Charles Davis £33.16s.2d. as well as a 3 gns 'advance' to W. Goldsmith. The returns on his share (250 copies at 4s.8d. each, wholesale) were £58.6s. (BB, p. 53).
ESTC t124790: L, 1302.a.36.
Travel–topography. London co-publishing.

838. Macdonald, Thomas.
A treatise on civil imprisonment in England; with the history of its progress, and objections to its policy, as it respects the interests of creditors, and the punishment, or protection of debtors. . . . By Thomas MacDonald, . . . London, printed for J. Murray, 1791.
xxviii,196p., 8vo. With a half-title. Price: 4s. in boards.
Entered in the Stationers' Company Register, 21 Apr. 1791, 'J. Murray. Whole'. Stock: 296 (W).
ESTC t090689: L, 518.h.16(2).
Law. Murray alone.

839. M'Donald, Andrew, 1755?–1790.
The miscellaneous works of A. M'Donald; including the tragedy of Vimonda, and those productions which have appeared under the signature of Matthew Bramble, Esq. with various other compositions, by the same author. London, printed for J. Murray, 1791.
viii,358,[4],82,[2]p., 8vo. With a half-title. Price: 6s.6d.
Vimonda is made up from sheets of the 1788 edition (item 672). Entered in the Stationers' Company Register, 7 June 1791, 'J. Murray, Whole'. Stock: 256 (W).
ESTC t092414: L, 80.i.13.
Drama. Murray alone.

840. Millar, John, 1735–1801.
An historical view of the English government, from the settlement of the Saxons in Britain to the accession, of the House of Stewart. By John Millar, . . . The second edition. London, printed by A. Strahan, and T. Cadell; and J. Murray, 1790.
vii,[9],565,[19]p., 4to. With a half-title and index. Price: 18s. in boards.
750 copies printed. Expenses: paper (112 reams) — £118.2s.6d.; printing — £67.10s.; advertising — £29.19s.6d. On 5 June 1795 there were 570 remaining: Cadell, 305; Murray, 265 (BB, p. 45; see Millar 1787, item 611). Stock: 6 (H); 273 (W).
ESTC t113336: L, 522.k.36.
History. London co-publishing.

841. Motherby, George, 1732–1793.
A new medical dictionary; or, general repository of physic. Containing an explanation of the terms, and a description of the various particulars relating to anatomy, physiology, physic, . . . By G. Motherby, M.D. . . . The third edition. Revised and corrected, with considerable additions, by George Wallis, . . . London, printed for J. Johnson; G. G. J. and J. Robinson; A. Hamilton, jun. and J. Murray, 1791.
x,388,393–738,[14]p., plates, 2to. The last seven leaves contain the index and explanations of plates. Pp. 389–392 omitted in pagination; but text and register are continuous. Price: £2.5s.
1000 copies printed. Murray bought a 1/8 share in July 1778. In March 1791 he paid George Robinson £106.5s. for paper and printing. The returns on his share (125 copies at 36s. each)

were £219.12s.6d. Shares sold 23 Dec. 1794: 1/ 16 to Longman for £40; 1/16 to Wilkie for £40 (BB, p. 7; see Motherby 1785, item 484). Stock: 1 (H).
ESTC t061354: L, 1832.d.25.
Medicine. London co-publishing.

842. Musaeus, C. A.
Popular tales of the Germans. Translated from the German. In two volumes ... London, printed for J. Murray, 1791.
Vol. 1: [3],xi,264p.; vol. 2: [3], 284p. 12mo. Price: 6s. in boards.
A translation by Thomas Beddoes of Musaeus's *Volksgeschichte der Deutschen* for which Murray agreed to pay Beddoes 30 gns., plus 10 gns. more should there be a second edn. (To Beddoes, 23 Aug. and 22 Nov. 1790). Sometimes the translation is attributed to Wm Beckford. Entered in the Stationers' Company Register, 8 Feb. 1791, 'J. Murray, Whole'. Stock: 34 (H); 324 (W).
ESTC t178187: O, Douce T 123–4.
Fiction. Murray alone.

843. Pagès, Monsieur de, (Pierre Marie François), 1748–1793.
Travels round the world, in the years 1767, 1768, 1769, 1770, 1771. By Monsieur de Pagès, ... Translated from the French. ... London, printed for J. Murray, 1791–92.
Vol. 1: xiv,289p.; vol. 2: iv,261,[2]p.; vol. 3: xxiv,303p., frontis. fold. table, 8vo. Advertisements in vol. 3 Price: vols. 1–2, 8s.; vol. 3, 5s. in boards.
Vol. 3 dated 1792. Entered in the Stationers' Company Register, 8 Feb. 1791, 'Murray'; vol. 3 entered 29 Oct. 1792. Stock: 25 2–vol. sets (W).
ESTC t093539: L, 10025.c.7.
Travel–topography. Murray alone.

844. Perfect, William, 1737–1809.
A remarkable case of madness, with the diet and medicines, used in the cure. By William Perfect, ... Rochester, printed for the author, and sold by W. Gillman, J. Murray, J. Evans and C. Forster, London, 1791.
[2],26p., 8vo. Price: 1s.6d.
ESTC t163261: C, Hunter.d.79.13(3).
Another issue:
52,[2]p., 8vo. With an errata slip and a final advertisement leaf.

ESTC n022327: DNLM, WZ260.P446r 1791.
Medicine. Agency–provincial.

845. Richter, August Gottlieb, 1742–1812.
A treatise on the extraction of the cataract. By D. Augustus Gottlieb Richter, ... Translated from the German. With a plate; and notes by the translator. London, printed for J. Murray, 1791.
xv,[1],214,[2]p., plate, 8vo. With a final advertisement leaf. Price: 4s.
A translation of *Abhandlung von der ausziehung des grauen staars*. Entered in the Stationers' Company Register, 30 Dec. 1790, 'J. Murray. Whole'. Stock: 8 (H); 599 (W).
ESTC t117573: L, 1186.i.5.
Medicine. Murray alone.

846. Robertson, George, d. 1791.
Memoir of a chart of the China Sea; including the Philippine, Mollucca, and Banda Islands, with part of the coast of New Holland and New Guinea. ... By George Robertson. [London], Printed for the author, and sold by J. Murray, Fleet-Street, 1791.
vi,134,[2]p., 4to. With a half-title and final advertisement leaf.
ESTC t154198: L, Tab.7.117.
Travel–topography. Agency–Murray alone.

847. Rousseau, Jean-Jacques, 1712–1778.
A treatise on the social compact; or the principles of politic law. By J. J. Rousseau, citizen of Geneva. A new edition. London, printed for J. Murray, 1791.
[12],249,[3]p., 12mo. With a final advertisement leaf.
A translation of *Du contrat social*; a reissue of the 1764 edition printed for T. Becket and P. A. de Hondt, with a cancel title page. The three pages of advertisements are for books published by Becket and de Hondt. Stock: 82 (W).
ESTC t136473: L, 1608/4490.
Philosophy. Murray alone.

**848. Russell, John, 1710–1796.
Theory of conveyancing. The second edition. By John Russell, with an Appendix. Edinburgh, printed for C. Elliot, sold by J. Murray, London, 1791.
xxix,[1],536p. 8vo. Price: 6s.6d.
No copy located. *English Review* 18 (Dec. 1791),

434–5. First published in 1788 (*ESTC* t112853). Entered in the Stationers' Company Register, 11 Nov. 1788, 'Author. Whole'. Stock: 2 (H). Law. Agency–Edinburgh.

849. Schrevel, Cornelis, 1608–1644.
Cornelii Schrevelii lexicon manuale Graco-Latinum & Latino-Gracum: studio atque opera Josephi Hill, Johannis Entick, nec non Gulielmi Bowyer, . . . ad calcem adjecta sunt sententia Graco-Latina, . . . Item tractatus duo: . . . Editio XV, prioribus multo auctior et emendatior. Londini, ex officina M. Brown. Sumptibus J. F. & C. Rivington; T. Longman; B. Law; T. Pote; W. Ginger; S. Bladon; C. Dilly, J. Johnson; G. G. J. and J. Robinson; H. Gardner; R. Baldwin; J. Nichols; J. Murray; T. Evans; W. Goldsmith; W. Otridge; P. Wynne; S. Hayes; Ogilvie and Speare; W. Lowndes; Scatcherd & Whitaker; W. Bent; G. & T. Wilkie; et C. Stalker, 1791.
viii,[680],176p., 8vo.
6000 copies printed. On 5 June 1783 Murray paid £4.10s for 100 books in 4000 at the sale of Catherine Caslon. He issued a note at three months to Wright & Gill for £9.9s. and at six months to Brown for £10.9s.9d. for paper and printing. The returns on his 1/40 share (150 books at 4s.4d. each, wholesale) were £32.10s. (BB, p. 34). The share was sold to G. Wilkie in Dec. 1794 for £15.5s. Stock: 35 and 6 (H); 34 (W).
ESTC n003607: ScCC, PA442.S35 1791.
Language. London syndicate.

850. Tassie, James, 1735–1799.
A descriptive catalogue of a general collection of ancient and modern engraved gems, cameos as well as intaglios, taken from the most celebrated cabinets in Europe; and cast in coloured pastes, white enamel, and sulphur, by James Tassie, modeller; arranged and described by R. E. Raspe; and illustrated with copper-plates. To which is prefixed, an introduction on the various uses of this collection, the origin of the art of engraving on hard stones, and the progres of pastes. . . . London: printed for and sold by James Tassie, and J. Murray. C. Buckton, printer, 1791. [French title page] Catalogue raisonné d'une collection generale, de pierres gravées antiques et modernes, tant en creux que camées, . . . moulées . . . par Jacques Tassie, . . . mis en ordre et le texte rédigé par R. E.

Raspe. Orné de planches gravées. . . . Londres, imprimé pour J. Tassie, et se vend chez lui et chez J. Murray. C. Buckton, impremier, 1791.
[8],lxxvi,[2],800,12,50,13,[2]p., 58 plates, 4to. With half-title. Price: £1.16s. in boards. Parallel English and French title pages and texts. With a list of subscribers. Explanation slip pasted to the verso of the final leaf of the subscribers' list and errata leaf.
With three supplements, each with separate pagination and register: 'Liste des cabinets & noms de possesseurs', 'Liste des graveurs anciens & modernes', and 'A reference from the numbers of the old catalogue to the new'. For the subscription proposal, see Tassie 1788, item 693. Large paper copies were also produced (21 to subscribers).
ESTC t140781: L, 787.l.17.
Arts. Agency–London.

851. Taylor, William, Manager of the King's Theatre, Haymarket.
A concise statement of transactions and circumstances respecting the King's Theatre, in the Haymarket. By Mr. Taylor, the proprietor. Together with the official correspondence upon the same subject, between . . . the Lord Chamberlain, and Earl Cholmondeley, &c. London, published by J. Debrett; T. Beckett; and J. Murray, 1791.
[4],46p., 8vo. With half-title. Price: 1s.
ESTC t031125: L, 641.d.31(21).
Drama. London co-publishing.

852. The second edition:
[4],48p. (pp. 21–28 are wrongly imposed), 8vo.
ESTC t001292: L, 8140.e.41(8).
Drama. London co-publishing.

852a. The third edition.
ESTC n050811: CSmH, 148044.
Drama. London co-publishing.

853. Trist, Jeremiah.
Historical memoirs of religious dissension; addressed to the seventeenth Parliament of Great Britain. By Jeremiah Trist, . . . Second edition. London, printed for J. Murray, 1791.
xvi,99,[1]p., 8vo. With a half-title.
ESTC t102942: L, 4136.b.8.
Religion. Murray alone.

854. Wade, John Peter, d. 1802.
Select evidences of a successful method of treating fever and dysentery in Bengal. By John Peter Wade, M.D. . . . London, printed for J. Murray, 1791.
xiii,[3],335,[1]p., 8vo. With a half-title. Price: 6s. in boards.
Entered in the Stationers' Company Register, 26 Oct. 1791, 'John Murray, Whole'. Stock: 428 (W).
ESTC t069644: L, 1170.g.6.
Medicine. Murray alone.

855. Whitaker, John, 1735–1808.
Gibbon's History of the decline and fall of the Roman Empire, in vols. IV, V, and VI, quarto, reviewed. By the Rev. John Whitaker, . . . London, printed for J. Murray, 1791.
[4],258,[2]p., 8vo. With an errata slip pasted to the verso of the second leaf, and a final advertisement leaf. Price: 4s. in boards.
Entered in the Stationers' Company Register, 26 Oct. 1791, 'John Murray'. Stock: 51 (H); 644 (W).
ESTC t079436: L, 589.f.9(3).
Religion. Murray alone.

1792

856. An analysis of the medicinal waters of Tunbridge Wells. London, printed for J. Murray, 1792.
viii,31,[1]p., 4to. Price: 1s.
ESTC t162793: Lrcs, (R) CR8/ANA.
Medicine. Murray alone.

857. The Asiatic miscellany, consisting of translations, fugitive pieces, imitations, original productions, and extracts from curious publications. By W. Chambers, Esq. and Sir W. Jones, . . . and other literary gentlemen, now resident in India. Calcutta, printed. London, re-printed for J. Murray, 1792.
[4],196p., plate, ill., 8vo.
Extracts from the first two numbers of *The Asiatick miscellany* published in Calcutta in 1785 and 1786. Stock: 83 (W).
ESTC n015949: CtHT-W, PJ409.A8 1792.
Miscellaneous. Murray alone.

858. An astronomical catechism, for the instruction and entertainment of young gentlemen and ladies. By a minister in the country for

the use of his own children. London, printed and sold by T. Wilkins, sold also by H. D. Symonds, and J. Bew, J. Murray, W. Richardson, A. Hamilton, and Mr. Vey, Ringwood, 1792.
[2],iii,[1],53,[1]p., plate, 12mo.
The Preface is signed: J. D.
ESTC t066982: L, 8562.aaa.18.
Education. London co-publishing.

859. [Beddoes, Thomas, 1760–1808.]
Alexander's expedition down the Hydaspes & the Indus to the Indian Ocean. London, sold by J. Murray; and James Phillips. Also by J. Edmunds, Madeley, 1792.
[2],viii,48,49*–54*,[3],50–90p., ill., 4to. With a half-title.
An extra gathering signed H* is inserted before sig. H; the text is continuous. Engravings by Edward Dyas, parish curate of Madeley in Shropshire; text composed by the daughter of J. Edmunds of Madeley, who printed the work.
ESTC t210317: Di, MR 46 K 1.
Another issue: excludes J. Edmunds from the imprint.
ESTC t142758: L, C.57.f.15.
Travel–topography. Provincial co-publishing.

860. Blumenbach, Johann Friedrich, 1752–1840.
An essay on generation. By J. F. Blumenbach, M.D. . . . Translated from the German. London, printed for T. Cadell; Faulder; Murray; and Creech, Edinburgh, [1792].
x,[2],84p., 12mo. With a half-title. Price: 2s.6d.
The translator's preface is signed 'A. Crichton, Nov. 23d, 1792'.
ESTC t061381: L, 1173.k.6.
Science. Edinburgh co-publishing.

861. Buffon, Georges Louis Leclerc, comte de, 1707–1788.
The natural history of birds. From the French of the Count de Buffon. Illustrated with engravings; and a preface, notes, and additions, by the translator. . . . London, printed for A. Strahan, and T. Cadell; and J. Murray, 1792–3.
Vol. 1. xii,[4],412p.; vol. 2. [vii],496p.; vol. 3. [xi],456p.; vol. 4. [xii],481p.; vol. 5. [xi],536p.; vol. 6. [xiii],585p.; vol. 7. [xii],530p.; vol. 8. [viii],448p.; vol. 9. [vi],502,[xxxviii],[2]p., 262 plates, 8vo. Price: £3.12s. in boards.
Translated by John Leslie, though often attrib-

uted to Wm Smellie (To Leslie, 13 Aug. 1790).
Vol. 1 is dated 1792, the rest 1793. 1000 copies
printed by Strahan, Hughs, Davis, Bensley and
Baldwin (To Cadell, 19 May, 1792). The presswork of Henry Goldney so poor that Murray
had to pay off this printer and have the part re-
done (to Henry Goldney, 3 Sept. 1792).
Murray's one third share of expenses totalled
£651.7s.4d. (Leslie was paid £112.11s. in all).
Murray sold 329 copies wholesale at £2.10s.
each, or £823.6s.8d. in total — a profit of
£171.19s.4d. (BB, p. 63; To Cadell, 28 Nov.
1791; To Watson 38; Co., 23 March 1792).
Entered in the Stationers' Company Register,
23 Feb. 1793 'A. Strahan, T. Cadell, & J. Murray.
Whole'. Stock: 2 sets (W).
ESTC t201253: E, Grindlay 386.
Another issue: Vol. 1 dated 1793.
ESTC t154791: L, 971.k.12.
Science. London co-publishing.

862. Cervantes Saavedra, Miguel de, 1547–
1616.
The history and adventures of the renowned
Don Quixote. Translated from the Spanish of
Miguel de Cervantes Saavedra. To which is
prefixed, some account of the author's life. By
T. Smollett, M.D. Illustrated with twelve new
copper-plates, elegantly engraved. The sixth
edition, in four volumes. London, printed for
F. and C. Rivington, T. Longman, B. Law, G. G.
J. and J. Robinson, J. Johnson, T. Cadell, R.
Baldwin, W. Richardson, W. Goldsmith, J.
Murray, J. Sewell, S. Hayes, W. Lowndes, J.
Debrett, W. Fox, D. Ogilvy, and Co. and W.
Miller, 1792.
Vol. 1: [4],xl,293p.; vol. 2: [1],314p.; vol. 3:
[1],xi,331p.; vol. 4: [1],322p., plates, 12mo.
2040? copies printed. On 31 Jan. 1782 at James
Macgowan's bankruptcy sale Murray paid £2.8s.
for a 1/60 share. On 10 April 1783 at the Globe
Tavern he paid George Robinson £1.10s. for a
1/32 share; on 5 June 1783 at Thomas Caslon's
sale he paid £1.12s. for a 1/36 share; and on 3
July 1783 at Thomas Evans's sale he paid
£1.11s.6d. for a further 1/32 share. In Sept.
1792 he paid Cadell £33.3s. for expenses. The
returns on his share (153 copies at 6s. each,
wholesale) were £45.18s. (BB, p. 28; see
Cervantes 1782, item 302). A further edition is
listed in BB, p. 28 for which no copy has yet
been found. On 2 Mar. 1792 Murray paid Cadell

13 gns. for expenses of a 1/32 share. The
returns on his share (63 copies at 6s. each,
wholesale) were £17.18s. Shares sold 23 Dec.
1794: 1/60 to Bangster for £1.7s.6d.; 1/36 to
Kearsley & Clark for £1.11s.6d.; 2/32 to
Otridge for 4 gns (BB, p. 28). Stock: 194 (W).
ESTC t059481: L, 12490.aaa.21.
Fiction. London syndicate.

863. Clark, John, 1744–1805.
Observations on the diseases which prevail in
long voyages to hot countries, particularly on
those in the East Indies; and on the same diseases as they appear in Great Britain. By John
Clark, M.D. . . . The third edition, revised and
enlarged. London, printed for J. Murray, 1792.
xxii,[4],567,[3]p.,tables, 8vo. With a final errata
leaf.
On 4 Jan. 1793 Murray paid Hall & Elliot
£42.11s.2d. and paid the author £50 for new
edition. Clark was apparently paid £50 for this
title and the one below (To Clark, 1 Feb. 1792).
Copyright sold May 1796 to Kay for 2 gns. (BB.
p. 55). Stock: 213 (W).
ESTC t185713: MRu, T1 C5.
Medicine. Murray alone.

864. Clark, John, 1744–1805.
Observations on fevers, especially those of the
continued type; and on the scarlet fever
attended with ulcerated sore-throat. By John
Clark, M.D. . . . London, printed for the
author: and sold by T. Cadell; and J. Murray,
1792.
xxviii,398,[2]p., 8vo. With a half-title, errata, and
advertisement.
ESTC n010818: MnU-B, Wang 616.92.C548.
Medicine. Agency–London.

865. [Disraeli, Isaac, 1766–1848.]
Curiosities of literature. Consisting of anec-
dotes, characters, sketches, and observations,
literary, critical, and historical. Second edition.
London, printed for J. Murray, 1792.
xi,[5],531,[15]p., 8vo. With a half-title, index,
and a final errata leaf. Price: 6s. boards.
Entered in the Stationers' Company Register, 13
Feb. 1792, 'Murray'.
ESTC n002979: MnSM, T828.D61.
Literary criticism. Murray alone.

866. A dissertation on the querulousness of

statesmen. London, sold by T. Longman, J. Murray, and J. Debrett, 1792.
[2],116p., 8vo. Price: 2s.6d.
ESTC t053798: L, 8135.d.22.
Politics. London co-publishing.

867. Donaldson, John, fl. 1790–1795.
Sketch of a plan to prevent crimes. By John Donaldson, Esq. London, printed for the author: and sold by J. Murray, 1792.
16p., 8vo. Price: 6d.
Entered in the Stationers' Company Register, 3 Dec. 1792, 'Author. Whole'.
ESTC t048411: L, 1129.h.22(4).
Politics. Agency–Murray alone.

868. The Edinburgh magazine, or literary miscellany, . . . Edinburgh, Printed for J. Sibbald. sold by Lawrie, Symington, and Co. Edinburgh; and J. Murray, London, 1792.
Vol. 15: 520p., 8vo., plates; vol. 16: Edinburgh, Printed for Lawrie and Symington, and sold by J. Murray, 1792. [ii],528, [2]p., 8vo., plates.
Published in monthly parts; title page, contents, and index issued every six months. Printed by Macfarquhar and Elliot, Edinburgh.
Primary location: E, NH 295.
Miscellaneous. Agency–Edinburgh.

869. Eighty-nine fugitive fables, in verse; moral, prudential, and allegorical. Original and selected. London, printed for J. Murray, 1792.
[2],viii,232p., 12mo. With a half-title. Price: 4s. bound.
ESTC t078511: L, 12304.bbb.25
Stock: 719 (H).
Poetry. Murray alone.

870. Emily; or, the fatal promise. A northern tale, in two volumes. . . . London, printed and sold by T. Wilkins. Sold also by H. D. Symonds, and J. Bew; T. Hookham; J. Murray; and W. Richardson; A. Hamilton; W. Drury; and W. Oulton, 1792.
vol. 1: [7],2–204p.; vol. 2: [3],2–215p., 12mo. Price: 6s.
ESTC t225440: L, RB23.a.9379.
Fiction. Agency–London.

871. The English review; or, an abstract of English and foreign literature. . . . London, printed for J. Murray, 1792.

Vol. 19: [1],[viii],480,[6]p., 8vo; vol. 20: [1],[viii], 480,[6]p., 8vo.
Published in monthly parts (priced at 1s.); title page, contents, and index issued every six months.
Primary location: NN, *DA.
Miscellaneous. Murray–with agency.

872. Fielding, Henry, 1707–1754.
The adventures of Joseph Andrews, and his friend Mr Abraham Adams. . . . By Henry Fielding, Esq. With prints by T. Rowlandson. Printed for J. Murray, London; and J. Sibbald, Edinburgh, 1792.
xx,331,[1]p. (pp. 147, 156 misnum. 146, 56 respectively), plates, 8vo.
ESTC n004257: CLU-S/C, PR3454.J77 1792.
Fiction. Edinburgh co-publishing.

873. Fielding, Henry, 1707–1754.
The history of Tom Jones, a foundling. By Henry Fielding, Esq. . . . Printed for J. Murray, London, and J. Sibbald, Edinburgh, 1792.
Vol. 1: xix, 230p.; vol. 2: xi,350p.; vol. 3: vii,316p., plates, 8vo.
A reissue of the sheets of Sibbald's 1791 Edinburgh edition. Twelve plates by Thomas Rowlandson. Stock: 18 (H).
ESTC n002590: CLU-S/C, PR3454.T59 1792.
Fiction. Edinburgh co-publishing.

874. Firishtah, Muhammad Qasim Hindu Shah Astarabadi.
The history of Hindostan, translated from the Persian. The third edition, in three volumes. . . . By Alexander Dow, . . . London, printed by John Murray, 1792.
Vol. 1: lxix,393p.; vol. 2: [14],429p.; vol. 3: [18],cx,450,[16]p., plates, ports.,map, 8vo.
A translation of Tarikh-i Firishtah. Vols. 1–2 contain the history written by Muhammad Kasim ibn Hindu Shah; vol. 3 is an original work by Alexander Dow. Murray paid 6 gns. for a 6/8ths share at the sale of Thomas Becket on 21 Jan. 1779 at the Queen's Arms. His profit is not recorded. The share was sold in May 1796 to Kay for 1 gn. (BB, p. 19). Stock: 7 sets (H); 30 (W).
ESTC n009057: CaBVaU, SpC DS436.A1F5 1792.
History. Murray alone.

875. Gay, John, 1685–1732.
Fables by the late Mr. Gay. In one volume complete. London, printed for J. F. and C. Rivington, B. and B. White, T. Longman, B. Law, G. G. J. and J. Robinson, T. Cadell, S. Blandon, R. Baldwin, J. Sewell, J. Johnson, H. L. Gardner, W. Goldsmith, J. Murray, W. Lowndes, W. Bent, J. Scatcherd, and J. Whitaker, G. and T. Wilkie, and E. Newbery, 1792.
viii,232p. (p. 212 misnum. 112), ill., 12mo. Price: 2s.
?4880 copies printed. Murray bought a 1/20 share at the Globe Tavern (John Crowder's sale) on 10 Sept. 1777 for £10.5s. which he paid to George Robinson on 16 Jan. 1778, and on 10 April 1783 at the Globe Tavern he paid Robinson £3.7s. for an additional 1/40 share. On 19 April 1792 Murray paid Thomas Longman £9.3s., his share of paper and printing. The returns on his share (366 books at 1s. each, wholesale), paid on 19 Apr. 1792, were £18.6s. (see BB, p. 9; Gay 1788, item 655).
Stock: 214 (W).
ESTC t013868: L, 12304.ccc.44.
Poetry. London syndicate.

876. Gowland, John, d. 1776.
An essay on cutaneous diseases, and all impurities of the skin. Proposing a specific, and, method of cure. By John Gowland, . . . London, printed for the proprietors, and sold by Mr. Johnson, and Mr. Murray, [1792?].
[2],37,[1]p., 8vo. With a half-title.
ESTC t058323: L, 1187.h.39.
Medicine. Agency–London.

877. Griffith, Richard.
A singular case of reproduction of the sphincter ani, and three other cases annexed; which illustrate the use of a fresh porter fomentation and seed poultice in the cure of mortification: addressed to J. Heaviside, Esq. . . . by Richard Griffith. London, printed for John Murray, 1792.
iv,36p., 8vo. Price: 1s.6d.
ESTC n026027: DNLM, 18th c.coll.
Medicine. Murray alone.

878. Hamilton, Alexander, 1739–1802.
Letters to Dr William Osborn, teacher and practitioner of midwifery in London, on certain doctrines contained in his essays on the practice of midwifery, &c. from Alexander Hamilton, . . . Edinburgh, printed for Peter Hill; and J. Murray, London, [1792].
[4],157,[1]p., 8vo. With a half-title. Price: 3s.
Dated at end: Edinburgh, Oct. 27, 1792.
ESTC t010794: L, 1178.h.11(1).
Medicine. Edinburgh co-publishing.

879. Hamilton, Alexander, 1739–1802.
A treatise on the management of female complaints, and of children in early infancy. By Alexander Hamilton, . . . Edinburgh, printed for Peter Hill; and John Murray, London, 1792.
xx,549,[1]p., 8vo. Price: 6s. in boards.
1500 copies printed. Expenses, £260.7s.: £100 to author; printing 35½ sheets, £44.10s.3d.; paper, £99.6d.; advertising, 15 gns; extras, £1.1s.3d. (BB, p. 61). Entered in the Stationers' Company Register, 21 May 1792, 'Author'. Stock: 6 (H); 320 (W).
ESTC t117281: L, 1177.c.7.
Medicine. Edinburgh co-publishing.

880. The history of Jane Grey, . . . with a defence of her claim to the crown. London, printed and sold by T. Wilkins; sold also by H. D. Symonds; T. Hookham; J. Murray; and W. Richardson, 1792.
xii,168p., plate, port., 12mo.
Edited by Thomas Wilkins. A reissue of the 1791 edition (item 827).
ESTC t204572: D, J.942054.GRE/1792.
History. London co-publishing.

881. Hunter, Henry, 1741–1802.
Sacred biography. Or the history of the patriarchs: being a course of lectures delivered at the Scots church, London Wall. By Henry Hunter, . . . The fourth edition. London, printed for the author, and sold by J. Murray; and James Dickson, Edinburgh, 1792–95.
Vol. 1: viii,420p.; vol. 2: xiii,[1],464p.; vol. 3: xvi, 493p.; vol. 4: xiii,464p.; vol. 5: xiii,[1],439,[1]p., 8vo. Price for the set: £1.10s.
Vol. 1 is dated 1792; the rest 1795. Vol. 5 contains a general index. The imprint to vol. 2 'printed for the author, and sold by H. Murray; and James Dickson, Edinburgh'; imprint to vol. 3 same as vol. 1; imprint of vol. 4 'printed for the author, by Ritchie and Sammells; and sold by J. Murray; and James Dickson, Edinburgh'; imprint to vol. 5 'printed for the author and

sold by Murray and Highley; and James Dickson, Edinburgh'. Stock: (H) 19 vol. 1; 13 vol. 2; 10 vol. 3; 24 vol. 4; 28 vol. 5. (W). 617 Vol. 1; 70 vol. 2 (22 fine paper); 332 vol. 4; 20 vol. 5. *ESTC* t098654: L, 1218.d.11,12,15. Note: Vols. 1, 2 and 5 only (pp. supplied from other copies). Religion. Agency–London.

882. Hunter, Henry, 1741–1802.
Sacred biography: being a sequel to the history of the patriarchs, in a course of lectures, delivered at the Scots church, London-Wall, containing the history of Deborah, Ruth, and Hannah. By Henry Hunter, D.D. Volume VI. London, printed for the author, by Ritchie and Sammells, and sold by J. Murray; and James Dickson, Edinburgh, 1792.
[6],xvi,537,[7]p., 8vo. With a half-title and final advertisement leaf. Price: 7s. in boards.
Stock: 9 (H); 932 (W).
ESTC t098657: L, 1218.d.16.
Religion. Agency–London.

883. Johnson, Samuel, 1709–1784.
A dictionary of the English language: in which the words are deduced from their originals, explained in their different meanings, . . . Abstracted from the folio edition, by the author, Samuel Johnson, A.M. To which are prefixed, A grammar of the English language, and the preface to the folio edition. The tenth edition. London, printed for J. F. & C. Rivington, L. Davis, T. Longman, B. Law J. Dodsley, C. Dilly, G. G. & J. Robinson, T. Cadell, J. Robson, W. Goldsmith, J. Bew, J. Murray, R. Baldwin, S. Hayes, G. & T. Wilkie, and C. Stalker, 1792.
[986]p., 8vo.
Information for this edition is not recorded (See Johnson 1790, item 772; BB, p. 10). Stock: 20, presumably of this edn. (H). Shares sold 23 Dec. 1794: 1/80 to Cadell & Davies for £10.5s.; 1/80 to Stockdale for £8.10s.6d.; 1/80 to Lowndes for £8.8s. (BB, p. 10). Further shares sold May 1796: 1/160 to Cadell for 6 gns.; 1/160 to Rivington for £6.10s.; and 1/160 to Rivington for £7 (BB, p. 67; see Addenda).
ESTC n028410: KMK, PE1620.J6 1792.
Language. London syndicate.

884. Johnson, Samuel, 1709–1784.
The works of Samuel Johnson, LL.D. A new

edition, In twelve volumes. With an essay on his life and genius, by Arthur Murphy, Esq. . . . London, printed for T. Longman, B. White and Son, B. Law, J. Dodsley, H. Baldwin, J. Robson, J. Johnson, C. Dilly, T. Vernor, G. G. J. and J. Robinson, T. Cadell, J. Nichols, R. Baldwin, N. Conant, P. Elmsly, F. and C. Rivington, T. Payne, W. Goldsmith, R. Faulder, Leigh and Sotheby, G. Nicol, J. Murray, A. Strahan, W. Lowndes, T. Evans, W. Bent, S. Hayes, G. and T. Wilkie, T. and J. Egerton, W. Fox, P. M'Queen, Ogilvie and Speare, Darton and Harvey, G. and C. Kearsley, W. Miller, B. C. Collins, and E. Newbery, 1792.
12 vols., plate, port., 8vo. Price: £3.12s. in boards.
Vol. 1, 'An essay on the life and genius of Samuel Johnson' by Arthur Murphy, also published separately in the same year (see Murphy, item 897). With an index in vol. 12. The plate is dated: Jany. 1st. 1787.
On 10 March 1791 Murray issued a three-month note for £25.1s.8d. He issued additional notes to Thomas Cadell on 19 Apr. 1792 at two and six months for £42.12s.9d. in all and paid Cadell a further £1.6s. on 2 July 1793 — a total outlay of £69.5d. On 10 Mar. he received £29.6s.8d., his share on 40 sets of Johnson's 'Lives'; on 19 Apr. 1792 he received £1.17s.11d., his share on 13 copies of Murphy's 'Essay' and £83.4s., his share on 32 sets of the 'Works' at £2.12s. each, wholesale. Finally, on 2 July he received £2.18s.4d., his share on 20 further copies of Murphy's 'Essay', at 2s.11d. each, wholesale — a nett profit of £48.6s.6d. (BB, p. 43; see Johnson's *Works* 1787, item 602). Stock: 16 (W).
ESTC t083955: L, qE/00428–00439.
Miscellaneous. London syndicate.

885. [Jones, John, 1766–1795].
The reason of man: with strictures on Rights of man, and other of Mr. Paine's works. Canterbury, printed and sold by Simmons, Kirkby and Jones, and J. Murray, London, 1792.
iv,28p., 8vo.
ESTC t046336: L, 8135 b.18(2).
Politics. Provincial co-publishing.

886. The second edition.
ESTC t168348: C, Syn.5.79.36/11.
Politics. Provincial co-publishing.

887. Keith, George Skene, 1752–1823.
Tracts on the corn laws of Great Britain, containing, I. An inquiry into the principles, . . . II. Application of these principles . . . III. Inquiry into the expediency . . . IV. Outlines of a new Corn Bill, . . . By George Skene Keith, . . . London, printed for J. Murray, and C. Elliot, Edinburgh, 1792.
[2],ii,36,38–43,[2]p.,fold. table, 8vo. Price: 1s.6d.
ESTC n005889: PU, 330.8.P753 v.65.
Law. Edinburgh co-publishing.

888. Leake, John, 1729–1792.
Practical observations towards the prevention and cure of chronic diseases peculiar to women: . . . To which are added, prescriptions, . . . By John Leake, . . . Seventh edition. . . . London, printed for Baldwin; Murray; and Egerton, 1792.
Vol. 1: viii,9–454p.; vol. 2: 423,[18]p., 8vo.
Vol. 1 was first published in 1777 as *Medical instructions towards the prevention and cure of chronic or slow diseases peculiar to women*; in 1781 a two–vol. edn of *Medical instructions* was published with the addition of 'Practical observations on the child-bed fever' as Vol. 2.
ESTC n012151: MBCo, 24.A.98.1792.
Another issue: London, printed for Evans; Murray; and Egerton.
ESTC n012152: DNLM 18thc. coll.
Medicine. London co-publishing.

889. Leake, John, 1729–1792.
A practical essay on diseases of the viscera; particularly those of the stomach and bowels, the liver, spleen, and urinary bladder in which their nature, treatment, and cure, are clearly pointed out and explained. By John Leake, . . . London, printed for Evans; Murray; Egerton; and Hookham, 1792.
xi,[1],442p., 8vo. Price: 6s.
Entered in the Stationers' Company Register, 24 May 1792, 'Author. Whole'.
ESTC t140685: L, 1190.k.5.
Medicine. London co-publishing.

890. [Le Sage, Alain René, 1668–1747.]
The adventures of Gil Blas of Santillane. A new translation, by the author of Roderick Random [Tobias Smollett]. Adorned with twelve new cuts, neatly engraved. In four volumes. The sixth edition. . . . London, printed for T.

Longman; B. Law and Son; G. G. J. and J. Robinson, J. Johnson, T. Cadell, W. Richardson, W. Otridge, J. Murray, W. Goldsmith, J. Sewell, W. Lane, T. Vernor, J. Scatchard and J. Whitaker, W. Lowndes, S. Hayes, G. and T. Wilkie, R. Faulder, W. Tenning, and R. Baldwin, 1792.
Vol. 1: xii,312p.; vol. 2: vi,263p.; vol. 3: vii,292p.; vol. 4: viii,276p., plates,, 12mo.
2000 copies printed. Murray paid £1.17s. for a 1/32 share at Thomas Becket's sale on 21 Jan. 1779 at the Queen's Arms. He paid £11.16s.10d. for paper and printing. The returns on his share (63 copies at 6s. each, wholesale) were £17.18s. Share sold 23 Dec. 1794 to Otridge for £1.5s. (BB, p. 25; see Le Sage 1782, item 311).
ESTC t143739: L, 12511.b.4.
Fiction. London syndicate.

891. A letter to the Members of Parliament who have presented petitions to the Honourable House of Commons for the abolition of the slave trade. By a West-India Merchant. London, sold by J. Sewell; J. Murray; and J. Debrett, 1792.
[4],84p., 8vo. With a half-title.
Reference: Sabin 34788.
ESTC t105992: L, 1600/1475.
Politics. London co-publishing.

892. Lind, James, 1716–1794.
An essay on diseases incidental to Europeans in hot climates. With the method of preventing their fatal consequences. By James Lind, . . . To which is added, an appendix concerning intermittent fevers. And a simple and easy way to render sea water fresh, . . . The fifth edition. London, printed for J. Murray, 1792.
xvi,357,[9]p., 8vo. Price: 6s.
750 copies printed. Murray paid £2.6s. for a half share at Thomas Becket's sale on 21 Jan. 1779 at the Queen's Arms. (He presumably already owned the other half). He paid out £59.18s. for paper, printing and advertising and received the copies which he sold for £131.5s., or 3s.6d. each. The copyright was sold in May 1796 to Kay for £2.5s. (BB, p. 16; see Lind 1788, item 668). Stock: 32 (H); 472 (W).
ESTC n002086: CaOTU, J.A. Hannah Coll..
Medicine. Murray alone.

893. Linné, Carl von, 1707–1778.
The animal kingdom, or zoological system, of

the celebrated Sir Charles Linnaus; class I. Mammalia: . . . being a translation of that part of the Systema natura, as lately published, . . . by Professor Gmelin of Goettingen. Together with numerous additions from more recent zoological writers, and illustrated with copperplates: by Robert Kerr, . . . London, printed for J. Murray; and R. Faulder, 1792.

xii,[30],400,[5],404–432,469–644p., plates, 4to. With a half-title. Price: 10s.6d. in boards. Vol. I, pts. 1, 2. No more published (see To Robert Kerr, 29 Oct. 1792) Part 1 comprises: 'Class I. Mammalia' with separate divisional title page; part 2, with separate half-title and divisional title page: 'Class II. Birds'. A printed slip is inserted after p. 432 explaining that it was impossible to complete the 'Systematic Catalogue of Birds', and that the sheets omitted will be delivered with the last part of the 'Class of Birds'. Vol. 1 pt. 2 entered in the Stationers' Company Register, 20 Dec. 1792, 'Author. Whole'. Stock: pt. 1, 181; pt. 2, 224 (W)

ESTC t080398: L, 435.f.2
Science. London co-publishing.

894. The looker-on: a periodical paper. By the Rev. Simon Olive-Branch, A.M. London, printed for T. and J. Egerton, Whitehall (where letters and other communications to the author are received). Sold also by J. Murray and J. Richardson, 1792[–93].

678p., 4to.
Edited by Wm Roberts. Issued in eighty-six numbers from 10 Mar. 1792 to 21 Dec. 1793. Individual numbers priced 6d. Kirby added as a selling agent to colophon of each number. No. 1 entered in the Stationers' Company Register, 9 Mar. 1792, 'T. & J. Egerton. Whole'; and other numbers regularly following.
Primary location: L, P.P. 5349.b.
Miscellaneous. London co-publishing.

*895. McArthur, John, 1755–1840.
A treatise of the principles and practice of naval courts-martial, with an appendix, containing original papers and documents illustrative of the text. London, printed for Whieldon and Butterworth, 1792.
xxviii,163,[1],cxlvii,[44]p., 8vo
ESTC t106171: L, 517.c.21
Military. London co-publishing.

896. Moises, Edward, 1716 or 17–1790.
The Persian interpreter: in three parts. A grammar of the Persian language. Persian extracts, in prose and verse. A vocabulary: Persian and English. By the Rev. Edw. Moises, . . . Newcastle, printed by S. Hodgson: sold by J. Sewell, Mess. Egerton, Mess. Payne & son, J. Murray, and T. Deighton, London; Mess. Prince & Cook, Oxford; Mess. Merrill, and W. Lunn, Cambridge; W. Tesseyman, York; and by W. Charnley, and R. Fisher, Newcastle upon Tyne, 1792.
[4],4,82,57,[69]p., 4to. Price: 10s.6d. in boards.
Part III, 'A vocabulary: Persian and English' is unpaginated. The final two leaves contain: 'Proposals for printing by subscription, the Persian poets, historians and moralists; . . . Also, A dictionary'.
ESTC t095375: L, 12906.g.9.
Language. Agency–provincial.

897. Murphy, Arthur, 1727–1805.
An essay on his life and genius of Samuel Johnson, LL.D. by Arthur Murphy, Esq. London, printed for T. Longman, B. White and Son, B. Law, J. Dodsley, H. Baldwin, J. Robson, J. Johnson, C. Dilly, T. Vernor, G. G. J. and J. Robinson, T. Cadell, J. Nichols, R. Baldwin, N. Conant, P. Elmsley, F. and C. Rivington, T. Payne, W. Goldsmith, R. Faulder, Leigh and Sotheby, G. Nicol, J. Murray, A. Strahan, W. Lowndes, T. Evans, W. Bent, S. Hayes, G. and T. Wilkie, T. and J. Egerton, W. Fox, P. M'Queen, Ogilvie and Speare, Darton and Harvey, G. and C. Kearsley, W. Miller, B. C. Collins, and E. Newbery, 1792.
[4],187,[1]p., 8vo. With a half-title. Price: 4s. in boards.
See Johnson's *Works* 1792, item 884; BB, p. 43. Entered in the Stationers' Company Register, 16 Mar. 1792, 'T. Longman & Partners. Whole'. Stock: 10 (H).
ESTC t087884: L, 1202.c.3(1).
Biography. London syndicate.

898. [O'Brien, Charles, calico printer.]
A treatise on calico printing, theoretical and practical: including the latest philosophical discoveries — any way applicable: — accompanied with suggestions relative to various manufactures. . . . [London], Printed for C. O'Brien, Bookseller, Islington and sold by Bew: Richard-

son: Murray: and the booksellers of Manchester, Glasgow, Dublin, &c., 1792–93.
Vol. 1: 103 unpaginated leaves; vol. 2: 151 unpaginated leaves. table, ill., 12mo.
A reissue of *The calico printers' assistant* of 1789–92, with the 12–page introduction and additional preliminary material in vol. 1 and new title pages to both vols. Vol. 1 entered in the Stationers' Company Register, 17 Aug. 1789, 'C. O'brien. Whole'; vol. 2 entered 10 June 1793.
ESTC t132216: L, 1651/621.
Another issue: both volumes dated 1792.
ESTC t073963: L, 1400.b.25.
Science. Agency–London.

899. Pargeter, William, 1760–1810.
Observations on maniacal disorders. By William Pargeter, M.D. Reading, printed for the author, and sold by Smart and Cowslade; J. Murray, London; and J. Fletcher, Oxford, 1792.
vii,[1],140p., 8vo. Price: 3s.
ESTC t002708: L, T.98(5).
Medicine. Agency–provincial.

900. Perry, William, lecturer in the Academy at Edinburgh.
The royal standard English dictionary. In which the words are not only rationally divided into syllables, accurately accented, their part of speech properly distinguished, . . . their true pronunciation, . . . To which is prefixed, a comprehensive grammar . . . The sixth edition. In which is now added the Scripture proper names, . . . By W. Perry, . . . London, printed for J. Murray, and Bell & Bradfute, and J. Dickson, Edinburgh, 1792.
[4],559,[1];36p., oblong 12mo. Price: 3s.
6000 copies printed at Edinburgh by Neill and Co. Murray purchased a ½ share in Aug. 1785 from Neill, printer at Edinburgh for 4 gns. His share of the expences were £58.2s.1d. (£43.8d. to Neill & Co. and £11.6d. to Wilson for printing; and £4.11d. to Bell & Bradfute for expenses). The returns on his share are not recorded (BB, p. 42). Bell & Bradfute ledger 6, item 417, records the purchase of paper from Auchindinny Paper Co. of 190 reams of second crown for £52.8s. (Edinburgh City Archive). Reference: Alston v. 296.
ESTC n048540: MBAt, TBMR: YED.P42.2.
Language. Edinburgh co-publishing.

901. The poetical epitome; or extracts, elegant, instructive, and entertaining, abridged from the larger volume: with a view to the improvement and amusement of young persons at classical and other schools. London, printed for Messrs. Rivingtons, Longman, Law, Dodsley, Whites, Johnson, Robinsons, Cadell, Sewell, Murray, Richardson, Baldwin, Bew, Goldsmith, Faulder, Hayes, Ogilby and Co. Bent, Scatcherd and Co. Vernor, Wynne, Wilkie, Lowndes, Evans, and Kearsley, 1792.
xii,532p., 12mo. With a half-title. Price: 3s.3d. bound.
Extracts from *Elegant extracts*, compiled by Vicesimus Knox. 6000 copies printed. For his 6/100 share of the expenses for this work and the *Prose epitome* (listed below), Murray paid out £48 (in two notes). On 25 Jan. 1792 he received £64.17s.6d. (360 books at 3s.7½d. each, wholesale), a profit of £16.17s.6d. Shares sold in May 1796 to Kay, Law, Murray, and Lee for £37.12s.6d. (BB. p. 39). Stock: 18 (H); 202 (W).
ESTC t120767: L, 1607/5132.
Poetry. London syndicate.

902. The prose epitome; or, extracts, elegant, instructive, and entertaining, abridged from the larger volume: intended to assist in introducing scholars . . . to an acquaintance with useful and ornamental knowledge. London, printed for Messrs. Rivingtons, Longman, Law, Dodsley, Whites, Johnson, Robinsons, Cadell, Sewell, Murray, Richardson, Baldwin, Bew, Goldsmith, Faulder, Hayes, Ogilby and Co. Bent, Scatcherd and Co. Vernor, Wynne, Wilkie, Lowndes, Evans, and Kearsley, 1792.
xxiv,456p., 12mo. Price: 3s.3d. bound.
6000 copies printed. See *Poetical epitome* (above); BB, p. 39. Stock: 18 (H); 200 (W).
ESTC n039970: MB, 6559.72.
Miscellaneous. London syndicate.

903. Robertson, Robert, 1742–1829.
Observations on fevers, and other diseases, which occur on voyages to Africa and the West Indies. By Robert Robertson, M.D. . . . London, printed for John Murray, 1792.
xvi,196p., 4to.
ESTC n010821: DNLM, 18th c.coll.
Medicine. Murray alone.

904. Robinson, Robert, 1735–1790.

Ecclesiastical researches: by Robert Robinson. Cambridge, printed by Francis Hodson; and sold by Johnson; Murray; Knott, London; and Lunn, Cambridge, 1792.
[20],643,[3]p., 4to. With an advertisement, list of errata, and list of subscribers.
ESTC t100368: L, 4530.f.8.
Religion. Provincial co-publishing.

905. Saint Quentin, Dominique de.
A poetical chronology of the Kings of England, from William the Conqueror to George the Third inclusive; preceded by a short chronological division of the history of England. The whole forming an introduction to the study of the history of this country, and particularly adapted to the chronological and historical game of England, published by Mr. Dudley Adams, Charing-Cross. Reading, printed and sold by Smart and Cowslade; sold also by Dudley Adams; Elmsly, and Murray, London, 1792.
[4],vii,[1],59,[1]p.,tables, plates, 12mo. With a half-title. Pp. 49–59 are the plates. Price: 1s.6d.
Preface signed: D. St. Quentin, begins: 'The following . . . have been chiefly extracted from the Gentleman's Magazine'.
ESTC t132778: L, 11643.aaa.20.
Poetry. Provincial co-publishing.

906. [Smollett, Tobias George, 1721–1771].
The adventures of Roderick Random. . . . A new edition. London, printed for B. Law, C. Dilly, G. G. J. and J. Robinson, T. Cadell, F. and C. Rivington, W. Goldsmith, W. Richardson, S. Hayes, W. Lane, R. Baldwin, J. Murray, G. and T. Wilkie, and W. Lowndes, 1792.
Vol. 1: xvi,280p.; vol. 2: xii,316p., plates, 12mo. 1500 copies printed. Murray bought a 1/32 share for £1.11s.6d. on 21 Jan. 1779 at the sale of Thomas Becket at the Queen's Arms. In Mar. 1792 he paid Thomas Cadell £3.14s.5d. for paper and printing. The returns on his share (47 copies as 3s. each, wholesale) were £7.1s. Share sold in May 1796 to Ogilvie for £10s.6d. (BB, p. 17; see Smollett 1780, item 268).
ESTC t055380: L, 1608/1512.
Fiction. London syndicate.

907. Thomson, James, 1700–1748.
The seasons, by James Thomson. A new edition. Adorned with a set of engravings, . . . To

which is prefixed, An Essay on the plan and character of the poem, by J. Aikin, M.D. London, printed for J. Murray, 1792.
xlv,[3],256p., plates, 8vo. With a half-title.
ESTC t051946: L, 11643.g.27.
Expenses for engraving totalled £93.14.10: £13.2s.6d. to Metz for 5 designs; £18 gns to Neagle for engraving 'Spring' and £21 for 'Winter'; 12 gns. to Medland for 'Autumn'; £21 to A. Smith for 'Summer'; £26.5s. to Heath for 'Musidora'. No other information supplied (BB, p. 57).
Poetry. Murray alone.

908. Trye, Charles Brandon, 1757–1811.
An essay on the swelling of the lower extremities, incident to lying-in women. By Charles Brandon Trye, . . . London, printed for J. Murray, 1792.
viii,80p., 8vo. Price: 2s.
Stock: 262 (W).
ESTC t061359: L, 1177.h.20.
Medicine. Murray alone.

909. Virgil.
The works of Virgil: translated into English verse by Mr. Dryden. . . . London, printed for J. Rivington and Sons, J. Robson, B. Law, T. Vernor, G. G. J. and J. Robinson, T. Cadell, J. Johnson, J. Murray, R. Baldwin, W. Flexney, P. Macqueen, C. & G. Kearsley, and L. Wayland, 1792.
Vol. 1: 324p.; vol. 2: 318p.; vol. 3: 285p.; vol. 4: 272,[108]p., plates, 12mo.
This edition includes 'The life of Pub. Virgilius Maro. Written by William Walsh, Esq.' and 'A short account of his person, manners, and fortune'. 1500 copies printed. Murray bought a 1/12 share for £6 at D. Cornish's sale on 17 Mar. 1782 at the Globe Tavern. In Mar. 1792 he paid £23.8s.9d. to Thomas Cadell for paper and printing. The returns of his share (125 copies at 6s. each, wholesale) were £37.10s. (BB, p. 13; see Virgil 1782, item 330). Share sold 23 Dec. 1794 to Otridge for £1.16s. (BB, p. 13). Stock: 47 (W).
ESTC t139439: L, 11355.aaa.32.
Poetry. London Syndicate.

910. Wade, John Peter, d. 1802.
Nature and effects of emetics, purgatives, mercurials, and low diet, in disorders of Bengal and

similar latitudes. By John Peter Wade, M.D. . . .
London, printed for J. Murray, 1792.
xii,286,[2],287–352p., 8vo. Price: 6s. in boards.
A variant has p. 186 misnum. 116. Entered in
the Stationers' Company Register, 21 May 1792,
'J. Murray, Whole'.
ESTC t069645: L, 1170.g.7.
Medicine. Murray alone.

911. Watson, Thomas, Presbyterian Minister at
Whitby.
Intimations and evidences of a future state. By
the Rev. T. Watson. London, printed for J.
Murray, 1792.
vii,[1],228,[4]p., 8vo. With two final advertise-
ment leaves. Price: 3s.3d. in boards.
Entered in the Stationers' Company Register, 25
Oct. 1792, 'J. Murray. Whole'. Stock: 89 (W).
The stock book lists a 1793 edition of which
there were 485 copies in the warehouse.
ESTC t145542: L, 698.f.24
Religion. Murray alone.

912. White, William, 1744–1790.
Observations on the nature and method of cure
of the phthisis pulmonalis; or, consumption of
the lungs: from materials left by the late William
White, M.D. . . . and now published by A.
Hunter, M.D. . . . York, printed by Wilson,
Spence, and Mawman; sold by G. G. J. and J.
Robinson, T. Cadell, B. White, J. Robson, and J.
Murray, London; and by all the booksellers in
York, 1792.
159,[1],26p., 8vo. Price: 3s.6d.
ESTC n010033: MBCo, Alpha Green Book
no.1.
Medicine. Agency–provincial.

913. Young, William, d. 1757.
A new Latin-English dictionary; containing all
the words proper for reading the classic writers;
. . . To which is prefixed, a new English-Latin
dictionary, . . . The eighth edition, . . . By the
Rev. Mr. William Young, . . . London, printed
for B. White and Son, J. F. and C. Rivington, T.
Longman, B. Law, W. Ginger, T. Pote, H.
Baldwin, J. Johnson, G. G. J. and J. Robinson,
R. Baldwin, T. Cadell, J. Sewell, J. Murray, T.
Evans, H. Gardner, S. Hayes, W. Bent, W.
Lowndes, G. and T. Wilkie, Scatcherd and
Whitaker, Vernor, Ogilvie and Speare, J. Evans,
and the executors of J. Knapp, 1792.

[1332]p., 8vo.
8000 copies printed. Murray bought a 1/64
share at the Globe Tavern from S. Crowder
on 10 Sept. 1777 for 10 gns. which he paid to
George Robinson on 16 Jan. 1778. He bought
an additional 1/80 share at Buckland's sale on
10 June 1790 for £8.13s. On 27 Jan. 1792 he
paid out £45.6s. for paper and printing. The
returns on his share (282 books at 4s.8d. each,
wholesale) were £65.16s. (BB, p. 10; see Young
1778, item 208; 1787 item 627). Shares sold 23
Dec. 1793: 1/64 to J. Walker for £11.14s. and
May 1796: 1/80 to an unidentified buyer for
£5.12s.6d. Stock: 58 (W).
ESTC t078079: L, 1560/1898.
Language. London syndicate.

1793

Beddoes, Thomas, 1760–1808.
A guide for self-preservation, and parental
affection; or plain directions for enabling people to keep themselves and their children free
from several common disorders. By Thomas
Beddoes, M.D. Bristol, printed by Bulgin and
Rosser, for J. Murray; and J. Johnson, London,
[1793].
24p., 12mo. Price: 3d.
ESTC t136212: L, 7391.aa.7.
Medicine. London co-publishing.

915. [Beddoes, Thomas, 1760–1808.]
The history of Isaac Jenkins, and Sarah his wife,
and their three children. London, printed for J.
Murray; and J. Johnson, 1793.
48p., 12mo. Price: 3s.
Entered in the Stationers' Company Register, 1
Jan. 1793, no name given; re-entered 9 Aug.
1793, 'J. Murray. Whole'.
ESTC t018477: L, 1457.c.34.
Fiction. London co-publishing.

916. The second edition:
ESTC t018473: L, T.444(2).
Fiction. London co-publishing.

917. Beddoes, Thomas, 1760–1808.
A letter to Erasmus Darwin, M.D. on a new
method of treating pulmonary consumption,
and some other diseases hitherto found incur-
able. By Thomas Beddoes, M.D. Bristol,
printed by Bulgin and Rosser; sold by J. Murray;
and J. Johnson, London; also by Bulgin and

Sheppard, J. Norton, J. Cottle, W. Browne, and T. Mills, Bristol, [1793].
67,[1]p., 8vo. Price: 1s.
ESTC n037552: MdBJ-W, RBR B3990n 1793.
Another issue: p. 67 is partly reset and the text extended to 72p. by a postscript dated 5th July, 1793.
ESTC t018371: L, 730 5.de.9(3).
Medicine. Provincial co-publishing.

918. Beddoes, Thomas, 1760–1808.
Observations on the nature and cure of calculus, sea scurvy, consumption, catarrh, and fever: together with conjectures upon several other subjects of physiology and pathology. By Thomas Beddoes, M.D. London, printed for J. Murray, 1793.
xvi,278,[2]p., 8vo. With a final leaf of advertisements and errata. Price: 4s. boards.
Entered in the Stationers' Company Register, 4 Dec. 1792, 'J. Murray. Whole'. Stock: 529 (W).
ESTC t117587: L, 1187.e.11.
Medicine. Murray alone.

919. Bell, Benjamin, 1749–1806.
A treatise on gonorrhoa virulenta, and lues venerea. By Benjamin Bell, . . . Edinburgh, printed for James Watson and Co. and G. Mudie; and J. Murray, London, 1793.
Vol. 1: xiv,453p.; vol. 2: viii,549,[1]p., 8vo. With half-titles. Price: 12s.
Entered in the Stationers' Company Register, 5 Jan. 1793, 'Author. Whole'. Stock: 10 (H).
ESTC t099544: L, 1175.l.17.
Medicine. Edinburgh co-publishing.

920. Berquin, Arnaud, 1747–1791.
The children's friend. Translated from the French of M. Berquin; complete in four volumes. Ornamented with frontispieces. A new corrected edition; with additions. London, printed for J. Stockdale; F. and C. Rivington; B. Law and Son; J. Johnson; C. Dilly; J. Murray; J. Sewell; and W. Creech, Edinburgh, 1793.
Vol. 1: xvi,296p.; vol. 2: 296p.; vol. 3: 300p.; vol. 4: 322p.; vol. 5: 278p.; vol. 6: 268p., plates. 12mo. With a final leaf of advertisements in vol. 2.
Translated by J. Cooper. ?2000 copies printed. The plates are dated 1787. In Sept. 1792 Murray paid Dilly £23.9d. and in May 1793, £47.3d. The returns of his share (224 copies at 12s. each,

wholesale) were £134.8s. In May 1796 1/8 share sold to Vernor Nov. 1794 (BB, p. 44). Stock: 6 (H); 168 (W).
ESTC t108208: L, Ch.790/61.
Education. Edinburgh co-publishing.

921. Biographia Britannica: or, the lives of the most eminent persons who have flourished in Great-Britain and Ireland, from the earliest ages, to the present times: collected from the best authorities, printed and manuscript, and digested in the manner of Mr. Bayle's Historical and Critical Dictionary. The second edition, with corrections, enlargements, and the addition of new lives: by Andrew Kippis . . . with the assistance of the Rev. Joseph Towers, LL.D. and other Gentlemen. Volume the fifth. London, printed by John Nichols, for T. Longman, B. Law, H. Baldwin, C. Dilly, G. G. and J. Robinson, J. Nichols, H. Gardner, W. Ottridge, F. and C. Rivington, A. Strahan, J. Murray, T. Evans, S. Hayes, J. Debrett, T. Payne, W. Lowndes, J. Scatcherd, Darton and Harvey, and J. Taylor, 1793.
xxxi,710p., Fo.
1250 copies printed (Strahan Ledgers at BL). Murray's name is not included in imprint of the first four volumes, 1778–1789. On 10 Oct. 1791 he paid £2.17s.6d. to Wilkie for a 1/32 share at Carnan's sale. He then paid the Robinsons' 'call' of £8 on 25 July 1791. On 31 Oct. 1793 he paid Robinson £17.3s.6d. and Nicholls £7.10s. for expenses. The returns on his share (40 copies of vol. 5 at 22s. each, wholesale) were £44. Share sold 23 Dec. 1794 to Kearsley for 2 gns (BB, p. 58).
ESTC t139263: L, 133.g.4–8
Biography. London syndicate.

922. Bristow, James, b. 1757.
A narrative of the sufferings of James Bristow, belonging to the Bengal Artilley [sic], during ten years captivity with Hyder Ally and Tippoo Saheb. Calcutta printed: London, re-printed for J. Murray, 1793.
vi,210p., 8vo. Price: 3s. in boards.
Entered in the Stationers' Company Register, 23 July 1793, 'J. Murray, Whole'. Stock: 320 (W).
ESTC t094616: L, 790.f.15(3).
Military. Murray alone.

923. Brown, William Laurence, 1755–1830.
The spirit of the times considered. A sermon,

preached in the English church at Utrecht, February 13, 1793, ... By W. L. Brown, ... London, printed for J. Murray, 1793.
[2],iii,[2],4–51,[1]p., 8vo. Price: 1s.
ESTC t049764: L, 695.f.2(1).
Religion. Murray alone.

924. Burton, John, 1745 or 6–1806.
Lectures on female education and manners. By J. Burton. Rochester, printed for the author, by Gilman and Etherington, and sold by the booksellers in Kent, James Evans, and John Murray, London, 1793.
Vol. 1: xii, 333,7p.; vol. 2. vii, 268p., 12mo.
Entered in the Stationers' Company Register, 8 Jan. 1793, 'Author. Whole'.
ESTC t116565: L, 1031.e.13.
Education. Agency–provincial.

925. The second edition:
London, printed for J. Johnson; J. Murray; and J. Evans, 1793.
ESTC n019872: CaBVaU, LC1441.B86 1793.
Education. Agency–provincial.

926. Clarke, Henry, 1743–1818.
Tabulae linguarum. Being a set of tables, exhibiting at sight the declensions of nouns and conjugations of verbs with other grammatical requisites essential to the reading and speaking of the following languages, viz. Latin Spanish Portuguese ... In eight parts. Part I. containing the Latin, Spanish, Portuguese, ... London, printed for the author and sold by Mr. Murray, 1793.
[9],iv–xxiv,32,[1],32–93,96–114,113–144,137–144,153–252,[12]p., 8vo. With a half-title noting T. Schofield, printer (at Liverpool). With errata, and advertisements.
At the foot of p. 252, 'End of the first part; or, vol. I'. No more published. Apparently printed in London and then, before publication, expanded by the insertion or addition of preliminary leaves, some leaves within the book and pp. 209–253 (on light blue paper), which were printed by Schofield. A variant issue: [i],[6],iii–xxvi. 252,[4]p.
Primary location: NN, KF 1793 88–8.
Language. Agency–Murray alone.

927. Debate on the expediency of cultivating sugar in the territories of the East India Company. With the speeches of Randle Jackson, and George Dallas, ... Reported by William Woodfall, ... [London], Printed by the reporter; and sold by B. and J. White, and H. Murray; J. Debretts; and J. Richardson, 1793.
[4],28p., 4to.
ESTC t200414: MRu, 942.073.P6Q.
Economics. London co-publishing.

928. De Lolme, Jean Louis, 1740–1806.
The constitution of England; or, an account of the English government; in which it is compared, both with the republican form of government, and the other monarchies in Europe. By J. L. de Lolme, ... A new edition, corrected. London, printed for G. G. J. & J. Robinson, and J. Murray, 1793.
[8],xvi,522,[18]p., plate, port., 8vo.
On 28 Apr. Murray issued notes (his share of expenses) to Robinson for £29.3s.4d. The returns on his share (250 copies at 4s.8d. each, wholesale) were £58.6s.8d. A 1/8 share was sold on 23 Dec. 1794 to Stockdale for £20 (BB, p. 24). Stock: 183 (W).
ESTC t110402: L, 1609/5576.
History. London co-publishing.

929. [Disraeli, Isaac, 1766–1848.]
Curiosities of literature. Volume the second. By I. D'Israeli. The second edition. London, printed for J. Murray, 1793.
[2],iii,[3],557,[15]p., plate, 8vo. With an index. Price: 7s. in boards.
Entered in the Stationers' Company Register, 4 Dec. 1792, 'J. Murray. Whole'. Stock: 226 (W).
ESTC t197694: MRu, 10477
Literary criticism. Murray alone.

930. [Disraeli, Isaac, 1766–1848.]
Curiosities of literature. Consisting of anecdotes, characters, sketches, and observations, literary, critical, and historical. The third edition, with large additions and considerable improvements. London, printed for J. Murray, 1793.
xv,[5],617,[15]p., 8vo. With an index. Price: 7s. in boards.
Entered in the Stationers' Company Register, 6 May 1793, 'J. Murray. Whole'.
ESTC t143344: Lu, Porteus.
Literary criticism. Murray alone.

931. [Disraeli, Isaac, 1766–1848.]
A dissertation on anecdotes; by the author of Curiosities of literature. London, printed for C. and G. Kearsley, and J. Murray, 1793.
vii,[1],83,[1]p., 8vo. Price: 2s.
ESTC t109208: L, 816.e.19(2).
Literary criticism. London co-publishing.

932. Donaldson, John, fl. 1790–1795.
A letter to the magistrates, burgesses, &c. of the royal burghs of Scotland. By John Donaldson, Esq. London, printed, for the author, and sold by J. Murray, 1793.
15,[1]p., 8vo.
Entered in the Stationers' Company Register, 18 Nov. 1794, 'Author. Whole'.
ESTC t065147: L, 601.aa.6(4).
Politics. Agency–Murray alone.

933. The Edinburgh magazine or literary miscellany, . . . Edinburgh, Printed for Lawrie and Symington, and sold in London by J. Murray and W. Boag, 1793.
Vol. 1: 496,[2]p., 8vo., engraved title page; plates; vol. 2: 508,2p., 8vo., engraved title page, plates.
A new series; published in monthly parts; title page, contents, and index issued every six months.
Primary location: E, NH 295.
Miscellaneous. Agency–Edinburgh.

934. The English review; or, an abstract of English and foreign literature. . . . London, printed for J. Murray, 1793.
Vol. 21: [1],[viii],480,[6]p., 8vo; vol. 22: printed for H. Murray: [1],[viii],480,[6]p., 8vo.
Published in monthly parts (priced at 1s.); title page, contents, and index issued every six months.
Primary location: NN, *DA.
Miscellaneous. Murray–with agency.

935. Fraser, Simon.
Reports of the proceedings before select committees of the House of Commons, in the following cases of controverted elections; . . . Heard and determined during the first session of the seventeenth Parliament . . . By Simon Fraser, . . . London, printed for J. Murray, C. Dilly, E. and R. Brooke, Whieldon and Butterworth, J. Debrett, and T. and J. Egerton, 1793.

Vol. 1: xiii,416,xxxiip.; vol. 2: [1],iv,xiv,456p., plates., maps, 8vo. Price: 6s.6d. in boards.
This is the 1791 edition with a new title page to vol. 1. The separate title page to vol. 2 reads 'Reports of the proceedings . . . during the second session of the seventeenth Parliament'.
ESTC n000016: TxU, JN1051 1793.
Politics. London co-publishing.

936. Gay, John, 1685–1732.
Fables by John Gay, with a life of the author, and embellished with a plate to each fable. London, printed by Darton & Harvey, for F. & C. Rivington, B & B. White, T. Longman, B. Law & Son, G. G. J. and J. Robinson, T. Cadell, S. Bladon, R. Baldwin, J. Sewell, J. Johnson, H. L. Gardner, J. Bew, W. Goldsmith, J. Murray, W. Lowndes, J. Scatcherd & Co. G. & T. Wilkie, & E. Newbery, 1793.
[2],xvi,256p., plates, 8vo. Price: 2s.
2040 copies printed. Murray bought a 1/20 share at the Globe Tavern (John Crowder's sale) on 10 Sept. 1777 for £10.5s. which he paid to George Robinson on 16 Jan. 1778, and on 10 Apr. 1783 at the Globe Tavern he paid Robinson £3.7s. for an additional 1/40 share (3/40 in all). On 3 Oct. 1793 Murray paid Wm Darton £25.16s.4d. for paper and printing. The returns on his share (122 copies Demy at 5s. and 31 Royal at 8s. each, wholesale), paid in Oct. 1793, were £42.18s. (see BB, p. 9; Gay 1792, item 875). Shares sold 23 Dec. 1794: 2/40 to Scatcherd for £5.15s.6d.; 1/40 to Stockdale for £3.5s.6d. (BB, p. 9). Stock: 116 'large 8vo (plates separate)' (H).
ESTC t013872: L, 12304.g.6.
Poetry. London syndicate.

*937. Gay, John, 1685–1732.
Fables by John Gay, with a life of the author, and embellished with seventy plates. . . . London, printed for John Stockdale, 1793.
Vol. 1: xi,225p.; vol. 2: vii,187,[1]p., plates, 8vo.
With a subscribers' list.
1500 copies printed. Murray had a 1/3 share. Total expenses were £900.6s., a cost of 12s. per copy. Prior to publication 375 were sold at £1.5s. each (148 to subscribers and 227 at a trade sale), realising £486.15s. The 'Life' was written by Charles Churchill for 3 gns. Twelve of the engravings are by Wm Blake. Three gns. were paid for each of what are in fact 71

engravings (BB, p. 58; loose sheet in BB detailing expenses; see Plate 25). Stock: 70 (W), presumably of this edition. A new edition with the text reset but using the same plates was issued in 1811 with a false 1793 imprint.
ESTC n009619: CLU-S/C, PR3473.F11 1793b.
Poetry. London co-publishing.

938. Goldsmith, Oliver, 1728–1774.
Dr. Goldsmith's Roman history, abridged by himself, for the use of schools. A new edition corrected. With copper plates. London, printed for Leigh and Sotheby; Scatcherd and Whitaker; Wilkie; Richardson; Murray; Goldsmith, 1793.
xii,300p., plates, 12mo.
3000 copies printed. Murray paid £7.10s. for a 1/12 share in Sept. 1791 at the sale of the late Lockyer Davis. In Oct. 1793 he paid £8.11s.10d. for paper and printing. The returns on his share (250 copies at 1s.6d. each, wholesale) were £18.15s. Shares sold May 1796: 1/24 to Cadell for £11.10s.; 1/24 to Kay for £11.12s.6d. (BB, p. 54). Stock: 14 (H); 334 (W).
ESTC n008963: MdAN, SpC uncat.
History. London syndicate.

939. Goldsmith, Oliver, 1728–1774.
The poetical works of Oliver Goldsmith, M. B. With an account of the life and writings of the author. A new edition. London, printed for T. Cadell; Scatcherd and Whitaker; G. and T. Wilkie, W. Miller; and J. Murray, 1793.
vi,xlii,151,[1]p. (p.35 misnum. 33), 8vo. With a half-title.
1000 copies printed. Murray paid Scatcherd 14 gns. in Mar. 1793 for 112 copies, which produced £22.2s.8d, a profit of £7.8s.8d. Shares sold May 1796 to Rivington for £8 (BB, p. 64). Stock: 37; 75 foolscap 8vo (H).
ESTC t146137: L, 11607.a.13.
Poetry. London syndicate.

940. Goldsmith, Oliver, 1728–1774.
The Roman history from the foundation of the city of Rome, to the destruction of the western empire. By Dr. Goldsmith. A new edition. . . . London, printed for Leigh and Sotheby, B. Law, G. G. J. and J. Robinson, T. Cadell, J. Murray, J. and C. Rivington, W. Richardson, T. Egerton, W. Goldsmith, and J. Scatchard, 1793.
Vol. 1: x,487p.; vol. 2: viii,501p., 8vo.
?1500 copies printed. Murray paid 14 gns for a

1/16 share in Sept. 1791 at the sale of the late Lockyer Davis. In March 1793 he paid £17.5s.6d. for expenses. The returns on his share (94 copies at 8s. each, wholesale) were £37.12s. Shares sold May 1796: 1/32 to Lee for £11.13s.6d.; 1/32 to Kay for 11 gns. (BB, p. 53). Stock: 5 (H); 60 (W).
ESTC t146149: L, 1609/2536.
History. London syndicate.

941. Gowland, John, d. 1776.
An essay on cutaneous diseases, and all impurities of the skin. Proposing a specific, and, method of cure. By John Gowland, . . . London, printed by J. Desmond, for the proprietors, and sold by Mr. Johnson, and Mr. Murray, [1793].
37,[1]p., 8vo.
Entered in the Stationers' Company Register 15 May 1793, 'R. Dickinson. Whole'.
ESTC n009263: TxU-M, RBR Pam.
Medicine. Agency–London.

942. [Griffith, Richard, fl. 1793–1804.]
Fables in verse: or, present life under different forms. London, printed for J. Murray, 1793.
[4],67,[1]p., 8vo. With a half-title. Price: 1s.6d.
ESTC t078513: L, 11658.b.14.
Poetry. Murray alone.

943. Haller, Albrecht von, 1708–1777.
Letters from Baron Haller to his daughter, on the truths of the Christian religion. Translated from the German. The second edition, corrected. London, printed for J. Murray, 1793.
xxxii,278,[2]p., 8vo. With a half-title and a final advertisement leaf.
A translation of *Briefe über die wichtigsten Wahrheiten der Offenbarung*. See Haller 1780, item 256. Stock: 12 (H); 700 (W).
ESTC t072771: L, 1490.aa.10
Religion. Murray alone.

944. Harrington, Robert, 1751–1837.
Chemical essays; being a continuation of my reflections on fixed fire, with observations and strictures upon Drs. Priestley's, Fordyce's, Pearson's and Beddoes's late papers in the Phliosophical [sic] transactions; and an answer to the reviewers. By Robert Harrington, M.D. London, printed for R. Faulder, J. Murray, J. Evans, and W. Creech, Edinburgh, [1793].

iv,92p., 8vo.
Dedication dated: July 10, 1793.
ESTC no16158: DNLM, 18th c.coll.
Science. Edinburgh co-publishing.

945. Hill, Edmund, gunpowder manufacturer.
Reply to the Report of the Committee of Ware-houses of the East India Company, on the subjects of saltpetre and gunpowder. Most respectfully submitted . . . by the gunpowder makers of London. London, printed for J. Debrett; John Murray; and W. Richardson, [1793].
26p., 4to.
Signed and dated: Edmund Hill. Apr. 25, 1793.
ESTC no37831: Lpro, PC.1/20/A31/4A pt.3.
Military. London co-publishing.

946. Hook, Archibald.
Major Hook's defence, to the action for crim-inal conversation, brought against him by Capt. Charles Campbell, and tried at Westminster, 26th February, 1793. London, printed for J. Murray, 1793.
lxv,[1],112,[1]p., 8vo. With an errata leaf. Price: 2.6d.
Entered in the Stationers' Company Register, 22 Apr. 1793, 'J. Murray. Whole'.
ESTC to64408: L, 1416.i.44.
Law. Murray alone.

947. Hunter, Henry, 1741–1802.
A sermon, preached Feb. 3, 1793, at the Scots church, London Wall, on occasion of the trial, condemnation, and execution of Louis XVI . . . By Henry Hunter, D.D. To which is subjoined, . . . a republication of a discourse on the rise and fall of the papacy; . . . By Robert Flem-ming, . . . London, printed for the author and editor. Sold by John Murray, 1793.
xii,32,220p., 8vo. Price: 3s.6d.
The discourse by Fleming has separate half-title and pagination. Entered in the Stationers' Com-pany Register, 9 Apr. 1793, 'J. Murray. Whole'.
ESTC to27134: L, 694.h.13(1,2).
Religion. Agency–Murray alone.

948. Johnson, Samuel, 1709–1784.
The Rambler. In four volumes. . . . The twelfth edition. London, printed for T. Longman, B. Law and Son, H. Baldwin, J. Robson, C. Dilly, G. G. J. and J. Robinson, T. Cadell, J. Nichols, F.

and C. Rivington, W. Goldsmith, J. Knox, J. Murray, W. Otridge, W. Lowndes, S. Hayes, G. and T. Wilkie, P. Macqueen, B. Collins, Hook-ham and Carpenter, Darton and Harvey, and R. Jameson, 1793.
Vol. 1: [4],322,[1]p.; vol. 2: [4],304; vol. 3: [4],319p.; vol. 4: [4],264,[32]p., port. in vol. 1; frontispiece plates to vols 2–4; advert. leaf in vol. 1, 12mo.
2000 copies printed. On 14 Aug. 1781 at John Hinton's sale Murray paid 4 gns for a 1/32 share. In July 1793 he paid £10.5s.1d. in expenses. The returns on his share (63 copies at 6s. each, wholesale) were 18 gns. (see John-son's *Rambler* 1789, item 726; BB, p. 28). Stock: 30 (W).
ESTC no13637: MnU, 824.J63 OR.
Miscellaneous. London syndicate.

949. Jones, John, 1766 or 7–1795.
The reason of man: with strictures on Paine's Rights of man, and some other of his writings. The third edition. By John Jones, . . . Printed at Canterbury, and sold by Simmons, Kirkby and Jones, and in London by J. Murray, 1793.
iv,28p., 8vo.
Another issue: Canterbury, printed by Sim-mons, Kirkby and Jones.
ESTC to46335: L, 8135 b.22(9).
Politics. Provincial co-publishing.

950. Jones, John, 1766 or 7–1795.
The reason of man: part second. Containing strictures on Rights of man, with observations on Mr. Erskine's defence of Mr. Paine, and thoughts on the war with France. By John Jones. Printed at Canterbury, and sold by Sim-mons, Kirkby and Jones, and in London, by J. Murray, and J. Stockdale, 1793.
[2],31,[1]p., 8vo.
ESTC to46334: L, 8135.b.22(9*).
Politics. Provincial co-publishing.

951. Latta, James, surgeon in Edinburgh.
A practical system of surgery. By James Latta, . . . Illustrated with cases on many of the sub-jects, and with copperplates. In three volumes. . . . Edinburgh, printed for G. Mudie, J. Elder, A. Guthrie, and J. & J. Fairbairn; J. Murray, and Ogilvie & Spiere, London, 1793–95.
Vol. 1: 2,505p.; vol. 2: xi,534p.; vol. 3: xiii,,708p., plates, 8vo. With half-titles.

Vols 2 and 3 are dated 1795, (See Latta 1794, item 996). Vol. 1 entered in the Stationers' Company Register, 31 Oct. 1793, 'J. Latta. Whole'. Certificate given Nov. 2. 1793'.
ESTC t147572: L, 782.g.16–18.
Medicine. Edinburgh co-publishing.

952. McBride, Duncan.
General instructions for the choice of wines and spirituous liquors. Dedicated to His Royal Highness the Prince of Wales. ... By D. M'Bride. London, printed by J. Richardson; J. Debrett; T.[*sic*] Murray; and other booksellers in town and country, [1793].
86,[2],16p., 8vo. Price: 2*s*.6*d*.
ESTC t064974: L, 713.c.35(1).
Miscellaneous. London co-publishing.

953. M'Donald, A., (Andrew), 1755?–1790.
Twenty-nine miscellaneous sermons. By A. MacDonald, ... The fourth edition. London, printed for J. Murray, 1793.
viii,403,[1]p., 8vo.
ESTC t090408: L, 4454.g.10.
Religion. Murray alone.

954. Murphy, Arthur, 1727–1805.
An essay on his life and genius of Samuel Johnson, LL.D. B Arthur Murphy, Esq. London, printed for T. Longman, B. White and Son, B. Law, J. Dodsley, H. Baldwin, J. Robson, J. Johnson, C. Dilly, T. Vernor, G. G. J. and J. Robinson, T. Cadell, J. Nichols, R. Baldwin, N. Conant, P. Elmsly, F. and C. Rivington, T. Payne, W. Goldsmith, R. Faulder, Leigh and Sotheby, G. Nicol, J. Murray, A. Strahan, W. Lowndes, T. Evans, W. Bent, S. Hayes, G. and T. Wilkie, T. and J. Egerton, W. Fox, P. M'Queen, Ogilvie and Speare, Darton and Harvey, G. and C. Kearsley, W. Miller, B. C. Collins, and E. Newbery, 1793.
[4],187,[1]p., 8vo. With a half-title. Price: 4*s*. in boards.
See Johnson's *Works* 1792, item 884; BB, p. 43.
ESTC t087884: L, T. 1563 (1).
Biography. London syndicate.

955. Pagès, Monsieur de, (Pierre Marie François), 1748–1793.
Travels round the world, in the years 1767, 1768, 1769, 1770, 1771. By Monsieur de Pagès, ... Translated from the French. The second edition, corrected and enlarged. ... London, printed for J. Murray, 1793.
Vol. 1: xx,300p.; vol. 2: xii,268p.; vol. 3: xxii,[1],303p., table, 8vo.
A translation of *Voyages autour du monde*. Entered in the Stationers' Company Register, 8 Feb. 1791, 'J. Murray. Whole'; vol. 3 entered 29 Oct. 1792. 16 sets, plus odd vols (H); 532 sets (W)
ESTC t146288: L, 10025.c.7
Travel–topography. Murray alone.

956. Perry, William, lecturer in the Academy at Edinburgh.
The royal standard English dictionary; in which the words are not only rationally divided into syllables, accurately accented, their part of speech properly distinguished, and their various significations arranged in one line; but, likewise, by a key to this work, ... To which is prefixed a comprehensive grammar ... The eighth edition. To which is now added the scripture proper names, ... By W. Perry, ... Edinburgh, printed for and sold by Bell & Bradfute, and J. Dickson; and J. Murray, London, 1793.
[4],568,36p., 18mo. Price: 3*s*.
10,000 copies printed at Edinburgh by Neill & Co. Murray purchased a ½ share in Aug. 1785 from Neill, printer at Edinburgh, for 4 gns. His share of the expenses paid 22 Nov. 1793 was £98.5*s*.4*d*. The returns on his share (5000 copies at 1*s*.6*d*., wholesale) paid in Dec. 1793 were £375 (BB, p. 42). Entered in the Stationers' Company Register, 6 Feb. 1794, 'Hester Murray 1 Half. Bell & Bradfute 1 fourth. Jas. Dickson 1 fourth'. Stock: 18 (H). Share sold May 1796 to Murray & Vernor for £19.7*s*.
ESTC t088676: L, 1212.b.5.
Language. Edinburgh co-publishing.

957. Pictet, François Pierre.
A letter to a foreign nobleman, on the present situation of France, with respect to the other states of Europe. By F. P. Pictet, citizen of Geneva. London, printed for Hookham and Carpenter; and sold by Sewell; Symonds; and Murray, 1793.
[4],103,[5]p., 8vo. With two leaves of advertisements. Price: 2*s*.6*d*.
A translation of *Lettre à un seigneur etranger, sur la position actuelle de la France*.
ESTC t038019: L, 8132.df.3(4).
Politics. London co-publishing.

958. Polwhele, Richard, 1760–1838.
Historical views of Devonshire. In five volumes. Vol. I. By Mr. Polwhele, . . . Exeter, printed by Trewman and Son, for Cadell, Dilly, and Murray, London, 1793.
xix,[1],192,191–214p. (pp. 191–192 repeated in pagination but text and register are continuous; p. iv misnum. vi), 4to. Price: 10s.6d.
No more published.
ESTC t130755: L, 289.i.12.
Travel–topography. London co-publishing.

959. Rutherford, William, 1745–1820.
A view of antient history; from the creation of the world to the rise of the Macedonian Empire. Including the progress of literature and the fine arts. And illustrated with a map of the antient world. In two volumes. By William Rutherford, D.D. Master of the Academy at Uxbridge. . . . The second edition. London, printed for J. Murray, 1793.
Vol. 1: x,450,[2]p., 8vo. With a plate, map, and advertsiement; Vol. 2: iv,528p. With a map.
Price: 14s. in boards.
The 1788–91 edn. with cancel title pages. Stock: 12 (H); 137, plus 347 vol. 2 only (W).
ESTC n068048. ScCC D59.R97 1793.
History. Murray alone.

**960. A sailor's address to his countrymen; or, an adventure of Sam Trueman and his messmate. London, Murray, 1793.
8vo. Price: 3d.
No copy located. *Critical Review* 9 (Oct. 1793), 235–6, describes this poem as 'Low, licentious, and unintelligible.'
Poetry. Murray alone.

961. Saunders, William, 1743–1817.
A treatise on the structure, economy, and diseases of the liver; together with an enquiry into the properties and component parts of the bile and biliary concretions: . . . By William Saunders, M.D. . . . London, printed by T. Bensley: and sold by G. G. and J. Robinson; J. Murray; J. Johnson; and T. Cox, Borough, 1793.
[4],232p., 8vo. Price: 4s. in boards.
Another issue (*ESTC* t054051) excludes 'printed by T. Bensley' in the imprint.
ESTC t218042: C Path.c.731.
Medicine. London co-publishing.

962. Shakespeare, William, 1564–1616.
The plays of William Shakspeare. In fifteen volumes. With the corrections and illustrations of various commentators. To which are added, notes by Samuel Johnson and George Steevens. The fourth edition. Revised and augmented (with a glossarial index) by the editor of Dodsley's collection of old plays [Isaac Reed]. London, printed for T. Longman, B. Law and Son, C. Dilly, J. Robson, J. Johnson, T. Vernor, G. G. J. and J. Robinson, T. Cadell, J. Murray, R. Baldwin, H. L. Gardner, J. Sewell, J. Nicholls, F. and C. Rivington, W. Goldsmith, G. and T. Wilke, J. and J. Taylor, Scatchard and Whitaker, T. and J. Egerton, E. Newbery, J. Barket, J. Edwards, Ogilvy and Speare, J. Cuthell, J. Lackington, J. Deighton, and W. Miller. 1793.
15 vols., plates, tables, 8vo. With half titles. Price: £6.15s.
1200 copies printed. Murray bought a 1/120 share at the Globe Tavern (D. Cornish's sale) on 17 Mar. 1778 for £9.15s. which he paid to George Robinson. On 14 Aug. 1781 at John Hinton's sale he purchased a 1/60 share for £7.17s.6d. and on 10 May 1783 he acquired a further 1/60 share (John Ridley's) for £9, which he paid to Thomas Evans. He paid £63.19s.1½d. to Wright & Co. for paper on 31 July 1791, and printing (to Henry Baldwin and Wright & Co.) £140.11s.7d. on 3 April 1793. Total expenses, £204.10s.8½d. The returns on his share (61 sets at £4.8s. each, wholesale) were £268.8s.8d., paid on 3 April 1793 (BB, p. 12; see Shakespeare's *Plays* 1790, item 791). Twenty-five fine paper copies were extra-illustrated with engravings published by E. and S. Harding, and include an 8pp. list with directions to the binder; also included is an additional quarter-sheet with a note by Steevens dated Nov. 10, 1794 and an instruction to the binder. Stock: 2 (H); 40 (W). Shares sold 23 Dec. 1794: 1/120 to John Clark for £6; 2/120 to Kearsley for £12. Shares sold May 1796 2/120 to Murray and Kay for £16.5s. (BB, pp. 12, 67; see Plates 41 and 42).
ESTC t033036: L, 681.f.1–15.
Drama. London syndicate.

963. Sterne, Laurence, 1713–1768.
The works of Laurence Sterne. In ten volumes complete. . . . With a life of the author, written by himself. . . . London, printed for J. Dodsley,

J. Johnson, G. G. J. and J. Robinson, T. Cadell, J. Murray, T. Becket, R. Baldwin, Hookham and Co. A. Strahan, W. Lowndes, W. Bent, G. and T. Wilkie, C. and G. Kearsley, and D. Ogilvie and Co., 1793.
Vol. 1: xx,[2],296p.; vol. 2: [iv],307p.; vol. 3: [iv],288p.; vol. 4: [iv],[7],264p.; vol. 5: [iv], 242p.; vol. 6: [xiv],[3]–284p.; vol. 7: [viii],276p.; vol. 8: [viii],280p.; vol. 9: xv,[4],208p.; vol. 10: vii,198p.; 8vo. plates, port.,ill., 8vo. With half-titles in all but vol. 10. The marble leaf is inserted in vol. 2, facing pp. 111–12.
1000 copies printed. In March 1793 Murray paid Cadell £37.18s.8d. for his 63/1000 share of paper and printing. The returns on his share (63 sets at 20s. each, wholesale) were £63. Shares sold 23 Dec. 1794 to Stockdale for £33.15s. (BB, p. 23 and Plate 27). Stock: 3 (H); 46 (W).
ESTC t014787: L, 1608/2569.
Fiction. London syndicate.

964. Thomson, James, 1700–1748.
The seasons, by James Thomson. A new edition. Adorned with a set of engravings, from original designs. To which is prefixed, an essay on the plan and character of the poem, by J. Aikin, M.D. London, printed for J. Murray, 1793.
xlv,[3],256p., plates, 8vo.
See Thomson 1792, item 907. Stock: 10 (H).
ESTC t172595: E, Hall.268.a.
Poetry. Murray alone.

965. [Trapp, Joseph, b. 1715 or 16.]
Observations on some late proceedings of the national convention of France. London, Murray, 1793.
23p., 8vo. Price: 6d.
No copy located. *English Review* 21 (March 1793), 229.
Politics. Murray alone.

966. Trapp, Joseph, b. 1715 or 16.
Proceedings of the French National Convention on the trial of Louis XVI. late King of France and Navarre; to which are added, several interesting occurrences and particulars . . . the whole carefully collected from authentic documents, and republished with additions, from the paper of the World. By Joseph Trapp, A.M. London, printed for the author; sold by

Messrs. Murray, Kearsley, and Wenman and Co; Ridgeway; Deighton; Downes and M'Queen; and at the World Office, 1793.
xii,214p., 8vo.
ESTC t212271: D, J.944035.TRA/1793.
Politics. Agency–London.

967. The second edition:
ESTC t075818: L,010665.l.38.
Politics. Agency–London.

968. The trial of Avadaunum Paupiah Bramin, (dubash to John Hollond, Esq; . . . and to his brother E. John Hollond, Esq; . . .) of Avadaunum Ramah Saumy, Bramin, . . . Sunkaraporam Vincatachillah Chitty, and Appeyingar Bramin; for a conspiracy against David Haliburton, Esquire, a senior merchant in the service of the East India Company, . . . To the trial is prefixed an address to the public by Mr. Haliburton, . . . London, printed for J. Murray, 1793.
[2],142p., 8vo. Price: 5s. in boards.
The 'Address' (p. 21) signed: David Haliburton, and dated: Fort St. George. July 30th 1792; First published in Calcutta in Nov., 1792, as 'The trial of Avadanum Paupiah'.
ESTC t072769: L, 1490.aa.16.
Law. Murray alone.

969. Wade, John Peter, d. 1802.
Nature and effects of emetics, purgatives, mercurials, and low diet, in disorders of Bengal and similar latitudes. By John Peter Wade, M.D. . . . London, printed for J. Murray, 1793.
xii,352p., 8vo.
Stock: 495 (W).
ESTC n004846: MnU-B, B615.73.W119.
Medicine. Murray alone.

970. Wade, John Peter, d. 1802.
A paper on the prevention and treatment of the disorders of seamen and soldiers in Bengal. Presented to the honourable court of East-India directors, in the year 1791. By John Peter Wade, M.D. London, printed for J. Murray, 1793.
[2],iii,[3],172p., 8vo. Price: 3s.
Stock: 7 (H); 549 (W).
ESTC t069343: L, T.103(2).
Medicine. Murray alone.

971. Watts, Isaac, 1674–1748.
Logick; or, the right use of reason, in the enquiry after truth. . . . By Isaac Watts, D.D. A new edition, corrected and improved. London, printed for T. Longman, T. Field, C. Dilly, T. Vernor, G. G. J. and J. Robinson, J. Murray, W. Otridge, W. Flexney, W. Goldsmith, S. Hayes, Ogilvy and Speare, and W. Anderson. 1793.
iv, 324p., 12mo.
?1000 copies printed. Murray paid 1 gn. for a 1/16 share on 10 June 1793 at Buckland's sale. He paid £4.2s.9d. for paper and printing. The returns on his share (71 copies at 1s.6d. each, wholesale) were £7.1s. Share sold 23 Dec. 1794 to Scatcherd for £2.5s. (BB, p. 18). Stock: 70 (W).
ESTC n002621: MChB, SpC BC61.W29.
Religion. London syndicate.

972. Webster, Charles, 1750–1795.
Facts, tending to show the connection of the stomach with life, disease, and recovery. London, printed for J. Murray; W. Gordon, P. Hill, and G. Mudie, Edinburgh, 1793.
[4],59,[1]p., 8vo. Price: 1s.6d.
Introduction signed: Charles Webster. 'Lectures on the Materia Medica read at Edinburgh several years since.' Entered in the Stationers' Company Register, 9 Aug. 1793, 'J. Murray, Whole'.
ESTC t014677: L, 784.l.17(3).
Medicine. Edinburgh co-publishing.

973. Wood, James, 1766–1822.
Thoughts on the effects of the application and abstraction of stimuli on the human body; with a particular view to explain the nature and cure of typhus. By James Wood, . . . London, printed for J. Murray; and W. Creech, Edinburgh; and sold by W. Charnley, R. Fisher, and S. Hodgson, Newcastle; W. Phorson, Berwick; J. Graham, Sunderland; R. Christopher, Stockton; and L. Pennington, Durham, 1793.
[8],78,[2]p.,tables, 8vo. With a final errata leaf. Price: 2s.6d.
ESTC t059530: L, 7561.c.62.
Medicine. Edinburgh co-publishing.

1794

974. The adjourned debate, which took place at the India-House in Leadenhall-Street, on Thursday, October 23, 1794. On the question for presenting an address to His Majesty, offering to raise three regiments for the publick service. Reported by William Woodfall. London, printed by the reporter, and sold (price 2s.) by J. Debrett; R. Faulder; F. and G. Egerton; Mrs. Murray, B and J. White, and T. Chapman; and J. Sewell, 1794.
58,[2]p., 4to. Price: 2s.
The original debate was A sketch of the debate, listed below.
ESTC t225497: L, RB.23.b.1611.
Politics. London co-publishing.

975. Beddoes, Thomas, 1760–1808.
Considerations on the medicinal use of factitious airs, and on the manner of obtaining them in large quantities. In two parts. Part I. by Thomas Beddoes, M.D. Part II. by James Watt, Esq. Bristol, printed by Bulgin and Rosser, for J. Johnson and H. Murray, London, [1794].
48,32,[2]p., plates, 8vo. With an errata slip and advertisement leaf. Price: 2s.6d.
The 'Proposal' is dated on p. 7: Sept. 30, 1794.
Part III was published in 1795.
ESTC t031516: L, B.489(3).
Medicine. London co-publishing.

976. [Beddoes, Thomas, 1760–1808.]
The history of Isaac Jenkins, and Sarah his wife, and their three children. The sixth edition. London, printed for H. Murray; and J. Johnson, 1794.
1–34p., 12mo. Price: 3s.
ESTC n032821: CLU-S/C0457.
Fiction. London co-publishing.

977. Beddoes, Thomas, 1760–1808.
A guide for self preservation, and parental affection. Third edition, corrected. By Thomas Beddoes, M.D. Bristol, printed by Bulgin and Rosser, for J. Johnson; and H. Murray, London, [1794].
24p., 12mo.
Preface dated: Aug. 26, 1794.
ESTC t136211: L, 1178.a.43.
Medicine. London co-publishing.

978. Beddoes, Thomas, 1760–1808
Letters from Dr. Withering, of Birmingham, Dr. Ewart, of Bath, Dr. Thornton, of London,

and Dr. Biggs, . . . together with some other papers, supplementary to two publications on asthma, consumption, fever, and other diseases, by Thomas Beddoes, M.D. Bristol, printed by Bulgin and Rosser: sold by J. Johnson; and H. Murray, London; also by Bulgin and Sheppard, J. Norton, J. Cottle, W. Browne, and T. Mills, Bristol, [1794].
[2],5,[1],48p., 8vo. Price: 1s.
ESTC t038486: L,T.182(4).
Medicine. Provincial co-publishing.

979. Bell, Benjamin, 1749–1806.
A treatise on the hydrocele, on sarcocele, or cancer, and other diseases of the testes. By Benjamin Bell, . . . Edinburgh, printed for Bell & Bradfute; and G. G. & J. Robinson, and J. Murray, London, 1794.
295,[1]p. 4 plates, 8vo. Price: 2s.6d. (wholesale). 500 copies printed. Murray owned a 1/3 share. Expenses totalled £46.2s.10d; profits, £62.10s. (BB, p. 65).
ESTC t099025: L, 1188.c.37(2).
Medicine. Edinburgh co-publishing.

980. Berquin, Arnaud, 1747–1791.
L'ami des enfans, par M. Berquin. . . . Londres, chez J. Stockdale; B. Law & fils; J. Johnson; C. Dilly; J. Sewell; F. & C. Rivington; H. Murray; & W. Creech, Edinburgh, 1794.
Vol. 1: iv,207p.; vol. 2: 206p.; vol. 3: 235,[4]p.; vol. 4: 212,[4]p., 12mo. With advertisements in vols. 2 and 3.
ESTC t133460: L, Ch.790/92.
Education. Edinburgh co-publishing.

981. Bristow, James, b. 1757.
A narrative of the sufferings of James Bristow, belonging to the Bengal artilley [*sic*], during ten years captivity with Hyder Ally and Tippoo Saheb. Second edition. Calcutta printed: London, re-printed for J. Murray, 1794.
vi,210p., 8vo. Price: 3s.
A reissue of the 1793 edition, with the title page reset. Stock: 80 (H).
ESTC t114170: L, 10056.ff.1.
Military. Murray alone.

982. Clarke, Henry, 1743–1818.
Practical perspective. Being a course of lessons, exhibiting easy and consise rules for drawing justly all sorts of objects. . . . By Henry Clarke.

London, printed for Messrs Ogilvy and Speare; Mr. Murray; and I. and W. Clarke, Manchester, 1794.
113,[1]p., plates, 8vo. Price: 4s.4d.
ESTC t222535: Csj, 2.24.86.
Education. Provincial co-publishing.

982a. A new edition. illustrated with fifty-five large copper-plates.
[12],113,[1],p., plates, 8vo.
ESTC t228402: Lng, Scientific.
Education. Provincial co-publishing.

983. The debates at the East-India-House, on Wednesday, the 17th of December, 1794, on the adjourned consideration of Mr. Twining's motion, 'That no director be allowed to carry on any trade or commerce to or from India, directly or indirectly, either as principal or agent'. Reported by William Woodfall. London, printed by the reporter, and sold by J. Debrett; R. Faulder; F. and G. Egerton; Mrs. Murray, B. and J. White, and T. Chapman; and J. Sewell, 1794.
[2],5–92,[2]p., 4to.
ESTC t091037: L, 8226.g.39(1).
Economics. London co-publishing.

984. Deletanville, Thomas.
A new French dictionary, in two parts: the first, French and English; the second, English and French: . . . To which is prefixed, a French grammar. By Thomas Deletanville. The third edition, carefully revised, much improved, and enriched with upwards of two thousand words, by Mr. Des Carrieres. London, printed for F. Wingrave, successor to Mr. Nourse; B. Law and Son; J. Johnson; C. Dilly; G. G. and J. Robinsons; W. Richardson; J.Scatcherd; J. Evans; H. Murray; and Vernor and Hood, 1794.
Vol. 1: [406]p.; vol. 2: [570]p., 8vo.
6000 copies printed: Murray bought a 1/16 share for £11.10s. on 26 Jan. 1792 at Robinson's sale of Wingrave's property held at the Horn Tavern. His share of the production costs were £64.1s.3d. The returns on his share (375 copies at 4s.6d. each, wholesale) were £88.7s.6d. Shares sold May 1796: 1/32 to Rivington for £7.10s; 1/32 to Lowndes for £7.10s. (BB, p. 62).
ESTC t127533: L, 1509/1157.
Language. London syndicate.

985. Disraeli, Isaac, 1766–1848.
Curiosities of literature. Consisting of anecdotes, characters, sketches, and observations,
literary, critical, and historical. The fourth edition. London, printed for H. Murray, 1794.
Vol. 1: [xx],618,[10]p.; vol. 2: [xii],583,[10],[2]p.,
plate, 8vo.
The title page to vol. 2 reads: 'Curiosities of
literature. Volume the second. A new edition,
with large additions and improvements'. Stock:
60 vol. 2 (W).
ESTC t145281: L, 11865.h.33.
Literary criticism. Murray alone.

986. The Edinburgh magazine or literary mis-
cellany, . . . new series. Edinburgh, Printed for
James Symington, and sold in London by J.
Murray and W. Boag, 1794.
Vol. 3: 484,[2]p., 8vo., engraved title page;
plates.
Published in monthly parts; title page, contents,
and index issued every six months.
Primary location: E, NH 295.
Miscellaneous. Agency–Edinburgh.

987. The English review; or, an abstract of
English and foreign literature. . . . London,
printed for H. Murray, 1794.
Vol. 23: [1],[viii],15,480,[6]p., 8vo. With a Prospectus outlining the new format under the
editorship of Wm Thomson.
Published in monthly parts (priced at 1*s*); title
page, contents, and index issued every six
months.
Primary location: NN, *DA.
Miscellaneous. Murray–with agency.

988. Fielding, John.
Fielding's new peerage of England Scotland &
Ireland; containing the descent and present
state of every noble family of the three kingdoms, with an index and their mottos translated. London, printed for John Murray, & J.
Stockdale, [1794].
[2],368,[4]p., plates, 24mo. The title page is
engraved and dated June 1794.
2000 copies printed. Murray's half share of the
expenses, £107.3*s*.3*d*. (BB, p. 64). No information on profits. Stock: 240 (W), letterpress (32
imperfect).
ESTC n006801: RP, W929.72.F459n.
Miscellaneous. London co-publishing.

989. Greenlaw, Alexander, 1754 or 5–1829.
A sermon preached at New-Brentford Church,
by the Rev. A. Greenlaw, on Friday, February
28, 1794, being the day appointed for a general
fast. Brentford, printed and sold by P. Norbury.
Also sold by Mrs. Murray; and Mr. Cook,
London, [1794].
24p., 4to. With a half-title. Price: 1*s*.
ESTC t177372: AWn, Summers Room.
Religion. Provincial co-publishing.

990. Grut, Thomas, b. 1769 or 1770.
A sermon, preached in the parish church of
Chesham, Bucks; on Sunday Nov. 16, 1794.
for the encouragement and support of Sunday
schools. By Thomas Grut, . . . Berkhamsted,
printed and sold at The Herald Office, by W.
M' Dowall. Sold also by H. Murray, F. & C.
Rivington, London. And by the booksellers in
Oxford, 1794.
iv,28p., 8vo.
ESTC t018000: L, 4473.e.14(4).
Religion. Provincial co-publishing.

991. [Hawkesworth, John, 1715?–1773].
The adventurer. . . . A new edition. Illustrated
with frontispieces. London, printed for J. Dods-
ley, T. Longman, B. Law and son, J. Robson, G.
G. J. and J. Robinson, T. Cadell, R. Baldwin, S.
Hayes, W. Goldsmith, W. Lowndes, G. and T.
Wilkie, R. Faulder, J. Deighton, W. Fox, E.
Newbery, and H. Murray, 1794.
Vol. 1: [4],468]p.; vol. 2: [4],444p.; vol. 3: [4],
455,[1]p., plates, 8vo.
Essays by John Hawkesworth, Joseph Warton,
Samuel Johnson and others. 1000 copies
printed. Murray bought a 1/32 share on 8
Apr. 1777 at the Queen's Arms for which he
paid 12 gns. to Edward Johnston. He bought
another 1/32 share at Becket's sale on 21 Jan.
1779 at the Queen's Arms for £2.5*s*. In 9 Mar.
1792 he bought a further 1/32 share at Rivington's sale for £4. The expenses for the edition,
paid to Thomas Cadell, were £26.15*s*.1*d*. Profits
on his share (71 copies at 7*s*.6*d*. each, wholesale)
were £26.12*s*.6*d*. Shares (3/32) sold 23 Dec.
1794 at Crown & Anchor sale for £6.8*s*.6*d*.
(see Hawkesworth 1778, item 186 and 1788,
item 659; BB, p. 1).
ESTC t123427: L, 1560/576
Miscellaneous. London syndicate.

992. Humpage, Benjamin.
Physiological researches into the most impor-
tant parts of the animal oeconomy. . . . By
Benjamin Humpage. London, printed for H.
Murray, and G. Mudie, Edinburgh, 1794.
iv,282p., 8vo. Price: 5s.
ESTC t098616: L, 784.k.11.
Medicine. Edinburgh co-publishing.

993. Hunter, Henry, 1741–1802.
The day of judgment. Two sermons, preached
at the Scots church, London-Wall, December
15th, 1793, recommending a collection toward
the relief of the weavers in Spitalfields, . . . By
Henry Hunter, D.D. London, printed for the
author, by T. Gillet. And sold by H. Murray;
and J. Johnson, 1794.
vi,57,[1]p., 8vo.
ESTC t059267: L, 4478.h.7(4).
Religion. Agency–London.

994. Imison, John, d. 1788.
A treatise of the mechanical powers. I. of the
lever, II. the wheel and axle, III. the pulley, IV.
the screw, V. the wedge, and VI, the inclined
plane. To which are added, several useful
improvements in mill work, bevel geer [*sic*],
friction, the best shape for teeth in wheels,
&c. By John Imison. The second edition corrected. London, printed for H. Murray, 1794.
[4],37,[3]p., 2 plates, 8vo.
The [1787] edn. (item 596) with a cancel title
page.
ESTC n063308: CaOHM, Disbd.
Science. Murray alone.

995. [Johnson, Samuel, 1709–1784.]
The Rambler. . . . The thirteenth edition.
London, printed for T. Longman, B. Law and
Son, H. Baldwin, C. Dilly, G. G. J. and J.
Robinson, T. Cadell, J. Nichols, F. and C.
Rivington, W. Goldsmith, H. Murray, W.
Otridge, W. Lowndes, S. Hayes, R. Faulder, G.
and T. Wilkie, P. MacQueen, B. Collins,
Hookham and Carpenter, Darton and Harvey,
Vernor and Hood, Cadell jun. and Davies, and
R. Jameson, 1794.
Vol. 1: [viii],462p.; vol. 2p: [viii],459p.; vol. 3:
[viii],407,[27]p., port. in vol. 1; frontispiece
plates to vols. 2–4, 8vo. Price: 12s.
This edition is not recorded at BB, p. 28 and is
possibly a new issue of the 1793 edition

(above). Murray's 1/32 share was sold 23 Dec.
1794 to Kearsley for £7.12s.6d. (BB, p. 28).
Miscellaneous. London syndicate.

996. Latta, James, surgeon in Edinburgh.
A practical system of surgery. By James Latta,
. . . In three volumes. . . . Edinburgh, printed
for G. Mudie, J. Elder, A. Guthrie, and J. & J.
Fairbairn; J. Murray, and Ogilvie & Speare, Lon-
don, 1794–5.
Vol. 1: [6],2,vii,505, vol. 2: xi,534p.; vol. 3:
xiii,708p., plates, 8vo. Price: £1.1s in boards.
Entered in the Stationers' Company Register 27
Apr. 1795, vols. 2 and 3, 'Author. Whole'.
ESTC n061422: MnU-B, B617.L355.
Medicine. Edinburgh co-publishing.

997. Moises, Hugh, 1773–1819.
An inquiry into the abuses of the medical
department in the militia of Great Britain,
with some necessary amendments proposed.
Addressed to the president and members of
the Militia Club. By H. Moises, . . . London,
printed for J. Murray, 1794.
[2],142p. (pp. 126 and 135 misnum. 26 and 153
respectively), 8vo. Price: 3s.
ESTC t056711: L, 8826.ff.42
Medicine. Murray alone.

998. A popular view of the effects of the
venereal disease upon the constitution: collected from the best writers. To which are prefixed, miscellaneous observations, by a
physician. Edinburgh, printed for Bell &
Bradfute; and G. G. and J. Robinson, and H.
Murray, London, 1794.
[4],205,[3]p., 8vo. With a half-title and final
advertisement leaf. Price: 3s.
ESTC t178408: C, Hunter.c.79.26/2.
Medicine. Edinburgh co-publishing.

999. Robinson, Pollingrove.
Cometilla; or views of nature. By Pollingrove
Robinson, Esq. London, printed for J. Murray,
1794.
xv,[1],262p., 8vo. Price: 3s.3d.
The 1789 edn. (item 740) with a cancel title
page. Pollingrove Robinson may be a pseudo-
nym. Stock: 275 (H).
ESTC n068065: ICU, RB PR5233.B32C7
Science. Murray alone.

1000. Sheldrake, Timothy, fl. 1783–1806.
Observations on the causes of distortions of the legs of children and the consequences of the pernicious means generally used with the intention of curing them; . . . By T. Sheldrake, . . . London, printed for Messrs. Egerton; Hookham and Carpenter; Lewis; Murray; Dilly; and sold at the author's house, 1794.
v,[3],95,[1]p., plates, 8vo. Price: 3s.
ESTC t041773: L, T.203(4).
Medicine. London co-publishing.

1001. A sketch of the debate, that took place at the India-House in Leadenhall-Street, on Wednesday, the 9th of October inst. on the following motion of William Lushington, . . . By William Woodfall. London, printed by the reporter, and sold by J. Debrett; R. Faulder; F. and G. Egerton; Mrs. Murray, B. and J. White, and T. Chapman; and J. Sewell, 1794.
36p., 4to.
ESTC t048416: L, 583.h.28(1).
Politics. London co-publishing.

1002. Smellie, William, 1697–1763.
A treatise on the theory and practice of midwifery. Elucidated with upwards of forty copper-plate engravings of anatomy, difficult labours, and instruments, and containing a copious variety of . . . cases. By W. Smellie, M.D. A new and corrected edition, in one volume, comprising the whole of what has hitherto made three. London, printed for the proprietors, and sold by Mess. Murray, Kay, and Otridge, 1794.
[2],484p., plates, 8vo. Forty tables are engraved on ten plates.
ESTC n014166: MBCo, 1.Msp.1794.1.
Medicine. London co-publishing.

1003. Smith, George, M.A.
A sermon preached at the Chapel of St. John, at Market Street, in the county of Hertford. On Friday, Feb. 28, 1794, being the day appointed for a public fast. By George Smith,, M.A. Rector of Puttenham in Hertfordshire, and curate of the said chapel. Berkhamsted, printed and sold at the Herald Office, by W. McDowall. Published and sold also by H. Murray, London, 1794.
[4],13,[1]p., 4to.
ESTC n067366: CtY-BR Mhc8 1797 Sm57.
Religion. Provincial co-publishing.

1004. Stedman, Charles, 1753–1812.
The history of the origin, progress, and termination of the American war. By C. Stedman, . . . In two volumes. . . . London, printed for the author; and sold by J. Murray; J. Debrett; and J. Kerby, 1794.
Vol. 1: xv,399p.; vol. 2: xv,449,[13]p., plates, maps, 4to. With half-titles. Price: 2 gns.
ESTC t114190: L, 601.l.21.
History. Agency–London.

1005. Thomson, James, 1700–1748.
The seasons, by James Thomson. A new edition. Adorned with a set of engravings, from original designs. To which is prefixed, An essay on the plan and character of the poem, by J. Aikin, M.D. London, printed for J. Murray, 1794.
xlv,[3],256p., plates, 8vo. With a half-title.
The plates are dated 1792. Printed on royal paper. At an unspecified date after Murray's death Cadell purchased 'the whole and coppers' for an unspecified sum (BB, p. 57). Stock: 370, 50 'with cuts' (W).
ESTC t007153: L, 1490.de.54.
Another issue: printed on Demy paper; the date in the imprint is in roman.
ESTC t137446: L, 11661.df.13.
Poetry. Murray alone.

1006. [Thornton, Robert John, 1768?–1837.]
Medical extracts. Being a concentrated view of some late discoveries in chemistry, and the new theory and practice of physic, thereby introduced. By a friend to improvements. London, printed for Robinson; and sold by Johnson; Dilly; Murray; Owen; and Cox, 1794.
[12],vii,[1],41,[3],xl,[2],45–126,335–360,127,126–134,[2]p., plates, 8vo. With a final advertisement leaf.
Thornton continued the work in 1795 and 1797.
ESTC n003563: MBCo, R128.7.T39.
Medicine. Agency–London.

1007. Vieyra, Antonio, 1712–1797.
A dictionary of the Portuguese and English languages, in two parts; Portuguese and English, and English and Portuguese: wherein I. The words are explained . . . II. The etymology of the Portuguese generally indicated from the Latin, Arabic, and other languages. . . . By Anthony Vieyra, . . . A new edition, carefully

revised and improved. London, printed for F. Wingrave, successor to Mr. Nourse; J. Johnson; J. Sewell; W. Richardson; R. Faulder; G. and T. Wilkie; H. Murray, 1794.
2 vols, unpaginated, 4to.
1000 copies printed. Murray bought a 1/16 share for 13 gns on 26 Jan. 1792 at Robinson's sale of Wingrave's property held at the Horn Tavern. He paid for production costs £40.5*s*.5*d*. The returns on his share (63 copies at 28*s*. each, wholesale) were £88.4*s*. — a profit of £34.5*s*.6*d*. (BB, p. 62).
ESTC t113570: L, 627.k.16.
Language. London syndicate.

1008. White, Thomas, b. 1753.
A treatise on the struma, or scrofula, commonly called the King's evil: in which the common opinion of its being a hereditary disease is proved to be erroneous; . . . By Thomas White, . . . The third edition. London, printed for the author; and sold by H. Murray; J. Walter; R. and T. Turner; and at the Dispensary, 1794.
[4],218,[2]p., 8vo. Price: 3*s*.
First published in 1784 (item 453).
ESTC t069344: L, T.103(3).
Medicine. Agency–London.

1009. Withers, Thomas, 1750–1809.
Observations on the use and abuse of medicine, with a view to the prevention and cure of diseases. A new edition. By Thomas Withers, M.D. . . . London, printed for C. Dilly; H. Murray; and Vernor and Hood, London; and sold by W. Tesseyman, York, and the booksellers of Oxford, Cambridge, Edinburgh, &c., 1794.
vii,[1],347,[1]p., 8vo. Price: 2*s*.
First issued in 1775 as *Observations on the abuse of medicine*.
ESTC n010858: DNLM, 18th c.coll.
Medicine. London co-publishing.

1010. Withers, Thomas, 1750–1809.
A treatise on the errors and defects of medical education: in which are contained observations on the means of correcting them. By Thomas Withers, . . . London, printed for C. Dilly; H. Murray; and Vernor and Hood, London; and sold by W. Tesseyman, York, and the booksel-

lers of Oxford, Cambridge, Edinburgh, &c., 1794.
v,[6],6–134p., 8vo. Price: 2*s*.
ESTC t010637: L, 10347.ee.8(4).
Medicine. London co-publishing.

1795

1011. Anderson, John, *c.* 1730–1804.
A practical essay on the good and bad effects of sea-water and sea-bathing. By John Anderson, M.D., . . . London, printed for C. Dilly; E. [*sic*] Murray; S. Silver, Margate; and all other booksellers in Town and Country, 1795.
[6],74p., 8vo. Price; 2*s*.
ESTC t027549: L,T.176(8).
Medicine. London co-publishing.

1012. Anderson, John, *c.* 1730–1804.
A preliminary introduction to the act of sea-bathing; wherein is shewn its nature, power, and importance; . . . By John Anderson, . . . Margate, printed for C. Dilly, and W. Murray, London; to be had at the libraries Margate, Ramsgate, and Broadstairs, 1795.
28,[2]p., 8vo. With a final advertisement leaf. Price 1*s*.
ESTC n020411: DNLM, WZ260.A5475p 1795.
Medicine. Provincial co-publishing.

1013. Balfour, Francis, fl. 1812.
A treatise on sol-lunar influence in fevers, &c. By Francis Balfour. Second edition, corrected and enlarged. Vol. I. London, printed for H. Murray, 1795.
xxii,306p., tables, 8vo. Price: 1*s*.6*d*.
ESTC t093704: L, 1168.i.12.
Medicine. Murray alone.

1014. Chambers, Ephraim, *c.* 1680–1740.
Cyclopaedia: or, an universal dictionary of arts and sciences. . . . By E. Chambers, F.R.S. With the supplement, and modern improvements, incorporated in one alphabet. By Abraham Rees, D.D. In four volumes. . . . London, printed for T. Longman, B. Law, C. Dilly, H. S. Woodfall, W. Domville, G. G. and J. Robinson, T. Cadell, R. Baldwin, W. Otridge, A. Strahan, F. and C. Rivington, W. Goldsmith, T. Payne, S. Hayes, W. Bent, G. and T. Wilkie, B. C. Collins, P. Wynne, C. D. Piguenitt, C. and G. Kearsley, W. March, A. Hamilton, T. Cadell, jun,

and W. Davies, W. Owen, H. Murray, A. Galbraith, and E. Johnson, 1795.
4 vols., unpaginated, plates, 20.
Originally issued in 89 parts (see Chambers, 1778, item 176, for publishing information; BB, pp. 8 and 51).
ESTC t210549: SSL, 030.d. SR.
Miscellaneous. London Syndicate.

1015. Chaumareix, Jean-Hugues Duroy de, 1763–1841.
Narrative of M. de Chaumereix, who escaped from the massacres of Aurai and Vannes, after the expedition of Quiberon. With observations on the public opinion in Brittany. To which is added a prospectus for pasigraphy, . . . London, from the printing-office of T. Baylis. Sold at Debrett's; Richardson's; J. Murray and S. Highley, and Wallis, 1795.
[2],46,4p., 8vo. The prospectus has separate pagination.
ESTC t134715: L, 9210.c.37.
Biography. London co-publishing.

1016. The debate at the East India House, on Friday, the 29th of May, 1795. On the several motions brought forward by Mr. Alderman Lushington, . . . Reported by William Woodfall. London, printed by the reporter, and sold by J. Debrett; Murray, and Co. B. and J. White, and T. Chapman; R. Faulder; Egerton, [1795].
77,[1]p., 8vo.
ESTC t140800: L, 9055.b.28.
Politics. London co-publishing.

1017. The debates at the East India House, on Wednesday, the 14th October, 1795. . . . To which is prefixed a summary of what passed at the quarterly General Court. On Wednesday, the 16th of September, 1795. Reported by William Woodfall. London, printed by the reporter, and sold by J. Debrett; R. Faulder; F. and G. Egerton; Mrs. Murray, B. and J. White, and T. Chapman; and J. Sewell, [1795].
66,18p., 4to.
Advertisement dated: Dec. 31, 1795.
ESTC t032170: L, 8023.1.11(3).
Politics. London co-publishing.

1018. The debates that have taken place at the East India House, on various important subjects, from January 24, 1793, to January 21,

1795. Reported by William Woodfall. London, printed by the reporter, and sold by J. Debrett; R. Faulder; F. and G. Egerton; Mrs. Murray, B. and J. White, and T. Chapman; and J. Sewell, [1795].
8,[4],vi,161,25,40,52,9,[1],92,[1],133p., in 8 parts, 4to.
ESTC t186673: C, Acton.b.25.354.
Politics. London co-publishing.

1019. The debates at the East India House, on Wednesday, the 13th of May last, on the following motion, made by Mr. Jackson, . . . and also on the motions brought forward by Mr. Lushington, on Friday, the 29th of May. . . . Reported by William Woodfall. London, printed by the reporter, and sold by J. Debrett; Murray, and Co. B. and J. White; R. Faulder; Egerton; and the book-sellers, near the Royal Exchange, 1795.
[4],138,179–223p., 4to.
Register and text are complete despite irregular pagination.
ESTC t009989: L, 583.h.28(3).
Politics. London co-publishing.

1020. Disraeli, Isaac, 1766–1848.
Curiosities of literature. Consisting of anecdotes, characters, sketches, and observations, literary, critical, and historical. The fourth edition. London, printed for H. Murray, 1795.
xvi,[4],618p., 8vo.
ESTC n044549: CaOLU SpC PN43.D5 1795.
Literary criticism. Murray alone.

1021. Dundonald, Archibald Cochrane, Earl of, 1749?–1831.
A treatise, shewing the intimate connection that subsists between agriculture and chemistry. Addressed to the cultivators of the soil, . . . By the Earl of Dundonald. London, printed for J. Murray and S. Highley, (successors to the late Mr. Murray), 1795.
Entered in the Stationers' Company Register, 31 Mar. 1795, 'Author. Whole'.
vii,[1],252p., tables, 4to. With a half-title.
Another issue: London: printed for the author, and sold by R. Edwards. March, 1795.
ESTC t160061: L, 1651/346.
Agriculture. Murray alone (with Highley).

1022. The Edinburgh magazine or literary

miscellany, . . . new series. Edinburgh, Printed for James Symington, and sold in London by J. Murray and W. Boag, 1795.

Vol. 4: 478,[2]p., 8vo., engraved title page; plates; vol. 5: Edinburgh, Printed for James Symington, and sold in Lonbon by H. Murray, 1795; 482,[2]p., 8vo., engraved title page; plates. Vol. 6: Edinburgh. Printed for James Symington, and sold in London by Murray and Highley, 1795; 480,[2]p., 8vo., engraved title page; plates.

Published in monthly parts; title page, contents, and index issued every six months.

Primary location: E, NH 295.

Miscellaneous. Agency–Edinburgh.

1023. The English review; or, an abstract of English and foreign literature. . . . London, printed for H. Murray, 1795.

Vol. 24: [1],[viii],480,[6]p. vol. 25: [1],[vi], 480, [6]p., 8vo;vol. 26: Printed for J. Murray and S. Highley. [1],[vi],480,[6]p.

Published in monthly parts (priced at 1s.); title page, contents, and index issued every six months.

Primary location: NN, *DA.

Miscellaneous. Murray–with agency.

1024. Euler, Leonhard, 1707–1783.

Letters of Euler to a German princess, on different subjects in physics and philosophy. Translated from the French by Henry Hunter, D.D. With original notes, and a glossary of foreign and scientific terms. In two volumes. . . . London, printed for the translator, and for H. Murray, 1795.

Vol. 1: [4], vi,v–lxiii,515p.; vol. 2: [6],viii,520,xx–viiip., plates, 8vo. Price: 16s. in boards.

First published in 1768 as *Lettres à une princesse d'Allemagne.* 1000 copies printed. Hunter received £113.8s. for the translation. Production expenses totalled £320.9s.9d. (BB, p. 68). Entered in the Stationers' Company Register, 14 Feb. 1795, 'Trustees of Jn. Murray 3/4. Dr. Hunter, 1/4'. BB, p. 68 lists Hester Murray, a 2/3 share and Hunter a 1/3 share. Shares sold May 1796, 2/3 to Murray & Vernor for £2.7s.

ESTC t100446: L, E/02063.

Education. Murray alone.

1025. Fiott, John, d. 1797.

Three addresses, to the proprietors of East-India stock, and the publick, on the subject of the shipping concerns of the Company. With their vouchers and documents. Originally published in 1791, 1792, and 1793. . . . By Mr. J. Fiott, . . . London, printed for F. and C. Rivington. J. Debrett; Mrs. Murray, B. and J. White; and W. Richardson, 1795. vii,[1],148,145*–148*,149–150,151*–160*,153–170,171*–181*, 17–2–194,[2],195–322p. (pp. 47 and 184 misnum. 48 and 186 respectively), table, 4to.

One address entered in the Stationers' Company Register, 26 Mar. 1791, 'J. Fiott. Whole'.

ESTC t095368: L, 8228.l.14.

Economics. London co-publishing.

1026. For all ranks of people, political instructions. Part I. On the bill of rights. . . . Part II. On a reform in parliament, and its probable consequences. Part III. On popular discontents. . . . London, printed for, and sold by, T. Cox. Also sold by Johnson; Murray; Manson; and Owen, 1795.

[2],19,[1];[2],29,[1];[2],22p., 8vo.

Each part has a divisional title page, separate register and pagination. Beneath imprint: 'Each part may be had separate, price sixpence'.

ESTC t105695: L, 1102.i.32.

Politics. Agency–London.

1027. Hewat, Alexander.

The firm patriot, and principal qualities which mark that fair and illustrious character, at the present juncture, in these realms. A sermon, for the fast day, February 25, 1795. By Alexander Hewat, D.D. London, printed for T. Cadell jun. and W. Davies (successors to Mr. Cadell); and H. Murray, 1795.

[4],32p., 8vo. Price: 1s.

ESTC t060285: L, 4471.f.71(3).

Religion. London co-publishing.

1028. Hunter, Henry, 1741–1802.

Sermons preached at different places and on various occasions; collected and republished in their respective order: . . . By Henry Hunter, . . . London, printed for the author; and sold by C. Dilly; Murray and Highley; and J. Johnson, 1795.

Vol. 1: vi,[2],363,[1]p.; vol. 2: [4],373,[3]p., 8vo. With half-titles and advertisement in vol. 2.

ESTC t098649: L, 4454.h.9

Religion. Agency–London.

1029. Letters addressed to the inhabitants of the ward of Farringdon without, on the subject of the late ward-meeting in St. Dunstan's Church, relative to the bill for suppression of seditious meetings: with strictures on the proceedings there. By an inhabitant of the ward who was present. London, printed for J. Murray and S. Highley, 1795.
52p., 8vo. Price 1s.
ESTC n068429: Or, Angus 42.e.17(d).
Politics. Murray (with Highley) alone.

1030. Mercier, Louis Sébastien, 1740–1814.
Fragments of politics and history. By M. Mercier. Translated from the French. In two volumes. . . . London, printed for H. Murray, 1795.
Vol. 1: xv,[1],484p.; vol. 2: vi,488p., 8vo. Price: 14s. in boards.
A translation of *Fragmens de politique et d'histoire*. The expenses for the edition, including translator's fee, came to £282.18s.9d. (BB, p. 68). Entered in the Stationers' Company Register, 14 Feb. 1795, 'Trustees of Jn. Murray. Whole'.
ESTC t123221: L, 1137.h.21,22.
Politics. Murray alone.

1031. One cause of the present scarcity of corn, pointed out, and earnestly recommended to the serious consideration of the people; as being, at the same time, a constant source of wretchedness to many individuals. By a physician. London, printed for W. Miller; and Mrs. Murray, 1795.
30p., 8vo. Price: 1s.
ESTC t043279: L, T.249(2).
Economics. London co-publishing.

1032. Pargeter, William, 1760–1810].
Formulae medicamentorum selectae. By the author of Maniacal observations. London, printed for H. Murray; and sold by J. Callow, 1795.
iv,58,[2]p, 12mo.
Primary location: C.
Medicine. Murray–with agency.

1033. Peart, E. (Edward), 1756?–1824.
The anti-phlogistic doctrine of M. Lavoisier critically examined, and demonstratively confuted. In which its absurdities are exposed, . . . To which is added an appendix, consisting of strictures on Dr. Priestley's experiments on the generation of air from water; and of criticisms on the remarks made by the reviewers on the author's former writings. By E. Peart, M.D. &c. London, printed for W. Miller, and Mrs. Murray, 1795.
vi,[2],151,[1]p., 8vo. Price 4s. in boards.
ESTC n005942: MBCo, 1.Mk.414.
Medicine. London co-publishing.

1034. Perry, Sampson, 1747–1823.
A disquisition of the stone and gravel; with observations on the gout, when combined with those disorders. By S. Perry, surgeon. The eighth edition. London, printed for the author, and published by Becket; Murray; Richardson; Crosby; and Southern, 1795.
106p., 8vo.
ESTC n028630: TxHMC, RBR Burbank.
Medicine. Agency–London.

1035. Perry, William, lecturer in the Academy at Edinburgh.
The standard French and English pronouncing dictionary; in two parts. Part I. French and English. Part II. English and French. Containing several thousand words not inserted in any folio or octavo dictionaries now extant, . . . By W. Perry, . . . London, printed for Murray and Co.; J. Stockdale; and Scatcherd and Whitaker, 1795.
ix,[3],351,[1];377,[3]p., 12mo. With a half-title. Price: 3s.
6000 copies printed. Murray had a one third share. Total expenses: £760.18s.5d. (Perry — £117.12s.; printing — £300.17s.; paper — £285.12s.; advertising — £36.17s.5d.) Murray's share: £253.12s.9d. Shares sold May 1794 to Scatcherd and Stockdale for £96 (BB, p. 63). Entered in the Stationers' Company Register, 11 July 1795, 'Trustees of J. Murray, J. Stockdale & Scatcherd & Whitaker. Whole'.
ESTC t087435: L, 626.a.32.
Language. London co-publishing.

1036. Saunders, William, 1743–1817.
A treatise on the structure, economy, and diseases of the liver; together with an inquiry into the properties and component parts of the bile and biliary concretions. By William Saunders, . . . Second edition. With considerable additions. London, printed and sold by J. Phillips;

sold also by G. G. and J. Robinson; J. Murray; J. Johnson; and T. Cox, Borough, 1795.
[4],xxvi,261,[1]p., 8vo.
ESTC no14038: DNLM, WZ260.S257t 1795.
Medicine. London co-publishing.

1037. Squirrell, Robert.
An essay on indigestion and its consequences, or advice to persons affected with debility of the digestive organs, nervous disorders, gout, dropsy, &c. . . . Also remarks on sea or cold bathing, . . . By R. Squirrell, M.D. London, sold by Murray & Highley, and by the author, No. 7, Denmark Street, Soho, [1795?].
[2],126p., 8vo. Price: 3s. in boards.
ESTC n65608: C-S, 616.3577.
Medicine. Agency–Murray alone.

1038. Taylor, John, d. 1808.
Considerations on the practicability and advantages of a more speedy communication between Great Britain and her possessions in India: with the outline of a plan for the more ready conveyance of intelligence over-land by the way of Suez; and an appendix, . . . By John Taylor, . . . London, printed for J. Murray and S. Highley, (successors to the late Mr. Murray), 1795.
[4],48,31,[1]p., 4to. With a half-title. Price: 4s.
ESTC t146368: L, 102.h.43.
Travel–topography. Murray (with Highley) alone.

1039. [Thomson, William, 1746–1817].
Observations on the importance of the East-India fleet, to the Company and the nation, in a letter addressed to . . . Henry Dundas, . . . By Thomas Newte, Esq. London, printed for J. Debrett; R. Faulder; F. and G. Egerton; Mrs. Murray, B. and I. White, T. Chapman; and J. Sewell, 1795.
[2],5–50p., 8vo.
Thomas Newte is William Thomson.
ESTC no12618: MdBJ-P, 954.H673.
Politics. London co-publishing.

1040. [Thornton, Robert John, 1768?-1837.]
Medical extracts. On the nature of health, with practical observations: and the laws of the nervous and fibrous systems. By a friend to improvements. . . . London, printed for Robin-

sons: and sold by Johnson; Dilly; Murray; Owen; and Cox, 1795.
Vol. 1: [16],[iii]-vi,134p.; vol. 2: [2],ii,[63],135]-334p.; Vol. 3: [69],361–556p., plates, 8vo.
The imprint in vol. 3 adds J. Johnson as a publisher and Manson to the list of agents. A fourth volume was published in 1797.
ESTC no03564: MBCo, 1.Ha.180.
Medicine. Agency–London.

1041. Townsend, Joseph, 1739–1816, Rector of Pewsey.
A guide to health; being cautions and directions in the treatment of diseases. Designed chiefly for the use of students. By the Rev. Joseph Townsend, . . . London, printed for Cox, Borough; and sold by Robinsons; Dilly; Murray; and Owen, 1795.
vi,[8],400p., 8vo. Price: 6s. in boards.
At foot of p. 400 'End of the first volume', but see next.
ESTC no30826: PPL, In Town 60409.0.
Medicine. London co-publishing.

1042. Second edition. London, printed for Cox; and sold by Robinsons; Dilly; Murray; and Owen, 1795–96.
vol. 1: vi,[viii],400p.; vol. 2: [viii],559,viiip., 8vo.
Vol. 2 title page, lacking edition statement, has imprint: Cox; and sold by Johnson; Robinsons; Dilly; Murray and Highley; and Owen.
ESTC no17911: MBU-M, Townshend 1795.
Medicine. London co-publishing.

1043. Ware, James, 1756–1815.
A copy of the appendix and notes, annexed to the third edition of Remarks on the ophthalmy, psorophthalmy and purulent eye; by James Ware, surgeon. London, printed for Charles Dilly; H. Murray; and J. Walter, 1795.
[4],32p., 8vo. Price 1s.
ESTC to06159: L, T.176(5).
See next but one.
Medicine. London co-publishing.

1044. Ware, James, 1756–1815.
An enquiry into the causes which have most commonly prevented success in the operation of extracting the cataract; with an account of the means by which they may either be avoided or rectified. To which are added, observations on the dissipation of the cataract, and on the

cure of the gutta serena. Also, additional remarks on the epiphora; or, watery eye. . . . By James Ware, Surgeon. London, printed for C. Dilly; H. Murray; and J. Walter, 1795. [4],vii,[1],172p., 8vo. With a half-title.Price 3s. *ESTC* t007131: L, T.107(2). Medicine. London co-publishing.

1045. Ware, James, 1756–1815. Remarks on the ophthalmy, psorophthalmy, and purulent eye; with methods of cure, considerably different from those commonly used; and cases annexed, in proof of their utility: also, the case of a gutta serena cured by electricity; by James Ware, surgeon. The third edition; with alterations, notes, and an appendix. London, printed for Charles Dilly; H. Murray; and J. Walter, 1795.

viii,179,[3]p., 8vo. With a final advertisement leaf. *ESTC* n012745: DNLM, W6.P3 v.910. Medicine. London co-publishing.

1046. Watson, James, Mr. Serjeant. Cursory remarks upon Mr. Twining's pamphlet, entitled Observations on the question, to be balloted for at the East-India-House, January 14, 1795. By Mr. Serjeant Watson. London, printed by W. Woodfall, for J. Debrett; R. Faulder; F. and G. Egerton; Mrs. Murray, B. and I. White, T. Chapman, and J. Chapman, 1795. [2],5–26p., 8vo. *ESTC* t108419: L, 8023.cc.46. Politics. London co-publishing.

'Books Printed For J. Murray' (Not Located)

The main sources are: 1. a 4–page advertisement from 1769 listing 11 titles (*ESTC* t135236: O, C.Pamph.1933.3*); 2. an 8–page advertisement from late 1773 listing 45 titles (*ESTC* t185935: O, Vet.A5c.2112.2); and 3. a 6–page advertisement from 1775 listing 27 titles (bound in the L copy of Craig, *Twenty discourses*, 1775, item 100 above). Entries are recorded exactly as they appear in the lists.

1047. 'Congreve's Works, printed by Baskerville, in 3 vol. large 8vo. with Copper-plates, a very elegant Edition. Price £1.1s. bound. The original Price of this Edition of Congreve's Works is £1.5s.' [1769 list, 6]

1048. 'Plutarch's Lives, translated by Mr. Dryden and others; a very neat Edition, in 9 vol. 18mo. with Heads. Pr. bound 18s.' [1769 list, 7].

1049 'An Ecclesiastical History from the Birth of Christ . . . translated from the French of Mr. [J. H. S.] Formey. Octavo, 2 Vols, bound in one. Price 7s.' [1773 list, 6; 1775 list, 16]. Only a London 1766 edition is located.

1050. 'The History of Clarissa Harlowe. By the late celebrated Mr. S. Richardson. A beautiful and uncommon Edition in Octavo. 7 Vols.

Price £1.8s. bound. At the End is contained a Collection of the Sentiments interspersed through the Work, omitted in the small editions' [1773 list, 8].

1051. 'The Art of Short Hand improved; being an universal Character adapted to the English Languge. . . . By David Lyle, M.A. Price 7s.6d.' [1773 list, 22] Only a 1762 edition is located.

1052. 'The Book of Martyrs, containing an Account of the Sufferings of the Protestant Martyrs in England, Scotland and Ireland: The Siege of Londonderry: The Spanish Invasion in 1588; Gunpowder Treason in 1605: The Fire of London 1666, &c. &c. Price bound 3s.' [1773 list, 24].

1053. 'The universal History from the earliest Account of Time, compiled from original Authors, illustrated with Maps, Cuts, and Chronological Tables, 7 Vols. Folio, Price £6.6s.' [1773 list, 25].

1054. 'A Treatise on the Parallactic Angle: with an appendix containing a complete Set of Solar and Lunar Tables. In Boards, Quarto, Price 3s.6d.' [1773 list, 26] William Sandby published an edition in 1766 (*ESTC* t072827).

1055. 'The Philosophical Principles of natural and revealed Religion, unfolded in geometrical Order. By the Chevalier Ramsay, Author of the Travels of Cyrus. Small Quarto, 2 Vols. Price £1.1s.' [1773 list, 27; 1775 list, 3]. Murray acquired several copies (on fine and ordinary paper) of this Foulis Press title in Apr. 1769 (Wm Kerr to JM, 23 June 1769).

1056. 'An Essay on the East India Trade. Price 1s.6d.' [1773 list, 29] NUC records a copy at Yale with a London 1770 imprint, but this copy is missing.

1057. 'An Inquiry, historical and critical, into the Evidence against Mary Queen of Scots; with an Examination of the Histories of Mr. Hume, and Dr. Robertson. Octavo, third Edition. Price 6s.' [1773 list, 34]

1058. 'An Essay on the Advantages of a polite Education, joined with a learned one. Price 1s.6d.' [1773 list, 35; 1775 list, 6]. The work, by Stephen Philpot, 'Printed for the author; and sold by W. Russell', first appeared in 1747.

1059. "The Choice Spirits Pocket Companion, or the Bucks Treasury; being a complete Collection of droll and humorous Songs, now in the highest Vogue among the Societies of Choice Spirits, Bucks, Free Masons, &c. Price bound 2s.' [1773 list, 36] Several works with similar titles were published but none identical.

1060. 'The Nunnery for Coquets; a Novel. Price 3s.6d.' [1773 list, 40]. A London edition 'Printed for T. Lowndes' appeared in 1771.

1061. 'The Ladies Miscellany; a new Work, consisting of entertaining Novels, Family Pictures, Flights of Fancy, Modern Characters, &c. 2 Vols. Price 6s.' [1773 list, 41] A Dublin edition in 2 vols. 'Printed for Thomas Walker' appeared in 1770.

1062. 'Brindley's beautiful Set of Classics, complete, in 24 Vols. very neatly bound. Price three Guineas. Note. The following Books may be had separate to complete Sets. Q. Curtius, 2 Vols. 6s; Catullus, 3s; Juvenal, 3s; Lucan, 2 Vols. 6s; Ovid, 5 Vols. 15s; Phoedrus, 3s; Tacitus, 4 Vols. 12s.' [1773 list, 42]. See Catullus 1774, item 75 above.

1063. 'Biblia Sacra ex Sebastiani Castellionis Interpretatione, ejusque postrema recognitione. In 4 tom. 12mo 10s.' [1773 list, 44] This work originally appeared in 1726–7.

Addenda

(These items have not been incorporated into the Tables and Figures.)

*[Fuller, Anne, d. 1790].
The convent: or, the history of Sophia Nelson. In two volumes. By a young lady. London, printed by T. Wilkins, 1786.
Vol. 1: 293p.; vol. 2: 320p., 12mo, Price: 6s
The *Critical Review*, 62 (Dec. 1786), 469, gives 'Murray' as bookseller.
ESTC t46879: L, N.2316.
Fiction. Agency-London.

Samuel Johnson, 1709–1784.
A dictionary of the English language: in which the words are deduced from their originals, explained in their different meanings, . . . Abstracted from the folio edition by the author, Samuel Johnson, LL.D. To which is prefixed, a grammar of the English language. The tenth edition. London, printed for. T. Longman, B. Law and son, J. Dodsley, J. Robson, C. Dilly, G. G. J. Robinson, T. Cadell, W. Richardson, R. Baldwin, W. Goldsmith, W. Lowndes, S. Hayes, Scratcherd and Whitaker, W. Bent, G. and T. Wilkie, F. Wingrave, and H. Murray, 1794. [960p.], 8vo.
Information not recorded in BB, p. 10, but see Checklist, item 883 for the 1792 tenth edition.
ESTC t083961: L, 1477.dd.5.
Language. London syndicate.

Index of Murray Publications

Entries are arranged by author or by title if anonymous. Multiple works by a single author in a given year are not indicated.

Abercrombie, John, 1784, 1787–88, 1791
Abstract of the trial of George Stratton, 1780
Account of the loss of His Majesty's ship Deal Castle, 1787
Account of the martyrs, 1776
Account of the Scots Society in Norwich, 1784, 1786
Addison, Joseph, 1788–89
Address to both houses, 1779
Adjourned debate . . . at the India-House, 1794
Adventures of George Maitland, 1786
Adye, Stephen Payne, 1769, 1772, 1778, 1785–86
Aikin, John, 1788
Ainsworth, Robert, 1790
Aitken, John, 1779, 1785, 1787, 1790
Alderson, John, 1788
Alves, Robert, 1778
Analysis of the medicinal waters of Tunbridge Wells, 1792
Anderson, John, 1786–88, 1795
Anderson, Walter, 1790
Andree, John, 1781–82, 1788, 1790
Argens, marquis d' (Jean Baptiste de Boyer), 1769
Ariosto, Lodovico, 1783
Arnot, Hugo, 1776–77, 1779, 1785
Articles exhibited by the knights, 1788

Articles . . . against Sir Elijah Impey, 1788
Asiatic miscellany, 1792
Astronomical catechism, 1792
Authentic memoirs, 1769
Bacon, Francis, Viscount St Albans, 1786
Balfour, Francis, 1795
Bannerman, Patrick, 1773
Baudelocque, Jean Louis, 1790
Beatson, Robert, 1786
Beccaria, Cesare, marchese di, 1769
Beddoes, Thomas, 1790, 1792–94
Bell, Benjamin, 1791, 1793–94
Bell, John, 1791
Bell, W., 1775
Benjamin Ben Jonah, of Tudela, 1783–84
Bennett, John, 1787, 1789
Bergman, Torbern, 1783–85, 1788
Berkeley, George, 1789
Berquin, Arnaud, 1787–88, 1793–94
Bettesworth, John, 1783
Biographia Britannica, 1793
Black, Joseph, 1777
Blackstone, Sir William, 1786
Blair, Hugh, 1784–85, 1787
Blane, Gilbert, 1785, 1788–89
Blumenbach, Johann Friedrich, 1792
Borthwick, George, 1775
Boutcher, William, 1775, 1778
Boyd, Robert, 1787

Boyer, Abel, 1783, 1786, 1791
Brand, Thomas, 1784–85, 1787
Breaks, Thomas, 1771, 1778
Brief account of a seminary established at Hampstead, 1787
Brisson, Pierre-Raymond de, 1789
Bristow, James, 1793–94
Brookes, Richard, 1778, 1782, 1786, 1790
Brown, John, 1773
Brown, John, M.D., 1787
Brown, William Laurence, 1788, 1793
Bruce, Peter Henry, 1780, 1782
Buc'hoz, Pierre-Joseph, 1775, 1779, 1784
Buffon, comte de (Georges Louis Leclerc), 1792
Burney, William, 1789
Burton, John, 1793
Butter, William, 1782–83
Campbell, Coll., 1784–85
Carlyle, Alexander, 1776, 1778
Carmichael, James, 1790
Carr, George, 1791
Carter, Francis, 1788
Carter, George, 1791
Cartwright, Edmund, 1771–72, 1777, 1779, 1783
Cary, Patrick, 1771
Cases, medical, chirurgical, and anatomical, 1788
Catullus, Gaius Valerius, 1774
Caylus, Madame de, (Marthe-Marguerite), 1770

Cervantes Saavedra, Miguel de, 1782, 1792
Chambaud, Lewis, 1782, 1789
Chamberlaine, William, 1784–85
Chambers, Ephraim, 1777–78, 1784–85, 1795
Chaumareix, Jean-Hugues Duroy de, 1795
Clark, Hugh, 1784
Clark, John, 1778–79, 1792
Clark, Samuel, 1775
Clarke, Henry, 1776–77, 1782–83, 1793–94
Clubbe, John, 1786
Coalitionist. A satire, 1783
Coley, William, 1785
Collins, Arthur, 1779
Colman, George, 1787
Combe, Charles, 1782
Cooke, James, 1784
Cornwell, Bryan, 1784, 1787–88
Crabbe, George, 1783
Craig, William, 1775
Crawford, Adair, 1779
Crébillon, Claude Propser Jolyot de, 1781
Cullen, William, 1772, 1776–81, 1785, 1791
Curry, John, 1772, 1775, 1786
Dalrymple, Sir David, 1776, 1779, 1790
Dalzel, Andrew, 1787, 1789, 1791
Dancer, Thomas, 1781
Davidson, David, 1789
De Lolme, Jean Louis, 1781, 1784–85, 1788–90, 1793
Dease, William, 1780
Debate at the East India House, 1795
Debate on the expediency of cultivating sugar, 1793
Debates at the East-India-House, 1794–95
Debates that have taken place at the East India House, 1795
Defoe, Daniel, 1784, 1791
Deletanville, Thomas, 1794
Dewell, T., 1784–85
Dialogue of the dead, 1770

Dickson, Adam, 1785, 1788
Disraeli, Isaac, 1791–95
Dissertation on the querulousness of statesmen, 1792
Dodd, James Solas, 1781
Donaldson, John, 1790, 1792–93
Douglas, Gawin, 1788
Dundonald, Archibald Cochrane, Earl of, 1795
Drysdale, William, 1787
Du Coudray, M. le chevalier, 1777–78
Dunbar, William, 1788
Duncan, Andrew, 1772–79, 1785–86
Edinburgh magazine and review, 1773–76
Edinburgh magazine, or literary miscellany, 1786–95
Eighty-nine fugitive fables, 1792
Elliot, Sir John, 1780
Emily; or, the fatal promise, 1792
English review, 1783–95
Epistle from John, Lord Ashburton, 1785
Epistle, in verse. Written from Somersetshire, 1789
Epistles, elegant, familiar, 1791
Equiano, Olaudah, 1789
Erskine, David Stewart, 1778
Essay to prove the insufficiency of a subaltern officer's pay, 1784
Ettrick, William, 1790
Euclid, 1776
Euler, Leonhard, 1795
Evans, Thomas, 1783–84
Evelyn, John, 1769
Every merchant not his own ship-builder, 1778
Ewing, Alexander, 1791
Extracts, elegant, instructive, and entertaining in poetry, 1791
Extracts, elegant, instructive, and entertaining, in prose, 1791
Falconar, Maria, and Harriet, 1788
Familiar letters from a gentleman, 1788
Fearne, Charles, 1770
Fénelon, François de Salignac de la Mothe-, 1769

Ferguson, James, 1778, 1785, 1790
Fergusson, Robert, 1773, 1788
Fielding, Henry, 1783–84, 1786, 1788, 1791–92
Fielding, John, 1794
Fiott, John, 1795
Firishtah, Muhammad Qasim Hindu Shah Astarabadi, 1792
Fitzgerald, Gerald, 1779
Fletcher, Charles, 1787
Florian, 1787–88
Fontana, Felice, 1787
Foot, Jesse, 1786
For all ranks of people, 1795
Fordyce, Sir William, 1774, 1777, 1785
Foreign medical review, 1779
Fraser, Simon, 1791, 1793
Frederick, II, King of Prussia, 1779
Fuller, Anne, 1787, Addenda
Fungus, Ferdinando, 1790
Galliard, Edward, 1773
Gardiner, John, 1784
Garrick, David, 1785–86
Gast, John, 1782
Gay, John, 1778, 1783, 1785, 1788, 1792–93
Gertrude; or, the orphan of Llanfruist, 1791
Girdlestone, Thomas, 1787
Godwin, William, 1784
Goldsmith, Oliver, 1774, 1779, 1784, 1786–87, 1790, 1791, 1793
Goldson, William, 1787
Gordon, Thomas, 1776, 1784–85
Gowland, John, 1792–93
Graham, Robert, 1788
Grant, Donald, 1771, 1779
Grant, James, 1790
Gray, Andrew, 1777
Gray, Thomas, 1776, 1778, 1786, 1790
Greenlaw, Alexander, 1794
Griffith, Richard, 1792
Griffith, Richard (poet), 1793
Grose, Francis, 1783
Grut, Thomas, 1794

Haller, Albrecht von, 1780, 1793
Hamilton, Alexander, 1775, 1781, 1792
Hamilton, James Edward, 1790
Hamilton, Robert, 1787
Hancock, Blyth, 1786
Happiness, a poem, 1790
Harrington, Robert, 1785, 1788, 1793
Harvey, John, 1769
Hastings, Warren, 1786–88
Hawkins, Sir John, 1787
Hawkesworth, John, 1788, 1794
Hayes, Thomas, 1783, 1785–86
Hederich, Benjamin, 1778, 1790
Henderson, William, 1789
Henry, the Minstrel, 1790
Heriot, John, 1787
Hewat, Alexander, 1795
Heysham, John, 1782
Higgins, William, 1789, 1791
Hill, Edmund, 1793
Hill, John, 1784
Hilton, William, 1773
Hints, on diseases that are not cured, 1781
Historian's pocket dictionary, 1789
History of Jane Grey, 1791–92
Hoblyn, Robert, 1769
Hodson, Thomas, 1784
Hoffmann, Friedrich, 1783
Hollingsworth, S., 1788
Home, Francis, 1780, 1782–83
Home, Robert, 1783
Homer, 1783, 1790
Homer, Philip Bracebridge, 1788–89
Hook, Archibald, 1793
Horace, 1778, 1791
Hough, John, 1778
Humpage, Benjamin, 1788, 1794
Hunter, Henry, 1783–88, 1792–95
Hunter, William, 1774, 1777
Imison, John, 1785, 1787, 1794
Inglefield, Ann, 1787

Inglefield, John Nicholson, 1783, 1787–88, 1790
Innes, George, 1783
Innes, John, 1776, 1778, 1779, 1783–84, 1791
Innes, William, 1790
Inquiry into . . . slavery, 1789
Jackman, Isaac, 1787
Jackson, Robert, 1791
Jackson, Seguin Henry, 1781
Jacob, Giles, 1782
James, I, King of Scotland, 1787
Jameson, Thomas, 1788
Jamieson, John, 1789
Johnson, Samuel, 1777–79, 1781, 1783–87, 1789, 1790, 1792–94, Addenda
Jones, John, 1792–93
Jones, Sir William, 1783
Jure divino, 1789
Juvenal, 1784
Kames, Henry Home, Lord, 1779, 1781–82
Kearney, Michael, 1776
Keith, George Skene, 1791–92
Kelso, Hamilton, 1786
Kemeys, John Gardner, 1783
Kentish, Richard, 1787, 1791
Kier, Adam, 1783
Kincaid, Alexander, 1790
La Fite, Marie-élisabeth, 1790–91
Langhorne, John, 1770–71
Languet, Hurbert, 1776
Lanségúe, M. de, 1791
Lassone, M. de, 1783
Latta, James, 1793–94
Laugier, Marc-Antoine, 1770
Laurie, John, 1776
Lavallée, Joseph, 1790
Lavater, Johann Caspar, 1787, 1789
Law, Edmund, 1770
Le Beau, Charles, 1776
Le Couteur, John, 1790
Le Sage, Alain René, 1782, 1792
Leake, John, 1787, 1792
Letter from a clergyman to the Bishop of Landaff, 1783
Letter from a lady, 1769

Letter from a Scotch nun, 1791
Letter to J. C. Lettsom, 1779
Letter to Mr. Dale Ingram, 1769
Letter to Philip Francis, 1788
Letter to Sir Richard Hotham, 1773
Letter to the author of Thoughts on the manners of the great, 1788
Letter to the . . . Lord Bishop of Landaff, 1783
Letter to the Members of Parliament, 1792
Letters addressed to the inhabitants, 1795
Lewis, Jenkin, 1789
Lieberkühn, Johann Nathanael, 1782
Lind, James, 1778–79, 1788, 1792
Linné, Carl von, 1792
Logan, John, 1787
London kalendar, 1783–88, 1790
London medical journal, 1781
London mercury, 1781
Longmate, Barak, 1784
Looker-on: a periodical paper, 1792
Lorgna, Antonio Mario, 1779
Lovat, Simon Fraser, Lord, 1785
Lucas, Henry, 1779, 1782
Luckombe, Philip, 1791
Lumley, Thomas, 1781
Lunardi's grand aerostatic voyage, 1784
Lysias, 1778
Lyttelton, George Lyttelton, Baron, 1768, 1774
McArthur, John, 1784, 1792
McBride, Duncan, 1793
M'Donald, Andrew, 1788, 1790–91, 1793
Macdonald, Thomas, 1788, 1791
M'Farlan, John, 1786
MacGilvray, John, 1787
Macintosh, William, 1782
Mackenzie, Alexander, 1790
M'Mahon, Thomas O'Brien, 1777
M'Nayr, James, 1789
Macpherson, R., 1783

Mair, John, 1773
Malcolm, Alexander, 1779
Manning, Henry, 1780
March, R., 1779
Marmontel, Jean-François, 1781
Maurice, Thomas, 1784
Mayow, John, 1790
Medical register, 1779
Mercer, Thomas, 1774
Mercier, Louis Sébastien, 1795
Middleton, Joseph, 1779
Millar, John, 1771, 1773, 1779, 1781, 1787, 1791
Millot, abbé, (Claude François Xavier), 1771
Milton, John, 1790
Mitford, William, 1784
Modern part of an universal history, 1780
Moir, John, 1784, 1786
Moises, Edward, 1792, 1794
Monro, Donald, 1778, 1780
Montagu, Lady, Mary Wortley, 1784, 1790
Morison, John, 1790
Mortimer, Thomas, 1789
Motherby, George, 1785, 1791
Murphy, Arthur, 1792–93
Murray, John, 1769, 1774, 1777, 1779, 1783–85, 1787–88
Musaeus, C. A., 1791
Navy leeches, 1769
New and general biographical dictionary, 1784
New topic of conversation, 1772
Nightingale, 1776
Nolan, William, 1786
Novelties of a year and a day, 1785
O'Brien, Charles, 1792
Observations on a pamphlet entitled A defence, 1783
Observations on the jurisprudence, 1785
Ode to the British empire, 1775
O'Gallagher, Felix, 1784, 1786
Ogilvie, James, 1786
Ogilvie, John, 1777, 1787, 1789
O'Halloran, Sylvester, 1772, 1778
One cause of the present scarcity of corn, 1795

Oswald, John, 1789
Pagès, Pierre Marie François, 1791, 1793
Palliser, Sir Hugh, 1779
Pargeter, William, 1792, 1795
Parkinson, Sydney, 1773, 1777
Parmentier, Antoine Augustin, 1783
Paterson, Samuel, 1788
Patrick, Simon, 1783
Peake, John, 1788
Peart, Edward, 1795
Perfect, William, 1783–84, 1787, 1789, 1791
Perfidious guardian, 1790
Perry, Sampson, 1777, 1779, 1785–86, 1789, 1795
Perry, William, 1774–76, 1780, 1788, 1792–93, 1795
Pictet, François Pierre, 1793
Pirie, Alexander, 1788
Plain reply to the strictures of Mr. Cumberland, 1783
Plan of re-union, 1778
Playfair, James, 1783
Playfair, William, 1787
Poetical epitome, 1792
Political magazine, 1785–89
Polwhele, Richard, 1793
Popular view of the effects of the venereal disease, 1794
Portal, Abraham, 1774–75
Pott, Percivall, 1790
Practical benevolence, 1785
Pratt, Samuel Jackson, 1777, 1782–83
Principles of law and government, 1781
Prose epitome, 1792
Quin, Charles William, 1790
Rameau, Jean Philippe, 1779
Ramsay, Allan, 1788
Rannie, John, 1789
Raspe, Rudolf Erich, 1786
Ray, John Mead, 1790
Reflections upon a late extraordinary promotion, 1788
Registrum Roffense, 1769
Renny, George, 1782
Report . . . to examine the physicians, 1789

Reports of cases concerning the revenue, 1776
Repository, 1771
Review of the history of Job, 1771
Review of the principal charges against Warren Hastings, 1788
Review of the proceedings against Lieutenant Charles Bourne, 1784
Richardson, George, 1778
Richardson, John, 1776–78
Richardson, William, 1774–75, 1780, 1784–86, 1788–89
Richter, August Gottlieb, 1791
Robertson, George, 1788, 1791
Robertson, James, 1783
Robertson, Robert, 1779, 1783, 1792
Robinson, Mary Darby, 1783
Robinson, Pollingrove, 1789, 1794
Robinson, Robert, 1792
Rollin, Charles, 1789
Ross, David, 1790
Rotheram, John, 1770
Rousseau, Jean-Jacques, 1779, 1791
Ruspini, Bartholomew, 1784, 1790
Russell, John, 1791
Rutherford, William, 1781, 1787–88, 1793
Sailor's address to his countrymen, 1793
Saint Quentin, Dominique de, 1792
Salmon, Thomas, 1785
Saunders, Robert, 1778
Saunders, William, 1777, 1782–83, 1793, 1795
Scheele, Karl Wilhelm, 1786
Schrevel, Cornelis, 1787, 1791
Schotte, Johann Peter, 1782
Scott, Helenus, 1782–83
Seally, John, 1788
Second letter to the Right Honourable Charles Jenkinson, 1782
Second report and address of the Philanthropic Society, 1789

Shakespeare, William, 1778, 1784–87, 1790, 1793
Sharpe, Gregory, 1769
Shaw, James, 1788
Shaw, William, 1780–82
Sheldon, John, 1784
Sheldrake, Timothy, 1794
Short journey in the West Indies, 1790
Simmons, Samuel Foart, 1780
Simson, Robert, 1775
Skeete, Thomas, 1786, 1788
Sketch of the debate, 1794
Sketch of the history, 1778
Sketch of the secret history of Europe, 1772
Smellie, William, 1778, 1794
Smith, George, 1794
Smith, Joseph, 1786
Smollett, Tobias George, 1774, 1780, 1792
Sonnets to Eliza, 1790
Spallanzani, Lazzaro, 1784, 1789
Speech . . . to the electors of Westminster, 1783
Spence, David, 1784
Spencer, John, 1772
Squirrell, Robert, 1796
Staehlin, Jakob von, 1788
Stedman, Charles, 1794
Sterne, Laurence, 1774, 1780, 1782–83 1788, 1790, 1793
Stevens, George Alexander, 1785–86
Stewart, Thomas, 1772
Stock, Joseph, 1776, 1784
Stuart, Gilbert, 1774, 1778–79, 1780, 1782–83
Swieten, Gerard, Freiherr van, 1776

Swinton, John, Lord Swinton, 1789
Sydney and Eugenia. A novel, 1790
Tassie, James, 1775, 1788, 1791
Taylor, Edward, 1784, 1785
Taylor, George, 1778
Taylor, John, 1795
Taylor, William, 1791
Thistlethwaite, James, 1776–77
Thomas, Andrew, 1789
Thomson, Alexander, M.D., 1781–82
Thomson, Alexander, 1788
Thomson, Frederick, 1790
Thomson, James, 1778–79, 1788, 1792–94
Thomson, John, 1775–76
Thomson, William, 1783, 1788–89, 1795
Thornton, Robert John, 1794–95
Thoughts on a fund for the improvement of credit, 1780
Timbury, Jane, 1788
Timour, 1783
Toleration and charity peculiar to the Christian religion, 1790
Townsend, Joseph, 1795
Trapp, Joseph, 1793
Trenck, Friedrich, Freiherr von der, 1788
Trial of Avadaunum Paupiah Bramin, 1793
Trist, Jeremiah, 1791
Trusler, John, 1785–86
Trye, Charles Brandon, 1784, 1787, 1792
Tucker, Nathaniel, 1776
Turnbull, William, 1786
Two remarkable letters, 1770
Tytler, James, 1788

Universal history, 1779
Urquhart, George, 1786
Vanity of fame. A poem, 1784
Vieyra, Antonio, 1794
Virgil, 1782, 1792
Voltaire, François Marie Arouet de, 1774, 177–77, 1788
Wade, John Peter, 1791–93
Wait, Robert, 1769
Wakefield, Gilbert, 1780
Walker, Robert, 1790
Wallis, George, 1781
Walpole, Horace, 1769
Walsh, Philip Pitt, 1787
Walwyn, B., 1781
Ward, William, 1778
Ware, James, 1795
Wastell, Henry, 1779
Watson, Daniel, 1769
Watson, James, 1795
Watson, Thomas, 1792
Watts, Isaac, 1793
Webster, Charles, 1793
Wells, the Rev. Charles, 1785, 1787
Whitaker, John, 1773, 1775, 1787–91
White, Thomas, 1784, 1787, 1794
White, William, 1792
Wilkie, William, 1769
Wilson, Andrew, 1783, 1788
Withers, Thomas, 1794
Wood, James, 1793
Wood, John, 1769
Works of the English poets, 1779, 1790
Wright, James, 1786
Young, Robert, 1787–88, 1790
Young, William, 1778, 1787, 1792

A Bibliography of the Pamphlets
Written by Murray

1. A | LETTER | FROM A | GENTLEMAN in EDINBURGH, | TO HIS | FRIEND in the Country: | OCCASIONED | By the late THEATRICAL DISTURBANCES. | [motto] Notwithstanding all that *Rousseau* has advanced so | very ingeniously upon Plays and Players, their | profession is, like that of a painter, one of the | imitative arts, whose means are pleasure, and | whose end is virtue. They both, alike, for a subsistence, submit themselves to public opinion. | SHENSTONE. | [double rule] EDINBURGH: | Printed in the Year MDCCLXVI. | [Price, TWO-PENCE.]

Signature: 8ᵛᵒ π A⁷
Pagination: [1] title; [2] blank; 3–16 text
Press figures: none
Copies: E (3), NjP, DFo. *ESTC* no19762
Notes: Halkett and Laing, *Dictionary of Anonymous and Pseudonymous English Literature* (iii, 264), erroneously attribute this work to Allan Ramsay, the Younger. Murray confirmed his authorship in a letter to Wm Gordon of Gordonstoun, 3 March 1766. The *Letter* itself is addressed 'To W******* G*****, Esq; at G———n' (p. 3).

2. A LETTER | TO | W. MASON, A. M. | PRECENTOR OF YORK, | CONCERNING | HIS EDITION OF | MR. GRAY's POEMS. | AND | THE PRACTICES OF BOOKSELLERS. | BY A BOOKSELLER. [motto] Sed quae reverentia legum? | Quis metus, aut pudor est unquam properantis avari?— | JUVENAL. | [double rule] LONDON, | PRINTED FOR J. MURRAY, (No. 32) FLEET-STREET. | MDCLXXVII.

Signature: 8ᵛᵒ [A]² B⁸ (±B3 or ±B3,6) C–D⁸ E⁴ F²
Pagination: [1] half-title: 'LETTER | TO | W. MASON, A. M. | [Price One Shilling.]'; [2] blank; [3] title page; [4] blank; [5]–56 text; [57]–64 Appendix
Press figures: 6–1, 16–2 (in third state copies only), 26–2, 33–4, 49–2, 58–1
Copies: Murray Archive (3), British Library (3), many institutional libraries. *ESTC* t004056
Notes: Judging from the occurrence of a cancel leaf B3 (pp. 9–10) in some copies and the press figure '2' on the verso of the conjugate leaf B6 (p. 16) in other copies, it is likely that there are three states of this work. The first state can only be inferred. In the second state B3 is a cancel, tipped onto the stub of the original B3. In the third state the conjugate leaf B3–6 has been replaced and the press figure '2' added to the verso of B6. Among twenty copies consulted, the second and third states are about equally represented, suggesting that the correction was made midway through the printrun. Just what textual change Murray (or the printer) made to either the recto or verso of B3 can only be speculated. In a effort at self-promotion, Murray may have added his own poetical

publications to the sentence: 'You will not aledge, that *The Traveller, The Deserted Village, Armine and Elvira, The Fables of Flora, The Minstrel*, or any poem in request, have been pirated' (p. 9). See Plate 44.

2.1. A LETTER to W. MASON, A. M. PRECENTOR OF YORK, from J. MURRAY, BOOK-SELLER, IN LONDON. [single rule] the second edition, corrected. [single rule] LONDON: Printed for J. Murray, (No. 32) Fleet-Street. [*sic*] M,DCC,LXXXVIII. [*Price* Six-pence.]

Signature: 8vo B–C^8
Pagination: [1] title; [2] blank, 3–32 text
Press figures: none
Copies: Murray Archive, Cambridge (Trinity), Yale, Harvard, Cornell. *ESTC* no33836
Notes: In this edition the style is somewhat improved and the invective toned down. For example, the 'barefaced Dodsley' of p. 29 in the 1777 edition becomes 'Mr. Dodsley' in this edition (p. 14); 'illiberal insolence' (p. 36) becomes 'illiberal manner' (p. 17). Also, notes are added on pp. 22–23.

3. AN AUTHOR'S CONDUCT | to the | PUBLIC, | stated in the behaviour of | DR. WILLIAM CULLEN, | His Majesty's Physician at Edinburgh, | [motto] Certainly there is little fairness in their dealings who have the | best of every bargain they make. The world may think them expert | as they get money, but it is impossible they can be honest. Real in- | tegrity proscribes all those stratagems of fraud and circumvention | which the covetous and cunning are eternally practising. | Moir's Sermons. | LONDON: | printed for j. murray, N° 32, fleet-street. | MDCCLXXXIV.

Signature: 8vo [A]^2 B–C^8 D^4 E^2
Pagination: [1] half-title, 'An Author's Conduct to the Public.'; [2] blank; [3] title; [4] blank; [i]–ii Advertisement; [1]–41 text; [42] blank
Press figures: none
Copies: Murray Archive, E (3), Eu, O, CtY
Notes: The E copy is uncut and measures 8.9 x 5.5 cm. The Eu copy is a presentation from Murray to Andrew Duncan. *ESTC* no15092. See Plate 45.

4. the | DEFENCE | of | INNES MUNRO, esq. | captain in the late seventy-third | or lord macleod's regiment of | highlanders, | against | *A CHARGE OF PLAGIARISM* | from | THE WORKS OF DR. WILLIAM THOMSON; | with the | ORIGINAL PAPERS ON BOTH SIDES. | [DOUBLE RULE] | LONDON: | printed for j. ridgeway, york-street, | st. james's square. | M.DCC.XC.

Signature: 8vo π^2 A–C^8 D^3.
Pagination: [i] title; [ii] blank; [iii]–iv Advertisement; [1]–33, 35–36, 36–51 text; [52]–54 Supplement.
Press figures: 2–3, 5–4, 38–3, 50–3
Copies: E (2); *ESTC* t186824
Notes: The E copy (1948.54(13)), presented by Murray to Alexander Fraser Tytler, includes Murray's annotations to pseudonymous articles reprinted in the pamphlet. See Plate 46.

Bibliography

Adams, Thomas R. *The American Controversy. A Bibliographical Study of the British Pamphlets about American Disputes, 1764–1783*, 2 vols. (Providence: Brown University Press for the Bibliographical Society of America, 1980).

Alden, John. 'Pills and Publishing: Some Notes on the English Book Trade', *The Library*, 5th series, 7 (1952), 21–37.

Alston, R. C. *A Bibliography of the English Language from the Invention of Printing to the Year 1800*. 10 vols. (Ilkley: Janus Press, 1974).

Alston, R. C., Robinson, F. J. G. and Wadham, C. *A Check-List of Eighteenth-Century Books Containing Lists of Subscribers* (Newcastle: Avero, 1983).

Altick, Richard D. *The English Common Reader: A Social History of the Mass Reading Public 1800–1900* (Chicago: University of Chicago Press, 1963).

Baer, Marc. *Theatre and Disorder in Late Georgian London* (Oxford: Clarendon Press, 1992).

Bald, R. C. 'Early Copyright Litigation and its Bibliographical Interest', *Papers of the Bibliographical Society of America*, 36 (1961), 81–96.

Ball, Johnson. *William Caslon, 1693–1766: The Ancestry, Life and Connections of England's Foremost Letter-Engraver and Type-Founder* (Kineton: Roundwood Press, 1973).

Barber, Giles. 'Books from the Old World for the New: The British International Trade in Books in the Eighteenth Century', *Studies on Voltaire and the Eighteenth Century*, 151 (1976), 185–224.

Belanger, Terry. 'Booksellers' Sales of Copyright. Aspects of the London Book Trade: 1718–1768' (doctoral dissertation, Columbia University, 1970).

—— 'Booksellers' Trade Sales, 1718–1768', *The Library*, 5th series, 30 (1975), 281–302.

—— 'From Bookseller to Publisher: Changes in the London Book Trade 1750–1850', in Richard G. Landon (ed.), *Bookselling and Book Buying. Aspects of the Nineteenth-Century British and North American Book Trade*, (Chicago: American Library Association, 1978), 7–16.

Bennett, Scott. 'John Murray's Family Library and the Cheapening of Books in early nineteenth century Britain', *Studies in Bibliography*, 29 (1976), 138–66.

Bentley, G. E. Jr. *Annotated Catalogue of William Blake* (Oxford: Clarendon Press, 1977).

—— 'Copyright Documents in the George Robinson Archive: William Godwin and Others 1713–1820', *Studies in Bibliography*, 35 (1982), 67–110. The archive itself is in the Manchester Central Library, MSS f. 091 A2.

Besterman, Theodore, (ed.) *The Publishing Firm of Cadell and Davies: Select Correspondence and Accounts 1793–1836* (Oxford: Oxford University Press; London: Humphrey Milford, 1938).

Bingham, Sylvester Hinckley. 'Publishing in the Eighteenth Century with Special Reference to the Firm of Edward and Charles Dilly' (doctoral dissertation, Yale University, 1937).

Blagden, Cyprian. *Fire more than Water: Notes for the Story of a Ship* (London: Longmans, Green & Co., 1949).

—— 'Booksellers' Trade Sales 1718–1768', *Library*, 5th series, 5 (1951), 243–57.

—— *The Stationers' Company: A History, 1403–1959* (London: George Allen & Unwin, 1960).

Blakey, Dorothy. *The Minerva Press, 1790–1820* (London: The Bibliographical Society, 1939).

Bonnell, Thomas. 'John Bell's *Poets of Great Britain*: The 'Little Trifling Edition' Revisited', *Modern Philology*, 85 (1987), 128–152.

Boswell, James. *Boswell's Life of Samuel Johnson, together with Boswell's Journal of a Tour to the Hebrides*, 6 vols ed. G. B. Hill, rev. L. F. Powell (Oxford: Oxford University Press, 1934–64).

Bourne, H. R. Fox. *English Newspapers. Chapters in the History of Journalism*, 2 vols (London: Chatto & Windus, 1887).

Brack, O. M. Jr. 'William Strahan: Scottish Printer and Publisher', *Arizona Quarterly*, 31 (1975), 171–91.

Brady, Frank. 'So Fast to Ruin: The Personal Element in the Collapse of Douglas, Heron, and Company', *Collections* of the Ayrshire Archaeological and Natural History Society, 11 (1973).

Brereton, Henry Lloyd. *Gordonstoun. Ancient Estate and Modern School* (Edinburgh: W. & R. Chambers, 1968).

Brewer, John, *et al. The Birth of a Consumer Society. The Commercialization of Eighteenth-Century England* (London: Europa, 1982).

Bullock, J. M. 'John Murray I. as an Author: Col. Robert Gordon', *Notes & Queries*, 11th series, 3 (Apr. 1911), 247.

Bushnell, George H. *Scottish Printers, Booksellers and Bookbinders, 1726–1775* (London: The Bibliographical Society, 1932).

Campbell, R. *The London Tradesman. Being a Compendious View of all the Trades, Professions, Arts . . . now Practised in the Cities of London and Westminster*, 3rd edn. (London: T. Gardner, 1757).

Carnall, G. C. and Nicholson, C. (eds.) *The Impeachment of Warren Hastings* (Edinburgh: Edinburgh University Press, 1989).

Carswell, John. *The Prospector. Being the Life and Times of Rudolf Erich Raspe 1737–1794* (London: Cresset Press, 1950).

Carter, John. *ABC for Book-Collectors* (London: Hart Davis, 1970).

Chapman, R. W. 'Authors and Booksellers', in A. S. Tuberville (ed.), *Johnson's England: An Account of the Life & Manners of his Age*, 2 vols (Oxford: Clarendon Press, 1933), ii, 310–30.

—— 'Eighteenth-Century Imprints', *The Library*, 4th series, 11 (1931), 503–04.

Chatterton, E. Keble. *The Old East Indiamen* (London: T. Werner Laurie, [1914]).

Clapp, Sarah. 'The Beginnings of Subscription Publication in the Seventeenth Century', *Modern Philology*, 19 (1931–32), 199–224.

Cochrane, J. A. *Dr. Johnson's Printer. The Life of William Strahan* (London: Routledge & Kegan Paul, 1964).

Cole, Richard Cargill. *Irish Booksellers and English Writers, 1740–1800* (Atlantic Highlands, NJ: Humanities Press, 1986).

Coleman, D. C. *The British Paper Industry 1495–1860* (Oxford: Oxford University Press, 1958).

Collins, A. S. 'Some Aspects of Copyright from 1700 to 1780', *The Library*, 4th series, 7 (1927), 67–81.

—— *Authorship in the Days of Johnson: Being a Study of the Relation between Author, Patron, Publisher and Public, 1726–1780* (London: Routledge, 1927).

—— *The Profession of Letters. A Study of the Relation of Author to Patron, Publisher and Public, 1780–1832* (London: Routledge, 1928).

Constable, Thomas. *Archibald Constable and his Literary Correspondents. A Memorial by his Son*, 3 vols (Edinburgh: Edmonston and Douglas, 1873).

Corbett, J. S. *England in the Seven Years' War: A Study in Combined Strategy*. 2 vols (London, 1907).

Couper, W. J. *The Millers of Haddington, Dunbar and Dunfermline: A Record of Scottish Bookselling* (London: T. Fisher Unwin, 1914).

Cross. W. L. *The Life and Times of Laurence Sterne*, 2 vols (New Haven: Yale University Press, 1925).

Curwen, Henry. *A History of the Booksellers. The Old and the New* (London: Chatto & Windus, 1873).

Darnton, Robert. *The Business of Enlightenment. A Publishing History of the 'Encyclopédie' 1775–1800* (Cambridge, MA: Belknap Press, 1979).

Dibdin, James. *The Annals of the Edinburgh Stage* (Edinburgh: Richard Cameron, 1888).

Dickins, Bruce. 'Doctor James's Fever Powder', *Life and Letters*, 2 (1929), 36–47.

Dickinson, H. T. *British Radicalism and the French Revolution* (Oxford: Blackwell, 1985).

Dickson, Robert. *Introduction of the Art of Printing into Scotland* (Aberdeen, 1885).

Doig, Andrew, *et al.* (eds.) *William Cullen and the Eighteenth Century Medical World* (Edinburgh: Edinburgh University Press, 1993).

Draper, John W. *William Mason. A Study in Eighteenth-Century Culture* (New York: New York University Press, 1924).

Dunbar, E. D. *Social Life in Former Days, Chiefly in the Province of Moray* (Edinburgh: Edmonston & Douglas, 1865).

Eddy, Donald D. *A Bibliography of John Brown* (New York: The Bibliographical Society of America, 1971).

Eisenstein, Elizabeth L. *The Printing Press as an Agent of Change*, 2 vols. (Cambridge: Cambridge University Press, 1979).

Ellis, Aytoun. *The Penny Universities. A History of Coffee-houses* (London: Secker and Warburg, 1956).

Ellis, Kenneth. *The Post Office in the Eighteenth Century. A Study in Administrative History* (London: Oxford University Press, 1958).

Ewen, C. L'Estrange. *Lotteries and Sweepstakes. An Historical, Legal, and Ethical Survey of their Introduction, Suppression, and Re-Establishment in the British Isles* (London: Heath & Cranton, 1932).

Feather, John. 'John Walter and the Logographic Press', *Publishing History*, 1 (1977), 92–134.

—— *The Provincial Book Trade in Eighteenth-Century England* (Cambridge: Cambridge University Press, 1985).

—— *A History of British Publishing* (London and New York: Routledge, 1988).

Febvre, Lucien and Martin, Henri-Jean. *The Coming of the Book. The Impact of Printing 1450–1800.* Trans. by David Gerard (London: N. L. B., 1971).

Fitschner, Linda M. 'Publishers' Readers, Publishers and their Authors', *Publishing History*, 7 (1980), 45–100.

Fleeman, J. D. 'The Revenue of a Writer: Samuel Johnson's Literary Earnings', in R. W. Hunt, I. G. Philip and R. J. Roberts (eds), *Studies in the Book Trade*, (Oxford Bibliographical Society, new series, 18, 1975, 211–230).

Foot, Miriam M. 'Some Bookbinders' Price Lists of the Seventeenth and Eighteenth Centuries', *De libris compactis miscellanea*, ed. G. Colin (Studia Bibliothecae Witockianae, 1; Aubel, Brussels, 1984), 273–319.

Forbes, William. *An Account of the Life and Writings of James Beattie*, 2nd edn., 3 vols (Edinburgh: Constable, 1807).

Forster, Antonia. *Index to Book Reviews in England 1749–1774* (Carbondale: Southern Illinois University Press, 1990)

—— *Index to Book Reviews in England 1775–1800* (London: The British Library, 1997).

Franklin, Colin. *Shakespeare Domesticated. The Eighteenth-Century Editions* (Aldershot: Scholar, 1991).

Gaskell, Philip. 'Notes on Eighteenth-Century British Paper', *The Library*, 5th series, 12 (1957), 34–42.

—— *A Bibliography of the Foulis Press*, 2nd edn (Winchester: St Paul's Bibliographies, 1986).

—— *A New Introduction to Bibliography* (Oxford: Clarendon, repr. 1974).

Gelduld, Harry M. [Jacob Tonson] *Prince of Publishers* (Bloomington: University of Indiana Press, 1969).

Genest, John (ed.) *Some Account of the English Stage from the Restoration in 1660 to 1830*, 10 vols (Bath: H. E. Carrington, 1832).

Goodman, Dena. 'The Hume-Rousseau Affair: From Private *Querelle* to Public *Procès*', *Eighteenth-Century Studies*, 25, No. 2 (Winter 1991–92), 171–201.

Graham, Walter. *English Literary Periodicals* (London: Nelson, 1930).

Gray, John M. *James and William Tassie. A Biographical and Critical Sketch with a Catalogue of Portrait Medallions* (Edinburgh: W. G. Paterson, 1894).

Greig, J. Y. T. (ed.) *The Letters of David Hume*, 2 vols (Oxford: Clarendon Press, repr. 1969).

Gunn, J. A. W. *Beyond Liberty and Property. The Process of Self-Recognition in Eighteenth-Century Political Thought* (Kingston: McGill-Queens University Press, 1983).

Hamilton, Henry. 'Failure of the Ayr Bank, 1772', *Economic History Review*, 8 (1956), 405–17.

Harlan, Robert Dale. 'William Strahan: Eighteenth-Century London Printer and Publisher' (doctoral dissertation, University of Michigan, 1960).

Harley, David. 'Honor and Property: the Structure of Professional Disputes in Eighteenth-Century English Medicine', in A. Cunningham and Roger French (eds.) *The Medical Enlightenment of the Eighteenth Century* (Cambridge: Cambridge University Press, 1990), 139–64.

Harris, Michael. 'The Management of the London Newspaper Press during the Eighteenth Century', *Publishing History*, 4 (1978), 95–112.

—— 'Periodicals and the Book Trade', in M. Harris and R. Meyers (eds.) *Development of the English Book Trade, 1700–1899*, eds. (Oxford, 1981), 66–94.

Hazen, A. T. *A Bibliography of the Strawberry Hill Press*, (New Haven: Yale University Press, 1942).

—— *A Bibliography of Horace Walpole*, (New Haven: Yale University Press, 1948).

—— 'One meaning of the Imprint', *The Library*, 5th series, 6 (1951), 120–23.

Henrey, Blanche. *British Botanical and Horticultural Literature before 1800*, 3 vols (London: Oxford University Press, 1975).

Hernland, Patricia. 'William Strahan's Ledgers: Standard Charges for Printing 1738–1785', *Studies in Bibliography*, 20 (1967), 89–111.

—— 'William Strahan's Ledgers, II: Charges for Papers, 1738–1785', *Studies in Bibliography*, 22 (1969), 179–95.

Hibbert, Christopher. *King Mob. The Story of Lord George Gordon and the Gordon Riots* (London: Longmans, Green & Co, 1958).

Higgs, Henry. *Bibliography of Economics, 1751–75* (Cambridge: Cambridge University Press, 1935).

Highley, Samuel III. 'The House of Murray', *The Critic*, 7–28 Jan. 1860.

Hof, Ulrich I. *Isaak Iselin und die Spätaufklärung* (Bern & München, [1967]).

Holloway, James. *James Tassie 1735–1799* (Edinburgh: National Galleries of Scotland, 1986).

Hopkins, Donald R. *Princes and Peasants: Smallpox in History* (Chicago: University of Chicago Press, 1983).

Howe, Ellie. *A List of Bookbinders 1648–1815* (London: The Bibliographical Society, 1950).

Howe, Ellie and Child, John. *The London Society of Bookbinders, 1780–1951* (London: The Bibliographical Society, 1952).

Kernan, Alvin. *Printing Technology, Letters and Samuel Johnson* (Princeton: Princeton University Press, 1987).

Kerr, Robert. *Memoirs of the Life, Writings and Correspondence of William Smellie*, 2 vols (London, 1811).

Knight, Charles. *An Old Printer and the Modern Press* (London, 1854).

—— *Shadows of the Old Booksellers* (London, [1865]).

The Kress Library of Business and Economics, 4 vols (Boston: Harvard University Printing Office, 1940–67).

Lackington, James. *Memoirs of the Forty-five First Years of the Life of James Lackington, Bookseller* (London, for the author, [1791]).

Landon, Richard G. 'Small Profits Do Great Things: James Lackington and Eighteenth-Century Bookselling', *Studies in Eighteenth-Century Culture*, 5 (1976), 387–99.

[Leigh, Richard A. A.] *The Story of a Printing House: being a Short Account of the Strahans and Spotiswoodes*, 2nd edn (London: Spottiswood & Co. 1912).

Lewis, Wilmarth S. (ed.) *The Correspondence of Horace Walpole*, 48 vols (New Haven: Yale University Press, 1937–83).

Lillywhite, Bryant. *London Coffee Houses* (London: George Allen & Unwin, 1963).

Longman, Charles J. *The House of Longman 1724–1800. A Bibliographical History with a List of Signs Used by Booksellers of that Period*, ed. J. F. Chandler, with an introduction and chapter on the history of the House of Longman, 1724–1800 (London: Longmans, Green and Co., 1936).

Lowe, Robert, Arnot, J. F. and Robinson, J. W. *English Theatrical Literature 1559–1900: A Bibliography* (London: Society for Theatre Research, 1970).

Lustig, I. S. and Pottle F. A. (eds.) *Boswell: The Applause of the Jury, 1782–1785*, (London: Heinemann, 1981).

Lutes, Richard. 'Andrew Strahan and the London Sharebook System, 1785–1825: A Study of the Strahan Printing and Publishing Records' (doctoral dissertation, Wayne State University, 1979).

Mackay, Charles. *Through the Long Day. Memorials of a Literary Life* (London: W. H. Allen, 1887).

Madden, Richard Robert. *The History of Irish Periodical Literature from the End of the 17th to the Middle of the 19th Century*, 2 vols (London: T. C. Newby, 1867).

Marston, Edward. *Sketches of some Booksellers of the Time of Dr. Samuel Johnson* (London: Sampson Low & Co., 1902).

Maslen, Keith and Lancaster, John (eds) *The Bowyer Ledgers: the Printing Accounts of William Bowyer, Father and Son* (London: The Bibliographical Society, 1991).

Matriculation Rolls for the University of Edinburgh: Arts, Law, Divinity (typescript, Edinburgh University Library, Special Collections).

Maxted, Ian. *The London Book Trades 1775–1800: A Preliminary Checklist of Members* (Folkestone: Dawson, 1977).

—— *The London Book Trades 1775–1800. A Topographical Guide* (Exeter, 1980).

Mayo, Robert D. *The English Novel in the Magazines 1740–1814* (Evanston, IL: Northwestern University Press, 1962).

McKenzie, D. F. *Stationers' Company Apprentices 1701–1800* (Oxford: Oxford Bibliographical Society, 1978).

McLachlan, Herbert. *Warrington Academy: Its History and Influence* (London, 1943).

Morison, Stanley. *John Bell, 1745–1831* (Cambridge: Cambridge University Press, 1930).

—— *The English Newspaper: Some Account of the Physical Development of Journals Printed in London between 1622 and the Present Day* (Cambridge: Cambridge University Press, 1932).

Mumby, F. A. *Publishing and Bookselling*, 5th edn rev. (London: Cape, 1974).

Murray, David. *Robert & Andrew Foulis and the Glasgow Press with some Account of the Glasgow Academy of Fine Arts* (Glasgow: Maclehose, 1913).

Myers, Robin (ed.) *Records of the Stationers' Company 1554–1920*, microfilm edn (Cambridge: Chadwyck and Healey, 1986).

Myers, Robin and Harris, Michael (eds) *The Development of the English Book Trade, 1700–1899* (Oxford: Oxford Polytechnic Press, 1981).

—— *Sale and Distribution of Books from 1700* (Oxford: Oxford Polytechnic Press, 1982).

—— *Author/Publisher Relations during the Eighteenth and Nineteenth Centuries* (Oxford: Oxford Polytechnic Press, 1983).

Nangle, B. C. *The Monthly Review, First Series, 1749–1789: Indexes of Contributors and Articles* (Oxford: Clarendon Press, 1934).

Nichols, John. *Literary Anecdotes of the Eighteenth Century*, 9 vols (London: for the author, 1812–16).

—— *Illustrations of the Literary History of the Eighteenth Century*, 9 vols (London, for the author, 1815–17).

Ogden, James. *Isaac D'Israeli* (Oxford: Clarendon Press, 1969).

Paston, George. *At John Murray's: Records of a Literary Circle 1843–1892* (London: Murray, 1932).

Patterson, Diana. 'John Murray, 32 Fleet Street. An Investigation of Publishing and Taste with a Catalogue of his Publications' (master's dissertation, University of Toronto, 1983).

Philips, C. H. *The East India Company 1784–1834*, 2nd edn (Manchester: Manchester University Press, 1961).

Plant, Marjorie. *The English Book Trade*, 3rd edn (London: Allen & Unwin, 1974).

Plomer, H. R., Bushnell, G. H. and Dix, E. R. *A Dictionary of Printers and Booksellers who were at Work in England, Scotland and Ireland from 1726 to 1775* (London: The Bibliographical Society, 1932; repr. 1965).

Pollard, Graham. *The Distribution of Books by Catalogue from the Invention of Printing to A.D. 1800* (London: Roxburghe Club, 1965).

Pollard, Mary. *Dublin's Trade in Books, 1550–1800* (Oxford: Oxford University Press, 1989).

Porter, Roy. *Doctor of Society. Thomas Beddoes and the Sick Trade in Late-Enlightenment England* (London: Routledge, 1992).

Pottle, F. A. and Wimsatt, W. K. (eds.) *Boswell for the Defence 1769–1774* (London: Heinemann, 1960).

Puller, F. W. *Marriage with a Deceased Wife's Sister Forbidden by the Laws of God and of the Church* (London: Longmans & Co., 1912).

Ransom, Harry. *The First Copyright Statute: An Essay on 'An Act for the Encouragement of Learning' 1710* (Austin: University of Texas, 1956).

Raven, James. *Judging New Wealth: Popular Publishing Responses to Commerce in England, 1750–1800* (Oxford: Clarendon Press, 1992).

Razzell, P. E. *The Conquest of Smallpox: the Impact of Inoculation on Smallpox Mortality in Eighteenth-Century Britain* (Firle: Caliban Books, 1977).

Rivington, Septimus. *The Publishing Family of Rivington* (London: Rivington, 1919).

Rodger, N. A. M. *The Wooden World. An Anatomy of the Georgian Navy* (London: Collins, 1986).

Rogers, Deborah. *Bookseller as Rogue: John Almon and the Politics of Eighteenth-Century Publishing* (American University Studies, Series IV, English Language and Literature, Vol. 28, 1986).

Roper, Derek. *Reviewing before the* Edinburgh *1788–1802* (London: Methuen, 1978).

Roscoe, S. *John Newbery and his Successors 1740–1814. A Bibliography* (Wormley, Herefordshire: Five Owls Press, 1973).

Rose, Mark. 'The Author as Proprietor: *Donaldson v. Becket* and the Genealogy of Modern Authorship', *Representations*, 23 (Summer 1988), 51–85.

—— *Authors and Owners: The Invention of Copyright* (Cambridge, MA: Harvard University Press, 1993).

Ross, Trevor. 'Copyright and the Invention of Tradition', *Eighteenth-Century Studies*, 26 (Fall, 1992), 1–27.

Rostenberg, Leona. 'Richard and Anne Baldwin: Whig Patriot Publishers', *Publications of the Bibliographical Society of America*, 47 (1953), 1–42.

The Rothschild Library. A Catalogue of the Collection of Eighteenth-Century Printed Books and Manuscripts Formed by Lord Rothschild. 2 vols (Cambridge: privately printed, 1954).

Sabin, Joseph. *A Dictionary of Books relating to America*, 29 vols (New York: Bibliographical Society of America, 1868–1936).

Sale, William M. *Samuel Richardson: Master Printer* (Ithaca: Cornell University Press, 1950).

Shaw, Graham. *Printing in Calcutta to 1800* (London: The Bibliographical Society, 1981).

Sher, Richard B. *Church and University in the Scottish Enlightenment. The Moderate Literati of Edinburgh* (Edinburgh: Edinburgh University Press, 1985).

—— 'Corporatism and Consensus in the Late Eighteenth-Century Book Trade: The Edinburgh Booksellers' Society in Comparative Perspective', in J. Rose (ed.) *Book History* (University Park: Pennsylvania State University Press, 1998).

Skinner, Robert T. *A Notable Family of Scots Printers* [The Donaldsons] (Edinburgh: T. & A. Constable, 1928).

Smiles, Samuel. *A Publisher and his Friends: Memoir and Correspondence of the late John Murray, with an Account of the Origin and Progress of the House, 1768–1843*, 2 vols (London: Murray, 1891). A one-vol. edn, rev. by Thomas Mackay, was published in 1911.

Smith, J. P. *James Tassie 1735–1799, Modeller in Glass. A Classical Approach* (London: Mallet & Son, 1995).

Somerville, Thomas. *My Own Life and Times, 1741–1814* (Edinburgh: Edmonston and Douglas, [1861]).

St Clair, William. *The Godwins and the Shelleys* (London: Faber and Faber, 1989).

Straus, Ralph. *Robert Dodsley, Poet, Publisher and Playwright* (New York: John Lane Co., 1910).

Sullivan, Alvin (ed.) *British Literary Magazines: The Augustan Age and the Age of Johnson, 1698–1788* (Westport, CT: Greenwood Press, 1983).

Sutherland, Lucy T. *The East India Company in Eighteenth-Century Politics* (Oxford: Clarendon Press, repr. 1962).

Todd, William B. 'The Printing of Johnson's *Journey*', *Studies in Bibliography*, 6 (1954), 247–54.

—— 'Pattern in Press Figures: A Study of Lyttelton's *Dialogues of the Dead*', *Studies in Bibliography*, 8 (1956), 230–35.

—— *A Bibliography of Edmund Burke* (Bury St. Edmunds: St. Edmundsbury Press, 1982).

Thomson, John. *An Account of the Life, Letters and Writings of William Cullen*, 2 vols (Edinburgh: Blackwood, 1859).

Tomalin, Claire. *The Life and Death of Mary Wollstonecraft*, rev. edn, (London: Penguin, 1992).

Tapp, W. H. 'John Donaldson: Enameller, Miniaturist and Ceramic Artist' *Apollo*, 36 (Aug. and Dec. 1942), 39–42, 55; 37 (Jan. 1943), 4–7, 22.

Trewin, John Courtenay, and King, E. M. *Printer to the House: The Story of Hansard* (London: Methuen & Co, 1952).

Trusler, John. *Memoirs of the Life of the Rev. Dr. Trusler, with his Opinions on a Variety of Interesting Subjects, and his Remarks, through a Long Life, on Men and Manners* (Bath: John Browne, 1806).

Tyson, Gerald. *Joseph Johnson: A Liberal Publisher* (Iowa City: University of Iowa Press, 1979).

Underwood, E. Ashworth. *Boerhaave's Men at Leyden and After* (Edinburgh: Edinburgh University Press, 1977).

Wallis, Philip. *At the Sign of the Ship: Notes on the House of Longman, 1724–1974* (London: Longman, 1974).

Ward, Robert E. *Prince of Dublin Printers. The Letters of George Faulkner* (Lexington, University of Kentucky Press, 1972).

Wark, Catherine Coggan. and Wark, R. E. 'Literary Piracy in the Eighteenth-Century Book Trade: The Cases of George Faulkner and Alexander Donaldson', *Factotum*, 17 (1983), 25–35.

Welsh, Charles. *A Bookseller of the Last Century, being some Account of the Life of John Newbery, and of the Books he Published, with a Notice of the later Newberys* (London: Griffith, Farran, 1885).

Werkmeister, Lucyle. *The London Daily Press, 1772–1792* (Lincoln: University of Nebraska Press, 1963).

Williams, Harold. (ed.) *The Correspondence of Jonathan Swift*, 5 vols (Oxford: Clarendon Press, 1963–72).

Wittenberg, Philip. *The Law of Literary Property*, rev. edn (Boston: The Writer Inc., 1978).

Zachs, William. *Without Regard to Good Manners: A Biography of Gilbert Stuart 1743–1786* (Edinburgh: Edinburgh University Press, 1992).

Index

A separate index to Murray's Publications is found on pages 410–14

ABC and Little Catechism, 53
Addison, Joseph, 79, 163, 217
advertising
  cost of, 86–7, 173
  at the end of books, 36–7, 57–8, 408–9, Plate 12
  in imprints, 29
  in newspapers, 26, 48, 62, 68, 86–7, Plate 31
Advocates' Library (Edinburgh), 102–3
Adye, Lieut. Stephen Payne, 28, 38–9, 46, 71, 113, 121, 222, 255
Agency bookselling, 29–32, 94, 107, 108
Aikin, John, 107, 284
Allan, David, 50, 106–7, 351, frontispiece
Almon, John, 301
America, 3, 38–9, 202, 209, 237
American Revolution, 157, 207, 221–6
Analytical Review, 83, 216, 247
Anderson, James, 210
Annual Register, 205–6
antiquarian books, 89–90
Argens, Jean Baptiste de Boyer, Marquis d', 28, 172
Arnot, Hugo, 68, 71, 165
Arthur, Archibald, 104
Atkins, Joseph, 225
auctions, 39, 54, 60, 84, 100, 103, 115, 195 *see also* trade sales
Ayrshire Bank (Douglas, Heron & Co.), 51

Baldwin, Henry, 36, 117
Balfour, John
  and Creech, William, 190, 194–5
  and London associates, 58, 97–9, 148, 208
  his paper mill, 97
  and Smellie, William, 98, 263, 265–6, 268, 271, 275
Bangour, Bernard Ward, Lord, 134–5
bankruptcies, 59–60, 118
Baskerville, John, 36, 106–7
Bathoe, William, 28, 257
Beattie, Rev. James, 157

Beccaria, Cesare, 29, 93
Becket, Thomas
  disputes with JM, 59–60, 86, 155–6
  sale of stock, 35–6, 59–60, 80, 155–6, 293–4, 297, 299–301, 306, 318, 349–50, 365, 368, 370, 382, 385, 388, 400
  and Scottish associates, 58
Beckford, William, 378
Beddoes, Thomas
  and cautious business practice, 51
  and the *English Review*, 210–14, 215
  History of Isaac Jenkins, 78, 155
  and Murray, Hester, 244
  and original non-fiction articles, 178–9, 236, 393
  and translations, 78, 173, 319–20, 333, 367, 378
beer, 43–5
Behn, Aphra, 55
Belfast, 48, 120–1
Bell, Andrew, 190
Bell, Benjamin, 88
Bell, John (author), 182
Bell, John (Edinburgh bookseller)
  and the archive of Bell & Bradfute, 40, 372–3, 387
  joint publications with JM, 29, 101–2, 121, 195, 372, 373, 387
  and Kincaid, Alexander, 29, 93
  selling arrangements with JM, 65, 88, 97, 101–2, 113–14
Bell, John (London bookseller), 60, 159, 201
Bennett & Hake, 38
Bensley, Thomas, 83, 359
Bentham, Jeremy, 267, 355
Bergman, Torbern, 173
Biblioteca Hoblyniana, 28
binding of books, 34–5, 104–6
Bingley, William, 36
Birmingham, 106–7
Black, Joseph, 11, 96
Blackstone, William, 203
Blake, William, 83, 392, Plate 23
Blane, Andrew, 190

Blane, Gilbert, 182, 226, 247
Boswell, James, 61, 64, 188, 214, 276, 369
Bowyer, William, 256, 262, 264, 269–70
Boyd, Henry, 69
Bradfute, John, 40, 101, 195, 372–3, 387
Bradley, Abraham, 111
Brand, Thomas, 176
Breaks, Thomas, 108
Brook, Abraham, 47
Brooke, Frances, 173
Brown, Alexander, 102
Brown, William Laurence, 162, 243
Buckland, James, 389
Buffon, Georges-Louis, Comte de, 85, 173
Burgess, William, 138
Burke, Edmund, 73, 229, 235, 269
Burns, Robert, 94, 96
Bute, John Stuart, 3rd Earl of, 21
Butters, Robert, 217, 361
Butterworth, Joseph, 299

Cadell, Thomas
    credit arrangements with JM, 37, 240–1
    disputes with JM, 84–5, 167, 193
    and Duché, Rev. Jacob, 163
    historical publications, 74
    joint publications with JM, 77–8, 280, 384, 393
    as a major publisher, 64–5, 84–5, 242
    and Mason's English Garden, 157
    and Scottish associates, 58, 96, 99, 193
    and Strahan, William, 85, 242
    and Thomson's Seasons, 402
Camack, John, 135–6
Cambridge, 93
Campbell, Ilay, Lord Advocate, 190
Campbell, James, 35
Campbell, R., 21
Caledonian Mercury, 138
Carlyle, Rev. Alexander, 225, 279
Carnan, Thomas, 390
Cartwright, Rev. Edmund, 29, 75, 112, 155–7, 203, 225, Plates 8, 10, 39
Caslon, Catherine, 313, 344, 374, 379
Caslon, Thomas, 381
Caslon, William, 304, 314, 317, 365, 371
catalogues, 54, 87–9, 181, Plate, 32
Cawthorn, George, 372
Chambers, Ephraim, 79–80
Chandler, Richard, 19
Chapman, William, 256, 260
Chapter Coffee House, 61, 291, 371
China, 16, 38
Charnley, William, 107–8, 259
Christie, James, 105
circulating libraries, 93
Clark, John, 182, 279, 285, 381

Clarke, Henry, 288
Cochrane (Cochran), James, 271
coffee houses, 82, 166, 168, 291, 371 see also taverns
congers, 54–6, 61
Congreve, William, 36
Cooper, Joseph, 337, 346
copyright, 52–62, 109–10
    Copyright Act (1710), 1, 55, 56, 58, 103, 109, 185
    Copyright Act (Ireland) (1801), 121
    see also Literary Property Decision
Cordwainers, Worshipful Company of, 25–6
Cornish, D., 283, 302, 325, 366, 388, 396
Cornwall, Bryan, 178
Court Miscellany, 14–15, 200
Court of Session (Edinburgh), 57, 190
Craig, Rev. William, 163–4
Crawford, Betty, 136
credit, 37, 39–41, 239–40
Creech, William
    and the Encyclopedia Britannica, 190–1
    joint publications with JM, 72, 88, 94–7, 121, 195
    and the Dillys, 157
    and the Edinburgh Magazine and Review, 203–4, 207
    and Elliot, Charles, 100, 195
    and the Literary Property Decision, 58–9
    and poor business practice, 96–7, 100, 243
    and Smellie, William, 98
Critical Review, 81, 95, 174, 209, 214
Cromp, Rev. Pierrepoint, 44, 260
Crowder, John, 279–81, 305, 307, 323, 332, 366, 383, 392
Crowder, Stanley, 389
Crown & Anchor (tavern), 245–6, 400
Cullen, Robert, 102
Cullen, Dr William, 94–6, 102, 105, 175–6, 191–5, 198, Plate, 45
Cumming, John, 93, 256
Cumming, Thomas, 111–12
Cunningham, John, 43–5, 103, 129
Currie, James, 210
Curry, John, 113

Daily Universal Register (later The Times), 190
Dalrymple, Sir Alexander, 234
Dalrymple, Sir David, Lord Hailes, 46, 63–5, 165, 270, 272
Dalrymple, Sir John, 51
Dancer, Thomas, 210
Dante, 69
Darwin, Charles, 4
Davies, Thomas, 318, 384
Davis, Lockyer, 377, 393
Davis, William, 279, 307, 332, 366
Debrett, John, 228
Defoe, Daniel Robinson Crusoe 72, 155
DeLolme, Jean Louis, 174

Dibdin, Thomas Frognall, 247
Dickson, Adam, 64
Dickson, James, 208, 275
Dilly, Charles
    and Beattie's *Minstrel*, 157
    disputes with JM, 69, 86, 114
    joint publication with JM, 61
    periodical ventures, 180, 201–3
Dilly, Edward, 86, 157, 201
D'Israeli, Isaac, 239, 244, 247
Dodsley, James
    and the American Revolution, 224
    and the *Annual Register*, 207
    and Beccaria's *Elementi di Economica Publica*, 29
    disputes with JM, 86, 186–8
    and Lothian's *History of the Netherlands*, 68
    and Lyttelton's *History of Henry II*, 23–4
    and Mason, William, 157, 186
    and Walpole's *Castle of Otranto*, 28
Dodsley, Robert, 32, 186
Donaldson, Alexander, 56–8, 187
Donaldson, John, 56–8, 104–5, 351, Plate 2c
Douglas, Heron & Co. (Ayrshire Bank), 51
Dow, Alexander, 118, 382
dramatic publications, 158, 164–5 *see also* theatre
Dryden, John, 55
Dublin
    and the Irish inheritance, 45–6, 49, 115–16, 123–4, 137–8
    Society of Dublin Booksellers, 116–17, 121
    trade by JM, 48, 62, 110–21, 182, 194
Duché, Rev. Jacob, 163
Duncan, Dr Andrew, 85, 94, 179–80, 205, 305
Dunlop & Wilson, 105

East India Company, 4, 133, 231–4, 236
Edinburgh, 6–7, 29, 31, 37, 91–103, 182, 250
    University of Edinburgh, 5, 7
Edinburgh Evening Courant, 190
Edinburgh Magazine and Review, 48, 121, 166, 190, 203–4
Edinburgh Pharmacopoeia, 113
Edmunds, J. and Miss, 380
Elliot, Charles
    joint publications with JM, 97, 99–101, 121, 176, 184, 187, 192–3
    and Macfarquhar, Colin, 330, 338, 374
    periodical ventures, 179, 203, 207, 263
    sales of stock, 100–1, 195, 371–3
Elliot, Cornelius, 101
Ellis, Joseph, 259
Encyclopaedia Britannica, 189–91
Enfield, Rev. William, 25, 82, 107, 122
English Review
    and the American Revolution, 226
    and the *Analytical Review*, 83, 216, 247
    and Creech, William, 95

    and the death of JM, 241, 244
    and JM's overall management, 208–16
    and international politics, 226, 235–6
    and Munro, Innes, 195–6, 216
    and Stuart, Gilbert, 168, 210
    and Trusler, Rev. John, 154
    and Whitaker, Rev. John, 170, 213–14
engravings and illustrations, 49–50, 106, 107, 157, 188, 239, Plate 23
Evans, Thomas, 200, 330, 336, 345, 368, 371, 375, 381
Evelyn, John, 28, 36
Evening Star, 195
Ewing, Thomas, 48, 88, 111–15, 260–1
Eyres, William, 107, 284

Falconar, Maria and Harriet, 228
Falconer, Rev. William, 19–20, 24, 155, 222
Faulkner, George, 111, 115
Fénelon, François de Salignac, 172
Fergusson, Robert, 7
fever powders, 46–8, Plate 14
fiction *see* novels
Fielding & Walker, 181
Fielding, Henry, 155, 164
Finlay, James (husband of Janet), 129–31
Finlay, Janet (née McMurray, Jenny), 7, 127–31, 136
Fitzgerald, Gerald, 157, Plate 40
Fletcher, Sir Robert, 71, 263
Flin, Lawrence, 115, 118
Foreign Medical Review, 178, 180, Plate 43
Fothergill, John, 276
Foulis, Andrew, Jr, 105–7, 289
Foulis, Robert and Andrew, 50, 104–6, 266, 269
Fox, Charles James, 212, 228, 232
French Revolution, 3, 228–31, 239, 240, 243
Fraser, Alexander, 324
Freeling, Francis, 43
French, John, 288, 290
Fuseli, Henry, 82–3

Galliard, Edward, 47, 263, Plate 14
Gallway, William, 134
Gardiner, John, 315
Gardiner, Thomas, 144
Gast, John, 72–4, 197, Plate 24
Gay, John, 13, 79, Plate 25
General Advertiser, or Morning Intelligencer, 206
General Evening Post, 87
Gentleman's Magazine, 7, 188, 209
George III, King of Great Britain, 103, 219, 223
George IV, King of Great Britain (the then Prince of Wales), 218
Gibbon, Edward, 72–3, 118, 170, 207, 213
Gillies, John, 74

Gilliland, Elizabeth (née McMurray), 7, 92, 125, 127–8, 130, 131, 136, 145, Plate 2b
Gilliland, James (husband of Elizabeth), 92–93, 96, 100, 128, 145, 208, Plate 2b
Gillray, James, 83, Plate 23
Gladwin, Francis, 236
Glasgow, 103–6, 129
Globe Tavern
  sales of the Caslons, 304, 313–14, 317, 344, 365, 371, 374, 379, 381, Plate 26
  sale of D. Cornish, 283, 302, 325, 366, 388, 396
  sales of the Crowders, 279–81, 305, 307, 323, 332, 366, 383, 389, 392
Godwin, William
  'Defence of the Rockingham party', 308
  and the English Review, 210, 212–14
  Instructions to a statesman, 315
  and Johnson, Joseph, 82
  and the New Annual Register, 207
  as a translator, 173, 324
Goldney, William, 277
Goldsmith, Oliver, 46, 62, 165, 174
Goldsmith, William, 371
Goodsman, David, 35, Plate 11
Gordon riots, 226–8
Gordon, Charles, 16
Gordon, Lord George, 226–8
Gordon, General Robert, 21, 222–4, 232–3
Gordon, Sir Robert (4th Bart.), 10, 232, 234
Gordon, Sir William, 10, 12, 15, 234
Gordonstoun Estate, Moray, 10
Grant, Rev. Donald, 162–3, 242
Gray, Thomas, 60, 99, 158, 184–9, Plates 16, 17
Griffith, Elizabeth, 258
Griffith, Richard, 176
Griffiths, Ralph, 81, 209 see also Monthly Review

Halhead, William, 118, 120
Halhed, Nathaniel, 236
Hamilton, Alexander, 113, 210, 260, 294
Hamilton, Archibald, 78, 81, 209
Harding, John, 27, 238
Harrison & Company, 60
Harvey, John, 29, 93
Hastings, Warren, 235–6
Hawes, William, 181
Hawkesworth, John, 85, 114
Hay, John, 120
Hellins, John, 210
Henderson, William, 358
Heriot, John, 153, 196, 340
Higgs, Samuel, 41
Highley, Samuel, 27, 238, 241–3, 245–9
Hill, John, 269
Hilton, William, 262
Hinton, James, 316, 325

Hinton, John, 369, 394, 396
Historian's Pocket Dictionary, 198
historical works, 72–5, 159, 165–72
'History of Sir Lancelot Edgevile', 14–15
Hoey, James, 116
Holcroft, Thomas, 210, 211, 355
Hollingsworth, S., 228
Holloway, Thomas, 83, 239, 246
Home, Dr Francis, 299
Home, Rev. John, 12
Horn Tavern, 399, 403
Hough, John, 164
House of Commons, 51
House of Lords, 58–9, 235
Hughs, Henry, 344
Hume, David
  historical works of, 70–73, 165, 169
  and Home's Douglas, 12
  and Millar's Distinction of Ranks, 70
  and Rousseau, Jean Jacques, 14, 15–16
  and Stuart, Gilbert, 206
Hunter, Rev. Henry, 69, 83, 164, 246
Hunter, Dr William, 78–9, 107, 131–2
Hutton, John, 190

illustrations see engravings
imprints
  as advertising, 29
  with the author's name, 67
  in joint publications, 66, 77–9, 81–2, 121
  mysterious 'Murray' imprints, 62, Plate 20
India
  political views of JM, 3–4, 224, 230, 231–7
  sales of books, 37, 43, 237, 243, 250
Inglefield, Capt. John, 141
Innes, William, 228
Ireland
  copyright laws, 56, 109, 121
  inheritance of JM, 29, 133–9, 223
  publishing activities of JM, 50, 72–3, 109–21, 204, 208
Iselin, Isaak, 175

Jackman, Isaac, 341
Jackson, Robert, 182
Jacobites, 6, 10, 230
Jamaica, 38, 182
James, Dr Robert, 46
Jamieson, John, 228
Jenkin, Caleb, 114–15, 119
Jenkinson, Charles, 301
Johnson, Joseph

and the *Analytical Review*, 83, 216, 247
and the French Revolution, 229
joint publications with JM, 77–8, 81–4, 173, 178, 246, 269, 359
and the *London Medical Journal*, 82, 181
and the *Theological Repository*, 202
Johnson, Samuel
  the *Adventurer*, 281, 349
  and Dalrymple, Sir David, 64
  Dictionary of the English Language, 324
  and Dr James's fever powders, 46
  and the *English Review*, 214
  Journey to the Western Isles of Scotland, 114
  and Ossian, 170, 297, 301
  and the *Plays of William Shakspeare*, 164–5, Plate 42
  proposed services for JM, 68, 175
  the *Rambler*, 163, 217
  as a Tory, 188, 209
  Works of Samuel Johnson, 340
  Works of the English Poets, 60–1, 159–60, Plates 18, 19
Johnson, William, 36
Johnston, Edward, 278, 281, 285, 298
Jones, John, 230
Jones, William, 203, 247
'Junius', 202, 222–3
Justamond, John, 210, 215

Kay, Thomas, 100, 371–2, 381–2, 385, 387, 393, 396
Kearney, Michael, 120, 165
Kearsley, George
  and De Lolme's *Constitution of England*, 295
  dispute with JM, 86
  at estate sale of JM, 245, 390, 396, 401
  joint publications with JM, 174, 381
  sale of title to JM, 295
Kennedy, Hellen, 136
Kenrick, William, 173
Kerr, Robert, 151, 386
Kerr, William
  advice to JM, 18–19, 22, 46, 92–3, 95, 127, 130
  and Creech, William, 95–6
  and the Irish inheritance, 133–4
  and the lottery, 46
  and the post office, 42, 92
Kerr, William, Jr, 142, 147, 149–50, 196
Kimber, Edward, 327
Kincaid, Alexander, 29, 40, 93–4
Kincaid, Alexander, Jr, 355
Kippis, Andrew, 207

Lackington, James, 74
Lane, William, 219, 373
Langhorne, Rev. John

and Cartwright's *Armine and Elvira*, 157, 261
The Crisis, 258–9
in the *Edinburgh Magazine and Review*, 203
Fables of Flora, 29, 111–12, 155–6
supply of beer from JM, 44
as a translator, 173, 260
Laugier, Abbé Marc-Antoine, 26, 58
Lavater, Johann Kasper, 69–70, 83, 199, 239, 358–9, Plates 21, 22a, 22b, 23
Law, Edmund, 57
Leland, John, 204
Leslie, John, 173, 210, 380
Leyden, 38
Licensing (or Printing) Act (1660), 53
Lind, James, 182
Lisbon, 38
Liston, Robert, 210
Literary Property Decision (1774), 1, 56–8, 191 *see also* copyright
Lizars, Daniel, 372
Logan, John, 210, 214
London Magazine, 187
London Medical Journal, 82, 181
London Medical Review, 247
London Mercury, 206–7
Longman, Thomas, 22, 32, 65, 67, 245, 373, 378
Lothian, Rev. William, 67–8, 224
lottery tickets, 46, 119
Louis XVI, King of France, 229–30
Lovat, Simon, Lord, 173
Lowndes, William, 362, 365
Lyttelton, George, Lord, 20, 22, 26, Plate 6

McArthur, John, 64
McDonald, Andrew, 164
MacDonald, Thomas, 40–1
Macfarlane, James, 35
Macfarquhar, Colin, 190, 330, 338, 374
Macgowan, James, 381
Macintosh, William, 195
Mackenzie, Henry, 217
Mackenzie, James, 100
McMurray, Robina *see* Ormiston, Robina
McMurray, Elizabeth *see* Gilliland, Elizabeth
McMurray, Janet *see* Finlay, Janet
McMurray, Jean (mother of JM), 6
McMurray, John *see* Murray, John
McMurray, Robert, 5–6, 8, 127, Plate 2a
Madison, Rev. James, 39
Magee, John, 48, 120
Malcolm, Alexander, 117
Malone, Edmond, 73, 164
Manby, Richard, 19
Mason, William, 157, 184–9, 190, 280, Plate 44
Mayne, John, 220
Mayne, Robert, 51, 225

Medical and Philosophical Commentaries, 48, 86, 94, 121, 179–80, 205, Plate 33
Medical Register, 180–1
medical works
  catalogues issued by JM, 88–9, 181, Plate 32
  and Creech, William, 95
  and Johnson, Joseph, 82–3
  published following death of JM, 244, 247, 249–50, Plate 48
  successful publishing by JM, 64, 159, 175–83
Merrill, T. & J., 29, 88, 93
Millar, Andrew, 36, 56–7, 84, 93
Millar, John
  Distinction of Ranks, 29, 36, 70, 105–6, 112, 165, 260
  and Glasgow University Library, 104
  Historical View of English Government, 78, 99, 343
  and Hume, David, 70
  and the Literary Property Decision, 58
  and Mason, William, 186
  and Stuart, Gilbert, 168
Miller, Robert, 39, Plate 13
Miller, William, 250
Millot, Abbé Claude François Xavier, 82, 112, 165, 173, Plates 29, 30
Mitford, William, 74, 165, 197
Monboddo, James Burnet, Lord, 190
Moncrieffe, Richard, 118–19, 208, 315
Montagu, Elizabeth Robinson, 255
Monthly Review, 48, 81, 95, 157, 174, 209, 214
Moore, John, 103–4, 210
Morning Chronicle and London Advertiser, 87, 200–1, 232, 234
Morning Star, 219
Motherby, George, 178
Motte Benjamin, 110
Mundy's Coffee House, 166, 168
Munro, Capt. Innes, 195–8, 216, 354
Murphy, Arthur, 304
Murray, Rev. Alexander (JM's uncle), 6, 8, 10–11, 41, 228
Murray, Alexander (printer), 271, 331
Murray, Archibald (JM's cousin), 225–6
Murray, Archie (JM's illegitimate son)
  advice from JM, 141, 144, 199, 229–30, 231, Plate 35b
  birth of, 2, 122
  education of, 139–41, Plate 35a
  inheritance, 242, 247
  and Murray, Hester, 2, 139, 144
  and Murray, John (the second), 150, 245, 248, 250
  naval career, 141–2, 250
Murray, Hester (JM's second wife)
  as a bookseller, 242–5
  and the death of JM, 240–6
  illnesses of, 13–14, 148, 240–1
  inheritance, 17, 142–3
  and Murray, Archie, 2, 139, 144
  and Murray, John (the second), 149, 151

  and Murray, Nancy, 9, 125, 126, 143
  relationship with JM, 2, 17, 127, 142–6
Murray, Jenny (JM's daughter), 145–6, 241, 245–7
Murray, John
  as an author, 4, 12–15, 42, 95–6, 186–7, 189, 191, 194–5, 196–8, 415–16
  birth of, 1
  chronology of his life, xvi–xv
  drinking of alcohol, 45–6, 124
  death of, 241–3
  education of, 7–8
  entertainment of friends, 27–8
  estate sale of, 245–6, Plate 47
  family tree, xvi–xvii
  illnesses of, 28, 146–7, 148, 226, 240–1
  infidelities of, 18, 122–5, 139
  and lodgers, 25
  marriages, 9, 143–4
  naval career, 2, 8–9, 18, 20, 27, 221
  other business ventures, 43–51
  portraits of, frontispiece, Plates 1, 2c
  property ownership, 136, 244
  purchase of Sandby's business, 19–22
Murray, John (bookseller of the same name), 77, 357
Murray, John ('the second JM')
  birth of, 144–5
  as a bookseller, 1, 243, 245–50, Plates 10b, 48
  and the death of JM, 241, 248
  education of, 149–52
  and Murray, Archie, 150, 245, 248, 250
  partnership with Highley, Samuel, 246–49
  portrait of, Plate 36
Murray, John & Brother (Leyden booksellers), 38
Murray, Mary Anne (JM's daughter), 148, 241
Murray, Nancy (JM's first wife)
  change of surname from McMurray, 21
  death of, 126–7
  illness of, 125–6
  and the infidelity of JM, 18, 122, 123
  inheritance, 16–17
  marriage to JM, 2, 9, 122
  move to Fleet Street, 22, 25
  pastimes of, 28, 45, 143
  running of the shop, 29
  separations from JM, 10–11, 122–5

navy *see* Royal Navy
Neill, Adam, 102, 333, 351, 370–1, 387, 395
Newbery, John, 7, 46
Newcastle, 107–8
newspapers, 36, 88, 201–3 *see also names of individual newspapers*
Nicoll, William, 82, 173
Nicolson, James, 298, 356
Noble, George, 242
North Briton, 202, 222

North, Frederick, Lord, 212, 223, 232
novels, 14–15, 72, 153–5, 158

Ogilvie, David, 360
Ogilvie, John, 157, 210
Ogilvie, William, 381
Ormiston, John (husband of Robina, below), 119–20, 132–3, 145, 147, 225, 241
Ormiston, Robert Murray, 242, 247
Ormiston, Robina (née McMurray, Binny)
  advice to JM, 17–18, 131–2, 162, 201
  birth of, 7
  and Finlay, Janet, 128, 130
  inheritance, 127–8, 136, 242
  marriage, 21, 119
  and Murray, Hester, 143
  and Murray, Nancy, 17–18, 125, 143
Ossian, 170, 297, 301
Otridge, William, 371, 385, 388

Paget, Henry (Hester Murray's second husband), 244–5
Paine, Thomas, 229–30
pamphlets
  on fever powders, 47
  on Home's *Douglas*, 12
  on politics, 228, 229, 230, 244
  written by JM, 12, 13, 42, 95–6, 186–7, 189, 191, 194–5, 196–8, 415–16, Plates 44–6
Parker, Sir Thomas, 273
Paxton, Archibald
  advice to JM, 11, 17, 19, 123, 241
  as executor of JM's will, 242
  friendship with JM, 125, 166
  and Murray, John (the second), 245, 248
Paxton, Jenny, 147
Paxton, John, 105, 144, 155
Paxton, William, 145
Peacock Tavern, 155, 166, 168
Percy, Thomas, 156
periodicals, 14, 87, 200–20 *see also names of individual periodicals*
philosophical works, 70
Pictet, François, 230
Piguenit, Caesar, 373
piracies, 53, 54, 113, 118, 184, 187, 190, 198
Pitcairn, Dr David, 146
Pitt, William, 212, 218, 228, 232, 235
plays, 164–5 *see also* theatre
poetry, 19, 60, 93, 104–6, 184–9, 215, 224, 155–60
Political Herald, 168
Political Magazine, 217
Portal, Rev. Abraham, 155, Plate 38
post office 'covers' ('franks'), 42–3, 225

Priestley, Joseph, 82
printing, 3, 34, 68, 98, 239
Protestant Association, 163, 207, 227–8
provincial booksellers, 29, 86, 91–108
Public Advertiser, 87, 232, 234
Pulteney, Sir William, 282

Quarterly Review, 250
Queen's Arms (tavern)
  sale of Becket, Thomas, 293–4, 297, 299, 300–1, 306, 318, 349–50, 365, 368, 370, 382, 385, 388, 400
  sale of Cadell, Thomas, 280, 323, 364
  sale of Johnston, Edward, 278, 281, 285, 298, 372, 400
Quicke, John, 256
Quin, Dr Henry, 49

Raeburn, Henry, Plates 2b, 2c
Rambler, 217
Rameau, Jean Phillippe, 117
Ramsay, Allan (poet), 93, 106
Ramsay, Allan (portrait painter), 12
Raspe, Rudolph Erich, 49–50
Repository: or Treasury of Politics, 202–3, 222
reprinting, 60, 109, 113, 121 *see also* piracies
Richardson, John (orientalist), 210, 229, 236
Richardson, John and William (printers)
  advice to JM, 19, 32
  joint publications with JM, 78, 259, 264, 277, 364, 371
  as a printer, 264, 273, 275, 277
Richardson, Samuel, 32, 80
Richardson, William (author), 75, 104, 210, 269
Ridley, John, 307, 332, 366, 369, 396
Rivington, Charles, 80, 371, 384, 393, 399, 400
Roberts, William, 210, 217
Robertson, Robert, 183
Robertson, Rev. William, 63, 71–3, 85, 167, 169
Robinson, George, 101, 155, 172–3, 277, 279, 287, 381
Robinson, Pollingrove, 155
Ross, James, 129, 133
Ross, Jean (mother of JM), 6
Rotheram, Dr John, 108, 195
Rotterdam, 38
Rouen, 38
Rousseau, Jean Jacques, 15–16, 117, 229
Royal Navy
  and the American Revolution, 221, 223
  naval career of JM, 2, 8–9, 18, 20, 27, 221
  sales of books, 37, 231, 250
Rutherford, Rev. William, 149–50

Samuel, John, 144
Sandby, William, 19–20, 22–3, 27, 54, 162, 255, 256, Plate 3
Savage, James, 50, 133–4
Scatcherd, James, 364, 371, 392, 406
Scheller, Immanuel Johann, 174–5
Scott, George, 202
Scott, Helenus, 237
sermons, 27, 35, 162–4, 170, 199, 225
Seven Years War, 8, 226
Sewell, John, 283
Shaw, Rev. William, 68, 276, Plate 9
Sherriff, Robert, 25
Sibbald, James, 330
Simmons & Kirby (printers), 376
Simmons, Samuel Foart, 180–1, 289, 296, 337, 361
Sims, James, 288
Skeete, Thomas, 182
Skinner, John, 210, 355
Skirving, William, 25
smallpox, 13–14, 145
Smellie, William
    and Balfour, John, 97–8, 265–6, 268, 271, 275
    and the *Edinburgh Magazine and Review*, 203–4, 263
    and the *Encyclopaedia Britannica*, 190
    and the *Medical Commentaries*, 179
    and sales of JM's catalogues, 88
    as a translator, 381
Smith, Adam, 11, 94, 278
Smith, Joseph, 103
Smith, Thomas, 32, 344
Smith, William, 111
Smollett, Tobias, 8, 14, 22, 81, 155, 209
Spectator, 79, 163, 217
St. Dunstan's Church, 19, 22, 143–4, 162, 219, 241, Plate 4
St. James's Chronicle, 87
Star, 218–20
Stationers, Company of, 22, 53, 56, 59, 230
Stedman, Charles, 225
Steevens, George, 164–5
Sterne, Laurence, 62, 80–1, 84, 155, Plates 27, 28
Stewart, Thomas, 164, 262
Stock, Joseph, 210
Stockdale, John
    credit arrangements with JM, 240
    at estate sale of JM, 245, 291, 371, 384, 391, 392, 397, 406
    and Gay's *Fables*, Plate 25
Strahan, Andrew, 78
Strahan, William
    estate sale of, 362
    ledgers of, 3, 40
    as a major publisher, 32, 242
    and Millar, Andrew, 85
    and Millot, Abbé, 260
    newspaper venture with JM, 201
    and Robertson, William, 167

and Scottish associates, 58, 93, 96
and Shaw, William, 293
Stuart, George, 7
Stuart, Gilbert
    advice to JM, 63–5, 81, 93, 193, 200
    alcohol drinking of, 44
    death of, 168
    and the *Edinburgh Magazine and Review* 166, 201–2, 203–5, 263, 265, 268, 271
    friendship with JM, 166–8, 233
    History of Mary Queen of Scots, 165, 167, 171, 189, 190
    and a history of the Netherlands, 224–5
    History of the Reformation, 71, 167, 189, 207, 227
    and 'Junius', 202
    newspaper articles of, 154
    and *Poems by Mr. Gray*, 272, 280
    and the *Political Herald*, 168
    and the *Repository*, 202–3
    as a reviewer, 169, 174, 210, 312
    and Robertson, William, 167
    as a translator, 173–4, 260, 295
    View of Society in Europe, 36
Stuart, Colonel James, 233
Stuart, Peter, 218–19
Stuart, William, 279
subscription libraries, 14
subscription publishing, 49, 68–70, 196, 239
Swediaur, François Xavier, 178, 303
Swift, Jonathan, 110
syndicate publishing, 79–82, 90, 155, 159, 164–5, 206, 244, Plates 18–19, 26–8, 37

Tassie, James, 48–50, 104–5, Plate 15
taverns and inns, 75, 82, 155, 166, 168, 400 *see also* Globe Tavern, Queens Arms
Taylor, Isaac, 156
Taylor, Robert, 234–5
Taylor, William, 164
theatre, 2, 11–13, 28, 123, 164, 209, 211 *see also* dramatic publications
Thomson, James, 56–7, 60, 107, 158
Thomson, William
    and the *English Review*, 210, 212–15, 241, 244, 247
    and the *London Mercury*, 206, 296
    The Man on the Moon, 155
    'Observations on the East India Fleet', 407
    Travels in Europe, Asia and Africa, 195–6
Timbury, Jane, 153, 354
Times, The, see Daily Universal Register
Tonson, Jacob, 56
Tory Party, 209
trade sales, 35–6, 88, 244–5 *see also* auctions, Globe Tavern, Queens Arms
translations, 29, 64, 69, 82–3, 85, 93, 112, 117, 153, 172–5, 178, 237
Trapp, Joseph, 230

Trist, Rev. Jeremiah, 210
Trusler, Rev. John, 149, 153–4, 198–9, 210, 217, 358
Trye, C. B., 182

Universal History, 165
Ussher, James, 260

Vernor, Thomas, 354, 364, 367, 405
Voltaire, François Marie Arouet de, 229, 278

Wade, John Peter, 67, 182
Wait, Rev. Robert, 28
Walker, John, 181, 371
Wallis, John, 117
Walpole, Horace, 28, 40, 187–8
Walter, John, 344
Ward, Caesar, 19
Warrington, 107, 284
Warton, Thomas, 114
Wayland, Levi, 350
Wedgwood, Josiah, 48
Weed, William, 27
Weemss, Ann, 16–17
Weemss, Hester *see* Murray, Hester
Weemss, Nancy *see* Murray, Nancy
Weemss, Capt. William, 11, 16–17, 18, 126, 142
Wells, Rev. Charles, 150
Wentworth, Viscount, 27
Wheble, John, 201

Whig Party, 188, 209
Whitaker, Rev. John
    friendship with JM, 66, 166, 168–70
    and Highley, Samuel, 243
    History of Manchester, 169–70
    Mary Queen of Scots Vindicated, 165, 170–2
    periodical writings, 202, 210, 213–14, 241
    rejection by JM, 239
    writing style, 71–2, 169, 202, 213
White, Benjamin, 24
White, Luke, 117–18, 120, 218–20, 243, 288
Wilberforce, William, 228
Wilkes, John, 21, 202, 222
Wilkie, George, 378–9
Wilkie, Thomas, 378
Williams, David, 297
Williams, Evan, 27, 238
Williams, James, 282
Wilson, William, 102, 131, 175
Wingrave, Francis, 399, 403
Wingrave, John, 35
Witherspoon, Rev. John, 270
Wollstonecraft, Mary, 82
Wombwell, Sir George, 234
Wood, James, 182
Wood, John, 28
Woodfall, Henry, 36
Woodfall, William, 200–1
Woolf, Virginia, 55
Wordsworth, William, 82

Yeo, John, 50
Young, Robert, 336

British Academy
Postdoctoral Fellowship Monographs

Since 1986, the Academy has operated a scheme of Postdoctoral Fellowships, designed to enable outstanding younger scholars to obtain experience of research and teaching in the university environment. In December 1995, the Academy launched a complementary scheme for the selective publication of monographs arising from its Postdoctoral Fellowships. Its purpose has been to assist individual British Academy Postdoctoral Fellows by providing a prestigious publishing opportunity that will be seen as a mark of excellence, and also to act as a showcase for the Postdoctoral Fellowship scheme itself. An annual competition has been held for the awarding of monograph publishing contracts. In the first three competitions, eight contracts were awarded.

PUBLISHED, OR IN PRESS

Patrick ffrench, *The Cut: Reading Bataille's* Histoire de l'œil   0-19-726200-7

Richard Gameson, *The Manuscripts of Early Norman England (c. 1066–1130)* 0-19-726190-6

D. K. Money, *The English Horace: Anthony Alsop and the Tradition of British Latin Verse*   0-19-726184-1

William Zachs, *The First John Murray and the Late Eighteenth-Century London Book Trade*   0-19-726191-4

Simon C. Smith, *Kuwait, 1950–1965: Britain, the al-Sabah, and Oil* 0-19-726197-3

IN PREPARATION (exact titles to be confirmed)

Wendy Mercer, *Xavier Marmier (1808–1892): A Critical Biography*

Stephen Rippon, *Transformation and Control: The Exploitation and Modification of Coastal Wetlands in Britain and North West Europe*

A. C. Scullion, *Women and the Scottish Theatre from the Restoration to 1851*

September 1998